The Great Ideas

Man
Mathematics
Matter
Mechanics
Medicine
Memory and Imagination
Metaphysics
Mind
Monarchy
Nature
Necessity and Contingency
Oligarchy
One and Many
Opinion
Opposition
Philosophy
Physics
Pleasure and Pain
Poetry
Principle
Progress
Prophecy
Prudence
Punishment
Quality
Quantity

Reasoning
Relation
Religion
Revolution
Rhetoric
Same and Other
Science
Sense
Sign and Symbol
Sin
Slavery
Soul
Space
State
Temperance
Theology
Time
Truth
Tyranny
Universal and Particular
Virtue and Vice
War and Peace
Wealth
Will
Wisdom
World

Array of photocells and light concentrators form part of sun-tracking photovoltaic system developed at Sandia Laboratories in New Mexico. The system is designed to seek and collect the maximum amount of available sunlight for direct conversion to electricity.

The
Great Ideas
Today

1980

Encyclopædia Britannica, Inc.

Chicago • London • Toronto • Geneva • Sydney • Tokyo • Manila • Seoul

"Toward a Sustainable Energy Future," by David J. Rose is a somewhat
shortened version of an address delivered by Dr. Rose at the Conference
on Faith, Science and the Future of the World Council of Churches held
at the Massachusetts Institute of Technology July 12–24, 1979. Copyright
World Council of Churches.
Reprinted by permission of the World Council of Churches, Inc.

A Doll's House by Henrik Ibsen, translated by R. Farquharson Sharp and
Eleanor Marx-Aveling, revised by Torgrim and Linda Hannas. © Revisions,
J.M. Dent & Sons, Ltd., 1958. An Everyman's Library Edition.
Reprinted by permission of the publisher in the United States, E.P. Dutton.

"The Dynamo and the Virgin," from *The Education of Henry Adams,* by Henry Adams.
Copyright, 1918 by the Massachusetts Historical Society.
Copyright, 1946 by Charles F. Adams.
Reprinted by permission of Houghton Mifflin Company.

Printed in the U.S.A. Library of Congress Catalog Number: 61-65561
International Standard Book Number: 0-85229-376-3
International Standard Serial Number: 0072-7288

Contents

A NOTE ON REFERENCE STYLE

In the following pages, passages in *Great Books of the Western World* are referred to by the initials '*GBWW*,' followed by volume, page number, and page section. Thus, '*GBWW*, Vol. 39, p. 210b' refers to page 210 in Adam Smith's *The Wealth of Nations*, which is Volume 39 in *Great Books of the Western World*. The small letter 'b' indicates the page section. In books printed in single column, 'a' and 'b' refer to the upper and lower halves of the page. In books printed in double column, 'a' and 'b' refer to the upper and lower halves of the left column, 'c' and 'd' to the upper and lower halves of the right column. For example, 'Vol. 53, p. 210b' refers to the lower half of page 210, since Volume 53, James's *Principles of Psychology*, is printed in single column. On the other hand, 'Vol. 7, p. 210b' refers to the lower left quarter of the page, since Volume 7, Plato's *Dialogues*, is printed in double column.

Gateway to the Great Books is referred to by the initials '*GGB*,' followed by volume and page number. Thus, '*GGB*, Vol. 10, pp. 39-57' refers to pages 39 through 57 of Volume 10 of *Gateway to the Great Books*, which is James's essay, "The Will to Believe."

The Great Ideas Today is referred to by the initials '*GIT*,' followed by the year and page number. Thus '*GIT* 1968, p. 210' refers to page 210 of the 1968 edition of *The Great Ideas Today*.

Preface

This is the twentieth issue of *The Great Ideas Today* to be offered since 1961, when there appeared the first in what has been an annual series of volumes intended for owners of *Great Books of the Western World*. The series was designed, as the original volume stated, "to examine the problems of today in terms of those books," and to "focus [their] wisdom ... on [contemporary] events and developments." By the "great ideas" were meant the ideas that form the structure of the *Syntopicon* and are the subjects of the "Great Conversation" that *GBWW* may be said to contain. These ideas, the first issue of *The Great Ideas Today* asserted, "constitute the intellectual implements which thinking men in every century must employ in order to understand the changing world in which they live." The underlying proposition on which the series has been based is that the great books, references to which are implicit and often explicit in the articles written by our contributors, cast light on contemporary world problems, on the on-going progress of the arts and sciences, and on a variety of special problems and issues which the series has over the years undertaken to consider.

Our symposium this year is devoted to world energy prospects, a subject hardly conceived of at the time the first issue of *The Great Ideas Today* was published, when the impending disappearance of recoverable fossil fuels did not yet loom as a world problem, and when little thought had been given to alternative energy sources. It is a subject with technical, economic, political, and social dimensions, all of which are discussed by our contributors, who have written widely on energy or on matters related to it.

The volume also contains three articles on the arts and sciences. One of these, by Seth Benardete, provides a profoundly original reading of Greek tragedy that offers encouraging evidence of the state of classical studies at the present time. A second article, by Francis Crick, who was asked to write of recent developments in the biological sciences, is devoted to the subject of genetic splitting and splicing, where extraordinary techniques have recently been developed. A third article, by Daniel Bell, is the second part of a two-part discussion (Part I appeared last year) of what has happened in the social sciences since the end of the Second World War and completes an instructive survey of this complex and increasingly technical field.

In addition, a special feature this year goes some way toward meeting the demands of readers who, notwithstanding that the books with which we are concerned are those of the Western world, insist that, given the world as it is now, we ought to provide some discussion of developments in the East. A lengthy and erudite essay by Hajime Nakamura, director of the Eastern Institute, Tokyo, and a specialist in Indian philosophy, draws from a wide variety of sources for an account of the idea of nature in the philosophy of both the East and the West. Professor Nakamura is well qualified for this difficult undertaking, and his discussion of Eastern traditions in particular will be of interest to readers who may not until now have known very much about them.

Following this essay, three "Additions to the Great Books Library" appear. They are a selection of the essays of Arthur Schopenhauer, whose major work, *The World as Will and Idea,* might well have appeared in *GBWW,* and who is a figure very much worth reading; *A Doll's House,* by Henrik Ibsen, a play that has lost nothing of its power in the century since it first appeared; and "The Dynamo and the Virgin," from *The Education of Henry Adams,* in which we are reminded of a conception of energy or force very different from the one now current in the world.

Finally, this year's volume contains a cumulative index of articles and reprints that have appeared in *The Great Ideas Today* since 1961.

PART ONE

A Symposium on World Energy Prospects

Introduction

S ave for one mention in connection with Chapter 54, "Mechanics," the term *energy* does not appear in the Syntopicon. It does not appear there because it does not appear, or appears hardly at all, in *Great Books of the Western World,* where there is no discussion of what we now mean by the word. What we mean is still partly a matter of mechanics, of course, as by extension it is one of psychology—that is, we mean what the Greek means, which is "work," or "force"—but fundamentally we have in mind something different. We are thinking as we use the term not of energy as such, but of the source from which energy comes. The cause of the action has taken the place for us of the action itself. By energy we mean fuel, which is to say, heat, and we mean heat not in the sense that would have interested Fourier, whose theory of the subject appears in *GBWW,* Volume 45, but in a sense that would have been important to Marx or Darwin. For the kind of heat we mean is the condition of our social existence and ultimately of our survival as human beings, and when we discuss the subject now, it is just that social existence and survival that we are thinking of.

That we should not have had such concern before the Industrial Revolution is in part because the amount of heat-energy required by the human race was then so small that the question of scarcity never arose. The population of the earth was itself small, and apart from domestic fires it needed large amounts of energy, chiefly wood, only for the blacksmith's forge or an occasional foundry. Now there are a great many more people in the world, and each one is sustained by an expenditure of energy that would have been unimaginable before the growth of the vast urban complexes and far-flung transportation systems on which most of us depend.

On top of that, the form of the energy we use has changed, derived as now it largely is from fossil fuels, which are nonrenewable deposits. For some two hundred years—more, if we count the deforestation and climatic changes brought about by earlier civilizations—the human race has been living off its capital in this respect, and in ever-increasing amounts. Our present concern reflects the fact that the end of that Golden Age of energy is now in sight. The earth is not going to supply us with its stored heat for very much longer. With certain possible exceptions, we shall have to capture what we need from the sun, and at a rate not appreciably greater than the sun can from day to day provide.

It is worth noting in this regard that, while the sun is sometimes spoken of as if it were an exotic, untried source of heat-energy, it is in fact the source of all the energy we have ever used, or ever can use. Coal, oil, wood, and even uranium are merely residual sun rays. In undertaking to use what we call solar energy, we are merely directing our attention to those sun rays that are now arriving upon the earth, as distinct from those that appeared a long time ago. It is not the source of energy, but its rate of replacement, that will be different in future.

The possible exceptions to such a future are the power we may be able to derive from nuclear fission and also from nuclear fusion — which is not yet a practical possibility, though the science by which it could be achieved is fairly well understood. Unhappily, nuclear fission has become the subject of intense opposition, the result of accidental malfunctions in power plants such as that which occurred not long ago at Three Mile Island, Pennsylvania, and of the difficulty in disposing of spent uranium, which remains radioactive for hundreds of thousands of years after its energy has been taken from it. Nor does the supply of uranium that such power plants would use promise to last indefinitely. This latter problem might be solved by what are called breeder reactors, of which none is now in operation in the United States, though a few function elsewhere in the world, but the objection to these is that, while they generate fuel and therefore have in theory a much longer life than ordinary fission plants, the fuel they generate is a kind of uranium that can be used for the production of atomic weapons.

Leaving that aside, what remains to be learned — or decided, so far as the matter is within our control — is just how far away the solar future is and what interim arrangements would be best to make. These last, in particular, are the subject of disagreement among the contributors to the symposium on world energy prospects that appears in this issue of *The Great Ideas Today*. The sharpest difference is that which lies between David J. Rose, of the Massachusetts Institute of Technology, who thinks that power derived from nuclear fission should be among such arrangements, and Amory Lovins, of the Friends of the Earth, who thinks that it should not. The underlying issues here, involving as they do social and environmental questions of a very serious kind, are difficult to resolve.

Other issues are hardly easier or less extensive. Among them is the economic question, or set of questions, raised by the fact that the remaining reachable supplies of fossil fuel in the world — chiefly petroleum — are for the most part located within a few nations from which the rest are obliged to purchase what they need, so that an enormous transfer of wealth is required. The question is whether the world economy can tolerate this vast exchange, coming as it does on top of an already serious balance of payments problem as between the industrialized and the developing countries. All that is considered in the present symposium by Ragaei El Mallakh, of the University of Colorado at Boulder, an authority on the subject who is among other things editor of *The Journal of Energy and Development,* a publication devoted to the consideration of such questions.

Further troubles are implicit in the political problems to which these economic forces may be said to give rise, and which at any rate, having arisen, vastly complicate the picture. Energy, at least petroleum energy, has not only become itself a point of division between have and have-not nations; it exacerbates the conflicts that already exist in the world. As supplies of oil and gas become smaller and therefore more expensive, the pressures within have-not nations whose economies are over-strained will become intense, while the temptation to transfer that pressure to richer countries — by trade limitations, for example—in the hope of extracting economic concessions, will be great. OPEC itself was a combination in restraint of trade (as we may call it) to which the countries of the Middle East (and certain others), which then were have-not nations, felt driven by the increasing gap between their condition and that of the industrialized world. But much more blatant pressures, not excluding internal revolutions and perhaps migrations of population (the flow of Mexicans seeking work into the United States across the southern border, like that of southern Italians into Germany for the same purpose, is perhaps a foretaste of things to come) are to be anticipated. Each of the contributors to the symposium expressed some anxiety as to the ability of the present regime in Saudi Arabia, which contains nearly half the world's known oil reserves, to survive in these circumstances. And of course it was partly this prospect which a decade ago inspired the so-called Trilateral Commission of industrialized nations to consider what measures those nations could take to protect themselves against the OPEC cartel, and which led to the formation of the International Energy Agency at the urging of Secretary of State Henry Kissinger in 1975. Both developments are discussed in the present symposium by Franklin Tugwell.

A further issue, perhaps more important than any of these others, though arising from them, is whether the kind of technological civilization which has now come about, at least in the West, can withstand the reduced supply of energy which nearly all contributors to the symposium agree will have to be accepted. With prudent management, the sun's rays can perhaps sustain us indefinitely, but if so, it will not be in the style to which we have become accustomed. Of course it may be a much greater style, even technologically speaking. It is far from clear that with less energy we must accept a reduced standard of living. Who knows what marvels of work we may be able to get out of small amounts of energy in the future? But assuming a reduced standard, we have perhaps already an indication of its rationale in such books as E. F. Schumacher's *Small is Beautiful.* Reflections in the same vein are offered in our symposium by Willis Harman, whose article is devoted to the proposition that reduced quantities of energy and altered energy technology will have profound effects upon the kind of lives we lead—in his view, for the better.

There are, of course, still other aspects of the subject that may occur to any reader of *Great Books of the Western World*. One is the fact that earlier civilizations were not deterred from great projects or diminished in their sense of destiny by the fact that they had available only a fraction of the energy that we in this century have had. Neither the Greeks nor the Romans felt themselves to be poor in this regard, nor did their relatively primitive command of energy resources prevent them from wielding enormous power in the world. It does not necessarily follow, therefore, that because we in our time—or rather, in times to come—may have to get along with less energy that we now have, or that we had until very recently, we must give up all pretensions to greatness, or to making a better life for the human race within the world we all inhabit. We can remember that the Egyptians built the pyramids, the Romans their aqueducts, and medieval Christendom its great cathedrals without benefit of the engines and the oils that we might suppose were necessary to such tasks.

This last may remind us that after all there have existed different kinds of energy in the world from anything we now recognize as such. Henry Adams points out, in the chapter from his autobiography called "The Dynamo and the Virgin" which is reprinted among the "Additions to the Great Books Library" in this issue of *The Great Ideas Today*, that there was in Christianity a force that was not the less prodigious for being perfectly intangible. The same thing could be said, of course, of any of the world's great religions. It would seem sensible to keep in mind that in the current discussion of energy we are talking about only one of the various kinds of force that make civilized life possible, that other kinds have been manifest in the past, and that the future is very likely to be one in which new and undreamed-of powers make the world go round.

Toward a Sustainable Energy Future*

David J. Rose

Professor of nuclear engineering at the Massachusetts Institute of Technology, David J. Rose is internationally known for his work in fusion technology, energy, nuclear waste disposal, and most recently for his concern with the ethical problems that arise from advances in science and technology.

Rose, who is Canadian by birth, has been interested in controlled nuclear fusion science and technology at least since 1958, when he went to M.I.T. from a position at the Bell Telephone Laboratories. In 1969, while at Oak Ridge National Laboratory, he began work on broader issues of energy technology and environmental affairs which he subsequently introduced as academic subjects at M.I.T., and which led him to researches in the flow of materials through society that have made him a recognized authority on the problems of nuclear waste disposal.

Subsequent involvement with nuclear policy matters for the federal government moved him to a deeper study of contemporary society, and since 1976 he has worked with the World Council of Churches to define the ethical issues underlying the search for what he calls "a just, participatory, and sustainable society."

A member of numerous professional organizations who has lectured and consulted on projects in many countries, Professor Rose was chosen as recipient of the 1979–80 Killian Faculty Achievement Award at M.I.T. in honor of his professional accomplishments and what the citation described as his "open, witty, and delightful relations with colleagues and friends."

* Condensed by permission from an article prepared for the World Council of Churches' Conference on Faith, Science and the Future, held at the Massachusetts Institute of Technology, Cambridge, Massachusetts, July 1979.

I. Introduction

The energy debate has been notorious and disheveled. Little of it has shown rational inquiry or intellectual development in which a structure of reason is gradually built, each new part securely placed atop the foundation of previous understanding. To borrow a phrase from a colleague, a better image of what has gone on would be that of a widening puddle.

Any reasonably complete discussion of energy involves issues of resources, technologies, ownership (and possession, which is not always the same thing), end uses, environmental impacts now and later, and social purpose; it also raises questions of growth, and of national and international stability; it leads to arguments for and against various future visions of society, to arguments about local and global justice, to differences over exploitive dominion as against stewardship, and more.

Such a panoply of issues tempts those who discuss such matters to apply a principle of selective inattention, whereby the investigator or advocate selectively ignores topics that embarrass him or that don't fit some preconceived idea. Each person tends to use up all the intellectual option-space (so to speak), with the ignored topics left to be handled by some *deus ex machina*.

Among the relevant considerations, some are pretty well fixed and therefore need to be factored in from the start. The principal ones are:

1. The traditional resources of energy, chiefly oil and natural gas, are disappearing; the remainder is becoming increasingly expensive and selectively out of the reach of various countries.
2. The world contains about four billion people and will have more later, barring some compulsive catastrophe. That works out to about two persons per hectare on agriculturally productive land (a hectare is approximately two and one half acres).
3. The nonindustrialized nations cannot follow the path of the industrialized ones under anything like the present distribution of energy resources, because of increasing cost and scarcity.
4. Large supplies of fossil combustible material remain, chiefly coal; but there are problems in the use of those.
5. Continued use of fossil combustible material at the present rate, let alone at increasing rates, will in a few generations cause severe global

environmental and climatic problems, dwarfing any that we have experienced hitherto.

6. Patterns of energy consumption do not change easily in the short term, but in the longer term many opportunities exist to use energy more efficiently and rationally, most prominently in the industrialized countries but also elsewhere.

7. The energy problem, like all large societal problems, contains sub-issues with different time perspectives, and the disparate responses required to suit different sectors and time perspectives often conflict.

8. In the long run—say, more than fifty years from now—the only major available energy options will be solar or nuclear power, each in various forms.

Does any option-space exist for the world in which some strategy with variations to match local regions and times takes these and other lesser issues into account?

We should not assume that a comfortable future will automatically come. Many early civilizations must have suffered energy starvation.[1] Viewing the landscape around Rome, or that of the ancient Greek cities, one notes the relative lack of trees; yet wood was the sole fuel for those societies. Plato says:

> Contemporary Attica may accurately be described as a mere relic of the original country . . . in consequence of the successive deluges which have occurred within the past nine thousand years . . . there has been a constant movement of soil away from the high altitudes . . . what remains of her substance is like the skeleton of a body emaciated by disease, as compared with her original relief. All the rich soft soil has moulted away, leaving a country of skin and bones.[2]

Plato's description is correct, but the reason he gives, like Toynbee's use of it to fit his challenge-and-response theory of civilizations, is not. The Greeks (and Romans, Phoenicians, etc.) themselves cut down the trees for firewood, to make charcoal for metallurgy, and so forth. Afterward, they introduced goats onto the land, completing the ruin, and so the Mediterranean littoral remains to the present day. Where are now the cedars of Lebanon? Cut down.

Gibbon, being more concerned with political and social events than with technology or engineering, nowhere mentions lack of energy as an Empire-dissolving force, yet it was so.[3] Exhaustion of wood and agricultural capacity within primitive transport distance of Rome must have contributed to the political unrest during the early Christian eras. European technology tended to move northward into the more ample forests of France and Central Europe. This tragedy of wood is now being repeated in India, Nepal, and other places where a potentially renewable resource is being turned into a virtually nonrenewable one.

Out of all this, we must seek for goals and methods that lead to a more just, participatory, and sustainable society. A good place to start a more detailed discussion combines the resource estimates and time perspectives indicated in items (1), (7), and part of (6), listed above.

II. Resources and time perspectives

Several recent estimates of the world's ultimate recoverable oil are in range of 2,000 billion barrels; that includes oil expected to be discovered well into the next century (e.g., more in Mexico). World production in 1978 was 60 million barrels per day, which would suggest a ninety-year supply, albeit under increasingly severe economic and technological conditions.[4] The proven (i.e., known and measured) world reserve of oil is much less, 720 billion barrels. Use of oil grew at about 6 percent a year in the period 1968–75; if that trend continued, the 720 billion barrels would be gone in seventeen years and the 2,000 billion in thirty years.

This growth rate will not continue. Nevertheless, many industrialized and developing countries have made plans that presuppose it. These shrivel as time passes. The most recent Shell energy forecast has world oil production increasing at an average rate of 3.3 percent per year in the period 1975–90.[5] Other groups forecast similarly.

The outlook for natural gas is similar, but for more regional use, because of the difficulty and expense of transporting it across the ocean. Estimated proven world resources of 2,500 trillion cubic feet correspond in energy content to 420 billion barrels of oil, about the same as the oil reserves themselves.

Uneven global distribution of oil and gas is too well known to need description here. However, substantial amounts remain to be discovered, and much of that will be in the nonindustrialized countries, because those places have not been explored to anywhere the same extent as the industrialized areas—for example, the United States and Europe.[6]

The energy resource and known reserves of coal are much larger. Estimates of world coal resource run about 10 trillion metric tons (energy equivalent to 40,000 billion barrels of oil) and proven reserves at present are about one-sixteenth of that amount. The largest deposits exist in the People's Republic of China, the United States, and the USSR, but surely very significant amounts await discovery elsewhere, including many developing countries.

These introductory statistics bring us to the topic of important time perspectives. Short-term expedients may foreclose serious long-term options, and each nation must take great care that its accommodation to today's realities does not limit its scope in dealing with the more distant future. For example, strong emphasis on expanding domestic oil production, without comparable attention to how it is to be used, may tend to deepen our dependence on oil and to intensify the harshness of the eventual and inevitable withdrawal. This is a special danger for countries that are now highly industrialized.

The shortest meaningful time perspective for serious social decisions in the private sector is determined by normal market expectations of rate of return on investments. This leads typically to time horizons usually of five years, rarely as great as ten years, in present industrial practice. Investments maturing later are much less attractive. Exploratory research aimed at distant returns can be justified, but the cost must be low by normal market rules. The political sector has a similar time perspective determined by the intervals between elections.

Recognizing this short time perspective leads to a better understanding of whether the 1979 energy shortage was "contrived" or "real." Almost all world oil studies—the World Alternative Energy Studies, the Organization for Economic Cooperation and Development, the Central Intelligence Agency of the United States, Exxon Corporation, and many others—assumed that the price of oil would either stay constant in real terms at the price prevailing at the time of the study (typically 1975–77) or would only rise slightly by 1990. Furthermore, few of them took any account of possible changes in attitude or government of the Mideast OPEC countries, despite many signs that changes were likely. Thus, the reduced output of Mideast oil, which in mid-1979 amounted to about 2 million barrels a day less than previously expected, represented a real unplanned shortage. At the same time, the oil-consuming countries did not cut back their use to match, and a real shortage of a few percent of world production has actually existed. Evidence that the near-term shortage exists, and that consumption is hard to reduce in the short term, comes from OPEC's ability since February 1979 to raise the price of oil at will, to $30 per barrel and more, with little effect on demand by all those who can afford it. In the economist's words, the short-term price elasticity of oil demand is small.

But in the somewhat longer term—say, five to twenty years—we are not running out of oil, provided that no attention is paid to the yet longer period when oil resources will indeed have been depleted. Thus the oil shortage can appear real or not, depending on one's time perspective. Meanwhile, conventional economic and political forces lead to increasing world use of oil (and gas), with too little regard for eventual consequences.

A still longer time perspective relates to developing and deploying new energy options: solar power, new and cleaner ways of using coal, advanced nuclear fission reactors and fuel cycles, and mature energy conservation technologies. That time depends somewhat on the technology, but it may be twenty years or more except under the most exceptional conditions and strong government incentives. Civilian nuclear power, for example, which received remarkable federal priorities, got under way in the United States in the early 1950s, and only by the early 1970s was it well enough developed to contribute 2 percent of the nation's electric power (the industrial momentum built up during that time led to a 12-percent contribution in 1978). The magnitude of such developments and the delay in their payoff place them outside the free market.

The disparity between the economic and technological time perspectives leads to market exploitation of existing options and neglect, possibly foreclosure, of potential new ones. Governments can correct this imbalance by either underwriting the long-term development as a nonmarket social good or constructing appropriate market signals—tax and other incentives, regulations, and so on—to stimulate development by the private sector. Governments in fact do both.

Several yet longer time perspectives are also important. The time to deplete a particular energy resource, so that it becomes too expensive for its accustomed uses, should exceed the time it takes to develop and deploy alternatives or to adjust to a social and technological position of doing without. Other important time perspectives are even longer. The urban and industrial infrastructures of civilizations, which heavily influence our energy use, can persist for centuries. Cities last for centuries and change fundamentally only over generations; most of them are now designed to operate on oil and natural gas, and can only be converted gradually to anything else.

The resource of solar power is not depletable (although we saw in the example of forest cutting how its mode of use can be destroyed). The energy resource in uranium is probably comparable to that in the world's oil supply, if the uranium is used in present-day nonbreeding reactors. However, in breeder reactors, the energy per kilogram is multiplied some seventyfold; by the same token, we could afford to pay about seventy times per pound as much for it, thereby obtaining the modest amount needed from abundant low-grade supplies. Then, the uranium reserves for nuclear fission would last millions of years. Similarly, deuterium for fusion reactors would also not run out in any foreseeable future. The problems of nuclear power are not depletion of the basic energy resource.

III. Rational utilization and increased efficiency

This title is better than "conservation" because it shows at a glance how the issue touches everybody. The broadest questions that can be asked about energy policy deal with the balance of emphasis between supply and conservation. In general, supply is relatively overemphasized, because the supply sector is simpler and better organized to provide its products and to receive and recognize rewards. Energy conservation tends to offer rewards that are received later in time by diffuse and ill-organized consumers. Thus, effective energy conservation requires either that a strong public awareness be generated, or that government financial incentive be provided, or both.

Energy conservation consists of two different categories of activity. The first is simple cessation of present waste; this reflects social concern and thoughtfulness and should become more general as people are made aware of the costs of waste. The second category concerns deeper changes in the economic structure, the designs of what we use, and public incentives. It is here that we focus principal attention.

Energy supply costs money, and the marginal cost of energy increases as more is demanded; however, in the relatively pristine field of rational utilization and increased efficiency much can be done, particularly in highly industrialized countries.[7] Related to energy conservation is the question of how energy use and GNP (a convenient but imperfect measure of public well-being) are related. In the short run, reducing energy consumed reduces GNP, but the long-term possibilities are much better. As capital equipment is retired it can be replaced by equipment designed to use less energy, though generally at higher cost.

The time scales for such transitions are different for different things. Well-built houses last a hundred years, but recent experience in residential energy conservation shows that old houses can be much improved and new ones satisfactorily heated by less than half as much energy. That comes out to halving the energy requirement per unit of service in one hundred years, or about 0.7 percent per year. Cars last on the average ten years, and the United States now requires that the fleet fuel efficiency of new cars almost double between 1976 and 1986. The life of industrial plants is intermediate, averaging about twenty years; new equipment uses typically perhaps three-quarters as much energy as the old. Applying those simple numbers, we find that industrial energy per unit output could be approximately halved in about forty-five years.

Further detailed analyses, taking into account these and many other replacement possibilities, suggest that overall energy used per unit of GNP could be as much as halved in forty–fifty years, with negligible effects on GNP. This means that conservation incentives, including rising energy costs, could lead to half as much energy being used in the year 2020 as is now used for today's national total of goods and services; or, the same amount of energy could accomplish twice as much. The detailed strategy for doing this would involve frequent reviews and appropriate corrections from time to time.

The key to effective energy conservation is planning for the long term. Attempts to induce efficiency by replacing houses, cars, and factories before they pass their useful lifetimes requires that useful things go unused, which in turn generally implies increase in energy consumption and decrease in GNP growth. As stated earlier and repeated here for emphasis, short-term energy consumption and GNP tend to be closely coupled (as experience in the 1973–74 oil crisis demonstrated), but over decades large beneficial changes can be made.

IV. Environmental catastrophe?

The chemical transformation of oil and coal—chiefly by burning them—has caused almost all the atmospheric pollution that is experienced today as well as much of the water pollution and has been an important cause of illness and death—for example, by heart and lung ailments. It is not yet possible to rank the various available energy sources precisely according to the relative severity of their impacts, and it may not be desirable to try. Different energy supplies meet different needs, so that their relative benefits—which must be set against their impacts—are not strictly comparable. However, there are grave reasons for special concern about the impacts of certain energy sources, given current energy projections. Especially important are the hazards of fossil fuel combustion. Local and regional hazards, for example, arise from emissions of nitrogen and sulfur oxides and particulates into the air. By far the most worrisome global hazard is the prospective buildup of carbon dioxide in the atmosphere, in part as a result of fossil fuel combustion, in part as a result of global deforestation and the oxidation of humus in the ground beneath.

Carbon dioxide (CO_2) comes unavoidably from burning carbonaceous material; there is no realistic means of control other than limiting the use of these fuels. Again, coal is the worst offender per unit of energy, though oil and natural gas, with about 70 and 50 percent, respectively, of coal's CO_2 emissions, also make important contributions.

Atmospheric CO_2 helps to regulate the temperature profile of the earth's atmosphere and surface. This happens because, although the atmosphere is transparent to the wavelengths of incoming solar radiation, atmospheric CO_2 and water vapor absorb the longwave infrared radiation (heat) reradiated from the earth's surface. They thus trap heat and raise surface temperatures; this is usually referred to as the greenhouse effect. Many analyses exist and all are in general agreement that although present accelerated destruction of the world's forest biomass and humus (chiefly in the tropics) now contributes appreciably to the CO_2 buildup, the major calamity would arise from the much vaster reservoir of fossil fuels, especially coal.[8] The present increase in atmospheric CO_2 is accurately and universally observed (e.g., at Hawaii and the South Pole). If present trends continue, the atmospheric carbon dioxide will double within two generations. Still in doubt is the actual effect on global temperatures, but almost all analyses predict an average warming between one and five degrees Celsius, with extra warming in the polar regions.

Government energy planning throughout the world virtually ignores this problem, but it presses now, because the fundamental changes that would constitute a remedy would take a long time. For example, global agriculture, by complicated geographic, social, and institutional arrangements, matches crops to particular areas. Experience shows that total production decreases in time of changing climate, because neither the pattern of land use nor the fertility can change rapidly enough to accommodate; the system has inertia. For example, if rainfall and other weather conditions suitable for growing wheat shifted from the Ukraine to Siberia, the wheat could not at once be grown, because the soil and other favorable conditions would take a long time to develop. And indeed, while the world energy problem is severe, the world food problem is even more critical, with fluctuations of a few percent in the global food production now bringing misery to many.

It is a hard task that lies ahead, to reduce substantially the combustion of coal, oil, and natural gas worldwide, in the face of growing demand for them, especially by developing countries. The options of solar power (probably without using biomass, so as to maintain photosynthetic carbon uptake at the highest practicable level), energy conservation (especially in industrialized countries), and nuclear power thus take on special significance. But the first and most difficult task may be to make people all over the world aware of the problem. No very effective institutional mechanisms appear available to deal with such global matters.

V. What are the long-term options?

Coal, oil, gas will not do, except during a relatively brief transition period. The idea of making large amounts of liquid or gaseous fuel from coal or oil shale becomes very unappealing. Biomass can be used selectively as fuel and sometimes with environmental benefit (e.g., urban and some agricultural wastes), but the penalties for overuse are severe. Geothermal and tidal power offer little hope except at a few special places. Thus we turn *a fortiori* to solar and nuclear power.

The long time it will take to develop and install solar or advanced nuclear power technologies, comparable to the time in which the classic fossil fuels must probably be phased out, provides a sense of urgency. A lively debate exists about whether the relative research and development priorities for the prospective long-term energy sources reflect proper social purposes. In this area, as in many other parts of the energy scene, we find people advocating options on social as much as on technical grounds. But the larger danger may lie in having too few rather than too many good energy options.

In what follows, it is important to note that many of the long-term options produce electricity as their most natural product. This fact bears strongly on the small-versus-large, diffuse-versus-concentrated debates now fashionable. All the nuclear systems are large, and while many of the solar technologies can be modular and small, the questions of interconnections and of backup energy sources lead us to the necessity of accepting substantial centralization. In all but the most primitivistic views of future society, one finds increasing centralization of energy supply and delivery. Even simple solar collectors, if they are efficient and cheap, will probably be made in large factories and depend on mature industries that produce the plastic and metal from which they are made.

Solar radiation is a diffuse source of energy, and large amounts of material are needed for collectors, storage devices, and so on. To build equipment that can capture and convert solar energy to useful forms requires capital investment embodying nonrenewable resources that are far from free, even though sunlight itself is free. The real attractiveness of solar power, besides its ubiquity, is the relative ease with which it can be transformed for a number of uses. However, this attraction has often been oversold by various high-technology schemes. A more realistic view is imperative.

Solar power, by convention, includes not only direct conversion of sunlight into useful forms but also hydroelectric power, winds, and biomass (organic matter). Discussions of this alternative thus tend to be extensive, since applications are diverse and options are hard to compare.

Low technology

The most immediately promising solar application is the production of low- and intermediate-temperature heat from about 70°C for domestic hot water to about 200°C for numerous commercial, agricultural, and industrial purposes. The simplest systems use flat-plate collectors like those on the increasingly familiar rooftop water heaters. More advanced systems use mirrors or simple lenses to concentrate the sunlight and provide higher temperatures. Most require little or no further science or advanced engineering; they will succeed if their design and construction are ingenious and simple enough to make them economically attractive. Another few years of rising oil and gas prices plus improvements in commercial solar systems should be sufficient for this technology to develop a strong commercial position.

High technology

In the past the solar energy program, partly through a history of influence by high-technology agencies, concentrated on tasks with formidable (but interesting) science and engineering problems. At this extreme, we find advanced photovoltaic conversion schemes, the power tower concept (in which a vast array of steerable mirrors focuses sunlight onto a boiler atop a several-hundred-meter tower), and ocean thermal electric conversion systems that exploit the temperature difference between the surface and the deeps of tropical ocean water.

One of the most promising technologies is photovoltaic electricity generation, which is technically feasible in a variety of installation sizes ranging from the individual household to large central station generators. Photovoltaic generators are technically feasible today and are used in space vehicles, in electrical equipment at remote locations, and so forth, where the high cost is justified. Wider applications must await either cost reductions of roughly an order of magnitude, for types in which the basic science is well understood (i.e., single crystals), or scientific development of potentially cheaper types (e.g., vacuum-evaporated thin films). A recent study by the American Physical Society predicts that development of such systems will be slow, providing no more than one percent of U.S. electric power by the year 2000.[9]

The power tower does not look promising. A planned ten-megawatt pilot plant in Barstow, California, will cost $120 million. It will be hard to replicate much more cheaply, because its costs depend so much on those of concrete, steelwork, mirrors, and so on, all of which represent well-developed technologies for which significant cost reductions cannot be expected. A particularly difficult engineering problem is the boiler atop the tower; it must withstand large and rapid thermal fluctuations as clouds pass over the field of mirrors.

Both the ocean thermal energy conversion scheme and, even more, the solar-power satellite scheme are unlikely energy options; they are very capital intensive and full of serious and poorly understood scientific and technical problems.

Windpower devices occupy an intermediate status, neither high technology nor low, and like most other solar technologies should be regarded as augmenting conventional power supply. The official line of development, which tends toward devices with vanes as large as the largest airplane wings, may not be the best approach. Much cheaper and more reliable devices can serve local areas; solid-state electric circuitry can match the electric output of any reasonable-size windmill to the frequency and voltage of power lines.

Many solar energy schemes would benefit from having associated energy storage systems for when the sun does not shine, and virtually all require backup sources for when the storage capacity is exhausted. There are many ways of providing storage, the need varying with the circumstances. A solar-electric system can be begun with its eventual storage system not yet in place, because the conventional electric grid can absorb the small fluctuations. In the long term the best form of storage in connection with solar energy is the production of fluid fuels that can serve as substitutes for hydrocarbons. A wide range of possibilities exists, ranging from making hydrogen by electrolysis of water to various photochemical processes. None has advanced to the point at which it can be seriously considered for engineering development. This is an important and hitherto neglected area for basic research and exploratory development.

VI. Nuclear power

This can be either fusion (joining hydrogen isotopes to produce helium in a super-hot plasma, as it is called), or fission of heavy elements, chiefly uranium or plutonium.

The sun is a fusion reactor, operating with an interior temperature of about 20 million degrees. Its particular mode of operation is much too slow for terrestrial uses: one charge of fuel takes 10 billion years to burn. Reaction times of the order of seconds at much lower density and much higher temperature are required for human purposes, using the less common isotopes of hydrogen—deuterium and tritium (which is mildly radioactive). The science of controlled fusion is fairly well understood, but the remaining (and larger) problems are technological: materials to withstand long-term bombardment by high energy neutrons, remote maintenance and repair of highly activated structures, recovery of tritium, which must itself be replenished in the reactor (in this sense a fusion reactor is a breeder, but of tritium, not uranium or plutonium). Those questions will not be answered in an engineering and economic sense before about the year 2000, so fusion can be looked upon as a possibility for the long term, whose probability of being useful is still uncertain.

With respect to fission, the debate is intense and sometimes proceeds with the finesse and charity of a duel in the dark with chain saws. It has involved governments, public interest groups, private interest groups, and has become the symbol of concern about high technology and the source of outrageous statements. The World Council of Churches appears conditionally in favor of it (under appropriate circumstances);[10] the National Council of Churches of Christ of the United States generally opposes it.[11]

What follows must be understood in the context of nuclear power incipiently withering away in the United States. New nuclear plants are still being built, but hardly any are being ordered, and all this was so before the much-publicized accident at the Three Mile Island plant near Harrisburg, Pennsylvania. Electric utility companies have been discouraged by uncertainty about the social or regulatory acceptability of nuclear power, about whether the federal government will be politically able to resolve the nuclear waste problem, and so forth. These institutional difficulties have been described at some length and are found in other countries as well.[12]

Many criticisms leveled against nuclear power have received so much notice that to repeat them here is unnecessary, and responding to them adequately would fill this book. The radioactivity from normal operation, including that associated with disposal of wastes, is not only small compared to the natural background but small compared to what comes from coal (uranium, for example, in the ash) and (surprisingly) natural gas (traces of radon).[13] But the largest health hazards of coal are not shared by nuclear power at all: sulfur and nitrogen oxides, polycyclic aromatic hydrocarbons and other carcinogens and mutagens, and the well-known miseries of coal mining.[14]

Although good technical solutions appear to exist for disposing of nuclear wastes, public acceptance in these matters is at a low ebb, reinforced in part by a history of relative disregard and nonperformance by many government agencies in the past.[15]

The Three Mile Island nuclear accident was very serious and will lead to changes in specific technological items, in training of reactor and power plant personnel, in management and regulation of nuclear power plants, and perhaps even in government ownership of large sectors of the U.S. electric generating facilities, an arrangement common in most other countries. The event will probably cause an extension of the *de facto* moratorium on ordering new nuclear facilities in the U.S., but whether the moratorium becomes *de jure* cannot yet be foretold.

A lesson to be learned from TMI is that even though the general accident sequence had been foreseen in the U.S. Reactor Safety Study,[16] neither the human elements that aggravated it nor the human ingenuity that prevented it from being worse were fully taken into account. Substantial and rational efforts must be made to minimize the probability of such accidents and to arrange the instrumentation and controls of reactors so that conditions are more rapidly and precisely judged and responded to.

The environmental and ecological problems of nuclear power—water and air pollution, for example—are small compared to those of most other energy sources.

Misassessment of these issues I have just mentioned shows the principle of selective inattention, stated at the beginning of this article. But what follows shows it even more.

A. Proliferation of nuclear weapons

Vertical proliferation, which means present nuclear weapon powers increasing the size or complexity of their nuclear arsenals, has virtually nothing to do with civilian nuclear power. What we are concerned with here is horizontal proliferation, where a country not now possessing nuclear weapons sidles or slides toward a nuclear weapons capability by virtue of the presence of civilian nuclear facilities in the land. This serious problem deserves serious attention.

A country that has no present civilian nuclear capacity, intending to build nuclear weapons, would find it much cheaper and faster to build small plants for that purpose than to build expensive civilian power facilities and then try to convert them. But a country that deploys civilian nuclear power, even with the best of intentions, can change its political intentions, and an existing facility certainly makes the transition to weapons easier. Hence the present concern over the Non-Proliferation Treaty, International Atomic Energy Agency inspections, control over use of nuclear fuel, and so forth.

But the other side of this logical coin is that if highly industrialized countries do not appreciably restrict their appetite for imported oil, thus making matters very difficult for developing countries, the latter will see themselves shut off from too many energy options through events over which they have no control. Thus, regional autarky, suspicion, and an attitude of go-it-alone (or with another supplier) builds up for installing nuclear power. Such attitudes, if commonly held, would lead to destabilization and enhanced danger of conflict. These matters have been discussed at length.[17]

The resolution, albeit difficult, of this problem is to remove the reasons why nations want to build nuclear bombs in the first place. The list of countries quite capable of building nuclear weapons which have decided not to do so is instructive: Australia, Canada, Italy, Japan, Sweden, Switzerland, West Germany, and probably a few more. Almost all are reasonably secure via international interdependence, and all have high enough standards of living to feel in no need to derail the international train of events in order to pick up pieces. The key, then, lies in promoting a cooperative international interdependence (but not based on concepts of neocolonialism); that in turn means paying more attention to the needs of the nonindustrialized countries.

B. Nuclear power as categorical evil?

The memory of Hiroshima and Nagasaki remains, and the shadow of ten thousand megatons darkens our prospects. But the evil lies not in the phenomenon of nuclear fission or in any chemical elements, all of them parts of Creation, but in the nature of man himself who, being given free will, can choose to build toward heaven or toward hell.

This involves high theology as well as high technology, and the issues need setting out. On the other hand, we have those who will claim that at the original Fall, evil entered what had before been a perfect world, and that ever since the world is different: trees are imperfect, man is sinful, and so are his works. The scope of human greed is eloquently set forth by Peter Rideman in the following passage:

> Now, however, as hath been said, created things which are too high
> for man to draw within his grasp and collect, such as the sun with the
> whole course of the heavens, day, air and such like, show that not they
> alone, but all other created things are likewise made common to man.
> That they have thus remained and are not possessed by man is due to
> their being too high for him to bring under his power, otherwise—so
> evil had he become through wrong taking—he would have drawn
> them to himself as well as the rest and made them his property.[18]

Since earliest times people have debated the question whether it is proper to mine the earth, raising issues similar to those today about technology in general and nuclear power in particular. Agricola, in his great sixteenth-century treatise on metallurgy *De Re Metallica*, summarizes the arguments up to that time, taking up these matters of social and moral purpose as the first priority. Regarding the opinions of those opposed to mining, he writes in part:

> First, they make use of this argument: "The earth does not conceal
> and remove from our eyes those things which are useful and necessary
> to mankind, . . . The minerals on the other hand she buries far

beneath in the depth of the ground; therefore, they should not be sought. But they are dug out by wicked men who, as the poets say, are the products of the Iron Age." Ovid censures their audacity in the following lines:

"And not only was the rich soil required to furnish corn and due sustenance, but men even descended into the entrails of the earth, and they dug up riches, those incentives to vice, which the earth had hidden and had removed to the Stygian shades. Then destructive iron came forth, and gold, more destructive than iron; then war came forth."

Another of their arguments is this: Metals offer to men no advantages, therefore we ought not to search them out. For whereas man is composed of soul and body, neither is in want of minerals. The sweetest food of the soul is the contemplation of nature, a knowledge of the finest arts and sciences, an understanding of virtue; and if he interests his mind in excellent things, if he exercise his body, he will be satisfied with this feast of noble thoughts and knowledge, and have no desire for other things. Now although the human body may be content with necessary food and clothing, yet the fruits of the earth and the animals of different kinds supply him in wonderful abundance with food and drink from which the body may be suitably nourished and strengthened and life prolonged to old age.[19]

Then a little later, again regarding iron, Agricola writes:

And next they raise a great outcry against other metals, as iron, than which they say nothing more pernicious could have been brought into the life of man. For it is employed in making swords, javelins, spears, pikes, arrows—weapons by which men are wounded, and which cause slaughter, robbery, and wars. These things so moved the wrath of Pliny that he wrote: "Iron is used not only in hand to hand fighting, but also to form the winged missiles of war, sometimes for hurling engines, sometimes for lances, sometimes even for arrows. I look upon it as the most deadly fruit of human ingenuity. For to bring Death to men more quickly we have given wings to iron and taught it to fly."[20]

An earlier quotation is from Timocreon:

O Unseeing Plutus, would that thou hadst never appeared in the earth or in the sea or on the land, but that thou didst have thy habitation in Tartarus and Acheron, for out of thee arise all evil things which overtake mankind.[21]

Agricola counters all these views by reminding the reader of the benefits accrued by use of metals: plows, for example, and useful tools of all sorts.

In the first place then, those who speak ill of the metals and refuse to make use of them, do not see that they accuse and condemn as wicked the Creator Himself, when they assert that he fashioned some things vainly and without good cause, and thus they regard Him as the

Author of evils, which opinion is certainly not worthy of pious and sensible men.[22]

My purpose in recounting all this is not to pretend that uranium and plutonium are iron but rather to reveal that similar debates have occupied the attention of thoughtful and eloquent people for millennia. We can see our present problems better after practicing on the perspectives available from history. Applied to the present nuclear debate, I see both promise and peril, and the dangerous imperfection of man, susceptible to the sins of avarice, over-ambition, and hubris. Despite these weaknesses, or perhaps because of them, I believe that resolution lies in seeking states of increasing grace and *caritas*, and accepting what is in Creation with an attitude of thanksgiving, dedicating the use of these things to the good of all and not for selfish gain. In a sense, we are junior partners in Creation and should be careful stewards over that part of it entrusted to us.

C. A paradigm of high technology, and therefore to be eschewed?

The previous paragraphs have dealt with this issue. Jacques Ellul is correct that "Techniques"—by which he means all of man's works—can and often do have unfortunate unforeseen consequences. But the absolutist tendency implicit in his attitude leads to other consequences just as unfortunate, or more so. The high technology of Roman iron is low technology for us. "Appropriate technology" would be a better phrase, provided the adjective truly referred to the context.

VII. What to do?

To move toward a more just, participatory, and sustainable civilization, and to take proper account of the outstanding circumstances described in the introductory section, there always was only one energy path, but we had to cut through the undergrowth of the previous sections in order to see it.

The industrialized countries, with their high energy use, economic power, and strong technological base, can control the energy future of the world so long as they can survive. They have the most to lose if global civilization starts to collapse, because, like Rome in the fifth century, they have so far to fall. They also have the greatest capability to alter their technological base, being able to utilize many sorts of technology—high, medium, or low—for the purpose. To them, any and all changes are "appropriate." Among the obviously appropriate changes are more efficient and rational uses of energy, for which more opportunity exists, and as a result of which large energy savings can gradually be made.

The developing countries, with their generally lower energy use and weaker economic and technological base, have less direct conventional control over the world's energy future but have a more justifiable call on whatever low- and intermediate-technology-based resources exist. For this reason, they have less to lose if the global civilization starts to collapse, because like those outside Rome in the fifth century, they live closer to the ground. Having fewer technological options available and more pressing needs, they find it more difficult to modify their energy strategies. The developing countries—all eighty-four of them, as of this writing—had only about one-third as much available oil to use in 1975 as did the United States alone.

Oil (and natural gas where it can be made available) is the fuel of choice for developing countries to start a determined program to reduce permanently their use of carbonaceous fuels—coal, oil, gas—through a combination of more rational and efficient energy use and a gradual accompanying shift to alternative energy resources, which are solar and nuclear. Both will be needed, and both tend to be more electric-oriented than the present mix of fossil fuels. Such a shift dramatizes the problem of how to live with nuclear power, but the problem was with us anyway and would not go away, no matter what some might wish. Perhaps recognizing its inescapability will aid in the resolution of it, which is in any event societal and moral. If solar power turns out to be as successful as we hope, and nuclear power turns out to be unnecessary, so much the better; nuclear power will then wither away naturally. In any case, a shift of a few percent per year toward these alternatives would be quite adequate, but it would not be easy, and it would certainly run counter to economic and political advice which was based on short time perspectives or narrow regional views.

The developing countries gain in several ways by this strategy. They get better interim access to oil and gas, which are more easily matched to their present economies than either nuclear power or the large solar schemes now being developed (though many small ones are broadly applicable), more affordable energy resources when they are needed most, and the chance to build a better civilization. As they develop, such countries will in turn need to shift to noncarbonaceous fuels; if everyone plans carefully, the buildup of carbon dioxide need not strain the global environment beyond its endurance. In all this, the developing countries should find it in their own interest to be energy-efficient also. If solar power wins here too, so much the better.

Such a strategy, whereby the industrialized countries would consciously switch their technological base, could avert the global CO_2 catastrophe in which everyone loses, but especially the highly organized societies. It would also go a long way toward making the developing countries full partners in the global enterprise of managing global affairs. That is important to us all, because people in many developing countries see themselves as standing at the side of a railroad track, watching the train of the industrialized nations going by at ever increasing speed, while they—the developing nations—are increasingly incapable of running alongside, let alone climbing aboard; then their only chance of gaining anything is to derail the train.

It would be better, and even in the interest of the industrialized countries, to have everybody on board the train, and to plan to operate it for the long term.

[1] Charles Singer, E. J. Holmyard, A. R. Hall, and T. I. Williams, *A History of Technology* (Oxford Univ. Press, 1954–58), vol. II in particular.

[2] Plato, Critias III A-C, as quoted by Arnold Toynbee, *A Study of History*, revised and abridged ed. (Oxford Univ. Press, 1972), p. 115 [*GBWW*, Vol. 7, p. 480 b–c].

[3] Edward Gibbon, *The Decline and Fall of the Roman Empire* [*GBWW*, Vols. 40 and 41].

[4] *Oil and Gas Journal*, Dec. 25, 1978.

[5] *The National Energy Outlook*, Shell Oil Company, Houston, Texas, July 1978.

[6] *Energy Needs, Uses and Resources in Developing Countries*, Report BNL 50784 (USA) by P. F. Palmedo, R. Nathans, E. Beardsworth, and S. Hale, Jr. (March 1978), contains a wealth of data.

[7] *See*, for example, "U.S. Energy Demand: Some Low Energy Futures" by the Demand and Conservation Panel, Committee on Nuclear and Alternative Energy Systems, U.S. National Academy of Sciences, in *Science* 200 (April 14, 1978): 142–52.

[8] For example, Minze Stuiver, "Atmospheric Carbon Dioxide and Carbon Reservoir Changes," *Science* 199 (1978): 253–58; U. Siegenthaler and H. Oeschger, "Predicting Future Atmospheric Carbon Dioxide Levels," ibid., 388–95; C. S. Wong, "Atmospheric Input of Carbon Dioxide from Burning Wood," ibid., 200 (1978): 197–200; J. H. Mercer, "West Antarctic ice sheet and CO_2 greenhouse effect: a threat of disaster," *Nature* 271 (1978): 321–25; J. S. Olson, H. A. Pfuderer, and Y-H. Chan, "Changes in the Global Carbon Cycle and the Biosphere," Oak Ridge National Laboratory (USA) Report ORNL/EIS-109 (September 1978), which lists 182 more references.

[9] *Principal Conclusions of the Amer. Phys. Soc. Study Group on Solar Photovoltaic Energy Conversion*, H. Ehrenreich, chairman; published by Amer. Physical Soc. (January 1979).

[10] See *Facing Up To Nuclear Power*, J. Francis and P. Abrecht, eds. (Edinburgh: St. Andrew Press, 1976). *See also* the World Council of Churches journal *Anticipation* Issues nos. 23 (November 1976), 24 (November 1977), 26 (June 1979), W. C. C., 150 Route de Ferney, Geneva, Switzerland.

[11] National Council of Churches of Christ, USA, May 1979.

[12] "Some Institutional Problems of the U.S. Nuclear Industry," T. L. Montgomery and D. J. Rose, *Technology Review* 81, no. 5 (March/April 1979): 53–62.

[13] *Radiological Quality of the Environment in the United States*, 1977 EPA—520/1-77-009 (September 1977).

[14] *See*, for example, "The Hazards of Conventional Sources of Energy," Health and Safety Commission Report of the British Government, April 1978; "Report of the AMA Council on Sources," *Journal of the American Medical Association* 240/20, (Nov. 10, 1978): 2193–95; "Nuclear Power—Compared to What,?" D. J. Rose, P. W. Walsh, L. L. Leskovjan, *American Scientist* 64 (1976): 291–99.

[15] *Management of Commercially Generated Radioactive Waste*, Report DOE/EIS-0046-D vol. 1, table 1.3.

[16] *Reactor Safety Study*, Report WASH-1400 (NUREG-75/014), United States, October 1975 ("The Rasmussen Report").

[17] "Nuclear Power, Nuclear Weapons and International Stability," D. J. Rose and R. K. Lester, *Scientific American*, April 1978, pp. 45–57.

[18] From "Account of Our Religion, Doctrine and Faith, Given by Peter Rideman of the Brothers Whom Men Call Hutterians" (c. A.D. 1545); as reprinted in *The Protestant Reformation*, ed. H. Hillerbrand (Harper, 1968).

[19] Georgius Agricola, *De Re Metallica* (1556); translated by Herbert and Lou Hoover (New York: Dover Publications, Inc., 1950), pp. 6–7. One of the most eloquent treatises and translations of all time.

[20] Ibid., 10–11.

[21] Ibid., 7.

[22] Ibid., 12.

Soft Energy Paths: How to Enjoy the Inevitable

Amory B. Lovins

Amory B. Lovins is an American consultant physicist who has lived in England since 1967. Educated at Harvard College and Magdalen College, Oxford, he has served since 1971 as full-time British representative of Friends of the Earth, Inc., an American nonprofit conservationist lobbying group. His field was originally experimental physics, but since 1970 he has concentrated on energy and resource strategy. Among his current clients are several U.N. agencies, the Organization for Economic Cooperation and Development (OECD), the U.S. Department of Energy, the Solar Energy Research Insititute, and the governments of California, Montana, Alaska, and Lower Saxony, as well as many other organizations in several countries. He is active in energy affairs at a technical and political level in about fifteen countries and has published seven books, several monographs, and many technical papers, articles, and reviews.

Dr. Lovins's earlier education was in music, classics, mathematics, linguistics, law, and medicine, among other subjects. He is married to Hunter Sheldon, a lawyer, forester, sociologist, and political scientist with whom he works on energy policy, and who before her marriage was assistant director of the California Conservation Project ("Tree People"), of which she was a cofounder, in Los Angeles. The Lovinses spend a portion of each summer in the White Mountains of New Hampshire guiding and doing landscape photography.

U ntil the late 1970s there was a broad industry-government consensus, remnants of which still linger, that the energy future should be like the past, only more so: that the energy problem is simply where to get more energy, of any kind, from any source, at any price, to meet projected demands. This view of the problem led to the vision of a solution—qualitatively like figure 1a for the United States and figure 1b for the United Kingdom—which might be called a policy of Strength Through Exhaustion. That solution is one in which increasingly scarce depletable fuels, both fossil and nuclear, would be mined faster and faster, then converted in increasingly complex and centralized plants into increasingly premium forms, especially electricity.[1]

There are many reasons such a policy does not work: some logistical, some political, and some straightforwardly economic. The first section of table I shows that the capital needed to build new energy systems to deliver

Figure 1a: Illustrative U.S. "hard" energy path

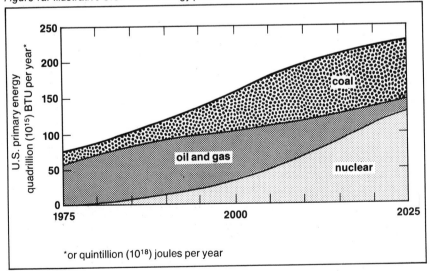

*or quintillion (10^{18}) joules per year

energy to final users at a given rate rises roughly tenfold as we go from the traditional direct-fuel systems on which our economy has been built to offshore, Arctic, and synthetic fuels. The further step to central electrification (power stations and grids) increases capital intensity about another tenfold. This roughly hundredfold total increase makes it impossible for any major country to use these big high technologies on a truly large scale—large enough to replace oil and gas. They are simply so expensive that they are starting to look rather like future technologies whose time is past. Their energy in turn is so expensive that people cannot afford to buy enough of it to pay for the plants.

Yet these are exactly the systems on which the "hard energy path" of figure 1 relies for most of its growth. Just the first ten years of such a program, as proposed by President Ford in January 1975, would have required the United States to invest in the energy sector over $1 trillion, three-fourths of it for electrification. Energy would have needed its present quarter of all discretionary investment, plus about two-thirds of all the rest. There would not have been enough money left to build the things that were supposed to *use* all that energy. Later, the burden of investment would have become even heavier. Putting billion-dollar blocks of capital into projects

Figure 1b: Illustrative U.K. "hard" energy path (Flowers Commission "official strategy," 9/76)

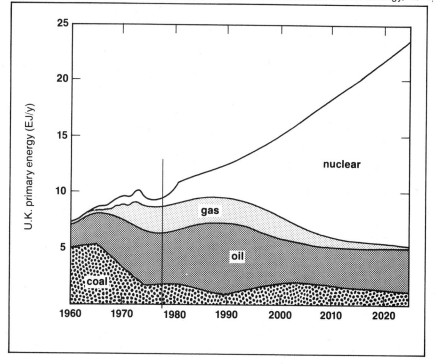

that take a decade to build would also have made inflation worse and utility finance severely unstable.[2] Every big power station built would directly and indirectly *lose* the economy something on the order of 4,000 net jobs by starving other sectors for capital. To add insult to injury, the mismatch between the most critical needs, such as liquid fuels for vehicles, and the main additional supplies which would be of electricity would make our oil problem even worse, while over half the energy growth would never even get to the final users because it would be lost in the process of conversion and distribution.

Such an approach to the energy problem would fail of its technical purpose and make our economic problems even worse. But at the same time it would create serious political problems, which appear to dominate the way we really make public policy decisions about energy. (We often

Table I. **Approximate Capital Investment to Deliver New Energy to U.S. End-Users**

Energy system[a]	Op. date	1976 \$/(BBL·DAY)[b]	Form supplied
HARD TECHNOLOGIES			
(Traditional direct fuels	1950s–60s	2–3,000	fuel)
Arctic and offshore oil and gas	1980s	10–25,000	fuel
Synthetics (coal/shale)	1980s	40,000	fuel
Central coal-el.	1980s	170,000	el.
Nuclear-el. (LWR)	1980s	235,000	el.
"TECHNICAL FIXES" TO IMPROVE END-USE EFFICIENCY			
New commercial bldgs.	1978	–3,000	heat/(el.?)
Common industrial and architectural leak-plugging, better home appliances	1978	0–5,000	heat & el.
Most heat-recovery systems	1978	5–15,000	heat
Bottoming cycles; better motors	1978	20,000	el.
Very thorough bldg. retrofits	1978	30,000	heat
TRANSITIONAL FOSSIL-FUEL TECHNOLOGIES			
Coal-fired fluidized-bed gas turbine with district htg. and heat pumps (COP=2)	1982	30,000	heat
Most industrial cogeneration	1979	60,000	el. & heat
SOFT TECHNOLOGIES			
Passive solar htg. (≤100%)	1978	<0–20,000	heat
Retrofitted 100%-solar neighborhood-scale space and water heat	1985	20–40,000	heat
Same, single house	1985	50–70,000	heat
300°C solar process heat	1980	120,000	heat
Bioconversion of farm and forestry wastes to alcohols/pyrolysis oil	1980	10–25,000	fuel
Microhydroelectric plants	1980	30–140,000	el.
Solar pond/Rankine engine	1979	120,000	el.
Wind-el. (Schachle/Riisager)	1979	70–185,000	el.
Photovoltaics (Patscentre CdS)	1980	110,000	el.

Source: A. B. Lovins, "Soft Energy Technologies," *Ann. Rev. En.* 3 (1978):477–517 (ref. 17).
[a]Empirical cost and performance data except synfuels.
[b]Enthalpic (heat-supplied) basis neglecting potential end-use efficiency.

claim to base such decisions on economics, but in practice we seem to base them on political expedience and then juggle the subsidies to make the economics work out to justify what we just did.) For example, financing tens or hundreds of billions of dollars' worth of unproved facilities that the market has never been willing to finance would require a strong central authority working outside the market—precisely what President Carter sought in 1979. Big, complex energy systems would presumably need big, complex bureaucracies to run them and to say who could have how much energy at what price. Centralized energy systems automatically give the energy and the social costs of getting it to different groups of people at opposite ends of the distribution system. The energy goes to Los Angeles and New York while the side effects go to Appalachia, the North Slope, Navajo country, Montana, Georges Bank. This is an arrangement considered admirable at one end but unjust at the other, so that by 1979 the United States already had more than sixty "energy wars" (serious and sometimes violent conflicts over siting facilities) going on between utilities or siting authorities and, for the most part, politically weaker rural people who do not want to live in a "zone of national sacrifice" for the benefit of people thousands of kilometers away. The Energy Mobilization Board being set up in 1980 to enforce such decisions more expeditiously seems bound to cause unmanageable strains on federalism.[3]

Another disturbing political feature of a hard energy path is that its increasing centralization and electrification make energy supplies much more vulnerable to disruption, whether by accident or malice. Vital energy supplies can be turned off by just a few people, altering the power balance between large and small groups. Societies that do not want to be turned off may need stringent social controls. It is also difficult to make democratic decisions about technologies with compulsory perceived hazards that are exotic, disputed, unknown, even unknowable; and governments seeking to guide such decisions are tempted to substitute "we the experts" for "we the people," elitist technocracy for democratic process. This is gratifying to the experts, but it may lead to a loss of legitimacy.[3] And over all these formidable political problems looms a larger threat of nuclear violence and coercion in a world where, we are told, a few decades hence we are supposed to have some tens of thousands of bombs' worth a year of strategic materials like plutonium running around as an item of commerce within the same international community that has never been able to stop the heroin traffic.

These are some of the simple, direct, first-order side effects of the hard-path approach, and they are still there even if the numerical details are altered within the same conceptual framework. And these problems in turn interact with each other to make a number of new, higher-order side effects which together suggest that the cheap and abundant energy this policy is supposed to produce is not cheap at all: we merely pay for it everywhere else.

Interactive side effects

Suppose, for the sake of argument, that Americans think energy ought to be cheap and therefore continue to subsidize it by over $100 billion per year to make it look cheap. It will then continue to be used wastefully, resulting in high oil imports that are bad for the dollar and American independence, worse for Europe and Japan, and disastrous for the Third World. That much is well known. But now the United States must earn the money to pay for the oil, and it has traditionally done this in three main ways:

- run down domestic stocks of commodities; this is inflationary, makes big holes in the ground, and leaves the forests looking moth-eaten.
- export weapons; this is inflationary, destabilizing, and immoral.
- export produce like wheat and soybeans; this turns the midwestern land markets upside down, probably raises food prices, and encourages us to mine the soil and groundwater.

The United States then—until the Afghanistan invasion—sold some of the wheat to the U.S.S.R., diverting Soviet investment from agriculture into military activities, so the United States had to raise its own military budget which is inflationary. (It had to do that anyhow to defend the sea-lanes to bring in the oil and to defend the Israelis from all those arms just sold to the Arabs—which suggests that the best form of Middle Eastern arms control might be American roof insulation.)

Because the wheat and soybeans then look important to the oil balance of trade, farmers feel driven to ever more water- and energy- and capital-intensive chemical agribusiness. This does in a lot of the natural life-support systems, encouraging still more artificial fertilizers, pesticides, herbicides, desalination, irrigation. The United States is presently mining Pleistocene groundwater in Kansas at twenty times the recharge rate. Average American soil loss is about twenty tons per hectare per year, over fifty in parts of the midwest. A dumptruck-load of topsoil passes New Orleans every *second*. The soil gradually burns out, dries up, blows away, washes away, loses interest—but who cares? At a ten percent discount rate, soil in fifty years is hardly worth anything.

Meanwhile, back in the cities, apparently cheap energy is substituted disproportionately for human skills, displacing people with black boxes. The economists praise this "increased productivity"—by which they mean the increased labor productivity of those people who have not yet been displaced—and tell us that we need more energy to fuel the economic growth that they say we need to employ the people whom we have just disemployed by this very process. So we increase poverty, inequity, alienation, crime, and try to spend money on crime control and health care; but we can't, because we already spent it on the energy sector, which is contributing to the unemployment and illness at which those investments were aimed.

At home, we drift gradually toward a garrison state, trying to protect ourselves from our homemade vulnerabilities. Abroad, rather than address rational development goals, we compete with our trading partners to export reactors, weapons, and inflation to the Third World. These things encourage international distrust and domestic dissent, entailing further suspicion and repression and heightening those same vulnerabilities. Meanwhile, burning more fossil fuels puts more carbon dioxide and other gunk into the air, so that we run the risk of destabilizing the world climate, on which marginal agriculture depends—not least in the midwestern breadbasket on which, by the next century, most people are supposed to be relying for food. Meanwhile, too, our nuclear programs are spreading bombs all over the place.[4]

The list goes on like this; but already it is clear that if such interactive side effects are added up, the sort of world they imply is one that we would not really want to live in. If, as proponents of the hard path state, there is no alternative to it, then the human prospect is indeed bleak. But there is quite a different way to look at the energy problem which makes more sense and leads in a nicer direction. I call it "soft energy path." Sketching it again in an indicative form—not as a precise forecast or recommendation but as a qualitative vehicle for ideas—its main elements might look like figure 2a for the United States and figure 2b for the United Kingdom.

The soft path has three main technical components: using energy very much more efficiently, intelligently using fossil fuels for a transition, and meanwhile rapidly deploying "soft technologies" (defined below). It differs from the hard path not only in how much energy is used and in what kinds of equipment we get it from, but also, most importantly, in its different implications for the political structure of society: a point to which I shall return. First, I must consider three questions: How much energy do we need? What kinds? Where should we get it?

Efficient energy use

It is by now widely accepted in most industrial countries that by insulating houses and by making more efficient cars and machines we can produce the same economic output as today with perhaps 20–30 percent less energy. But the opportunities for wringing more work from our energy are vastly greater than that, even if we use only "technical fixes" listed on Table I— well-known, currently economic technical measures that have no significant effect on life-styles. There are, of course, two ways to use less energy: to curtail or eliminate the services it provides (rooms colder in winter and warmer in summer, dimmer lights, carless Sundays), or to provide unchanged or even expanded services with less energy by using it more productively. The latter type of savings is the only one considered here. They are quite different: insulating your roof does not mean freezing in

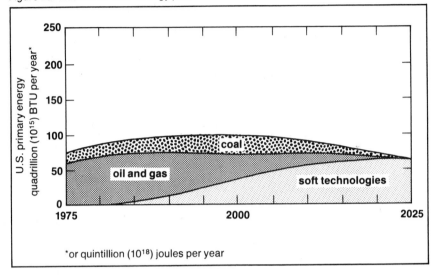

Figure 2a: Illustrative "soft" energy path

the dark, although they are on occasion—perhaps deliberately—confused.

The first firm indication of how far the scope for higher energy productivity had been generally underestimated came only in January 1979, when Gerald Leach and his colleagues published their detailed and ratproof calculations[5] of how to use energy more efficiently in about 400 sectors of the British economy, at a cost of savings that is generally less than the present price of North Sea gas (a very weak economic test). These savings sufficed to treble British primary energy efficiency: real GNP could treble over the next fifty years or so while total British energy use slightly *declined,* simply by using energy in a way that saves money.

My colleague David Olivier then asked what the saving would be if its cost were less, not than present dwindling fuels, but than long-run replacements for them such as the synthetic-fuel plants and power stations now being ordered. His careful work showed a further doubling of efficiency—a trebled GNP with a halving of total energy use—without nearly approaching his economic target, at which the full saving might be nearer eightfold than sixfold.[6] Broadly similar results confirming a cost-effective severalfold efficiency improvement came in during 1979 from many other countries, including Denmark, Sweden, Switzerland, France, West Germany, the United States, and Canada.[7] Why this greater-than-expected scope for saving energy? Partly because the new 1979–80 studies are more detailed than any done previously: they look, in many cases, at literally hundreds of opportunities throughout the economy, thus adding up very many individually small savings, most of which were previously ignored. But these studies also take fuller account of recent technical progress in using energy more productively.

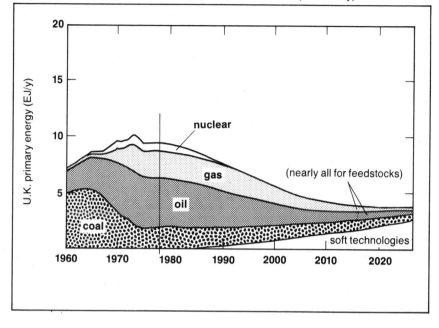

Figure 2b: Illustrative U.K. "soft energy" path (D. Olivier 3/80, preliminary)

It is now technically straightforward and highly cost-effective, for example, to make buildings so heat-tight (with insulation, vapor barriers, and heat exchangers) that they need essentially no space heating even in sub-Arctic climates, and to fix up many existing buildings to nearly that standard. Recent innovations, such as hybrid drive, make it equally easy to build big, comfortable cars that get more than five times the mileage of an average U.S. car in the 1980 fleet. The new generation of jet aircraft being flight-tested in 1980 is about twice as efficient as the existing fleet. Properly sizing, coupling, and controlling industrial electric motors roughly doubles their practical efficiency. Properly designing household electrical appliances roughly quadruples their efficiency at no loss in convenience. Adding up such improvements throughout the economy makes it *not only possible but also economically efficient* to maintain present Western European levels of per-capita economic activity with a total per-capita energy budget of less than one kilowatt—typically about one-fifth the present European and one-twelfth the present North American level. Maintaining such economic activity throughout a completely industrialized world of 8 billion people would require no more energy than the world uses today.[8]

Nor are the rates at which such savings are imagined unreasonable. Leach's trebled efficiency improvement, for example, could be achieved at a more or less linear rate over fifty years (about the retirement date of a major energy supply facility ordered now) if the savings were implemented *more slowly* than they acually were in Britain in the late 1970s. During

1973–78, 72 percent of new U.S. energy supplies came from more efficient use—$2\frac{1}{2}$ times as much as from all supply expansions combined—so that without trying hard, and before the 1978 National Energy Act could work, energy conservation gave the United States twice as much energy-"supplying" capacity, and gave it twice as fast, as synthetic-fuel advocates claim they can do (at ten times the cost if their plants work at all).[9] Even more surprisingly, between 1973 and 1978 the nine EEC countries got 95 percent of their new energy supplies from more efficient use.[10] This is a dramatic comparison of the effects of millions of individual actions in the market with those of a few centrally planned supply projects, including the entire European nuclear program.

It is important to emphasize that the severalfold saving described above does not assume any significant changes in how we live, where we live, or how we run our society. It assumes massive economic growth of a traditional heavy-industrial kind, a "spherically senseless" assumption which makes no sense no matter which way one looks at it, but which I have made anyway for the sake of argument. People who wish to Los Angelize the planet will find a soft energy path the most efficient method to meet the resulting energy needs. People who think today's values or institutions imperfect, on the other hand, are welcome to assume some mixture of technical and social change which will make the energy savings even easier; but the "pure technical fix" assumed here has not done that.

Indeed, this argument merely takes seriously the classical market-economics criterion—to which many analysts pay lip service—of providing our energy services in the cheapest way (omitting all "externalities" as a conservatism). An authoritative analysis of the results of using this criterion in the decade or so prior to 1978, in the light of 1978 energy prices, has found that Americans would then have bought about 28 percent less oil than we did (cutting oil imports in half), bought about 34 percent less coal than we did (eliminating Western strip-mining), bought about 43 percent less elec-

Table II. Evolution of Approximate Forecasts of U.S. Primary Energy Demand in the Year 2000 ($q/y \equiv 10^{15}$ BTU/y $\sim$ EJ/y) (1978 rate $\sim$ 78 q/y)

Year of forecast	Beyond the pale	Source of forecast		
		Heresy	Conventional wisdom	Superstition
1972	125[a]	140[b]	160[c]	190[d]
1974	100[e]	124[f]	140[g]	160[h]
1976	75[a]	89[i]–95[j]	124[g]	140[h]
1978	33[k]	63[m]–77[m]	95[n]–96[m]–101[p]	123[q]–124[r]

a Lovins speeches
b Sierra Club
c U.S. Atomic Energy Commission
d other federal agencies
e Energy Policy Project "ZEG"
f Energy Policy Project "TF"
g U.S. Energy R&D Admin. (ERDA)
h Edison Electric Institute

i von Hippel & Williams (Princeton Univ.)
j Lovins, *Foreign Affairs*, 9/76
k Steinhart (Univ. Wisc.) (for 2050)
m CONAES I-III (for 2010) (*Science*, April 14, 1978)
n USDOE, 9/79, $32/bbl (1977 $)
p Weinberg (IEA-Oak Ridge) "low"
q USDOE, 9/79, $18 & $25/bbl av.
r Lapp (believes E/GNP fixed)

tricity than we did (so that over a third of today's power stations would never have been built), and paid about 17 percent less than we did pay for the energy services we actually received.[11]

The speed with which these conclusions are seeping into official policies is illustrated for the United States (analogously to most countries) by table II, a sociological matrix classifying forecasts of future energy needs (mainly for the year 2000) by date and source. It is a diagonal matrix, with successively lower forecasts becoming one notch more "respectable" every two years, so that the highest 1978 forecast is below the lowest 1972 forecast. The 1980 forecasts now in press fit the same pattern. And we have nowhere near hit bottom: even the lowest entries do not reflect the recent discovery that an energy-conscious materials policy could roughly treble national energy efficiency, and the latest European technical studies[8] imply a long-run U.S. energy need—even with increased affluence—around 10–15 quads, or about one-sixth current levels.

Technology is the answer! (But what was the question?)

It is not necessary to accept this figure, however, to see that if long-term energy needs will be comparable to or below today's, rather than much higher as was earlier feared, then soft technologies can play a proportionately larger and earlier role (fig. 2). By "soft technologies" I mean *diverse* energy sources that are *renewable* (running on sun, wind, and farm and forestry residues), that supply energy in the *scale* and *quality* appropriate to the task, and that are relatively understandable to the user (perhaps in the spirit of a pocket calculator, which is a very high-technology device, but is a tool rather than a machine: I run it, it doesn't run me, and even though I can't make one, I can decide about my use of it).

The question of appropriate scale has given rise to much misunderstanding by people who do not understand its purpose: to minimize the costs (including the social costs) of distribution. Appropriate scale does not mean everything has to be small: it would be just as silly to run a smelter with little wind machines as to heat houses with a reactor. Careful examination, both in energy and in other fields, reveals that the real economies of scale in direct construction costs are often counterbalanced or reversed for most applications (since most energy uses are quite dispersed) by previously uncounted *dis*economies of scale. These include the costs and losses of distribution; inability to use mass production; increased unreliability and need for backup; longer construction time (increasing vulnerability to cost escalation, interest charges, changes in technology or regulatory requirements, and errors in demand forecasting); the political costs mentioned earlier (centrism, autarchy, vulnerability, technocracy, inequitable allocation of costs and benefits); siting problems; loss of diversity, increasing the likelihood and consequences of failure; encouragement of oligopoly; reduced relevance to Third World development; reduced personal responsibility for technologists; increased policy influence of promotional constituencies; and decreased scope for fundamental innovation in technologies that are less fun to do and too big to play with. The first four of these increasingly subtle types of costs are in principle quantifiable, and credible efforts to quantify them have cast serious doubt on whether *net* economies of scale in traditional energy systems are in fact positive.[12]

At least as important as appropriate scale is appropriate energy quality. Though traditional policy treats demand as homogeneous, there are in fact many different forms of energy whose different prices and qualities suit them to different applications. It is the applications that matter: we want comfortable rooms and other real goods and services, not raw electricity or oil for its own sake. Whereas planners of a hard energy path suppose that the more energy we use, the better off we are, and that more energy of whatever kind will meet the need, the object in a soft path is rather to seek just the amount and type of energy that will do each particular task in the cheapest, most effective way. An excess of energy beyond what we require to accomplish our social goals measures not success but failure—failure to do our tasks with an economically efficient minimum of energy, using elegant frugality in both the quantity and the quality of energy we select for each use. This ideal—economy of means, and the right tool for the job—is the basis of all good engineering and the only philosophy consistent with either economic rationality or common sense.

As table III shows, most—in Europe, roughly three-quarters—of all delivered energy needs are for heat, mainly at low temperatures. Most of the rest is portable liquid fuel to run vehicles. Only about 8 percent represents the special, premium uses that need electricity and can give us our money's worth from it, for this very high-quality form of energy is correspondingly expensive: on a heat basis, delivered electricity from a newly ordered power station in the United States (and similarly abroad) will cost over $130 per barrel oil equivalent, or four times the 1980 OPEC crude

Table III. **Percentage of Total Delivered Energy (Heat Supplied Basis) Required in Various Forms in Selected Industrial Countries Around 1975**

Form required	U.S.A.	Japan	Sweden	U.K.	France	F.R.G.	Av.W.Eur.
Total heat	58	68	71	66	61	75	71
<100°C	35	22	48	55	36	50	45
100–600°C	15	31	14	6	14	12	13
>600°C	8	15	9	5	11	13	13
Portable liquids	34	20	19	26	29	18	22
Electricity-specific	8	10	10	8	10	7	7
industrial motors	5	7	6	4	6	4	4
other electrical*	3	5	4	4	4	3	3
(Supplied as electricity)	(13)	(16)	(18)	(14)	(12)	(13)	(11)

*Lights, electronics & telecommunications, electrochemistry, electrometallurgy, household nonthermal appliances, electric rail, arc-welding.

oil price.[13] Such a price might be worth paying for to run motors, appliances, lights, electronics, smelters, railways, and other such premium uses; but all these "electricity-specific" uses, totaling today typically 8 percent of all delivered energy needs, are already oversupplied by current electrical deliveries, as shown in the last line of table III. Still more electricity can therefore only be used for low-temperature heating and cooling (as the surplus has already been used), which is like cutting butter with a chain saw or using a forest fire to fry an egg. It is inelegant, messy, dangerous, and extremely expensive.

Since the energy supply problem is overwhelmingly—typically about 92 percent—a problem of heat and of portable liquid fuels, more electricity is much too expensive (and also too slow) to be a rational response. Arguing about what kind of new power station to build is like shopping for brandy to put in your gas tank, or antique furniture to burn in the furnace. It is completely the wrong question, even though in most countries it accounts for roughly three-fourths of all energy investment and of energy research funds. Our real, unsaturated needs are for heat and vehicular liquids, uses for which new electricity (and usually old electricity too) is grossly uneconomic:[2,14] so much so that if you have just built a new nuclear power station, you will probably *save money* by writing it off and never operating it. Why? Because its output can be used only for heat, but all it is worth paying for heat is what it costs to provide it in the cheapest way. This means draft-proofing, insulation, heat exchangers, greenhouses, etc., which typically cost less than the *running costs alone* for a nuclear plant; so you are better off not running it. (Under American conditions, socializing the sunk capital cost by writing it off at the taxpayers' expense would probably save the country money too, since if the plant did operate, people would probably have to pay even more money in the form of excess running costs plus unpaid federal tax subsidies plus utility profits.[4])

If we are running out of oil, should we not then build power stations? No; that is like being short of bread and cheese and hence substituting beef-steak. If we do not build a nuclear power station, will we not then have to build an oil-fired power station instead? No; that would be like substituting caviar for the beefsteak. Well, then, how about a coal-fired power station instead? No; it does not matter which kind of new power station will send out the cheapest electricity, since *none* of them can come close to competing in either cost or speed with the *real* competitors: efficiency improvements and passive solar heating (in which the building itself captures and stores solar heat rather than using special collectors: this works better than flat-plate collectors, especially in cloudy climates, and costs a small fraction as much). We should thus seek to do in the cheapest way the end-use tasks that we would have done with the oil and gas if we had had them in the first place.

The importance of this end-use orientation is vividly illustrated by a sad story from France, involving what energy planners call a "spaghetti chart" (stylized in fig. 3). Around 1976 the energy conservation planners in the French government started at the right-hand end of the chart, asking how best to heat buildings, their single biggest end-use need. They concluded that the worst way was with electricity, even with heat pumps, so they had, and in principle won, a battle with Électricité de France, as a result of which electric heating is supposed to be discouraged or even phased out because it is so wasteful of money and fuel. Meanwhile, down the street, the energy supply side of the French government started at the left-hand end of the chart, saying: "Look at all that nasty oil going into our country! We want to replace that oil; oil is energy; we must need some other kind of energy. Voilà! Reactors give us energy: we'll build reactors all over the place." But they paid little attention to what happened after that, and so the two sides of the French energy policy establishment proceeded on opposite assumptions about what problem they were trying to solve. Early in 1979 these

Figure 3: A schematic, stylized "spaghetti chart"

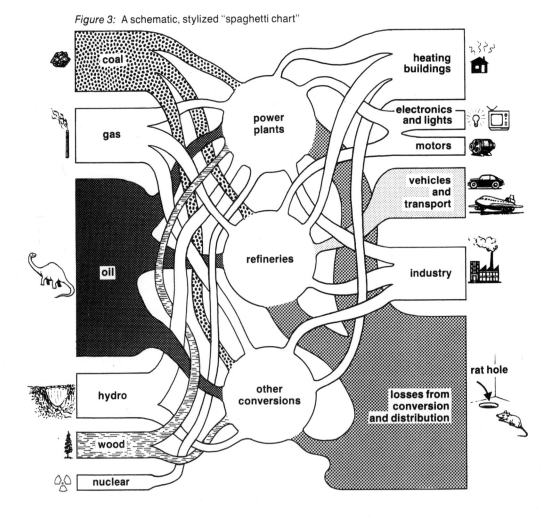

conflicting views collided in the middle: the Ministry of Industry suddenly realized that the only way to sell most of the planned nuclear electricity would be for electric heating, which they had just agreed not to do. Which end of the spaghetti chart we start on, what we think the problem is, is not an academic abstraction; it determines what we buy.

If we want more electricity, we should exhaust opportunities in order of increasing price, by:

- eliminating pure waste (like lighting empty offices at headache level);
- replacing with efficiency improvements and passive solar measures the electricity now used for low-temperature heating and cooling;*
- making motors, lights, appliances, smelters, etc., cost-effectively efficient;
- industrial cogeneration, combined-heat-and-power stations, bottoming cycles that make electricity from low-temperature waste heat, modern wind machines, microhydroelectricity, solar ponds and Rankine engines, filling empty turbine bays at existing dams.

Only after all these would we even think about building new central power stations.

Just the first three items would enable us to support the present life-styles and level of economic activity of the United States (or of many other countries, including Sweden, France, Switzerland, and Canada) with less than a third as much electricity as they now use. The United States would then need no thermal power stations of any kind, but only present hydro, microhydro, and wind power; and the other countries named would all be net exporters of electricity based on present hydro capacity alone.

Likewise, if we want to replace oil relatively quickly, there are only two important ways to do it: make the buildings much more efficient,[15] and get the inefficient cars off the road. Indeed, it would be cheaper than making synthetic fuels to save oil by having the United States Treasury pay from half to all the cost of giving people free diesel Rabbits in return for scrapping their Brontomobiles; or to pay people up to about $200 cash grant for every mile per gallon by which their new car can improve on the efficiency of a scrapped Petropig.[4,16] In contrast, building power stations is the slowest and costliest known way to displace oil.[14]

Soft technologies

These criteria for new energy supplies still do not determine, however, how to replace dwindling oil and gas not just with savings but with new supplies. Having been raised as a high technologist, I had always believed the gospel of nuclear power and synfuels until, during 1976–78, I shopped around for

---

* This is why some U.S. utilities offer to come in and insulate your electric water-heater free: they can resell the electricity saved without having to build a costly new plant to make it.

the best present renewable energy sources which are already in or entering commercial service: devices which are already here and do not require further research. These soft technologies turned out to be sufficient to meet essentially all long-term energy needs in every industrial country so far studied; not only the United States and Canada but also fuel-poor, energy-rich countries such as Britain, France, Germany, Denmark, Sweden, and even Japan.[7] The technologies assumed[17] were only the best present art in

- active and passive solar heating, and passive solar cooling, of efficient buildings;
- solar process heat for industry (contrary to popular belief, collector designs are available which can provide 500–600°C under load on a cloudy day in the winter in northern Europe);
- efficient processes for converting present farm and forestry wastes (but not special crops) to alcohols and pyrolysis oil to run efficient vehicles;
- present hydroelectricity;
- microhydroelectricity, often by rehabilitating abandoned small dams; and
- a modest amount of windpower in appropriate sites.

The analyses did not assume such innovations as cheap solar cells (photovoltaics), even though they will almost certainly be here in the early 1980s before we know what to do with them. The prospect that extraordinarily rapid recent technical progress will continue was ignored. And again contrary to a widespread misconception, the problem of storing energy from the intermittent renewable sources is already solved: it is much *less* difficult than the truly intractable problem of energy storage in a hard energy path,[8,17] provided that one has done the cost-effective conservation measures first. For example, even in a very harsh climate, all the space- and water-heating needs of a cost-effectively heat-tight house can be met, using no backup, with a solar system five to ten times smaller and much simpler than most analyses say would be needed for partial coverage, because those studies assume a solar-heated sieve: there is a strong synergism between heat-saving measures and the design of a cheap solar system which needs so little storage that its storage for 100 percent coverage is cheaper than backup would be without it.[8,17]

Conservative economic comparisons of soft and hard technologies, based on empirical cost and performance data, have shown both under American[17] and European[6] conditions that while the soft technologies are not cheap, they are cheaper than not having them. They may cost more or less than present oil and gas but cost generally less in capital cost (table I) and several times less in delivered energy price (table IV) than the hard technologies that would otherwise have to be built to replace that oil and gas, even weighting the comparison with half-a-dozen conservatisms in the sense least favorable to this result.[17]

That is not the way governments currently make economic comparisons of this sort. They instead compare the supply systems they like (power stations and synfuels) with each other while comparing conservation and solar investments with the historically cheap and often heavily subsidized oil and gas—a test the hard technologies would fail by a much wider margin. If we symmetrically compare all investment opportunities with each other, we find, as a Harvard Business School study[18] has authoritatively confirmed, that the best buys are efficiency improvements, after which come soft technologies, then synfuels, and, costliest of all, new power stations. Historically, the United States and most other countries have taken these options in reverse order, worst buys first.

There is increasing evidence that soft technologies are not only cheaper but also faster than hard technologies: that they return more energy, money, and jobs sooner per dollar invested. This is because they take days, weeks, or months to build, not ten years; they diffuse into a vast consumer market (like snowmobiles, pocket calculators, and CB radios) rather than

Table IV. **Approximate Delivered Energy Prices to U.S. End-Users, Calculated from Empirical Cost and Performance Data (Except Synfuels) Using Conservative Assumptions that Favor Hard over Soft Technologies**

Energy form	Energy system	1976 $/GJ	1976 $/BBL[a]
Subsidized	Natural gas	1.9	11
historic	Coal	2.1	12
fuels (U.S.	#2 fuel oil	2.8	16
regional av.,	Propane	4.4	25
end 1976)	Taxed regular gasoline	5.3	31
	Electricity (residential)	8.7	51
Low-temperature	Improved end-use efficiency,		
heat (35% of	passive solar heat	−0.2–1.4	−1–8
all U.S. end-	100% solar (neighborhood)	1.2–2.5	7–14
use needs)	1976 natural gas/furnace	2.8	16
	1976 #2 fuel oil/furnace	4.1	24
	100% solar (single house)	2.9–4.1	16–24
	Synthetic gas/furnace	5.0–6.4	29–37[b]
	LWR/long-storage heat-pump	7.4	43
	LWR/resistive heater	17.5	101
Process heat	1976 direct coal	2.8	16
(23% of all	Synthetic gas/furnace	6.2	36[b]
U.S. end-use	300°C Winston solar/buffer stor.	7.3	43
needs)			
Portable liquid	Char-oil from Tatom mobile pyrolyzer,		
fuels (34% of	free 50%-wet feedstock	0.8–1.1	5–6
all U.S. end-	Alcohol bioconversion	1.4–4.8	8–28
use needs)			
Electricity	Microhydroelectric	1.7–8.0	10–46
(8% of all U.S.	Solar pond/Rankine engine[c]	6.9	40
end-use needs)	Wind (Schachle/Riisager)		
	with 10-h storage ($6.3/GJ)	10.5–17.2	61–100
	Photovoltaics (Patscentre		
	CdS) with 10-hour storage[c]	7.5	43
	LWR	17.5	101

Source: A. B. Lovins, *Annual Review of Energy* 3 (1978):477–517 (ref. 17).
[a]$/Barrel crude-oil heat equivalent (5.8 GJ) @ 100% conversion eff.
[b]USDOE estimates are ~$40/bbl or $7/GJ.
[c]Solar pond/Rankine and photovoltaics are not assumed in Lovins's soft-path analysis.

requiring tedious "technology delivery" to a narrow market (like reactors and steel mills); and since they come in dozens of categories, each held back by institutional problems largely independent of the others, the dozens of relatively slowly-growing individual "wedges" of soft technology can add up by strength of numbers to rapid total growth—unlike monolithic technologies held back everywhere at once by the same problems.

Nonetheless, essentially complete reliance on soft technologies might take four or five decades to achieve, and meanwhile we shall need to use fossil fuels, briefly and sparingly, for a transition. We should use them in special technologies that are clean, efficient, and designed to plug soft technologies into later. For example, the Swedish national program of installing district heating grids in cities is rapidly implementing a policy of designing the hot-water pipes so as to facilitate a later switch to solar seasonal-storage district heating (which costs only about half as much as active solar heating for individual buildings[17]). Likewise, quite clean ways of burning coal (notably fluidized-bed combustion and recent developments in baghouses with dry sorbents) could help to displace oil and gas now burned under industrial boilers over the next few decades.

The incremental investments of a soft path—in efficiency improvements, soft technologies, and transitional fossil-fuel technologies—would lead to a very different energy future, not by wiping the slate clean, but by starting where we are and doing different things from now on. A soft path does not abolish big technologies: it says that they have an important place which they have already filled up, and that we can take advantage of those we have (like the existing electric grid) without multiplying them further. It is not an anti-technology program; it involves exciting technical problems, but of a different and perhaps unfamiliar kind: seeking devices sophisticated in their simplicity, not in their complexity.

Comparing the paths

The two paths look quite different in an indicative graphical form (figs. 1 and 2), but most of the difference is in the efficiency not of end-use but of the energy system itself (fig. 4). The hard-path primary energy growth goes mostly to conversion and distribution losses that produce no welfare. But in the soft path, matching supply to need gradually squeezes out most of these losses, and extracting several times as much work from each unit of delivered energy yields more delivered functions—goods and services—than in the hard path, even though total energy use is much lower. A soft path does more with less, saving money in the process.

The same diversity that helps to make a soft path faster than a hard path also reduces the risk of technical failure: that risk is spread over dozens of relatively simple things already known to work, rather than put into complicated big coal-gas plants and fast breeder reactors that aren't here and

Table V. **Two Ways to Make 2×10^8 kg/y of Fixed Nitrogen**

Characteristic	Western-style coal-fed fertilizer plant	Indian-style gobar gas plants
Number of plants	1	26,150
Capital cost (10^6)	140	125 (~60 with Chinese tech.)
Foreign exchange (10^6)	−70	0
Direct employment (10^3)	1	131
Energy balance (TW-h/y)	−0.1	+6.35

Source: A. K. N. Reddy, Indian Institute of Science, 560012 Bangalore.

may or may not work. The soft path is environmentally more benign, and hedges our bets on climatic risks by getting out of the fossil-fuel-burning business as fast as possible.[8] Further, it is suited not only to urban and industrial societies but also to modern development concepts, as table V neatly encapsulates: while saving capital and foreign exchange, expanding employment, and providing improved fertilizer, biogas plants can produce enough clean and efficient fuel to meet virtually all of a village's cooking, lighting, and pumping needs (half India's total energy needs today), displacing the inefficient burning of dung, which sends all the nitrogen and most of the heat up in blinding smoke, and of firewood, which has brought about deforestation in many developing countries and so caused devastating erosion. No doubt the power of this development tool is what induced China to install over nine million biogas plants during 1972–78. And as a final geopolitical benefit, the soft path also provides strong leverage against proliferation of nuclear weapons.[4]

Perhaps the most important contrast between the hard and soft paths, and the one that most defines them, is political. Each path entails difficult political problems of very different kinds: in the hard path, centrism, inequity, vulnerability, technocracy; in the soft path, pluralism, getting used to doing through billions of individual choices what we would otherwise have done with a few big projects. The idea that in a problem as complex and fine-grained as energy, central management may be more part of the problem than part of the solution will doubtless be a traumatic adjustment for central managers. There is no free lunch: some lunches are just cheaper than others. There is no energy future free of social problems; we must choose which types of problems we prefer. Those of a soft path seem so much more tractable—and more so in the future, not less—that if its economic and political advantages were allowed to show themselves, such a path would largely implement itself through existing market and political processes.

Indeed, I am no longer concerned with whether we shall end up with something like a soft path, but rather with how difficult we shall make it for ourselves. Will we get there smoothly by choice, or disruptively under compulsion of circumstances when nothing else works? If we wish the former, there are three important ways we can facilitate the transition:

- Clear away a long, messy list of "institutional barriers" (market imperfections)—silly rules and customs which prevent people from using energy in a way that saves money. These include obsolete building codes and mortgage regulations, restrictive utility practices, inequitable access to capital (a problem I think can be rather easily solved[2,19]), split incentives between builders and buyers or between landlords and tenants, and poor access to information.
- Stop subsidizing conventional fuels and power: the United States now provides tax and price subsidies of over $100 billion per year, a very expensive form of self-deception. The California 55 percent solar tax credit is less than the federal tax subsidies being offered to Alaskan

Figure 4a:

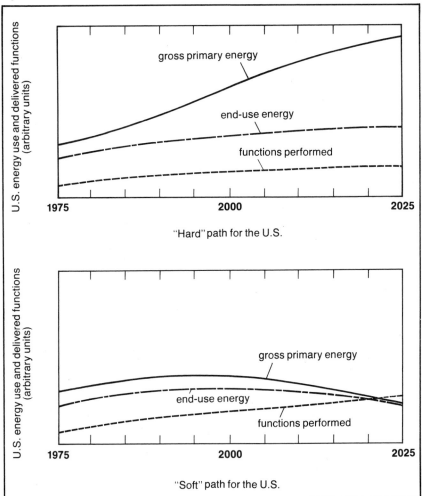

gas, so that after both are subsidized at great public expense, solar heat that is actually cheaper than gas looks more expensive.
- Move gradually and fairly toward charging ourselves for depletable fuels what it will cost us to replace them in the long run.[19] Alternatively,

Figure 4b:

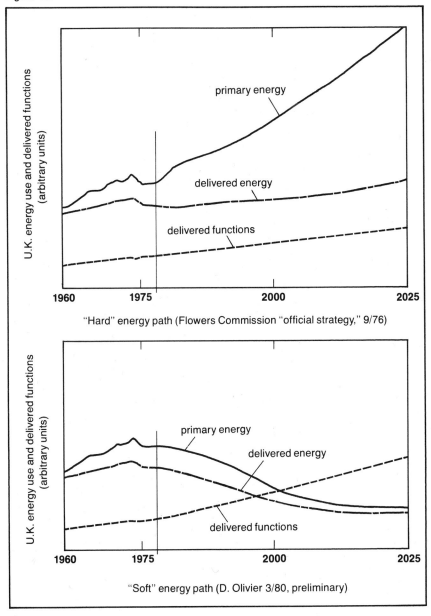

"Hard" energy path (Flowers Commission "official strategy," 9/76)

"Soft" energy path (D. Olivier 3/80, preliminary)

allocate our energy investments as if we had done this already,[2] so evading the awkward problem of tariffs that are both just and economically efficient.

It is not easy to do any of these three things; only easier than not doing them. But if done right, they can command broad political support, for unlike the hard path, the soft path has advantages for almost every constituency. It offers jobs for the unemployed, capital for businesspeople, savings for consumers, chances for small business to innovate and for big business to recycle itself, better national security for the military, environmental protection for conservationists, exciting technologies for the secular, a rebirth of spiritual values for the religious, world order and equity for globalists, energy independence for isolationists, radical reforms for the young, traditional virtues for the old, civil rights for liberals, states' rights for conservatives. It does not, perhaps, satisfy Westinghouse, which has not yet grasped its opportunities and hence wrongly sees it as a threat, but it does run with, not against, our political grain.

A soft path cuts across the ideological disputes that have been stalling energy policy. The Congress of the United States, for example, has already spent three years saying that before we can even start on an energy policy we must agree on price versus regulation, capitalism versus socialism, Jefferson versus Hamilton, the role of the oil companies, the future shape of our society. We have never agreed about any of those things, and we never will. (Life would be dull if we did.) But if we make such agreement a prerequisite for energy policy, hell will freeze over first, maybe literally. In a soft path, however, such disputes hardly matter. If you are an economic traditionalist, most concerned with what's cheapest for you, you can put up your solar system because it's cheaper than not doing it. If you're a worker, you might want to build it because it gives you more and better jobs than building power stations. If you're an environmentalist, you could build it because it's benign, or if you're a social transformationalist, you could build it because it's autonomous. So what? It's still the same collector. You don't have to agree, before or after, about why you built it.

There is an overwhelming consensus in most countries that efficient energy use and appropriate renewable sources are desirable, but there is no consensus on anything else in energy policy, and none is in sight. So perhaps we should push hard on the things we agree about, because they're enough, and then we can forget the things we don't agree about, because they'll be superfluous. We have never tried to design an energy policy around an existing consensus, but it seems long past time we started.

Yet the time left us to do that is short, because although the two paths are both illustrative and embrace infinite variations on a theme, there is a sense in which they are mutually exclusive. This does not mean that hard and soft *technologies* are *technically incompatible*. They're not: there is nothing technical to stop you from putting solar panels on a reactor (it might even work better), and figure 2 shows hard technologies coexisting with soft during a fifty-year transition. But that transition takes place within a social and political context which gives rise to three kinds of exclusivity:

- cultural (each world makes the other harder to imagine);
- institutional (each accretes thick layers of laws, organizations, and customs that inhibit the other); and
- resource competition (every year, dollar, barrel of oil, hour of work, and bit of skill used for one cannot be used for the other).

Where we are today is a fine example: many people cannot imagine any approach to the energy problem except what they've been doing for the past thirty years; copious habits and rules left over from the cheap-oil era are locking us into more of the same; past lopsided resource commitments have manifestly restricted today's options. Continuing these processes threatens to push the soft-technology wedge in figure 2 so far into the future that before we can get to it, the fossil-fuel bridge to it will have been burned.

We ought to be choosing one or the other of these paths before one has foreclosed the other (or before proliferation has foreclosed both). We should ask where we want to be in fifty years and then work backward from our goal to see how to get there smoothly, rather than continue by incremental ad-hocracy, one power station at a time, not asking where we're going. And we should be using the relatively cheap fossil fuels and the cheap money made from them, thriftily, to capitalize a transition to our ultimate energy-income sources, because once that cheap fuel and money are gone, we shall not have another chance to get there.

To grasp what Pogo called these "insurmountable opportunities," we must appreciate that the big, difficult, important, exciting issues in energy policy are not at all too complex or too technical for ordinary people to understand, although they may well be too simple and too political for many technical experts to understand. This realization, and the actions that spring from it, are already going far to solve the energy problem, not from the top down but from the bottom up. Our governments may be the last to know, especially in the diverse, pluralistic societies where grass-roots action has most scope. In early 1980 in the United States, for example, we are approaching our 200,000th solar building, of which half are passive (and half those were made by adding greenhouses to existing buildings). From a quarter to all of the new housing starts in our more solar-conscious communities are passive solar. Over 150 factories in New England and over 40 percent of the houses in northern New England (over half in rural Georgia) have switched from oil and gas to wood. Over half the states have fuel alcohol programs. Over forty main wind-machine companies supply an explosively growing market whose two largest sales in 1979 (to state governments) totaled $235 million. Noting that a system of simple government grants had led the people of Nova Scotia to insulate half their houses in one year, the people of Fitchburg, Massachusetts, designed a program of door-to-door citizen action to do the same in five weeks. (It actually took them seven weeks.) A rich array of renewable and conservation measures is implementing itself through private initiative, simply because it is the only thing people can find that makes economic and political sense. Empirical experience of what actually works is proving abundantly that most people are pretty smart, and, given incentive and opportunity, can go very far to solving their own energy problems, just as they have always solved problems. In that philosophical premise, the Jeffersonians and the market economists appear to be vindicated.

Yet this approach requires governments to approach their task with greater humility: to seek to facilitate and get out of the way. The type of leadership we most need in energy is that stated by Lao-tzu some 2,500 years ago:

> Leaders are best when people scarcely know they exist;
> not so good when people obey and acclaim them;
> worst when people despise them.
> Fail to honor people, they fail to honor you.
> But of good leaders who talk little,
> when their work is done, their task fulfilled,
> the people will all say: "We did this ourselves."

---

[1] The thesis of this article is presented and documented in detail in my *Soft Energy Paths: Toward a Durable Peace* (Harper Colophon, N.Y., 1979; Pelican, U.K., 1977). An updated restatement for less technical readers, by L. Hunter Lovins, is to be published in 1980 by Friends of the Earth [FOE] (124 Spear St., San Francisco, CA 94105) as *Energy Unbound: Your Invitation to Energy Abundance*. FOE published in 1979 a compendium of the two dozen or so best critiques of the thesis, with my responses: *The Energy Controversy: Soft Path Questions and Answers*. More detailed references supplying the rich technical background—necessarily only sketched in this article—are in the sources cited in notes 7, 8, and 17. A continuous update (bimonthly from January 1978) is provided by the International Project for Soft Energy Paths (IPSEP, c/o FOE as above): *Soft Energy Notes,* a newsletter available by subscription and distributed in over eighty countries. A reprint of the first seven issues, through July 1978, is available free as report DOE/PE-0016/1 from the Office of Solar Policy, Office of Policy & Evaluation, USDOE, Mail Stop 7E-088, Forrestal Bldg., Washington, D.C. 20585.

[2] Indeed, even under perfect or no regulation, utilities that keep building power stations will go broke. *See* my "Electric Utility Investments: *Excelsior* or Confetti?" March 1979 paper for E. F. Hutton conference, available from IPSEP, in press in *Journal of Business Administration* (Vancouver), 1980; and *Proceedings of the Conference on Energy Efficiency and the Utilities: New Directions,* California Public Utilities Commission (San Francisco), 1980.

[3] I have argued this further in my "Democracy and the Energy Mobilization Board," *Not Man Apart,* pp 14–15, February 1980, FOE. *See also* the pioneering work (e.g. "Energy Wars and Social Change," 1979) of Prof. Luther Gerlach (Dept. of Anthropology, 200 Ford Hall, University of Minnesota, Minneapolis, MN 55455). On the general problem of how to make energy decisions, *see* Council on Science & Society, "Deciding About Energy Policy" (CSS, 3/4 St. Andrew's Hill, London EC4V 5BY, U.K., 1979); my "Cost-Risk-Benefit Assessments in Energy Policy," *George Washington Law Review* 45 (August 1977): 911–43; and, on welfare economics, Peter Junger's "A Recipe for Bad Water," *Case Western Reserve Law Review* 27 (Fall 1976): 3–335.

[4] This thesis, outlined in chapter 11 of *Soft Energy Paths*, is expanded in "Nuclear Power and Nuclear Bombs" in the July 1980 issue of *Foreign Affairs*; *see also Nature* 283 (1980):817–23.

[5] Leach *et al.*, *A Low Energy Strategy for the United Kingdom*, International Institute for Environment & Development (10 Percy St., London W1, U.K.) and Science Reviews Ltd. (London), 1979.

[6] Work to be published in 1980 by Earth Resources Research Ltd. (40 James St., London W1, U.K.).

[7] *See* refs. 8 and 14; my "Re-Examining the Nature of the ECE Energy Problem," *Energy Policy* 7 (September 1979): 178–98; the proceedings of the May 1979 Rome conference on soft energy paths, in preparation by IPSEP, 1980; and frequent reports of individual studies in *Soft Energy Notes*.

[8] A compact summary of results and references, up to date at mid-January 1980, is my "Economically Efficient Energy Futures," review paper for the March 1980 Münster International Workshop on Energy/Climate Interactions, available from IPSEP, and in press in W. Bach *et al.*, eds., *Energy/Climate Interactions* (Reidel, Dordrecht, 1980). *See also* Solar Energy Research Institute (Golden, Colorado 80401) "Sustainable Prosperity: An Efficient Solar Future," May 1980 draft report to USDOE. This report proposes a decrease of a quarter in total energy use and nearly half in nonrenewable fuel use while real GNP increases by two-thirds during 1980–2000.

[9] Vince Taylor, "The Easy Path Energy Plan," 1979 (*see also* "Energy: The Easy Path" [1979], Union of Concerned Scientists [1384 Massachusetts Ave., Cambridge, MA 02238]).

[10] J. Saint-Geours *et al.*, "In Favour of an Energy-Efficient Society," EEC (Brussels), 1979, Annex 2, p. 1 (*cf* p. 2).

[11] Roger Sant, "The Least-Cost Energy Strategy," Energy Productivity Center, Mellon Institute (Suite 1200, 1925 N. Lynn St., Arlington, VA 22209), 1979.

[12] The issues in this paragraph are explored in depth in chapter 5 of *Soft Energy Paths*, pp. 483–89 of ref. 17, and the sources in ref. 8, note 75.

[13] For details, see *Soft Energy Paths*, chapter 6; my letters in *Science* 201 (1978): 1077–78 and 204 (1979): 124–29; the Appendix to ref. 14; and, updating it, Charles Komanoff (475 Park Ave. S., 32d floor, New York, NY 10021), "Cost Escalation at Nuclear and Coal Power Stations," submitted to *Science*, February 1980.

[14] A. B. Lovins, *Is Nuclear Power Necessary?*, FOE (9 Poland St., London W1V 3DG, U.K.), 1979; also available from IPSEP.

[15] Marc Ross & R. H. Williams, "Drilling for Oil and Gas in Our Buildings," PU/CEES-87, Center for Environmental Studies, Princeton University (Princeton, NJ 08540), 1979.

[16] A. B. Lovins, "Shortcuts to U.S. Energy Conservation," letter, *NY Times*, Jan. 1, 1980.

[17] ———, "Soft Energy Technologies," *Annual Review of Energy* 3 (1978): 477–517, Annual Reviews Inc. (Palo Alto, CA) (also available from IPSEP). For fascinating historical background, *see also* Ken Butti and John Perlin, *A Golden Thread: 2500 Years of Solar Architecture and Technology*, (New York: Cheshire/Van Nostrand Reinhold, 1980).

[18] Robert Stobaugh & Daniel Yergin, eds., *Energy Future* (New York: Random House, 1979).

[19] A. B. Lovins, "How To Finance the Energy Transition," 1979, available from IPSEP. Some U.S. utilities even give zero-interest conservation loans, repayable only when you sell your house, because doing so saves them many millions of dollars.

The Energy Crisis and Foreign Policy: The Diplomacy of Transition

Franklin Tugwell

Senior Analyst of the Energy Program, Office of Technology Assessment, United States Congress, on leave from Pomona College and Claremont Graduate School, where he teaches government, Franklin Tugwell has been concerned with energy policy, especially as it affects the economics of developing nations and the politics of Latin America, for a number of years. A consultant to the Trilateral Commission, he has published a monograph (with John C. Sawhill and others), *Energy: Managing the Transition* (1978), based upon the commission's energy discussions. He has also written on *The Politics of Oil in Venezuela* (1975) and was a contributor to *Search for Alternatives: Public Policy and the Study of the Future,* published in 1973. He was a member of the Energy Committee of the Atlantic Council for 1979–80.

Mr. Tugwell, who received his doctorate from Columbia University in 1969, was twice given awards for excellence in teaching at Pomona College and has lectured widely elsewhere. He has also contributed to symposiums and has been a member of a variety of public and private groups which have met to consider problems of public policy. While working in Washington with the Office of Technology Assessment, he makes his home in Reston, Virginia, where he lives with his wife and two children.

Introduction

O f all that we have learned from the energy crisis, perhaps the most startling lesson is that our technical civilization has bound us together with starving Indians and Islamic zealots in a system of relationships that we are unwilling to do without. Economic damage has been slight compared with the profound shock of this new knowledge. Energy interdependence startles us because we can do little about it at a price we are willing to pay, and because this, in turn, reveals that we have joined a struggle over the biosphere itself that will go on and on.

These observations help place the topic at hand—the conduct of energy diplomacy by the United States—in proper perspective. Studies of energy policy too often focus narrowly on domestic necessities, neglecting the fact that this is ultimately an international problem and that the best solutions are likely to be found in practical measures of international cooperation. What, then, has American foreign policy contributed? Has the United States provided responsible leadership to the other industrialized countries in responding to the energy challenge? Has our policy helped the developing nations cope with the consequences of rapidly rising prices? What should American policy be in the future? In responding to these questions it is useful to begin with the initial American reaction to the recent Arab oil embargo, and with the gradual awakening to the implications of energy dependence and depletion that followed.

From collective security to transition management

The complicated events that led up to the "oil shock" of 1973 drew little notice in the capitals of the industrialized countries. Oil prices had been edging upward since the Caracas OPEC meeting in 1970, but signs of a fundamental transformation of power relationships in world petroleum affairs were widely ignored. Indeed, many Americans were unaware that the United States had become a major importer of crude petroleum and refined products.[1] It is not surprising, therefore, that, with the launching of the OAPEC embargo, the energy "crisis" was perceived in the United States primarily as a diplomatic/security threat, a challenge to the flexibility and freedom of action of the government in the conduct of great-power diplomacy, especially in the Middle East.[2] The Arabs had discovered and successfully deployed an "oil weapon" in their struggle with Israel, and the principal goal of American policy was to protect against, and neutralize, this weapon.[3] Having defined the crisis in these terms, American policymakers then moved quickly to develop initiatives that would respond to it.

Domestically, this took the form of Operation Independence, a plan to make the country entirely self-sufficient in energy resources by 1980. It is sobering to recall the optimistic assessment of the energy picture that underlay the projections of Operation Independence. This was a time of energy speculation of the most unreliable kind, and it merits careful study, especially for those inclined to place confidence in the "latest" estimates of the costs of new technologies or of reserves of undiscovered hydrocarbons. The fact is that the control of energy (except nuclear power) in America, and in much of the world, had been largely a private preserve, in which the role of the public sector was to facilitate and support the activities of private corporations. The government had no independent source of information regarding the oil market or the energy reserves of the world and had developed no contingency plans for the kind of energy emergency that occurred, this despite the fact that embargoes had been tried twice before, albeit unsuccessfully, in Middle Eastern conflicts. For five decades, as the industrial world came to rely increasingly on petroleum for its energy requirements, private companies had supplied that product reliably, in growing quantities, at declining prices. Aside from some complaints about monopolistic practices, there was little reason for the American government to challenge their reign. Thus, in 1973, the Nixon administration felt confident that the private sector could still handle the problem and would respond by quickly increasing the production of new energy in the United States. Offshore oil and gas, and then later oil shale, would provide the answer, "breaking the back of the energy crisis." The United States could become energy-independent once more, destroying the effectiveness of the oil weapon.

The next step was to bring the developed consuming countries together to guarantee their collective security against embargo. Accordingly, Secretary of State Henry Kissinger, in a series of skillful steps, shepherded Japan, Canada, and most of the non-Communist European countries to the signing of the International Energy Program (IEP) and, later, to the establishment of the International Energy Agency (IEA).[4] At the outset of this effort, a concern of the United States was the growing inclination of key oil-importing countries such as Japan and France to break ranks and seek special deals with the OPEC group in order to secure oil supplies. For their part, many of these countries, led by France, feared that consumer cooperation for self-defense would engender a climate of "confrontation," thereby increasing Arab commitment to the use of embargo as a weapon. In order to calm these fears, the United States agreed to broaden the focus as well as the mandate of the consumer group to include a commitment to work toward the less threatening long-term goal of producer-consumer cooperation in energy. Although this gesture did not satisfy the French, who refused to join the group, it did permit the formal establishment of the IEA in 1975.

Although very few Americans have even heard of the IEA, it nevertheless represents an important innovation in economic diplomacy. Among other things, it binds the United States, by treaty, to define its energy security in collective terms; as a result, the United States is legally obligated to share its oil with the eighteen other member countries in time of emergency, and its involvement is to be automatic, in the sense that the American government has waived the right to decide, unilaterally, whether it will do so or not.[5]

The IEA collective security program is based upon a plan for emergency sharing designed to distribute available supplies equitably among member countries during a crisis and to provide a coordinated program of oil stockpiling. The agreement is designed to be activated automatically in the case of a cut in supplies of at least 7 percent. The first line of defense, in this situation, is demand restraint—each country has agreed to formulate a program by which consumption can be dampened on an emergency basis—to be followed by drawdown of emergency stockpiles. These stockpiles, by agreement, are to be enlarged annually until 1980, when each member has agreed to have an equivalent of ninety days of imports in actual storage. The last step is the allocation of supplies, if necessary, among members. An emergency information system has been established to collect operational data from member countries and oil companies during the crisis. In practice, the allocation of oil would be accomplished by means of orders, issued by the IEA itself, to tankers on the sea, redirecting them as needed to equalize access to supplies. The system has been tested twice, in the energy equivalent of "war games" in 1976 and 1978, and a number of improvements have been made as a result.

In addition to establishing a collective security mechanism, the IEA group also agreed to set up a financial "security net," in the form of a loan program of $25 billion, to assist countries that might be unable to handle oil payments, and to establish what was called a "minimum safeguard price" for imported oil. The latter measure was in response to the concern, expressed by many, that new investments in energy would not be forthcoming in the amounts needed for fear that OPEC would collapse and prices would return to pre-embargo levels. Accordingly, after lengthy negotiations, a $7 per barrel figure was agreed to by member countries. In practice, of course, this has never been invoked, nor has the implementation of the price floor been further discussed, although some analysts continue to argue that price reductions are possible.

How successful has this strategy of consumer self-defense been? In view of the obstacles that had to be overcome, quite successful. A recent study of the Emergency Program has concluded that, assuming stockpile obligations are met, the program would provide an effective short-term defense against most kinds of supply disruptions, such as those caused by civil war or embargo. For example, should the IEA lose 9 percent of its supply (as was the case with the 1973–74 embargo), and assuming demand restraint measures are effective and import levels are equivalent to those of 1976, 60 days of net imports in stock would last some 1,800 days, or nearly five years. Should OPEC producers seek to force greater losses and cut their exports by a full 60 percent—a very difficult action for many of the members of that organization—they would be able to force a supply loss of some 20 percent. But even a cut of this magnitude would take a year to deplete 60 days of IEA stocks.[6]

To be sure, problems remain: the stockpile program, notably in the United States, is behind schedule; drawdown and demand-restraint programs remain to be formulated; and any long-drawn-out embargo would almost surely create conflicts between countries such as Britain, with plenty of oil, and Japan, which imports nearly all its energy. But the collective security arrangement has almost certainly forced the OPEC countries to reassess the likely costs of using the embargo weapon and has probably led many of the principal oil exporters to conclude that a targeted embargo, one aimed at one or a small number of consuming countries, would be both difficult and expensive to mount with any hope of success.

While American leaders worked to strengthen the consumer alliance, important changes were taking place in the oil world. On the one hand, it became evident that another embargo was less and less likely to occur. A number of OPEC countries, most notably Saudi Arabia, had begun to accumulate vast currency surpluses, and by investing this money they became increasingly enmeshed in the Western economic system, on which they were dependent to keep their assets viable for future generations. In doing so, of course, they acquired a stake in the health of that system; an economic crisis thus became a threat to themselves as well. This transformation in the definition of Saudi self-interest was important to the United States, which at the same time actively sought to establish a "special relationship" with the royal family of that kingdom. Also important in changing the ambience of oil politics was the progress in U.S.-sponsored Arab-Israeli peace talks.

American diplomatic success in energy affairs was accompanied by growing disillusionment at home, however. The dream of energy independence accomplished by unleashing the creative forces of private industry gave way to growing frustration as it became clear that imports had continued to grow even as prices soared. Even more surprising, American oil companies, disregarding any concern for security, had actually increased the proportion of oil imported from precisely the Arab countries that had embargoed the United States. (*See* Chart I.) Pessimistic reassessments of the amounts of cheap domestic oil and gas left in the ground led the government to the

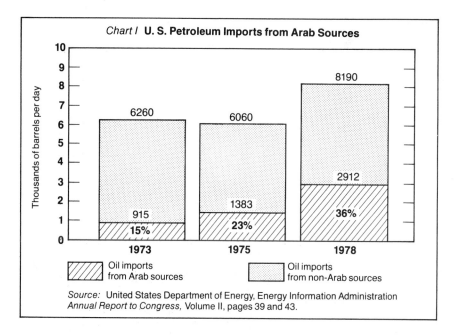

Chart I **U. S. Petroleum Imports from Arab Sources**

Thousands of barrels per day

Year	Value	Arab %	Arab imports
1973	6260	15%	915
1975	6060	23%	1383
1978	8190	36%	2912

Oil imports from Arab sources

Oil imports from non-Arab sources

Source: United States Department of Energy, Energy Information Administration *Annual Report to Congress,* Volume II, pages 39 and 43.

conclusion that, in all probability, production of these fossil fuels would never again reach the levels of the recent past, that America was in fact on the downward slope of the depletion process. And replacements would be expensive, much more expensive than was first thought. The energy crisis, in short, was not a temporary foreign-policy crisis but a full-fledged global transition process that would affect every facet of life as the world moved to a mix of more expensive sources of energy. During this transition, petroleum would for many years remain essential; its use was embedded in the fabric and infrastructure of the economy, and the United States would continue to be tied to the world oil economy.

For energy diplomacy this redefinition of the crisis, eventually codified in clearcut terms in the two National Energy Plans of the Carter administration, forced a reassessment of the nature of the threat facing the country, and of appropriate responses.[7] Long-term dependence on imported oil meant that the Western economic system would be forced to rely for many years on one of the most unstable regions of the world. A secure supply at prices that change only gradually would continue to be essential. This was a key lesson of the 1973–74 crisis. Careful analysis has revealed that the industrial world can almost surely absorb the cost of higher energy prices without serious instability, provided those increases occur gradually.[8] It is sudden increases in price that are so damaging. To be sure, there might be problems in the transfer of funds, and the developed nations would have adjustments to make. But as long as everyone has time to adapt, seek out new sources, and make new capital investments, the transition can be handled.[9] A precipitous change, in contrast, could bring disaster to everyone:

Table I. **OPEC: Crude Oil Production Capacity: 1979** (*in thousands of barrels per day*)

Country	Production capacity	Current production	Country	Production capacity	Current production
Africa*	900	900	Libya*	2,200	1,990
Ecuador	225	220	Neutral Zone*	600	545
Gabon	225	210	Nigeria	2,200	2,185
Indonesia	1,650	1,580	Qatar*	600	455
Iran	5,500	3,600	Saudi Arabia*	9,500	9,500
Iraq*	3,500	3,300	United Arab Emirate*	2,430	1,830
Kuwait*	2,500	2,250	Venezuela	2,400	2,330
			Total	**34,430**	**30,895**

Source: Central Intelligence Agency, *International Energy Statistical Review*, Nov. 28, 1979.
*Indicates Arab members of OPEC.

spurting inflation, severe international debt and recycling problems, a paralysis and even collapse of development efforts in the Third World.

As this picture of the larger threat to world order came to be widely accepted by the leaders of the industrial democracies, a series of forecast studies—by the Central Intelligence Agency (CIA), the IEA itself, and several private groups—warned it was possible that the market for oil would force a price crisis by the early 1980s, or even sooner.[10] Because of consumers' inability to switch away from oil, any insufficiency of supply at even the new higher prices might lead to sudden, uncontrolled price escalation. This, in turn, might set world consumers against each other, trying to outbid each other for available oil. The IEA system made no provision for such a circumstance and would provide no help. Developing countries might find themselves left out entirely, so limited was their purchasing power. Many would be forced to shut down energy-intensive industries completely. Political analysts foresaw the possibility of political instability in many of these countries, as well as in such European countries as Italy, Greece, Turkey, and the new Iberian democracies. The example of the 1930s appeared increasingly applicable.

But how to prevent this? In the short term, clearly, one answer was to fend off a shortage by stifling the growth of demand. Here the IEA system again proved useful. The Secretariat of the IEA drew attention to conservation needs and supervised an assessment of the progress of individual members in setting, and meeting, their targets by slowing the growth of imports and developing alternative sources of energy. In addition, the Governing Board of the IEA issued a set of "principles" that member countries pledged to follow in the conduct of energy policy, and it announced agreement on a group-import target designed to prevent a shortfall from developing.[11] The Iranian revolution, which brought an unexpected decline in available supply, increased the urgency of these efforts and led to the adoption of specific individual-country import limitation targets. These were announced at a special ministerial-level meeting in December 1979. President Carter at this time pledged to limit the flow of foreign oil into the United States to 8.5 million barrels per day, well below the 10 to 12 million barrels per day forecast by many earlier studies.

In the effort to restrain demand, the United States has been the focus of attention because of the sheer size of its energy consumption and because of widespread agreement that there is ample opportunity for conservation in this country. American oil consumption in recent years has accounted for more than half of the total IEA figure, and American automobiles consume one-ninth of all the petroleum produced in the world every day. (*See* Table II.) Like Saudi Arabia among the producing countries, the United States is the "swing" consumer.

But the American citizen has been more difficult to convince of the reality of the energy transition. A long era of declining energy prices, a traditional distrust of political leaders and large corporations, an isolationist impulse following the Vietnam nightmare—these and other things made it difficult for national leaders to convince the public that sacrifices would be needed because of a shortage that might develop sometime in the future. To most Americans, high energy prices were and are the problem, not the solution; Arabs and, probably, oil companies are the villains.

Reflecting these public misgivings, adjusting to the energy transition has been a painful and drawn-out process for the president and the Congress. Repeatedly, the national legislature has rejected strong measures and integrated programs proposed by the executive, giving the appearance of helplessness and incompetence in the face of grave threats to the economic welfare of the country.

OPEC and the West: prospects for accommodation

This, then, is about where we stand today. While conservation is likely to reduce the immediate danger of a price crisis, it remains clear that demand growth will eventually catch up with supply, even at the new, higher OPEC prices set in 1979 and 1980.[12] A defensive alliance of industrial democracies alone simply cannot cope with the task of managing a global energy transition; organized demand restraint can help, but such a job can only really be handled by joint bargaining and planning involving both producers and consumers. In general, a commodity agreement of some kind, based on a common definition of the overall character of the price and supply transition, is the best means of institutionalizing such a process.[13] Is this, then, the appropriate objective of American energy diplomacy? Is it possible to imagine such an agreement in the foreseeable future?

In order to answer these questions, it is helpful to begin with a more careful characterization of the price transition itself and of the orientation of those countries in a position to influence it. The latter may be divided into at least three clusters: the IEA group, led by the United States; the

Table II. **Estimated Imports of Crude Oil and Refined Products: 1978**
(*in thousands of barrels per day*)

	U.S.	Japan	Canada	Western Europe
Algeria	635	7	...	428
Bahrain	3	36	...	4
Egypt	20	negl	...	41
Iraq	75	153	25	1,552
Kuwait	11	508	...	799
Libya	741	3	...	978
Qatar	64	108	...	191
Saudi Arabia	1,228	1,712	133	3,049
Syria	7	...	...	76
United Arab Emirates	424	484	...	807
OAPEC	3,208	3,011	158	7,925
Ecuador	64	...	1	...
Gabon	49	...	...	63
Indonesia	599	657	...	26
Iran	771	852	110	2,053
Nigeria	984	...	...	734
Venezuela	876	6	222	207
OPEC	6,521	4,490	491	10,887
Canada	318	...	...	19
Mexico	469	...	...	...
Other	890	821	174	2,101
Total	8,228	5,347	665	13,128

"moderates" in OPEC, led by Saudi Arabia and including Kuwait, Qatar, and the United Arab Emirates; and the remainder of the OPEC member-ship, most of which tend to be price "hawks" to one degree or another.[14] Political as well as economic differences divide the two groups within OPEC, but the most important distinction is in the need for income and in the projected lifetime of reserves. Chart II presents an illustration of the price strategies each of these groups would prefer. The key assumption in this chart is that a price transition of some kind *will occur,* that is, that the price of oil will rise until it reaches a hypothetical "zone" in which purchasers will begin to choose alternative sources of energy rather than pay a still higher price for an additional barrel of oil. This zone is depicted as a broad one, partly because different users may be willing to switch to alternatives more readily than others, and partly because the alternatives themselves will vary in cost and attractiveness. The actual location of the zone, of course, is a best guess; its location will remain unknown until prices reach it, an important continuing source of uncertainty in energy decision-making. The IEA group would prefer a gradual transition—over as long as ten to twenty years, if possible—to assure plenty of time to adapt, develop alternatives, and prevent economic instability. Saudi Arabia and the price "moderates" prefer rapid, but not destabilizing, movement to the price of alternative energy sources. Their moderation stems from their concern for the world

West Germany	France	U.K.	Italy	Nether- lands	Spain	Other Western Europe
199	75	7	82	11	25	29
...	...	4	...	...	...	...
8	8	25	...	...	...	...
58	411	180	379	80	116	328
44	48	226	212	149	37	83
307	67	31	304	36	114	119
12	84	9	17	18	11	40
294	803	281	455	324	326	566
29	47	...	...	...	...	...
131	194	81	80	76	91	154
1,082	1,737	844	1,529	694	720	1,319
...	...	...	...	...	...	...
22	23	...	3	8	...	7
17	...	...	2	...	...	7
347	209	185	294	325	173	520
207	162	39	21	200	4	101
26	15	24	47	9	39	47
1,664	2,091	1,063	1,896	1,236	936	2,001
3	...	...	...	2	1	13
...	...	...	...	...	...	...
1,144	348	504	466	482	66	1,652
2,848	2,494	1,596	2,362	1,720	1,003	3,666

Source: Central Intelligence Agency, *International Energy Statistical Review*, Nov. 28, 1979.

economy, in which they have a stake, and their strong desire for political stability in the non-Communist world. Their differences with the IEA stem from their determination to obtain the best possible return for their non-renewable resources before these resources are gone.

The price "hawks" are spending all they can earn, and their reserves have a more limited lifetime. They are aware that oil consumers cannot switch away from petroleum quickly, that an aggressive pricing policy, aimed at obtaining the most income, involves raising prices well above the replacement range in the short term and allowing it to sink back down to this range only as the alternatives actually come on line. Since they have little invested abroad, their concern for the welfare of the Western economic system is secondary; in some cases, such as post-revolutionary Iran, actual damage to that system would appear to have become a tacit secondary goal on political grounds.

In simplified outline, then, these are the positions that must be reconciled if the world petroleum economy, and thereby the energy transition itself, is to be managed. Interestingly enough, the key conflict is not between OPEC and the West but between the two groups of OPEC countries. Contrary to its reputation, OPEC is, and has always been, a very weak organization. Its Secretariat is virtually powerless to control member countries, and for practical purposes the organization itself exists only during the actual

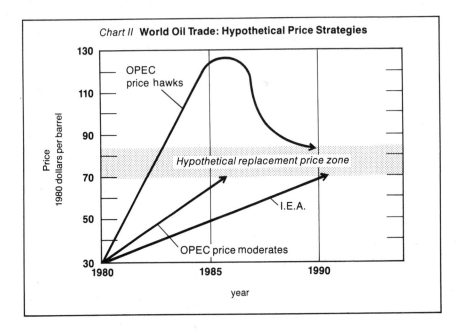

Chart II **World Oil Trade: Hypothetical Price Strategies**

ministerial meetings twice a year. It is not, and never has been, a true cartel. When OPEC was founded in 1960, its creators, Venezuelan Minister of Mines Juan Pablo Pérez Alfonzo and Saudi Sheikh Abdullah Tariki, hoped to form a strong governing mechanism that could set both production levels and prices for the world oil system. But internal divisions proved overwhelming, and neither goal has been attained.

OPEC's principal success, insofar as the market is concerned, has been in establishing a floor under prices, but only after market forces, politically driven, have moved prices upward. Thus, in the 1973–74 crisis the OAPEC embargo gave OPEC the opportunity to follow the market and peg prices at much higher levels. The tightened market that followed the Iranian revolution created a similar opportunity.

Because OPEC cannot control supply, management of the world petroleum economy has fallen by default to Saudi Arabia. With reserves estimated at nearly one-fifth of the world total, Saudi Arabia is in the most favorable position, by varying its production level, to adjust for changes by its fellow OPEC countries and thereby to control supply in such a way as to promote the prices it prefers. In recent years, partly because of the slackening of demand, Saudi production capacity has exceeded its actual output, allowing it to open its valves and sell more whenever it so chose. Since the price hike of 1973–74, Saudi Arabia has consistently used its reserve position in this way and has been opposed by the price "hawks" led by Iran. While pursuing this strategy, it stressed to the United States that its moderation was based on the expectation that the United States would pressure the Israelis to come to terms with the Arabs.

For a number of years the Saudis were successful in their attempt to manipulate the market. Taking into account inflation, oil prices remained stable and may actually have decreased slightly in the years 1973–78. However, the Iranian revolution, and the consequent tightening of the market, made the Saudi position untenable. Spot market prices soared as buyers sought to fill company stocks for the winter of 1979–80, and most OPEC members broke ranks with the Saudis and took advantage of the panic to raise their official selling prices. As the December 1979 OPEC meeting approached, the Saudis negotiated a common price level with other moderates and Venezuela but were unable to convince the rest of the membership to accept their position. Therefore, no agreement was possible, and the price "hawks" left Caracas hoping to use the opportunity to push prices upward and establish a much higher floor, while the Saudis left determined to increase production beyond the 9.5 million barrels per day they had set as a ceiling, in order to stabilize the market. The approach of recession and the impact of newly enacted conservation measures in the United States may allow the Saudis to succeed in their objective, at least for a year or two.

Although it will still be much more costly than they would like, the IEA countries nevertheless would be happier to see the Saudi strategy triumph within OPEC than to face the swift escalation of prices desired by the hawks. For their part, the Saudis are determined to maintain control of the world oil system for as long as they can. Unfortunately, dependence on the Saudis to fine-tune the energy market, even with the assistance of conservation policies in the United States and elsewhere, is hardly a secure or satisfactory alternative. In the first place, the Saudis may not succeed. Depending on their estimates of the price increases that can be achieved, price "hawks" may be willing to cut production substantially to counter Saudi production increases and force prices upward rapidly.[15] Other countries, such as Iran, may be willing to sacrifice earnings in the short run to accomplish this goal.

Nor is it certain that the Saudi government will continue to pursue this strategy. The governing elite of that nation, recruited from an extended royal family with several thousand members, has been divided for years about the best way to develop the country. Some members feel that it would be best to leave as much oil in the ground as possible, exporting only enough to pay for imports. At prices like those reached in 1980, this might mean cutting production by as much as a third. The reasoning is clear: money not spent immediately must be invested, but at the rates of inflation that Western economies have experienced in recent years these investments depreciate faster than they grow. In other words, some of their earning power is lost. That amounts to a kind of payment, by future generations, to keep the world economy stable and strong. Many Saudis clearly doubt that this is justified, and there is no way to anticipate a possible change in that country's policy.[16]

The Saudi government has spent very large sums on an internal development strategy that depends heavily on the success of a plan to manufacture and export petrochemicals and refined products. On the advice of Western experts, the government is hoping in this way to decrease its dependence on crude oil sales, and to build the foundation for a domestic economy that can compete in world markets when the oil begins to run out. Recently, however, a number of analysts have raised doubts about this strategy, suggesting that in fact the Saudis will be unable to produce petrochemicals and refined products at competitive prices and sell them in markets that are already struggling with an overcapacity. Should that turn out to be the case, after so many years of careful planning and enormous investments, there can be little doubt that Saudi elites will reconsider the value of their ties to the United States and their sacrifices in behalf of the Western economic system.[17]

Finally, there is always the possibility that the Saudi government may itself succumb to the political instability that has always accompanied rapid economic development and social modernization. Western analysts often argue that this polity, because of its control by an extended royal family, is not a typical developing nation and is therefore less likely to be overthrown. That may be true. The analytical literature on the politics of modernization, however, strongly suggests that a monarchical regime, under conditions of rapid economic change, is inevitably unstable.[18] Indeed, it is the opinion of this writer that rapid, destabilizing political change in Saudi Arabia is almost certain within the next five to ten years, and when it comes it will almost surely bring with it a sweeping reorientation of development priorities, foreign policy, and oil-export policy.

To conclude, then, reliance on the ability and willingness of the Saudi regime to manage the oil market to avoid the dangers of a radical price increase is almost certainly a poor gamble. The chances are simply too great that the gradual price strategy advocated by Riyadh cannot be maintained and that prices will shoot up, either all at once or in ratchet-like steps, to devastating levels that make even current charges seem moderate. In view of this conclusion, what can the United States do? Before addressing such a question, let us consider briefly the plight of still another group of countries, the oil-poor developing nations, as they face this difficult transition process. For, precisely because the threat to them is greatest of all, they may be able to change the context of OPEC decision-making in ways unavailable to the IEA group.

Energy and development

The seventy-odd non-OPEC developing countries pose a special challenge to American energy diplomacy. Although these countries currently produce and consume small amounts of oil on a world scale—they account for 7 percent and 12 percent respectively of production and consumption—their need for energy of all kinds is the most urgent and will grow most rapidly in the future. And as is so often the case with unequal power and wealth, these countries can be expected to pay the greatest direct and indirect human cost for future energy "crises." Certainly that has been the case to date.

Although precise estimates are difficult, it is generally accepted that the oil-poor, less developed countries (LDC's) suffered an immediate overall reduction in their economic growth of about 2.5 percent as a result of the 1973–74 price increase. To this must be added the indirect damage caused by the price-induced recession, which cut demand for their exports, and by the energy-driven increases in the prices they paid for imported goods and services.[19] Because their growth rates were low anyway, for many countries this amounted to a direct expropriation of their entire economic gains for the year. Ironically, the damage was greatest to those countries that seemed to be doing the best job of dragging themselves out of poverty, since the most energy intensive period of economic growth is usually that in which the basic infrastructure of the country is being put in place. At this stage many countries use twice as much energy—usually liquid fuels—as countries that are already economically developed.

To a certain extent, the impact of the 1973–74 price increase was both masked and alleviated by the availability of loans derived from recycled OPEC gains. Financial transfers to the developed countries doubled between 1973 and 1976, mainly in the form of loans from commercial banks seeking an outlet for their funds. In theory, such loans present an opportunity to obtain development capital and can be considered beneficial. But this is true only if the funds can be used to generate growth and income beyond the interest charges and repayment obligations. Unfortunately, in many cases the funds remaining after payment for energy imports were used instead to finance the maintenance of current consumption levels—it is hard and politically dangerous for the government of a country deep in poverty to ask its citizens to cut back—leaving the countries involved deeply in debt and short of foreign exchange, but with little prospect of earning enough to finance future payments of interest and principal. As a result, many countries are in fact worse off than they were in 1973. In addition, many large international banks, having tripled their holding of LDC long-term debt since 1973, find themselves much more vulnerable to energy price increases. A blow to LDC economic growth and foreign exchange earnings has become a threat to them as well. Accordingly, banks are now reluctant to lend more, thus increasing the sensitivity of the developing nations to further price increases. This alarming pattern of mutual interdependence is a new and powerful motivation in energy diplomacy.

The 1973–74 crisis itself occurred at a time when many developing nations were hoping to use the United Nations as a forum to promote a dialogue between themselves and developed countries concerning the entire system of international economic relations. To many LDC's, the OPEC action in increasing the price of exported oil represented precisely the kind

65

of defensive step they felt all developing nations should consider. Accordingly, there was broad agreement among these countries that they could not side with the industrialized countries in their conflict with OPEC. United States hopes for a broad alliance between the IEA group and the oil-poor LDC's in the North-South Conference on International Economic Cooperation proved ill-founded, despite the obvious economic self-interest binding the two groups of countries.

Disappointed, American policymakers have tended to ignore the urgency of the energy problems of the oil-poor LDC's. Although, as we shall see, there is a certain cruel logic in this, what may appear to make sense in the short term may turn out to have been mistaken in the long run. Because they will be an important source of financial instability, and because they will be the largest incremental users of liquid fuels to the end of the century, the developing nations present some important opportunities. Many of these countries have untapped energy sources, both conventional and unconventional, and as a group they surely contain most of the world's undiscovered oil and gas. Whatever they do to develop their indigenous energy sources of all kinds will tend to ease the competition for OPEC supplies, making the strategy of price "hawks" more difficult.

As a group, developing nations may be able to move ahead more quickly to the era of renewable energy, partly because they must often bear the full price of imported oil for new energy, and partly because they often have not yet fully committed themselves to the capital intensive infrastructure—pipelines and electrical grids—associated with conventional fuels. The United States, through AID, the Department of State, and the Department of Energy, is involved in several small programs designed to assist LDC's in the planning of their energy sectors and in developing small-scale, decentralized renewable energy technologies. Unfortunately, these are very small programs and have been highly fragmented administratively. In considerable degree, too, they have reflected the negative attitude of many U.S. energy administrators toward renewable energy, and the message communicated is that the "sun and dung" technologies are for the poor while the rich intend to continue using nonrenewable hydrocarbons for themselves.

Despite these obstacles, a number of developing nations have decided to move ahead quickly in the development of renewable energy. Several are following the lead of Brazil, for example, in installing alcohol fuel distilleries, and others are investigating the use of small electric generators and anaerobic digesters to process animal wastes for gas for cooking and lighting. Many of the new solar technologies, however, such as photovoltaic conversion systems, are really space-age technologies, and the developing nations are often unable to design and mass-produce them without help. For many of the oil-poor countries, also, the largest single source of renewable energy, forest biomass, has already been depleted by citizens seeking firewood to replace expensive kerosene as a cooking fuel.

The United States has likewise given only lukewarm support to the development of conventional oil and gas supplies in the developing nations. The problem here is both institutional and ideological. The discovery and production of these fuels requires large amounts of capital and access to skills now largely controlled by private companies, many of them American. The leaders of most developing countries are reluctant to provide attractive terms and guarantees to these companies, preferring to develop their own natural resources wherever possible.[20] The United States has tended to side with the oil companies in the sense that it has been reluctant to support initiatives that would circumvent them. A good example of this is found in the career of a proposal by the World Bank to make capital available for the development of LDC conventional energy. Although there were conflicts within the United States government over this idea, the United States in the end was only willing to support this initiative insofar as it did not conflict with the interests of the international companies. The World Bank program has been established and is expected to contribute some $1.2 billion to development efforts in LDC's. But the goal of the program is to serve as a catalyst; the major funding for oil and gas exploration and drilling must still come from other sources.

Here the issue of company attitudes toward the energy crisis requires some comment. The role of the companies has changed rapidly in the years since 1970, and this change is often overlooked. For the most part, the oil companies no longer own concessions but serve instead as intermediaries in the oil market, buying oil from government companies and marketing it in the rest of the world. Because they are now heavily dependent on the good will of producing governments for access to crude, they must often be prepared to respond to the demands of those governments even when the interests of the legal "home" government might be damaged. In addition, because they are intermediaries and because many of them have large continuing interests in domestic production in the United States—soon to be price decontrolled—they can be expected to benefit directly from world price increases. The point here is that the old image of large "American" multinationals whose interests are very close to those of the United States government must be scrutinized carefully. No identity of interests here can be assumed in advance. This applies also to the behavior of these organizations in the oil-poor developing nations.

In part because of the standoff between LDC governments and reluctant oil companies, there has been little exploration and drilling for oil and gas in the LDC's. As research geophysicist Bernardo Grossling has discovered in his tally of company activities, 77 percent of all drilling for oil in the world has been done in the United States, and the concentration of efforts in this country continues in both drilling and geophysical exploration, despite the substantial increases of prices since the early 1970s. Indeed, as the table reveals, there was actually less exploratory activity in the developing nations in 1976 than there was in 1971. This trend is unfortunate.

Table III. **Exploratory Drilling for Petroleum in Developing Countries and the United States[a]**

Number of Wells
(In parenthesis: percentage with respect to 1971 figure)

Region or country	Relative prospective area	Years: 1971	1972	1973	1974	1975	1976
Africa & Madagascar[e]	1.62	251	224	179	189	212	171
		(100)	(89.2)	(71.3)	(75.3)	(84.5)	(68.1)
Latin America	1.53	538	542	488	506	408	439
		(100)	(100.7)	(90.7)	(94.1)	(75.8)	(81.6)
S & SE Asia Ext.	1.01	214[c]	199[b]	295[d]	251	300[b]	208[b]
		(100)	(93.0)	(137.9)	(117.3)	(140.2)	(96.3)
United States	1.00	6,922	7,539	7,466	8,619	9,214	9,234
		(100)	(108.9)	(107.9)	(124.5)	(133.1)	(133.4)

Source: Bernardo F. Grossling, *A Long-Range Outlook of World Petroleum Prospects*, prepared for the Subcommittee on Energy of the Joint Economic Committee of the U.S. Congress, March 2, 1978.
[a]Estimated from data in *Am. Assoc. Petroleum Geologists Bull.*, Foreign Developments issues, and North American Drilling Activity issues, 1972–77.
[b]Data for India and Afghanistan not available.
[c]Data for Burma not available.
[d]Data for Afghanistan not available.
[e]The yearly fluctuations for this region are much influenced by incompleteness of the data. On the other hand, the five-year trend is significant.

In the meantime, of course, the energy supply prospects for oil-importing developing countries have steadily worsened. How, and whether, many of these countries will manage the price increases of 1979–80 is a serious concern throughout the world financial community. The oil import bill facing this group of nations, about $3 billion in 1973, is likely to soar over $40 billion in 1980.[21] And, as mentioned, private banks are now reluctant to increase their exposure by lending to finance oil imports. Unable to borrow, unable to expand domestic supplies of energy in the short term, many developing nations will simply have to defer consumption and, quite literally, suffer the loss.

As might be expected, Third World solidarity has begun to crumble under these pressures. At the recent meeting in Havana of the putatively "nonaligned" nations, a group of consumers, led by Jamaica and India, won agreement from the OPEC countries to discussions, most probably in the United Nations, about future world oil price and supply. Clearly, there is a new consciousness among the OPEC members that the support they have enjoyed is eroding quickly. It is unclear at the time of this writing, however, where these efforts will lead. For example, the OPEC group may try to work out special arrangements to compensate poor importers—by establishing, for example, a two-tiered system of prices. On the other hand, the time may be approaching when serious discussion of a world oil commodity agreement may again be possible. Such conferences take a year or more to prepare and, if the North-South dialogue can be a guide, may last several years as well. For hard-pressed importing LDC's, therefore, the immediate prospect is grim indeed.

Conclusion

As is the case with most foreign policy matters, it is difficult to provide neat, satisfying measures of success or failure in the conduct of energy diplomacy. Any assessment of performance must rely primarily on qualitative judgments regarding the need for action, the relative availability of different options, and the degree of vigor and perceptiveness with which the government has pursued these.

Coming to grips with the energy crisis has been especially difficult for the United States because it involves an acknowledgment that what seemed at first a temporary obstacle to the conduct of great power diplomacy was in fact much more: the first steps in a global adjustment to long-term energy depletion. To the short-term problem of embargo, the American response was rapid and effective. The International Energy Agency is now in place, and the usefulness of the "oil weapon" has been blunted. But the threat of a disruptive price transition continues, and it is a threat to all countries that consume oil and whose economic welfare is tied in some way to the capitalist world system. The United States has found this more difficult to handle; indeed, the current approach, to align ourselves tacitly with the price moderates in OPEC, is unlikely to prove satisfactory for long. But what alternatives are available?

One part of the answer is domestic, and here America is well served by a president willing to risk his political future by forcing the economy to accept, through price deregulation and other measures, the truest measure of scarcity: higher prices. This challenge will continue to test the American political system, for the risk will continue greater than most domestic interests will acknowledge. Conservation, rapid investment in renewable energy, attention to energy stockpiles—all are necessary, and will remain politically dangerous. Success may well depend on the government's ability to convince the American public that there is a better way to calculate the cost of imported oil than the price at the gas pump.[22]

But the larger challenge is still found at the international level. And the time may be approaching, despite bitter political conflicts in the Middle East, when the environment may be more conducive to cooperative, constructive initiatives because of the growing mutual awareness that the international energy system is a collective enterprise in which unrestrained conflict and self-interest may damage everyone. The key to this change, sadly, is likely to be the awful plight of the developing countries. Pressure from that quarter is more likely to break the resolve of the price "hawks" within OPEC than any number of appeals and threats from the wealthy West. The changed strategic climate following the Soviet invasion of Afghanistan may also contribute to a new OPEC willingness to cooperate with Europe, America, and Japan.

Even a marginal improvement in the prospects for an international commodity agreement in oil is important enough to be taken seriously. For the United States, the principal challenge in preparing for negotiations is in building a consensus within the IEA regarding the character of the "price" bridge to the future. This means, among other things, giving up the dream of an OPEC collapse and a return to cheap oil. More important, it also means extending the range of diplomatic vision to encompass global transition issues, for other crises await us as we encroach upon the biosphere's carrying capacity, and any wisdom we can accumulate from our experience with energy is badly needed.

---

[1] The United States became a net importer of petroleum in 1948, but imports remained at low levels until the 1960s. In 1970 domestic production of oil reached a peak and has continued to decline gradually since. It will probably continue to drop as the resource moves toward eventual depletion in the next century.

[2] OAPEC, the Organization of Arab Petroleum Exporting Countries, was the organization that instituted an oil embargo in 1973, principally directed at the United States because of American support for Israel in the war that was in progress at the time.

[3] For an interesting review of the development of U.S. policy in these early days, *see* Henry R. Nau, "The Evolution of U.S. Foreign Policy in Energy: From Alliance Politics to Politics-as-Usual," prepared for the annual convention of the International Studies Association, Feb. 22–24, 1978.

[4] The IEA currently has nineteen members: Austria, Belgium, Canada, Denmark, West Germany, Greece, Ireland, Italy, Japan, Luxembourg, The Netherlands, New Zealand, Spain, Sweden, Switzerland, Turkey, the United Kingdom, and the United States. Norway maintains a special limited membership.

[5] Only the belief that the United States would not actually be called upon to share its oil convinced a reluctant Congress to authorize American involvement in the IEA system.

[6] Edward W. Krapels, *Emergency Oil Reserve Programs in Selected Importing Nations* (London: unpublished mss., 1977). *See also* John Sawhill, et. al., *Energy: Managing the Transition* (New York: The Trilateral Commission, 1978).

[7] For a clear and articulate statement of America's energy quandary, *see* Executive Office of the President, *National Energy Plan II*.

[8] For an estimate of the direct and indirect impact of the 1973–74 oil price increases in the United States, *see* ibid., pp. I–7.

[9] Well-written statements of these adjustment problems can be found in Sam H. Schurr, et. al., *Energy in America's Future: The Choices Before Us* (Baltimore, Md.: Johns Hopkins University Press for Resources for the Future, 1979), and Hans H. Landsberg, et. al., *Energy: The Next Twenty Years* (Cambridge, Mass: Ballinger, 1979).

[10] *See*, for example, Carroll L. Wilson, Project Director, *Energy: Global Prospects 1985–2000* (New York: McGraw-Hill, 1977).

[11] Among the most important principles are ones that pledged members to: (1) formulate specific national energy programs with import reduction a central goal; (2) allow domestic energy prices to rise to levels that encourage conservation and development of alternatives; (3) place strong emphasis on research, development, and demonstration; (4) plan for means, other than decreased oil consumption, to handle a possible supply shortfall.

[12] For an articulate review of prospects, *see* Walter Levy, "The Years that the Locust Hath Eaten: Oil Policy and OPEC Development Prospects," *Foreign Affairs* (Winter 1978/1979).

[13] Precisely such an arrangement has been proposed in a study by Øystein Noreng. *See* his *Oil Politics in the 1980s: Patterns of International Cooperation* (New York: McGraw-Hill, 1978).

[14] Venezuela has, among the latter, been the most "moderate," seeking to serve as a mediator where possible. But its interests incline it toward the high-price group.

[15] The key variable here, of course, is the willingness of consumers to pay more rather than do without. In the short run it is entirely possible that a decision to produce less may be more sensible for an OPEC member. An excellent discussion of the motivations within OPEC can be found in Dankwart Rustow and John Mugno, *OPEC: Success and Prospects* (New York: New

York University Press, 1976). *See also* Charles Doran, *Myth, Oil and Politics* (New York: The Free Press, 1977).

[16] In fact, the Saudis have not increased their actual production capacity in recent years by as much as many oil experts expected, and they have cut down their projected export levels substantially. As time goes by, this compromise between those who would export more, to control prices, and those who would wait may break down as the volume needed to manage the market increases.

[17] On this issue, *see* Louis Turner and James Bedore, "Saudi and Iranian Petrochemicals and Oil Refining: Trade Warfare in the 1980's?" *International Affairs* (London), October 1977.

[18] *See* Samuel P. Huntington, *Political Order in Changing Societies* (New Haven: Yale University Press, 1968).

[19] For more details on the energy problems of developing nations, *see* Edward R. Fried and Charles L. Schultze, eds., *Higher Oil Prices and the World Economy: The Adjustment Problem* (Washington: Brookings Institution, 1975), and Harold van B. Cleveland and W. H. Bruce Brittain, "Are the LDCs in Over Their Heads?" *Foreign Affairs* (July 1977).

[20] The problem is especially acute where there may be deposits of oil or gas too small to attract company interest because of the low likelihood that any surplus will be available for export, but which might make an important difference to the country's own development prospects.

[21] *See* the comments by World Bank President Robert McNamara as reported in *The Energy Daily*, Thursday, October 4, 1979.

[22] On this point, *see* Sam H. Schurr, et. al., *Energy in America's Future: The Choices Before Us* (Baltimore, Md.: Johns Hopkins University Press for Resources for the Future, 1979); and Daniel Yergin and Roger Stobaugh, eds., *Energy Future* (New York: Random House, 1979).

Energy: The International Economic Implications

Ragaei El Mallakh

Ragaei El Mallakh, who is professor of economics at the University of Colorado, Boulder, is an authority on the economics of energy, particularly as they affect, or emanate from, the Middle East, a part of the world he has studied extensively.

Born in Egypt, where he took degrees in both law and commerce at the University of Cairo, Professor El Mallakh won a Fulbright fellowship to the United States in 1951 and took advanced degrees in economics at Rutgers University before going to the University of Colorado in 1956. The department of economics there specializes in resources, energy, development, and international economics and has the largest number of graduate students in economics from energy-producing countries of any institution of higher learning in the United States. From it has evolved the International Research Center for Energy and Economic Development (ICEED), of which Professor El Mallakh is director.

Professor El Mallakh is the author of numerous books, articles, and monographs in his field, among which the most recent are full-length studies of the oil economy of Qatar and of trade and investment in Kuwait. A contributor to many conferences and organizations devoted to energy economics, he was chairman of the First Annual Conference of Energy Economists at Washington, D.C., last year, where he delivered the keynote address.

Experience of the seventies

The decade of the 1970s was one in which the world became aware of energy's critical role in the operation of the global economy. That ten-year span saw sweeping economic changes. The United States became the largest single oil importer, when formerly it had been self-sufficient in this energy source. The price per barrel of "marker" crude rose from $1.80 on January 1, 1970, to $26 on January 1, 1980. The clear distinction between the developed or industrialized and the so-called Third World or developing countries was obliterated. Rising oil prices fed inflationary trends in the OECD (Organization for Economic Cooperation and Development) nations. The non-oil-exporting developing countries were even less able to absorb the shock of energy price increases, so that, for some, economic progress was halted. Together, the LDC's (less-developed countries) paid $11.4 billion more for their purchases of oil in 1975 than in 1970. Considering the size of the gross national product of these economies and the tight foreign exchange requirements, this figure reflects a greater burden than that on the advanced economies of $62.8 billion, which was their increased oil bill for the same period. Moreover, many of the major oil-exporting nations, such as Kuwait, Libya, Saudi Arabia, and United Arab Emirates, found themselves in a new category—wealthy but not industrialized and far from economically developed. Take, as an example, the United Arab Emirates, which in 1970 did not exist as an independent state. Near the close of the seventies, the per capita GNP (gross national product) of this small country was much higher than that of the United States, West Germany, and Japan, and almost three times that of the United Kingdom.

Nor did the decade end on a note of stability. In 1979 the specter of the 1973–74 disruptions and quadrupling of oil prices reappeared. The price of marker crude (Saudi Arabia light of 34° gravity, upon which other OPEC oils are pegged depending upon gravity, sulfur content, and locational advantage to markets) rose from $13.34 per barrel on January 1, 1979, to $26 per barrel as of January 1, 1980. In absolute terms, this is a larger increment than the $8.75 per barrel leap between June 1, 1973, and January 1, 1974, in the wake of supply dislocations caused by the Arab oil embargo. These prices are, or were, for oil tied up in medium- to long-term delivery contracts which traditionally account for upwards of 95 percent of world-traded crude oil. A disturbing phenomenon discernible in 1979 and early 1980 is the shift by some producing countries away from the medium- and long-term contracts to the spot market, where the price is subject to no controls and has jumped at times to more than $45 per barrel. This trend indicates a desire on the part of some oil exporters to exploit the instability in the supply/demand balance and to expand the spot market itself. Furthermore, a number of OPEC producers (e.g., Kuwait, Algeria) have announced production cutbacks as a conservation measure and to slow any price erosion.

There have been definite and, from the consumer viewpoint, positive responses to the stimuli of oil prices and supply disruptions. Prior to the fateful 1973–74 period, global demand for oil had been increasing at approximately 6 percent annually. This historical trend underwent significant change, in part through policy (conservation, regulation), in part from indirect causes, as the market function (higher oil prices) or on account of general conditions (the economic slowdown in the OECD). By 1976 free world oil demand had fallen below the 1973 level. With rising economic activity, worldwide oil demand grew at between 2 and 3 percent annually from 1976 to 1979.

Given the predominance of petroleum, the time required to bring new or additional energy sources on stream, and the lag between the formulation of conservation measures and their implementation, it is clear that the overall global energy balance remains fragile. That fragility is likely to last for much of the 1980s. With respect to supply, OPEC output has remained at about the same level, ranging from 31 million barrels per day (b/d) in 1973 to between a high of 31.3 million b/d in 1977 and a low of 27.2 million b/d in 1975 (reflecting the global recession). This steadying of OPEC production is indicative of both the gradual increase in non-OPEC output and the reduced oil demand growth.

Conservation has played its part as well for exporters (reduction of output) and importers (lowered consumption). The impact of OECD conservation efforts was first apparent in the European states and Japan, and the United States was under pressure from the other industrialized countries to match their lowered consumption rates. American performance of late has been encouraging. The United States has kept its 1979 net oil imports to 7.77 million b/d, well below the 8.2 million b/d ceiling to which the nation was committed by President Carter at the Tokyo summit in mid-1979. This points to a 1.3 percent decrease in net oil imports, which compares favorably to gains in the same year in net imports by Japan (5 percent), West Germany (5.5 percent), and France (5.8 percent).

This reduction in U.S. oil imports can be traced to several factors, among them price-induced conservation and the implementation of certain governmental policies and regulations such as those requiring greater fuel efficiency in autos. Traditionally, the transportation sector's share of American energy has been the largest in final demand (greater than industrial and household and commercial sectors), in contrast to the consumption patterns prevailing throughout the OECD members. This is traceable to the relatively low prices for gasoline and diesel fuel in the United States. For instance, in July 1974, retail prices for regular gasoline (in American dollars per gallon) ranged between 52.9 cents and 65.9 cents within the United States, $1.318 in France, $1.265 in West Germany, $1.747 in India, $1.69 in Italy, $1.361 in Japan, $1.47 in oil-exporting Norway, and $1.25 in the United Kingdom. Only in 1979 did the price of gasoline in the U.S. rise to the levels prevailing elsewhere half a decade earlier. Recent American drops in consumption, then, seem something of a catch-up to the price-induced conservation experienced earlier in the industrialized bloc. In 1979 domestic demand in the United States for oil products declined 1.6 percent, with demand for gasoline off 5.2 percent over the previous year, this being the lowest level since 1976.

OPEC's economic role

OPEC's initial posture was defensive. Excess productive capacity worldwide, output decisions largely in the hands of the foreign concessionaire companies, and the massive crude oil and natural gas production of the United States which served to set world oil prices, all combined to form a buyer's market. In 1959 and 1960, the operating companies unilaterally slashed posted crude oil prices; the latter year saw the birth of OPEC, with Saudi Arabia, Iran, Iraq, Kuwait, and Venezuela as midwives.

OPEC's first decade of existence was characterized primarily by a drive to halt the erosion in prices, to raise producer-nation revenues per barrel through changes in income tax rates and accounting procedures, and to wrest more advantageous financial concession arrangements, ensuring a certain level of exploration activity. The organization's membership increased to thirteen countries.

As the 1970s opened, OPEC shifted its focus to such issues as expanded participation to assert more control over production levels and to move into aspects of the oil industry other than the lifting of crude only, that is, into downstream operations in refining, transportation, and marketing. National oil companies in the producing countries were given a larger role in most areas of operation. Throughout the remainder of the decade, outside forces, such as declining U.S. domestic petroleum output and rising world consumption, joined with producer-country nationalizations of, or drastically increased participation in, the operating concessionaire companies (thereby putting production decisions in the hands of the OPEC states) to alter radically the equation in international oil trade. A seller's market emerged, and the producing countries now had the power to raise or lower output levels to keep the supply/demand balance tight, prices up, and the seller's market intact.

Two issues of overriding concern to the OECD and developing bloc importers alike arose in the 1970s and will continue in the 1980s. They are supply security and the staggering balance-of-payments problem. Clearly, OPEC's production is the key to stability in international oil supply; in 1979, as seen in table I, OPEC accounted for 60 percent of available free world oil. The 1985 range of OPEC output projections given in that table falls between a low of about 55 percent and a high of 62 percent of total available free world oil. Underlying output forecasts for OPEC is the massive proved reserves represented by that body, in 1980 accounting for approximately 435.6 billion barrels or 80 percent of free world reserves and 68 percent of the global total (including the communist bloc). Saudi Arabia alone has one-quarter of the total world proved reserves of oil.[1] The tenuous supply condition which marked the close of the seventies changed from a mild surplus in 1977–78—mistakenly regarded as a glut sufficient to restrain price increases—to a shortage in 1979 brought on by the reduction in Iranian exports of around 2 million b/d; this wreaked havoc on the pricing structure. The precarious supply picture is likely to go on throughout the next decade since some of the major OPEC states (Libya, Kuwait, Saudi Arabia, the United Arab Emirates, and, to a lesser extent, Algeria and Iran) can cut back output and exports to keep the world oil market tight without concomitant budget tightening at home.

While the OECD and the oil-importing developing countries are vulnerable to supply pinches and financial burdens due to upward spiraling oil import bills, OPEC members are vulnerable in their overwhelming dependence on a single commodity for revenues and foreign exchange earnings. The major fear of the large-scale oil exporters is that a too-rapid exploitation of their nonrenewable resource may leave them essentially "oil-less" before sufficient development and diversification of their economies can be achieved. This basic concern is linked to a critical economic problem confronting such key producers as Saudi Arabia, Kuwait, Libya, and the United Arab Emirates—the present absorptive capacities of their economies.

The developmental impact of the vastly expanded oil revenues has been conditioned by the absorptive capacities of respective producer countries. A workable definition of absorptive capacity for capital investment might be in terms of the minimum expected rate of return yielded by an investment that is acceptable to the investor. Since the governments of the oil-exporting nations are the primary investors, the absorptive capacity of these economies for revenues is determined by the minimum rate of return on investment acceptable to the government. Social as well as economic and political benefits can figure in determining the acceptability of investment returns.

All OPEC members suffer to varying degrees from absorptive capacity constraints, despite the current account deficits of some. The bottlenecks causing these constraints can be traced to basic conditions of underdevelopment, specifically the lack of technology, shortages in skilled labor, deficiencies in entrepreneurship, inefficient bureaucracies, and inadequate institutional frameworks. Moreover, some OPEC countries, among them several of the largest exporters, have traditional desert economies which are remote from large-scale modern agricultural and industrial development.

The limitations of absorptive capacity may be seen in the experience of Kuwait, which has the longest history of oil-generated capital surplus. Today, Kuwait's ability to absorb funds domestically is already curtailed because most of the capital-intensive infrastructure and industrial projects are now in place: highways, telecommunications, water supplies, ports, government buildings, refineries, gas-gathering systems and liquefaction plants, and petrochemical complexes. Left with surplus funds, Kuwait has turned to foreign investment. However, there is increasing uncertainty over this alternative approach to the channeling of funds which cannot be absorbed domestically into foreign economic ventures. In recent years, sizable currency fluctuations, especially in the dollar—long the currency of oil payments—and the pound sterling, along with galloping worldwide inflation, have called into question the wisdom of many investments made by Kuwait in the 1970s, including short- and long-term commercial bank liabilities denominated in the dollar or pound sterling. Unless the recycling of such surplus funds can bring positive or better returns, these economic conditions are a disincentive to maintaining, let alone increasing, oil production which generates revenues in excess of domestic absorptive capacity.

As the 1980s begin, the short-term picture is not overly bright. The doubling of oil prices in 1979 has led to a new OPEC surplus of oil revenues over their import bills, reaching possibly in excess of $110 billion in 1980, or more than double the surplus of the previous year. Facing the national and international monetary institutions—commercial banks, central banks, and the International Monetary Fund (IMF)—is their second massive recycling task; the upcoming job is of a far greater magnitude than that following 1973–74. It would not be surprising if the IMF were to increase dramatically its role, particularly with regard to the developing or Third World. By its function in blunting wild fluctuations in the balances of payments of its member nations, the International Monetary Fund can, through lending, diminish the possibility of a return to excessive protectionism and trade wars.

Simply stated, because of the oil price increases, money from both industrialized and developing oil importers flows to OPEC, which can absorb only a limited amount through imports of goods and services from its oil-trading partners; the vast majority of OPEC imports emanates from the industrialized OECD. What does not return through trade from the OPEC states to other nations becomes subject to redistribution. Some funds can be moved through investment into foreign economies, but the real losers are those Third World states which have limited investment appeal to most OPEC countries and which are largely raw material producers themselves.[2]

Energy supply options

One of the first options available to increase the global supply of energy is to develop new sources of oil and natural gas. Given the high prices obtaining now for petroleum and the political tremors and uncertainties wracking the Persian Gulf, exploration is becoming more attractive in sites where costly climatic and geologic conditions exist and in areas where the presence or absence of commercially exploitable petroleum reserves is a complete question mark. Alaskan and North Sea oil development began when prices were relatively low, putting these ventures then in the high-cost category.

By far the most probed regions on the basis of exploration and development wells drilled are, in descending order: the United States (more than 2 million wells); the U.S.S.R. (about half a million); Europe (some 200,000); Canada (approximately 150,000); and Latin America (100,000). Less than 50,000 such wells have been drilled in each of the remaining regions of Africa, the Middle East, China, South and Southeast Asia, Japan, and Australia/New Zealand.[3] Of course, some of these countries or regions are considered to contain a greater share of the world's potentially petroliferous areas than others, a factor not reflected in the frequency of well-drilling to date. As an example, almost half of the potential petroleum-bearing area is located in the Third World—the Middle East, China, South and Southeast Asia, Africa, and Latin America—yet exploration activities there, including even that in OPEC states, account for under 5 percent of such work globally. Thus, the less-developed countries may hold the key to future oil supply. Oil exploration in the Third World has suffered in the past from the lack of adequate data and from political uncertainties inherent in periods of independence movements and nation-building. New technology and the incentive of high oil prices could spur greater interest on the part of both the Third World non-OPEC nations and the oil-hungry OECD seeking to diversify and expand oil supplies. Some non-OPEC developing countries, such as China, Malaysia, Egypt, and Peru, have at present an oil production capacity which can be expanded, and new finds have been made in others, including Guatemala and Sudan. In addition, improved recovery techniques, better reservoir management, and deeper drilling can extend the lives of existing sources in OPEC, the OECD, and the Soviet Union.

The second major option involves expansion of alternatives to oil. As enumerated in table II, these sources in 1979 accounted for some 46 percent of total OECD energy consumption. If natural gas, which is a petroleum product often produced in conjunction with crude oil, is pulled out of the nonoil sources, then the contribution of these alternatives in 1979 drops to only some 27 percent of the OECD's energy consumption.

Once the brightest star on the energy horizon, nuclear power has become something of an embarrassment to its proponents because of waste disposal problems, frequent shutdowns, increasing uranium costs, and cost overruns in plant construction; the unfortunate Three Mile Island near-disaster may

Table I. **1985 Free World Oil Production** (*in million barrels per day*)

	1979	1985
OECD (including natural gas liquids—NGL)		
United States[a]	10.7	9.1–10.3
Canada	1.7	1.5—1.7
Western Europe	2.5	3.5—4.5
Japan	b	b
Australia/New Zealand	0.4	0.3—0.4
OECD total	15.3	14.4–16.9
Non-OPEC less-developed countries (including NGL)		
Latin America	3.0	4.3—5.5
Africa	0.9	1.2—1.7
Asia and Middle East	1.4	1.7—2.2
Total non-OPEC less-developed countries	5.3	7.2—9.4
OPEC		
Saudi Arabia[c]	9.6	8.8–10.5
Iran	3.0	3.5—4.5
Iraq	3.4	3.0—4.0
Kuwait[c]	2.5	1.8—2.3
United Arab Emirates	1.8	1.8—2.2
Libya	2.0	1.8—2.3
Nigeria	2.3	2.0—2.5
Venezuela	2.3	1.7—2.3
Indonesia	1.6	1.5—1.9
Algeria	1.1	0.8—1.0
Ecuador	0.2	0.2—0.2
Gabon	0.2	0.2—0.2
Qatar	0.5	0.5—0.5
Total crude oil	30.5	27.6—34.4
Natural gas liquids	1.0	1.5—1.8
Total OPEC oil and natural gas liquids	31.5	29.1–36.2
Additional possible OPEC reductions		3.0
Reduced OPEC production allowing for contingencies		26.1–33.2
Net exports (imports) of centrally planned economies	0.8	(0)–(1.0)
Total available free world oil	52.8	47.7–58.5

Source: John C. Sawhill, deputy secretary, U.S. Department of Energy, testimony before the Senate
Foreign Relations Committee, United States Congress, reprinted as special supplement,
Petroleum Intelligence Weekly, March 10, 1980, supplement p. 7.

[a] U.S. oil consumption based on Department of Energy February 1980 assessment, including U.S.
territories; other OECD oil consumption estimates based on 1979 assessments by OECD countries.
[b] Negligible.
[c] Includes share of jointly administered Neutral Zone.

have been the last straw. Safety and environmental concerns led to the moratorium declared in 1979 on new American nuclear plant construction. The questioning of nuclear power is prominent not only in the United States; plebiscites have been or will be held on the issue of future nuclear development in many European countries. Although expansion of nuclear energy has not been halted, it has definitely been slowed. The European Community plans envisaged 130 nuclear power stations by 1990; an optimistic forecast now would be for some 100 plants by that year.

Coal output in the OECD underwent a sharp decline after World War II, when cleaner burning oil and natural gas were both plentiful and cheap. Revitalizing that industry has not proved as easily and quickly managed as was thought possible in the mid-1970s. The obstacles have included safety standards, transportation bottlenecks, and environmental controversies over strip mining. For instance, large quantities of clean-burning, low-sulfur coal are found in the western United States where environmental concerns are strong and where the distance to the eastern industrial centers is substantial. While the United States has the world's largest coal reserves, imports of this fossil fuel in 1979 were on the order of 3 million tons, almost double the 1977 level and markedly higher than the 47,000 tons in 1972. The chief reason given by the utilities for these imports is the high rail transport costs within the United States; a typical haul from Wyoming to Texas cost $19.25 per ton in early 1980 compared with $10.93 per ton in 1977.

Solar power remains limited by technology at present to its applications in space heating and cooling and in water-heating systems. Even this application is often of a secondary or complementary backup nature to other systems. As a clean and renewable source of energy, solar power will make its main contribution in the future when technology can lower its cost or other energy forms undergo sufficient price increments to make it competitive. Research and development (R&D) must be continued if solar power is to meet even a modest portion of world energy demand by the year 2000.

Oil shale development still lags, traceable primarily to the absence of low-cost technology, to environmental concerns, and to inadequate water resources in the western United States, where the shale deposits are located. Synfuel (oil and/or gas) from coal liquefaction and gasification as well as gas from unconventional sources remain primarily in the infant stage. Besetting most of the nonpetroleum energy alternatives are three inhibiting factors: cost of production, length of payout period, and technical "bugs" in commercial-scale operations. Most of the alternative energy systems remain primarily at the laboratory technology or pilot plant level, where the full impact cannot be assessed of possible logistical snags and of safety and environmental issues entailing potentially higher costs than expected. To these impediments in developing other nonpetroleum energy sources must be added the reality of lead times, which vary between seven and ten years in most cases and which, under existing inflationary pressures, make cost estimation even more difficult. Thus, the mid-1980s increase in the share of nonpetroleum (oil and natural gas) sources in OECD energy consumption (33 percent) given in table II, while appearing modest, could prove to be, in fact, an upper limit because of these constraints.

Scenarios for the 1980s

Possibly the most damaging course for the United States in the coming decade would be to repeat the vacillation and the inability to formulate energy policy which characterized the seventies. Accounting for almost half of the OECD's and a third of the world's energy consumption, the United States has a critical responsibility in this area. The United States is also the largest single producer of energy, and its performance is equally crucial on the supply side of the global energy equation. The energy problem has been further compounded by hostile attitudes and misconceptions, often based on inadequate information. Public opinion polls have shown a consistent lack of belief in the depth and persistence of the shortages or potential shortages in energy; the causes are variously ascribed to manipulations by the oil industry, greed of OPEC members, or bungling by the U.S. government.[4] This is further borne out by the poll results from 1974 into mid-1979, indicating only about half of the public recognized that at present about 50 percent of the U.S. oil supply is imported. Moreover, energy, and specifically oil, price increases have been singled out as the domestically and politically acceptable explanation for U.S. inflationary woes.

This downplays the other very real causes of inflation: declining productivity, greater governmental regulation, and economic rigidities reflected in wage-price spirals. While energy prices are undoubtedly a factor in inflation within the United States and other OECD nations, they are not the only or possibly even the major factor. Such industrial economies as Germany and Japan, both more heavily dependent upon imported oil and for a longer period than the United States, have a better handle on inflation as well as stronger currencies. And the rate of industrial inflation is cited by OPEC members as the reason for price hikes in an attempt to keep the real value of their oil-generated revenues stable. The oil exporters complain of sky-rocketing import bills for capital equipment essential for their economic development programs and for consumption goods. OECD members' inflation rates take on a moderate cast when compared with those obtaining in many OPEC economies, where some have registered 30 percent or higher annually over the last five years.

Squeezed within this vicious circle are the less-developed countries in which the majority of the world's population lives.

The past decade has shown an oddly impulsive reaction to the energy

Table II. **1985 OECD Energy Demand and Supply: Base Case**
(*in million barrels per day of oil equivalent*)

	1979	1985
Natural gas consumption		
United States	9.7	9.2
Canada	1.0	1.2
Western Europe	3.7	4.6
Japan	0.4	0.9
Australia/New Zealand	0.2	0.3
OECD total	15.0	16.2
Coal consumption		
United States	7.1	9.6
Canada	0.3	0.5
Western Europe	4.9	5.5
Japan	1.0	1.3
Australia/New Zealand	0.6	0.8
OECD total	13.9	17.7
Nuclear		
United States	1.3	2.9
Canada	0.2	0.3
Western Europe	0.8	2.2
Japan	0.3	0.5
Australia/New Zealand	...	...
OECD total	2.6	5.9
Hydro/geothermal/other		
United States	1.5	1.8
Canada	1.0	1.4
Western Europe	1.7	2.2
Japan	0.3	0.4
Australia/New Zealand	0.2	0.2
OECD total	4.7	6.0
Total OECD nonoil energy consumption		
United States	19.6	23.5
Canada	2.5	3.9
Western Europe	11.1	14.5
Japan	2.0	3.1
Australia/New Zealand	1.0	1.3
OECD total	36.2	46.3
Oil consumption[a]		
United States	18.7	18.4
Canada	1.9	2.1
Western Europe	14.8	16.0
Japan	5.6	6.3
Australia/New Zealand	0.8	0.8
OECD total consumption	41.8	43.6
OECD stock build-up	1.0	0.4
Total OECD oil demand	42.8	44.0
Total OECD energy demand	79.0	89.8

Source: John C. Sawhill, deputy secretary, U.S. Department of Energy, testimony before the Senate Foreign Relations Committee, United States Congress, reprinted as special supplement, *Petroleum Intelligence Weekly*, March 10, 1980, supplement p. 7.

[a] U.S. oil consumption based on Department of Energy February 1980 assessment, including U.S. territories; other OECD oil consumption estimates based on 1979 assessments by OECD countries.

problem—both in sufficient physical supply and the monetary aspects—in postures of confrontation, ad hoc decisions, lack of medium- and long-term planning, and a failure to move collectively. Neither oil-importing nor exporting nations have been exempt, as witnessed in OPEC's inability to come up with a unified price in 1979.

An alternative course would involve a coordinated, multifront attack on the energy problem in three areas. First, alternatives to oil must be more vigorously developed, but with a realistic acceptance as to time frame. The 1980s will likely see an intensification of investment in energy R & D with supply repercussions appearing in the 1990s. Alternatives to oil are not necessarily deemed a threat to OPEC; reduction of oil consumption in power generation by utilities and in heating will extend the life-spans of existing petroleum reserves, thus allowing this source to be utilized for a longer period of time as a petrochemicals feedstock and for the hard-to-replace uses in transportation. Second, conservation can and should be a positive method of easing supply pressures by lowering demand, particularly in the transportation sector. The price mechanism and incentives are beginning to bring noticeable results in conservation. Third, the sorely needed coordinated action should recognize the interdependence of the consumer-producer relationship. A collective importing-nation approach or that by a collective exporter bloc has done little either to stabilize prices, to stabilize the value of oil-generated funds, or to spur the production of nonoil alternatives. Coordination, if not cooperation, between energy exporters and importers could serve to stabilize supply and allow for orderly price increases with moderation. Further coordination could join OPEC capital with OECD technology to ensure continuing energy supplies in the long term through wider petroleum exploration activities worldwide as well as by research and development into the coming era of diversified and renewable energy systems.

---

[1] These proven reserves estimates are taken from the widely accepted source *Oil and Gas Journal*, December 31, 1979, pp. 70–71.

[2] A short treatment of the monetary upheavals and absorptive capacity issue is offered in Ragaei El Mallakh, "Where Does the OPEC Money Go?" *The Wharton Magazine*, Winter 1980, pp. 34–39.

[3] This aspect has been studied by Peter R. Odell, "A Personal View of 'Missing Oil'," *Petroleum Economist*, January 1980, pp. 21–23.

[4] U.S. public perceptions of the energy problem and the ramifications for conservation and policy formulation have been traced by Rene D. Zentner, "The Myth of Energy Conservation," in *Energy Options and Conservation* (Boulder, Colorado: International Research Center for Energy and Economic Development [ICEED], 1978) and "The Energy Crisis Revisited: Policy Options for the '80s," in *New Policy Imperatives for Energy Producers* (Boulder: ICEED, 1980).

World Energy and the Challenge to Industrial Civilization

Willis W. Harman

Willis W. Harman, who was trained in physics and took a doctorate in electrical engineering from Stanford University, has in recent years devoted himself to social policy analysis and futures research, principally at SRI International, where he is associate director of the Center for the Study of Social Policy. His work at SRI has involved research into alternative futures and the analysis of energy policy and other major social problems, subjects on which he has written a number of papers. He has been a consultant to the National Goals Research Staff of the White House and also to the Conference Board in New York and was a member of the Technical Advisory Board of the U.S. Department of Commerce from 1973 to 1977.

Dr. Harman has been active also in the Association for Humanistic Psychology and served for a time as both a member of the executive board and of the editorial board of the *Journal of Humanistic Psychology*. In 1978 he became president of the Institute of Noetic Sciences in San Francisco, founded in 1973 to advance the state of intuitive knowledge, creativity, and subjective experience. He has recently published a book, *An Incomplete Guide to the Future* (1979), summarizing what he feels he learned during his first ten years in the field of futures research.

The world energy situation in brief is:

(a) The industrialized world will not have the fossil fuel energy to continue on its present path, and there will not be renewable energy sources developed in time to substitute.

(b) The developing world will not have the energy to develop in the pattern of the industrialized world.

(c) There will soon be global awareness of these facts.

All the rest is commentary. It revolves around what responses will be made to this situation.

The world becomes ever more dependent on supplies of oil and natural gas which are rapidly approaching a state of scarcity. There are no substitutes for these fuels that do not impose high economic, environmental, and social costs. The shift to renewable sources must be made eventually and the later the shift starts the more difficult it will be; however as long as there remain any reasonably cheap fossil fuels, economic rationality militates against development of renewables. Eventual reduction in average per-capita energy-use rate seems both prudent and probably inevitable; yet the effects of this on productivity and material standard of living make the prospect look dismal.

Within this picture there is much room for argument—and much argument. Isn't there enough oil and gas for decades to come—and enough coal for centuries? What about new synthetic fuels? How about nuclear power? And fusion? And photoelectric breakthroughs?

We must look into those questions, of course. But then we need to go on and examine why the world energy situation is far more fundamental than simply a matter of what energy sources are developed.

A conventional view of world energy supply

Modern industrial society is designed to run on petroleum and natural gas. Massive road-building dwarfs all other public works; automobile production is central to the economies of the most highly industrialized nations. An enormous chemical industry depends upon natural gas as its basic raw material. Only England and West Germany among industrialized countries derive less than two-thirds of their energy needs from oil and gas. As earlier societies had been shaped by the advent of new energy sources—draft animals, sailing ships, waterwheels, coal—so modern industrial society is shaped by its energy sources. Urbanization and agribusiness alike depend upon cheap, easily transportable liquid and gaseous fuels.

Although estimates vary tremendously, the total energy potentially available in fossil fuels around the world is probably something of the order of 10^{23} joules. Of this about two-thirds is in the form of coal and lignite. Around a fifth is petroleum and natural gas, and something like another fifth is heavy oil, oil shale, and tar sands. Of the total world supply of recoverable fossil fuel energy, approximately 1/400 is used up every year at the present rate. The vast majority of the present use, over two-thirds, is oil and gas. World oil production will turn downward in the next ten to twenty years, and there will be severe regional shortages before that. World natural gas production will peak out a little later, but still only decades away.

During the last quarter century world fuel consumption tripled, oil and gas consumption quintupled, and electricity use grew nearly sevenfold. Such trends cannot be sustained indefinitely, especially the trend with regard to oil and gas. Clearly there has to be a shift of energy sources in the near future—from oil and gas to something else. There may also have to be changes in the ways and amounts in which energy is used.

The substitute fuel most obvious because of its relative plenitude is coal—both for direct energy supply and for conversion to synthetic liquid and gaseous fuels. But there are fundamental environmental problems attending both the extraction and the combustion of coal. Underground mines may cause surface lands to subside; there are also problems with mine drainage contaminating streams. Surface mines pose severe problems of land reclamation, particularly in arid and semi-arid regions. Coal combustion produces emissions of fly ash, sulfur oxides, toxic metals, and carcinogenic organic compounds.

Another candidate group of synthetic fuels includes heavy oil, oil shale, and tar sands. Because of the heat required in extraction of these fuels and, in the case of the latter two, the amount of material that has to be moved or disposed of, costs and environmental problems are high.

There is still another problem that arises from the burning of fossil fuels, no matter what kind. That is the potentiality of climate shifts associated with the buildup of carbon dioxide in the atmosphere. Carbon dioxide from the combustion of fossil fuels is eventually absorbed in the process of photosynthesis by plants, in the formation of carbonates in water, and in other ways. However, this is a very slow process compared with the rate at which it is currently being produced. As a result the level of carbon dioxide concentration in the atmosphere has been going up steadily with the increase in combustion of fossil fuels. It has gone up something like 10 percent since the turn of the century and if present trends continue would double by around 2020. The resultant effects on climate would be significant (if unpredictable in detail) due to the "greenhouse effect," a capturing of solar energy that would otherwise have been reflected back out into space. Some countries might gain from the climate changes; some would undoubtedly lose as rainfall and temperature patterns shift. Desertification is already a serious global problem; it tends to worsen with any shift in rainfall patterns because soil destruction is a much more rapid process than soil formation.

Not too long ago it was widely assumed that nuclear technologies would be available to take over energy supply functions as oil supplies began to give out. As is well known, it turns out that nuclear fission and breeder technologies lack public acceptance on safety grounds, and fusion power will apparently not be available nearly as soon, nor as cheaply, nor as "cleanly" as was expected.

Solar energy is another story. In the first place, there is already a tremendous amount used. All the waterpower and windpower however used throughout the world is solar power. So is all the firewood. Furthermore, all homes and buildings and their outside environments are primarily solar heated. Were it not for the heat of the sun they would be at a temperature of some 240°C below zero; only the last few degrees of "room temperature" are provided by oil or gas. The usual energy accounting methods predispose us to overlook the extent of our existing dependence on solar energy. Its potential contribution is great, even in the relatively near term. Solar energy systems can easily and satisfactorily be used to warm homes and work places, dry grain, or provide industrial process heat. Most of the fuel burned around the world provides heat at temperatures solar collectors could easily achieve. Solar electricity and higher temperature heat are already economically competitive in much of the Third World.[1]

Nevertheless, to shift to major dependence on solar energy would involve a tremendous capital investment and many years. If nuclear power is not going to be socially acceptable, and if fusion is problematic, it will be necessary for the world to move in the direction *both* of rapid conversion to renewable sources and of restructuring industrial society to use far less energy than present projections suggest.

If industrialized societies face difficult energy problems, the energy crisis of the Third World is even more severe. Traditional energy sources — principally firewood, charcoal, and forage for draft animals — are growing scarce and expensive. Where ecological carrying capacities have been exceeded, forests are receding and grasslands are becoming deserts. Third World deforestation is advancing rapidly, and with it the erosion of topsoil; where this has silted up reservoirs still further problems result. Dependence of developing countries on world oil supplies has been increasing, and these countries are in a poorer position than the industrialized nations to absorb or offset the adverse economic impacts of rising oil prices.

The above discussion summarizes some of the conventional arguments about world energy problems and policies. Now we need to take a broader and more fundamental look at these matters.

The sobering lesson of entropy

The conventional portrayal of the economic process as a self-sustaining, circular flow between "production" and "consumption" (or in more elaborated form in input-output tables) is seriously misleading in one very important respect. It encourages neglect of the fact that the economy requires inputs from the environment—energy and resources—and spews back into the environment waste heat and waste materials. This important general property of the economy is related to the Entropy Law of thermodynamics.

This law states essentially that (a) all kinds of energy are gradually transformed into heat, and heat flows by itself only from a hotter to a cooler region (never in reverse), so that it tends to get more and more dissipated and unavailable to do mechanical work; and (b) matter, too, is subject to an irrevocable dissipation (with one exception, to be mentioned just below). Entropy is a measure that can be thought of as an index of unavailable energy (energetic entropy) or of material dissipation (material entropy). The tendency of order (e.g., the arrangement of materials in a house) to become disorder (e.g., scattered by a tornado) can be counteracted through the directed use of available energy (e.g., by picking up the fragments, transporting them to the original spot, and reassembling them). This is the exception noted above—energetic low entropy can be exchanged for material entropy, thus reversing the natural tendency toward dissipation.

The world economy can be accurately said to run on low entropy (*see* figure). It requires as inputs the low entropy of high quality energy (mainly from fossil fuels and the sun) and of concentrated material resources (e.g., rich ores, hydrocarbon feedstocks). The economy exudes high entropy in the form of waste heat and rubbish. Life processes in the environment restore some of this waste to a low-entropy form (e.g., plants converting carbon dioxide to plant structure); the remainder accumulates.

The greater the economic activity, the greater the amount of low entropy required by the economy, and the greater the amount of high entropy cast forth into the environment. This is true despite recycling (which uses up low entropy) and "pollution control," which may convert noxious wastes into less undesirable ones but does not eliminate the waste (although it may cause it to accumulate in a less undesirable location). The inexorability of the situation was well stated by economist Georgescu-Roegen: "'Bigger and better' motorcycles, automobiles, jet planes, refrigerators, etc. *necessarily* cause not only 'bigger and better' depletion of natural resources but also 'bigger and better' pollution."

Thus it is no accident, but rather a fundamental characteristic of the economy, that material resource use and energy use have risen essentially proportionally with measures of economic activity such as the GNP. All but a few percent of the energy use has been from fossil fuels and will continue to be so well toward the end of the century, despite the longer term promise of the "inexhaustible" sources. It is also fundamental that whatever is accomplished in the way of making waste products less noxious, the total amount of waste of one form or another will tend to go up with total economic activity (including the activity of pollution control).

Basic trends of industrial society

Industrial society has been characterized by a number of trends, which have accounted for its benefits and achievements but also lead toward its most basic problems. These include:

- *Industrialization of production,* i.e., subdividing work needed to produce goods and services into elemental increments, and organizing and managing these increments toward the goals of productivity and efficiency.
- *Automation,* the further organizing of work so that it can be performed by energy-driven, self-operating machines.
- *Economization of human activities,* including them increasingly in the mainstream monetized economy.
- *Rising influence of materialistic science,* i.e., the search for knowledge guided by the principles of objectivity and causality and embodying the prediction and control values of technological exploitation.
- *Pragmatic values* predominating, with the individual free to seek his own self-interest, as he defines it, in the marketplace; economic rationality increasingly prevailing in social decisions.
- *Material progress,* both as an observable trend and as a declared goal, implying man's expanding control over nature and his unlimited ability to understand the universe from the data provided by his physical senses. (One aspect of material progress, reduced mortality as a result of improved diet and public health measures, contributed to a dramatic rise in world population.)

As Mumford,[2] and White,[3] and others have argued, these trends are intimately related to an underlying image of man-in-the-universe, involving materialistic values and an ethic of man dominating the rest of nature.

That image of man, and those trends, have brought us to a "new scarcity" of:

- Fossil fuels and other sources of energy
- Mineral and nonmineral resources
- Natural fresh water
- Arable land and habitable space
- Waste-absorbing capacity of the natural environment
- Resilience of the planet's life-supporting systems.

Although they are somewhat interdependent and exchangeable, we are simultaneously approaching the planetary limits for all these resources. This is not necessarily to say that shortages in all of them are imminent, but neither are the limits infinitely far away.

The new scarcity differs fundamentally from age-old scarcities of food and shelter. The latter were "solved" in the past through geographical expansion and technological achievement. The new scarcity is more a *consequence* of technological and industrial advances (which have affected both the size of populations and the per-capita impacts).

Thus the industrialized world faces an essential dilemma. Not only has present industrial society been shaped by the trends of technological and industrial advance, economic growth, and rising influence of materialistic science. It has been assumed that continuation of these trends was essential to resolution of the problems of poverty and hunger in the Third World, unemployment, pollution, and the other difficulties of managing the increasingly complex world production and distribution system. But now it is becoming apparent that continuation of these trends may actually impede achievement of such social goals as spiritual satisfaction, meaningful life work, wholesome physical and social environment, fair distribution of the earth's resources, and manageability of the life-supporting ecosystems. The nature of this dilemma seems to demand fundamental system change—yet the one thing we clearly do not know how to accomplish is basic system change without risking serious social disruption.

Some characteristics of a whole-system view

In recent years we have come to learn—or perhaps relearn—something fundamental about the health of the individual human being. Health is a function of the whole organism—of body physics and biochemistry; of attitudes and emotions; of thoughts and perceptions. Illness only seems to be a collection of symptoms, or a disease "caused" by bacteria or virus. It is also a consequence of lowered body immunity to ever-present viruses, and the lowered immunity in turn is related to attitudes and emotions. Some attitudes—resentment, hostility, frustration, anxiety—promote illness; other attitudes—humor, joy, peace, love—promote healing and wellness. But attitudes relate to perceptions of oneself and the environment; and the perceptions are functions of beliefs. Thus some kinds of beliefs are unwholesome; other beliefs foster wholeness and wellness. There is little gained by treating symptoms or even diseases alone, if the underlying cause lies equally in the person's self-perception and basic beliefs.

It is thus with the health of social systems. Some problems are like a cut finger that can be healed with the help of a Band-Aid. Other situations such as the energy-environment-economic complex of problems are really whole-system malfunctions and will be resolved only by some sort of whole-system response, including self-perception, prevailing values, and underlying beliefs.

The true dimensions of the present challenge are seen when the energy crisis is viewed in long historical perspective. High per-capita energy use is not only characteristic of modern society but it is part of a pattern that involves social institutions, life-styles, production systems, and guiding societal goals and values. This pattern had its roots far back in history, and if it changes, it will change in all its aspects.

The long-term multifold trend which led to modern industrial society first became visible in the societies of Western Europe some eight or ten centuries ago, in the latter stages of the Middle Ages. It has since spread to affect every region of the globe. The rise of capitalism, the development of science, industrialization, the wedding of science and technology, modern concepts of economic development, all are aspects of the playing out of this trend. As suggested earlier, the dilemmas of the present world can be viewed as manifestations of approaching the end of that particular path and entering a new era.

This long-term modernization trend began with a change in the dominant belief system of Western Europe which initiated a progressive secularization of values that has continued up to the present day. There began a tendency to organize activities rationally around impersonal and utilitarian values and patterns, rather than having these prescribed by social and religious tradition. Related to this was the new concept of material progress —the idea that man can, through his own efforts, improve his physical environment. Both of these tendencies, although weak at first, represented distinct breaks with medieval thought.

As this multifold modernization trend gained momentum, especially after the mid-nineteenth century, it generated the characteristics of modern industrialized society. The production of goods, and then services, and then more and more of human activities, became "industrialized." Management became optimized with respect to such technical and economic criteria as efficiency and labor productivity. Economic rationality came to predominate more and more in social and political decision-making, to the extent that economic values became a pseudo-ethic shaping society's choices. Knowledge came to be ordered more and more according to the prediction-and-control values of materialistic science—that is to say, knowledge came increasingly to be valued because it would generate manipulative technology. The prestige of materialistic science grew so powerful during the first half of the twentieth century that it almost seemed as though there were no other kinds of legitimate knowledge. We heard of the "warfare between science and religion," from which science emerged the clear victor.

Premises, premises . . .

But then a funny thing happened on the way to the future. Whereas prior to the mid-sixties only the rare voice had ever been raised to caution against where the multifold modernization trend was leading us, by the seventies such alarms were commonplace. From Alvin Toffler's *Future Shock* and

Jacques Ellul's *The Technological Society* to Robert Heilbroner's *An Inquiry into the Human Prospect* the problems as well as the opportunities of industrial society were seen to lie in the basic characteristics of this long-term trend.

This reexamination took place at the most fundamental level with respect to the basic premises which had underlain science and society for many decades. Not only was there a kind of respiritualization of society apparent (sporadic, and taking many bizarre forms, to be sure) and a questioning in the culture of the ultimate authority of materialistic science; among a minority group of scientists as well, the arguments by which science had thrown out religion, spirituality, a valid sense of values, and apparently even consciousness, had begun to seem less valid than to an earlier generation. This change of mind among some scientists resulted largely from two developments — the discovery that there is far more going on in our unconsious mental processes than in our conscious mind, and the persistence of the so-called psychic phenomena which seem inexplicable on the basis of physicalistic models. These latter, although explained away many times on the basis of error or fraud, refused to stay swept under the rug.

There is an immense array of evidence suggesting that ordinary consciousness comprises the most minute fraction of the total activity of the mind. This unconscious activity covers a vast spectrum ranging through autonomic functioning, reflexes, dreaming, psychoanalytic defense mechanisms, habitual behavior, memory search, pattern recognition, conceptualization, "hunches" and intuition, creative imagination, and religious/ mystical experience. Some of this activity is primarily inferred; some sporadically comes into consciousness and is experienced more directly. In biofeedback training, for example, the individual finds (with the aid of some form of feedback signal) that unconsciously he "knows" how to dilate capillaries and change blood flow in his fingertip, to relax muscle tensions causing headaches, to change brain-wave patterns and accompanying subjective states. Suggestion, expectation, and felt need have far greater power to influence perception and behavior than is ordinarily assumed. The phenomena of repression and hypnosis illustrate how individuals and whole cultures are susceptible to self-deception. The reality perceived tends to be a consequence of the reality believed, as well as the other way around. As Abraham Maslow emphasized in an inconspicuous little book on *The Psychology of Science*,[4] the form assumed by the science or systematized knowledge of any society tends to be a cultural artifact, "a product of the human nature of the scientist."

A second development also calls into question the success of an earlier generation of scientists in dismissing religion as pre-scientific superstition, and proclaiming that all of the world's religious traditions were based on illusion. That is the staying power that psychic research proved to have. The program of the 1979 annual meeting of the American Association for the Advancement of Science included a landmark session on consciousness, "remote viewing," and psychokinesis—topics that could not have crashed the gate fifteen years ago. The same topics were the central focus of an international colloquium on "Science and Consciousness" sponsored by the French government in Cordoba, in October 1979.[5] (We should be clear, however, that a very significant fraction of the scientific community, perhaps a majority, still do not acknowledge the research findings claimed for this field to be credible.)

The essential implication of this field of psychic research is that mind is not brain. Mind is not limited in ways implied by models of the physical brain, even quantum-mechanical and holographic ones. The research on "remote viewing"—perceiving a scene not visible to the physical eyes—and on precognition and retrocognition suggests that effects of mind are not limited by distance or physical time in ways that physicalistic models of mental functioning would suggest.[6] Several researchers have extended the principle of biofeedback training outside the person's body—demonstrating that unconsciously he "knows" (just as with the capillary dilation) how to move an object at a distance by focusing his mind on it, but until very sensitive feedback indication of that motion is provided the ability is denied and seems not to exist.[7] The dramatic implication of this sort of psychokinetic phenomenon is that ultimately mind is predominant over the physical. And, not least important, recent research on telepathic communication suggests that we have knowledge of what is going on in another mind with whom we are in rapport, even when this knowledge is not accessible to the conscious awareness. (In one such experiment a flashing strobe light stimulus in one person's eyes produces an electrical component in the brain wave of another, remote and isolated, who has no conscious awareness of whether the strobe light is flashing or not.) Minds are joined in ways not accounted for by any physical explanation.

The premises, values, and goals implicit in our Judeo-Christian heritage —and indeed those implicit in all religious traditions—had been strongly challenged by materialistic science. But now not only in a "re-spiritualizing" culture, but also in significant fringe areas in science, with recognition of the vast extent of unconscious mental functioning and of phenomena not accounted for in materialistic science, the whole matter of basic premises and guiding values is undergoing reexamination.

The contradictions of modern society

If the changing view of science is the most fundamental level at which the viability of a hyper-modernized, hyper-industrialized world is challenged, it by no means stands alone. Numerous contradictions of modern society point to the need for and the imminence of major restructuring.

Modern industrialized society implicitly assumes the consumption of scarce resources to be the ultimate source of enjoyment; economic measures, which are commonly taken to indicate social effectiveness, are essentially measures of this consumption. Yet on a finite planet this assumption must inevitably lead to increasing competition and conflict, not only with one another but with nature itself. We are inclined to forget how recent was the value shift by which we all became no longer ashamed to be called "consumers." Two generations ago frugality was still a virtue and hedonistic consumption was a vice. If we were suddenly to become frugal again, the economy would collapse. Yet the entropic writing on the wall is clear: Frugal we must become.

Modern society rightly considers employment, i.e., satisfying social roles in which the person makes an appreciated contribution, to be essential to its citizens' well-being. But employment tends to be seen as a by-product of economic production. The overwhelming proportion of recognized social roles in modern society are connected to jobs — having a job, being married to someone who has a job, or training to get a job. However, with modern means of industrial production many of these jobs have ceased to be meaningful and satisfying. Furthermore, as planetary limits to further material growth are approached and as economic rationality pushes for further automation of production, the number of jobs will fall far short of the number of persons who want and need satisfying social roles. This fundamental contradiction is masked under statistics on the problems of unemployment and underemployment, and the unrealistic hope is promulgated that the contradiction will somehow be resolved by economic measures.

Economic and technological growth have brought new problem-solving capabilities; yet they have recently shown themselves to have increasingly *problem-generating* consequences. Each year we seem to be presented with still more analyses and portrayals of the threats to quality of life, and even to survival, by the continuation of the material-growth-oriented mode of thinking and behaving.

Economic and technological growth brought, through the exploitation of developments in basic science, many unintended benefits. These seem overshadowed these days by the unintended negative consequences of further technological development and application (e.g., threats to health from synthetic chemicals, disruption of natural balances).

Economic and technological growth brought a rise in the material standard of living for hundreds of millions, liberating them from the struggle for bare subsistence and vastly expanding their range of choice. Paradoxically, however, the institutions required to implement these technologies have proven to have enslaving characteristics of their own (e.g., through dominance of large institutions, imposition of economic rationality on more and more aspects of life).

Economic and technological growth have supported democratic processes — modern communication and transportation facilities and inexpensive printed material are among the most obvious ways. Yet new and alarming democracy-threatening aspects have begun to appear. Three examples will suffice. It is becoming apparent what threats to civil rights and liberties would be posed by major dependence on nuclear power—behavior conditioning procedures for the elite guardians of dangerous nuclear fuels and waste to insure their dedication to their task, mandatory psychiatric examinations for persons in sensitive positions. New surveillance possibilities inviting misuse are inherent in widespread use of credit cards and electronic funds transfer, wherein complete tracking of a person's movements becomes possible through his purchases. Most importantly, perhaps, though subtle, the very momentum of economic and technological growth tends toward the automatic making of decisions which appropriately belong in the political process.

The contradictions extend to the global level. World distribution of food, income, and wealth is far more uneven than is the distribution in any single country, even those with the most notoriously unjust political orders. That is a sobering fact in the light of the relationship between inequitable distribution and social stability, and the observation that economic and demographic forces seem inexorably to worsen global maldistribution. The rich "North" partakes of a feast that the world's limited resources cannot sustain while the teeming populations of the impoverished "South" remain trapped in a remorseless cycle of poverty, illiteracy, deprivation, and high birthrates. The threat of ultimate "wars of redistribution" grows ever closer.

The contradiction inherent in the armaments race (with Third-World countries spending more on armaments than on health and education combined—in some cases over half the GNP) and the nuclear impasse between the superpowers is so obvious as to require little comment. If a marriage counselor were told by his clients that they had "solved" their marital problems by sleeping with loaded pistols under their pillows, he would question their sanity. Yet when whole nations do the equivalent, the insanity somehow becomes acceptable.

Most fundamental of all the contradictions, because it underlies all the others, is that noted above, in the basic premises of industrial civilization. The deepest value commitments and the ultimate goals of all societies that ever existed come from the profound inner experiences of some groups of people—religious leaders, prophets, mystics, poet-philosophers, or in some visionary cultures the majority of the adult population. Modern industrial society, almost alone in history, has come to focus so obsessively on the kind of knowledge that leads to technology, to the ability to manipulate and control, that it largely ignores and even seems to deny knowledge of another kind—knowledge of the world of inner experience that leads to the highest goals and deepest value allegiances of humankind. Preoccupied with "know-how," it has neglected the understanding of what is ultimately worth doing.

The plausibility of whole-system transformation

These inherent contradictions of modern society comprise one reason it is plausible that we might be in the early stages of one of the major transformations of human history. The period since the Middle Ages has been, in the time sweep of history, a great leap from low to high ability to affect the physical environment—to affect it intentionally, to better our lot, but also unintentionally, provoking increasingly severe insults. The progress now needed is in terms of improving our ability to choose wisely what those powers are to be used for. That progress is of a significantly different character from progress in physical technologies. Thus we might expect on those grounds tendencies toward a marked deflection from the long-term trend of industrial society.

A second reason the transformation is plausible comes from the proliferation of social movements since the mid-sixties. These movements—environmental protection, conservation, human rights, human potential, holistic health, appropriate technology, feminist, and so on—are coming to perceive themselves, and to be perceived, as not representing solely the causes they espouse, but also, in the aggregate, a massive force for fundamental social change. Marilyn Ferguson in her book *The Aquarian Conspiracy*[8] begins: "A leaderless but powerful network is working to bring about radical change.... This network is the Aquarian Conspiracy. It is a conspiracy without a political doctrine. Without a manifesto. With conspirators who seek power only to disperse it—whose strategies are pragmatic, even scientific, but whose perspective sounds so mystical that they hesitate to discuss it.... Broader than reform, deeper than revolution, this benign conspiracy for a new human agenda has triggered the most rapid cultural realignment in history."

Viewed in the aggregate, these social movements amount to a powerful and growing force to deflect continuation of the long-term modernization trend. They have a counterpart in the Third World in the form of an "alternative development" or "liberatory development" thrust, proposing an alternative to modernization in the sense of striving to become like high-consumption Western (or Communist) industrialized societies. "Liberatory development" would place the emphasis on human liberation and well-being, on human kinship with all life, on self-reliance of developing peoples, and on preservation of cultural values—rather than on predominantly economic goals and mindless adoption of Western technology.

One tactic of these social movements is to challenge the legitimacy of institutions or institutional behaviors. The power of such a challenge has already been felt since World War II by imperialist nations forced to free their political colonies, by electric utilities and the nuclear power industry, by the U.S. government in the case of the Vietnam War, and by multinational corporations in areas ranging from safety and consumer protection issues to corporate social responsibility to relations with Third World countries.

There is a third kind of evidence for plausibility of the transformational hypothesis. Sociological studies of past periods of revolutionary change in various societies indicate that typically there are precursors which follow remarkably similar patterns. These precursors are in the form of certain social indicators which rise some time prior to the revolutionary change period and subsequently decline. In part this may be because they are indicators of a deeply underlying anxiety. Among these indicators are alienation from the institutions of society; rate of mental illness; rate of violent crime; rate of social disruption and use of police to put down dissension; tolerance of hedonistic behavior, particularly sexual; religious cultism; and economic inflation.[9] All of these indicators may appear at other times, but the pattern as a whole seems to be characteristic of the early stages of revolutionary change. All of them have risen since the mid-sixties.

Yet a fourth reason for believing not only that a social transformation is under way, but that it is one of the most thoroughgoing and profound in history, lies in the challenge to basic premises discussed earlier. At the deepest level of the societal structure every society forms around some basic paradigm, some tacitly assumed set of fundamental beliefs about man, society, the universe, and the source of authority. Very rarely in history has this basic world view gone through rapid and fundamental change. Perhaps the last two times in Western society were the end of the Roman Empire and the end of the Middle Ages. Speaking of the latter, Lewis Mumford in his *The Transformations of Man* reminds us how dramatic was the value shift involved: "All but one of the seven deadly sins, sloth, was transformed into a positive virtue. Greed, avarice, envy, gluttony, luxury, and pride were the driving forces of the new economy." In the realm of beliefs the shift was equally dramatic. From the medieval perception of a cosmos alive in every portion, with parts interrelated in a "great chain of being" and a hierarchy of transcendency, prevailing opinion went to the post-seventeenth-century scientific view of regular phenomena in a "dead" universe devoid of mental or spiritual properties. All institutions of society were intimately involved in these changes—both being shaped by the evolving world view and also helping to shape it.

Mumford and others see industrialized society heading toward another great transformation, possibly much more rapid than the last. In the coming transformation it is the scientific/industrial paradigm that is challenged, and the centuries-old trend of modernization whose deflection is at issue.

Concluding remarks

In the preceding discussion we have emphasized the chain of linkages from society's basic premises to individual and institutionalized values to the characteristics of industrial society, predominant among which is the profligate use of energy. The point is, the energy dilemma of the world will never be resolved by energy policies and technologies—only by a whole-system response.

This is not a pessimistic observation—nor an optimistic one. It simply clarifies the nature of our options. If the observation is accurate, most of the options in political vogue will not work. There are others, not presently receiving serious consideration, that will work—at least in the sense of being in the evolutionary pattern toward a viable global society.

Let us return to where we began and rephrase the initial synopsis. The world energy situation in brief is:

(a) The industrialized world is in a transition *from* high and growing per-capita consumption of energy, predominantly from oil and natural gas, *to* lower per-capita energy consumption, coming to an increasing extent from renewable sources. This transition may be quite rapid; if so, it will be for environmental and social reasons rather than because of actually running out of either fossil or nuclear fuels. The transition involves not simply change in energy practice and policies; it involves whole-system change.

(b) The developing world will not have the energy to develop in the pattern of the present industrialized world. Either the Third World and the industrial world will join in partnership to create a new global order, or there will be increasing and increasingly unpleasant confrontations between the developed and the developing peoples.

(c) There is growing global awareness of the worsening energy dilemma. If that awareness can be transformed into awareness of the need for whole-system change on a global scale, the transition may resemble not a "fall of the industrial empire" but a metamorphosis.

The metamorphosis of a larva to become an adult insect begins with the degeneration of much of the larval tissue. Simultaneously there is a proliferation of growth around other special cells termed "imaginal cells" that assume the role of prefiguring portions of the new creature that will eventually emerge from the pupal shell. The transformation is profound, but nonviolent. Perhaps the metamorphosis of the industrial world to some new trans-industrial global order has already begun—with thousands of intentional communities and "alternative development" organizations and social movements and voluntary associations playing the role of "imaginal cells," linked by a vaguely defined and emergent set of beliefs about what comprises a viable and satisfying global future.

The world energy situation will get worse before it gets better. It may eventually get better, more because of dramatically reduced energy "needs" than because of the development of new and exotic energy sources. But if so, a lot of other things will have changed in the process.

[1] Denis Hayes, *Rays of Hope: The Transition to a Post-Petroleum World* (New York: W. W. Norton, 1977).

[2] Lewis Mumford, *The Transformations of Man* (New York: Harper and Brothers, 1956).

[3] Lynn White, Jr., "The Historical Roots of Our Ecological Crisis," *Science* 155, no. 3767 (March 10, 1967).

[4] Abraham H. Maslow, *The Psychology of Science* (New York: Harper and Row, 1966).

[5] Marilyn Ferguson, "European Conference Explores 'Paradigm Crisis,'" *Brain-Mind Bulletin* (Los Angeles) 4, no. 24 (Nov. 5, 1979).

[6] Russell Targ and Harold Puthoff, *Mind-Reach: Scientists Look at Psychic Ability* (New York: Delacorte, 1977).

[7] Robert Jahn, "Psychic Processes, Energy Transfer, and Things That Go Bump in the Night," *Princeton University Alumni Weekly* 79, no. 7 (Dec. 4, 1978), pp. S-1 through S-12.

[8] Marilyn Ferguson, *The Aquarian Conspiracy: Personal and Social Transformation in the 1980s* (New York: St. Martin's Press/J. P. Tarcher, 1979). Ferguson is not alone in observing this network phenomenon. For example, two anthropologists, Luther Gerlach and Virginia Hine, out of their research on a wide range of political, social, and religious movements, observe the emergence of a new institutional form which they term a "segmented polycephalous integrated network (SP[I]N)." (V. H. Hine, "The Basic Paradigm of a Future Socio-Cultural System," *World Issues*, April/May 1977, pp. 19–22.) This institutional form has extended to include a vast diversity of social, political, and religious movements having seemingly disparate ideals and objectives but through the 1970s developing the consciousness of a single "New Age" front (Mark Satin, *New Age Politics* [New York: Dell, 1979].)

[9] This list of leading indicators of revolutionary change is based on several works including particularly E. A. Tiryakian, "A Model of Societal Change and its Lead Indicators," in *The Study of Total Societies*, ed. S. Z. Kalusner (New York: Doubleday, 1967), and D. C. Schwartz, "A Theory of Revolutionary Behavior" in *When Men Revolt and Why*, ed. J. C. Davies (New York: Free Press, 1971).

PART TWO

Current Developments
in the
Arts and Sciences

On Greek Tragedy

Seth Benardete

Recently appointed professor of classics at New York University, where he has taught since 1965, Seth Benardete is known in his field as a man of formidable learning and intelligence whose writings on classical literature and philosophy are looked forward to with special interest and respect. Though most of these have been brief, in the fashion of learned articles, they include longer studies of Herodotus and of Sophocles' *Antigone*, the latter in three parts published by the magazine *Interpretation* in 1975. Professor Benardete also contributed translations of Aeschylus' *Suppliant Maidens* and *Persians* to the University of Chicago Press series of Greek drama edited by Richmond Lattimore and David Grene, the edition on which most students now rely.

Born in New York City and educated at the University of Chicago, from which he received a doctorate in 1955, Professor Benardete was a Junior Fellow at Harvard and taught at St. John's College and at Brandeis University before going to N.Y.U. He is an editorial advisor for both *Interpretation* and *Ancient Philosophy* and is referee for the *American Journal of Philology, Classical World,* the State University Press at Albany, and Wesleyan University Press.

I

Of all literary forms tragedy and comedy alone seem to make a natural pair. They are natural in that they designate something not merely in letters but in life, and they are a pair in that, taken together, they seem to comprehend the whole of life, not just some aspect of it. We recognize as much when we speak of "the tragedy and comedy of life," which is a phrase as old as Plato.[1] At the same time, tragedy seems to raise a claim that by itself it is the truth of life. Aristophanic comedy, at any rate, is parasitic on tragedy, and Plato suggested that the artful tragic poet is a comic poet as well, but not the other way round.[2] Yet tragedy's claim to be the truth of human life does not mean that this truth is wholly sad. As we know, there is also gaiety in human life, which is neither outweighed nor subsumed by its sadness: we laugh at least as much as we weep, and it would be a severe moralist who would trace all our laughter to pain. Or, to put it differently, while tears are the natural ground of tragedy, from which tragedy can never wholly cut itself loose, tears by themselves seem to be inadequate as a sign for the whole of human life. Tears, one might say, have to become synecdochal if they are to signify so much; and they cannot become synecdochal unless they are informed by art. "The tragic sense of life" stands in need of tragic poetry.

The universality at which tragedy aims holds especially for Greek trage-dy. Unlike Old Comedy, Greek tragedy is presented as if it had no author; its illusoriness is complete. Thus its perspective appears to be absolute, that is, appears to be without perspective. No one represents unequivocally the wisdom of the poet in Greek tragedy; everything that might detract from its absoluteness is usually suppressed, and this is done so systematically that some effort is required to notice what has been suppressed. Although the stories of tragedy like its language are taken from heroic epic, the word *hero* in the Homeric sense does not occur in the extant plays. The legends of tragedy are not legendary; its re-presentation of the past is shadowless. Monarchical rule had long ceased in Athens (the word *king* survived as the name for a magistrate who no longer ruled the city), yet tragedy has nothing but kings and queens for its protagonists; the people are hardly more conspicuous in tragedy than they are in Homer.[3] Its women move as freely in the open as its men; and there is hardly a line in Aeschylus or Sophocles to remind the audience that their own women are confined strictly to the home. Again, whatever its origins might be, tragedy as we know it is Athenian; but the stuff of tragedy is not. Thebes looms larger than Athens; when Aristophanes has Aeschylus boast that his *Seven Against Thebes* once filled the audience with martial spirit, he is sharply reminded that the Thebans are his beneficiaries.[4] The greatest single event in Athenian history, one in which the Athenians would legitimately take pride and to which we ourselves can hardly be indifferent—the defeat of the Persians at Salamis—is shown to them as a Persian catastrophe, and in order to make it all the more unrelieved, Aeschylus has the Chorus pretend that Darius never mounted an expedition against Greece and Marathon did not take place. On the other hand, Sophocles must have seemed as enigmatic as the Sphinx when he attributed to Oedipus's grave an eternal power to defend Athens from attack, for the audience would have been hard put to it to remember any such occasion. Were they to believe that at some future time Sophocles would be vindicated? But if it comes to that, if the role of the Areopagus was a political issue at the time of the *Oresteia* (458 BC), what political lesson could Aeschylus have conveyed in revealing that its first trial ended in a hung jury and that Athena spoke for the acquittal of someone who pleaded guilty to the charge of matricide?

The placelessness and timelessness of Greek tragedy remind one of Plato's *Republic*, in which Socrates presents the best city in speech. There, not only does the ever-present urgency of the problem of justice occasion the best city in speech, its being utopian is readily granted to be a consequence of its beauty. The beauty of Greek tragedy, however, is a nightmare, in which the terrible is not abstracted from but distilled. Greek tragedy is, as it were, the offscourings of Socrates' city. The criminality against which the city has devised its strongest prohibitions is the setting for tragedy's celebration of its protagonists. Tragedy prosecutes as it praises. It crosses the beautiful of epideictic oratory with the justice of forensic oratory, but it wholly fails to join them with the good of deliberation.[5] Tragedy simply suspends the political good, even while its horizon is the city's. Aeschylus's Clytaemnestra could have swung the Chorus of elders to her side had she but seen fit to link Agamemnon's injustice in his killing of their daughter with the general injustice of the Argives' suffering at Troy, for which the Chorus are convinced Agamemnon deserves punishment. But she refuses to condemn the war, despite the fact that her enticement of Agamemnon to walk on rich embroideries can only be designed to provoke the people's resentment at his impious and barbaric squandering of the royal wealth. Clytaemnestra muffs her chance to found a regime that would combine authority with consent. The killing of Agamemnon exhausts her (1568–76); it serves Aegisthus but neither herself nor the people she has ruled for ten years. She lets Cassandra divert the Chorus from the political issue of the war to the inherited fate of the Atreidae, even though this entails that Iphigeneia's sacrifice, about which Cassandra knows nothing, be forgotten and Clytaemnestra herself appear to be a common adulteress.[6]

Cassandra's diversion of the *Agamemnon*'s initial theme seems to be typical of tragedy. The plague that affects all of Thebes is due, we are told, to the murder of its former king; but Oedipus becomes so enthralled, as are we, by the riddle of his origins that he never learns from the sole eyewitness of Laius's death whether in fact he is guilty of regicide. The city would have been satisfied if Oedipus's discovery had been so limited but, as matters turn out, it has only his inference to rely on, and even at the end we do not know whether his exile is still needed as a civic purification. We realize here, as elsewhere, that we have become estranged from the city's primary concerns, and that what has estranged us is the sacred. The sacred loses its political place in tragedy. "First and Fifth," Aristotle says, is the care of the divine;[7] it is fifth for the city and first for tragedy. Prior to its admission into the city, the city attenuates the sacred. In the *Antigone,* where there is a conflict between divine and human laws, Teiresias reaffirms the sacredness of burial without vindicating Antigone (1016–22, 1070–71). He interprets the divine law as applicable to each and every corpse; he does not limit the obligation to the family, ignoring the fact that Antigone would not have done what she did if Polyneices had not been her brother. The first stasimon of the play allows for civility to be part of the uncanniness of man; but to be devoted to the sacred strikes the Chorus, when they first catch sight of Antigone, as a demonic monstrousness, and, after they have heard her defend the sacred, they detect in her her father's bestial savagery (376, 471–72); she is, of course, the daughter of Oedipus. We recall that Aristotle distinguishes between moral and heroic virtue, and their respective opposites, vice and bestiality.[8] Tragedy looks away from moral virtue—the pairs of vicious extremes are the subject of comedy—and toward heroic virtue, which, without the mean of moral virtue, ceases to be the opposite of bestiality. Antigone herself speaks of her criminal piety; literally, she says she stops at nothing in the performance of holy things (74). Antigone shatters the single limit which the first stasimon ascribes to man (death), and she shatters it by becoming at one with the sacred. The sacred shines through Antigone not despite the fact that she is the offspring of an incestuous union but because of it. Out of the family that violates the family comes the defender of the family's inviolability. "Antigone" means antigeneration.

At the beginning of his *History,* Herodotus identifies human happiness with political freedom and greatness (I.5.3–4). He goes on to indicate that justice is incompatible with such happiness (I.6.2; 14.4), and he then illustrates their incompatibility with the story of Croesus. After having made Lydia into an imperial power, Croesus invited the Athenian Solon to inspect his treasury and then asked him whom of those he had seen did he judge to be the happiest. Solon's answer was Tellus the Athenian: Athens was well off, his sons were beautiful and good, they had made him a grandfather, he himself was well-off by Athenian standards, and his end was most brilliant, for in an engagement with Athens's neighbors he routed the enemy and died most beautifully, in return for which the Athenians buried him at public expense at the spot where he fell and honored him greatly. (Note that in this judgment the private goods are dependent on the public good and fully in harmony with it. The sacred is absent.) Croesus, however, is not satisfied and asks Solon whom of those he had seen he would put in second place. Solon does not answer this question, for he now does not speak as an eyewitness but reports a story, one in which the beautiful and the political good are absent. The story concerns Cleobis and Bito, two Argive brothers whose livelihood was adequate and whose bodily strength was such that they had both won contests. It is not said that Argos, where they lived, was well-off, or that they were beautiful. On a day sacred to Hera, their mother—she must have been a priestess—had to be conveyed to the sanctuary, but the oxen could not be found and time began to run out, so that Cleobis and Bito yoked themselves to the cart and dragged it forty-five stades. "Observed by the festival gathering," Solon relates, "the best end of life befell them, and the god showed in their case that it is better for a human being to be dead than to live." These verbs of seeing and showing are deceptive, for just as the story is only hearsay, the cause of what follows is speech and what follows is itself ambiguous. The Argive men blessed the strength of the youths, the Argive women blessed their mother for having such sons, and she, overjoyed by their deed and its acclaim, stood before the statue of Hera and prayed to the goddess to grant her sons whatever is best for a human being to obtain. The brothers lay down in the temple and never got up again, and the Argives, on the grounds that they had proved to be best, made statues of them and dedicated them at Delphi (I.31).

Solon tells these two stories as if the moral common to them both—no one is to be judged happy before he is dead—could conceal their differences. These differences constitute the double frame of Greek tragedy: the political in its innocent autonomy, and the sacred in its subversion of that innocence. The last words of Aeschylus's *Seven Against Thebes,** which are the last words of the trilogy (the first two plays are lost), give perfect expression to this doubleness but do not resolve it. The Chorus of maidens divides between those who side with Antigone in her resolution to bury Polyneices and those who side with the city that prohibits it. The first group says: "Let the city injure or not the mourners of Polyneices; we shall go and join in his burial, we his escorters; for this is a grief common to the [human] race, and the city praises the just things differently at different times." The second group replies: "But we shall side with him (Eteocles), as the city and the just jointly praise. For after the god and the strength of Zeus he checked the city of Cadmeans from being overturned and being swamped altogether by a wave of foreigners." Nothing better indicates the difficulty if not the

---

* *GBWW*, Vol. 6, p. 39.

impossibility of any resolution than that the partisans of the city speak of the gods while the others are silent about them, yet the sacred still lurks in their appeal to a common humanity.

Herodotus's Solon did not leave it simply at distinguishing two kinds of happiness; he went on to warn Croesus not to believe that their combination was possible (I.32.8–9). Croesus failed to heed Solon; confronted with the growing power of the Persians, he consulted the Delphic oracle as if his own political greatness could concern Apollo. When Croesus later tells Cyrus that he wants to charge Apollo with deception, Cyrus laughs (I.90.3). Croesus, however, though his happiness was not unalloyed even before he met Solon (one of his sons was mute), so much identified happiness with empire and freedom that even the subsequent loss of his other son, for whom he mourned in idleness for two years, did not force him to acknowledge his misery (I.46.1). Only after the capture of Sardis, when he was about to be burned alive, did he remember Solon. Croesus was immune to tragedy. Its elements were at hand but not the recognition of them. That the same men are not always prosperous was all that he learned from Solon (I.207.1).

Croesus's immunity to the tragic is all the more surprising because he had a part in a complete tragedy. Adrastus, the son of the Phrygian king, accidentally killed his own brother. Banished, he came to Croesus to ask for purification according to law (Lydian law, Herodotus says, is in this respect close to Greek law); and once purified, he lived at Croesus's expense. The inescapable, however, which was latent in his own name (Adrastus means just that), overtakes him in the guise of Croesus's son Atys, whose name signifies Doom. A wild boar was devastating the fields of the Mysians; they requested Croesus to send them his son along with hunters and hounds. Croesus granted the rest but denied them his son, for a dream had warned him that an iron spear would kill Atys. As a consequence of that dream, Atys's marriage had been hastened, all iron weapons in the palace had been transferred to the women's quarters, and he himself was forbidden to join in any military expedition. Informed of the dream, Atys argued that a boar's tusks were not of iron and that his enforced detention shamed him in the eyes of his bride and fellow citizens. Croesus then relented, but he insisted that Adrastus accompany his son to guard him against highwaymen. Adrastus agreed reluctantly to repay the kindness of Croesus, and when the boar was cornered, he aimed at it, missed, and hit Atys instead. Croesus then called upon Zeus the god of purification to witness what he had suffered at the hands of Adrastus, and he called on the same Zeus as god of the hearth and of comradeship, since the stranger whom he had welcomed he had cherished to be his son's murderer and had sent him as a bodyguard only to discover in him his greatest enemy. Adrastus himself appeared before Croesus and surrendered to him, urging him to slay him over the corpse of Atys, recounting his double misfortune and concluding that life was not worth living. Croesus took pity on Adrastus and forgave him; "but Adrastus, the son of Gordias the son of Midas, he who was the murderer of his own brother, and the murderer of his purifier, when the grave site of Atys was deserted, in recognition of the fact that he was the most weighed down with misfortune of all the men he knew slew himself over it" (I.45).

The specifically tragic element in this story is the law's incompetence to absolve Adrastus of the double guilt he experiences despite his innocence. Greek tragedy is concerned with those experiences of the soul which are situated on the other side of the frontier of the law. Although Oedipus tells the men of Colonus that he is "pure by law" (548) and beats back Creon's attempt to fasten guilt upon him, yet when Theseus returns his daughters to him, and Oedipus in his gratitude asks him to extend his hand so that he can touch and kiss his head, "if it is sanctioned," he checks himself and says, "What am I saying? How could I in my misery be willing to touch a man with whom no stain of evil dwells?"[9] Tragedy is not possible if the law is experienced as asserting the complete coincidence between Ought and Is.[10] The Persians, Herodotus says, deny that anyone has yet killed his own father or mother, but as often as such an event has occurred, they say there is an absolute necessity that if the matter is examined thoroughly it will always be discovered that the offspring was either supposititious or the consequence of adultery, for everything the Persians are forbidden to do they are forbidden to say (I.138).[11] Or as the Roman jurist Papinian puts it: "Any acts which offend against pious reverence, reputation, or our shame, and to speak generally are done in contravention of morality, must be believed to be acts which we not only ought not, but cannot, do."[12] And if neither Persia nor Rome admits of tragedy, Christianity no less precludes it. The pagan historian Zosimus tell us—his accuracy is not in question here—that Constantine murdered his son Crispus on suspicion of his having committed adultery with his stepmother Fausta, and when Helen, the mother of Constantine, took this hard, Constantine consoled her by having Fausta burned in her bath; but when he asked the priests for purification of his crimes and was told that no rite of purification was capable of cleansing him, an Egyptian from Spain informed him that Christianity absolved any crime, and the impious who converted were at once free of sin (II.29.3). The tragic consists in what is both impossible for morality and forgivable by a religion of salvation.[13] Tragedy discloses the inevitability of the morally impossible for which there cannot be any expiation.

Herodotus tells another story that is in point. The Egyptian king Psammenitus had ruled for six months when Cambyses took him captive and made trial of his soul. He had his daughter dressed as a slave and sent to carry water along with other noblemen's daughters; and while they passed by their fathers with wails and cries, which were echoed by those who saw them, Psammenitus looked, understood, and bowed his head to the ground. When they had passed by, the king's son with two thousand other boys of the same age, with their necks in halters and their mouths bridled, were likewise exhibited on the way to their death; and though the rest of the Egyptians wept at the sight, Psammenitus behaved as he had with his daughter. But when one of his drinking companions, now reduced to a life of beggary, happened to pass by—he was not part of Cambyses' experiment —Psammenitus shouted aloud, called him by name, and struck himself on his head. Called upon to explain his actions, the king said, "Son of Cyrus, the evils that are my own were greater than lamentation, but the sorrows of a friend deserved my tears: he has fallen from great happiness to beggary on the threshhold of old age."[14]

If silence is the proper form of private grief, tragedy is not only paradoxical because it imitates action in speech but—and particularly—because it gives voice to silence. Aeschylus managed at least twice to keep his protagonists silent for an entire play within a trilogy.[15] The *logos* of silence is the rhetorical equivalent in tragedy to its thematic transgression of the law. Their equivalence can be shown by means of a passage in Plato's *Philebus*. Socrates cites seven occasions when the soul experiences by itself a mixture of pleasure and pain. They are anger, fear, longing, *thrênos*, love, envy, and jealousy (47e1–2). *Thrênos* is plainly out of place, for whereas the others are all unmediated passions of the soul, *thrênos* is the expression of a passion. It is not grief at the death of someone—that is *penthos*—but a song sung at a funeral. A *thrênos* is no less conventional than is the occasion of its utterance, but as the phrase "to be in mourning" suggests, the conventional face of grief is inseparable from whatever is in fact experienced. The tragic poet can neither strip grief of its conventions without having it fall silent altogether nor leave it to its conventions without failing to articulate it. Grief, however, not only baffles the poet, it attracts him, and in just the way Socrates indicates: the pleasure that accompanies its expression betrays the pain of the original grief. The *thrênos* induces in us an innocent guiltiness that deepens the experience from which it relieves us. Poetry thus assumes the task of purification which the law itself can neither do nor acknowledge the need to do.

Poetry, according to Aristotle, has a double base in our nature.[16] We learn by imitating others and take pleasure in images as images. We impersonate and keep our distance, are both actors and spectators. Our sociality is a function of our emulation, and our delight in images of our curiosity. The imitative arts thus bring together without truly uniting them man's natural desire to know and his nature as a political animal. That from which the morality of the city makes him avert his eyes is brought before his eyes in an image. The image transgresses the moral and yet pleases. Aristotle's two examples are paintings of loathsome animals and corpses; they correspond respectively to comedy and tragedy, of which in turn there is the dung beetle of Aristophanes' *Peace* and Sophocles' Antigone, who in scorning her sister's offer to die with her says, "My soul has long been dead" (559–60).

How the image succeeds in preserving the law while canceling it is not easy to say. Aristotle suggests that this is due to the illusory equation it effects between the artfulness of the image and the purposiveness of the imaged. The image is the image of a natural teleology.[17] Antigone, accordingly, would be the *telos,* the artful perfection, of the corpse. The guard who brings Antigone before Creon, who has forbidden burial to her brother, likens her to a bird that on seeing her bed bereft of its nestlings bursts out with a piercing cry of lamentation (423–27). Polyneices' corpse stripped of its ritual dust affects Antigone in the way in which the loss of her brood affects the mother bird. As Sophocles develops this figure, the corpse is Antigone's nest, the dust her young. The corpse now stands tenantless; it was occupied when Antigone clothed it in dust. Again, the corpse is lifeless now that it no longer houses the dust. And still again, the life of the corpse is the dust, and the dust is Antigone's. It was her life that the guards brushed off Polyneices. She alone was not affected by the stench of his rotting corpse.[18]

The beautiful image of the ugly is but one aspect of tragic poetry; the other is the beautiful image of the beautiful, or the praise of the noble. Tragic poetry reserves its praise for those whose nobility appears to be without calculation. The self-evident impossibility of joining the good with the noble—the prudence of Ismene or Chrysothemis with the nobility of Antigone or Electra—seems to be the unexamined premise of tragedy. Perhaps, however, tragedy only starts from that premise in order to question it without incurring the suspicion that its questioning is due to rancor. Goethe's criticism of Antigone's last defense, in which she narrows the grounds of her action, suggests as much.[19] Aristotle, in any case, seems to imply that though tragedy is the proper form for those poets whose natures are noble, the manner of their praise does not issue in admiration but in pity and fear. Pity and fear are the truth of praise. When Caesar entered Rome his sole opponent was Quintus Metellus, who barred his access to the public treasury. Metellus stood his ground, even when Caesar threatened to kill him on the spot; but he yielded when Caesar added, "Young man, it was harder for me to say it than to do it." Bacon characterizes this as "A speech compounded of the greatest terror and greatest clemency that could proceed out of the mouth of man."[20] Our experience of tragedy is not unlike that compound. The fear of Metellus is in a sense the pity of Caesar.

Pity is for those who do not deserve their suffering, whose suffering is sensed to be in excess of what they did and who they are. Pity thus assumes a moral universe—Ought and Is are in agreement—in which an exception has occurred. The exception, moreover, is experienced not as a sign of the difference between "for the most part" and "necessity" but rather as no less deliberate than the presumed coincidence of virtue and happiness. The suffering is understood to be punishment. There are gods. To interpret the punishment as disproportionate, however, is to presuppose that all that has happened is separable from to whom it has happened, whereas in tragedy it is shown that no such separation is possible; to undo the one is to undo the other. Where suffering and being fully match, there is the experience of fate, of which the most superficial sign, and consequently the deepest one as well, is the significance of tragic names. The victim of fate can *be* if and only if he suffers what he ought not to suffer. Our pity therefore draws us reluctantly to will his annihilation. Our pity ends in our own terror. At the very moment that Oedipus at Colonus has had confirmed his new-found security—Theseus had just restored his daughters to him—the Chorus say, "Not to be born surpasses every account."[21]

This saying of the Chorus is a hard-won acquisition for them. Through their experience they are forced to coin the proverbial. And what holds for the Chorus holds for tragedy in general. It too renews the ancient. It brings to light those experiences which no longer seem to be possible as experiences. It must therefore transport us. The here and now must drop away. We experience this displacement—this *ekstasis*—as enthusiasm, the indwelling of a god, of which the fundamental moods are pity and fear.[22] The condition for the possibility of tragedy is post-Promethean, but what it presents is pre-Promethean man, for whom death is before his eyes and there is neither art nor hope. In taking us outside ourselves, tragedy makes us experience our total dependence on gods. The abyss over which they suspend us reveals our need of them.[23] Tragedy unfolds the significance of Athena seizing Achilles by the hair when he draws his sword to kill Agamemnon;[24] it does not concern itself with Odysseus, who, trapped in the cave of the Cyclops, draws his sword but checks himself.[25]

We may recall the nursery rhyme, "Hush-a-bye, baby." Its recitation is meant to accompany an imitative performance of itself. The baby is first rocked as if he were in a cradle on the top of a swaying tree; he is then dropped at the very moment at which the song presents hypothetically the breaking of the tree's branches; but since the baby's fall is then checked, the song's hypothesis is at the last minute denied to be possible. The nurse who induces the terror relieves the terror. The terror is induced presumably out of a sense of the baby's unfocused anxiety that can only be soothed if it is first translated into a terror the source of which is made known.[26]

The enchantment of tragedy works something like that. It gives a name to the nameless. Man's mortality gets paired with and yet separated from the immortality of the gods. Death thus ceases to be the negation of life without entirely ceasing to be what it is. It is both willing and unwilling to be called by the name of Hades. The Chorus who declare that not to be born is best do so immediately after they assert that death is an ally who exacts at last the same from all, "when the hymnless, lyreless, danceless fate of Hades comes to light";[27] and in the next stasimon they invoke and revere, "if it is sanctioned," Persephone "the non-evident goddess" and Hades, whose very name means unseen (1556–78).

II

These remarks on the general conditions for Greek tragedy are very far from comprehending its variety, let alone the particular ways in which a tragedy arrives at the revelation of the tragic. The individual tragedy shapes the universally tragic. If the *Antigone* represents the conflict between state and individual, it first represents the conflict between a city's decree and a divine law; and it further represents the city's decree as an arbitrary decision of its ruler and the divine law in a specific interpretation of it; and finally the ruler is Creon, who proves to have modeled his understanding of the city on the family, and the defender of the divine law is Antigone, who is in love with death. Thus the closer one looks at the action and actors of a tragedy, the less manifest the tragic as such becomes. We are forced therefore to look at anything within a tragedy that sounds like the universally tragic in light of the action that has prompted its utterance. Our nearest example is the Chorus's saying, in *Oedipus at Colonus,* that "Not to be born surpasses every account." Their interpretation of Oedipus's experience is not neutral to his experience; it has been refracted through their own experience, which images but does not duplicate exactly his experience. Oedipus, after all, has stated at the beginning of this play that his sufferings, along with time and the noble, have taught him to be content (7–8). His contentment seems to be an acceptance of his experience: he would not now choose not to have been born. Perhaps, then, the Chorus need time before they can echo Oedipus's contentment, and if they are deficient in nobility they may never be able to bring themselves to affirm it.

The Oedipus of *Oedipus the King* is a riddle to himself; the Oedipus of *Oedipus at Colonus* is a riddle to everyone else. The first scene of the play contains so many mysteries that almost in desperation one concludes that Oedipus has become his own oracle. Oedipus's first words are a question: "Daughter of a blind old man, Antigone, to what region have we come, or the city of what men?" Does Antigone not know that her father is old and blind (cf. 21–22)? Is there a signpost that Antigone has just read? Could they have come to a region that is not a city of men, or to a city that is not a region? Oedipus does not wait for an answer but asks another question: "*Tis,*" he begins. It might mean "Who?", or "What region?" or "What city?" "Who/What," he asks, "will welcome the wanderer Oedipus today with meagre gifts—he asks for little, receives still less, and this suffices me?" Does Oedipus always identify himself by name when he begs? Does the "Who" have to be human, and the "meagre gifts" food and lodging (cf. 104)? And of whom does he ask this question? Antigone cannot know anymore than he does. Does he abruptly turn to talk to himself? Why does he ask for more than he finds sufficient? Is the still proud Oedipus trying out the role of humility? The "we" of his first question has become "Oedipus" at the beginning of his second question and "me" at the end. When he turns back to his daughter he deepens his mysteriousness. "If, daughter, you see any seat, either at profane places or at groves of gods, set and establish me, so that we may learn by inquiry where we are." If it makes no difference where he is seated, why does Oedipus note the difference? Why should his being seated make it possible to find out where they are? He has not yet asked whether the place is inhabited (27–28). Does he mean that if it is a profane place it is not the place he has been looking for, and if it is sacred it might be?

"We have come as strangers," he says, "to learn from citizens, and to practice whatever we are told." And yet, despite this admission of ignorance, no sooner does Antigone inform him that she knows by sight that a city is far off and by conjecture that they are in a sacred place—the place they are in is less plain than the place they are not—than Oedipus asks her, "Can you tell me where we are?" Antigone, to our surprise, knows the answer: "Athens, at least, I know, but not the place." And then to turn our surprise to bewilderment, Oedipus says, "Well, every wayfarer told us that much." Oedipus knew all along that he was in Attic territory. Why, then, did he ask at the beginning what city they had come to if his ignorance extended only to the place? And, finally, if he is so willing to do what he is told, why does he at once defy the first inhabitant he meets? Indeed, he has already planned to defy the citizens, for of the alternative—profane places or groves of gods—"profane" (*bebêla*) means literally that which it is permitted to walk on, and hence "sacred groves of gods" must mean a place whose access is forbidden. Oedipus is now prepared to violate the sacred knowingly.

The riddles of the opening cluster around the knowledge of place, and the knowledge of place is embedded in Oedipus's own name—"Know-where." Can Oedipus himself have been the place he was looking for (cf. 1520–23)? We learn at the end of this play that the place of his disappearance is not to be known to anyone, for though Theseus presumably knows —how, if he covered his eyes at the last minute and Oedipus disappeared without a trace?—and transmitted his knowledge to his successor, Athens is now, in the time of the audience for whom the play was written, a democracy and no longer can have a custodian of this secret. "Know-where" has become "Nowhere" (cf. 1649).

However this may be, the riddles continue. The native of Colonus forbids Oedipus to ask any more questions before he leaves the place where he is, "for you occupy a place not sanctified for trespass." Is there a connection between out-of-placeness and questioning? Oedipus complies by asking two questions: "What is the place? To whom of the gods is it held to belong?" The stranger then ignores his own prohibition and answers both questions: "A place untouchable and uninhabited. The goddesses in whom terror dwells occupy it, daughters of Earth and Darkness." Antigone was mistaken; the place is not inhabited. Could there be two places? Oedipus then asks what the awesome (*semnon*) name of the goddesses is; plainly, he is eliciting the name he wants to hear—*Semnai*—the distinctive epithet of the Furies at Athens and their name in the oracle he has (89); but, he is told, "the people (*leôs*) here would call them the all-seeing Eumenides; elsewhere, different names are beautiful." Oedipus must have come to the wrong place; but Oedipus decides otherwise: "Well, may they graciously (*hileô*) welcome the suppliant, since I would no longer depart from this place." Oedipus is going to stay regardless of whether the Furies are gracious or not, for whereas the name Eumenides points directly to the word *eumeneis* (kindly-disposed), Oedipus chooses to substitute an equivalent word of the same metrical shape that puns on "people" (cf. 486). Does Oedipus need the graciousness of the people more than the kindness of the gods? It is striking, in any case, that Theseus does not need to consult an oracle to confirm Oedipus's interpretation; indeed, neither Theseus nor anyone at Colonus is ever told the oracle. Oedipus's defiance now shakes the native's confidence; he decides not to expel Oedipus "apart from the city." What city? It cannot be Athens, for the inhabitants of Colonus have total control over this place (78). Is Colonus then a city too? If it is, then the situation into which Oedipus has stumbled must be shortly after Theseus had consolidated all of Attica under the sovereignty of Athens, when the country towns were stripped of their political independence but their sacred places were left intact.[28] Oedipus, however, has now violated the sacred, and since we never learn whether Ismene managed to perform the elaborate rites of purification before Creon seized her, Oedipus might remain polluted to the end; during the interval in which Ismene would be performing the ceremony, the Chorus learn of Oedipus's crimes (510–48). We are made to wonder, in any event, whether Theseus needs the violation of the sacred, for if, on the one hand, the place of Oedipus's disappearance is not to be approached (1760–63), and, on the other, that place is not to be known, transgression is inevitable. Oedipus, "pure by law," brings to Athens the permanence of guilt.

We are not yet done with Oedipus the riddle. After the native of Colonus has allowed him to stay where he is, Oedipus asks him, "What is the place in which we have come?" (52). Had not Oedipus already asked this question (38)? Is this yet another place? The native, in any case, does not repeat himself: "The whole place is sacred. Awesome Poseidon occupies it. The Titan god, the fire-bringer Prometheus, dwells in it; and the place you tread upon is called the bronze-footed threshhold of this land, the bulwark of Athens. The neighboring fields claim the horseman Colonus as their founder, and all in common have his name." "This land" does not refer to Colonus; it is not even clear whether it includes Colonus. The root of Athens is not in Athens; the root of Athens, it turns out, is in Hades (1590–91). Colonus is many places together bound in name to, and apart in being from, Athens: the native distinguishes between what the place is called and its *synousia*. "It is this sort of place, stranger, not honored in speeches but more by a being together (*synousia*)."

Oedipus, in staying in this place and refusing to go to Athens, grants Athens "the greatest gift of his *synousia*" (647). Oedipus seems to be needed in order to weaken the apartness of Colonus without fully assimilating Colonus to Athens. He says he is sacred (287). The togetherness and apartness of Colonus are expressed in the first stasimon in which Oedipus, on the authority of Theseus, is finally welcomed by the Chorus. The first strophic pair is devoted to Colonus, the second to Athens. Their connection is only made at the beginning: "You have come, stranger, to the best dwelling on earth of this land of good horses, gleaming-white Colonus" (cf. 694, 700). The difference between "earth" and "this land" recalls Socrates' noble lie: the warriors of his best city are to believe that the earth is their mother, and they must, "as about their mother and nurse, deliberate about the land in which they are and defend it if anyone attacks it, and on behalf of the rest of their fellow citizens think of them as brothers and earth-born."[29] The earth is literally their mother, the land is *as if* it is their mother. The land is an image of the earth. Yet the image prevails over the imaged as soon as it is a question of war. Oedipus has come as well in order to be an eternal defense against the attack of strangers. The stranger-citizen (cf. 637–38), who becomes the sacred place that is nowhere, is the link between Colonus and Athens. "Pity," he says to Athens, "this wretched image of Oedipus the man" (109–10).

The native has explained to Oedipus the place or places where he is. Oedipus asks, "Does anyone dwell in these places?" "Of course. They are named after this god." Do we not know this already? But Oedipus has listened better than we have. The neighbor said only that the neighboring fields bear the name of Colonus; and Oedipus, who saw through the metaphor of the riddle, is now inclined to interpret everything literally. The demesmen of Colonus are at one with their deme; in some sense, they are already what Oedipus is going to become. According to the first stasimon, Dionysus, the Muses, and Aphrodite inhabit Colonus, and there are no men. Colonus the god is Colonus the place: Colonus means "Hill." When Antigone descries Creon, she says: "O plain, well-endowed with praises, now it is your task to make manifest these so-brilliant words" (720–21). She too realizes that Colonus is its people; what she does not realize is that Oedipus set out from the start to separate them, for without separation there can be no unity of Athens. As soon as the native had left, Oedipus disobeyed him once more. Told to remain where he had come to light (77), Oedipus ordered Antigone to conceal him.[30] Oedipus now goes out of his way to compound his original transgression. When the Chorus enter and cannot find him, Sophocles makes them speak as if he could not avoid violating verisimilitude; they say they must neither look nor speak when they pass by the grove. But they are speaking, they are looking; and they are doing both because Oedipus, by concealing himself, has made them commit his crime. Not only that, but on their entrance they say, "Look! Who was he? Where does he dwell? Where has the out-of-place one darted, the most

115

insatiate of all? Look! Seek him out! Search everywhere! The old man is a wanderer, a wanderer, not of this place, for otherwise he would not have entered the not-to-be-trodden grove." Oedipus, they say, is guilty of trespass and reveres nothing (134), and Oedipus, they say, is innocent, for he must be ignorant. Oedipus's concealment has made the Chorus rehearse the twofold experience of his own crimes, and they are made to do so while they commit knowingly a crime of their own. When Oedipus pops up at them, it would not be surprising if they took him to be at first one of the Furies. Oedipus beseeches them in these words: "Do not behold me the lawless."[31] To behold Oedipus is to see reflected their own impiety.

We are now in a position to answer our original question. Why do the Chorus assert that not to be born is best just after Theseus has proved by deed that Oedipus is henceforth secure? The Chorus do not leave it at what is truly best; there is a second best: "And, once one has come to light, to go there quickly from where one has come is by far the second best; since as soon as youth has passed, youth that brings airy thoughtlessness, what labor wanders far outside? What toil is not there within?" The Chorus find youth tolerable because of youth's ignorance; they identify knowledge with evil: "murder, civil factions, strife, battles, and jealous resentment." Knowledge brings with it the city; it is what Oedipus brought them when he took away their innocence. "Not to be born surpasses every account (*logos*)" because non-being is without *logos;* and *logos,* they have learnt from Oedipus, goes with being. The stranger brings *logos.*[32] The being-together (*synousia*) of themselves with Colonus is no longer possible without *logos.* In the first stasimon, their praise of Athens, unlike that of Colonus, calls attention to their own speaking and their knowledge of the difference between hearsay and autopsy. Their praise of Athens includes her arts.

III

The Chorus's praise of Athens points back to the anomalous place of Prometheus the fire god in the sacred setting of Colonus (54–56). Colonus is not quite as artless and pre-political as is suggested by the unhewn and natural rock upon which Oedipus first sits (19, 192). How the arts affect the human condition is the theme of Aeschylus's *Prometheus Bound,* in which we find Prometheus chained to a rock by Zeus as a punishment for his service to men. The gift of arts there is but one of Prometheus's three crimes; the other two are his rescue of men from their annihilation and his cure of their despair. The relation that obtains among his three crimes is not at once clear, even though Prometheus puts them together in his talk with the Chorus (228–54). We are given to understand that as soon as Zeus usurped his father's throne he distributed among the gods who had sided with him various offices and honors, but he assigned no special role to men and planned to destroy them entirely before he produced a new race. Prometheus does not explain what lay behind the plan of Zeus, but on the basis of what Prometheus himself tells us about man's pre-Promethean misery, Zeus's plan does not seem to be altogether unreasonable. Prometheus's pity should not dissuade us from looking at ourselves pitilessly. To be pitiless is to be, according to the Chorus, "iron-hearted" (242), and iron is a Promethean gift. The Chorus, at any rate, do not praise Prometheus for his rescue of men; they do, however, praise him for his second crime.

> Prometheus. I stopped mortals from seeing death as their lot in front of
>   them.
> Chorus. What remedy did you find for this disease?
> Prometheus. I settled blind hopes in them.
> Chorus. You gifted mortals with a great benefaction.
> Prometheus. Besides this, I gave them fire.
> Chorus. And now mortals who live for a day have flame-faced fire?
> Prometheus. Yes, and from it they will learn many arts.

Mortals once saw death as their lot in front of them; they could not have simply foreseen the day of their death (as it is usually translated), for then Prometheus would not have been compelled to give them blind hopes; he only would have had to take this faculty away. Prometheus made death invisible (Hades). The pre-Promethean situation of man was the constant awareness of death, and as this made any activity based on future expectations impossible, which is the presumption of any productive art, Prometheus had to remove men's oppressive sense of their own mortality before the arts could become useful. Mortals are ephemeral (*ephêmeroi*), according to the Chorus; they live in the light of day in which they once saw themselves as only mortal. But Prometheus's gift of fire, coupled with blind hopes, means the replacement of this natural light by artificial light, whose purpose is precisely to conceal the original horizon within which men live. The price paid for the arts is blindness.

The Chorus believe that to see death before one's eyes is a disease, and that Prometheus benefited men in settling blind hopes in them. On the other hand, the Chorus ask in wonder whether men have fire, but they seem not to regard it as a great benefit to them; only Io, for whom the arts are of no use, will address Prometheus as though she thought it is (612–13). The Chorus are immortal, and it would not be strange if they thought fire was primarily a benefit to the gods. Without fire, men could not have sacrificed to Olympian gods; if they sacrificed at all, they could only have poured libations and offered first fruits. And if one thinks of the technical expression, "fireless sacrifices," which are sacrifices to the Fates and Furies, it is fitting that pre-Promethean man, haunted by his own mortality, should appeal to the only gods who as far as he knew controlled his life and death. In any case, such fireless sacrifices would necessarily assign a higher if not exclusive position to the chthonian gods: even the immortal gods would

117

have made men think of death. No wonder, then, that Zeus when he assumed power had no regard for those who could neither please nor displease him.

Prometheus's three crimes not only change radically the condition of men but also the relation of men to the gods. Prometheus's reflection on this latter change is embodied in his description of the arts; but before we turn to that, we must consider how Prometheus viewed his effect on simply human life. The order in which he has presented the arts is not at first clear (450–503), for the fact that number, though the "chief of contrivances," is third in his list shows that it is not in a self-evident position. Men originally lived in the dark; their caves were sunless and they did not know how to make houses whose windows faced the sun. Their emergence from caves into the sun naturally leads Prometheus to describe the art of distinguishing the seasons. The night-sky gave them clear signs for discrimination, but since the risings and the settings of the stars are sometimes still "hard to discern," Prometheus gave them numbers, which are the only sure way of marking the seasons; and as numbering is useless unless one remembers accurately, it is joined with the invention of letters. Thus the first four arts form a whole: (1) openness (houses), (2) the seeing of the sky in its differences (astronomy); (3) the precise discrimination of the stars' movements (number); (4) the precise recording of these movements (letters). The fifth and central art is the taming of animals, which partly is necessary for agriculture and hence dependent on the preceding three arts. The mention of horses suggests ships, the horses of the sea, and Prometheus then reflects on his own situation in which he has no device to release himself from his pains; for if Prometheus saved men from the flood sent by Zeus by advising Deucalion to build a ship, his own helplessness would now especially come home to him.

The Chorus next interpose and compare Prometheus to a bad physician who cannot cure himself. Prometheus is thus provoked into describing medicine. Medicine deals with symptoms, which are the predictive signs of disease, and hence Prometheus couples it with prophecy, also an art of interpreting signs which can be either good or bad. The phrase that closes his account of prophecy—"These are the sort of things"—would seem to indicate that metals, the ninth and last invention, are on a completely different plane. The connection with what preceded seems at first purely verbal: "the signs that arise in fire" were previously dark, and just as Prometheus gave men eyes by which to see them, so he showed them the benefits hidden in the earth. But if one considers that metallurgy is the only art mentioned that essentially needs fire (apart from certain kinds of divination), and that "the signs that arise in fire" could equally well describe the way in which one judges in smelting the state of a molten batch, metals are the fitting climax to the Promethean arts of prophecy. The last four arts, however, are much harder to see in their inner unity than the first four.

Taming of animals might have led Prometheus to reflect on mastery in general, and from the mastery of the sea he might have got to the mastery of disease, and that in turn may have led him to the mastery of chance through divination. The discovery of metals, then, would be related to the previous three arts somewhat as housebuilding was related to astronomy, number, and letters. As housebuilding meant the coming out into the open of men, which entailed in turn the arts of discrimination and accuracy, so metallurgy, as the art of bringing out into the open things which are not naturally out in the open, would entail the three preceding arts that make use of hidden characteristics of the sea, the earth (herbs), and fire (sacrifices).

Prometheus first described men as clear-sighted in the face of death, and his own activity as one of blinding; but in the account of the arts he presents men as originally blind and the arts as means to bring them out into the light. The contradiction is traceable to Prometheus's failure to state what he believes to be the nature of man. Men were previously *nêpioi*, he says, and he made them sensible and in control of his arts. If we take *nêpioi* literally, Prometheus claims that men were originally unspeaking; but beings without speech and sense can hardly be considered men at all, and Prometheus only says that he showed them how to write. If, however, *nêpioi* means only foolish, as it usually does, then his claim to have given men those arts they are capable of finding out for themselves seems unfounded. The art of astronomy is altogether different from the gift of fire. Men might never be so favored as to find out how to make fire (cf. 367–69), but as long as they can see and reason they can discover the order in the movement of the stars. And again, if men can speak and thus make distinctions, they can count, and no Prometheus would be necessary to instruct them.

What the silence of Prometheus about the nature of man implies is revealed in a remark that at first looks like a merely grammatical curiosity. Among the ways of divination is ornithoscopy: "I discriminated for them accurately the flights of crook-taloned birds, whichever are on the right by nature and those on the left (488–90)." The last phrase is constructed in such a way that "by nature" cannot be taken to refer to the birds on the left. "On the right" means by extension propitious, but "on the left" literally means "of good name," and only because one recognizes it as an euphemism for "unpropitious" does it mean "on the left." The words for left and right are themselves signs that have to be interpreted. The right is right by nature, but the left is only sinister by name; but since they are correlative terms, right and left as propitious and unpropitious have suppressed the distinction between nature and convention. That distinction is not operative for men, for it has been replaced by art; consequently, the distinction between speech and language cannot be drawn. Prometheus does not distinguish between the natural numbers and the conventional signs of letters. The fourth art (letters) and the eighth (divination) equally show that

Prometheus, in bringing men into the light, has not revealed all the distinctions to be found in the light, and that the ambiguous status of speech and reason in his account is founded on the blindness he first gave to men. It is impossible to reconcile his giving men blind hopes as well as the art of divination unless their belief that they accurately know this art is in fact the basis of their blind hopes. Men first lived in chaos and were like the shapes of dreams (448–50), but Prometheus showed them how to tell which dreams were fated to turn out true. Men do not altogether awaken under Prometheus's guidance but still live in a twilight. They now believe they can tell apart "reality" from "dream," but "reality" is only the reality of dreams. "I opened the eyes of mortals," Prometheus says, but only so that they could see the signs concealed in fire and not the light of the sun. For Prometheus makes no distinction between the "hard to discern" risings and settings of the stars and the "hard to discern" cries of birds (458, 486). But men as surely lack the complete art of divination as Prometheus possesses it. The arts that illuminate the human world are embedded in all-encompassing darkness.

The list of the arts begins with man's emergence into the open and ends with the bringing to light of metals. Within this framework of light, the central art is something of an anomaly. The verbs Prometheus uses to describe his ways of giving each art are those of showing, distinguishing, and discovering (altogether thirteen times); but in the case of taming, the verbs are surprisingly direct: "I yoked" and "I led" (462, 465). Taming apparently is not an art that can be taught in speech; Prometheus has to show it in deed. And what holds for the tamer holds for the tamed: it must learn by suffering. Prometheus thus alludes as fastidiously as he can to the need for force and compulsion in taming, for even in his medicine there are only "gentle remedies" (482). The taming of Prometheus himself, which is constantly described in terms of subduing a horse, is sufficient proof that persuasion does not suffice. Prometheus, who pities even the fate of the monstrous Typhon (352), is inclined to discount and reject compulsion—he calls horses "lovers of the reins" (465)—but his tacit admission of its necessity raises the question whether the same relation that holds between men and beasts should not also obtain between gods and men. The gods, as beings of a different order, may have to rule by force. It is "the bit of Zeus" that compelled Inachus to eject "by force" his daughter Io from house and country (671–72). That the gods need to use force would be perhaps the major concession Prometheus will later make in being reconciled with Zeus. The very condition of his release—the continuation of the reign of Zeus— means that he can no longer simply please Io and by implication the rest of mankind (cf. 756–70). "Violence" is here as a silent actor in the first scene, because Prometheus does not yet understand it. Prometheus now, however, regards not men but the new gods as savage, and the gods are shown to be at best indifferent; Oceanus never mentions men. The tyranny of Zeus must be moderated if human life is to become tolerable, and Prometheus offers a way to make the gods as philanthropic as himself. Sacrifices are a way to tame the gods, for they give the gods a reason for taking an interest in them. The first effect that sacrifices had, one can imagine, was to persuade Zeus to abandon his plan of destroying the race of men, for Prometheus, though he saved it once from a flood, surely could not have saved it from the onslaught of thunderbolts.

These implications behind Prometheus's list of the arts do not suffice to explain its dramatic function. Why does it occur between the Oceanus-scene and the arrival of Io? Just prior to Oceanus's coming, Prometheus told the Chorus to stop bewailing his present troubles and hear the future that awaited him (271–73), yet Oceanus's arrival not only delays this relation for the moment but puts it off until Io comes. Oceanus must somehow have made Prometheus meditate on the past and remember the arts he gave to men. "Do not think," he tells the Chorus, "that I am silent out of wilful pride and disdain, but I devour my heart in deep reflection to behold myself thus outraged" (436–38). Prometheus's thoughts are on the arts, and if not thoughts of remorse they are almost of despair. To the Chorus's confident belief that once released he will be as strong as Zeus (508–10), he replies that he is not thus fated to lose his chains, "for art is far weaker than necessity" (511–14). This looks at first as if it only meant, "My art is weaker than the compulsion of Zeus" (cf. 107), and hence Prometheus's list of the arts would be his way of acknowledging his own weakness; but were this its primary sense, it would not have led the Chorus to ask, "Who then is the helmsman of necessity?" The general form of Prometheus's assertion makes it applicable to Zeus as well: "His art too (these chains) is weaker than necessity." The Chorus phrase their question personally; they do not ask, "What then is master of (stronger than) necessity?" They sense at once that art no more than necessity is a purely abstract noun. The Fates and Furies are necessity; and since Zeus is weaker than they, the conclusion seems plain: not Prometheus but Zeus essentially is art.

The ordering of human life through the arts parallels the ordering of the world that Prometheus accomplished on Zeus's accession to the throne. The empire of Zeus would also have been surrounded by darkness. Indeed, this empire, in which each god has a specific task, is presented in the first scene, where Zeus is shown to control both the art of metalworking (Hephaestus) and the art of taming (Force and Violence). But Zeus, who has assigned a share to every god, turns out to have only a share on his own. There is something for which he has no art. The three Fates and their executive arm, the Furies, have no part in the arts of Zeus. Zeus's defect consists in his ignorance of generation. He does not know that if he marries Thetis she will have a son that will overthrow him. Zeus, then, lacks the art of the Fates or generation. Their art is weaving. Of the three human needs—food, clothing, shelter—Prometheus mentions arts that satisfy the first and third but not the art of weaving. As the only female art does not appear among the arts of mortals, so it is not counted in the technocracy of Zeus. When Zeus did learn Prometheus's secret, he generated nonsexually Athena, the goddess of weaving. The perfect product of art, who solves the problem of generation among the gods, solves it also for men: by virtue of her being motherless, she later tips the scales in favor of Orestes.[33]

IV

The tragic poets are masters of presenting deadly thought in the garb of innocence. Their words float long before they sink in and terrify. They seem to have learned how to do this from Homer. When Hector returns to Troy and goes to upbraid Paris at home, Helen says to him: "Come, enter, brother-in law, and sit upon this seat, since especially the toil of war has occupied your heart on account of myself a bitch and the original offence of Paris, upon whom Zeus did place an evil fate, in order that hereafter we may be the subject of song for men who will be."[34] Homer lets Helen divine that the Trojan War, which had its ground in the Achaeans' vindication of sacred right, finds its ultimate end not in the heroes' glory, but in Homer himself.[35] Aeschylus's *Oresteia* likewise begins with the Trojan War and the issue of right; the evils it has caused puzzle the *Agamemnon*'s Chorus; but those evils seem to be overcome through the establishment of right at Athens, until we hear Athena say, "Let there be foreign war! It is at hand with no effort at all. Therein will be some dread love of glory."[36] Has matricide been condoned just to have Athens no longer be aware of the issue of right? The Furies have not vanished; they have gone underground. "Surely, the grace of the gods is violent."[37]

One of the means by which the terrible beauty of tragedy gets indicated without actually speaking out is the incoherent. Be it by a word out of place, a sentence, an argument, or an entire scene, suddenly we are startled and filled with unease. In the course of her third defense, Antigone says, "If I had been the mother of children, or my husband died and wasted away, never would I have undertaken this toil despite the citizens. On account of what law do I say this? If my husband died, I would have had another husband, and a son from another man, if I had lost my husband." This speech is doubly incoherent, for not only does it seem to mar Antigone's nobility, it presupposes that the death of a hypothetical son requires the death of a hypothetical husband; but that could only hold if her husband were her son. Antigone can imagine herself to be, against the meaning of her name, a mother; but she cannot imagine any family other than her own. Similarly Hippolytus in Euripides' play of that name, appears to argue brilliantly for his innocence when he perceives that his outraged father has just read Phaedra's letter traducing him, until we realize that he does not know the charge against him is rape and he is proving that he could not have been a seducer. Hippolytus's misogyny has betrayed him, for it has made him believe that rape is impossible.

Other examples come to mind. Medea, in that play by Euripides, has long been planning the murder of her children; Aegeus, the king of Athens, arrives, and first in learning from him that men consult oracles for the sake of having heirs, and then in gaining from him the promise of Athens as a place of refuge, she resolves to execute her plan. Medea takes the motiveless appearance of Aegeus as a divine confirmation of her justice. Chance looks like providence. How else can one explain the perfect coincidence between her own safety and the meaning of her crime? A barbarian takes it upon herself to exemplify for the Greeks their own belief that the punishment for perjury is the annihilation of one's family.[38] The Chorus in *Antigone* remark on Haemon's entrance that he is Creon's younger son and thus obliquely refer to Megareus (1303), whose sacrificial death in appeasing the wrath of Ares has just now helped to save Thebes.[39] It would seem, then, that Creon has already shown that he rules in accordance with his own laws: he has given up his son for the sake of his fatherland. Yet he has decided not to glorify Megareus's death but has strangely chosen Eteocles' as the highest form of patriotism. His fall would surely gain in poignancy if the loss of his elder son underlay his hatred of Polyneices and Antigone. Creon, however, never refers to Megareus, and he gives no indication that he has ever experienced suffering. If the death of Megareus meant nothing to him, the death of Haemon and Eurydice will not either; and what looks like the fitting punishment for his crimes will altogether miss its mark.

Perhaps the most beautiful of all choral odes is the parodos of the *Agamemnon*. Twelve Argive elders begin by singing of the expedition against Troy and their own age that exempted them from military service; they then recount Calchas's interpretation of an omen that occurred at Argos prior to the setting sail of Agamemnon and Menelaus; his interpretation foretold the sacrifice of Iphigeneia and the sack of Troy. The rest of their song describes vividly the sacrifice of Iphigeneia at Aulis, but they insert between the omen and the sacrifice an account of Zeus's justice that begins, "Zeus whoever he is." At first we are swept along by the Chorus, but we are soon nagged by a strange omission on their part: they fail to state what crime Agamemnon committed in punishment for which he had to sacrifice his daughter. They move directly from a sign to that of which it is a sign without their speaking of a cause. Do they believe that a sign can double as a cause? We then notice that the Chorus cut off their description of Iphigeneia's sacrifice just before her throat was slit: "What happened next I neither saw nor shall I say (247)." Contrary to our own reasonable surmise that the Chorus never left Argos, they now inform us that they were at Aulis and averted their eyes at the last minute; but if they were there and yet not part of the army, it seems necessary to conclude that the Chorus escorted

Iphigeneia from Argos to Aulis. In the insert, between the omen and the sacrifice, they ascribe to Zeus the establishment of the law, "By our suffering understanding." Understanding is guilt: "There drips instead of sleep before the heart a distress that remembers the pain" (179–80).

At the same time, then, that we learn of the Chorus's complicity, we learn that they put no trust in anything but what they can see with their own eyes. They are acutely sensitive in regard to morality and extremely skeptical in regard to evidence. They doubt everything they hear but do not see.[40] They do not believe Clytaemnestra when she reports the fall of Troy; they find the perfectly plain visions of Cassandra very hard to follow; and they decide not to help Agamemnon, when they hear his cries, because at least half the Chorus are not certain what they mean (1346–71). Their skepticism, however, is at odds with their morality, for hardly anything they see conforms self-evidently with their morality. Their morality needs to be grounded in knowledge of cause, but all they know of Zeus is his name; he is only a likeness (cf. 160–65, 1486). Their silence, then, about what caused Agamemnon to sacrifice Iphigeneia embodies their probity and distress. This does not mean, however, that the Chorus cannot see how detestable Aegisthus is, and they are prepared to fight him (1651); but Clytaemnestra, despite Cassandra's best effort to blacken her, baffles them to the end (1560–61).

The disparity between the Chorus's morality and their reliance on eyesight alone seems to be resolved, if not for them then for us, in the *Choephoroe*, where Orestes sees before his eyes the Furies, and guilt thus becomes visible. Its visibility, however, seems to entail a diminution of its power; it is no longer an experience of the soul that the law cannot reach.[41] The Furies terrify Orestes, but they do not succeed in bringing about his remorse. Orestes never regrets what he did. Guilt made visible separates the fear of future punishment from the impossible wish to undo one's crime. The Furies' manifestation is thus indispensable for Athena's establishment of right in the form of law. The Furies become the Kindly Ones in becoming pure instruments of punishment. Law deters through its sanctions; it is indifferent to the curative power of remorse. Law has nothing to do with the tragic. It cannot care less whether or not Clytaemnestra has bad dreams. The Chorus of the *Choephoroe* are the first to anticipate the conclusion of the *Oresteia*. Sent by Clytaemnestra to appease with libations those below the earth, they are afraid that they *will* be appeased and that Clytaemnestra will not have to pay for her crime (21–83). Guilt cannot redeem; it is a luxury of the successful criminal (cf. 841–43). Orestes too is disturbed lest Clytaemnestra has managed to appease his father, for he, Electra, and the Chorus have conjured Agamemnon to come into the light and join with them against his enemies (459–60), but Agamemnon has failed to appear. Accordingly, Orestes, even after he has resolved to act (514), hesitates. He has to know what prompted Clytaemnestra to send libations; that they are, as he says, "less than her fault" (519), does not entail that they did not suffice to turn aside Agamemnon's wrath and baffle his epiphany (cf. 461). The dream cannot mean what the dream-interpreters, who engaged themselves to speak "from god" (39–42), made it out to mean. And when we hear the dream, we are puzzled as to how it could have admitted of any other interpretation than Orestes' (527–50). Clytaemnestra dreamed that she gave birth to a snake, and when she offered it suck it bit her on the breast and drew blood. Who else could the snake be than Orestes? The sole wrinkle in Orestes' straightforward interpretation is one line, which is ordinarily taken to say—it assumes an unexampled hyperbaton—that she anchored the snake like (*dikên*) a child in swaddling clothes but could possibly mean that in the swaddling clothes of a child she anchored just punishment (*dikên*). The child, then, would not be Orestes but Iphigeneia, and the interpreters would have told Clytaemnestra that the sacrifice of Iphigeneia does not now sanction her father's murder. It is, in any case, remarkable that Clytaemnestra, when she defends herself before Orestes, does not mention Iphigeneia (cf. 242).

Orestes has no qualms about having killed Aegisthus; he believes he had the law behind him (989–90), but he does not believe that Apollo's oracle is as compelling as the law; his reasons for obeying the oracle are not unmixed (298–305). The Athenian jury too did not find Apollo's case altogether convincing. This is truly astonishing. There stood before them the ugliest and the most beautiful gods, and they could not make their verdict unanimous. The attraction men have to the ugliness of punishment has never been more vividly conveyed.[42] Athena arranged for a contest in which it was shown that the Olympian gods could never wholly gain the worship of men. In persuading the Furies to become part of the new political order of Athens, Athena placed within that order a reminder that men do not have the capacity to recognize fully the justice of Zeus.[43] Athena's wisdom thus partly consists in the admission that men cannot know her wisdom as wisdom. This admission lies behind her persuasion of the Furies. The Olympian gods will not punish Athens for its failure to reverence them with all its heart, with all its might, with all its soul. She asks the Furies to make the same concession (795–96). The visible gods of the city relax their grip on the soul, for the human undecidability of Orestes' case signifies the inevitability of human error—the acquittal of the unjust and the condemnation of the just—for which there is to be no punishment. The city that subsequently condemned Socrates postponed his execution until the sacred ship *Salaminia* could return from Delos. It purified itself *hosiou heneka,* which literally means "for the sake of the holy," but came to mean "for form's sake." By the same token, once the gods have sanctioned public error within the city, the city can obviously kill its foreign enemies without any qualms. The Trojan War can now take place. All that the city perhaps still needs is the supplement of tragedy.

The *Choephoroe* is divided into two unequal parts, a high and a low. The high part goes up through the first stasimon (652), the low contains the killing of Aegisthus and Clytaemnestra. The first part looks at matricide in the element of divine command and moral duty, the second part presents matricide as it is. Orestes needs his friend Pylades to remind him of Apollo's oracle (900–4). The disjunction between the two parts cannot be missed if one keeps together the last words of the first stasimon—"deepcounseling Fury"—with Orestes' first words in the execution of his plan—"Boy! Boy!" (653). The Chorus say that deepcounseling Fury is introducing Orestes into the palace, but Orestes has to shout and knock like any figure on the comic stage in order to get admitted.[44] Not even Euripides, as far as we know, ever went this far in violating tragic decorum. Tragic decorum simply does not suit the brutal business of a mother's murder: the urine and feces of the infant Orestes are more consonant with it (749–60). So are slaves. The Nurse who speaks about the mindless beast that Orestes was is but one of three such who between them make possible Orestes' actions. The Chorus of slave women persuade the Nurse, in as miraculous a way as Athena does the Furies, to suppress part of Clytaemnestra's order in repeating it to Aegisthus (766–82); and the cries of the slave who discovers Aegisthus's corpse get Clytaemnestra to come out of the women's quarters unarmed and unescorted (877–84). The house of Atreus is freed by slaves. Orestes did not anticipate any of the difficulties they manage to overcome; indeed, the very phrase—"Where is the stranger from?"—which he had imagined would die in Aegisthus's throat before he could utter it, is spoken by the slave doorkeeper (575, 657). Orestes, moreover, did not even expect to be welcomed, "since the house is inspired by evils" (570), let alone be welcomed by his mother. In the entire rehearsal of his contingency plans, he never mentioned Clytaemnestra. "Mother" never crosses his lips until he says, "Pylades, what shall I do? Shall I shrink from killing my mother?" (899).

Perhaps, however, what most distinguishes the second from the first part of the play is the absence of Electra. She does not speak after Orestes asks the Chorus about the dream; she has no part in the murder (554). Orestes spares Electra against her will and the expectation of the Chorus (473, 481–82; cf. 279). The incoherence of his plan seems to be a way of freeing her from even the charge of conspiracy.[45] Orestes faces the Furies alone because he has arranged to face his mother alone. If, however, he had strictly complied with the oracle, he would never have faced his mother at all; he would have killed her as he had Aegisthus (and Clytaemnestra had killed Agamemnon), without ever revealing why she was to be killed and who he was (cf. 555–59, 831–32). Orestes, however, cannot bring himself to act as if he is the pure executor of the law, anymore than he can let Electra participate in the killing. That Apollo defends him anyway, despite his disobedience, is a sign perhaps of the violent grace of the Olympian gods.

V

Sophocles' *Oedipus the King* seems to be the most systematically ambiguous of all Greek tragedies. It admits of two entirely different interpretations, neither of which seems to be a deeper version of the other. The first interpretation takes its bearings from Oedipus, the second from the plot. For the first the plot is nothing but an instrument of disclosure; and whatever difficulties there are in it do not detract from the showing of Oedipus. The second interpretation refuses to ignore the knots that complicate the plot unnecessarily. We begin to wonder whether Sophoclean irony truly consists in our knowledge and Oedipus's ignorance, or rather in our own ignorance of which we never become aware. Each interpretation has to be worked out separately from the other before they can be joined together to illuminate what is darker than either Oedipus or the plot—the gods.

Any interpretation of Oedipus has to face this riddle: what is the necessary connection between Oedipus's solution to the riddle of the Sphinx and Oedipus's two crimes? This riddle, to which Oedipus gave the answer "man," was, what walks on four legs in the morning, two at midday, and on three at evening? Is the answer that Oedipus gave the cognitive equivalent to the actions of patricide and incest? That Oedipus is, as the Chorus say, the paradigm of man—he shows that beneath all the show man is nothing but show (1186–96)—does not seem to require that he know what walks on four feet in the morning, two feet in the afternoon and three in the evening. The universality that Oedipus supposedly represents sits awkwardly with his uniqueness; *he* never crawled on four feet or walked on two. A sign, however, of their connection is his name. His name means either "Swollen Foot" or "Know-Where."[45a] Inasmuch as it identifies him either as his body or his mind, it identifies him as both: the two identifications might be the same. When Oedipus explains his self-blinding, he adds that had there been a way of closing off his hearing, he would have done that, too. "For the mind to dwell outside of evils is sweet" (1389–90). Oedipus assumes that his mind would vanish with his seeing and hearing; indeed, he has already identified Teiresias's blindness with his deafness and his mindlessness (371). Oedipus, therefore, through his denial of any separation between body and mind, can identify happiness with ignorance and knowledge with misery. His wish to be a Lucretian "blind body" agrees not only with Iocasta's assertion that to live at random is best but with his own boast that he is the son of Chance (977–79, 1080). To see through seeming—the riddle—is to discover that there is nothing but seeming: the king is his father, his wife his mother. Oedipus saw through the riddle but not through the form of the riddle, in which man's distinguishing feature was a corporeal one that changed in number but not in kind.

Oedipus is first challenged to reflect on the connection between the Sphinx and the plague in the first scene. A priest describes his petitioners:

"You see what ages we are who sit at your altars: some do not yet have the strength to fly far, others are priests heavy with age—I am of Zeus—and others are a chosen band of still unmarried men" (15–19). Oedipus is here confronted with a divergent solution to the riddle, whereby aged priests replace the aged and bachelors replace man the biped. The sacred and the sexual, neither of which was in either the riddle or its solution, are now in front of him. Not only, then, is the prohibition against incest encoded here in its inconspicuousness and thereby imitated, but by contrast a link is hinted at between the solution "man" and the asexual and the nonsacred. That link is made explicit in the first stasimon of the *Antigone*, where the gods do not pose any limit for man and man in his uncanniness is a neuter "this" (334). It would seem that Oedipus does not know what his solution means, which is that man as he understands him is independent throughout his life; the sacred involved in his beginning (incest-prohibition) and the sacred involved in his end (burial) do not pertain to man as man. Oedipus, in any case, does not now reflect on the absence of any women before him, let alone on the nature of the plague: "The city is wasting away in the earth's seed-pods of fruit, it is wasting away in the herds of cattle, and the aborted births of women (25–27, 171–73)." That barrenness is the way in which the city is being punished for harboring a regicide does not puzzle him. It is as if he had never heard of the old wives' tale that links incest and degenerate offspring. As the son of chance, coincidence is for him without significance. In his first speech he called all those assembled before him, despite the disparity in their ages, children (1, 6).

Oedipus soon defines himself: "Children to be pitied, you have approached me desiring what is known and not unknown to me. I know well that all of you are ill, and though you are ill there is not one among you who is as ill as I am, for your distress comes to you alone and by yourself, but my soul groans together for the city, for me, and for each one of you" (58–64). Oedipus takes it for granted that he is unique; he is the only one who can bridge the gap between the city and the individual: he inserts "me" between the "the city" and "you" (singular). He thereby implies that he is different from both the extremes that he joins together. He comprehends both the public and the private, while remaining a separate one. Asked by Creon whether he is to report the oracle to Oedipus alone inside or to the assembly, he replies, "Announce it to all. I bear a grief for them more than for my own soul (93–94)." The soul of Oedipus discounts the soul of Oedipus. He is the uniquely selfless self. He alone has nothing to hide.

The objectivity of his solution to the riddle is of a piece with the disinterestedness with which he accepted the city's gift of the monarchy and the queen (383–84). His indignation at Teiresias's silence is the result of Teiresias's refusal to help the city—Teiresias never says "city," Oedipus speaks of it five times—and the old man's harping on himself: Teiresias says "I" eight times to Oedipus's once (396). The sacred is indifferent if not hostile to the city. Teiresias pretends that had he known why Oedipus summoned him he would not have come (316–18). Oedipus, on the other hand, is devoted wholly to the city. His chance success of solving the riddle, Teiresias tells him, destroyed him. "It's no concern of mine," Oedipus replies, "if I saved this city" (443). His open anger testifies to the purity of his public-spiritedness; he does not stop to calculate, as Creon does, how to combine the profitable with the noble (595). There is for him only the city, since he *is* the city (625–30).

Oedipus's transparency extends even to his language. He speaks all the time as if he knew from the start what he set out to discover. Creon says that Laius was killed by highwaymen, Oedipus picks it up with "highwayman" (122, 124). "Since I now have," he tells the Chorus, "the rule which he had before, and have his bed and wife, in whom we both did sow, common would be the offspring of common children if his family had not been unfortunate; but as it is, chance swooped upon his head; but in exchange for this, just as if for my own father, I shall fight on his behalf" (258–65). Oedipus cannot speak metaphorically; everything he says is literally true. Such literalness would seem not only to do away with poetry but with dreams. The imaginary would be reality. That which Iocasta tells him has already happened to many—in their dreams they slept with their mother—has already happened to him without dreaming (981–82). Oedipus has nothing private to turn to, away from others. His destruction of the family is therefore the indispensable means for grounding his own self-understanding. Oedipus did unwittingly what he would have had to do knowingly if he was going to be what he says he is. He finds, however, that he cannot will retroactively the condition that defines him. His self-blinding seems to be an attempt on his part to restore the private condition he destroyed: Creon grants him his wish to be allowed to touch his daughters (1466–77). "It is holy," Creon had told him, "only for those in the family to see and hear the evils of the family" (1430–31). Oedipus has become opaque (1326).

This interpretation of Oedipus's fate makes him out to be a root of the city that the city needs but cannot afford to have represented. Thebes is autochthonous. Its present generation is the offspring of the dragon teeth that Cadmus once sowed (1). The Thebans as Thebans have only one mother; they are therefore fraternally bound with one another and isolated from everyone else. Oedipus's son Eteocles in Aeschylus's *Seven Against Thebes*, appeals to the citizens to defend their "dearest nurse, Mother Earth" (16; cf. 422–26, 476); he does not ask them to defend their "natural" parents. The fraternity of the Thebans, however, necessarily entails incest, for any weakening in the sense of mother weakens the justice of their claim to Theban territory. And yet to treat the claim literally is to accept Oedipus's criminality: "How in the world, how in the world, could your father's furrows have put up with you in silence for so long?" (1210–12). The Chorus's question admits of an answer if his father's furrows are not Iocasta, but insofar as they are Iocasta, Oedipus has violated the indispensable condition for the existence of the city, the prohibition against endogamous marriages. That prohibition allows for the bonding of the city's families qua families but not for the bonding of the citizens qua citizens, which can only be effected if the prohibition against incest that holds for each family does not hold for the city as a whole. Oedipus's identification of himself with the city cancels of necessity that prohibition, and that cancellation in turn makes Oedipus the one true citizen of Thebes. Oedipus is the tyrant (873–82) whose illegitimacy legitimates the city.

Oedipus's blindness seems to be set off against a neutral background of Theban awareness. He alone does not know where he stands; everyone else is in place. His way is solely a way of self-discovery, for no else needs to be exposed. We are first compelled to question this when Creon tells Oedipus that Laius was the former king: "I know by hearsay, for I have not yet seen him" (105). We are so bemused by our being one-up on Oedipus that we fail to weigh carefully Creon's reply: "[The oracle] now plainly orders us to punish by force his murderers (106–7)." Oedipus is told for the first time that Laius was murdered;[46] and if Creon is reporting accurately, the oracle used the plural "murderers." The plural is for the moment not troublesome, but Oedipus's ignorance of Laius's murder is. Since only the sequence — Laius's murder, Oedipus's arrival at Thebes — is necessary to the plot, not the interval between them, Oedipus could have taken the road to Daulia after the killing rather than have continued on his way to Thebes. A lapse of a year or so would not have altered anything essential, and it would have made the Thebans' silence, to say nothing of Iocasta's and Creon's, much more plausible; as it is, the squeeze on time brings in its train a more serious awkwardness. Laius left Thebes in order to consult the oracle at Delphi (115); he told no one of the purpose of his journey, but it is easy enough to suspect that he wanted to have it confirmed that he had indeed thwarted the oracle. His action on the road strengthens this suspicion, for, according to Oedipus, when Oedipus was passing by the cart, after he had struck in anger the driver, Laius (if it was he) without provocation aimed a blow at Oedipus's head. Laius, it seems, was taking no chances that this young man might be his son.

However that may be, Laius left Thebes prior to the coming of the Sphinx, and Oedipus arrived at Thebes just after the coming of the Sphinx. Oedipus only now learns of this sequence. Creon agrees that if highwaymen or a highwayman killed Laius, the assassination must have been planned at Thebes; no one would have dared such a crime unless he had been bribed (124–26). Laius's assassination must have had a political purpose, and only Oedipus's timely solution of the riddle forestalled a *coup d'état*. Since Creon alone stood to gain by Laius's death, and since Creon had suggested that the king tell him in secret of the oracle, Oedipus's accusation against Creon is not a sign of his ungovernable temper but a display of his shrewdness. Oedipus is rightly puzzled by the Thebans' failure to investigate Laius's murder. Creon's excuse would only deepen his suspicions. "The complex-singing Sphinx led us to forego what was not evident and examine what was at our feet" (130–31). In itself, the excuse is plausible; but in the given time-span it almost suffices to convict Creon (cf. 566–67). Within days if not hours of the posing of the riddle, the riddle was solved (736). The allusion in Creon's words to Oedipus's condition has distracted us; it would not have distracted Oedipus, who would not understand why the Thebans had not put him to this second test. "Even if the matter was not divinely ordained," he tells the Chorus, "it was not proper for you to let it go unpurified" (255–56). That Oedipus did not connect the killing of Laius with the availability of the Theban throne should not surprise us, given that he was ignorant of the former; but that the Thebans were never puzzled by the coincidence of his arrival with the report of Laius's death should surprise us. If Oedipus had to conclude either that the Thebans were incapable of putting two and two together, or that he must have stumbled on a conspiracy, who but a madman would not have chosen to err on the side of reason?

Sophocles has combined an ironic linguistic surface that holds no riddles for us with an ironic structure of actions for which we have no guide. He has made us experience the collapse of the coherence of seeming: the dreamworld is not Oedipus's but our own. We are turned into Thebans, for whom nothing has to make any sense. Iocasta must have long noted the close resemblance Oedipus bears to Laius (743), but she casually mentions it as if it were of no significance. There is no necessity, after all, that resemblance entail consanguinity. The servant who escaped from Laius's retinue saw no reason why he should denounce Oedipus. He was so afraid apparently that his lie would be exposed—there was no band of highwaymen—that he preferred to let a regicide be king; indeed, since he must have known that the baby he declined to kill had grown up to be prince of the royal house of Corinth, it must be said that he preferred to allow Oedipus to commit incest rather than to be known as a liar. As the sole survivor from Laius's retinue, he would have been no doubt reluctant to tell the truth, for the suspicion would have been strong that he had abetted a single assassin; but in the face of the alternative—an incestuous regicide on the throne at Thebes—his silence seems inexcusable. He must have convinced himself that the violation of the law, no matter how sacred the law is, does not count as long as it is not publicly known. He asked leave of Iocasta so that he would not have to face Oedipus with his guilty knowledge (758–62); but he believed, as does Oedipus, that even here the saying holds good, "out of sight, out of mind."

"It is best to live at random, as much as one can. Don't fear marriage with your mother. Many mortals have already even in dreams slept with their mother. But to whomever these things are as nothing, he bears his life most easily" (979–83). This principle, which Iocasta lays down, presumably only to cajole Oedipus out of his terror of the oracle, simply formulates the universal practice among the Thebans. Since the events of the play seem to refute the principle, Sophocles has checked us from wondering whether or not the Thebans have any evidence for their adherence to it.

Of the three ways of access to the truth, two are divine, one human. Apollo cannot be compelled, Oedipus says, to yield up any more than he has; Teiresias knows the truth but cannot or will not offer any way of verifying it; the servant who was an eyewitness lies. That "many" cannot be equal to "one" is Oedipus's ultimate refuge (843). As long as that inequality holds, Oedipus is not guilty of regicide. Iocasta's confidence in its truthfulness seems to be grounded on nothing more than her equation of public knowledge with truth: "Know that this was expressly said, and he cannot cast it out again: the city heard it, not I alone" (848–50). Oedipus's confidence, on the other hand, is grounded more firmly. His own account cannot possibly be squared with his guilt, for he states that at the crossroads he slew them all (813). No one escaped, for if one had escaped, the coincidence of the five in Laius's retinue and the five in Oedipus's story, with one fugitive from each group, could not but have convinced Oedipus that he had indeed slain Laius. Iocasta, moreover, gives two versions of the crucial sequence. The first conforms with our belief: the city was informed of Laius's murder shortly before Oedipus was declared king (736–38). But twenty lines later, Iocasta inverts the sequence: "When [the servant] returned from there (i.e., the place where Laius was murdered) and saw that you had the throne and Laius was dead, he took me by the hand and begged me to send him to the fields and pastures of the flocks" (758–61). Oedipus, then, had already solved the riddle, won the throne, and married the queen before the city knew that Laius had been murdered.

This sequence certainly saves the morality of the servant, who might well believe that no harm is done if both mother and son remain ignorant. But his morality is saved at a preposterous cost. Laius's murder would now have to have been proclaimed to everyone but Oedipus. And yet, is this more difficult to believe than the accepted version, that with nothing to hide, no one at Thebes ever hinted at Laius's murder? We know that Iocasta did not wear mourning at her wedding. But, the objection runs, this alternate sequence means that in the course of a single day two retinues of five men each, each with one mule-cart and one herald, passed the same spot on the road to Delphi. Is *this* more difficult to believe than that the servant who fled from the scene just happened to be the servant to whom Laius had intrusted the baby Oedipus? And that the Corinthian messenger who came to report Polybus's death just happened to be the shepherd to whom Laius's servant handed over the baby Oedipus? Once coincidences are accepted, one more or less cannot matter. It would not have troubled either Iocasta or the city that with Laius still alive she was committing bigamy. Iocasta certainly feels no guilt that, if the oracle delivered to Laius were false, she and Laius were guilty of the gratuitous murder of their son.

Either Oedipus killed his father and married his mother, or he married his mother but did not kill his father. In the former case, the oracle is vindicated, in the latter it is not. In the former case, the gods would seem to be malevolent, ready to have a man violate their own sacred laws in order to prove that their oracles are true. Oedipus had assumed that the prophecy was conditional: if he went back to Corinth he would fulfill the oracle. And the gods surely cannot believe that the clarity of divine prohibition is less revealing of themselves than the obscurity of oracular pronouncements. Even if one grants that the more the law becomes "second nature" the less its author is recognized, there still seems to be no necessity that the revelation of the legislator be at the expense of the authority of the legislation. Oedipus, at any rate, does not need to be punished in order to know that the prohibition against incest is sacred: "Never, never, O holy majesty of the gods, might I see that day, but might I vanish before I see the taint of such a calamity upon me" (830–33; cf. 863–73).

If, on the other hand, Oedipus did not kill Laius, there would be no actual connection between the oracle that limited the cause of the plague to Laius's murder and Oedipus's detective work. The gods would thus have let Oedipus make that connection on his own. He alone would be responsible, through error, for discovering his crimes. It seems at first that Teiresias's presence argues against this, but Teiresias, for all the effect he has, could just as well have remained silent about both Oedipus's patricide and incest. Neither Oedipus nor the Chorus ever mention that part of the prophecy, Oedipus because he believes it agrees with the oracle he had already construed, the Chorus because, being Thebans, they never notice anything. Teiresias, of course, could not have anticipated that he would be so ignored, but Teiresias contradicts himself. He states on his entrance that had he known why he was summoned he would not have come; and he states on his exit that he has said all that he had come to say (447).

Teiresias, apparently, provoked Oedipus so that he could pretend to blurt out in anger what he had planned to say all along. If so, his plan backfired; Iocasta and Iocasta alone made Oedipus afraid through her wish to prove to him the unreliability of oracles. Oedipus himself, moreover, initiated his own fate by believing a drunkard rather than his putative parents. If Oedipus had been a true Theban he would have shrugged off the drunkard's remark; and if Corinth had been Thebes, a rumor about his illegitimacy would never have spread (779–86). The threat that the rumor posed to the Corinthian monarchy reinforced Oedipus's own unease. The gods, it seems, use simply human experiences as such in order to accomplish their end. These experiences are enthusiastic: they have the gods within them and are wholly independent of the truth or falsity of oracles and divines.

Admittedly, the story of Oedipus does not look as if it deals with the human at all; rather, it seems to present man with an inhuman choice. Either everything happens by chance and nothing is intelligible, or nothing happens by chance and everything is intelligible, but with this proviso: the possibility of discovering the pattern is remote, for it too depends on chance, and the pattern once discovered is sure to make life unlivable. There are either no gods or gods whose graciousness solely consists in guaranteeing that we shall never find out that they exist.

To believe in chance is to be inspired by grace. We must wish for the Theban condition. This wish, however, can not only never be granted us, for Oedipus has destroyed its possibility once and for all, but the disenchantment of the Thebans cannot be a matter of regret. One wonders, then, whether Oedipus is altogether disenchanting: he does not kill himself. The Chorus do not know why Oedipus chose a life of blindness rather than death. Oedipus explains: "Had I gone to Hades, I do not know with what eyes I would in seeing have beheld my father, nor in turn my miserable mother, to both of whom I have done things that deserve more than hanging (1371–74)." Oedipus's unwilled crimes uncover in him an autonomous element of shame. Shame is the human experience that reveals the gods. Oedipus now knows that Hades exists. Hades is the god of whom a man like Oedipus alone can have any experience (cf. 972, 987). It needs crimes as terrible as his to infuse human shame with divinity.

Oedipus can now enlighten the Thebans. The Chorus had told us, though no one, not even Teiresias or the priest of Zeus had remarked on it, that the corpses of the plague's victims were being left unburied (180–89; cf. 29–30). The Thebans' disregard of this divine law is of a piece with the rest of their practice; the Chorus make it plain that only women—wives and aged mothers—bewailed the absence of due burial rites. Faced, then, with the Thebans' invincible ignorance and undefiant impiety, the gods found that Oedipus was indispensable: he charged Creon with the task of burying Iocasta (1446–48). That the divine law of burial is the underground theme of the Oedipus story is suggested both by his daughter's sacrificial defense of it and his own peculiar end. Oedipus, who believed he was his own origin, is the only man who ever buried himself.[47]

Oedipus's shame is that which distinguishes him from the virtuous man (*epieikês*), who Aristotle says should not be the subject of tragedy.[48] At the end of his analysis of the moral virtues (apart from justice and prudence), the last one of which is wittiness or "educated insolence," Aristotle denies that shame belongs to the virtuous (*epieikês*), regardless of whether some things are truly shameful and others only thought to be shameful. The virtuous man will not do either because he ought not to do either; and even if he does, he will not have willed it, and shame can only be for what is willed.[49] Oedipus's shame, on the other hand, is for what he neither willed nor can will; it can only be ascribed to his imaginative experience of that which puts an inviolable limit to his seeing. Hades the invisible re-covers the nakedness of his parents. The prohibition against incest thus comes together with the command to bury the dead. They are united in Hades, through Hades, and by Hades, for without Hades, parents cease to be anything but sexual beings and corpses cease to be anything but carrion. In guarding man against man's possible bestialization (through incest and cannibalism), Hades sanctifies the so-called humanity of man. This function of Hades is due almost entirely to the poets; it is their gift to the city and its laws.[50] Homer has Achilles say, after he has seen a perfect likeness of the dead Patroclus, "So even in the house of Hades soul and image are, after all, something."[51] Hades is the locus of the reality of the image; it is the natural home of the poet.

VI

Of the four philosophers who have discussed tragedy, two are ancient, two modern. For Plato and Aristotle, *Oedipus the King* was the paradigmatic tragedy, for Hegel it was *Antigone,* and for Nietzsche, Euripides' *Bacchantes.* Plato and Hegel agree at least in setting tragedy against the background of the city, for both detect in the sacred an unassimilable albeit indispensable element of the city, and Aristotle too, insofar as his morally virtuous man is to be proof against the tragic experience of Oedipus, can be grouped with them; but Nietzsche's acount of tragedy does not seem to take its bearings by the sacred city. His theme is rather the poet than the poem. Accordingly, *The Bacchantes* is his play, for it is in a sense the same Dionysus who schemes to reveal himself to the Thebans and is the god of the Attic theater. *The Bacchantes* is almost a tragedy about tragedy: it begins with the god's explanation of his human disguise. Unless the god of the theater goes masked, he cannot reveal himself to be the god he is.

The paradox of a concealed god attempting to become manifest shows up in the various formulations that Dionysus gives of his purpose. "I have come," he begins, "the son of Zeus, Dionysus, to the land of the Thebans" (1–2); but two lines later he says, "Transformed from a god into a mortal shape I am here at the stream of Dirce and the water of Ismenus." He then tells us that Thebes is the first Greek city he has come to, after he had established his dances and rites throughout Asia Minor, "in order that I might be a god manifest to mortals" (22).

Now, either the cult itself or the initiatory rites of the cult sufficed elsewhere to reveal Dionysus, whereas Thebes must learn not only that it is uninitiated in his rites but that his defense of his mother consists in his coming to light for mortals as a god she bore to Zeus (39–42). The Dionysian creed has a codicil at Thebes: Dionysus is a god born from a mortal woman. But the action of *The Bacchantes* is that Pentheus, the King of Thebes, is at war with Dionysus; he excludes him from his libations and prayers, "on account of which I shall point out to him and all the Thebans that I am born a god" (47). Dionysus does not want any special worship at Thebes, but he cannot gain acceptance there unless he treats it as a special case. Once he has settled things at Thebes, he will move on, "showing myself," as he says; "but if the city of Thebans in anger seeks with arms to drive the bacchants from the mountains, I shall join forces with the maenads: it is for this purpose I have altered into a mortal form and changed my shape into the nature of a man (50–54)." Pentheus's war against Dionysus, then, requires the disclosure of Dionysus; Pentheus's war against his crazed followers requires the concealment of Dionysus. Since, however, Dionysus's own actions abort the second possibility and yet do not strip him of his disguise, Pentheus seems to be punished for not seeing through what was designed to be opaque. Pentheus suffers for Dionysus's frustration of his own plan.

The worship of Dionysus cannot consist with the recognition of Dionysus. The Chorus worship Dionysus according to convention (430–33, 712, 890–96); they hear but never see Dionysus (577, 590). Pentheus comes to obey Dionysus, but he then sees him as a bull (920–22); he does not submit to him as Dionysus. Belief and knowledge are of different orders; their inconvertibility is a lesson that Dionysus too has to learn. Although he sees the smoldering ruins near the palace, which bear witness to his mother's vain attempt to see Zeus as he is in himself, he does not realize their application to himself (6–9).[52] Tempted by Hera to confirm by autopsy that Zeus was truly her lover, and thus to confute her sisters' claim that she had imputed to Zeus her own disgrace, Semele prevailed on Zeus to show himself and was burnt to a crisp for her presumption. The gods, however native, are forever strangers; they can cease to be strangers if they are willing to give up their being for their being believed. Dionysus testifies to the primacy of the latter in the course of his report to the Chorus on how he eluded Pentheus: "Thinking he was binding me, [Pentheus] could not touch me, but, fed on hopes, he found a bull in the stall, where he had led me, and tried to shackle its knees and hooves, breathing out his anger, dripping sweat from his body, and biting his lips; and I sat by and quietly looked on. At this moment Dionysus came and rattled the palace and lit a fire at the tomb of his mother; and Pentheus when he saw it, thinking the palace was on fire, rushed about in distraction, ordering his servants to bring water, and every slave was engaged but all in vain; but Pentheus, dropping this task, seized a sword and rushed into the palace—as if I had escaped—and then Dionysus, as it appears to me, I speak only belief, made an apparition in the courtyard; and Pentheus rushed at that and stabbed the brilliant air, as though he were slaying me" (616–31).

There are altogether four gods in this account: (1) the god who speaks, (2) the god who certainly rattled the palace, (3) the god who apparently made (4) an apparition of (1). Pentheus confounded the first with the fourth Dionysus, but the first is a disguise of the second; the fourth too, then, in being no more an illusion than the first, must be indistinguishable from it. Did Pentheus go after the real apparition of Dionysus, and is the Dionysus who now speaks its illusory double (cf. 286–97)? Perhaps Dionysus himself cannot tell; his words, "as it appears to me, I speak only belief," could express his own uncertainty as to whether he really did make an image of an image; but possibly the fourth Dionysus, no less than the third, is only in speech: the first Dionysus would have had to invent him in any case if he were going to remain incognito to the Chorus.

The puzzle Dionysus has set for himself, trying to do what Zeus could not, comes out clearly in his first confrontation with Pentheus. Dionysus asserts that his own initiation occurred face to face with Dionysus. Pentheus asks what visible aspect the rites (or instruments) of initiation have. Dionysus replies: "The uninitiated are not to know what cannot be said" (472). Pentheus then asks what benefit is conferred on those who sacrifice. Dionysus replies: "It is not allowed for you to hear, but it deserves to be known" (474). Pentheus cannot know before he is initiated; he refuses to be initiated before he knows. He must have belief prior to knowledge; his conversion cannot be grounded on either present evidence or promised good.

The stubbornness of Pentheus is amazing. Not one miracle opens his eyes. His servant reports that the bacchants bound in a public prison had had their shackles loosened of their own accord, "and keys unlocked the door without mortal hand" (448). This first miracle Pentheus does not even comment on; the second miracle—his bound prisoner escapes—puzzles him enough to ask how he did it, but not enough to wait for an answer (642–46). The third miracle—the burning of his palace and the collapse of some of its beams—gets him to call his servants, but he himself soon loses any interest in it. The fourth miracle, again a report—that one bacchant when she struck a rock with the thyrsus opened up a gushing spring, another produced a fountain of wine, still others scratched the soil and got milk, and honey dripped from ivy-covered thyrsi—all this provokes his servant to say, "If you had been there, the god you now blame you would have approached with prayers" (711–2); but Pentheus does not even bother to argue him out of his delusion. The fifth miracle hardly has a parallel in Greek literature. "At the appointed time the bacchants shook their thyrsi for bacchic rites, invoking Iacchus with collective voice the son of Zeus; and the whole mountain joined in bacchic revelry and every beast, and nothing was not in motion" (723–27). A mountain dances; Pentheus is unaffected. The sixth miracle consists in the rout of his men, and the seventh in the utter destruction of a village (728–64). These last two events only serve to convince Pentheus that the women could not resist heavy-armed troops (780–86); they do not convince him that a god is behind them.

Euripides did not assign such stubbornness to Pentheus merely to comment on miracles; he also wanted to present through Pentheus our own condition as audience. We are asked to imagine Pentheus as a spectator who comes to the theater after the *The Bacchantes* has begun; he has not heard the prologue but must still try to figure out the plot without Dionysus's help. We are further asked to imagine that Pentheus comes without a program; indeed, he has never been to the theater before. The collapse of the palace is for him neither a miracle nor its image; it is crushed cardboard. A stagehand pulled some strings, he does not know exactly how, but if he wanted he could learn the trick too. We, however, without even thinking about it, see triple: there is Dionysus, there is Dionysus disguised as a man, there is a man playing the disguised Dionysus. The play does not work unless we believe in exactly this way, but we would be very hard put to it to persuade the naive Pentheus we have imagined that he must believe as we do. That is the difficulty Dionysus solves: he persuades the reluctant spectator Pentheus to become part of his drama. He gets him to imitate a bacchant, and once caught up in his role he is ripe for conversion. The conversion of Pentheus is the paradigm of the willing suspension of disbelief.

Dionysus deters Pentheus from sending armed troops against the Theban women. It is not clear why he should prefer to destroy Pentheus alone and unarmed; the effect is to diminish the miraculousness of Pentheus's destruction and therefore to suggest either that Pentheus armed is proof against conversion or that Pentheus, unmoved by ostentatious miracles, must be converted in another way. Pentheus promises the stranger he will sacrifice all the women, "as they deserve" (796); the stranger predicts a shameful rout; Pentheus gets exasperated and will not listen any longer; the stranger proposes another way, whereby he will bring back the women without arms; once more Pentheus scorns the stranger and calls for his arms. Pentheus's arms act as almost a magical charm against enchantment, and inasmuch as Pentheus is presented as if he were the only active male citizen of Thebes—Cadmus and Teiresias sound like doddering drunkards —his armor can be said to stand in for the city. The enchantment of the city is his sole protection against the enchantment of the stranger.

Pentheus begins to be disarmed when Dionysus asks whether he would not want to see the women sitting together in the mountains (811). Over and above the latent prurience of Pentheus, to which Dionysus appeals, the pleasure Pentheus would obtain from the painful sight of drunk women is due to his quietly contemplating their future punishment. Dionysus objects that they will track him down if he goes in secret; Pentheus sees at once that secrecy belongs to the kind of rites that the stranger is introducing and is not consonant with the openness of the politically noble; but he forgets that punishment, no matter how just, is not necessarily noble. Dionysus appears to go along with Pentheus's revised plan, but he orders him to dress up in women's clothes. Pentheus is shocked. After having been reminded of the noble, he is urged to be shameless. Dionysus explains: "Lest they kill you if you are seen there as a man." Pentheus accepts the explanation; despite his armor, he is suddenly afraid of being killed. Pentheus panics. The cause of panic was the fourth of the seven attributes that Teiresias assigned to Dionysus: "He has a share as well in Ares: terror flusters an army under arms and at its station before it touches a spear" (302–4).

Panic is groundless fear. It is itself the cause of the result which it fears. It makes inevitable the possible and brings about the conviction of fate: *The Bacchantes* is the only extant play of Euripides in which the word *chance* does not occur. But to say that Dionysus is the cause of causeless fear is to say no more than that the disguised Dionysus is the cause of Pentheus's panic. Pentheus panics through the stranger's recommendation of extreme caution. Terror parading as unmanly moderation is Dionysus's specialty: the true miracle of the bacchants is their chastity, sobriety, and decency (686–88, 940). Pentheus experiences his fear as reasonableness (826); what still holds him back is shame (828); even as he enters the palace he still hesitates to follow Dionysus's counsel. Euripides has brought Pentheus to the point of conversion and stopped; even though Dionysus promises the Chorus that Pentheus will be punished, he still has to invoke himself in order to make Pentheus senseless, "for if he is of sound mind he will never be willing to put on female dress" (851–52). Since the next scene shows Pentheus fully converted, Euripides seems to have denied us the very moment of conversion;[53] all we see and hear is the result: "Bring me through the middle of Thebes: I am the only man among them who dares this" (961–62). Prior to his conversion, Pentheus had to be assured that Dionysus would lead him through Thebes unobserved (840–42); now he boasts that he has achieved the peak of manliness. Pentheus comes to terms with his panic by representing his adoption of female dress as courage. He is now too manly to need the trappings of manliness. To be unafraid of disgrace covers the formula for both shamelessness and courage, but while the formula seems to sponsor the defiance of convention, it conceals death under convention. Death is a kind of bashfulness that Pentheus has outgrown. He is now too noble to prevail over women by force (953). That is now his sober interpretation of his former fear that they would kill him.

Euripides' showing of fear is the pendant to Sophocles' showing of shame; and just as shame is the passion with which Aristotle ends his account of the moral virtues, so fear is the passion with which he begins: the blush of shame and the paleness of fear comprehend the moral virtues. Courage, however, unlike shame, is for Aristotle a virtue, but it gives him the most trouble. Courage is the only virtue which he admits can also be spoken of in five spurious ways.[54] Political courage, which shame partly constitutes, is the highest form of these phantoms. But what is true courage is left unexplained. It must be in the service of the noble, but what the noble could be that on the field of battle transcends the sacred fatherland and yet is not an "ideal" seems to resist definition. Not only does courage alone fail to bear the sign of virtue—its performance must be with pleasure ($1117^{b}15$–16)— but courage is shadowed by Hades, and Aristotle allows that Hades' existence might affect the way in which human happiness is judged ($1100^{a}10$– 30, $1101^{a}22$–$1101^{b}9$). Fear and shame, then, are a kind of residue in virtue as virtue is ordinarily understood; they are accordingly the tragic passions.

Their resistance to enlightenment is a function of their inextricable involvement with Hades, and Hades is the soul of tragedy.

Agathias in his *Histories* (2.30–31) tells the following story. Seven Greek philosophers, dissatisfied with the prevailing opinion about God (i.e., Christianity), and falsely informed about the state of Persia, that its people were just and its ruler Plato's philosopher-king, decided to leave the place where the laws forbade them from living without fear and to settle in Persia, despite its alien and incompatible customs. Although they were royally entertained, they found that neither the Persians nor their king lived up to what they had heard; and on their journey back—the Persian king stipulating in his treaty with Byzantium that they were to be left alone regardless of their opinions—they came across the corpse of a man lately dead, tossed aside, in accordance with Persian customs, without burial. Out of compassion for the lawlessness of barbarian law, and in the belief that it was not holy to allow, as far as it lay in their power, nature to be wronged, they had their attendants prepare the body for burial and then bury it in a mound of earth. That night one of the philosophers had a dream: a man whom he did not know and who bore no resemblance to anyone he knew, but for all of that with an august countenance and the beard and dress of a philosopher, seemed to address him with the following injunction: "Do not bury the unburiable; let him be prey to dogs. Earth, mother of all, does not accept the mother-corrupting man." Neither the dreamer nor his comrades could make anything of the dream; but on continuing their journey, and the lay of the land being such that they were compelled to retrace their steps, they came across the corpse they had buried the day before lying naked on the ground, "as though the earth of its own accord had cast it up and refused to save it from being eaten." Thunderstruck at the sight, the philosophers made no further attempt to perform any of the burial rites. They concluded that the Persians remain unburied as a punishment for their committing incest with their mothers and are justly torn apart by dogs.

This story measures the distance between us and Greek tragedy. When Gibbon retold it, he followed Agathias in all particulars but one: he omitted any mention of what befell the philosophers on their journey back. The sacred did not fit readily into his opposition between superstition and enlightenment.

---

[1] *Philebus* 50b3 [*GBWW*, Vol. 7, p. 630b].

[2] *Symposium* 223d3–6 [ibid., p. 173c].

[3] Euripides experimented in his last play, *Iphigenia at Aulis*, with having the protagonist wholly invisible: the army with its demagogic leader never appears, but nonetheless determines the action. The army is the locus of morality which needs to punish Paris in order to deter other wives from following the way of Helen (543–57) [*GBWW*, Vol. 5, p. 429d].

[4] *Frogs* 1023–24 [ibid., p. 576c].

[5] Cf. *Republic* 604c1–d2 [*GBWW*, Vol. 7, p. 432d].

[6] [*GBWW*, Vol. 5, p. 68c] Even more striking than this mistake of Clytaemnestra is her acceptance of the role in which Cassandra has imaginatively cast her (*Agamemnon* 1497–1504) [ibid., p. 67d]. She needs the support of the divine in order to ground her sense of right, even though the right supported by the divine (Thyestes' curse) does not ground her right (Iphigeneia's sacrifice).

[7] *Politics* 1328^{b}11–12 [*GBWW*, Vol. 9, p. 532d], cf. *Nicomachean Ethics* 1145^{a}10–11 [ibid., p. 394d].

[8] *Nicomachean Ethics* 1145^{a}15–33 [ibid., p. 395a].

[9] Sophocles *Oedipus at Colonus* 1132–34 [*GBWW*, Vol. 5 p. 124c–d].

[10] Cf. Plato *Republic* 378c7 [*GBWW*, Vol. 7, p. 321c].

[11] Cf. Sophocles *Oedipus Tyrannus* 1409 [*GBWW*, Vol. 5, p. 112a].

[12] *Digest* XXVIII.7. 1 1 5.

[13] Racine indicates this in the following way. Although he follows closely either Seneca or Euripides in his *Phèdre*, he departs from both in adding to Théramène's account of Hippolyte's death the fact that when the monster came out of the sea, everyone else took refuge in a neighboring temple and was saved, "without arming themselves with a useless courage" (V. vi), but Hippolyte went out and faced it. This departure from his sources is connected with another, apparently formal change: Hippolyte is no longer chaste but secretly in love with Aricie, who has been forbidden by Thésée to have any suitors. Hippolyte's horror at Phèdre's confession of love for him arises from his recognition that he too has broken the law no less than she: the decree of his father and the prohibition against incest are equivalent. *Phèdre* is the last play on a pagan theme that Racine wrote; he retired shortly afterward to Port-Royal and drew his inspiration for his dramas from the Bible.

[14] Herodotus III.14.10 [*GBWW*, Vol. 6, p. 92b].

[15] Aristophanes *Frogs* 911–20 [*GBWW*, Vol. 5, p. 574d].

[16] *Poetics*, chapter 4 [*GBWW*, Vol. 9, pp. 682–83].

[17] *On the Parts of Animals* 644^{b}22–645^{a}36 [ibid., pp. 168c–169b].

[18] 409–12 [*GBWW*, Vol. 5, p. 134d]; cf. Euripides *Suppliants* 760–68, 941–47 [ibid., p. 265a].

[19] "There is a passage in *Antigone* which I always look upon as a blemish, and I would give a great deal for an apt philologist to prove that it is interpolated or spurious. After the heroine has, in the course of the piece, shown the noble motives for her action, and displayed the elevated purity of her soul, she at last, when she is led to death, brings forward a motive which is quite unworthy and almost borders upon the comic." Goethe then summarizes the passage, 905–12 [ibid., p. 138d]. "This is, at least, the bare sense of the passage, which in my opinion, when placed in the mouth of a heroine going to her death, disturbs the tragic tone, and appears to me to be very far-fetched—to savor too much of dialectical calculation." *Conversations with Eckermann*, pp. 227–28 (tr. Oxenford, London, 1901).

[20] *Of the Advancement of Learning*, I.vii.28 [*GBWW*, Vol. 30, p. 25c].

[21] Sophocles *Oedipus at Colonus* 1224 [*GBWW*, Vol. 5, p. 125c].

[22] Plato *Ion* 535b1–c8 [*GBWW*, Vol. 7, p. 145a]; Aristotle *Politics* 1342^{a}7 [*GBWW*, Vol. 9, p. 547d].

[23] Cf. Plato *Symposium* 215c1–6 [*GBWW*, Vol. 7. p. 169c–d]; *Minos* 318b5–c1.

[24] *Iliad* I.188–222 [*GBWW*, Vol. 4, p. 5a–b].

[25] *Odyssey* IX.299–305 [ibid., p. 232b].

[26] Cf. Plato *Laws* 672b3–c5 [*GBWW*, Vol. 7, p. 672c–d].

[27] *Oedipus at Colonus* 1220–23 [*GBWW*, Vol. 5, p. 125c].

[28] Cf. Thucydides II.15–16 [*GBWW*, Vol. 6, p. 391c].

[29] *Republic* 414e2–6 [*GBWW*, Vol. 7, p. 340c–d].

[30] The obscurity of the Greek seems justified only if Oedipus wants to pun on his own name: "out of the way foot"—*ex hodou poda*—sounds like *Oidipodâ*.

[31] The usual translation assumes an unexampled construction: "Do not behold me as lawless."

[32] Herodotus's second book is devoted to Egypt. Although it contains many stories, there are only three (they all involve Greeks) told in dialogic form. The first story concerns Paris and Helen—his violation of the sacred; the second concerns Amasis, a usurper, who acts in an unroyal manner; and the third also concerns Amasis, who is moved to speak because, he believes, a Greek woman from Cyrene has bewitched him (II.112–15; 173.2–4; 181) [*GBWW*,

Vol. 6, pp. 71a–72a; 86b; 187c–188a]. Speech comes with the departure from law: the Egyptians are excessively pious, according to Herodotus, and avoid the adoption of foreign customs (II.37.1; 91.1) [ibid., pp. 56d; 91c]. Sophocles calls our attention to Egypt at lines 337–41, a passage that is modeled on Herodotus II.35.2 [ibid., p. 56c].

[33] *Eumenides* 657–66, 736–38 [*GBWW*, Vol. 5, p. 88b–c, d].

[34] *Iliad* VI.354–58 [*GBWW*, Vol. 4, p. 43d]; cf. *Odyssey* VIII. 579–80 [ibid., p. 228c].

[35] Cf. Euripides *Helen* 36–41 [*GBWW*, Vol. 5, p. 298b].

[36] *Eumenides* 864–65 [ibid., p. 89d].

[37] *Agamemnon* 182; cf. 1206 [ibid., p. 54a; p. 65a].

[38] Hesiod *Works and Days* 282–85.

[39] *Antigone* 626–27 [ibid., p. 136c].

[40] Cf. 475–98, 988–93 [ibid., p. 57b–c, p. 62c].

[41] This effect is acknowledged indirectly by Cicero: "Do not believe, Senators, that, as you see on the stage, wicked men by the onslaught of the gods are terrified by the burning torches of the Furies. His own deceitfulness, his own criminality, his own wickedness, his own reckless-ness put his mind in disarray. These are the furies, these the flames, these the torches." (*In Pisonem* 20 (46)." In Euripides' *Orestes*, the difference between "conscience" and "god" appears in the following way. Menelaus is shocked to find a filthy and unkempt Orestes after the murder of his mother. He asks him, "What illness is destroying you?" Orestes replies, "Intelli-gence (or conscience), because I know the terrible deeds I have done." Menelaus is perplexed, partly no doubt by the use of "intelligence" to explicate illness. "What are you saying? Clarity, you know, is wisdom, not obscurity." Orestes: "Pain is what is particularly destroying me." Menelaus: "The reason for that is that the goddess is dreadful but all the same curable (395–99)." The goddess Pain is both manageable and intelligible; "intelligence" is neither.

[42] Cf. Plato *Republic* 439e6–440a3 [*GBWW*, Vol. 7, pp. 352b–353b].

[43] *Eumenides* 616–21 [*GBWW*, Vol. 5, p. 87c].

[44] Cf. Aristophanes *Acharnians* 395, *Clouds* 1145 [ibid., pp. 459d, 502c].

[45] Orestes is consistent on this point. His delay in revealing himself to Electra makes sense only if he never had any intention to reveal himself. His placing a lock of hair on his father's tomb almost betrayed him (he did not suspect that Clytaemnestra and Aegisthus had forbid-den anyone to pay his due respects to the corpse (cf. 429–50); but Electra concluded (fortunate-ly for Orestes) that the lock meant that Orestes would not or could not return (cf. 167, 179–84); but the two sets of footprints that she then noticed forced her to realize that Orestes must have come himself and not just sent a messenger. This forced Orestes to show himself, though Electra does not recognize him (211). Why Aeschylus crossed the perfectly correct reasoning of Electra with false imaginings is a question that goes to the heart of tragic poetry.

[45a] The messenger from Corinth (924–26) ends his first line with *mathoim' hopou* ("I would learn where"), his second with *Oidipou* ("of Oedipus"), and his last with *katisth' hopou* ("you know where"), all of which point to "Oedipus" as meaning Know Where (*Oida pou*) (cf. 1036).

[46] Cf. Aristotle *Poetics* 1460ª27–31 [*GBWW*, Vol. 9, p. 696c].

[47] Cf. *Oedipus at Colonus* 1520–21, 1599 [*GBWW*, Vol. 5, p. 128a, c].

[48] *Poetics* 1452ᵇ34–36 [*GBWW*, Vol. 9, p. 687c].

[49] *Nicomachean Ethics* 1128ᵇ10–33 [ibid., p. 375d–376a].

[50] Horace says: "Sacred Orpheus, the interpreter of the gods, deterred savage men by terror from slaughter and loathsome food (i.e., cannibalism); he is said on account of this to soothe tigers and fierce lions" (*Art of Poetry* 391–93). Horace points to the complete coincidence in the highest poetry between the useful ("deterred by terror") and the pleasant ("soothe"); cf. 333–44.

[51] *Iliad* XXIII.103–4 [*GBWW*, Vol. 4, p. 162b].

[52] Euripides' *Alcestis* presents a not dissimilar lesson for Apollo. He gave his son Asclepius the power of resurrection; Zeus killed him; Apollo in anger killed the Cyclopes, in punishment for which he had to serve Admetus as a slave. Apollo rewarded the friendly treatment he received at the hands of Admetus by getting the Fates to postpone his death if he could find someone willing to die in his place. His father and mother refuse the privilege, his wife Alcestis accepts. Apollo did not understand why Zeus had disapproved of his gift of immortality; consequently, he tried to get around what he took to be Zeus's jealousy. Zeus lets him learn by a demonstration that the relations men have with one another cannot bear this kind of divine interference. Alcestis no sooner makes an offer that loses its grace if she demands recompense than she manages to make Admetus's future life intolerable (347). The demand

for justice is on the part of men stronger than love with no strings attached (cf. 299–302, 336–39). The abuse that Admetus heaps on his father for his unwillingness to die for him loses all its cogency as soon as one imagines that he was addressing his mother. Zeus adds another lesson: not Apollo's son Asclepius but his own son Heracles resolves the difficulty into which Apollo has fallen.

[53] Euripides does vouchsafe us something: the choral ode that intervenes between Pentheus's entrance into and exit out of the palace is devoted to punishment and happiness (862–911): the satisfaction that the punishment of enemies gives fills the gap between the complete freedom from need that men want (and Dionysus promises) and the median contentment that is granted to them. We learn after Pentheus's death that Cadmus's one regret at the outcome is that Pentheus will no longer address him affectionately as he asks, "Who wrongs you, old man? Who dishonors you? Who disturbs and troubles your heart? Speak, so that I may punish, father, the one who wrongs you" (1320–22) [*GBWW*, Vol. 5, p. 351b].

[54] *Nicomachean Ethics* 1116ª15–17 [*GBWW*, Vol. 9, p. 362b–c].

The Explosion of Biological Information

F. H. C. Crick

On any list of the important biologists of our time, Francis H. C. Crick takes eminent place. He is best known for the work that led in 1953 to discovery of the molecular structure of DNA, the substance that exercises hereditary control over life functions, for which, along with James D. Watson and Maurice Wilkins, he subsequently received a Nobel Prize. Since then, he has gone on to researches which have made it possible to locate the position of specific amino acids on a protein molecule, and which have determined the code for each of the twenty amino acids normally found in protein and the way in which the cell ultimately avails itself of the DNA code to build proteins—both of which have bearing on the procedures described in the following article.

Professor Crick, whose training was in physics and mathematics rather than biology, was employed at the Medical Research Council Laboratory of Molecular Biology, housed in the Cavendish Laboratories at Cambridge University, from 1949 to 1977. In the latter year he was given an appointment to the Salk Institute for Biological Studies at San Diego, where he now spends his time in teaching and writing. He has published a book about the new biology that he did so much to create, *Of Molecules and Men* (1966).

The complexity of biology

The complexity of biology is to some extent a matter of everyday observation. Even a child living in a city knows something about animals and plants. A fish is very different from a sparrow and neither of them is anything like a cabbage. Our own bodies, although we tend to take them for granted, seem quite complicated objects to us, especially if something goes wrong with them. The insides of a human being seem to have at least as many parts as the insides of an automobile.

What this naive view of biology does not take into account is just how immense the complexity is. As we learn more about the living world we discover that not only are there many different types of fish, amphibia, reptiles, birds and mammals, of which we see only a tiny fraction in even the largest zoo, but that in addition to these familiar vertebrates there are many invertebrates as well, among which are large ones, such as the lobster and the octopus, and many small ones, such as the million or so species of insects. Plants also are extremely various, from the familiar flowering trees and bushes of our streets and gardens, down to mushrooms, lichens, and fungi of all sorts. Less visible are the microorganisms, both protozoa and bacteria, many of which can scarcely be seen with the naked eye. Even smaller are the viruses, parasites which can multiply only within a living cell, and which straddle the borderline between the living and the nonliving.

As if this catalog were not enough, we must remember that, of all the species of organisms which ever existed on the earth, the great majority are now extinct. Not only are there no woolly mammoths anymore, the entire world of dinosaurs has vanished, as have many other strange creatures known to us only from fossils. The total number of species that ever existed must run into many billions.

When we look closely at the individuals of one particular species we find, at least for higher organisms, that although they look roughly the same, they are really all different from each other, though the differences may be small. This is most obvious to us from our knowledge of human beings, no two of whom look alike to us unless they are identical twins. More detailed studies of individuals show this impression to be well founded. Leaving aside differences produced by upbringing, we can easily show that individual people (twins aside) are genetically unique. Thus even within a species there is considerable genetic variability.

Finally we need to look more closely at the complexity of a single individual. Modern biochemistry has shown convincingly that organisms are far more complicated than our superficial impressions would suggest. A small bacterium, which we can hardly see unless we use a high-powered microscope, is a carefully organized self-reproducing chemical factory with thousands of distinct components, each one built with precision at the atomic level. One of our own cells is even more complex, and our tissues and organs, built of many cells cooperating together, are necessarily still more elaborate. Our bodies are not constructed of uniform chunks of "flesh," built on the scale of everyday life. They are delicately engineered at a level which is far too small for us to see. If they were not, they could not carry out the many complex operations needed for survival.

The world of biology, past and present, is vast, both in its detail and in its variety. It would take a huge number of parameters to describe it adequately. But do we need to have all this information in order to understand biology? Is it not enough to understand the general laws which govern biological behavior, provided we have sufficient well-studied examples to illustrate them? To some extent it is, and yet we must remember that biological laws are not exactly like the basic laws of physics. The latter operate mainly on relatively simple objects, such as electrons, which show little variety. One electron is indistinguishable from any other electron. Other physical laws, such as Newton's Law of Gravity, are true for more complex objects because the property studied—in gravity, it is mass—is strictly additive under a wide variety of conditions. Biological laws are rather different. It would perhaps be better to refer to them as mechanisms (the mechanism of natural selection, for example). They tend to be less compelling than physical laws, with curious complications and exceptions. For that reason we must study many more examples than would otherwise be necessary. Perhaps the most important difference is that the laws of physics are the same everywhere in the universe, whereas, if there is life on other worlds, it is unlikely that the major generalizations of biology here will all be true there. Much of biology, especially at the molecular level, is frozen history and might well be different in important respects if it all happened a second time.

In this essay I shall not attempt to grapple with the complexity of biology as a whole. The information explosion of the title refers to molecular information, and even this is restricted to the two major families of macromolecules, the nucleic acids and the proteins. As everyone knows, our understanding of DNA, RNA, and proteins has increased enormously during the past three decades. What is less well known is that within the last few years a new wave of techniques has accelerated by a large factor the rate at which we can acquire biochemical information of this sort. We stand on the brink of a great expansion of fundamental biological knowledge, only the first fruits of which have been harvested. This expansion promises to give us many new insights into the control and evolution of biochemical processes and to provide us as well with supplies of important molecules, for medical and other purposes, which were hardly imagined possible even ten years ago.

Classical molecular biology

To understand what is being discovered, we must first sketch what we already know. A preview of much of this can be found in parts of the article by John Platt in *The Great Ideas Today* 1968, especially the section headed "The Molecular Basis of Life." A more detailed but less lively description can be found in any modern textbook of biochemistry. Here, only a broad sketch of the outlines will be attempted.

Imagine you could observe a living cell at molecular resolution. What would you see? Almost all cells are surrounded by an oily flexible membrane that prevents the molecules inside the cell from leaking outside. This membrane has special gates and pumps to introduce molecules from the surrounding fluid into the cell, or to hasten the exit of others. Many plant cells and bacterial cells have a rather rigid cell wall outside this membrane to support it and assist it in its activities.

Inside the cells of higher organisms are several kinds of organelle, such as mitochondria, lysozomes and, above all, the cell nucleus which houses the chromosomes that carry the genetic information. Such a cell also has internal membranes, arranged in a complicated manner. A bacterial cell usually has none of these. Much of it consists of a thick salty solution of molecules and aggregates of molecules of many shapes and sizes. More elaborate cells also have a lot of this complex molecular soup.

How big are these molecules? If we define an organic molecule as a set of atoms held together by strong bonds (meaning they rarely if ever break at room temperature), then we notice a remarkable thing. The great majority of them are either large or small; there are rather few of intermediate size. To be more precise, molecules having less than a hundred atoms are common, as are those with thousands or tens of thousands of them, but molecules of intermediate size, having a few hundred atoms, are rather rare.

There is a good reason for this. Each organic molecule in a cell is built up or broken down in simple steps. Typically a group of just a few atoms will be added or removed at each step. This explains why there are so many different small molecules. But what about the big molecules? It turns out that the most important macromolecules are made by stringing certain small molecules end to end, in a semi-repetitive manner. They are often mass-produced on a production line. A special molecule of intermediate size would usually have to be custom-made. Very many distinct operations would be required to synthesize it, and for this reason such molecules are comparatively rare.

Proteins

The majority of large molecules in the cell belong to the protein family. A typical protein is a fairly compact structure, rather globular in shape, containing some thousands of atoms, each one held in a special position in the molecule. Many proteins are enzymes, that is, they are catalysts which speed up one particular chemical reaction in the cell. Without the protein, the reaction would proceed at a negligible rate. With it, the reaction goes very rapidly, the protein being unchanged at the end of the reaction, so that it can act over and over again. Moreover it acts accurately (that is, with very few side reactions) and discriminatively (without attacking closely related molecules).

Proteins as a class are very versatile. While many act as enzymes, others form structures, and some, such as the myosin in muscle, do both. The protein collagen is the main component of tendon and skin; keratin of hair; silk fibroin of silk. Other proteins form the various molecular pumps we find in membranes. In most cases where high molecular specificity is required, a protein has been evolved to fulfill the role.

The secret of proteins is that they are not initially synthesized as compact structures. Each protein really consists of a long, regular backbone to which small side-groups are joined at regular intervals and which then folds on itself to produce the intricate three-dimensional shape needed for its highly specific function. The structure is held together by the cooperative interaction of many weak bonds, which depend on the neat way the different parts of the molecule fit together. Boil a protein and the thermal jostling will often be too much for such delicate packaging. It will then unfold and become disordered. Indeed, one of the main functions of cooking is to denature proteins by heat to make them easier for us to digest.

The single polypeptide chain of a protein is synthesized by the cell, using special biochemical machinery, by joining head to tail small molecules called amino acids, chosen from a standard set of twenty kinds and supplied by the metabolic machinery of the cell or obtained directly from its food. A typical protein has several hundred of these amino acids all strung together in a particular order. It is this order which determines the individual nature of each protein and allows it to fold up correctly so that it can have the necessary chemical groups adjacent to each other at special places on the surface. The information needed to synthesize any particular protein is thus the order of the amino acids in its polypeptide chain.

We can now see more clearly why the molecules in a cell tend to be either large or small. Those large molecules which are enzymes act as catalysts whose main job is either to turn small molecules into closely related ones or to string them together to make larger ones. The cell is a chemical factory that contains many small components produced by machine tools which are themselves constructed by joining certain small components together in a particular order.

The nucleic acids

As is well known, the amino acid sequence of a particular protein cannot be copied directly from an existing protein. There is no mechanism to do this. Instead, the sequence information is carried on another macromolecule called messenger RNA (ribonucleic acid). This in turn is usually the working copy of another, closely related, macromolecule called DNA (deoxyribonucleic acid), which embodies the master copy of the genetic information of the cell.

RNA and DNA also have a regular backbone with side groups at regular intervals (though the two backbones are slightly different), but in this case there are only four common types of side groups. These four types are generally known by their initial letters. DNA has A (adenine), G (guanine), C (cytosine), and T (thymine). RNA also has A, G, and C, but instead of T it has the closely related U (uracil). It speaks the same language as DNA but a different dialect. The biological information we shall be considering will be mainly the sequence of the four bases: A, G, C and T (or U) in DNA (or RNA) and to a lesser extent the amino acid sequences of proteins. Since the nature of a cell is largely determined by the proteins it produces, we see that this molecular information is indeed at a very basic level.

Naturally, there must be a dictionary to connect the four-letter language of the nucleic acids with the twenty-letter language of the proteins. That dictionary is called the genetic code, by analogy with the Morse code (*see* fig. 1). The sequence of letters of nucleic acid are read in groups of three at a time, starting at a special point. There are sixty-four such triplets (4x4x4). Of these, sixty-one are allocated to one amino acid or another, the other three standing for "end chain." (The signal for "begin chain" is a little more complicated.) The genetic code has so far been found to be identical in all organisms—animal, plant, bacteria, or viruses—with the exception of mitochondria, the little energy-producing organelles found in higher organisms. Mitochondria have their own DNA and their own machinery for protein synthesis. It has recently been discovered that their code differs from the usual one in a few triplets. It remains to be seen whether other exceptions to the "universal" genetic code will be discovered.

DNA, as is now well known, is usually a double helix, consisting of two

The Genetic Code

First Position (5′ End)	Second Position				Third Position (3′ End)
	U	**C**	**A**	**G**	
U	Phe	Ser	Tyr	Cys	**U**
	Phe	Ser	Tyr	Cys	**C**
	Leu	Ser	Term[a]	Term	**A**
	Leu	Ser	Term	Trp	**G**
C	Leu	Pro	His	Arg	**U**
	Leu	Pro	His	Arg	**C**
	Leu	Pro	GluN	Arg	**A**
	Leu	Pro	GluN	Arg	**G**
A	Ileu	Thr	AspN	Ser	**U**
	Ileu	Thr	AspN	Ser	**C**
	Ileu	Thr	Lys	Arg	**A**
	Met	Thr	Lys	Arg	**G**
G	Val	Ala	Asp	Gly	**U**
	Val	Ala	Asp	Gly	**C**
	Val	Ala	Glu	Gly	**A**
	Val	Ala	Glu	Gly	**G**

[a] Chain terminating (formerly called "nonsense").

		Ala	Alanine	Leu	Leucine
U	Uracil	Arg	Arginine	Lys	Lysine
C	Cytosine	Asp	Aspartic acid	Met	Methionine
A	Adenine	Asp N	Asparagine	Phe	Phenylalanine
G	Guanine	Cys	Cysteine	Pro	Proline
		Glu	Glutamic acid	Ser	Serine
		Glu N	Glutamine	Thr	Threonine
		Gly	Glycine	Try	Tryptophan
		His	Histidine	Tyr	Tyrosine
		Ileu	Isoleucine	Val	Valine

Figure 1. Each amino acid is known by a three- (or four-) letter abbreviation of its name. Each entry in the table corresponds to a triplet of bases on the messenger RNA. Thus AUG stands for methionine. The signal(s) for chain initiation are not shown here.

long polynucleotide chains wound round and round each other. Rather surprisingly the two chains are antiparallel rather than parallel. That is, if the sequence of atoms in one backbone is considered to run upward, that of the other chain runs downward. At every level a side group (called a base) of one chain is paired with the side group opposite it on the other chain. The pairing is highly specific, only certain base pairs being allowed: G pairs with C, A pairs with T. Any base can follow any other base on one chain, but if the sequence of bases on one chain is given, that of the other is rigidly determined because of the base-pairing rules.

This base pairing enables the cell to copy DNA (or RNA) by separating the two chains and allowing each separate chain to act as the template for the synthesis of a new companion. It is a really beautiful mechanism, though the details of the process are more complicated than this simple description would suggest. The base pairing is also used in the process of making a single-stranded copy of the RNA of some limited stretch of a long DNA molecule, since A pairs with U (in RNA) in a way similar to A with T.

DNA molecules are usually very long. Even a small virus may have as many as 5,000 bases or base pairs, depending upon whether its nucleic acid is single-stranded or double-stranded. The bacterium *E. coli* has about three million base pairs in its DNA, all in one big circular molecule. The DNA of one of your own cells contains some six billion base pairs, though this is not all in one piece but is dispersed among the various chromosomes. The total length of this DNA is about two meters, all of which has to be folded up within the cell nucleus, a structure less than one hundredth of a millimeter in diameter.

Proteins come in all sizes, but a "typical" polypeptide chain might be 300 amino acids long, thus needing 900 bases to code for it. Allowing some extra sequences at the beginning and the end, we see that the messenger RNA for such a protein might have a little over a thousand bases. Naturally, some messages are shorter than this and some are very much longer, depending on the size of the protein coded. A small virus, 5,000 base pairs long, might be expected to code for about half-a-dozen proteins, assuming they were all of average size. That is the sort of number which is actually found in those cases that have been studied carefully. It may not sound very large, but some viruses of this size are quite capable of killing an infected animal or giving it a lethal cancer, using only that limited amount of genetic information.

A similar calculation suggests that the DNA of *E. coli* probably codes for several thousand different proteins. Our own cells can code for many more but, as we shall see, not quite as many as the bare figures would indicate.

The flow of information

The word *information* can be used in many ways, some more precise than others. Here I propose to use it only in a very restricted sense to mean the *sequence information* in nucleic acids and proteins. Since these macromolecules are constructed using only a limited alphabet (four letters for the nucleic acids, twenty letters for proteins), this usage has at least the virtue of being fairly precise. It leads us to ask how information can flow between the three families of macromolecules, DNA, RNA, and protein.

One of the major generalizations of molecular biology (known as the Central Dogma) is that only certain transfers are possible. Information can flow from DNA to new DNA, as in DNA replication. In the replication of

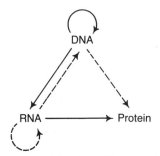

Figure 2. A simple diagram to represent the Central Dogma. The arrows represent the possible flows of detailed sequence information. The solid lines represent the most common transfer: the dotted lines those found less frequently. The *absence* of some arrows embodies the central dogma: that information of this type never flows *out* of protein.

certain RNA viruses, we find the flow RNA to RNA. Within one nondividing cell the major flow is from DNA to RNA and then from RNA to protein. (James D. Watson has used the term *Central Dogma* for these flows alone, but such a usage is undesirable.) Under special circumstances we may find the flow RNA to DNA and even from single-stranded DNA to protein, though this latter process can only be made to occur under artificial conditions and is both inefficient and inaccurate. What we never find are the flows from protein to protein, or from protein to either DNA or RNA (*see* fig. 2). Correctly stated, the Central Dogma says that when (sequence) information has got into protein *it cannot get out again.*

It is important to realize that the Central Dogma only summarizes what has been found in biological systems at the present time. For example, it says nothing of what might have happened in the past and in particular at the origin of life. Nor does it in any sense imply that proteins cannot interact with nucleic acid, since we have abundant evidence that some of them do. What it says is that the detailed information in the sequence of the amino acids in such a protein can neither be copied exactly nor translated into a corresponding detailed sequence of bases along a piece of nucleic acid. It does not say anything about the control of the *rate* at which these flows take place, only whether the sequence information can or cannot be transferred under the appropriate conditions. It is, at bottom, a negative statement, but a very powerful one nevertheless. There is no known exception to it.

One other feature of information flow is important. That is the multiplication of information, or, more strictly, the multiplication of the number of *copies* of a fixed amount of information. The genetic material (usually DNA) is usually doubled at each step. A cell divides into two daughter cells, each of which receives identical copies (mutations aside) of the genetic material of the mother cell. This process can happen over and over again. After ten successive divisions there will be just over a thousand copies ($2^{10} = 1,024$); after twenty divisions, a million copies. Notice that the process is "geometrical." It is not simply a single copying process, repeated over and over again, as in the printing of a newspaper or book. Each copy itself acts as the instructions for two or more new copies. The fertilized egg may contain just two copies of a particular gene, one from the egg and one from the sperm. The mature adult, after forty or more successive cell doublings, will possess many trillions of copies. Moreover, if that gene is active in a certain subset of cells, that stretch of DNA will control the production of perhaps a thousand or more molecules of messenger RNA. Each such messenger RNA may act as instructions for the production, on the ribosomes in the cytoplasm, of some thousands of copies of the particular protein which it codes. If there is a mistake (a mutation) in both of the original pair of genes, these will be magnified many, many times in the finished protein. A small change of a few atoms in just one or two DNA molecules may produce a drastic change in many grams of protein in the adult. It is not surprising that the magnified effect of this atomic alteration can in some cases have a devastating effect on the organism. The base sequence of DNA coding for β-hemoglobin in those human beings who inherit sickle cell anemia differs by only a single base pair in each of the two genetic copies, yet this minute change is usually enough to kill the unfortunate possessor before his or her teens.

So much for the broad outlines of classical molecular biology. The reader will notice that although we have described how information flows between the macromolecules and have given the rules which control these flows (the base-pairing rules and the genetic code), nothing at all has been said about the details of the information contained in any particular macromolecule, apart from the sort of molecular lengths involved. In fact some authors use the words *the genetic code* to mean the actual message contained in genetic DNA or RNA rather than (as I have done) the dictionary used to translate from the four-letter languages to the twenty-letter language. It is a remarkable historical fact that the flow and rules governing them were worked out using only tiny bits of detailed sequence information, often only three bases long. This was because, at that time, the methods for sequencing proteins were rather slow and those for the nucleic acids (especially DNA) either very laborious or nonexistent. The recent development of new sequencing methods has made it possible to determine experimentally DNA sequences hundreds or thousands of base pairs long, thus increasing by a large factor our detailed knowledge of genetic information. To these methods we must now turn.

Recent developments

In order to sequence a macromolecule, it is necessary to have enough of it and to have it reasonably pure. For nucleic acid, this represents formidable problems. It is true that some RNA molecules are small. The transfer

RNA molecules which are an essential part of the machinery of protein synthesis are only about seventy or eighty bases long. There are substantial numbers of them in each cell, so that their purification is possible, even though there may be thirty or more distinct types in one cell; not surprisingly, they were the first nucleic acid molecules of appreciable length to be sequenced. It is when we turn to genetic nucleic acid and, in particular, to the DNA of the chromosomes, that the problems arise. For most genes, there are only one or a few copies per cell. This, chemically speaking, is an infinitesimal amount. Even as little as one microgram (a millionth of a gram) of a substance of molecular weight 600,000 (corresponding to about a thousand base pairs of DNA) contains a trillion molecules. In addition, most DNA is extremely long.

We can overcome both of these difficulties to some extent by studying small viruses, but even 5,000 base pairs of DNA is far too long to sequence at one go. We see immediately that four things are required: (1) we must be able to cut a DNA molecule at particular points to obtain it in shorter pieces; (2) we then need to fractionate these many pieces from each other, to obtain each one of them in a pure form; (3) in addition, we need fairly large amounts of each pure component; it has turned out that in many cases the best way to do this is to start from one single molecule of DNA and arrange for it to be magnified biologically; and (4) finally, it is necessary to have a rapid method of sequencing such that sequences 100 or 200 bases long can be obtained in a single experiment. Our knowledge of molecular biology is now so extensive that it has proved possible to achieve all these aims, though new methods have had to be developed to do this.

Methods of separation

The power of these methods springs from several causes. The invention of chromatography and in particular paper chromatography has led over the years to many similar methods for separating molecules, in either one or two dimensions, using a thin layer of material, either in the form of a permeable sheet (such as paper) or as a special gel. Other devices use tall vertical columns containing material in the form of a packed suspension of a powder or small beads of various kinds. In all these methods a small portion of a solution containing the molecules to be separated is deposited at one place. Liquid is then made to flow past this point, carrying the dissolved molecules along with it. Conditions are chosen so that the different kinds of molecule are delayed by different amounts as they flow along together so that after they have traveled a sufficient length, usually some centimeters or tens of centimeters, they are strung out one behind the other and thus separated.

The method of electrophoresis, in which electrically charged molecules are pulled through a solvent by an applied electrical field, has also been adapted to work in sheets of paper or layers of other materials. In this method, molecules with a net positive charge will travel in one direction while those with a net negative charge will go in the opposite one, and molecules with no net charge will stay at the point of origin. Broadly speaking, molecules having a bigger net charge or a smaller size will travel faster than the others.

After this separation in one direction, it is often possible to achieve a second separation at right angles to the first one, either by simply turning the paper so that the second flow (using a different solvent or a different method) is perpendicular to the first one, or by transferring the molecules lying on the strip obtained from the first flow by "blotting" the strip onto another sheet of material, again so that the direction of the second separation is at right angles to that of the first. By this means the separation in the first dimension can be on the basis of, say, molecular size, while that of the second may perhaps be due to the electric charge carried by the molecules. Many combinations of methods are possible. As a result the molecules which started all together in one small drop, often in one corner of the paper, will at the end of the double run be spread out, well separated, over the two-dimensional surface of the paper or gel.

The weakness of many of these methods is that only small amounts of material can be handled before the system becomes saturated and the separation inefficient; if too much material is used, a spot will often "tail" to give a smear. It is therefore necessary to use special methods to detect the molecules as they lie separated on the paper or gel. Originally this was done by using some chemical stain to make the colorless spots visible. Molecules which absorb ultraviolet light were detected by taking a photograph of the separation using an ultraviolet lamp as illumination. In some cases fluorescent stains could be used. A very powerful method has turned out to be the use of radioactive tracers. If the starting materials can be made radioactive, either by obtaining them from cells grown using radioactive chemicals for food or by tagging them at some later step in the experiment with a radioactive atom or group of atoms, then minute amounts can be detected by taking an autoradiograph of the dried sheet containing the separated molecules. The autoradiograph will show the different spots as dark marks (due to the effect of the radioactivity on the photographic emulsion) standing out against a transparent background. By viewing such photographs with a special viewing box (to provide a uniform bright light), quite faint spots can be detected. The molecules can often be identified merely by their position on the gel, and, if necessary, the spots can be cut out of the sheet (using the photograph as a guide) and their material dissolved out of them, so that further experiments can be done on each separated component. By these means, as we shall see, very remarkable experiments have become possible, mainly because complex mixtures, often of rather similar molecules, can be separated very effectively even though the amounts of material used are very small.

Enzymes as tools

The second important tool used by modern molecular biologists is the enzyme. In classical organic chemistry a chemical reaction was carried out by mixing two or more fairly pure chemicals, often in some carefully chosen solvent, allowing them to react together and then separating the products of the reaction both from each other and from any unused starting material. Even in the most successful reactions, yields were seldom very high, and side reactions (that is, unwanted reactions which take place due to a lack of specificity in the reacting molecules) were often a nuisance.

The advantages of enzymes are twofold. They can carry out reactions under very mild conditions (indeed conditions have to be mild or the enzyme itself would be damaged) and they are highly specific. Side reactions are usually negligible. For this reason it is usually unnecessary to add special chemical groups (called protecting groups) to the molecule being processed to prevent the more obvious side reactions. The disadvantage of enzymes is that they cannot be produced at will to carry out a particular chemical step. The enzyme must occur in Nature. It has to be first discovered and then purified, at least to some extent. When few enzymes were known, this was a considerable handicap, but now that many different enzymes have been purified from many different sources, some rather unexpected (for example, snake venom or horseradish), it is often possible to design the experiment to take advantage of the enzymes available. In some cases a deliberate search has been made to find more enzymes of a particular general type by devising special screening techniques and examining many organisms, often microorganisms, to see if they appear to possess such an enzymatic activity. This screening can often be done on intact organisms or on organisms simply broken open without the necessity for any purification. If, in a particular case, some enzymatic activity is found, then an attempt can be made to grow larger quantities and to purify the enzyme. Again, modern methods of handling and purification are now much more powerful and versatile, so that this is not nearly as difficult a job as it was in the past.

An enzyme is rather like a very fine pair of hands on a molecular scale. It acts so delicately because its structure has been refined by many millions of years of natural selection; the cell, too, has a need for chemical tools which act rapidly and selectively. By holding chemical groups in very precisely defined positions it can control the possible chemical reactions much better than a human chemist, who in most cases can only mix chemical reagents together in the same vessel and allow them to react by bumping against one another in all possible ways as they diffuse about in the solvent.

Matching molecules of nucleic acid

A third tool used in these investigations depends on the way the bases of nucleic acid form pairs. This again can be highly specific. The pairing is used in two ways. If an enzyme is involved, as in the replication of DNA, the pairing is usually very accurate indeed. Mispairing is usually negligible. However, two separate single strands of nucleic acid, having complimentary base pairs, can under certain conditions be made to join together in solution to form a double helix. Here the pairing may not always be quite so precise, since in most cases so many base pairs are involved that an occasional mispairing will make little difference.

The power of this latter method comes from the ability of a piece of nucleic acid, having a particular base sequence, to diffuse rapidly and so to seek out and combine with its partner strand in a mixture of many other single-stranded nucleic acid molecules having different base sequences. The conditions are chosen so that a molecule cannot pair too easily with another one. Only when it finds a molecule with the correct (or almost correct) complimentary sequence will the two join together and zip up to form a double helix. As we shall see, this enables the experimenters to pick out one particular length of nucleic acid even when it is mixed with a host of others. In addition, by using the electron microscope, this act of molecular recognition can be observed at the level of single molecules; with suitable shadowing, one can not only see nucleic acid molecules, looking rather like very long pieces of fine string, but can tell which stretches are double-stranded and which single-stranded. Moreover, this technique only needs infinitesimal amounts of material.

Cutting nucleic acid specifically

One of the most fortunate discoveries of molecular biology has been that of the restriction enzymes. The details of their natural function need not detain us. It suffices to say that a particular restriction enzyme will cut DNA only at very special places. For example, one known as Eco RI recognizes only the sequence

$$5' \ldots . \mathrm{G}{\downarrow}\mathrm{A\ A\ T\ T\ C} \ldots . 3'$$
$$3' \ldots . \mathrm{C\ T\ T\ A\ A}{\uparrow}\mathrm{G} \ldots . 5'$$

the two arrows showing exactly where the cuts are made. Although restriction enzymes had been known for some time, it was only in the last ten years or so that it was realized that they act in this particular way. If the base sequence of DNA were random, or approximately so, then such an enzyme would cut DNA into a whole variety of sizes, the average length of the pieces being about 4,000 bases. By this means, lengths of DNA, perhaps millions of base pairs long, could be cut into a well-defined set of pieces of many different lengths.

Once it was realized that enzymes of this type existed, and how important they might be, a deliberate search was made to discover more of them. As a result we now have 50 or 60 distinct types of restriction enzymes, each with a different specificity. Some need only four or five base pairs, rather than six, as the recognition signal, so that they cut DNA in rather more places. Such a battery of tools allows the research team to play tricks of all sorts. They can, for example, cut a selected stretch of DNA, perhaps from a small virus, using two or more restriction enzymes with quite different specificities, applying them separately, together, or in succession. This often allows them to put all the resulting fragments in a definite order and thus produce, on a coarse scale, a "map" of the DNA. Or they may want to cut the DNA at or near a particular point—perhaps the origin of DNA replication —and, with luck, may be able to find one particular restriction enzyme which will do this; or they may need, for some purpose, to cut the DNA of a small virus in one place only. Again, by trial and error the researchers may be able to find just the enzyme for the job, even though they may have, as yet, no knowledge of the exact base-sequence of this DNA.

Having cut the DNA into a whole set of pieces, it is often necessary to separate them so that each one in turn can be sequenced. To do this, the researchers will usually use a fractionation method which sorts the molecules according to size. This is likely to be successful if there are not too many pieces of DNA to be separated, as otherwise quite different pieces of DNA which, by chance, have the same, or nearly the same, length will run together. This problem becomes acute if the whole genome of a higher organism is being used. A typical restriction enzyme may break human DNA into roughly a million distinct pieces. Clearly some other approach is needed if the research team is to obtain, out of this complex mixture, the single piece of DNA required.

Biological magnification

It is here that biological magnification becomes useful. Starting with DNA fragmented into many pieces, obtained either by using a restriction enzyme or by the rather coarse method of breaking the DNA (at random points) by mechanical shear, the experimenter manipulates this mixture, using enzymes as tools, so that each piece of DNA is inserted into a special place in the DNA of, for example, a small virus which attacks an easily grown bacterium. (Such a virus is called a bacteriophage, or phage for short.) This mixture of viruses, each with its own genes plus one inserted piece of DNA, is then used to infect a population of bacteria, but with the bacteria in numerical excess, so that most of those bacteria which are attacked are infected by one virus only. The mixture is then plated out, at fairly high dilution, on a lawn of uninfected bacteria lying on top of nutrient jelly in a flat dish. After incubation, the lawn of bacteria appears as if motheaten, being covered with small, circular, translucent areas. Each area represents a place where an infected bacterium has fallen onto the plate and multiplied many times, thus killing all the host bacteria in that small region and leaving a clear hole in the lawn of growing and dividing bacteria. Each plaque, as these holes are called, contains many, many identical copies of the virus which originally fell there. Each of these copies contains both its own DNA and the piece of inserted DNA.

We are now faced with the following problem. We have obtained many plates, each with many plaques. With luck one of these plaques, and perhaps only one of them, will contain a copy of the exact piece of DNA we are looking for. But how are we to find, out of so many, just the one we want?

To do this we need a probe that will recognize the DNA we want and no other, together with a rapid method of screening all the plaques with this probe. A probe often used is the messenger RNA related to the gene we are looking for or, more likely, some DNA which is a copy of this messenger RNA, again made using enzymes and biological magnification. If we can obtain this material radioactive and reasonably pure, then we can use it to screen each phage plaque to see which one contains DNA which will combine specifically with our radioactive probe. I will omit the details of the manipulation which, though ingenious, are relatively straightforward. Suffice it to say that by taking known methods and improving them, it is now possible, given a suitable probe, for one person to screen as many as a million phage colonies in less than a working week. The few phages which have the desired DNA show up as dark spots on autoradiographs taken of special replicas of the original plates. These plaques can then be picked. That is, using a toothpick the experimenter can transfer phages from the indicated plaque in the appropriate place to a test tube where they can be increased by further growth in bacteria. The rate of biological magnification is considerable, since each bacterium infected with a single phage can, in the space of twenty minutes or so, produce several hundred identical copies. Thus, starting with a single phage, it is possible to grow overnight, in a small test tube of bacteria, as many as a billion identical, or almost identical, copies of that phage. Once the right DNA molecule has been identified, amounts of this DNA sufficient for sequencing can be grown relatively easily.

The DNA needed (the extra piece originally inserted) must now be clipped away from the rest of the DNA of the phage, again by the use of a suitable restriction enzyme, and this DNA must be purified away from the rest, but usually this step is not especially difficult. We now have—pure, and in appreciable amounts—one particular piece of DNA, perhaps that containing a single human gene. This opens the way to a determination of its precise base sequence. The method just sketched in outline is only one of the many methods available today. All of them combine ingenious methods of cutting and joining DNA with the use of biological magnification and, often, rapid screening methods to select the molecule one wants from a rather random and complex mixture. Even though the reader has not been given the exact details of the methods used, he or she may be able to appreciate how powerful they are. To be able to select one single copy of one macromolecule from a host of very similar ones, and then to multiply it many times and purify it, is a remarkable achievement. Without these new methods we would have no hope of studying the chemical details of our own genes.

Methods for rapid sequencing

Having obtained a pure stretch of DNA, possibly one or two hundred base pairs long, it is now necessary to sequence it. There are two main methods of doing this, each with several variations, but they all have one thing in common. They depend on being able to sort out, on a specially thin gel, a set of fairly similar nucleic acid molecules having many different lengths. Thus a single-stranded DNA having, say, 71 bases can be easily resolved after a run on such a gel from one having one extra base or one fewer. The general method is to do four separate experiments, one for each of the four bases, and run the results side by side on the same gel. Consider the experiment which concentrates on the base adenine (A). By one device or another it is arranged that only chains which end in A are present at the end of the incubation. Thus if, starting from a fixed point, the 76th, 80th, and 82nd base is A, then chains of length 76, 80, and 82 will be present, whereas those with lengths 77, 78, 79, and 81 will be absent. Thus the *position* of the spots on the gel, after the chains have all been spread out, will say exactly where the A's are. If we have three similar experiments, one for G, one for C, and one for T, then we can see, for each position, what base was present in the original sequence.

How is this done? The methods vary, but I will describe one. If the DNA is double-stranded, the two strands of the DNA are first separated from each other by gentle heating, to make them come apart, followed by purification. Then, one strand is used as a template for the enzymatic synthesis of a new strand. A special primer is used to make sure the synthesis always starts at the same place in the sequence, and the new DNA chain is made radioactive by supplying the enzyme which controls the process with radioactive precursors. There are naturally four such precursors, one for A, one for G, one for C, and one for T.

To this mixture is added a small amount of a chemical related to the A precursor which I will call A'. This is so like A that the enzyme will put it in place of A, should A' present itself to the enzyme, but it is so designed that no further base can be added once A' has been inserted at the end of the growing chain. Thus the chain will stop growing whenever an A' is incorporated. Since A is present in excess the new chain will contain A in many places, but some chains will be shorter than others, since by chance they will have received A' (and thus stopped growing) at an early stage in their synthesis. By a careful choice of the amount of A', *all* lengths ending in A will be represented in the final mixture of chain lengths. Only minute amounts of material need be used, since the position of the spots on the final gel can be obtained by autoradiography.

The whole experiment is usually done twice, using first one of the single-stranded DNA's as a template and then the other. Thus the sequence is effectively obtained twice over as an insurance against possible mistakes. In all, eight separate incubations are necessary, and if the eight products are then run side by side on the special gel the exact base-sequence can be read off, twice over, from the autoradiograph of the result. By methods of this general type, sequences of up to a hundred base pairs can be easily obtained and, with care, the method will deal with sequences as much as several hundred base pairs long. With modest equipment and expense, an experienced laboratory worker can obtain DNA sequences at the rate of several hundred base pairs a week.

These methods, which are still being developed and improved, are now in use in all the leading molecular biology laboratories. In fact, such was the eagerness to use the new sequencing techniques that results obtained using one method were published even before the exact details of the method had had time to get into print. They have been applied not only to small viruses and mitochondria but to selected pieces of the chromosomal DNA from higher organisms, including man himself. Similar methods are being developed for RNA, though it is more usual to make a DNA copy of the RNA molecule, using a special enzyme called reverse transcriptase, and then sequence this DNA copy.

A small virus

When all this has been done, what does the result look like? To bring home to the reader what one is up against, the DNA sequence of a small virus—a bacteriophage called ϕX 174—is shown in figure 3. This was obtained by Fred Sanger and his colleagues at Cambridge, England. The genetic material of this virus happens to be circular single-stranded DNA, so bases are shown rather than base pairs. It is just 5,386 bases long. In fact, Sanger's group has sequenced this virus twice, the second time using an improved method, and has also sequenced a related virus, G4, of similar size.

At first sight, one is baffled to the point of irritation. A sequence of such

```
GAGTTTTATCGCTTCCATGACGCAGAAGTTAACACTTTCGGGATATTTCTGATGAGTCGAA
AAATTATCTTGATAAAGCAGGAATTACTACTGCTTGTTTACGAATTAAATCGAAGTGGAC
TGCTGGCGGAAAATTGAGAAAATTCGACCTATCCTTGCGCAGCTCAGAAAGCTCTTACTTT
GCGACCTTTCGCCATCAACTAACGATTCTGTCAAAAACTGACGCGTTGGATGAGGAGAAG
TGGCTTAATATGCTTGGCACGTTCGTCAAGGACTGGTTTAGATATGAGTCACATTTTGTT
CATGGTAGAGATTCTCTTGTTGACATTTTAAAAGAGCGTGGATTACTATCTGAGTCCGAT
GCTGTTCAACCACTAATAGGTAAGAAATCATGAGTCAAGTTACTGAACAATCCGTACGTT
TCCAGACCGCTTTGGCCTCTATTAAGCTCATTCAGGCTTCTGCCGTTTTGGATTTAACCB
AAGATGATTTCGATTTTCTGACGAGTAACAAAGTTTGGATTGCTACGACCGCTCTCGTG
CTCGTCGCTGCGTTGAGGCTTGCGTTTATGGTACGCTGGACTTTGTGGGATAACCCTCGCT
TTCCTGCTCCTGTTGAGTTTATTGCTGCCGTCATTGCTTATTATGTTCATCCCGTCAACA
TTCAAACGGCCTGTCTCATCATGGAAGGCGCTGAATTTACGGAAAACATTATTAATGGCG
TCGAGCGTCCGGTTAAAGCCGCTGAATTGTTCGCGGTTTACCTTGCGTGTACGGCGCAGGAA
ACACTGACGTTCTTACTGACGCAGAAGAAAACGTGCGTCAAAAATTACGTGCGGAAGGAG
TGATGTAATGTCTAAAGGTAAAAAACGTTCTGGCGCTCGCCCTGGTCGTCCGCAGCCGTT
GCGAGGTACTAAAGGCAAGCGTAAAGGCGCTCGTCTTTGGTATGTAGGTGGTCAACAATT
TTAATTGCAGGGGCTTCGGCCCCTTACTTGAGGATAAATTATGTCTAATATTCAAACTGG
CGCCGAGCGTATGCCGCATGACCTTTCCCATCTTGGCTTCCTTGCTGGTCAGATTGGTCG
TCTTATTACCATTTCAACTACTCCGGTTATCGCTGGCGACTCCTTCGAGATGGACGCCGT
TGGCGCTCTCCGTCTTTCTCCATTGCGTCGTGGCCTTGCTATTGACTCTACTGTAGACAT
TTTTACTTTTTATGTCCCTCATCGTCACGTTTATGGTGAACAGTGGATTAAGTTCATGAA
GGATGGTGTTAATGCCACTCCTCTCCCGACTGTTAACACTACTGGTTATATTGACCATGC
CGCTTTTCTTGGCACGATTAACCCTGATACCAATAAAATCCCTAAGCATTTGTTTCAGGG
TTATTTGAATATCTATAACAACTATTTTAAAGCGCCGTGGATGCCTGACCGTACCGAGGC
TAACCCTAATGAGCTTAATCAAGATGATGCTCGTTATGGTTTCCGTTGCTGCCATCTCAA
AAACATTTGGACTGCTCCGCTTCCTCCTGAGACTGAGCTTTCTCGCCAAATGACGACTTC
TACCACATCTATTGACATTATGGGTCTGCAAGCTGCTTATGCTAATTTGCATACTGACCA
AGAACGTGATTACTTCATGCAGCGTTACCGTGATGTTATTTCTTCATTTGGAGGTAAAAC
CTCTTATGACGCTGACAACCGTCCTTTACTTGTCATGCGCTCTAATCTCTGGGCATCTGG
CTATGATGTTGATGGAACTGACCAAACGTCGTTAGGCCAGTTTTCTGGTCGTGTTCAACA
GACCTATAAACATTCTGTGCCGCGTTTCTTTGTTCCTGAGCATGGCACTATGTTTACTCT
TGCGCTTGTTCGTTTTCCGCCTACTGCGACTAAAGAGATTCAGTACCTTAACGCTAAAGG
TGCTTTGACTTATACCGATATTGCTGGCGACCGTGTTTTGTATGGGCAACTTGCCGCCGCG
TGAAATTTCTATGAAGGATGTTTTCCGTTCTGGTGATTCGTCTAAGAAGTTTAAGATTGC
TGAGGGTCAGTGGTATCGTTATGCGCCTTCGTATGTTTCTCCTGCTTATCACCTTCTTGA
AGGCTTCCCATTCATTCAGGAACCGCCTTCTGGTGATTTGCAAGAACGCGTACTTATTCG
CCACCATGATTATGACCAGTGTTTCCAGTCCGTTCAGTTGTTGCAGTGGAATAGTCAGGT
TAAATTTAATGTGACCGTTTATCGCAATCTGCCGACCACTCGCGATTCAATCATGACTTC
GTGATAAAAGATTGAGTGTGAGGTTATAACGCCGAAGCGGTAAAAATTTTAATTTTTGCC
GCTGAGGGGTTGACCAAGCGAAGCGCGGTAGGTTTTCTGCTTAGGAGTTAATCATGTTT
CAGACTTTTATTTCTCGCCATAATTCAAACTTTTTTTCTGATAAGCTGGTTCTCACTTCT
GTTACTCCAGCTTCTTCGGCACCTGTTTTACAGACACCTAAAGCTACATCGTCAACGTTA
TATTTTGATAGTTTGACGGTTAATGCTGGTAATGGTGGTTTTCTTCATTGCATTCAGATG
GATACATCTGTCAACGCCGCTAATCAGGTTGTTTCTGTTGGTGCTGATATTGCTTTTGAT
GCCGACCCTAAATTTTTTGCCTGTTTGGTTCGCTTTGAGTCTTCTTCGGTTCCGACTACC
CTCCCGACTGCCTATGATGTTTATCCTTGAATGGTCGCCATGATGGTGGTTATTATACC
GTCAAGGACTGTGTGACTATTGACGTCCTTCCCCCGTACGCCGGGCAATAACGTTTATGTT
GGTTTCATGGTTTGGTCTAACTTTACCGCTACTAAATGCCGCGGATTGGTTTCGCTGAAT
CAGGTTATTAAAGAGATTATTTGTCTCCAGCCACTTAAGTGAGGTGATTTATGTTTGGTG
CTATTGCTGGCGGTATTGCTTCTGCTCTTGCTGGTGGCGCCATGTCTAAATTGTTTGGAG
GCGGTCAAAAAGCCGCCTCCGGTGGCATTCAAGGTGATGTGCTTGCTACCGATAACAATA
CTGTAGGCATGGGTGATGCTGGTATTAAATCTGCCATTCAAGGCTCTAATGTTCCTAACC
CTGATGAGGCCGCCCCTAGTTTTGTTTCTGGTGCTATGGCTAAAGCTGGTAAAGGACTTC
TTGAAGGTACGTTGCAGGCTGGCACTTCTGCCGTTTCTGATAAGTTGCTTGATTTGGTTG
GACTTGGTGGCAAGTCTGCCGCTGATAAAGGAAAGGATACTCGTGATTATCTTGCTGCTG
CATTTCCTGAGCTTAATGCTTGGGAGCGTGCTGGTGGTGATGCTTCCTCTGCTGGTATGG
TTGACGCCGGATTTGAGAATCAAAAAGAGCTTACTAAAATGCAACTGGACAATCAGAAAG
AGATTGCCGAGATGCAAAATGAGACTCAAAAAGAGATTGCTGGCATTCAGTCGGCGGACTT
CACGCCAGAATACGAAAGACCAGGTATATGCACAAAATGAGATGCTTGCTTATCAACAGA
AGGAGTCTACTGCTGCGCGTTGCGTCTATTATGGAAAACACCAATCTTTCCAAGCAACAGC
AGGTTTCCGAGATTATGCGCCAAATGCTTACTCAAGCTCAAACGGCTGGTCAGTATTTTA
CCAATGACCAAATCAAAGAAATGACTCGCAAGGTTAGTGCTGAGGTTGACTTAGTTCATC
AGCAAACGCAGAATCAGCGGTATGGCTCTTCTCATATTGGCGCTACTGCAAAGGATATTT
CTAATGTCGTCACTGATGCTGCTTCTGGTGTGGTTGATATTTTTCATGGTATTGATAAAG
CTGTTGCCGATACTTGGAACAATTTCTGGAAAGACGGTAAAGCTGATGCTGATTGGCTCTA
ATTTGTCTAGGAAATAACCGTCAGGATTGACACCCTCCCAATTGTATGTTTTCATGCCTC
CAAATCTGGCTTTTTATGGTTCGTTCTTATTACCCTTCTGAATGTCACGCTGATT
ATTTTTGACTTTGAGCGTATCGAGGCTCTTAAACCTGCTATTGAGGCTTGTGGCATTTCTA
CTCTTTCTCAATCCCCAATGCTTGGCTTCCATAAGCAGATGGATAACCGCATCAAGCTCT
TGGAAGAGATTCTGTCTCTTTTCGTATGCAGGGCGTTGAGTTCGATAATGGTGATAGTATG
TTGACGGCCATAAGGCTGCTTCTGACGTTCGTGATGAGTTTGTATCTGTTACTGAGAAGT
TAATGGATGAATTGGCACAATGCTACAATGTGCTCCCCCAACTTGATATTAATAACACTA
TAGACCACCGCCCCGAAGGGGACGAAAAATGGTTTTTAGAGAACGAGAAGACGGTTACGC
AGTTTTGCCGCAAGCTGGCTGCTGAACGCCCTCTTAAGGGATATTCGCGATGAGTATAATT
ACCCCAAAAAGAAAGGTATTAAGGATGAGTGTTCAAGATTGCTGGAGGCCTCCACTATGA
AATCGCGTAGAGGCTTTGCTATTCAGCGTTTGATGAATGCAATGCGACAGGCTCATGCTG
ATGGTTGGTTTATCGTTTTTGACACTCTCACGTTGGCTGACGACCGATTAGAGGCGTTTT
ATGATAATCCCAATGCTTTGCGTGACTATTTTCGTGATATTGGTCGTATGGTTCTTGCTG
CCGAGGGTCGCAAGGCTAATGATTCACACGGCCGACTGCTATCAGTATTTTTGTGTGCCTG
AGTATGGTACAGCTAATGGCCGTCTTCATTTCCATGCGGTGCACTTTATGCGGACACTTC
CTACAGGTAGCGTTGACCCTAATTTTGGTCGTCGGGTACGCAATCGCCGCCAGTTAAATA
GCTTGCAAAATACGTGGCCTTATGGTTACAGTATGCCCATCGCAGTTCGCTACACGCAGG
ACGCTTTTTCACGTTCTGGTTGGTTGTGGCCTGTTGATGCTAAAGGTGAGCCGCTTAAAG
CTACCAGTTATATGGCTGTTGGTTTCTATGTGGCTAAATACGTTAACAAAAAGTCAGATA
TGGACCTTGCTGCTAAAGGTCTAGGAGCTAAAGAATCAGGTAATTCCAAAGCTTTATACG
TGTCGCTACTTCCCAAGAAGCTGTTTCAGAATCAGAATGAGCCGCAACTTACCAAGTCGGGTTACG
TGCTCACAATGACAAATCTGTCCACGGAGTGCTTAATCCAACTTACCAAGCTGGGTTACG
ACGCGACGCCGTTCAACCAGATATGAAGCAGAACGCAAAAAGAGAGATGAGATTGAGGC
TGGGAAAAGTTACTGTAGCCGACGTTTGGCGGCGGCAACCTGTGACGACAAATCTGCTCA
AATTTATGCGCGCTTCGATAAAAAATGATTGGCGTATCCAACCTGCA
```

a length, consisting of only four letters without obvious intervals or punctuation marks, does not allow its important features to jump to the eye. Not surprisingly, some scientists, used to thinking of living organisms in rather grosser terms, have been horrified by the detail and the obscurity of the message. But it is important to realize that it is at this level that the commands of life are spelled out. Unless we are able to master this strange new language we shall never understand how living things operate. The information in these viral instructions is enough to allow the virus to take over the synthetic machinery of the host cell, make many copies of itself, not only of its own DNA but also of the protein box which houses that DNA, and then to kill the cell, so that numerous virus particles are released into the surrounding medium. The polio virus has a similarly limited number of bases (no doubt in time its sequence, too, will be determined), and yet it can cripple or even kill a human being.

Many of the signals contained in nucleic acid sequences are still not easy for us to read clearly. There are sequences which indicate where DNA replication should start, others which tell the enzymes which produce RNA copies where to begin transcribing, and yet others for certain control proteins to attach to. But there is one type of signal we can read with great ease. That is the signal of the sequences which, when translated using the genetic code, control the amino acid sequence of a protein. Fortunately, for many viruses, mitochondria, and bacteria, most DNA has this function, so we can understand fairly well what many of those sequences of four letters imply. Yet even for a simple virus like ϕX 174, the results were not quite what was expected.

Normally, one long continuous stretch of DNA will be transcribed to form a single messenger RNA molecule. This usually has an untranslated run of bases at its beginning, followed by some hundreds of bases which are translated, three bases at a time, into the amino acid sequence of a polypeptide chain. Following this, there is usually a shorter, untranslated length of RNA. Like a movie film, the message has both a lead-in and a similar length at its end. These long stretches of DNA, each of which is transcribed onto a messenger RNA molecule, are separated by shorter sequences which contain the instructions for starting and ending transcription, and also those which control the *rate* at which that particular message is transcribed. In bacteria the situation may be slightly more complicated, since one messenger RNA may code for several successive polypeptide chains, but such a combined message is never found in higher organisms.

Figure 3. The base sequence of the small bacterial virus known as ϕX 174, written as English is written, each line from left to right and then the lines from top to bottom. The letters A, T, G, and C symbolize the four kinds of base found in the single-stranded DNA of the virus. This DNA is actually circular, so the bottom of the sequence shown joins onto the top.

The concept of phase

To understand what was different in the virus ϕX 174 it is necessary to grasp the idea of "phase." As we have seen, in translation the message is read three bases at a time, beginning at a designated starting point. If, for some reason, the reading frame is displaced one base to the right (or one to the left), the whole grouping of the message into triplets is altered and the resulting polypeptide chain will be completely different from the usual one. If this happens at some point in the translation process, then we say that the message is being read "out of phase." There are, in all, six possible ways of reading in triplets a message coded on double-stranded DNA, three readings off one chain and three others (in the reverse direction) off the complementary chain. These six readings will all be quite different from one another.

Normally, only one of these is used to code for a polypeptide chain. Since, out of the sixty-four codons, no less than three stand for "end polypeptide chain," a *random* sequence of bases will, on the average, have a stop triplet every twenty amino acids or so. This is usually true of all the five out-of-phase readings of a stretch of coding DNA. Only in the correct reading frame are chain-terminating triplets rare, since polypeptide chains are usually several hundred amino acids long and yet require only one terminating triplet. If, by mutation, such a triplet is accidentally created in the middle of the coding sequence, the translation will terminate there and only a part of the polypeptide chain will be produced. This will usually be rejected by natural selection, because in most cases a protein with such a truncated chain will not function correctly.

Notice that if, by mutation, one base pair is accidentally omitted from the DNA in the middle of a coding sequence, then the whole reading of the message after that point will be altered and the resulting protein is unlikely to perform properly. The same is true if an extra base pair is accidentally added to the sequence. Some environmental mutagens have just this effect and indeed alterations of this sort may be at the root of many cases of chemical carcinogenesis. It seems highly likely that multiple alterations to DNA, at special places, are the cause of most forms of cancer.

Gene compaction

The DNA of ϕX 174 is known to code for at least nine proteins, one being the main protein of the viral capsid (the box which contains and protects the DNA). Most of the other proteins have the various special functions needed to assist the growth of the virus. From certain genetic experiments the approximate positions of the genes for these proteins had been located on the DNA. It was discovered, when the exact base sequence of the DNA was determined, that in more than one case the coding sequences over-lapped somewhat. That is, the same stretch of DNA was being used to code one polypeptide chain in one phase and another polypeptide chain in a different phase. Because the phase was different the two amino acid sequences were quite different from one another (*see* fig. 4).

```
···Lys    Glu    Trp    Asn    Asn    Ser    Leu    Lys    Thr···
··· A A A G A A T G G A A C A A C T C A C T A A A A A C T ···
          Met    Glu    Gln    Leu    Thr    Lys    Asn···
```

Figure 4. A stretch of the DNA of the virus φX 174 which is read in two distinct phases. The base-sequence is the middle line. The top line shows how it codes for part of the A protein. The bottom line shows the coding for the beginning of the B protein. On the corresponding messenger RNA molecules T would be replaced by U.

Such a possibility had been considered before, but it had always been thought improbable because it implied, in many cases, that changing a base pair at a particular point altered an amino acid in *two* distinct proteins. This would impose restrictions on the possibilities open to natural selection and thus make it more difficult for it to act efficiently. Why, then, did it occur in this virus?

The most likely answer is that the size of the viral DNA is limited by the size of the box (the capsid) which has to contain it. Since the virus cannot obtain more information by making its DNA longer, it pushes genes as close together as possible and even uses one piece of DNA for two genes, the advantages of having more genetic information offsetting the disadvantages associated with double readings. Moreover, it does not need to use extra DNA for the job. This is an additional advantage since extra DNA means, other things being equal, a higher overall mutation rate, and this higher rate of making mistakes might be more than the virus could cope with. Extra DNA also means that the virus cannot replicate quite as fast as it would if it had less.

A detailed study of the sequences has suggested that, of the two readings, one was the original one, the other evolving later. Presumably the virus, by accident, tried out the second reading and found that it made a polypeptide chain which, however inefficiently, helped its reproduction. Natural selection would then act to improve this new protein while disturbing the function of the original one as little as possible. Evolutionary arguments are always difficult to prove but, whatever the historical sequence, there is no doubt that today φX 174 has DNA sequences which code for more than a single protein. In fact, in one or two places the overlapping is so extensive that one particular base pair manages to be part of triplets used to code for three different polypeptide chains, each of which might be several hundred amino acids long.

Genes in higher organisms

Three other small viruses have had extensive work done on their sequences. They, too, are about 5,000 base pairs long, but their genetic material is double-stranded DNA, whereas ϕX 174 used single-stranded DNA. These viruses attack not bacteria but the cells of various mammals, and with certain hosts they are oncogenic; that is, they give the animal cancer. Growing in a mammalian cell they are able to use certain processes only found in the cells of higher organisms. These little viruses are not very complex objects compared with the host cells in which they operate, and it might be thought easier to consider them first before passing to a description of chromosomal genes. As it turns out these viruses, too, seem to need to keep down their total content of DNA; they therefore use a trick which has not, as yet, been found in chromosomal genes. Although most of the chromosomal genes so far studied tend to be larger than the average viral gene, they are in one sense simpler. For this reason we will consider them first.

A general remark should be made at this point. The word *gene* can, at the moment, only be used in a loose way. In bacteria we have a fairly clear idea of how DNA functions, but the complexities are such that *gene* is not a concept which can be defined very simply. In higher organisms we do not, as yet, fully understand how DNA expresses itself; the exact meaning of the word is thus uncertain. In spite of this, it is useful to have a word to describe, however vaguely, this unit of genetic expression, and I use *gene* when convenient in this general sense.

Repetitive sequences

It has been known for some time that there are types of DNA sequences in higher animals and plants which are not found in bacteria. The most unexpected of these are the highly repetitive sequences. There may be stretches, many millions of base pairs long, which consist of a sequence of a small number of base pairs repeated over and over again with the minimum of variation. Perhaps that found in certain crabs is the most striking. It consists of a multitude of consecutive repetitions of the sequence AT, with only an occasional G or C mixed in. Certain crabs have 10 percent of their DNA in this nonsense sequence, and one has as much as 40 percent. Not surprisingly, these sequences are not transcribed into RNA. Nobody knows their exact function. Not all simple sequence DNA is as simple as this, semi-exact repeats of, say, seven bases or eleven bases being more common than repeats of two. Most higher organisms have appreciable amounts of such DNA, often possessing several different sorts. In most cases they are widely distributed over the various chromosomes, often near the centromeres, the little chromosomal organelles which are involved in chromosome movement. It is surmised that simple sequences exist to perform some "housekeeping" function (a term probably invented by a male), meaning that we don't know exactly what this function is but feel it can't be too important.

Simple sequence DNA is only the extreme case of a whole family of repetitive sequences, in most of which the repetition is longer and less precise. These less repetitive sequences, often called "intermediate repetitive," are more widely dispensed in the DNA, and many of them are transcribed. Their function therefore is likely to be more interesting but, although there are many facts and plenty of speculation, it is not yet known what they do.

Excess DNA

The other surprising feature of the DNA of higher organisms is the very large amount of it found in certain species. Certain plants, such as lilies, or certain amphibia, such as salamanders, have much more DNA than we do, sometimes as much as twenty times more. It seems ridiculous to suppose that a salamander is a more complex organism than a human, or that one salamander needs far more detailed genetic information than a similar one in another region. Again, it is surmised that the bulk of this DNA is unlikely to have a primary function. One has the impression that if an organism can accommodate extra DNA, without a serious handicap to its way of life, it will do so. It is not like a virus, the amount of whose DNA is limited because it must fit into a rather rigid protective container. An organism with more DNA usually has bigger cells, and these cells tend to divide more slowly, but there is no obvious spatial limit to the size of its set of chromosomes.

Of course, the chromosomes of higher organisms are not made purely of DNA. They possess a considerable amount of protein. Much of this is used to construct small molecular beads, called nucleosomes, on which the DNA is wound, since to fit into the nucleus the DNA must be folded extensively. There are many other proteins as well, but the function of most of them has not yet been discovered. Bacteria, too, have protein associated with their DNA, but whatever its function there is certainly less of it.

Nuclear RNA

There is another striking difference between the nucleic acid of higher organisms and bacteria. In higher organisms almost all the DNA lies in the nucleus of the cell. No protein synthesis takes place there, all the machinery for protein synthesis (ribosomes, transfer RNA, etc.) being in the surrounding cytoplasm. The messenger RNA, transcribed off the DNA in the nucleus, must therefore pass through the pores of the nuclear membrane to the cytoplasm before it can direct protein synthesis. It has been known for some time that the situation cannot be quite as simple as that, because there is extensive RNA with unusual properties in the nucleus. This RNA is, on the average, considerably longer than messenger RNA. It contains base sequences which are not found in messenger RNA, and yet it seems to be, at least in part, the physical precursor of the RNA messages in the cytoplasm. This material, known by the clumsy name of the heterogeneous nuclear RNA (or hnRNA for short), is not found at all in bacteria that have no nucleus or nuclear membrane. In fact, so eager are the bacterial ribosomes to translate messenger RNA that they hop onto it and start translating it into protein even before its transcription from the DNA is completed. A partly synthesized molecule of messenger RNA will have a string of ribosomes attached to it, busily making protein, while the growing end of the RNA is still attached to the DNA being transcribed.

Bacteria, then, are very different from higher organisms. They do not have long complex molecules of hnDNA and they have no appreciable excess of DNA. They do not contain repetitive sequences of any sort, except for those genes which control the production of certain structural RNA molecules. These types of RNA (ribosomal RNA, transfer RNA, etc.) are needed in such large amounts that their genes have to be present in multiple copies. It is therefore not surprising that the viruses of bacteria are somewhat different from those of higher organisms, for many of the operations needed to produce a virus are carried out by the chemical machinery of the host cell which it has commandeered for its own use.

Introns and exons

At the present time only a very few genes, in a very few higher organisms, have been examined in detail. The coverage has been sparse and patchy in the extreme. Thus, any generalization of these preliminary results must be regarded as very tentative. In spite of this, the new information has such striking features that not all of it is likely to be freaky.

Fortunately, those genes which have been studied have in most cases been tackled by more than one group of experimenters so that we can double-check many of the results. Consider first the protein ovalbumin. This is the main protein in the white of an egg. It is synthesized in large quantities in the oviduct of a laying hen. It consists of a single polypeptide chain 385 amino acids long. The messenger RNA for this protein has been sequenced by the usual technique of making a DNA copy and sequencing that. It has the expected 1,155 bases coding for the protein, with a stretch of 67 bases before and no less than 637 bases after the coding sequence. When the genetic DNA came to be studied, a very surprising result was found. The gene was several times the predicted length. More detailed

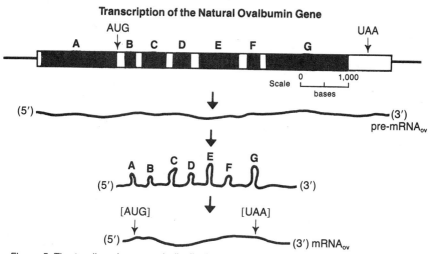

Transcription of the Natural Ovalbumin Gene

Figure 5. The top line shows symbolically the structure of the region of DNA which is transcribed onto RNA. The white regions show the stretches which end up in messenger RNA (the exons); the black regions the stretches which are spliced out (the introns). The second line shows the initial RNA transcript. The third and fourth lines show symbolically how the seven introns (marked A to G) are spliced out to give the final messenger RNA (mRNA). The total length of the gene on the DNA is about 7,550 base pairs. The mRNA is only 1,859 bases long. The total length of the seven black regions is more than three times the total length of the eight white regions.

studies showed that the expected base sequence on the DNA, instead of being continuous, was interrupted no less than seven times by apparently nonsensical sequences, often hundreds of base pairs long (*see* fig. 5). It was like finding a series of advertisements interrupting the text of a short story.

The stretches of DNA which did not code for the protein are now called "intervening sequences," or "introns," while the parts which end up on the messenger RNA are called "exons," because they are expressed. It was then found that what the cell did was to make a complete RNA transcript of the whole stretch of DNA, both introns and exons (this transcript forming part of the hnRNA in the nucleus), and then proceeded to cut out the introns while splicing the RNA exons together to form the message which was then exported to the cytoplasm. The discovery of introns, and the splicing mechanism for removing them, came as a complete surprise, for nothing like them had been found in the earlier work on bacteria or bacterial viruses.

The function, if any, of the extra DNA in the introns is obscure. It seems unlikely that these sequences are ever translated to form polypeptide chains, since stop triplets are frequent in all three phases of reading. Some of these sequences, after they have been clipped out, may conceivably be used for other purposes, such as gene control, but it seems likely that most of them are broken down so that their components can be recycled. In the case of ovalbumin it has already been shown that for one intron there is a minor difference in sequence between individual chickens, even though the chickens are of the same breed.

Another protein whose genes have already been intensively studied is hemoglobin. This is the major protein in red blood cells, whose function is to carry oxygen from the lungs to the tissues. It has four polypeptide chains, two called α and two β. Each type has a separate gene, usually on different chromosomes. There are a whole family of β-like polypeptide chains. Some are used only in the fetus, others only in the adult. All these genes appear to be related, since the amino acid sequences they produce are similar though distinct. The β-like genes usually lie close together on one stretch of DNA. All the globin genes probably evolved from a common ancestral gene. Several of them have been sequenced, or partly sequenced, in a number of mammals, including man, so it is possible to make comparisons.

As with ovalbumin, it is found that globin genes contain introns, though there are not as many as there are in the ovalbumin gene. What is striking is that all the globin genes studied so far have exactly two introns and that, in effect, they occur in exactly the same two positions in all of them, though the length and composition of the introns varies considerably between the different genes and between the same gene in different species.

This strongly suggests that these two introns are very old in their evolution, probably several hundred million years. The successful introduction of a new intron or the complete elimination of an existing one seems to be a very rare event. On the other hand, the results on the insulin gene show that in some cases such an event can occur. The rat has two related genes for insulin (strictly for the precursor protein, from which insulin is derived, called preproinsulin). One of these has two introns, whereas the other has only one. A detailed comparison with other mammals suggests that this loss or gain of an intron (whichever it was) took place very roughly 30 million years ago, since it appears likely that before that time both genes had a common ancestor.

The gene for the light chain of γ-globulin has an interesting feature. Gamma-globulin has to be excreted by those cells which produce it. To get outside the cell it has, at some point, to pass through a membrane. Most likely it does this while its polypeptide chain is still being synthesized. The initial part of this chain has a sequence of about a couple of dozen amino acids, many of which are hydrophobic and thus tend to prefer environments like the fatty inside of a membrane. This initial stretch of polypeptide chain (known as the signal peptide) is cut off shortly after synthesis, when the bulk of the chain has passed through the membrane and no longer requires the signal peptide. It is significant that one of the introns on the DNA is placed very close to the sequence coding for the junction between the signal peptide and the rest of the chain. The positioning of the intron in this case seems to be more than a coincidence.

The immune system, which produces antibodies against foreign macromolecules and thus protects us from infection, is too complicated to describe here in detail. Two points only need be made. The polypeptide chains involved are coded by genes which appear to have arisen in evolution by tandem duplication. For example, the heavier of the two types of polypeptide chains in the γ-globulin molecule consists of four "domains," joined together end to end. The amino acid sequence of each domain is different from that of the others, but the similarities suggest that the domains are all related and, in the distant past, that they evolved from a common ancestral gene of about one quarter the length. It is significant that there are introns in the present gene which lie just at those points in the DNA sequence that correspond to the boundaries between these polypeptide domains.

The other remarkable discovery which has come from a study of the DNA sequences of these unusual polypeptide chains is that the arrangement of the DNA is not the same in the cells producing γ-globulin as it is in the germ line (that is, in egg and sperm). In the latter the single polypeptide chain is mainly coded for by two distinct stretches of DNA widely separated from each other on the chromosome. Such cells produce no γ-globulin. In those cells which do synthesize the protein, these separated DNA sequences are brought much closer together, so that one stretch of DNA of moderate length contains them both. In other words, the *DNA sequences* must have been rearranged at some stage during the development of the organism from the fertilized egg. The details of this fascinating process, which are only just being unraveled, are too complicated to describe here, though we know that the exact rearrangement can be different in different cells of the body. This special mechanism, which so far has not been found in other more mundane genes, helps to provide the immense variety of related proteins which are needed to recognize the many unknown intruding molecules that are found in infections of various kinds.

Mammalian viruses

We can now return to viruses and consider those small mammalian viruses which have already been sequenced or partly sequenced. In many ways the most interesting one is Adenovirus, but this is so complex that I shall leave it on one side and instead concentrate on three related viruses, called SV40 (Simian Virus 40), polyoma, and BKV, a human papovavirus. All three are double-stranded DNA viruses containing about 5,000 base pairs. All have been sequenced completely, SV40 having been done independently by two separate groups of workers. They all grow in the cells of one particular mammal or another, and all of them, in other animals, can produce a cancer. That is why so much work is being done on them.

As in the case of the bacterial virus, it is found that genes are pushed together, one stretch of DNA being used to code more than one protein. One such stretch is read in the same phase to produce two proteins having related amino acid sequence but of different lengths. It is also read in another phase to code part of the polypeptide chain of a third protein having a completely different amino acid sequence. This reading of a piece of DNA in more than one phase is just what was found in φX 174.

Since the host cells of these viruses have introns in their DNA and also contain in the nucleus the enzymatic machinery for splicing them out of RNA transcripts, it is no great surprise to find that all three viruses possess introns. And yet, on reflection, if their DNA is limited, why do these small viruses not reduce their introns in size or eliminate them entirely? Instead of doing that, the virus has evolved a neat way of using introns to obtain more useful genetic information. The part of the viral DNA which is responsible for "transforming" certain host cells (that is, loosely speaking, producing cancer) is called the T region, since it codes for at least two proteins known as T (big T) and t (little t). The exact details vary between the viruses, so I shall give here only an outline description, omitting certain complications. As their names imply, little t is a small protein, big T being about four times as large. The remarkable thing is that the initial RNA transcript is the same in each case. If it is unprocessed it will produce the smaller protein, t, since even though the message is very long there is a stop triplet in it which terminates the t protein. However, there is a potential intron in this region. That is, the RNA transcript may sometimes be spliced to remove a stretch of RNA. This process eliminates a stretch of coding RNA and with it the stop triplet at its end. When the ribosomes in the cytoplasm translate this slightly shorter message they make a much longer protein, T, since there is no stop codon in that phase till toward the end of the message.

The important point is that by either splicing the RNA or not the system can make either T or t. These two proteins both start with the same amino acid sequence, but after the first hundred or so residues their sequences are quite different. In fact, the arrangement is even more elaborate than this, for there may be a third protein (middle T) which can be produced by a different splice, part of whose sequence is read out-of-phase to the reading which produces part of T.

These viruses, then, do not discard introns. They turn them to their own advantage by using them to obtain more proteins from their limited amount of DNA.

So far, no such device has been found in a chromosomal gene, probably because there is no obvious restriction on the amount of chromosomal DNA. If a chromosomal gene did arise which, by alternative methods of splicing, could produce two distinct proteins, one would expect that, in the course of evolution, the gene would be duplicated on the chromosome, one copy then specializing in one protein and the second copy in the other one.

A possible exception might be the genes coding for proteins of the immune system, but here the variety is produced by chopping and joining the chromosomal *DNA*, rather than by manipulating the RNA transcript, since each particular cell produces no more than one type of polypeptide chain even though it does so in large quantities. The variety the body needs is produced between cells, not within them.

The distribution of introns

I have mentioned briefly some of the genes which have already been sequenced, but these are only a sample of what has been done and more results are coming in almost every week. This rapid flood of detailed information has already led to surprising realizations, the most important of which are that there is a widespread occurrence of introns in higher organisms and a compaction of genes, by one means or another, in viruses. When we come to consider the origin and function of introns, however, we realize how much more we shall have to learn before we can approach an understanding of that process. So far, no introns have been found in bacteria or bacterial viruses, but for all we know there may be some classes of bacteria that still have them.

Most of the genes examined in higher organisms are of a special type. They produce a protein in large amounts in some particular type of differentiated cell. Are there also introns in the bread-and-butter proteins which are found in all sorts of cells? We know that some genes (those for the five kinds of histone) have no introns at all, at least in two invertebrates. Is this a peculiarity of this class of protein or are there many other examples? Are there higher organisms without any introns? So far, only one has been found in the little fruit fly, *Drosophila*, on which so much genetic study has been done over the years. Are many more there to be found, and are they perhaps smaller and rarer than those in organisms with much more DNA in their chromosomes?

The base sequences of those introns which have been studied in related genes strongly suggest that they drift very rapidly in evolution, both in composition and in length. This might imply that most of an intron has no essential role to play in the life of the organism. However, a few preliminary experiments suggest that without its introns a gene may not function correctly. Exactly what this implies remains to be seen. One obvious hypothesis is that the entire processing step needed to remove an intron can only be done conveniently when the transcription of the RNA is physically separated from its translation into protein. This happens in higher organisms because of the nuclear membrane, whereas in bacteria the two processes can proceed together. This idea, if correct, would explain why higher organisms have introns while bacteria appear to lack them. It would predict, however, that mitochondria (which have their own DNA but no nuclear membrane) should have no introns. None have been found as yet in human mitochondria but there appear to be several in those of yeast cells. The reason for this difference is obscure.

Whatever their function, it is important to realize that in most cases introns are remarkably large. If we average those chromosomal genes so far studied which code for protein, then the total length of DNA in all these introns is several times the total in exons. Speaking loosely, in these genes there is more nonsense than sense. This clearly needs an explanation of some sort.

The origin of introns

In spite of the paucity of information, there are already two broad theories about how introns arose in evolution. The more obvious one is that originally genes had no introns. With the evolution of mitosis and a nuclear membrane, introns for the first time became possible. Introns appeared in genes because a special process existed which could insert stretches of DNA at certain places. Of course, such an insertion would normally make nonsense of the gene, but possibly the very act of insertion in the DNA created signals (special base sequences) which, when transcribed into RNA, allowed the splicing mechanism to clip out the RNA of the inserted sequences, so that the message could still function correctly. Whatever the details, the idea is that the intact gene existed first and the introns were subsequently added to it.

The second idea, which we owe to W. Gilbert and S. Tonegawa, is more ingenious. It is proposed that genes which started later in evolution were never at any time coded without interruptions. The gene was born with the introns in it. The suggestion is that such genes were put together from several existing sequences elsewhere in the genome which were shuffled around in evolution till they accidentally came together to code for the new polypeptide chain. It is argued that it would be easier to shuffle exons in this way if they were moved about with an intron fragment at either end, since this would make the exact positions of cutting and joining together less critical.

Such a theory would naturally explain why introns, in some cases, occur at the borders between discrete protein domains and would also occur near the junction between signal peptide and the rest of the polypeptide chain. A signal peptide is a good example of the evolutionary advantages of this mechanism. Suppose that certain conditions arise such that a protein hitherto used only inside cells could usefully be secreted for use outside them. Rather than evolve a new signal peptide afresh, it would seem easier to tack onto the beginning of the gene a length of DNA which already codes for a signal peptide elsewhere in the genome. Exon shuffling, guided by natural selection, would be just the mechanism to achieve this arrangement.

Against the theory is the fact that not all introns appear to be between protein domains, but perhaps we have the wrong preconceptions about domains in such cases. Clearly we shall need many more sequences to decide between these two ideas. It may turn out that both are correct. When an organism has many introns it seems very likely that exon shuffling will occur, whereas in the earlier stages of evolution, when introns were perhaps scarcer, exon shuffling would be more difficult and the insertion mechanism might have been more prevalent.

It should be realized that, at the moment, we do not know when introns first arrived on the scene. Several authors have suggested that introns originally existed in the very simplest organism, or even nearer to the origin of life when organisms as we know them hardly existed. They argue that the ancestors of bacteria had introns but that, as competition became more intense and very fast replication became advantageous, the bacteria gradually discarded their introns so that they could multiply more quickly and outgrow their relations, till eventually no introns were left. Higher organisms, it has been suggested, do not always need rapid growth, and in such cases the introns would be retained. It may take a while before we can discover exactly what happened in evolution, especially at times as long as a billion or so years ago.

Selfish DNA

There still remains the problem of the function of introns. There seems a fair possibility that these DNA sequences may, in most cases, have no function whatsoever, existing only for their own sake. To use a catch phrase, their DNA might be simply Selfish DNA. This term was suggested by the idea of the Selfish Gene, but the two ideas are different. The theory of evolution by natural selection is no respecter of persons. In a population it is not the individual that survives nor, in a sexually breeding population, even his exact combination of genes. What survives are the individual genes, in the sense that the genes of the new generation are (mutation aside) exact copies of certain genes in the previous one. If the function of a gene confers a selective advantage, in one way or another, it is likely to be passed on. Otherwise it will, in time, be eliminated.

What distinguishes selfish DNA from a selfish gene is that it can multiply and spread within the genomes of single individuals and that, in the ideal case, selfish DNA has no phenotypic function at all. Why, then, is it not eliminated? The answer must be that elimination, being partly due to chance, is a slow process and that the selfish DNA sequences are able to spread not merely through the population but through the genome of a single individual, even though they confer no advantage on the organism that carries them. If we postulate that, by one mechanism or another, certain DNA sequences can increase their number by moving around on the chromosome, fitting in now here, now there, then we see that even without a function such sequences might survive. Of course, if they colonize the chromosomes too successfully they will eventually burden them with so much DNA that the organism will be handicapped. If the selfish DNA spreads indefinitely the organism will probably become extinct, together with its selfish DNA. Thus there will be selection against any DNA sequences which spread too rapidly. For a stable arrangement a balance must be struck between the tendency for the DNA to increase and the burden its presence puts on its host. Since a lot of junk DNA tends to slow cells down, we would expect that organisms whose life-style demands rapid growth or a short life cycle would select against selfish DNA, by one means or another, more effectively than would those organisms that have a more relaxed way of life. This may explain why introns appear to be either small or absent in *Drosophila*, which has a very short life cycle.

This idea of selfish DNA has yet to be adequately tested, but it does seem to have the capability of explaining why some organisms have so much more DNA than others, a fact that otherwise seems completely nonsensical. This extra DNA is probably not all within genes, in the form of introns, but exists between genes as well, as one would expect if selfish DNA moved around indiscriminately. If the basic idea is correct, it will be important to discover the various mechanisms by which some DNA can increase and migrate. In this picture the DNA of a chromosome is not a rather fixed entity in evolution. Sequences are continually increasing, moving about, and being eliminated. From time to time an intron may grow in size as some other DNA sequence is inserted within it. At other times a part of it may suddenly be deleted, so that on this extended time scale each intron will be in a state of flux. Occasionally an intron may be deleted entirely and disappear at that place but that would be a very rare event, since for it to occur the beginning and the end of such a deletion would have to be positioned very exactly.

This is not to say that all introns have no function. It seems almost certain that, even if most introns effectively did nothing when they first originated, some of them, simply by being there, will have acquired a function in the course of evolution. Such introns may then be difficult to delete without damage to the organism. How many introns in fact serve some useful purpose remains to be discovered.

Introns as genetic markers

Whatever the function of introns, it seems certain that they will be extensively used as genetic markers, especially for evolutionary studies. Once a particular piece of DNA has been obtained pure and in reasonable amounts, it is easy to use it to screen for similar DNA in the individuals of the same or related species. In order to demonstrate a difference, exact sequencing is not always necessary. The simpler method of showing that a restriction enzyme cuts the DNA differently may suffice in some cases. Because intron sequences tend to drift rather rapidly in evolution, we may expect that they will not always be exactly the same in all individuals. This has already been found for one of the ovalbumin introns in chickens and for one hemoglobin intron in man. It would be surprising if there were not such variation in many other human introns. At the moment, genetic differences between human beings are scored in different ways. The preferred method at the molecular level was to study proteins, either by electrophoresis or by amino acid analysis. It will be interesting to see to what extent DNA sequencing will replace these earlier techniques. Before long we may see anthropologists penetrating the jungles of Brazil or New Guinea to take blood samples from indigenous tribes so that they can sequence the DNA of certain key human genes. We may expect to learn a lot about the history and prehistory of human migration and interbreeding by these new techniques.

While the drift of base sequences in an intron may provide evidence on the shorter evolutionary time scales, the appearance, disappearance, or change of length of introns may act as suitable markers when longer periods are of interest. The amount of valuable information lying concealed in living organisms, awaiting only the attention of competent investigators, is enormous. The methods, once developed, are so rapid and (relatively speaking) so inexpensive that it will be difficult to know where to stop, such is the wealth of detail which might be explored. We may expect to see results on many genes in many individuals in many different species.

The control of genes

The main thrust of present research is not so much to unravel the course of evolution but to discover the way organisms function now, and especially how they develop from the fertilized egg to the adult individual. Here, one of the major unsolved problems is that of the control of genes, for it is obvious that some genes act in some cells and not in others. The problem is complicated by the three-dimensional structure of nucleoprotein, the combination of chromosomal DNA with special proteins. However, it seems likely that some of the signals used will depend mainly on the base sequence of the DNA, and these we shall have in abundance. Hopefully, the detailed study of mutations which alter these functions, together with experiments on purifed cell components in the test tube, will eventually tell us how chromosomal genes are turned on and off, how hormones work, and how whole sets of genes are coordinated. We also need to know whether the processing of the hnRNA (and splicing in particular) is also subject to control mechanisms which alter the rate at which messenger RNA is produced and, as a consequence, the rate at which a particular protein is synthesized. All this basic biological knowledge should, in the end, help us to understand better certain intractable medical problems (cancer being a good example) and perhaps lead us to invent cures for them.

Possible risks

The new methods are also important for the production of macromolecules for medical or commmercial purposes. Detailed sequencing is not always needed in such cases. It is the manipulation by enzymes, particularly restriction enzymes, and the use of biological magnification which have made possible this type of genetic engineering. There have been legitimate worries about the possible dangers of such techniques, but it now appears that, in their desire to avoid trouble, the scientists most closely concerned overestimated the possible risks involved. Unfortunately the general public, unused to such candor and such caution on the part of "experts," took this to mean that the risks must really be appreciable and the dangers serious. Some sections of the public and the press showed a degree of anxiety amounting almost to hysteria. The plain fact is that the numerical value of the risk is unknown and is likely to remain so. The chance of producing and releasing a dangerous pathogen is undoubtedly extremely low, but it could be argued that, if this did happen, whole populations might be devastated. Yet danger also exists from known diseases like the plague, and modern medical and hygienic methods have shown that such infections can be contained. For this reason they are usually not as serious now as they were in the past. It seems likely that if, by some remote chance, a new infection were accidentally produced by manipulating DNA, it would be inherently no worse than the plague and could be contained in a similar way by public health measures. Taking all factors into consideration, the chance of a large-scale catastrophe seems extremely remote, especially if reasonable safety precautions are employed as a matter of routine.

Human beings tend to fear unknown dangers more than familiar ones. For this reason they may worry about remote hypothetical infections while living happily with quite appreciable risks, such as those from automobiles or from smoking cigarettes, because these are well known. Other dangers cause no worries because people are hardly aware of them. The risk of acquiring from an animal a pathogen lethal to human beings is as difficult to estimate as the likelihood of danger from recombinant DNA, but few people fuss about keeping pets or visiting the zoo because of the risk of such an infection. Yet it is known that in the past human beings have been killed by diseases caught from animals such as parrots or monkeys, while no microorganism produced by the new methods has yet harmed a single person, let alone killed anyone.

Fortunately, not everybody has overreacted to these unknown risks, and average citizens and their representatives have shown that, given time, they can face up to the issue in a more balanced way. Nor did every country overreact. What alarmed the American public so much was taken quite calmly by the Swiss, who normally are regarded as, if anything, overendowed with an excess of sober good sense. There is something ridiculous in American molecular biologists having to go to Switzerland to do experiments considered unsafe in the land of pioneers and free enterprise.

A dramatic danger which never seems to materialize soon becomes a bore, even if the risk is appreciable, as it is for a severe earthquake in San Francisco. The public's interest shifts to other things. The lesson which might be drawn from this episode is that while scientists venturing into the unknown should act responsibly, it is also important that they not let their legitimate worries alarm the general public unnecessarily.

Future applications

It is too early to say exactly what impact these new methods will have on the production of useful organisms and biochemicals. Several interesting proteins have already been produced, but new results are coming in so rapidly that any summary would be out of date even before this book was printed. Much work is also in progress to produce modified organisms, especially microorganisms, having functions they did not possess before, such as nitrogen fixation. These involve very complex genetic engineering. Any account of them must wait for the future. Even in simpler cases certain technical problems still need to be overcome. Messenger RNA from a higher organism will not always work in bacteria because the latter use different signals to attach ribosomes to the message. With a little ingenuity this particular difficulty can be circumvented but there are several others. For example, the best way for the bacterial cell to secrete the required protein into the surrounding medium, thus making its purification easier, has still to be found.

At the moment, the major uncertainty concerns which macromolecules are worth producing, other than those needed for research purposes. There is little obvious commercial demand for nucleic acids as final products; the obvious molecules to go for are proteins. The problem is, which proteins. At first sight, insulin for diabetics would appear to be a good target but there is a snag. It happens that insulin from domestic animals, such as cows or pigs, is so like human insulin that it can be used by most diabetics without undesirable side reactions. At present, insulin is obtained from slaughterhouse material so that it is relatively cheap. Whether insulin grown in bacteria will be able to compete with it in price is uncertain.

At the other extreme is growth hormone. Here the animal equivalent is not acceptable to humans. Yet the demand for growth hormone (to cure certain types of dwarfism, among other things) is, by commercial standards, very small, and by itself it would hardly justify the development costs.

One protein which might be extremely valuable is interferon, which gives a broad protection against viral infection. Here again the protein must be the human variety. The technical problem in this case is that the messenger RNA for interferon, which is needed to start the whole process, is only present in minute amounts. It has recently been announced that this difficulty has been overcome. It now seems likely that interferon for medical purposes may become available on a large scale before too long.

To judge from past experience, the full potential of a new and powerful technique is not always appreciated in the initial stage of its development. A safe prediction would be that eventually most of the applications of DNA manipulation will be for purposes which have not yet been considered. Just how fast these will come along remains to be seen. It appears almost certain that in the long run the production of new sophisticated biochemicals will have a very considerable impact not only on medicine and industry but on our everyday life.

The storage of information

The information explosion will have other consequences. Even now it is difficult to keep track of all the nucleic acid sequences being reported. There is a clear need for some central organization to collect them and store them on a computer, so that they can be made available to scientists on request. This is already done for the amino acid sequences of proteins. It would be wise to have people doing such work who were interested in the sequences and mildly fanatical about their accuracy, as otherwise mistakes will tend to accumulate. It is worth noting that an appreciable fraction of the DNA sequences known at the moment has been sequenced at least twice, often by independent groups. This is no bad thing, especially for sequences which are of wide general interest.

There will also be a need to store, in one way or another, the organisms that contain special DNA. This is relatively easy for viruses and bacteria which can be kept at very low temperatures or frozen. Whether they should be stored centrally is not easy to decide. There is as yet no clear convention as to when scientists should make a useful organism available to others in the field. The broad principles are agreed. The research team has an exclusive right to the initial use of a new molecule or organism, especially if it took them a lot of work to construct it. Eventually they should make it available to other interested scientists, for otherwise it may be impossible for others to check their results, an essential feature of the scientific method. This presents no special logistic difficulties. The researchers need only hand out a few organisms to any one individual, because from these many more can be grown with comparative ease. The problem is, when should they release them? It might be a sound rule for editors of learned journals to refuse to publish a paper unless the authors agreed to make available, from the date of publication, any special biological material of this type which was used in the experiments described in the paper. In any case, the sequences of nucleic acid and protein are not the only molecular information which will need to be collected and stored. Other examples are the atomic coordinates of the three-dimensional structures of proteins and nucleic acids, obtained by X-ray diffraction of crystals.

The storage of materials

A more difficult problem arises in cases where we wish to store not merely information but organisms, cells, or molecules. This presents formidable difficulties for higher organisms such as mice or men, though it is technically possible to store their sperm or even some of their cells. Scientists working on small organisms used for intensive genetic analysis have already had the problem of how to keep in stock many thousands of mutant strains. Even though certain cells or small animals can be kept frozen for some time, the cost of carrying many specimens soon becomes appreciable. For most bacteria and viruses the problem is technically a little easier, but the number of useful strains and mutants has already reached such large quantities that it seems impractical to try to keep them all.

It is not very rewarding to store protein molecules as such, since they cannot be replicated in any straightforward way. Nucleic acid molecules are, by comparison, relatively easy to maintain, especially if they are conveniently joined onto the DNA of a phage. One particular type of protein is of special interest. An important recent development is that of monoclonal (or monospecific) antibodies. These are pure antibody molecules (proteins) obtained by the ingenious technique of fusing an antibody-producing cell with a cancer cell to make the combination immortal, so that it can be grown in culture indefinitely. From one such cell a population is grown that makes only a single antibody rather than the very mixed antibodies made by injecting an antigen into a whole animal. To obtain the type of antibody required, screening methods have to be used. These are at present somewhat laborious, though we may hope that they will become easier in the future. Monoclonal antibodies are a powerful tool for recognizing molecules, especially macromolecules, which fit onto their surface. Again, many varieties will be produced, in laboratories all over the world, and some system will have to be worked out so that they can be made available to as many scientists as possible, either by distributing the relatively pure protein secreted by each type of cell or, more likely, by sending out small numbers of the cells themselves for others to grow up and harvest the antibody. This is clearly much more of a problem to organize than just storing sequences on a computer.

The combinatorial principle

We have seen that at the molecular level the information explosion in biology is mainly concerned with highly specific macromolecules and especially with the exact sequence of their components. Much of this flood of results comes from the new rapid methods for obtaining these sequences but, as stressed in the introduction, we must have these results because there is an immense variety of biologically significant molecules, the sequences of which we need to know if we are to understand the living world in depth. What does this variety spring from? At bottom it is a result of the combinatorial principle. Consider a stretch of DNA a mere 200 base pairs long—the sort of length that can be sequenced, with a little skill, on a single gel. How many possible sequences are there? The answer is 4^{200} or approximately 10^{120}, which is the number one followed by 120 zeros. That is vastly more than the number of fundamental particles in the entire universe, usually thought to be about 10^{80}. The number of possible sequences for the DNA of a small virus, some 5,000 base pairs long, is quite beyond our comprehension. It is an easy calculation to show that in the entire history of the earth the vast majority of these sequences would *never* have occurred, at any time, even in as small an amount as one molecule. By any normal standards the number of possible sequences of this length can be considered infinite. It is this, at bottom, which has allowed Nature to become complex and has made necessary the immense amount of detailed work that faces any molecular biologist today. Without this complexity creatures like ourselves, able to pose these fundamental problems and to search, often successfully, for answers to them, could not exist.

A world which did not use chemistry to exploit the combinatorial principle would be effectively a dead world, for without the unlimited variety made possible by combinatorial methods a versatile replication system would hardly be possible. It is one of the great advantages of organic chemistry (that is, the chemistry of carbon) that it lends itself so well to constructing molecular combinations, mainly because carbon is tetravalent and joins so well onto other carbon atoms. In our present world a tremendous accumulation of biological information cannot be avoided if we are ever to understand just how living organisms (ourselves included) carry out their many complex functions and how, over more than a billion years, they evolved to produce the fantastic variety of creatures alive today.

Further reading

A good general introduction to molecular biology is James D. Watson's *Molecular Biology of the Gene*, 3rd edition, published by W. A. Benjamin, Inc., 1976. For a more detailed account of introns and exons there is my survey article "Split Genes and RNA Splicing," in *Science*, volume 204 (April 20, 1979), pages 264–71. A very readable book on recent ideas about genes is *The Selfish Gene* by Richard Dawkins, Oxford University Press, 1976.

The Social Sciences Since the Second World War—Part Two

Daniel Bell

Daniel Bell, who contributed the first part of this two-part essay to *The Great Ideas Today* last year, has perhaps as close to a comprehensive grasp of the social sciences as anyone now alive can claim. His own contributions to the field include: *History of Marxian Socialism in the United States* (1952); *Work and Its Discontents* (1956); *The End of Ideology* (1960); *The Reforming of General Education* (1966); *The Coming of Post-Industrial Society* (1973); *The Cultural Contradictions of Capitalism* (1976); and other writings. He is at work on three further books: *The Exhausted Isle,* a study of modern British society; *Teletext and Technology,* on the new networks of knowledge and information which have been created in our time; and *The Return of the Sacred,* dealing with the argument as to the future of religion.

Among numerous professional and public commitments, Mr. Bell has served as a member of the President's Commission on Technology, Automation, and Economic Progress (1964–66), and as chairman for the commission of the Year 2000 for the American Academy of Arts and Sciences. With Irving Kristol he was founder and for ten years co-editor of *The Public Interest,* served two terms on the editorial board of *The American Scholar,* has been a member of the board of editors of *Daedalus* since 1970, and was on the editorial board of *Fortune* magazine from 1948 to 1958. He has taught at the University of Chicago, at Columbia University, and at Harvard, where since 1969 he has been professor of sociology.

In the twenty-five years after World War II, from 1945 to 1970, the social sciences seemed to be on the verge of presenting a set of comprehensive paradigms which would not only provide coherent theoretical schemas to order the bodies of human knowledge but would also provide reliable guides to social policy and planning through the new research techniques and the adoption of mathematical and quantitative modes that hitherto had been associated largely with the physical sciences. The prime example of this was economics. Not only had neoclassical economics (as formulated by Alfred Marshall) become joined to the work of John Maynard Keynes in a new synthesis (associated largely with the name of Paul Samuelson) but the development of new methods of macroeconomic analysis—e.g., the gross national product and national income accounts developed by Simon Kuznets, Colin Clark, and Richard Stone, the input-output matrices of Wassily Leontief, the econometric models by Lawrence Klein, the formulation of linear programming by George Dantzig, and the measurement of technological change by Edward Denison and its integration into economic theory by Robert Solow—all promised the completion of a set of intellectual tools which, as the phrase went, would allow policymakers to "fine tune" the economy.

Other social science developments held out similar promise. The yoking of cybernetics, linguistic theory, cognitive psychology, and computer science seemed to foreshadow a new discipline that could successfully "model" the mind as well as society. Culture and personality theory, initiated by Ruth Benedict, proposed to show how patterns of culture were reflected in modal personality types, and thus to demonstrate the interactions of social behavior. Structural-Functionalism in sociology, a theory identified primarily with Talcott Parsons, sought to build a "general theory" of society by identifying the mechanisms of integration in cultural and social systems. And, in government, the large-scale expenditures in social-policy programs and research indicated an aim to show that social experiments and evaluation of policy could give us a more secure basis of policy judgment on health, education, welfare, housing, manpower training, and interracial issues.

Most of these promises—as discussed in Part One of this essay, in *The Great Ideas Today* 1979—have gone unrealized. In some instances, as in economics, the science became more elegant in its mathematical formulations but seemed less able to deal with the more complex socioeconomic reality. The "general systems" approach, as promised by cybernetics and computers, seems to have been too grandiose, and while some important and significant advances have been made in such areas as computer applications to cognitive learning (e.g., the work of Seymour Papert at M.I.T.), the more ambitious claims have been toned down. In anthropology the "culture and personality" emphasis has almost vanished, as subsequent work has shown that the premises were too simplistic, that culture patterns could not be described in "holistic" terms, and that a theory of "personality dynamics" could not be sustained. Structural-Functionalism in sociology, while a towering intellectual effort to provide a complete morphology of society and, in the history of social thought, a major effort to work out the logic of Max Weber and Émile Durkheim through a set of comprehensive categories which could encompass the entire range of social actions, was an effort that many sociologists felt was too abstract and could provide no direct ways to deal with sociographic or empirical issues. And the experiments in social policy, by and large, proved to be failures, though few persons could agree upon the reasons. Some social scientists pointed out, quite justly, that a number of these programs had been trumpeted by the government as "social science" when there was little science in them, either in warranted theory or in reliable data. Conversely, policymakers claimed that the social scientists themselves had been too schematic and abstract in their approaches and had failed to understand the *political* nature of social policy, both as a process in government and in terms of popular reaction. Whatever the reasons—and these will be matters for the historians to adjudicate—the fact remains that a sobering or disillusioning mood began to prevail in this area as well.

In the 1970s the social sciences went off in two divergent directions. On the one hand (if one was pessimistic) one could say that there was a splintering of the fields; or (if one was optimistic) one could say that the social sciences had retreated to more mundane, more empirical, and "smaller," more manageable problems of research, all in the hope eventually of finding some warranted generalizations with which one could reknit the disciplines. In most fields, certainly, there had been significant advances in quantitative modes of research and in sophisticated mathematical tools, and these were now being applied assiduously to trace out in a precise way the specific variables which researchers felt were important in solving their problems. In the sociology of medicine, for example, there have been striking advances in epidemiology that relate the incidence of disease to different segments of populations. And in the study of social mobility, there have been painstaking regression models and path analyses to show exactly how factors such as parent's occupation, cultural advantage, schooling, I.Q., and the like affect the chances of individuals to get ahead in the society. In effect, what has happened has been the spread of "empiricism" and a retreat from grand theory—though critics of these efforts argue that without theory, empiricism can only multiply results endlessly, and that to wait for some "pattern" to emerge is to submit to the fallacy of inductivism.

On the other hand, there were, in the 1970s, major new synoptic attempts to provide some master keys to the understanding of social behavior (it is an incorrigible impulse in science), and these efforts themselves have provoked new and often savage disputes. In this past decade, one can identify four major developments in the social sciences:

(1) The emergence of sociobiology as an effort to unify all social behavior through the parameters, genetically based, that govern kin selection, territoriality, division of labor, group size, etc., through a fusion of ethology, ecology, population genetics, and neo-evolutionary theory.

(2) The multiplicity of new paradigms in macroeconomics in the work of Herbert A. Simon, Harvey Leibenstein, and Thomas Schelling.

(3) New schools of neo-Marxism, bringing forth a plethora of new approaches that, by and large, still bog down in exegetical and textual quarrels as to what Marx "really" said or meant.

(4) Structuralism, a term which is quite diffuse but which has been used to describe the work of Lévi-Strauss in anthropology, Piaget in psychology, Roland Barthes in literature, Louis Althusser in Marxism, Jacques Lacan in psychoanalysis—and a host of epigones who have carried the word into almost every domain of knowledge.

It would be nigh impossible, within a short space, and for a general audience, to survey the myriad number of empirical studies that have sprouted in the social sciences in the last decade, and even more difficult to draw any large generalizations.

What this essay attempts to do is to explore these four developments and to conclude with the question whether the dream of a unified social science or some master system is possible.

1. Sociobiology

In her *Patterns of Culture* (1934), Ruth Benedict set forth the foundations of anthropology, if not of all the social sciences, in terms of two propositions: the uniqueness of the human species, as against other species, in shaping social behavior; and, given the extraordinary diversity of culture patterns, the relativism of culture. She wrote:

> There are societies where Nature perpetuates the slightest mode of
> behaviour by biological mechanisms, but these are societies not of men
> but of the social insects. . . . Not *one* item of his tribal social
> organization, of his language, of his local religion, is carried in his
> germ-cell. . . . Man is not committed in detail by his biological
> constitution to any particular variety of behaviour. The great diversity
> of social solutions that man has worked out in different cultures in
> regard to mating, for example, or trade, are all equally possible on the

basis of his original endowment. . . . We must accept all the implications of our human inheritance, one of the most important of which is the small scope of biologically transmitted behaviour, and the enormous rôle of the cultural process of the transmission of tradition.[1]

Little more than forty years later, a man who had made his reputation with a powerful book on insect societies, E. O. Wilson of Harvard, brought forth a new book, *Sociobiology: The New Synthesis* (1975), which promised the creation of a major new discipline that would relate the social sciences to biology and explain fundamental patterns of social life through the theoretical principles of neo-Darwinian evolutionary biology. The premise of the proposed discipline denied the "uniqueness" of the human species, accepted the wide variety of human behaviour, but interpreted that diversity in evolutionary terms as a form of species strategy that was consistent with principles underlying the adaptation of other species. Wilson even proposed (to take one small example) that homosexuality may be related to species' adaptive mechanisms, which seek to strengthen the gene pools of a species. Sociobiology sought to establish two claims: that one could not ignore the role of biology—in particular, of genetics—in explaining some fundamental and universal constants of human behavior; and that a unified theory could explain some constants in group behavior, such as territoriality, sexual mating patterns, aggressive responses, in the chain of evolutionary species, and that aspects of these theories could be applied to human social behavior when considered in a long evolutionary perspective.

Greeted at first with an acclaim so rapid as to take almost all observers by surprise, Wilson's work also became the storm center of a controversy so vehement as to earn a place in the annals of intellectual history. Yet *Sociobiology* did not emerge out of the blue. It was, as the subtitle of the work indicated, an attempt at a new synthesis. Over the previous forty years a number of new theories and ideas had developed in ethology, ecology, and population genetics, and it was the effort to derive some underlying principles from all these and give them precise formulation, in many instances in mathematical form, that gave Wilson's work its distinction. To understand its novelty, and the nature of the controversy, one has to sort out the intellectual strands in his writings and to clarify the ideological fears they have aroused.

Traditionally, animal or bird behavior was thought to consist of simple responses, some of them innate and some learned, to a stimulus or signal, e.g., an attack, or a courtship signal. But the work of certain ethologists, notably Konrad Lorenz, Nikolaas Tinbergen, and Karl von Frisch (all of whom won the Nobel Prize in 1973), established a new view of animal behavior. They showed that animals have an innate capacity for complex acts in response to simple stimuli, i.e., that the response is not on a one-to-one basis, but involves a variety of possible responses, and that certain behavior patterns are inherited. In other words, genetically determined responses must be subject to the pressures of natural selection, and innate behavior must evolve. Thus, for example, a motor pattern involved in a context of feeding could evolve into a ritualized form as a signal, as in courtship or an attack; thus it could change from a noncommunicatory act to a communicatory act, presumably under the selective pressures of the environment; and these new, adaptive patterns would then be utilized by later biological members of the species.

In a different context, the Scottish ecologist V. C. Wynne-Edwards published a book in 1962, *Animal Dispersion in Relation to Social Behaviour,* in which he suggested, as David Barash put it, that virtually all social behavior—including dominance hierarchies, securing of territories, flocking in birds, herding in mammals—are regulatory devices to relate population levels of the group to the ecological limits in the availability of food. Barash writes: "It had long been recognized that socially subordinate individuals often fail to breed and that overpopulation in nature is rare. Wynne-Edwards suggested that social congregations serve to inform individuals of the local population density, so that individuals could avoid overpopulation by regulating their own breeding accordingly."*

The weakness of many of these ethological studies, however, is that they are based on naturalistic observation and do not explain the way innate behavior evolved, i.e., the genetic mechanisms. Moreover, as the influential book of George C. Williams, *Adaptation and Natural Selection: A Critique of Some Current Evolutionary Thought* (1966), points out, natural selection has to explain how the process operates not through the group but through the individual, since it is the individual who transmits the genetic pattern. This problem becomes the bridge to the next strand.

This second strand is the work in population genetics that began in the 1940s and is summed up in the neo-Darwinism associated with Theodosius Dobzhansky, George Gaylord Simpson, and Ernst Mayr. (It is summed up in Mayr's magisterial book, *Populations, Species, and Evolution* [1970].) Classical Darwinism was based on two postulates: the idea of the common descent of all mammals, including man, from one ancestral species, in a long chain of being; and the idea of natural selection, to explain the enormous variation of species, as an adaptive mechanism to the environment. But Darwin had no notion of the source or mechanism of variation, of the way in which hereditary information is transmitted from parent to offspring through the genes. Mendel made his discoveries in 1865, but these were largely ignored or unknown until rediscovered in 1900.

The new Darwinian synthesis, or neo-Darwinism, as it is now called, starts out with the uniquely different individuals who are organized into interbreeding populations. Given this premise, every biological individual has a dual component: the *genotype* (the full component of genes, not all of which may be expressed) and the *phenotype* (the observable properties of the

---

* *The Wilson Quarterly,* Summer 1977, pp. 109–10.

organism, as they have developed out of the genetic inheritance *and* the responses to the environment). The genotype is part of the gene pool of a specific interbreeding population, but it is the individual, the phenotype, that competes with other phenotypes for reproductive success.

Not only is the emphasis on the individual, or phenotype, central, but the very concept of the species as a fixed *type*, qualitatively distinct from other types, is called into question. Every interbreeding population—called a *deme*—is a statistical distributed set of genes in the gene pool, a set of variations, the "cluster" of which, or the statistical "mean," is an abstraction, since only the variant individual has reality. The importance of the gene pool lies in the distribution of variations, but it is the success or failure of the single individual that "advances" the different traits in the gene pool. As Mayr writes:

> In a population of thousands or millions of unique individuals some
> will have sets of genes that are better suited to the currently prevailing
> assortment of ecological pressures. Such individuals will have a
> statistically greater probability of surviving and of leaving survivors
> than other members of the population. It is this . . . step in natural
> selection that determines evolutionary direction, increasing the
> frequency of genes and constellations of genes that are adaptive at a
> given time and place, increasing fitness, promoting specialization and
> giving rise to adaptive radiation and to what may be loosely described
> as evolutionary progress.[2]

Classical Darwinian theory held that every organism fights for its own survival, and the chance to reproduce. But that theory could not explain why some organisms help other members of their kind. A prairie dog barks when it sees a predator. The alarm gives the other dogs a signal and a chance to escape but calls attention to the animal that utters it and thus reduces its chances of survival. How does one explain this "altruistic" action? A solution was proposed in 1964 in two articles by the British geneticist W. D. Hamilton ("The Genetical Theory of Social Behaviour," in the *Journal of Theoretical Biology*, vol. 7, 1964). Hamilton pointed out that "altruistic behavior" is actually a case of ensuring the survival of those who share *common* genes. Natural selection is supplemented by "kin selection," i.e., the occurrence of altruistic behavior increases with the closeness of the benefici- ary: the more genes that are shared by common ancestry, the more likely does behavior tend to be altruistic. Hamilton's work predicted that altruistic and cooperative behavior would be found more frequently in the interac- tions of related than of unrelated individuals, and this has been confirmed by observation. Thus, evolutionary adaptation takes place not by the surviv- al of the individual but through the efforts of kin, apparently genetically motivated, to ensure the survival of their close kind.

This addition of the theory of kin selection made possible a closer fit between evolutionary behavior and social theory and gave biologists a bridge from insect societies to primates and, they have argued, to human behavior.* And while kin selection is the most dramatic innovation, providing the third major strand, there are still other bridges that biologists have proposed to span the range of social behavior in studies of territoriality, mating systems, and communication as basic social phenomena.

Sociobiology is the effort to provide this synthesis. As Wilson remarks in his book:

> Biologists have always been intrigued by comparisons between societies of invertebrates, especially insect societies, and those of vertebrates. They have dreamed of identifying the common properties of such disparate units in a way that would provide insight into all aspects of social evolution, including that of man. The goal can be expressed in modern terms as follows: *when the same parameters and quantitative theory are used to analyze both termite colonies and troops of rhesus macaques, we will have a unified science of sociobiology.* (p. 4, emphasis added)

Wilson admits that such comparison may be facile, and a deliberate oversimplification, but he points out how impressed he has been with the functional similarities between insect societies and troops of monkeys. He writes:

> Consider for a moment termites and monkeys. Both are formed into cooperative groups that occupy territories. The group members communicate hunger, alarm, hostility, caste status or rank, and reproductive status among themselves by means of something on the order of 10 to 100 nonsyntactical signals. Individuals are intensely aware of the distinction between groupmates and nonmembers. Kinship plays an important role in group structure and probably served as a chief generative force of sociality in the first place. In both kinds of society there is a well-marked division of labor....

Sociobiology, as Wilson outlines it, would deal with the effective population size of groups with common genetic features, and the nature of the gene flow between them. "The principal goal of a general theory of sociobiology," he writes, "should be an ability to predict features of social organization from a knowledge of these population parameters combined with information on the behavioral constraints imposed by the genetic constitution of the species."

In his book of more than 600 double-column text pages, Wilson explored every form of animal society from machinelike colonies of jellyfish to

---

* As Hamilton points out, the highest degree of cooperation is displayed by colonies of genetically identical cells that make up the human body. And as John Maynard Smith comments:

"It is important to note that these concepts apply to organisms incapable of recognizing degrees of relationship. In species that usually live in family groups a gene causing an individual to act altruistically towards members of its own community will increase in frequency even if the individuals carrying it cannot recognize family members."

screeching chimpanzees, dealing with topics from time-energy budgets to mating patterns and kin selection, all in twenty-six chapters. The twenty-seventh chapter dealt with man. Admitting the much greater degree of plasticity of human social organization, Wilson, more tentatively, also insisted that one could raise the question whether there might be genetic predispositions for both class position and religion, since individuals "are absurdly easy to indoctrinate—they *seek* it." In a later book, *On Human Nature* (1978), Wilson restates the issue in more general but stronger terms. He writes: "if the genetic components of human nature did not originate by natural selection, fundamental evolutionary theory is in trouble. At the very least the theory of evolution would have to be altered to account for a new and as yet unimagined form of genetic change in populations. Consequently, an auxiliary goal of human sociobiology is to learn whether the evolution of human nature conforms to conventional evolutionary theory." (pp. 33–34)

The criticism of the sociobiology project has been both ideological and intellectual. The first arose in left-wing and liberal circles that feared sociobiology would become an ideology for racism and conservatism, as an aspect of Social Darwinism had been in the late nineteenth and early twentieth centuries. There were several reasons for the fear. In the previous decade and a half, works popularizing some of the findings in ethology, such as Robert Ardrey's *African Genesis* (1961) and *The Territorial Imperative* (1966), as well as Desmond Morris's *The Naked Ape* (1967), had argued that aggression, territoriality, and hierarchy (i.e., the pecking order in animals) were innate or "natural," and that utopian or liberal ideas about the possibility of changing human nature were fallacious. More to the point, a number of psychologists had begun to argue that achievement in school was due primarily to I.Q. and that remedial and other programs for the disadvantaged might fail or be costly unless this fact were taken into account. The psychologist Arthur Jensen argued that there was a distinct difference in the modal scores of black and white populations. Richard Herrnstein sought to place the problem not on the basis of group or race but simply of differences in I.Q. and argued that 80 percent of an individual's I.Q. is derived from inheritance (technically, in any large group of persons, 80 percent of the variance could be attributed to genetic inheritance), so that if social standing were equalized, or a policy of equality of result created by government policies were instituted, those with the higher I.Q. would come to occupy higher positions in society.

The introduction of the I.Q. issue, the debate on school achievement and equality, and the allegations of the schools' failure to improve the standing of minority and disadvantaged children all combined to rouse in liberal and left groups the fear that biological arguments were being used to justify cuts in governmental social programs and to subtly introduce questions of racial inferiority. While it is true that some conservatives did raise the question of genetic incapability as a reason for attacking Great Society programs, the validity of the sociobiology argument became, for a while, almost hopelessly entangled in these political and ideological questions.

The intellectual case for or against the claims of sociobiology to embrace social behavior within the framework of neo-Darwinian principles rests on three theoretical issues. One is the question whether the principle of kin selection in its strong forms operates within human groups as it does within other species; two, the question whether the variability of human cultures is a function of a distinctively new principle of consciousness; and three, related to the second but possessing logical autonomy, the question whether, even if there were shown to be some genetic foundations for specific behavioral patterns, the biological "level of explanation" is not more adequate to explain behavior than psychology and sociology—technically, the question of "reductionism."

The fundamental calculus of sociobiology—the adaptive role of kin selection—is based on the proposition that, as Wilson has put it, a person has 50 percent of his genes held in common with a full sibling and that altruistic behavior by that sibling would favor those genes, so that "the altruistic genes will spread through the population." The calculus has been attacked by S. L. Washburn, who writes:

> A parent does not share one half of the genes with its offspring; the offspring shares one half of the genes in which the parents differ. If the parents are homozygous for a gene, obviously all offspring will inherit that gene. The issue then becomes, How many shared genes are there within a species such as *Homo Sapiens?* . . . Individuals whom sociobiologists consider unrelated share, in fact, more than 99 percent of their genes. It would be easy to make a model in which the structure and physiology important in behavior are based on the shared 99% and in which behaviorally unimportant differences, such as hair form, are determined by the 1%.*

And Marshall Sahlins, the cultural anthropologist, has argued that kinship behavior in human societies does not follow the genetic calculus, that "marriage rules" are highly variable, and that genetic sharing decreases far more rapidly than social obligations in any human social system.

In one sense, the parties to the debate are talking past each other. The sociobiologists tend to look for what they regard as universals in human culture and seek to root these in some kind of genetic predisposition. The anthropologists concentrate on the wide variety of human traits. Thus, in *On Human Nature,* Wilson cites a study by the anthropologist George P. Murdock that lists almost eighty activities, from age-grading to weather control, "that have been recorded in every culture known to history and ethnography," while the anthropologist Marvin Harris, in an attack on sociobiology, states: "George Peter Murdock's *World Ethnographic Atlas* con-

---

* "Human Behavior and the Behavior of Other Animals," *American Psychologist,* May 1978, p. 415.

tains forty-six columns of variable cultural traits. Over a thousand variable components per society can be identified by using the alternative codes listed under these columns. No two societies in the sample of 1,179 have the same combination of components."*

To put the question as culture versus biology, however, is not only wrong but misleading. The more difficult question is: in what way does genetic inheritance limit the ranges of human behavior; or again, in what way does genetic predisposition facilitate what kinds of change? In short, what does the human "biogram" allow us to do or not to do?

Wilson accepts the idea of variability. In his *Sociobiology* he writes: "The parameters of social organization, including group size, properties of hierarchies, and rates of gene exchange, vary far more among human populations than among those of any other primate species. The variation exceeds even that occurring between the remaining primate species." But he then goes on to argue: "The hypothesis to consider, then, is that genes promoting flexibility in social behavior are strongly selected at the individual level. But note that variation in social organization is only a possible, not a necessary consequence of this process." And, in fact, in *On Human Nature* Wilson concludes: "I believe that a correct application of evolutionary theory also favors diversity in the gene pool as a cardinal virtue. If variation in mental and athletic ability is influenced to a moderate degree by heredity, as the evidence suggests, we should expect individuals of truly extraordinary capacity to emerge unexpectedly in otherwise undistinguished families...."

If the argument were left only on the "species" level, there would probably have been little dispute and little excitement over sociobiology. Where the issue becomes more problematic is the effort of many sociobiologists to specify gene-controlled behavior traits that are shared with Old World primates, and gene-controlled behavior traits that are specific to human beings. Wilson, for example, mentions incest avoidance, male bonding, territoriality, semantic symbol language that develops in the young on a relatively strict timetable, specific facial expressions and other features as genetically restricted, and insists that "to socialize a human being out of such species-specific traits would be very difficult if not impossible, and almost certainly destructive to mental development."† It is in the definition of such "species-specific traits," and the exact degree of determinism, that the intellectual heat of the debate has centered.

The issue of reductionism is a double one. In one dimension it is the fear that sociobiology will deflate man by seeing behavior as either genetically predisposed or as a strategy to enhance one's own kind of genes. As Wilson, who is a scientific materialist, has said: "We are likely to see some of our

---

* *Cultural Materialism: The Struggle for a Science of Culture* (New York: Random House, 1979), p. 124.

† Edward O. Wilson, "Biology and the Social Sciences," *Daedalus*, vol. 2 (Fall 1977), p. 132.

most exalted feelings explained in terms of traits which evolved. We may find that there is an overestimation of the nature of our deepest yearnings."

The second aspect of reductionism is more methodological and goes to the core of some central questions in the philosophy of science: namely, whether the level of explanation of a sociological question (e.g., the kinds and varieties of human groups, or the layout of roads, or the patterns of exchange between persons) is fully answerable in sociological terms, or whether such an answer requires, as well, the "reduction" of that explanation to psychological levels (e.g., of individual motivations and desires) and of that, in turn, to biological levels of genetic codes—some writers (e.g., Francis Crick) arguing that biological explanations themselves have to be reduced to physical-chemical laws.

Wilson has argued the need for some kind of biological reductionism. He has written:

> The full phenomenology of social life cannot be predicted from a knowledge of the genetic programs of the individuals alone. When the observer shifts his attention from one level of organization to the next, *he expects to find obedience to all of the laws of the levels* below. But upper levels of organization require specification of the arrangement of the lower units, which in turn generates richness and the basis of new and unexpected principles. The specification can be classified into three categories: combinatoric, spatial, and historical.[3]

Yet, as the anthropologist Clifford Geertz has pointed out, the reductionist approach inherent in sociobiology—which seeks to explain human social behavior in terms of broad principles applicable to ants as well as to humans—is derived from a defective philosophy of science, based on a hierarchical concept of disciplines. Geertz has proposed thinking of these questions in "parallel" terms, and in his inimitable way he has offered "clowning" as an example. A clown's skill is a disposition, which depends upon certain kinds of neurological complexities and muscular developments, and, since some aspects of facial expressions may be genetically determined (though whether it would be possible to ascertain this is another matter), biologists could provide some understanding. At the same time, clowning might be discussed in the psychoanalytical context as tendencies to exhibitionism. Or, in the context of social institutions, as implying that circuses are a social mode to play out roles. Or, in connection with certain cultural traditions, as an instance of modes that mimic clumsiness. As Geertz points out, one can discuss the various aspects of clowning behavior and increase one's understanding of its varied meanings without making any claims to higher or lower levels of explanation.[4]

For all the furor, it is quite clear that in the next decade the relation of biology to the social sciences will become more intimate. One can seek, as the sociobiologists do, for the broad principles that underlie some presumed constants of all living group behavior. Or one can focus, as anthropology does, on the relation of cultural evolution to biological evolution. As Marvin Harris has put it: "It took billions of years for natural selection to create specialized adaptations for fishing, hunting, agriculture; for aquatic, terrestrial, and aerial locomotion; and for predatory and defensive weaponry, such as teeth, claws and armor. Equivalent specialties were developed by cultural evolution in less than ten thousand years. The main focus of human sociobiology ought therefore to be the explanation of why other species have such minuscule and insignificant cultural repertories and why humans alone have such gigantic and important ones."*

Wilson himself agrees in the concluding sentences to his essay on "Biology and the Social Sciences" that "Biology is the key to human nature, and social scientists cannot afford to ignore its emerging principles." He adds, however, that "the social sciences are potentially far richer in content. Eventually they will absorb the relevant ideas of biology and go on to beggar them by comparison."

2. Economics

The regnant "paradigm" in economics in the quarter of a century after World War II was Keynesianism, a doctrine which, in the large, asserted that government intervention could manage the economy through fiscal policy. In the 1970s the consensus as to this had fallen apart. The rock on which that paradigm broke, as Sir John Hicks, the Nobel laureate, sought to show in *The Crisis in Keynesian Economics* (1974), was inflation. But more was at stake for the science itself than the embarrassment of being unable to deal with the most crucial public-policy issue facing a society. What the new discussions brought back into question were the fundamental relationships of analysis and the fundamental terms of inquiry: the fundamental relationship between microeconomics, or the behavior of individuals (with the firm seen as an individual), and macroeconomics, or the aggregates in the economy as a whole; the fundamental terms of "equilibrium," or the idea that relationships between basic variables (e.g., wages-prices, consumption-investment) return to some balance after markets are cleared of a "natural growth rate" for an economy, and the idea of "maximization," or that rational behavior can be defined by saying that individuals do act to optimize their gains and will choose that path of action which will achieve the greatest gain.

The classical framework of analysis of equilibrium began with Say's Law of Markets, which, crudely put, states that "supply creates its own demand." The idea that inadequate demand could be a cause of unemployment was unlikely, since human wants were deemed to be insatiable, and supply would generate the demand through the circular flow of payments from

---

* *Cultural Materialism*, p. 125.

suppliers to consumers or investors. Temporary gluts or shortfalls might always occur, but this would be adjusted through the movements of wages and prices for each market. Neoclassical economists, following Marshall, refined the explanation of Say's Law by using marginal analysis to show the determination of the level of real output. A producer would never seek to offer a worker a wage greater than the value of the added output his labor could produce, so that the number of workers hired by a firm would be set at the point where the marginal cost would equal the marginal output. And by the same reasoning, as John Bates Clark sought to show in his *Distribution of Wealth* (1899), the same principle would apply to the markets for all factors of production, not only to wages but to rents and returns of capital (interest and profit) as well. Clark's "conclusion was that under perfect competition each factor would inexorably receive a return precisely equal to its contribution, and Clark could demonstrate that each factor would receive a [return] equal to the value of the marginal product."[5]

If a money wage was too high, competitive pressure would drive that wage down to the price where the employer would be able to hire a person; if money wages were "sticky," an employer would not hire workers so that unemployment was a "partial equilibrium" at those levels.

In neoclassical theory, a cut in money wages was the same as a cut in real wages because the price level remained unchanged. The level of money wages did not determine the price level, but vice versa. The price level itself (i.e., the *general* price level) was determined by the quantity theory of money, which was accepted by every neoclassical writer. (The prices for individual commodities, i.e., relative prices, might fluctuate for natural or exogenous reasons, from droughts for food, to cartels for oil.) So long as the total quantity of money was held steady, the general price level could not rise, though individual prices, of course, would adjust to each other, under the general "ceiling" conditions. (Thus, having to spend more for fuel oil would force a cut in the spending on some other products.) But almost all neoclassical economists—indeed, the thought goes back to David Hume—believed in the rough proportionality between changes in the stock of money and changes in the general level of prices in the economy.

The neoclassicists made a fundamental distinction between the *real* value of money and the *nominal* value. The real value expresses the actual magnitudes the money can command (tangible items, such as houses, or capital plant, or art works), or what the money can buy in the marketplace. Nominal value is simply the amount of money expressed in a monetary unit, such as the dollar. (To be a "millionaire" would not mean much if a million dollars only bought a cup of coffee, as happened with the German mark in the 1920s.) The general price level is a nominal magnitude. Quantity theorists argued that people act to maintain some level of *real* balances. If the relation between the nominal and the real balances moved out of line, prices would rise (because people would seek to lower their holdings of money) until the nominal money balances would be equal in real terms to the desired or customary level of real balances. In short, a fall in the value of money as prices rose, or a rise in real income, would return the system to equilibrium.

The relation between money, prices, and income was described in a "transactions" model by the American economist Irving Fisher, and in a "cash-balance" method by the neoclassicists at Cambridge. A crucial modification of the monetarist argument was made by the Swedish economist Knut Wicksell, who argued that money could not be treated purely as a commodity, as the cash-balance approach did. He emphasized the growing role of credit and indicated the mechanism by which changes in the quantity of money influenced interest rates, which, in turn, influenced flows of investment and savings. Wicksell thus showed how the interest rate became the equilibrating instrument for the supply and demand for capital.

The neoclassical economists understood that there were often sharp price fluctuations in the real world, and that purely monetary or nominal events, such as a big gold strike, could have real effects in the short run. But they believed that such economic fluctuations were transient, or that monetary distortions after a while would leach away, since underneath these top-of-the-wave turbulences was a basic equilibrium mechanism. The logic of market-oriented equilibrium economics was, if perturbations occurred, to let them run their course, since adjustments (even at times painful ones) would "wring out" the excesses.

Keynesian theory introduced a number of substantial modifications in neoclassical theory. One was the observation that the perturbations, or transient deviations from the equilibrium, could last a long time and have devastating social effects. And, even where there was unemployment or excess capacity in an economy, as in a depression, the price levels were more or less "sticky," and nominal levels therefore had a substantial impact on real quantities. Under full employment, the divorce between nominal events and real quantities would return. Once all capacity, plant and labor, was utilized, additional nominal expenditure would then raise the price levels, and the control of inflation would then be in the power of the monetary authorities to expand or limit the money supply, in order to compress the nominal levels back to the "real" price levels.

In short, what the Keynesians argued was that "natural" equilibrium would not take place in the market economy (or, if it did, it would be at a "partial equilibrium" of high unemployment or unused capacity) and that government fiscal policy intervention was necessary to redress the balance. Inflation was not seen as an issue because inflation was not seen as deriving from a rise in nominal money wages beyond the real price level.

The missing equation in this picture of the relation of wage levels to unemployment and inflation was the famous Phillips Curve, which, as Robert Solow has wryly observed, provided more employment for economists, after its results were published in 1958, than any public-works enterprise since the construction of the Erie Canal. A. W. Phillips, an economist at the

London School of Economics, had matched unemployment rates in Britain between 1862 and 1957 with changes in hourly wage rates. Solow has described its import:

> Notice that he was comparing the rate of change of wages, a nominal quantity, with the percentage of the labor force out of work, a real quantity. If there were no long-run connection between real events and nominal events, then there ought to be no relation between those two time series. If the crude dichotomy in the Keynesian picture were a good description of the world, then the rate of wage inflation ought to be near zero for anything but full employment. And in times of full employment, if there were any to be observed, there ought to be substantial inflation.
>
> What Phillips found was really pretty astonishing. The simple bivariate relation, relating only one real and one nominal variable, held up very well over a very long time during which the nature of British industry and labor changed very drastically. Here was evidence for a strong, and apparently reliable, relation between the nominal world and the real world. It did not appear to be a short-run transient affair, as the mainstream macroeconomics of the 19th and early 20th centuries would have suggested. It seemed not to be a simple dichotomy between less-than-full employment and full employment, as the casual picture of the early 1950s might have suggested. It seemed to say quite clearly that the rate of wage inflation—and probably, therefore, the rate of price inflation—was a smooth function of the tightness of the aggregate economy.[6]

Phillips's study had been a "straight" empirical one. But the theoretical implications for public policy—and for Keynesian economics—were worked out by Paul Samuelson and Robert M. Solow. In their article "Analytical Aspects of Anti-Inflation Policy," in the *American Economic Review* of May 1960, the two M.I.T. economists assembled an analogous time series for the United States. While there were divergences, the postwar data did show a "curve" of the same qualitative shape, and Samuelson and Solow posited a hypothetical relation between the rate of price inflation and the unemployment rate: "This shows the menu of choice between different levels of unemployment and price stability as roughly estimated from the last twenty-five years of American data," they wrote.

The relation known as the Phillips Curve, and its generalization by Richard Lipsey, won immediate and widespread acceptance in American economic thinking. It served, as Franco Modigliani has put it, "to dispose of the rather sterile 'cost-push'–'demand-pull' controversy." It also served to reinforce the idea that one could now "manage" the economy even more decisively because of the "menu" of choice. But the inflation of the 1970s, and especially of the last five years, which have been double-digit years for the most part, has proved recalcitrant to public policy and is a difficult problem for the Keynesian economists.

One can point to a number of specific "perturbations" which conjoined to create this inflation. In the United States the Johnson administration during the Vietnam War had stepped up government spending but refused to compensate for the military expenditures by higher taxes. The "oil shock" of 1973 and after quadrupled and then quintupled energy prices. A series of crop failures in the Soviet Union pushed up food prices. A worldwide synchronization of rising demand and a shortage in primary processing capacity conjoined in the early 1970s. The simultaneity of all these events burst the twenty-five-year worldwide economic expansion which had more than doubled world industrial output.

But in the resulting recession, and in the slow but steady recovery in the U.S., *both* a high level of inflation and an unacceptable level of unemployment have persisted. That is the great theoretical—and seemingly insuperable—puzzle. To put the question within the framework we have been discussing, the Phillips Curve has gone flat, and the idea of a trade-off—of reducing inflation by increasing unemployment, or increasing jobs at the cost of more inflation, the "menu of choice"—has seemingly vanished. As Robert Solow points out in his 1979 essay:

> Most of the serious estimates suggest that an extra 1 percent of unemployment maintained for one year would reduce the rate of inflation by something between 0.16 and 0.5 percent. That trade-off is not very favorable. We also know that the inflationary process involves a great deal of inertia; that is, it takes a long time for the economy to pass from one member of the family of Phillips curves to a lower one, at least under normal circumstances. For instance, an extra 1 percent of unemployment maintained for three years would reduce the inflation rate by something between 0.5 and 1.75 percent. (An extra point of unemployment for three years costs the economy about $180 billion of production, which makes this a very expensive way to reduce the inflation rate.)
>
> We know those two things, albeit in a tentative and gingerly way. What we don't know ... is why the inertia is so great, why those Phillips Curves are so flat. That is, we do not know what bits of our social and economic structure would have to be changed in order to change those relationships. (Ibid., pp. 44–45)

The inadequacies of Keynesian macroeconomic policy have produced two divergent responses. One is a swing back to monetarist theory. Its argument is that given a constant money supply or a fixed rate of expansion in accordance with business activity, equilibrium forces *will* reassert themselves. It seeks to minimize government intervention, in particular those by the Federal Reserve Board to "time" the expansion or contraction of money in order to affect the price level.

The other response has been that of the "post-Keynesians" and is built on the theoretical work of such Keynes associates as Joan Robinson and

Piero Sraffa, as well as the Polish economist Michal Kalecki, who, independent of Keynes, had come to similar conclusions.

The monetarist argument has been identified principally with Milton
Friedman, a Nobel laureate and the leader of the so-called Chicago School.
Friedman opened his attack in 1967 in his presidential address to the
American Economics Association, in which he reasserted the distinction
between real and nominal magnitudes, emphasized the "permanent income hypothesis" (i.e., the idea of "real balances" as the basis of monetary
theory), and attacked the Phillips Curve hypothesis. Friedman restated the
argument that changes in the quantity of money caused output and price
changes, and that in the short run the stock of money was not a neutral
reflector of varying demands but a determinant of such demands.

Friedman's major policy prescription was that the monetary authorities,
once they have wrung out the excess money in the system (by reducing the
money supply or having the government reduce its own spending, which
he regards as a prime source of inflation), should set a fixed level of money,
plus an additional growth rate, say three percent, consonant with the "natural growth" potential of the society. Within that framework, individuals and
firms would make their own self-adjusting decisions, based on relative
prices, for their own needs and wants. But, through the control of the
quantity of money, the general price level would be kept relatively stable.

A number of questions emerge about the Friedman prescriptions. One
has to do with the definitions of money itself. The stock of money is usually
calculated in terms of two measures: M-1, or cash in circulation plus money
in checking accounts, and M-2, which is M-1 plus time deposits, such as
savings accounts and negotiable certificates of deposit by corporations and
banks. The argument is that the structural change in the nature of the
credit system (from the spread of interest-bearing checking accounts to the
volatility of credit because of easily available credit cards), plus the large
"overhang" of Euro-dollars—that is, the several hundred billions of U.S.
dollars that float around outside the United States and are used as a basis
for new dollar loans by foreign banks—all make the question of monetary
measurement more difficult and variable.

A second, and perhaps greater, difficulty is that there seems to be an
"uncoupling" between money supply and interest rates, so that business
behavior seemingly is less affected by these controls than has been assumed.
As Lester Thurow has pointed out:

> Business investment functions are probably the best example of this
> phenomenon. In classical economic theory, rising interest rates lead to
> less investment and falling interest rates lead to more investment.
> Much to the shock of initial investigators, econometric equations found
> either no effect or the exact opposite to be true. Investment was not

affected or went up when interest rates went up. Econometricians immediately went back to their computers to find an investment function where interest rates would be statistically significant and appear with the right sign. All such efforts failed.[7]

The experiences of the economy in 1977–1978 seem to have borne out these apprehensions. From April 1977 to June 1978 the Federal Open Market Committee of the Federal Reserve System tightened credit substantially by raising the federal funds rate that commercial banks charge each other for loans to balance their accounts from $4\frac{3}{4}$ percent to $7\frac{3}{4}$ percent — an increase of almost 65 percent — yet the growth rate of the money supply did not slow down. During 1978 the basic money stock (currency and demand deposits) kept rising until October and in the next thirteen weeks declined at a 1.1 percent annual rate, but the velocity, the rate at which the stock of money turns over, increased during the final quarter at an astonishing 9 percent annual rate. The rise in interest rates in that year, reaching a high of 13 percent by the year's end, led many economists to forecast a downturn in construction. Yet this did not happen. One reason may be illustrated by the remark of a builder quoted in the *Wall Street Journal* (January 24, 1979): " 'I don't adjust to interest rates,' says Ray Huffman, a San Diego builder. 'My materials cost 1% more each month. I can't afford to lose rent and lose depreciation by not building. . . .' "

The persistence of these attitudes has turned increasing attention to a new, young group of economists who have been building what is called Rational Expectations theory. The premise of the monetarists is that money *counts;* the premise of the new school is that money does not count, because individuals have learned from past experience to *discount* what is happening, and to proceed, on the basis of the information they have, to borrow or not borrow, independent of the momentary monetary rates, in accordance with their judgments of their advantage.

The idea was first put forth by John Muth in 1961 but was elaborated and given powerful technical elaboration by Robert Lucas, of the University of Chicago, in 1972, when he sought to build a notion of stochastic or random shock effects into econometric models, in order to see how such unanticipated effects or reverse movements, particularly in money supply, affected price results in output and employment. Lucas's argument was that such effects are transitory because they are nominal, that money is only a veil in the short run, and that once these shocks are discounted, the classical long-run postulates hold. In effect, Lucas was seeking a way to "discount" the effect of the "discounting" of public decisions by a skeptical public. He was saying that the distrust of governmental measures, fiscal and monetary, was based on a rational calculus of real balances. Through some spectacular mathematical pyrotechnics, a return to the Marshallian notion of equilibrium was being brought about, based on "real" values or, more specifically, on rational expectations.

One can put the problem in simpler, more mundane terms. When the money stock is first increased, people find themselves with more dollars than before and tend to assume that they are wealthier. Businessmen are deceived by distorted price signals, consumers by the number of extra dollars. Thus they act as if this is so, and a rise in output may result. Or, as Lucas puts it: "Everybody thought he was gaining on everybody else. But everybody was wrong. When the true situation becomes clear and real values reassert themselves, people find they have overspent and overborrowed. So when the government tries the same tactic again, the response is far different. When expansionary monetary policy is used repeatedly over time, the kick is lost. There is no stimulating effect on output. Expected expansions come out as inflation and nothing else."

The fact that individuals learn quickly to discount government actions results in an unforeseen collective effect which negates the very intentions the government tries when it tries to alter the economy's course by fiscal or monetary interventions. What, then, should the government do?

The policy argument built around the rational-expectations concept is not that actions of government cannot affect production and employment. They can and do, but only when they surprise people. But to use the old homily, once burnt, twice shy. Or, to use the modern idiom, to get a greater "high," one needs a larger "kick." The crucial point is that government actions which are based on the necessity for surprise can, in the end, only lead to increasing distrust on the part of the polity.

The "rational expectation" view is that some cyclical swings in production and employment are inherent in the *micro* level of the economy which no government *macro* policies can or should attempt to smooth out. This is based on the argument that macro-policy can only deal with aggregates and cannot "fine tune" or choose between the individual decisions of consumers or firms. On the theoretical level, it is based on the assumption that a business cycle is, to some extent, an inextricable aspect of a market economy, because individuals will react differently to price signals, particularly when random shocks (e.g., shortages, sudden price jumps, etc.) lead to a short-term misreading of the signals and to wrong calculations of profit. If misread by enough persons, the changes will create a cumulative swing in output until the misreading is realized, and retrenchment and readjustment set in. Since random shocks to prices and markets are inevitable, because of natural catastrophes or man-made actions, these erratic swings are inevitable. In attempting to meet these, however, the government becomes not the solution but part of the problem, for if the "political discount rate" (i.e., mistrust) is higher than the "economic discount rate" (the nominal expectation of what future costs will be), the actions by government only cause larger and larger perturbations.

It is at this point that Lucas rejoins Friedman on the monetarist conclusions. As regards inflation, monetary authorities should announce, and stick to, a policy that would bring the rate of increase in the general price level to some specified figure, and thereafter monetary policy should seek to reduce uncertainty by maintaining a steady and consistent rate in the growth of the money supply, so that people could build these expectations into their judgments and act accordingly.[8]

The post-Keynesian movement that developed in Anglo-American economics in the 1970s is a complete turn from the monetarist, rational-expectations group and even from the neoclassical school of economics. It rejects general equilibrium theory on the ground that, however elegant, a "timeless" general theory cannot help us understand the variegated changes in modern economic systems. The starting point for the understanding of the economy, the neo-Keynesians assert, is not relative prices which determine distribution but the distribution of income, which determines what will be commanded and produced. The distribution of income is not regarded in the manner of the marginalists, however, for whom each factor in production receives a return proportional to its contribution, but, in the past, as a function of custom, and, in the present, as a consequence of power relations in the market. Inflation is an outcome of the conflict of organized groups for larger shares of the income.

In pure theory, it is a return to the classical economics, as reformulated by Piero Sraffa, with its emphasis on production and the reproduction of the means of production, as the key to the understanding of fundamental economic processes, rather than the subjective utilities of consumer demand. Lionel Robbins had redefined economics as the allocation of scarce resources among competing ends; the neo-Keynesians insist that economics has to deal, first, with growth and investment. On the empirical side, their theory emphasizes institutional relations—the power of organized groups, the character of changes in technology—as the framework of decisions. It differs from orthodox Keynesianism in its emphasis on investment and the long-run processes of the reproduction of the economy, rather than the short-term readjustments (the partial equilibrium of Marshall) of the economy through demand. It differs from Marxist economics in that it eschews the debate over the labor theory of value, the definition of groups in the society necessarily in class terms, and on the idea of the inevitable breakdown of capitalism. It draws much of its inspiration from the group of Cambridge economists who worked with Keynes, such as Sraffa, Joan Robinson, and Nicholas Kaldor, and from economists whose ideas had paralleled Keynes or extended Sraffa, such as Michal Kalecki and Luigi Pasinetti. In the United States a group of younger economists, led by Paul Davidson, Alfred S. Eichner, and J. A. Kregel, have sought to propagate these ideas. They have begun the *Journal of Post-Keynesian Economics,* and a series of essays expounding their point of view appeared in 1978 in the economics magazine *Challenge.*

The starting point for post-Keynesian analysis is the question of growth, or "economic dynamics," as against "economic statics," or the equilibrating mechanisms of an economy with competitive or imperfectly competitive markets. The initial postwar effort to set forth the lineaments of a theory was made by the Oxford economist Roy Harrod (the biographer of Keynes) and formalized by the M.I.T economist Evzey Domar. The Harrod-Domar formula, which they sought to integrate into neoclassical theory, states that the growth rate of an economy (a dependent variable) is determined by the propensity to save (roughly, the rate of savings) and the incremental capital-output ratios, that is, the increases in the productivity of capital. Harrod posited what he called a "warranted" rate of growth—a rate of growth of demand and investment to keep all capital fully utilized—and a "natural" or "potential" rate of growth, which would be sufficient to employ a growing labor force plus any increase in labor productivity. Any shortfalls in these baseline rates would lead to unemployment; any rates that outstripped the growth of capacity and the absorption of a new labor force would create inflation.

A number of technical, empirical, and institutional questions arose over the utility of the Harrod-Domar model, even though it seemed to provide a satisfactory framework for analysis. One was the fact that, as in all such macro-models, capital and labor are considered as aggregates and homogeneous, returns to scale are taken as constant, and consumer tastes and production technologies are considered as unchanged. Yet in any dynamic economy few of these assumptions used in neoclassical theory hold. More to the point: in a dynamic economy, the motor of growth is technology. And how can one "convert" technological change into these standard constants? The problem is how to use such a model, even as a simplified framework, for descriptive analysis or policy decisions.

A different question, raised by the post-Keynesians (in John Cornwall's book *Modern Capitalism*, 1977), was whether a capitalist economy could grow at a rate equal to the warranted and natural rates, thus maintaining full use of capital capacity and full employment.

The crux of the problem is how investment proceeds. In neoclassical theory, savings determine investment, and this is based on the willingness of individuals to forgo current consumption in order to get a satisfactory return (through interest or profit) on their savings. The post-Keynesians believe the reverse: it is investment that determines savings. Based on the work of Kalecki, they argue that investments are financed in large measure out of retained earnings, by profits, and that in oligopolistic situations, firms set their markups sufficiently high so that they can generate sufficient flow from internal sources. (This, for example, is the "standard volume" concept of pricing used by General Motors, as explained by Alfred P. Sloan in his book *My Years With General Motors*.) The empirical issue, then, is the degree of market power of the large corporation to "administer" prices and to adjust production to a set rate of return on investment.

The centrality of investment leads, in post-Keynesian theory, to an argument about distribution, or how incomes are set in the economy. The post-Keynesians reject the view that the income of labor is determined by marginalist principles at the microeconomic level in the labor market. They argue, as did Keynes, that since labor does not know, or cannot choose, the real wage at which it would be employed, nominal wages play the central role in labor's demands. They base a theory of income distribution (derived from essays of Joan Robinson and Nicholas Kaldor, in the *Review of Economic Studies,* 1956) on the argument that an increase in the economic growth rate, because of the higher level of investment, necessarily increases the share of profits in the national income, at the expense of wages.

According to this reasoning, changes in demand, both aggregate and in sectors, are due more to changes in income than to changes in relative prices, and income itself is determined by the market power of contending groups. The rate of inflation is determined, at one end, by the rate of increase of nominal money wages relative to labor productivity—an argument that has recently been reemphasized by Richard Kahn, Keynes's oldest associate at Cambridge, in defending the relevancy of Keynesian theory to the contemporary situation, and in particular to Great Britain. At the other end, it is determined by the ability of large corporations to control the markup of their prices, and even to cut output, rather than price, to maintain their profit ratios. In this analysis, inflation is seen primarily as a cost-push phenomenon: When governmental authorities intervene, particularly through monetary measures, to reduce the money supply, the conflict between the organized groups to safeguard their "market shares" becomes more intense.

The policy prescriptions that follow from such an analysis are an argument for an "incomes policy," a set of wage-and-price controls which would deal not only with aggregate levels but necessarily with the relative wage and price structure between industries and occupations. Basil J. Moore, a post-Keynesian theorist, has written:

> If the government is forced to put itself in the position of regulating wage increases, it will soon be pushed into taking a position not only on appropriate life-cycle income profiles, but also on appropriate relative wage structures among occupations. From there it is but a short step to specifying the appropriate incomes for rentiers and entrepreneurs, and the very foundations of the system will be fundamentally challenged. In order for a modern capitalist system with collective bargaining to avoid stagflation, it becomes necessary to achieve a consensus about equitable relative incomes—and it is precisely this which seems beyond our present political competence.[9]

Most of the orthodox Keynesian economists accept the argument that institutional factors are largely responsible for inflation or instability, without going to the extent of accepting the elaborate theoretical scaffolding of Sraffa or Kalecki. They regard the synthesis of Marshall and Keynes, reformulated by Samuelson and Solow, as a valid model of the economy—*outside* the political system. In the real world, of course, they recognize the crucial role of the political system and seek to produce policy prescriptions through an examination of the interplay of both. But as economists they believe that a pure theory can still be created and serve as a fiction or an "as if"—as if individuals behaved in accordance with the maximizing precepts of rational behavior.

By way of empirical analysis, Charles Schultze, the present chairman of the Council of Economic Advisors, published a monograph in 1959 for the Joint Economic Committee of the Congress, *Recent Inflation in the United States,* which argued that if wages and prices become so sticky that they cannot move downward, inflation is bound to occur. William Nordhaus, a former member of the Council, in an essay on "Inflation Theory and Policy," in the *American Economic Review* of May 1976, posits a "dual economy" model. In one sector there are "auction markets," where supply and demand and flexible prices obtain, as in commodity markets, agricultural products, securities markets, and some internationally traded goods. In the other, there are "administered markets," where the market power of buyers and sellers can limit price movements—in much of manufacturing, utilities, government sectors, and labor markets. The logic of this argument has led economists such as Arthur Okun, Henry Wallich, and Sidney Weintraub to propose that government use tax-incentive policies (TIP) to penalize or reward corporations or firms that set prices or wages beyond a flexible guideline. Yet increasingly, as Edward Tufte and others have pointed out (*Political Control of the Economy,* Princeton University Press, 1978), there is also a "political business cycle," whereby governments, in order to retain popularity, will spend or adjust their budget policies to the timing of elections rather than to the economic business cycle and so create a host of economic problems for the society. As Assar Lindbeck has put it:

> The present 'crisis' in the Western economies is not, I think, mainly a
> 'crisis' in economics, though we economists have no doubt
> overestimated the stability of macroeconometric behavior functions.
> The main problem is not that we are unable to understand analytically
> what is happening, but rather that the institutional changes and the
> discretionary policies that are necessary for macroeconomic stability
> seem to be politically difficult to implement.[10]

And yet—though the subject is far beyond this essay—the fundamental problem may be the very character of economic theory as its major practitioners have fashioned it. Why theory? Because theory directs one to what to see, to the choice of the relevant variables, to the statement as to what is essential about the character of a subject.

Economic theory, by and large, is based on the model of classical mechanics and seeks to create a science in the image of the natural sciences. The model of classical mechanics leads to the idea of an equilibrium, in which natural forces seek to assert themselves and restore economic relations to a balance, the fulcrum of which is perfect competition.* It seeks to be a science by putting its propositions in axiomatic form and setting forth the parameters of different kinds of action so as to create a general, timeless theory and a set of covering laws which would stipulate the range and type of possible actions.

Yet the crucial question is whether economics can be such a science, even within the framework of its self-imposed ordinance of excluding exogenous actions. One can acknowledge, yet put aside, the question of stochastic disturbances, or random shocks, since there may be, as Robert Lucas has attempted to show, ways of building such stochastic disturbances into a model and thus accounting for them. The larger questions are epistemological ones.

Economics deals with "human actions," but it presupposes a definition of rational self-interest as the basis of fictions, or prediction, as if these actions were like laws of physical motion. The result is, basically, a mechanistic view of human behavior. (And Marx, too, in *Kapital,* assumed he could decipher the "laws of motion" of capitalism.) Yet it is not at all clear that this is true, nor, certainly, that prediction is possible—especially if it is based on expectations of human behavior. To put it more formally, as G. L. S. Shackle does in his book *Epistemics & Economics* (Cambridge University Press, 1972), the economic theorist can choose either "rationality" or "time." The theory that rejects time can set forth propositions such as subjective marginalism, and partial or general equilibrium. But the introduction of time not only produces uncertainty but also necessitates understanding the behavior of non-rational actions if it is to deal with the choices human beings make.

One can reformulate the question, as I sought to do several years ago in *The Coming of Post-Industrial Society:*

> The theoretical virtue of the market is that it coordinates human interdependence in some optimal fashion, in accordance with the expressed preferences of buyers and sellers (within any given distribution of income). But what ultimately provides direction for the economy, as Veblen pointed out long ago, is not the price system but *the value system of the culture* in which the economy is embedded. The price system is only a mechanism for the relative allocation of goods and services within the framework of *the kinds of demand* generated. Accordingly, economic guidance can only be as efficacious as the cultural value system which shapes it.[11]

To put the issue in terms of an older philosophical debate, the question is whether economics is *theoretical* or is *practical knowledge*, whether it is a

---

* The idea of treating a social system as a "state of equilibrium" was put forth by Vilfredo Pareto (*The Mind and Society,* p. 66), and through the intermediation of L. J. Henderson, the Harvard physiologist, influenced Talcott Parsons and his work in sociology. But it is no accident, so to speak, that Pareto was initially an economist and an engineer.

natural or a moral science. The predicaments of the last ten or so years and the crisis in economic theory have made that question a central one for the social sciences.

Conventionally, economics is divided into two broad sectors: macro- and microeconomics. Macroeconomics deals with the large magnitudes of gross national product, savings, investment, the money supply, etc. Most of the policy discussions of the economy are within a *macro* framework. Microeconomics is concerned with individual decisions (by persons or firms) in response to prices in markets, on the basis of preferences or wants relative to supply and demand. Macroeconomics, then, is the aggregated behavior of thousands and millions of such individual decisions, as registered by price transactions, and the postulates of microeconomics—the assumptions regarding the behavior of individuals—underlie the conceptual framework of macroeconomic theory.

Neoclassical microeconomic theory is utilitarian. It makes some specific assumptions regarding the actions, if not the motivations, of human beings. What it assumes is that such decisions are rational (i.e., the means chosen seek to fulfill the ends); that they are based on relevant information of alternative prices in markets; and that decisions are made so as to maximize or optimize gains (or efficiency) and to minimize losses (or costs). More formally, these actions can be expressed in "utility preference schedules," or can be "scaled" in a consistent rank order, so that individuals can judge the relative costs or worth of their decisions. Out of these schedules come the more technical tools of economics such as "indifference curves," which means that at roughly equal prices substitutions can take place between different preferences for comparable goods, "production functions," or the different mix of capital or labor at relative prices; or "opportunity costs," meaning that the choice of a resource to one use at an expected gain has to be measured against what may be forgone by an alternative use, etc.

This form of behavior, called "rational action," is usually contrasted with that in a "traditional society," where prices may be set by custom, or factors in production used by habit, or where markets are haphazard or dictated by political rules.

Macroeconomic theory has been challenged in recent years, not only by the argument that the theoretically closed system of interacting variables becomes less meaningful because of the greater role of "exogenous" factors, such as political decisions, but equally by challenges to the postulates of microeconomics itself. Is there such an animal as "economic man," or such conduct as "rational behavior"?

One way of dealing with the question is to say that "rational conduct" is simply a normative standard, an "as if," a theoretical construct of what allocation and distribution would be like *if* people did behave that way; and as a normative standard, it is a measure against which to judge the shortfalls of actual or nonrational conduct. But such an argument eludes the issue by failing to account for the ways individuals actually do behave. Most economists think of their discipline as a positive science, which is both descriptive and explanatory, and they do seek to justify their postulates not just as ideal models but as empirically grounded justifications. They believe man is *Homo economicus* in the arena of production and consumption. It is at this point that the debate in microeconomics in recent years has broken open.

At one end are economists such as Gary Becker of the University of Chicago who argue that not only do individuals act to maximize their gains, that the utilitarian postulates are valid, but that this economic approach can be applied to a wider range of human behavior including areas such as crime or marriage that are usually thought of as noneconomic. For Becker, in fact, economics is not a subject matter, but an approach, an argument that is summed up in his book, *The Economic Approach to Human Behavior* (Chicago: University of Chicago Press, 1976; p. 8). "Indeed," he writes,

> I have come to the position that the economic approach is a
> comprehensive one that is applicable to all human behavior, be it
> behavior involving money prices or imputed shadow prices, repeated
> or infrequent decisions, large or minor decisions, emotional or
> mechanical ends, rich or poor persons, . . . patients or therapists,
> businessmen or politicians, teachers or students. The applications of
> the economic approach so conceived are as extensive as the scope of
> economics in the definition given earlier that emphasizes scarce means
> and competing ends.

Becker and a number of other economists who share this approach argue that maximizing behavior and stable preferences are not simply primitive assumptions but are derivable from the natural selection of adaptive evolutionary behavior, as human beings have evolved over time. These economists have found in sociobiology a support for their arguments. In fact, Jack Hirshleifer, of the University of California of Los Angeles, in an essay "Economics From a Biological Viewpoint," believes that "the fundamental organizing concepts of the dominant analytical structures employed in economics and sociobiology are strikingly parallel."[12]

These versions of "economic man" have been challenged by a number of different social scientists who unite in believing that the postulates of rationality assumed by the utilitarian economists are too abstract and are not demonstrated in actual behavior. One of the earliest and most general challenges was made by Herbert A. Simon, who, though a political scientist and a writer initially on organization behavior, won the Nobel Prize in economics in 1978. In *Administrative Behavior* (3rd ed. 1976), Simon wrote:

> Economic man has a complete and consistent set of preferences that
> allows him always to choose among the alternatives open to him; he is
> always completely aware of what these alternatives are; there are no
> limits on the complexity of the computations he can perform in order

to determine which alternatives are best; probability calculations are
neither frightening nor mysterious to him.

But such assumptions of rational choice, argued Simon, have little relation
to flesh-and-blood humans. The chief difficulties—and here Simon was
drawing on his work in computer science—are the human limits on memory and computing power, and the multiple and conflicting goals in problem-
solving.

Against the idea of "economic man," Simon proposed the idea of "bounded rationality." In this he focused on three themes. He proposed that
alternatives be discovered through a search in which only a relatively *few*
alternatives were considered. Against the scaling of utility preferences in a
complete ranked order, he proposed a two-valued utility function, simply
satisfactory or unsatisfactory, and subsequent choices followed like branch-
ing of a tree from a choice regarding the outcome of the previous decision.
In place of the economist's emphasis on choice as a constant set of *new*
decisions made for each problem (or in response to price), decisions were
seen as a combination of habitual premises and rules that were modified
only over the long run.

While these were technical arguments within decision theory, Simon
applied them principally to organizational behavior. The notion of "organizational efficiency," derived from "maximizing" or "optimizing" notions,
was not applicable to the behavior of organizations. Any organization had
conflicting sets of goals; the criteria for success were difficult to agree upon;
and most managers rarely acted to maximize their operations, if only
because the costs of obtaining all the relevant information were too high
or too time-consuming. Instead, what organizations did more typically was
to "satisfice"—to follow a course of action that was not necessarily "the best,"
but good enough to avoid unacceptable levels of trouble. The crucial point
was that an organization was not simply an "entrepreneur" but a complex
decision-making system of bargains, and one could not understand the
behavior of organizations, including economic decisions, without understanding that complexity.[13]

One could argue, in defending the "rational choice" argument, that if an
organization itself is a congeries of individuals, each would still seek to
maximize his own advantage within the firm, and that while the organization might not be responding fully to the "outside environment" in optimizing its behavior, the decisions might reflect the outcomes and bargains of
its major participants. This is the assumption, for example, of J. Kenneth
Galbraith in *The New Industrial State* (1967), in which he argues that the
"technostructure" or the ruling bureaucracy within the organization acts to
safeguard its own interests, as against maximizing the profits of a firm for
its shareholders.

But a different argument, within the logic of microeconomic theory itself,
is mounted by Harvey Leibenstein of Harvard in his *Beyond Economic Man:*

A New Foundation for Economics (Harvard University Press, 1976). For Leibenstein, cost minimization is the exception rather than the rule in most firms, and in contrast to the idea of *allocative efficiency,* which is used in neoclassical economics, Leibenstein substitutes the terms *X-efficiency* and *X-inefficiency,* i.e., the deviation between the optimal levels of effort from the firm's "rational" viewpoint and the actual levels that individuals achieve. The difference in degree is the "X-efficiency" in the system.

Simply put, Leibenstein argues that in most activities, habit, routine, and entrenched conventions shape the normal course of behavior. For him, the critical measure of efficiency in an organization is the amount and nature of *effort* that an individual makes, and that effort, as such, is not a variable in standard micro theory. In short, for Leibenstein, nonmaximization should be the standard assumption of economic theory, and maximization only a special case. In this emphasis on habit and institution, Leibenstein has gone back to Veblen to recast a theory of microeconomic behavior.

In a very different sense, the postulates of microeconomics have been challenged by Thomas C. Schelling of Harvard in an imaginative book, *Micromotives and Macrobehavior* (New York: Norton, 1978). The basic assumption of economics is that macrobehavior is a *linear* addition of all the individual microdecisions. But for Schelling, what the individual seeks for himself, in the aggregate, often turns into a nightmare. Or, to put it in another way, the "aggregate" is a qualitatively distinct phenomenon from the actions of "individuals."

Schelling draws his models from the commonplaces of everyday life. If a wreck occurs on a highway, cars passing in the opposite lane will slow down to look; all cars in that lane, subsequently, will back up; each car gets a "ten-second" look, yet it costs the entire line ten minutes for that ten-second look. In a gasoline panic, individuals will begin arriving at a gas station at 6:30 A.M. though the station does not open until 7:00. But if each person seeks to arrive even earlier than the other, if enough persons are determined to beat the average, the average itself will get earlier in a "self-displacing prophecy." Each individual is reacting to the expected behavior of the group, but the group is the sum of the individuals. Thus the average arrival time is a "statistical consequence of the behavior [it] induces." Similarly, a tolerant individual may not resent a black family moving into his neighborhood, yet when that number begins to increase, the fear about the fall of property values, induced by the thought that another white neighbor may move, induces the first individual to leave. In short, interacting expectations may be self-fulfilling or self-negating. The same distribution of micromotives can lead to widely divergent macrophenomena, either of greater participation or of withdrawal.

The crucial point is that societal outcomes, when they are the sum total of interacting individuals, often lead to outcomes which none of the individuals desires. The well-known illustration is Garrett Hardin's example of the "tragedy of the commons" (*Science,* Dec. 13, 1968, pp. 1243–48), where a shared resource, a grazing area, is used by each individual for his own maximizing advantage until in the end the resource is destroyed. If a single individual withholds his cows to preserve the grass, he gains no advantage, but the others do. Conversely, in other situations where goods are public or collective (e.g., a trade-union collective-bargaining contract), an individual who does not pay for the outcome may yet receive it and become a free rider. In short, since interacting individuals, acting only on "micromotives," are unlikely to coordinate their activities, some group or collective action is needed. Schelling concludes:

> A good part of social organization consists of institutional arrangements to overcome these divergences between perceived individual interest and some larger collective bargain. [The collective bargain above is for everyone to graze fewer cows so the pasture survives.] Some of it is market-oriented—ownership, contracts ... and a variety of communications and information systems. Some have to do with government—taxes to cover public services.... More selective groupings—the union, the club, the neighborhood—can organize incentive systems or regulations to try to help people do what individually they wouldn't but collectively they may wish to do. Our morals can substitute for markets and regulations in getting us sometimes to do from conscience the things that in the long run we might elect to do only if assured of reciprocation [pp. 127–28].

In sum, if economic activities are social processes, can one have an adequate theory of economic behavior outside the framework of a comprehensive sociological theory? It is a question that economists and sociologists will be pursuing in the next decade.

3. Neo-Marxism

In the 1960s and 1970s, one saw a surprising upsurge of Marxist politics and neo-Marxist thought on a scale largely unexpected, following the sense of an exhaustion of radical ideas in the West by the end of the 1950s.* Three developments may have accounted for this change.

---

* Since I am prominently identified with the theme of the "end of ideology," which received considerable attention in the early 1960s, it is not amiss to point out that many persons have read the argument from the title of my book, not from its contents.

The book dealt with the "exhaustion of political ideas in the Fifties," which is the subtitle of the book, and states two propositions: One, that a "new generation, with no meaningful memory of these old debates and no secure tradition to build upon" is searching yearningly and desperately for "a cause" to build new faiths. And two, "that while the old nineteenth-century ideologies and intellectual debates have become exhausted, the rising states of Africa and Asia are fashioning new ideologies with a different appeal for their own people.... The ideologies of the nineteenth century were universalistic, humanistic, and fashioned by intellectuals. The mass ideologies of Asia and Africa are parochial, instrumental, and created by political leaders." See *The End of Ideology* (Glencoe, Ill.: The Free Press, 1960, rev. ed. 1962), pp. 40, 373.

One was the emergence of a large number of third-world countries such as Cuba, Vietnam, Cambodia, Mozambique, and Angola, which called themselves Marxist, and an array of other countries, as diverse as Southern Yemen, Afghanistan, Libya, or Algeria, which called themselves in one form or another socialist. The paradox is that little of this emerged out of classical Marxist theory, which, in its Western evolutionary framework, saw socialism as the next, higher stage after capitalism. These were almost all former colonial peasant societies which had come under the leadership of young elites that were seeking to transform them from the top, through state direction. Their leaders, like Calibans, had learned a language and used it to curse. Their Marxism was a rhetoric of anti-imperialism and a technique for political mobilization.

A second reason was the youth upsurge in the 1960s, in the Western industrial countries, against Establishment and Authority. There was an emphasis on spontaneity and "doing one's thing," on participation, on communitarianism, and an attack on materialism and consumerism. Its root impulse, thematically, was on the grosser features of capitalist society, and its initial impacts were in culture (or, more specially the "counterculture") and on the quality-of-life issues in politics, particularly ecology and the environment. Sometimes parallel and sometimes intertwined were the drive of the blacks for civil rights and the demand by women for equal rights. Intellectually inchoate and populist in temper, as the young radicals of the 1960s began to move into the institutions, particularly the universities, and as the recession of the 1970s seemed to herald the economic decline of the Western countries, many of the younger scholars turned to various forms of neo-Marxism to refine their ideas and to explore a more coherent kind of social analysis.

The third reason, somewhat independent at first, yet finally providing a new foundation, was the independent scholarship in Marxist studies that had begun to emerge in the 1950s and the publication of many of the texts of Marx that had been suppressed or ignored by the predominant Communist monopoly in the publication of Marx's works during the years following the Russian Revolution. The "rediscovery" of forgotten Marxist writers of the 1920s, such as Lukács, Gramsci, and Korsch, or the sudden emergence of the "Frankfurt School," including Horkheimer, Adorno, Marcuse (and as a younger follower Jürgen Habermas), all provided the basis for a tremendous industry of publication of older texts, intense discussion of their ideas, and tremendous outpouring of exegetical arguments as to what Marx really meant, or the relevance of Marx to the day.

It would take an essay as long as these two parts combined merely to sketch the diverse issues and the many revisionist quarrels in a dozen different fields which this new burst of intellectual energy produced. In any philosophical world view grounded in a faith system, such as Christianity, the minute dissection of "the Word" assumes a fateful character. As in

Christianity, where if the wrong *letter* is employed (*homoiousian* as against *homoousian*) one risks loss of salvation, so, in Marxism, the slightest doctrinal deviation risks derailing the Revolution from the track of History.

And the difficulty of Marxism was—and is—that definitive texts are lacking. Even today there is no complete set of all the writings of Marx and Engels. And when they are completed, the problems will not change because of the contradictory dilemmas that Marx faced in wrestling with crucial philosophical issues: the questions of voluntarism (in which men make their own history) versus determinism; an activity theory of knowledge versus a copy theory of knowledge; human nature as possessing an essence (*Wesen*) or a human nature that changes as a consequence of the growth of men's technical powers.[14]

The striking thing is that few if any of the early philosophical works of Marx—*The German Ideology* and the *Economic-Philosophical Manuscripts*, written before 1847, and the sketchy but massive sociological treatise, the so-called *Grundrisse*, or Outlines of National Economy (1857–59)—not only were not published in Marx's lifetime but did not even appear until a half-century after his death—the first two in the 1930s in German (and much later in English) and the last in the 1950s in German. Marx completed only the first volume of *Das Kapital;* the other two volumes were arbitrarily organized by Engels, while a large sheaf of auxiliary materials, the *Theorien über den Mehrwert* (Theories of Surplus Value), were published in four volumes only after the death of Engels by his literary executor, Karl Kautsky, and still remain incompletely translated into English. Even the early English translations of many of Marx's works, including *Kapital*, are clumsy and inexact and only now are being redone.

The first generation of Marxian theoreticians, among them Kautsky, Lenin, and Plekhanov, knew little if any of the early works. Their conceptions of Marxism derived from the first codification of Marx's work, the book by Frederick Engels, *Anti-Dühring*, and from the pamphlet derived from it, *Socialism, Utopian and Scientific*. Engels was largely dismissive of the early works, and when asked by a visitor in 1893 why he did not publish them, Engels remarked that one needed a knowledge of Hegel to understand them, that many were now obscure in their metaphysical jargon, and that his important task was to complete the publication of *Kapital*, which he regarded as the major achievement of Marx.

Regarding the early philosophical works: in 1876 Engels wrote a long review essay of a book by a man named Starcke, on Feuerbach, Marx's immediate intellectual mentor, which he published as *Ludwig Feuerbach and the Outcome of Classical German Philosophy*. To this he appended the fragmentary and incomplete (they are little more than gnomic jottings) paragraphs of Marx called the "Theses on Feuerbach," which Engels regarded as the most "meaty" of those older philosophical statements.

One curious result is that concepts which, in the past twenty years, have seemed to be inextricably associated with the name of Marx were almost completely unknown and never appeared in the writings of the first generation of Marx's expositors. The most striking is the concept of *alienation*. The term does not appear in any of the writings of Engels, Plekhanov, Kautsky, or Lenin. The entry on "alienation" in the authoritative *Encyclopaedia of the Social Sciences* (1931) deals only with "alienation of property," as a legal term, while the biographical entry on Marx (1933), by Karl Korsch, a major Marxist philosopher, does not mention the term. The magisterial study by Sidney Hook, *From Hegel to Marx* (1936), a meticulous study of the development of Marx's thought from Hegel through the various left-Hegelian writers to Marx, carries only a passing reference to the term, and the word itself, *alienation*, does not appear in the index of the book.

Yet in the major writings on Marx in the 1960s and after, the term *alienation* is regarded as the central concept in Marx's thought. The major work by the French Catholic writer, Père Jean-Yves Calvez, *La Pensée de Karl Marx*, is a 600-page book in which it is used as the organizing theme to explore all of Marx's work. This is equally true of the work of Iring Fetscher, the German scholar. And the theme has been used by more popular if less exacting writers such as Bertell Ollmann and Richard Schacht.

All this has given rise to an exegetical debate as to whether there was a *continuity* in Marx's thought, or a rupture. David McClellan, a prolific writer on the subject and a recent biographer of Marx, argues that there is a consistency and continuity to Marx's thought, especially, he points out, as the term *alienation* is used in the *Grundrisse*. Writers as diverse as Sidney Hook and Louis Althusser argue, for different intellectual reasons, that there was a "break" in Marx's writings, though each dates it differently. For Hook, the term *alienation* was a product of German romanticism, which Marx himself later mocked, and had disappeared because Marx, beginning with *The German Ideology*, sought to locate social relations in more exact class terms. For Althusser, the decisive break comes with the writing of *Kapital*, which he regards as the basis of Marx's "scientific" work, as against philosophy. For an outsider, these may seem puzzling and only doctrinal quarrels, yet to the extent that doctrine shapes or justifies large intellectual structures, let alone political movements, in the beginning—and in the end—is the Word.

The difficulty with all this is compounded by the fact that on *any* single major concept associated with the name of Marx there is no single unambiguous definition of the terms involved. The phrase *historical materialism* was never used by Marx but was coined by Engels. The term *dialectical materialism* was never used by either Marx or Engels but was created by the Russian Marxist Plekhanov.

Let us take a key idea. Marxist sociology can probably be summed up in a single sentence: "All social structure is, fundamentally, class structure." That is Marxism's strength; it is also its problem. To say that all social divisions in society are derived from class is to give one a powerful prism on social behavior. It posits a single axis that divides basic interests; it identifies different world views (even truths) and different life-styles in class terms. The difficulty is that the statement is more metaphoric than denotative. It begins to founder when one asks: what does one mean by class?

Marx, in fact, uses the term *class* in five different ways. Even when, most broadly, class is related primarily to the structure of production, as the essential classes (i.e., the large bulk of tradesmen, professionals, priests, officers, and government employees are placed outside the productive process and supported by the "value" produced by the workers), the boundary definitions are vague. Who belongs to the working class? Is it only production or factory workers? Where does one fit in clerical and technical personnel? What of managers who are salaried individuals yet run the enterprises? Who are "the capitalists"? What does it mean to "own" property? Who owns the mutual insurance companies that possess the largest aggregate of disposable capital in the United States? And who "owns" A.T.&T. or Exxon or General Motors, the largest capitalist corporations in the country?

No wonder that even committed Marxists are baffled. The exploration and reinterpretation of Marx have gone into every field—philosophy, aesthetics, history, sociology, and economics. One should distinguish, again, the political and moral criticism of capitalism from a radical standpoint (and the validity this might have) from the effort to ground a new philosophy and social science out of the thought of Marx. It is these latter efforts that will be touched upon, if necessarily briefly.

The major starting point has been philosophy. Here, what has been termed "classical Marxism" has been the subject of the most heated debate and thoroughgoing revision. Classical Marxism, as put forth by Engels, emphasized a "copy theory of knowledge," i.e., that what we know is a reflection of the external reality. This, of course, was a mechanistic position, since materialism was the foundation of knowledge, and to show change, even in nature, it was held that "matter" moved "dialectically." Engels also sought to cast Marxism in a "scientific" vein, according to the mode of the time, by emphasizing determinism and "laws" of society almost on the model of physics—an effort that found its doctrinal support in Marx's brief methodological assertions in the Author's Prefaces to *Kapital* that he was not describing capitalism empirically but as abstractions are used in the physical sciences, and that he was seeking to identify the "laws of motion" of capitalism.

Yet, as George Lichtheim, one of the early independent scholars of the subject, pointed out in his *Marxism: An Historical and Critical Study* (London: Routledge & Kegan Paul, 1961), this "scientistic" view clashed with the early writings of Marx, which contained an "activity theory of knowledge" that was rooted in the development of consciousness.

What Lichtheim was summing up was a view, expressed in more technical ways, that Marx's ideas were directly rooted in Hegel, and that this had radically different consequences for understanding Marx than the deterministic reading by Engels. The question whether Engels had radically revised Marx, or whether Marx himself had surrendered some of his early views, bedevils Marxist debates today.

Marxist philosophy in the last decade and a half has centered on the thoughts of four views: that of György Lukács, the Hungarian philospher; the "Frankfurt School," which includes Max Horkheimer, Theodor Adorno, Herbert Marcuse, and, as a later votary, Jürgen Habermas; Jean-Paul Sartre, the French existentialist who sought to graft Marxist thought onto his earlier writing; and the French philosopher Louis Althusser.

Lukács, who has been the most influential (and enigmatic) Marxian critic, had in 1923 published a book entitled *History and Class Consciousness* in which, without knowing directly of the early writing of Marx, he "intuited" on the basis of his reading of Hegel a different view of Marx from the orthodox view prevailing at the time. But Lukács, in 1923 and later in 1930, was forced, ignominiously, to recant the book and, as a devoted Communist, he forbade any reprint of it. For many years it led a subterranean existence as an esoteric text, in part because of its "gnostic" inference that the intellectuals were the true, inner elite of the vanguard, a theme that Thomas Mann depicted in his portrait of Lukács as Naphta, the Jesuit revolutionist, in *The Magic Mountain*. Lukács derided dialectical materialism as simply "inverted Platonism," without any philosophical foundation, but he also gave a radical interpretation to the theory of historical materialism. For Lukács, there was no "independent" view of reality and history outside of "class views," and knowledge, therefore, was always class-bound. But if this was the case, which view was "true"? For Lukács, the view of the proletariat was true—even if the proletariat itself did not hold that view—because in the immanent development of consciousness, the proletariat was the "human subject" that alone could achieve universality, the consideration of reason, this being, for Lukács, something historical.

The question whether there is a *marche générale*, of History, and more, whether Stalinism, despite its "excesses," was "historically progressive," was the inner debate that wracked the Commmunist intelligentsia. If morality is only class morality, from what standpoint could one condemn the forced collectivization and the concentration camps? How does one know in which direction History is marching and whether "the Party," as embodied in the current leader, is on the course dictated by the "cunning reason"? Lukács himself was always ambiguous, publicly, about Stalinism. Though he became a minister in the short-lived cabinet of Imre Nagy, during the Hungarian Revolution of 1956, and was arrested and deported when the Russian troops crushed the dissident Communist rebellion (Nagy himself was shot), Lukács never wavered in his support of the ultimately "progressive" role of the Russian Revolution.

The Frankfurt School was never communist—Adorno once said of Lukács that "[He] tugs vainly at his chains and imagines their clanking to be the forward march of *der Weltgeist*" (the world-spirit), though Marcuse, in his book *Soviet Marxism,* was more ambiguous regarding the "historical" role of the Russian Revolution.

The Frankfurt School, founded originally at that university, saw as its main task the development of "critical theory." By this it meant an attack on positivism, and the development of a "negative dialectic," i.e., the exposure of the retrograde features of "bourgeois" Enlightenment philosophy, such as its emphasis on egoism and individualism, the uncritical view of "progress," and, in particular, the role of "technological rationality" as the basis of functional efficiency. The attacks on technology and on mass culture were the central themes of Marcuse, particularly in *One-Dimensional Man,* and of Adorno in collections of essays, such as *Prisms.* Positivism was seen as the acceptance of existing empirical reality as truth.

If one asks from what standpoint it is that one makes the criticisms, the answers become more uncertain. Formally it was the idea of Reason, expressed in different ways. For Adorno, it was the idea of "authenticity"; for Marcuse, as in his book *Eros and Civilization,* it is the lifting of all "repression" so that libidinal energies are freed for creative tasks; for Jürgen Habermas, who has attempted the most thoroughgoing critique of contemporary philosophy (in his *Knowledge and Human Interests*), it is the effort to achieve "undistorted communication." Where for Francis Bacon, in his *Novum Organum,* men were divided by the "idols of the tribe," the "idols of the market," and so forth, for Habermas it is no longer the direct exploitation of the worker by the capitalist that inhibits the rational development of the productive capacity of the society but the nature of science and technology itself. As he writes in his book *Toward a Rational Society:*

> ... technology and science become a leading productive force, rendering inoperative the conditions for Marx's labor theory of value. It is no longer meaningful to calculate the amount of capital investment in research and development on the basis of the value of unskilled (simple) labor power, when scientific-technical progress has become an independent source of surplus value, in relation to which the only source of surplus value considered by Marx, namely the labor power of the immediate producers, plays an ever smaller role.[15]

The "critique" of science in its various positivist guises becomes, then, one of the main tasks of philosophy. The positive goal, however, is to achieve "inter-subjectivity," or common understandings among men, and only when all ideological and communication "distortions" are eliminated can men begin to define their "knowledge-constitutive interests," those which give them true insight into their authentic needs.

For Sartre, too, in his *Critique de la raison dialectique,* the problem of "standpoint" is crucial. Sartre, too, reasserts the Hegelian principle that History unfolds the truth about man, and he rejects the "copy theory of knowledge" of Engels—and of Lenin, who followed this in his *Materialism and Empirio-*

Criticism. The first limitation of Marxism, argues Sartre, is its failure to put forth a theory of "mediation," or how one moves from the abstract "concepts" about nature and history to the concrete lives of individuals and the specificity of events—the themes that existentialism had taken as primary. Marxism, argues Sartre, has failed because it subordinates individuals to a preconceived schematism. The second limitation is the materialist dialectic, which roots the historical process in nature, where, for Sartre, the ontological vantage point is the dialectical movement of men to freedom. What inhibits freedom, says Sartre, is scarcity, which, in a theme going back to Hobbes, forces men to treat each other as instruments or things, or as "others." The dialectic of history is *altérité* (otherness), and *alienation* as created by scarcity. Since these divide men, the standpoint of judgment, of emancipation, is that which creates "wholeness" or the ensembles of totality in human relations.

The major thrust of almost all neo-Marxian philosophy was to return to Hegel, and to the historicism that is at its core. But Hegel's historicism presents three problems: it sees the world in dualistic terms, e.g., subject and object, spirit and matter, nature and history, etc.; it posits an immanent process of unfolding in which these dualities become resolved at "higher" levels of unity; and it holds, necessarily, that man has no nature but a history. But if so, what is the thread of understanding from the past to the present? In a simple sense, if human nature today, because of greater consciousness or technical powers, differs from that of ancient Greece, how do "we" understand one another? For Hegel, as for Marx, Greek art represented the "childhood" of the human race.

In his early writings, Marx had sought to *overcome* philosophy by the revolutionary union of theory and practice (e.g., the theses on Feuerbach), but the "later" Marx, or Engels, rejected this dualism by investing his faith in science—though, as George Lichtheim remarks, "he left it to Engels to complete the circle with the construction of a materialist ontology which reads the dialectic back into nature."[16]

What Louis Althusser, the French communist philosopher, has sought to do is to repudiate the Hegelian and historicist interpretations of Marx and to restore the "scientific" method which he believes Marx created in *Kapital*. For Althusser, the early writings represent a "humanist" Marx who simply becomes entangled with the problems of subjectivity. What he proposes as distinctive about Marx is the emphasis on the structure of relations, the *Darstellung*, as the independent object of study within the mode of production. In short, à la mode, what Althusser has given us is a "structuralist Marx" to replace the Hegelian Marx. It is a topic to which we shall revert in the next major section, on structuralism.

Marxian social theory has had three components. One, rooted in the early philosophical writings, is the idea that socialism is the fulfillment of the Enlightenment, the overcoming of all dualities (in philosophy, of subject and object, spirit and matter; in the social world, of mental and physical labor, town and country labor), the "realization" of History in the universalization of human society. As Marx remarked, in his essays on *The Jewish Question,* bourgeois society had brought political emancipation in the freedom of property and the freedom of religion, whereas socialism would mean human emancipation, or the freedom from property and the freedom from religion. Man's command over nature would be matched by his command of his own fate.

The second component of traditional Marxism, beginning with the *Poverty of Philosophy* and extending through *Kapital,* is a structural analysis of capitalism as an integral system of commodity production, which, because of competition and the changing organic composition of capital (i.e., the shrinking base of labor), must come into crisis and eventually give way, owing to the social character of production, to socialism.

The third component, which found its most mechanistic exposition in Engels, is a general theory of society in which all social structure is conceptualized on the basis of a substructure and superstructure; in which the mode of production is seen as determining all other social relations; and in which class positions within the mode of production (read back into history, as well) become the basis of the polarization of society.

Of these three components, the first derived from an evolutionary Hegelian vision which saw increasing rationality and the growth of self-consciousness as the motor forces of history. While the normative views of socialism from this vision may remain as utopia, as history or philosophy they are patently deficient.

The second view surely had great analytical power in dealing with capitalism from 1750 to 1950, but it is questionable whether the actual theoretical formulations remain valid in the state-directed and post-industrial worlds of the latter part of the twentieth century. Capitalism as a socioeconomic system may decline, but it is questionable whether it will do so for the reasons that Marx, rather than, say, Schumpeter (in his *Capitalism, Socialism, and Democracy*), adduced.

As to the "general theory of society," the mechanistic and positivist formulations going back to Engels have increasingly been abandoned; the inadequacy of reading pre-capitalist and certainly non-Western societies in class terms has been recognized; and the fumbling efforts to redefine mode of production as crossed by "social formations" all attest a dissolution of what had once been, at least, a straightforward determinist theory of society.

What is most striking, perhaps, has been the inadequacy of Marxist theory to explain "Marxist" societies. By what Marxist categories does one explain the deep tensions between the Soviet Union and China, or the violent, eruptive outbreak of hostilities between Vietnam and Cambodia? If one takes the Soviet Union as a society that has existed now for more than sixty years, how does one explain the new class structure of that society with the growth of new, privileged strata? In 1957 Milovan Djilas, the former Yugoslav communist leader, wrote *The New Class,* in which he argued that the bureaucracy in the Soviet Union had become the basis of a new class system; but Marxism has never had an adequate theory of the nature of bureaucracy. Lenin, in *State and Revolution,* argued that under socialism, administrative tasks would be so simplified that any person could take his turn in the administration of the State. Max Weber, writing at the same time but more presciently, argued in *Economy and Society* that socialism would become even more bureaucratic than capitalism because of the technical nature of administration and the requirements of planning. More recently, two Hungarian sociologists, György Konrád and Iván Szelényi, based on their experiences in Hungary, published a book, *The Intellectuals on the Road to Class Power: A Sociological Study of the Role of the Intelligentsia in Socialism* (New York: Harcourt Brace Jovanovich, 1979), which argues that the intelligentsia has become a new class, but one that invariably comes into conflict with the political party elite. From the Soviet Union through Yugoslavia to Cuba, what the various studies of different Communist societies fail to explore is the *rebirth* of inequality after the revolutions and the institutionalization of that inequality into new systems of privilege. A primitive explanation goes back to functionalist theory, e.g., that the "time" of a manager is worth more than that of a worker, since he has greater responsibilities for coordination, and that greater privileges such as an automobile and chauffeur need to be provided for him than for the worker. That may explain the inequality of *functional position,* but not necessarily why the advantages to the individuals in those positions are passed on to their children. A more promising explanation is that, though private property has been eliminated as a source of privilege in "socialist" societies, given the technical nature of the societies, skill, or "intellectual capital," or "cultural capital," becomes the main source of differentiation, and its advantages are passed on differentially to the children in the society. In effect, there is (as Bakunin and Machakski argued long ago) a "functional" reason why the intelligentsia are the inevitable privileged class under socialism; and this gives some pith to the gnomic remark of Alvin Gouldner, in his book *The Future of Intellectuals and the Rise of the New Class* (1979), that "Marxism is the false consciousness of the intelligentsia."

While no final word can ever be said on a doctrine as protean as Marxism, one should call attention to the three-volume work by Leszek Kołakowski, *Main Currents of Marxism: Its Rise, Growth, and Disillusion* (Oxford: The Clarendon Press, 1978). Kołakowski was in the late 1950s the most brilliant Marxist philosopher in Poland, one of the organizers of the paper *Po Prostu* that inspired the Polish upheavals in 1956, and, until 1968, when expelled from the post, he was Professor of the History of Philosophy at the University of Warsaw. Since then he has been, principally, a Fellow of All Souls College,

Oxford. The *Main Currents* is his major, synoptic effort to treat Marxism as the history of a doctrine. The first volume deals with the "Founders," the second, the "Golden Age," with the first generation of exegetes, and the third, the "Breakdown," with both Stalinism and the major neo-Marxist philosophers such as Lukács, Gramsci, Marcuse, and others. There is no single thread which runs through the 1,500 pages of detailed exposition and philosophical glosses; it is a patient effort to sort out the variety of conflicting formulations and judgments. Yet in the Epilogue Kołakowski, who had been hailed twenty-five years ago as the most brilliant Marxist philosopher of his generation, permits himself some personal reflections. He writes:

Marxism has been the greatest fantasy of our century. It was a dream offering the prospect of a society of perfect unity, in which all human aspirations would be fulfilled and all values reconciled. . . .

To say that Marxism is a fantasy does not mean that it is nothing else. Marxism as an interpretation of past history must be distinguished from Marxism as a political ideology. No reasonable person would deny that the doctrine of historical materialism has been a valuable addition to our intellectual equipment and has enriched our understanding of the past. True, it has been argued that in a strict form the doctrine is nonsense and in a loose form it is a commonplace; but, if it has become a commonplace, this is largely thanks to Marx's originality. Moreover, if Marxism has led towards a better understanding of the economics and civilization of past ages, this is no doubt connected with the fact that Marx at times enunciated his theory in extreme, dogmatic, and unacceptable forms. If his views had been hedged round with all the restrictions and reservations that are usual in a rational thought, they would have had less influence and might have gone unnoticed altogether. As it was, and as often happens with humanistic theories, the element of absurdity was effective in transmitting their rational content. . . .

As an explanatory 'system' it is dead, nor does it offer any 'method' that can be effectively used to interpret modern life, to foresee the future, or cultivate utopian projections. Contemporary Marxist literature, although plentiful in quantity, has a depressing air of sterility and helplessness, in so far as it is not purely historical. . . .

The influence that Marxism has achieved, far from being the result or proof of its scientific character, is almost entirely due to its prophetic, fantastic, and irrational elements. Marxism is a doctrine of blind confidence that a paradise of universal satisfaction is awaiting us just round the corner. Almost all the prophecies of Marx and his followers have already proved to be false, but this does not disturb the spiritual certainty of the faithful, any more than it did in the case of chiliastic sects: for it is a certainty not based on any empirical premises or supposed 'historical laws', but simply on the psychological need for certainty. In this sense Marxism performs the function of a religion, and its efficacy is of a religious character. But it is a caricature and a bogus form of religion, since it presents its temporal eschatology as a scientific system, which religious mythologies do not purport to be.

4. Structuralism

In a UNESCO volume published ten years ago, intended to sum up the state of our knowledge in the "social and human sciences," the noted Swiss psychologist Jean Piaget wrote:

> One of the most general trends of avant-garde movements in all the human sciences is structuralism, which is taking the place of atomistic attitudes or 'holistic' explanations (emergent wholes).[17]

What may have been an avant-garde movement ten years ago is today a flood tide. Structuralism seems to have swept through almost every area of literary and social-science studies, producing a huge literature in which the names of Piaget in psychology, Claude Lévi-Strauss in anthropology, Jacques Lacan in psychoanalysis, Louis Althusser in Marxist studies, Michel Foucault in epistemology and the history of ideas, and Jacques Derrida and Roland Barthes in literature are especially distinguished. Looming in the background are the works of Ferdinand de Saussure and Roman Jakobson and the revolution in linguistics associated with their names, a revolution whose ideas about the nature of language and the system of signs undergird almost all the diverse work in the various disciplines that have been called structuralist. Yet among these writers, as among those who seek to expound or popularize their doctrines, one finds almost no agreement as to what structuralism *is*. "What is structuralism," writes Roland Barthes:

> It is not a school of thought, or even a movement, for most of the authors habitually associated with this word do not feel in any way bound together by a common doctrine or cause. It is hardly a well-defined term: *structure* is a word of long standing (derived from anatomy and grammar) which today suffers from excessive use.*

And if one turns to the highly lucid work by Howard Gardner, *The Quest for Mind: Piaget, Lévi-Strauss and the Structuralist Movement*, one finds Gardner disclaiming definition at the start:

> The fact is, I think, that it is not possible to define the movement with any precision, any more than it is to delineate clearly a field called social psychology or behavioral genetics. Writers have tended to apply the term 'structuralism' either to a hopelessly vague field of literary analysis, to all contemporary French intellectual thought which is not

---

* Quoted in Jean-Marie Benoist, *The Structural Revolution*, (London: Weidenfeld and Nicolson, 1978), p. 1.

avowedly existentialist, or to the writings of any and all scholars and critics who call themselves structuralists. Certainly none of these approaches is wholly satisfactory. Add to the confusion that no two structuralists, not even Lévi-Strauss and Piaget, define 'structure' in the same way, and one wonders why the term has not been publicly banned or appropriated by Newspeak.[18]

Gardner may have spoken from hindsight, for in looking at a trendy anthology entitled *The Structuralisits from Marx to Lévi-Strauss,* one might say that Newspeak had been quick to seize the day. The editors, Richard T. and Fernande M. De George, open their introduction by remarking:

> Structuralism has been described as a method, a movement, an intellectual fad, and an ideology. Each of these characterizations is in part valid. For structuralism is a loose, amorphous, many-faceted phenomenon with no clear lines of demarcation, no tightly knit group spearheading it, no specific set of doctrines held by all those whom one usually thinks of as being associated with it. It cuts across many disciplines—linguistics, anthropology, literary criticism, psychology, philosophy. For some it gives hope of uncovering or developing a common basic approach to the social sciences, literature and art which would unify them and put them on a scientific footing, much as the 'scientific method' grounds and unifies the physical sciences.*

After which these editors proceed to locate the roots of structuralism in the nineteenth century in the thought of Marx, Freud, and de Saussure:

> What Marx, Freud and Saussure have in common, and what they share with present day structuralists, is a conviction that surface events and phenomena are to be explained by structures, data and phenomena below the surface. The explicit and the obvious is to be explained by and is determined—in some sense of the term—by what is implicit and not obvious. The attempt to uncover deep structures, unconscious motivations, and underlying causes which account for human actions at a more basic and profound level than do individual conscious decisions, and which shape, influence and structure these decisions, is an enterprise which unites Marx, Freud, Saussure, and modern structuralists.[19]

Unhappily, such claims dissolve any distinctive meaning to structuralism, for the idea of an underlying structure—the distinction between appearance and reality—is co-extensive with the entire history of Western philosophy, especially gnosticism and mysticism. In the pre-Socratics, beginning with Thales, we have the effort to find an underlying substance to the diversity of elements, and these were variously located as air, earth, water, or fire; and with these were associated the qualities of wet, dry, hot, or cold,

---

* An unfortunate figure of speech, since the avant-garde movement in the philosophy of science, from Paul Feyerabend to Stephen Toulmin, denies the distinctiveness of something called "the scientific method."

so the cross-classification of elements and properties (e.g., fire is hot and dry, etc.) gave one a substructure to the physical world. Plato's divided line distinguished between the visible (sensory) and the intelligible (conceptual) and saw knowledge as a movement from the one to the other. Aristotle saw the hidden design of any object in its "entelechy," the movement to the realization of its immanent form; this biological theme was later recast by Hegel and Marx in the idea of "necessity" as the realization of History. And for Kant, the categories of understanding—basically space and time, which were the intrinsic properties of mind—organized the flux of experience into intelligible concepts.

If one seeks to understand the distinctiveness of structuralism, one has to see it as a movement with a specific *epistemological* program, no matter how diverse its various applications. One can, perhaps, identify six elements of this program.

1. *The search for invariant relations on the model of the natural sciences.* The starting point here is Galileo. In reacting against the "essentialism" of Aristotle, who looked for the qualitative differences between phenomena and classified these as *types,* Galileo introduced the idea of a field. Specifically, Galileo did not study "concrete" objects but their abstract properties, not a falling body but attributes such as mass, acceleration, velocity, and the like, and he sought to find the quantitative relations between these properties which would govern any specific body. Structuralism makes no distinction between the natural and human sciences and, as we shall see, claims to find isomorphic structures between physical and psychological phenomena.

2. *Against historicism, or "diachronic" analysis,* structuralism rejects the idea that a phenomenon is to be understood through its genesis. In one variant it sees "history" as contingent and variable and therefore without a distinct pattern; in another version, as too deterministic, like a Hegelian scheme. (For Hegel, only the West had a history, for only the West had a "rational" development and was not bound to nature; all other social forms were "frozen.") Structuralism rejects the idea that the character of a phenomenon is to be understood as derived from its historical context.

3. *Against subjectivity.* Classical philosophy had no concept of a theory of the "knowing subject," an individual who is the judge of knowledge. Plato, indeed, denied the idea of such an individual. Knowledge was located in the "predicates," the ideal forms under which particulars were subsumed. With Descartes we find the problem of the "knower" replacing that of the "known" as the problem for philosophy, a dualism of mind and body, and an implicit relativism in which the vantage point of the knower becomes the starting point of inquiry. With subjectivity we also find a radical humanism, as in existentialism, in which the individual person, his free will and his responsibility, becomes the source of truth—for him or her.

Structuralism seeks to replace the human subject—the individual or the thinking consciousness, the transcendental ego—as the unit of study with the *relations* between individuals, the products and objects of the interactions, and the linguistic code and invariant structures as the knowledge which has intelligibility. One can say that it is the supremacy of the code over that which is codified (the content), the synchronic over the diachronic, the model over the diverse facts.

4. *The congruence of a linguistic structure as the embodiment of the modes of thought and the relational rules derived from them with all other modes of cultural or social relations.* Common to almost all structuralism is the idea, derived from de Saussure, that language is an ordered system of signs, a distinct system with its own rules and properties that can be stated without reference to historical or extra-linguistic factors, like the rules of chess that govern the system of play. With this in mind, Lévi-Strauss argues that all cultural phenomena should be considered in terms of signs. And, indeed, for him society is interpretable as an "ensemble" of three different kinds of communication — the exchange of messages, the exchange of commodities (i.e., goods and services), and the exchange of women (i.e., marriage and kinship rules) — each of which is distinct, but all together make a common structural field. Within this view, social anthropology, economics, and linguistics are all subsumed under the common rubric of the semiotic.

5. *The argument, though more true of Lévi-Strauss and Piaget (and, in a different context, of Noam Chomsky), that the underlying structure of mind is rational.*

In the history of ideas, this has two radical consequences. One is to abolish the distinction between the savage and the modern as two different types of thought, the one ruled by magic and the other by science, or, in the older distinction of Lévy-Bruhl, between the pre-logical and logical. For Lévi-Strauss, the savage mind is as logical as the modern, but in its own mode. For example, in his study of *Totemism* (Boston: Beacon Press, 1963), Lévi-Strauss insisted that the totem of a clan was not a magical or animistic symbol for some abstract taboo, but a means of enforcing marriage rules, since the function of the totem was to identify the clan of a person and to enforce rules of endogamy and exogamy; in short, it was a logical way of enforcing the incest taboo.

The second consequence is a paradox regarding structuralism's nineteenth-century forebears. For the past hundred years, a single, powerful conception infused almost every doctrine in the social sciences. This was the idea that under the surface appearance of a world of rationality was an underlying structure of irrationality. For Marx, underneath the formally free exchange of commodities in accordance with rational self-interest lay the anarchy of the market and the reduction of men to things. For Freud, beneath the veneer of civilization (the social superego) was the turbulent, aggressive id. For Pareto, under the logical system of thought were the residues of sentiment. For Max Weber, under the rational calculation of means to ends was a functionalized world where the means became the ends in themselves. It was this convergence, if not consensus, which gave force to the apprehension about the nature of man and the fragile character of society.

But in the view of Lévi-Strauss and Piaget (and Noam Chomsky), behind the disorder and the flux of the world, beneath the large varieties of culture and the extraordinary number of languages, is a substructure of rationality and order. The common source is the character of linguistics and the properties of mind. For Chomsky, mind has the innate power to generalize rules, while language itself, grammar and syntax, has a set of properties embedded in deep structures which can be intuited and generalized by the mind. For Lévi-Strauss, what defines culture is the ability of mind to make necessary, logical distinctions; beneath the wide range of social relations are a limited number of cross-ties, while, despite the diversity of cultures, there is a limited set of invariant forms that can be deciphered and made intelligible by transformational rules.

If this is so, it is in a crucial respect a return to Kant. For Kant, philosophy was the imposition of logical order on factual disorder. Knowledge is not the "orders of fact," which can never be verified, but the "matters of relations," and these relations themselves, the categories we use to organize experience, are innate properties of mind.

6. *The tendency to Formalism.* Within anthropology, it was Radcliffe-Brown who argued that structure is of the order of fact, derived from the observation of each particular society. Anthropology, then, could be a natural science built up from induction. But for Lévi-Strauss, such an effort is hopeless, for it cannot map the variety of order or reduce it to manageable proportions. For Lévi-Strauss, social structure "has nothing to do with empirical reality but with the models which are built up after it." What the anthropologist does is to elaborate a language "and to account with a small number of rules for phenomena held until then to be entirely different. Thus in the absence of an inaccessible factual truth, we [arrive] at a truth of reason." In effect, structuralist thought consists not in identifying a recurrent content under a variety of literary forms but "in perceiving invariant forms within different contexts."[20] In an essay on the Slavic linguist Vladimir Propp, Lévi-Strauss denies the charge. He writes: "Contrary to formalism, structuralism refuses to set the concrete against the abstract. . . . *Form* is defined by opposition to material other than itself. But *structure* has no distinct content; it is content itself, apprehended in a logical organization conceived as property of the real."[21] But this begs the question for Lévi-Strauss insists that a myth can never be properly understood by its *manifest* content but by the *imputed* relations, or homologies, established by the analyst.

In this regard, Lévi-Strauss is following the logic of Roman Jakobson and his associates in the so-called Prague School of Linguistics, who searched for the basic building blocks of language in the units of sound (phonemes), and who postulated a small set of distinctive features required to produce a sound which would account exhaustively for all sounds used in the languages of the world. In his study of kinship, which anthropology takes to be the fundamental unit of social organization, Lévi-Strauss reduced all the multitudinous systems and elaborate rules to three structures and two forms of exchange, each dependent on a single differential, the harmonic or disharmonic character of a given regime. All principles of kinship came down to relations between rules of residence and rules of descent.

In these areas, and later, more extensively, in his analysis of myth, Lévi-Strauss makes the fundamental argument that the content of any relationship is idiosyncratic, and what is crucial is the structure of the relationship itself. Once these structures are identified, the anthropologist can seek for the transformation rules that would allow him to identify the limited number of forms under which the relations could be subsumed.

It would be exhausting and far beyond my limitations of space to go into the specifics of the work of men as prolific as Piaget, who has written or collaborated on more than fifty books and hundreds of articles, or Lévi-Strauss, whose four volumes of *Mythologues* alone deal with several hundred myths, or Jacques Lacan, whose talent for neologism bursts the bounds of the French language itself, or Louis Althusser, the Marxist who has repudiated the early writings of Marx as Hegelian, and who rests his claim that Marxism is a science on a structuralist reading of *Das Kapital*—let alone into the linguistic sources of their works, or the literary expositors who have extended the ideas of semiology into all domains.

It is not the specific content of these works that is important but the intention and reach of structuralism, which seeks to capture no less than the "dream of reason" by constructing a general theory of the human mind. In classical philosophy there was an effort to identify the first principles which would be controlling of all other distinctions in the analysis and classification of phenomena, an effort which dominated philosophy from Aristotle to Aquinas. In Descartes the dream of reason was to perfect an *organon,* a method, that would tie together the realm of abstraction with the realm of real-world space, an organon that Descartes thought he had achieved in the union of algebra and geometry that today is called analytical geometry. In the social sciences the dream of reason was the effort of Auguste Comte to find the laws of thought that would explain the stages of the human mind, from the theological to the metaphysical to the positive stage of human knowledge. Marx thought, at least in the extravagant claims made by Engels, that he could uncover the laws of social development, as Darwin had elaborated the principle of biological evolution. In contemporary sociology Talcott Parsons thought he could build a general theory of action whose four components — the organismic, the personality system, the social system, and the cultural system—could provide a complete morphology of social relations. Structuralism is the latest and, in some ways, the most ambitious of these efforts.

One of the reasons why structuralism has been somewhat alien to Anglo-American thought is that the English tradition of philosophy, the dominant weight until recent years, has been one of skepticism, of empiricism, and, especially under the influence of Russell, of *analysis* in which the intention of philosophy is to clarify meaning by clarifying terms through an examination of the way words work in sentences. But even there one comes up against the wall of the later Wittgenstein, who insisted that there is no constitutive correlation between our language and the world it is supposed to denote, select, reflect, and that we cannot establish an isomorphic relation between words and what they refer to. One accepts rules as conventions, but rules are constructed and can be changed.

Structuralism is really a *logique* in which the model is mathematics, and like mathematics it is less interested in content than in relations (just as algebra replaces numbers with symbols to make the relations more manipulable) and in the combinatorial modes which expand the number of relations. In its method, structuralism follows the logic of set theory, in which elements and transformations are placed in formal mathematical terms. Piaget, in particular, has been influenced by the Bourbaki (a fictitious name given to a circle of French mathematicians), who have been collectively publishing an encyclopedic work on basic mathematical structures which seeks to axiomatize all mathematical propositions. Piaget has also suggested, in his essay on Psychology in the UNESCO volume, that it is pointless to distinguish between social logic (inter-individual or collective actions) and individual logic since both are governed by common logico-mathematical structures (p. 246). And Lévi-Strauss in his *Elementary Structures of Kinship* has argued that "the laws of thought, primitive or civilized, are the same as those which find expression in physical reality and in social reality, which is simply one of their aspects." For Piaget, just as there is a congruence between mathematics and physical reality, there is the congruence of mathematics, language, and the structure of human thought.

What is one to make of all this? Is it a Library of Babel which, in the image of Borges, is "limitless and periodic," so that "if an external voyager were to traverse it in any direction, he would find, after many centuries, that the same volumes are repeated in the same disorder (which, repeated, would constitute an order: Order itself)"? Or is it a new *organon,* the key to the deciphering of knowledge?

For Lévi-Strauss, his conclusions are not "factual truths" but the "truths of reason." This very rationalism by reduction is the heart of one of the arguments about the validity of the argument. Sociological relativists reject the idea of an emergent human nature. Functionalists do not accept the proposition that the coherence of culture lies in some analogical structures rather than in the actual interdependencies of daily life. Materialists scorn the mentalistic approach, while evolutionists and humanists (each in a different way and for different reasons) may see a principle of "emergence" in human powers or in the nature of consciousness that is not captured in the logical sets of combinatorial mathematics.

There are other questions. When Lévi-Strauss breaks apart the Oedipus story and shows its homologous relationship to myths in cultures far removed, or when Edmund Leach, in an ingenious structuralist interpretation of Genesis and other stories in the Bible (the Abraham/Isaac story and the Jephthah/daughter story in Judges), shows, by "transformation rules" (God is changed to Father, virgin son to virgin daughter), that the stories are binary opposites, is one deciphering a code or *imposing* a code on these stories? How does one judge? Like serial music, it may only be a matter of ingenious recombination.

There is, perhaps, a different aspect to these efforts, which goes to the heart of the question whether the social sciences can become closed systems on the model of the natural sciences, or whether they remain bound to the humanistic disciplines, with their emphasis on the diversity of human responses and the variety of meanings which constitute the richness of the human imagination. Perhaps there is a way to thread this argument: it is to say that there *are* cultural universals but that these universals are not the underlying formal patterns or structures of action but the existential predicaments that confront all human beings and all human groups in the consciousness of their days. One can say that all human groups respond to some modal situations: the fact of death, the character of tragedy, the nature of love, the definition of courage, the idea of reciprocity, and the like. The *responsa* they give is the *history* of human culture, in all its variety, but in the essential understanding of life, the questions are recurrent and always the same.

---

[1] Ruth Benedict, *Patterns of Culture* (Boston: Houghton Mifflin, 1934), pp. 12, 13–14, 15.

[2] Ernst Mayr, "Evolution," *Scientific American,* September 1978, pp. 52–53.

[3] E. O. Wilson, "Biology and the Social Sciences," *Daedalus,* Fall 1977, p. 137; emphasis added.

[4] I take the example from a summary of a workshop discussion on Sociobiology and the Social Sciences held by the American Academy of Arts and Sciences, March and April, 1977.

[5] "The Intellectual Gantry of Neoclassical Economic Policy," chap. 2 in William Breit and Roger L. Ransom, *The Academic Scribblers* (New York: Holt, Rinehart and Winston, 1971), p. 14. I have profited as well from the review "Monetarism: A Historic-Theoretic Perspective," by A. Robert Nobay and Harry G. Johnson, *The Journal of Economic Literature,* June 1977.

[6] Robert M. Solow, "What We Know and Don't Know About Inflation," M.I.T. *Technology Review,* December 1978/January 1979, p. 38. Mr. Solow's witty account is recommended for the story of his adventures with the Phillips Curve.

[7] Lester C. Thurow, "Economics 1977," *Daedalus,* Fall 1977, pp. 83–84.

[8] On the literature on monetarism, *see* the essay by Nobay and Johnson, op. cit. Milton Friedman's theories are put forth in *Studies in the Quantity Theory of Money* (University of Chicago Press, 1956), and his Presidential Address, "The Role of Monetary Policy," *American Economic Review,* March 1968. The essays by Robert Lucas that brought attention to his theories are "Expectations and the Neutrality of Money," *Journal of Economic Theory,* April 1972, and "Understanding Business Cycles," Supplement to *Journal of Monetary Economics,* 1977. In addition to the fine exposition in the 1977 Annual Report of the Federal Reserve Bank of Minneapolis, there is a popular but oversimplified account of the "Rational Expectations" school in "The New Down-to-Earth Economics," *Fortune,* Dec. 31, 1978.

[9] Basil J. Moore, "A Post-Keynesian Approach to Monetary Theory," *Challenge,* September/October 1978, p. 52. For an overview of the subject, *see* Alfred S. Eichner and J. A. Kregel, "An Essay on Post-Keynesian Theory: A New Paradigm in Economics," *Journal of Economic Literature,*

December 1975. Also, Michal Kalecki, *Selected Essays on the Dynamics of the Capitalist Economy,* 1933–1970 (Cambridge University Press, 1971); Joan Robinson, *Essays in the Theory of Economic Growth* (London: Macmillan, 1962); Alfred S. Eichner, *The Megacorp and Oligopoly* (Cambridge University Press, 1976).

[10] Assar Lindbeck, "Stabilization Policy in Open Economies with Endogenous Politicians," *American Economic Review,* May 1976, p. 18.

[11] Daniel Bell, *The Coming of Post-Industrial Society* (New York: Basic Books, 1973), p. 279.

[12] *The Journal of Law and Economics,* April 1977, p. 2.

[13] For Simon's major work, see *Adminstrative Behavior,* 3rd ed. (New York: Free Press, 1976, expanded with a new Introduction); *The New Science of Management Decision* (Englewood Cliffs, N. J.: Prentice-Hall, 1977); *Models of Man* (New York: John Wiley, 1957). Of the technical papers, the two most apropos are: "Theories of Bounded Rationality," in C. B. McGuire and Roy Radner (eds.), *Decision and Organization* (Amsterdam: North-Holland Publishing Co., 1972), and "From Substantive to Procedural Rationality," in S. J. Latsis (ed.), *Method and Appraisal in Economics* (Cambridge: Cambridge University Press, 1976).

[14] For a discussion of these questions, *see* my essay, "The Once and Future Marx," in the *American Journal of Sociology* (vol. 83, no. 1, July 1977), reprinted in my book, *The Winding Passage: Essays and Sociological Journeys, 1960–1980* (Cambridge, Mass.: Abt Books, 1980).

[15] Jürgen Habermas, *Toward a Rational Society* (Boston: Beacon Press, 1970), p. 104.

[16] George Lichtheim, "Sartre, Marxism, and History," in *Collected Essays* (New York: Viking Press, 1973) p. 378.

[17] Jean Piaget, "General Problems of Inter-disciplinary Research and Common Mechanisms," in *Main Trends of Research in the Social and Human Sciences: Part One: Social Sciences* (Mouton/Unesco; Paris, The Hague: 1970), p. 479.

[18] Howard Gardner, *The Quest for Mind* (New York: Alfred A. Knopf, 1973), pp. 9–10.

[19] *The Structuralists: From Marx to Lévi-Strauss,* edited by Richard T. and Fernande M. De George (New York: Anchor Books, Doubleday & Co., 1972).

[20] *Structural Anthropology,* vol. II (New York: Basic Books, 1976), p. 21.

[21] Ibid., p. 115.

PART THREE

The Contemporary Status of a Great Idea

The Idea of Nature, East and West

Hajime Nakamura

Hajime Nakamura, chairman of the department of Indian philosophy and literature and director of the Eastern Institute, Tokyo, and professor emeritus at the University of Tokyo, has gained international reputation as a student of Japanese and Indian philosophy and letters. His writings in English include *Ways of Thinking of Eastern Peoples: India, China, Tibet, Japan* (1964); *A History of the Development of Japanese Thought from 592 to 1868* (1967); and *Religions and Philosophies of India* (1973). In Japanese he has published a *History of Vedanta* and *Early Buddhism* (both in five volumes), among other works.

In many of these writings, as in the present article, Professor Nakamura takes the position that intellectual and social developments within any given culture are to be found in other cultures as well, and that the student will find common human themes in all of them. Professor Nakamura is the first writer from outside the Western tradition to be published in *The Great Ideas Today*.

What is nature?

The term *nature* is known to everybody, but the concept of nature is hard to define. Many different words for it are to be found in the languages of the Far East, such as Chinese, Korean, and Japanese. The English word *nature* is derived from the Latin *natura*, which means "birth," "origin," "natural constitution or quality of a thing," and that in turn is derived from the verb *nasci*, to be born. *Nature* in common English use has fundamental meanings, as follows:

1. the essential character of a thing; quality or qualities that make something what it is; essence;
2. inborn characters; innate disposition; inherent tendencies of a person;
3. kind; sort; type; as when we say "things of that nature."

It is with these meanings in mind that we shall discuss the idea of "nature" first in the different contexts of various Eastern traditions.

Natural phenomena and the deities that preside over them

In the first stage of the development of human intelligence, natural phenomena were personified in various countries of the East. I shall confine myself mainly to the mythologies of ancient India and Japan, with only occasional references to other contexts.

The mythologies reflected in the Indian *Rgveda* and the *Avesta* of Iran have many points of similarity, e.g., in the names of gods and other terms — indicating that both mythological systems had a common source in ancient times. Both mythologies had a god associated with the sun, a deity called the "son of waters," and a divine being connected with *soma*. From the earliest Indian and Iranian texts it is clear that the united Indo-Iranian peoples recognized two classes of deity, the Vedic *asuras* or Avestic *ahuras*, on the one hand, and the Vedic *devas* and Avestic *daevas* on the other.[1] The former were conceived initially as mighty kings, drawn through the air on their war chariots by swift steeds, benevolent in character, and almost entirely free from guile and immoral traits.[2]

The texts indicate that Vedic man's religious experience was focused on this world. There was a correlation between the world of nature, the cosmos, and man's own communal life. People made sacrifices to the gods, and natural phenomena themselves were either deified or at almost every point were regarded as closely allied to the holy or sacred. The Vedic seers delighted in sights of nature and were lost in the wonders of natural phenomena; to them, the wind, the rain, the sun, the stars were living realities and were inextricably a part of spiritual life. Many of the hymns are not addressed to a sun-god, a moon-god, a fire-god, or anything of the sort, but to the shining sun itself; the gleaming moon in the nocturnal sky, the fire blazing on the hearth or on the altar, or even the lightning shooting forth from the cloud were all manifestations of the holy or numinous. This spiritual interpenetration of the phenomena of nature and man's corporeal life can be regarded as the earliest form of Vedic religion.

Such an attitude also characterizes Shintō. The religion of early Japan emphasized gratitude to the beneficent forces of nature while also to some degree appeasing the malevolent forces. These forces were indiscriminately called "kami," which is usually translated as "gods" or "deities."

Subsequent to this stage there occurred various speculations regarding the meaning of the religious life. Vedic poets sought to penetrate the essence of natural phenomena. They projected their own experiences into divine images and sought to explain phenomena by causes analogous to their own experience. Natural phenomena were gradually sharpened, transformed into mythological figures, even into gods and goddesses.

The higher gods of the Ṛgveda are almost entirely personifications of natural phenomena, such as Sun, Dawn, Fire, Wind. In India the sun was deified as Sūrya.

> Sūrya (cognate in name to the Greek Helios) is the most concrete of several solar deities. As his name also designates the luminary itself, his connection with the latter is never lost sight of. The eye of Sūrya is often mentioned. All-seeing, he is the spy of the whole world, beholding all beings and the good or bad deeds of mortals. Aroused by Sūrya, men pursue their objects and perform their work. He is the soul or guardian of all that moves and is fixed. He rides in a car, which is generally described as drawn by seven steeds. These he unyokes at sunset:
>
> When he has loosed his coursers from their station,
> Straightway Night over all spreads out her garment. (i. 115,4)[3]
>
> Sūrya rolls up the darkness like a skin, and the stars slink away like thieves.

Another solar deity, Savitṛ, known as the "Stimulator," "represents the quickening activity of the sun. He is preeminently a golden deity, with golden hand and arms and a golden car. He raises aloft his strong arms with which he blesses and arouses all beings, and which extend to the ends of the earth. He moves in his golden car, seeing all creatures on a downward and an upward path. He shines after the path of the dawn. Beaming with the rays of the sun, yellow-haired, Savitṛ raises up his light continually from the east. He removes evil dreams and drives away demons and sorcerers. He bestows immortality on the gods as well as length of life on man. He also conducts the departed spirit to where the righteous dwell. The other gods follow Savitṛ's lead. Savitṛ is extolled as the setting sun:

Borne by swift coursers, he will now unyoke them:
The speeding chariot he has stayed from going.
He checks the speed of them that glide like serpents;
Night has come on by Savitṛ's commandment.
The weaver rolls her outstretched web together
The skilled lay down their work in midst of toiling,
The birds all seek their nests, their shed the cattle:
Each to his lodging Savitṛ disperses. (ii. 38)

He was in ancient times invoked at the beginning of Vedic study and is still repeated by every orthodox Hindu in his morning stanza prayers:"

May we attain the excellent
Glory of Savitṛ the god,
That he may stimulate our thoughts. (iii. 62,10).

"Prosperer," Pūṣan, "seems to be the beneficent power of the sun, manifested chiefly as a pastoral deity. His car is drawn by goats and he carries a goad. Knowing the ways of heaven, he conducts the dead on the far path to the fathers. He is also a guardian of roads, protecting cattle and guiding them with his goad. The welfare he bestows results from the protection he extends to men and cattle on earth and from his guidance of mortals to the abodes of bliss in the next world."[4]

Viṣṇu is

one of the two great gods of modern Hinduism. He seems to have been originally conceived as the sun personified. The essential feature of his character is that he takes three strides, which doubtless represent the course of the sun through the three divisions of the universe. His highest step is heaven, where the gods and the fathers dwell.

For this abode the poet expresses his longing in the following words (i. 154, 5):

May I attain to that, his well-loved dwelling,
Where men devoted to the gods are blessed:
In Viṣṇu's highest step—he is our kinsman,
Of mighty stride—there is a spring of nectar.[5]

The religious rites of worshipping sun, water, and other natural elements are still widely practiced in India.

In later Hinduism, sun-worship became an important religious rite. In the Purāṇas, mention is made of royal families who claimed to be the descendants of the sun. The Buddha himself was said to have belonged to a family descended from the sun (ādicca-bandhu). In Japan the sun was deified as the goddess Amaterasu-Ō-Mikami (lit. the Heaven-Shining-Great-August Deity), who was worshiped as the ancestor of the imperial family. It was thought that the sun at midday was deified. The myth of the solar ancestry of the imperial clan was widely accepted among the various clans resident in Japan, including many clans of Chinese and Korean descent. This tendency was not lacking in India. The sun-goddess of Japan, however, was regarded by most Shintō believers as a real or actual historical personage, whereas the sun-god of India was not. Of the Greeks it is said: "Every Greek philosopher, whatever he may have come to think in adult life, had been taught in childhood to regard the sun and moon as gods; Anaxagoras was prosecuted for impiety because he thought that they were not alive."[6]

The dawn likewise came to be extolled in the Vedas as Uṣas, a beautiful and shy maiden. In the West we have Eos, and Aurora, and we find a Japanese counterpart in the goddess Waka-hirume-no-mikoto, the deification of the rising sun. In the Vedas the moon was worshiped as Soma, which means the soma plant and its juice, being personified. In Japan moon-worship was not strongly evident, but the divine figure Tsuki-yomi-no-mikoto is pertinent.[7]

In India the wind was worshiped in the Vedas as Vāyu or Vāta, and the storm as the Maruts. We find counterparts to Vāyu and Vāta in China and Japan also.[8] In Japanese classics the moon-god was regarded as a male deity with the name of Tsukiyomo-no-otoko. There is a rain-god described in the Ṛgveda. (v. 83)

The Vedas deified the waters as Āpas goddesses. In Japan it is likely that waters themselves were not deified, but it was supposed that a deity lived in them. In India the goddess of the lake, Sarasvatī, appeared at an early stage. Worship of her was adopted by Vajrayāna Buddhism, and she was ultimately introduced into Japan to be adopted as a folk deity under the name of "Benten." Worship of her is still prevalent among the Japanese populace.

The names of these deities in both India and Japan, and also in many other countries,[9] still indicate their origins. For example, the Lithuanian god of thunder, called Perkunas, is etymologically identical with the Vedic god of rain, Parjanya. Many prominent figures of mythology of ancient peoples have proceeded from personifications of natural phenomena.[10]

Heaven was personified and deified as the Vedic Dyaus; its counterpart in Greek religion was the phonetically equivalent Zeus (= Dyaus). The latter, however, was a much more complex figure, more like a human being than the Vedic Dyaus. The Ṛgvedic poets addressed the Heavenly Father with the vocative form "Dyauṣ pitaḥ"[11] (O Father Heaven!), which is equivalent to the Greek Zeus "pater" and Latin "Jupiter" (Jovis Pater = fatherly Jove). In ancient China, Heaven was the chief deity. The Chou king called himself "Son of Heaven," and the Chou justified their conquest of the Shang dynasty on the grounds that they had received the "Mandate of Heaven" (T'ien-ming). They were thus mediators between man and nature.[12] In Japanese mythology, heaven was not a god but the region where the gods reside, quite different from Dyaus or Varuṇa of India or Zeus of Greece. It has an essential place in Japanese mythology, however. Compared with other traditions, the worship of heaven did not develop fully in India.

The earth is called a mother in the Ṛgveda. This was the case also in Greek religion, but not in ancient Japan. Heaven and earth were often invoked together in the hymns of the Ṛgveda in dual as Dyāvāpṛthivī. In Thessaly, Zeus was worshiped along with his female counterpart, Dione, but Dione was later forgotten. The idea of Heaven and Earth being universal parents probably goes back to remote antiquity, for it is common to the mythology of China and of New Zealand and can be inferred in Egyptian mythology. Izanagi and Izanami in Japanese mythology may have been the deifications of heaven and earth, but there remains no trait which definitely allows such a conjecture.

The fire-god Agni (cf. Latin: ignis; cf. English: ignition) is preeminently the god of sacrifices in India. In Japan the fire-god was worshiped under the name of Kagu-tsuchi (radiant father) or Ho-musubi (fire-growth). The idea of fire as all-pervading was common to both ancient India and Japan, but it is difficult to identify the special feature of the fire-god of the ancient Indians. Although fire was essential to the sacrifices of the Indo-European races, the god Agni, so popular in the religion of the Ṛgveda, gradually lost his preeminence. A conception of fire as the fundamental principle of the universe, as was held by Heraclitus, did not occur among Hindu philosophers, who sought rather a quiet and calm mental condition.

The warlike Indra, of the Vedic Indians, was in earliest times undoubtedly a king among gods. In this respect he corresponds to Zeus of the Greeks, or Jupiter of the Romans. Indra did not, however, like Zeus act as the righteous judge. This characteristic is also missing in Japanese mythology. It is said that the gods of Japanese mythology do not judge, a restraint which has played a large role in the legal thought of East Asian countries. (One exception is Yama, who was the ruler of the dead in Vedic mythology. In the great Epic he became judge of the dead. This figure was introduced into Chinese Taoism and then into Japanese popular belief. He is call "enma," the Japanese transliteration of the Sanskrit word "Yama." But in China and Japan he was regarded as somewhat alien to the common people in general.)

In Japanese mythology some counterparts to Indra can be found, for instance, the god of thunder, "Narukami." The storm-god Susaowono-mikoto killed an eight-headed dragon with a miraculous sword, which is said to have been transmitted by the imperial family as a symbol of sovereignty. His strong and occasionally outrageous character is quite similar to that of Indra. However, where Indra is completely a god, Susaowono-mikoto is god and man simultaneously and appears in an historical setting as a relative of the ancestor of the Japanese imperial family.

The Vedic pantheon sometimes was called "all the gods" (Viśve Devāḥ). On one occasion "all the gods" were numbered at 3,339, reflecting the three spheres of the world: the earth, the air, and the sky. In ancient Japan there was a similar notion of "myriads of gods" (literally "eight million gods," Yao-yorozu-no-kami-gami). The number of Shintō deities constantly fluctuates. Some are forgotten and later reestablished under new names; or again, wholly new gods are added to the pantheon. The characters of these myriad gods are ill-defined. Analogous to the division between the Olympian gods and the mystery gods in Greek mythology, however, a division was made between the children of the storm-god and the deities associated with the sun-goddess (*Amaterasu-Ō-mikami*). In Japanese mythology the "realm of the visible" belongs to the latter and "the domain of the invisible" to the former.

The gods of the Ṛgveda were invited as guests on oblations. They took food and drank wine; they were invoked, flattered, propitiated, and pleased. Men had direct communion with gods without any mediation; the gods were looked upon as intimate friends of their worshipers. They were addressed with such phrases as "Father Heaven," "Mother Earth," "brother Agni." There was a very intimate personal relationship between men and gods, and every daily phenomenon was regarded as dependent on the gods. In like manner, Japanese villagers sometimes prayed to individual deities, sometimes to special categories of deities, and sometimes to the gods generally. The prayer comprised petitions for rain, for good harvests, for protection from earthquake and conflagration, for children, for health and long life to the sovereign, and for peace and prosperity in the nation. To some extent the physical aspect of the Ṛgvedic gods is anthropomorphic, as is the case with the Greek gods—head, face, eyes, arms, hands, feet, and other portions of the human frame are ascribed to them—yet their forms are often shadowy and their limbs or parts are often simply meant figuratively to describe their activities. Thus the tongue and limbs of the fire-god are simply his rays, while his eye represents the solar orb. The gods were not always moral in their character. They often shared human weakness and were easily pleased by flattery. They conferred benefit in exchange for oblation offered to them. In one hymn the gods discuss what they should give. "This is what I will do—not that, I will give him a cow or shall it be a horse? I wonder if I have already had some wine from him."[13] A simple law of give and take prevails.

In the Homeric religion we find the gods arranged in a hierarchy, organized as a divine family under a supreme god. Like the Vedic gods, they are personal, but they are not vague and indefinite beings; they are concrete and individual deities of robust and sharply defined personality. They are not spirits but immortal beings of superhuman body and soul, conceived as glorified men. Such an elaborate hierarchy of gods with specific personalities is quite different from the Vedic conception of the gods.

One might suspect that the Vedic gods represent an earlier phase of the development of mythology, but the individual character of each Vedic god was not clear even in later periods. The difference was not that of stage of development but rather that of the respective conceptions of god. The gods in Indian myths had little personality, and ultimately orthodox Hindu thinkers came to deny them all individuality. For example, Indra, who received much respect in the Ṛgveda, came to be regarded as only a common name (a godly being who occupies that position is called by the name of "Indra"); he was not an individual person.[14] In this connection, and having to do with the individuality of the gods, we may point out that before the rise of Buddhism, Brahmanism had no idols. Indian art can be traced chiefly from the time of the Maurya dynasty, when Buddhism flourished. Shintōism, also, had practically no idols, not because the ancient Japanese were especially enlightened, but because they had no high art before sculpture and painting were introduced from China, and because they only very feebly assigned an individual character to each god. It was after the introduction of Buddhism that Japanese art flourished.

A feature characteristic of Shintōism is the fact that many Japanese gods are regarded as historical and human beings of superior quality. For the ancient Japanese the mythical world and the natural world interpenetrated one another to the extent that human activities were explained and sanctioned in terms of what *kami*, ancestors or heroes, did in primordial time. The whole of human life and the cosmos was accepted as sacred, permeated as it was taken to be by the *kami* nature. (Indeed, notwithstanding the ban on natural deities in the Jōdo Shin sect of Japan, the actual national religion of the Japanese has been essentially a nature-religion, with its pantheon consisting of nature-gods.) On the other hand, Indian gods had nothing to do with history. Indian gods were regarded as ancestors in some cases. But they were not involved in historical development, even up to the days of Hinduism.

The figures of gods in native religions were not wiped away in Asia as in the West. According to the genuine teaching of Buddhism, a monk should practise for *avhat*-ship, for his own deliverance. Nevertheless, it is evident that the Buddhist ought to maintain amiable relations with all beings, "expanding" sentiments of compassion and benevolence in the ten cardinal directions. Hindu gods were tolerated and some of them were sanctified.

A multitude of gods resides in natural objects, early Buddhists believed.

In later Buddhism it was regulated that the saint must honor the deities "who haunt the spot where he has taken his abode," so that the best way of honoring the deities is "to give them the merit of his gifts to the brethren, good men of good control."[15] Finally, natural gods came to be tolerated in Buddhist countries.

Love of natural beauty

The term *nature* means, in some cases, natural scenery, including the plants and animals that are part of it. Love of nature is conspicuous in Eastern traditions, which in that respect have something in common with the German. Indeed, "sentimentality and feeling for Nature are the common property of German and Indian poetry," Maurice Winternitz, the noted Indologist observes, "whilst they are foreign, say, to Hebrew or Greek poetry." To which he adds: "Germans and Indians love descriptions of Nature; and both Indian and German poets delight in connecting the joys and sorrows of man with the Nature which surrounds him."[16]

Nature holds a much more important place in Sanskrit plays than in the Greek and modern drama. Characters are surrounded by nature, with which they are in constant communion. They move in the midst of mango and other trees, creepers, lotuses, and pale-red trumpet-flowers, gazelles, flamingos, bright-hued parrots, and Indian cuckoos, which are often addressed by them and form an essential part of their lives. The influence of nature on the minds of lovers is much dwelt upon. Prominent everywhere in classical Sanskrit poetry, these elements of nature are most abundant in the drama.[17]

In order to understand Indian poetry thoroughly, the reader must have seen the tropical plains and forests of Hindustan steeped in intense sunshine or bathed in brilliant moonlight; he must have viewed the silent ascetic seated at the foot of the sacred fig tree; he must have experienced the feelings inspired by the approach of the monsoon; he must have watched beast and bird disporting themselves in tank and river; he must know the varying aspects of nature in different seasons; in short, he must be acquainted with all the sights of an Indian landscape, the mere allusion to one of which may call up some familiar scene, or touch some chord of sentiment, as in the *Meghadūta*, a beautiful lyrical gem by Kālidāsa.[18] It is apparent that in writing this lyrical poem the poet aimed at immortalizing in verse the various places and scenes which he had visited and whose beauty had charmed his gaze. Even in the second part, in which he has to give the "message," he fills the major portion of it with a descriptive picture of Alakā, its environs, and the gay sports of its denizens, making each stanza a piece of masterly miniature painting.[19]

The poem "Ṛtusaṃhāra," also by Kālidāsa, is a "highly poetical descrip-

German and Eastern traditions share sentiments for nature. An example of this feeling in German art can be seen in *The Flight Into Egypt* by Martin Schongauer ca. 1445–1491.

The Japanese love mountains, rivers, flowers, birds, grass, and trees, and represent them in the patterns of their *kimonos*. They are fond of the delicacies of the season and keep their edibles in natural forms as much as possible in cooking.

The Japanese regard for nature is manifest in the dwarf trees, grown with an artist's eye for shape, which are placed in their homes together with flowers.

tion of the six seasons into which classical Sanskrit poets usually divide the Indian year. Among glowing descriptions of the beauties of nature, interspersed with erotic senses, the poet adroitly interweaves the expression of human emotions. Perhaps no other work of Kālidāsa manifests so strikingly the poet's deep sympathy with nature, his keen powers of observation, and his skills in depicting an Indian landscape in vivid colours.

"The poet dwells longest on the delights of spring, the last of the six seasons. It is then that maidens with *karnikāra* flowers on their ears, with red *asoka* blossoms and sprays of jasmine in their locks, go to meet their lovers. Then the hum of intoxicated bees is heard and the note of the Indian cuckoo; then the blossoms of the mango-tree are seen; these are the sharp arrows wherewith the god of the flowery bow enflames the hearts of maidens to love."[20]

In the "Amaruśataka," another Sanskrit poem, the bright eyes and beauty of Indian girls find a setting in scenes brilliant with blossoming trees, fragrant with flowers, gay with the plumage and vocal with the song of birds, diversified with lotus ponds steeped in tropical sunshine and large-eyed gazelles reclining in the shade.[21]

Even Indian ascetics, who diverted themselves from earthly life, composed poems in praise of nature. They enjoy and extol nature as the sanctuary beyond worldly sensuous attachments, afflictions, and bondages. In their case, nature is conceived as something opposed to human elements, and a means of deliverance from them.

In China there exist many poems that express appreciation of natural beauty, by which we feel blessed. In general, the Japanese, too, love mountains, rivers, flowers, birds, grass, and trees, and represent them in the patterns of their *kimono*. They are fond also of the delicacies of the season, keeping their edibles in natural forms as much as possible in cooking. Within the house, flowers are arranged in a vase and dwarf trees are placed in the alcove; flowers and birds are engraved in the transom; simple flowers and birds are also painted on the sliding screen; and, in the garden, miniature mountains are built and water is drawn. The literature is also closely tied up with warm affection for nature. "*Makura no Sōshi*" (Pillow Books) begin with general remarks about the four seasons and then go into the description of the scenic beauties of the seasons and human affairs.[22]

This sentiment for nature, which contributed to the sympathetic heart of the Japanese people and their love of order in communal life, may be due partly to the influence of the land and climate and to early attainment of a settled agricultural civilization. Everywhere in Japan there are passable mountain ranges, rich in streams and lakes; the land was favorable to settled abodes and the development of communal life. The mild climate, the variety of scenery, the rich flora and sea-products and the remarkable absence of beasts of prey—these combined contributed greatly to the development of a peace-loving and docile disposition and to an ability to establish order and attain solidarity.

The love of nature, in the case of the Japanese, is tied up with their tendencies to cherish miniature forms and treasure delicate things. Contrast the Japanese love of individual flowers, birds, grass, and trees with the British enjoyment of the spacious view of the sea, the Dover Cliffs, and the countryside.[23] Such aesthetic preferences of various nations are culturally significant traits of their respective peoples.

Yet in this respect the Japanese love of nature differs somewhat from the Chinese attachment to the rivers and mountains. The point may be illustrated by a comparison of the following two poems. Dōgen, the Japanese Zen master (13th century A.D.), writes:

Flowers are in Spring, Cuckoos in Summer,
In Autumn is the moon, and in Winter
The pallid glimmer of snow.

The land, climate, and early attainment of a settled agricultural civilization may have influenced the Japanese sentiment for nature.

In contrast to Japanese enjoyment of individual flowers, birds, and blades of grass is British love of the countryside as a whole scene.

Compare the Chinese verse of "Wu-men-Kuan" ("Gateless Gate," by Wu-men Hui-k'ai):

A Hundred flowers are in Spring, in Autumn is the moon,
In Summer is the cool wind, the snow is in Winter;
If nothing is on the mind to afflict a man,
That is the best season for the man.

In the Chinese, the word *cuckoos* of the Japanese is replaced by *cool wind*, which gives an entirely different effect. The cool wind and cuckoos are both sensible objects, but the former gives the sense of boundless remoteness, while the latter suggests something limited, almost cozy.

The Japanese garden typically exemplifies the Japanese interest in expressing natural scenery on a miniature scale. In this respect, the Indians are quite different. They too love nature and construct gardens (udyāna, ārāma) where they plant grass and trees and lay out wells and springs, but they rarely try to imitate natural rivers and mountains on the smaller scale.

In Japanese temples and elsewhere there are sometimes "gardens without flowers." This might seem preposterous in the eyes of Westerners. This is the object which the Japanese landscape-gardener sets before him, to suggest some famous natural scene in which flowers may or may not appear. In some gardens all has been arranged as if molded by the hands of nature itself; structure and decoration in no way vie with nature but are kept in harmony with it. Spectators thus feel as if they have been placed in a secluded recess within the bosom of nature.

What the Japanese call *hako-niwa* is a whole landscape-garden compressed into the microscopic limits of a single dish or flowerpot,—paths, bridges, mountains, stone lanterns, etc., all complete—a fanciful little toy. It symbolizes a view of the natural world. Japanese people tend to like *hako-niwa*-like things.

In all this there is no inkling of a view that regards the natural world as cursed or gruesome. Dōgen says: "There are many thousands of worlds comparable to the sūtras within a single spade of dust. Within a single dust there are innumerable Buddhas. A single stalk of grass and a single tree are both the mind and body (of us and Buddhas)."[24]

Nor is there anything of the kind of pessimism to be found in Occidental people. In the West, pessimism means a weariness with existence in this world. In the case of the Japanese, it means to be wearied only of complicated social fetters and restrictions from which they wish to be delivered. Consequently, the sense of pessimism is dispelled as soon as one comes to live close to the beauties of nature, far apart from human society. Saigyō (1118–90), though he had escaped from the world, enjoyed contemplating the moon, hills, streams, and flowers, and spending the rest of his life traveling around on foot. Kamo Chōmei (1155–1216), wearied as he was of this world, enjoyed nature and was contented, living a life of seclusion in

To Westerners, pessimism means a weariness with existence in this world. To the Japanese it means weariness of social fetters and restrictions. Pessimism is dispelled as soon as one comes close to the beauties of nature, far apart from human society.

his hermitage. Saint Gensei (1623–68) of Fukakusa and, more recently, Ōtagaki Rengetsu also enjoyed nature, despite the fact that they hated to mingle in worldly affairs. Pessimism in these cases takes the form of an attachment to nature.

> Changeable is this world,
> So may be the cherry blossoms,
> Falling in my garden." (Manyō-shū, v. 1959)

> Brief is this mortal life —
> Let me go and seek the Way,
> Contemplating the hills and streams undefiled!"
> (Manyō-shū, v. 4468)

Love of plants and animals

In a number of Asiatic traditions, plants and animals have been objects of human love. Plants are frequently invoked as divinities, along with waters, rivers, mountains, heaven, and earth. The cult of trees and other plants is very widely practiced throughout India.

"The *soma*, the most important plant of the *Ṛgveda*, is described as growing on the mountains, and must have been easily obtainable. [In later periods]... it was brought from long distances, or substitutes had to be used on account of its rarity. Thus the identity of the original species came to be lost in India. The plant now commonly used is evidently" quite different.

"Among large trees the most important is the *Aśvattha* ("horse-stand") or sacred fig tree (*Ficus religiosa*). Its fruit (*pippala*) is described as sweet and the food of birds. Its sacredness is" apparent, "for its wood was used for soma vessels and no Hindu would dare to utter a falsehood beside it. Now called Pīpal, this tree is the abode of Brahmā, or of the triad of Hindu gods, Brahmā, Viṣṇu, and Śiva. It is worshiped by pouring water at the roots, by daubing the trunk with red ocher, by fastening rags or threads to the branches, and by circumambulation. Buddhists worship it as the Bo-tree, under which Gautama Buddha attained perfect wisdom.

"The tree most characteristic of India, shading a large area with its wide-spreading foliage, is the Nyagrodha ('growing downwards') or banyan (*Ficus Indica*)." It is especially sacred to Viṣṇu. "With its lofty dome of foliage impenetrable to the rays of the sun, and supported by many lesser trunks as by columns, this great tree resembles a vast temple of verdure fashioned by the hand of Nature."

Among other sacred plants, the *Kuśa* grass is preeminently holy among Hindus for its close association with the Vedic sacrifice. The lotus flower, symbolizing unstained purity, has been esteemed as the national flower throughout all religious traditions. The holy basil *tulasī* or *tulsī* (*Ocymum*

Among sacred plants the lotus has been esteemed throughout all religious traditions as a symbol of purity.

sanctum), a small shrub which may be found growing in the courtyard of most Hindu houses, and which is the most sacred plant of modern India, is believed to be animated by Lakṣmī, the wife of Viṣṇu, or by Sītā; the entire worship of many high-caste Indian women consists in its daily circumambulation with offerings of rice and flowers. And the *mango*, the *bel*, or wood-apple, and the *nīm* tree, the leaves of which are prophylactic against disease and snakebite, are likewise holy and receive worship generally or at certain times.

Japan has been rich in vegetation, and the Japanese are devoted to the worship of plants. Everywhere, from the forested mountain to the fertile plain, the ancient Japanese saw exuberant vegetation, and they called their land, with its farms and rice fields, "the luxuriant country of the plain of reeds and fresh young ears of rice corn." A curious legend relates how Susanowo, by pulling out the hairs of his body and scattering them, produced trees useful for all kinds of buildings and different kinds of fruits. The vegetable world was worshiped above all because it represented the essential food of the people, being therefore the necessary basis of all social order; worshiped also was the material of houses, from the thatch of the cottages to the precious wood of the temples.

Within the Indian tradition, animals also contribute to mythological and religious conceptions. The cow, of course, figures largely in Hinduism. The bull or cow is a sacred animal, owing, no doubt, to its preeminent utility, and should not be slain; in fact, *aghnyā* ("not to be killed") is a frequent designation of the cow. One of the reasons for the Indian Mutiny was that Sepoys became angry when they came to know that grease of such animals was used on cartridges.

Other animals worshiped in India have been the "horse, conspicuous in the Ṛgveda as drawing the cars of the gods, and as representing the sun under various names (in the Vedic ritual the horse was regarded as symbolic of the sun and of fire)." Also, the sacred goose of Brahmā, the *garuḍa*, the mythical eagle or vulture of Viṣṇu, the *nandin*, or bull, of Śiva, the tiger of his wife Durgā, the rat of Gaṇeśa, the parrot of Kāmadeva the god of love, share the reverence due to the gods with whom they are associated.

Among wild animals, the tiger now survives only in the wooded hills to the south of the Gujarāt peninsula, but still familiar to the Indians is the lion (simha), whose roar is the characteristic on which they chiefly dwell. The king of beasts was conventionally familiar in Indian literature, and his old Sanskrit designation is still common in Sikh and Hindu names in the form of Singh.

"Among the noxious animals of the *Ṛgveda*, the serpent is the most prominent. This is the form which the powerful demon, the foe of Indra, is believed to possess." "When the Aryans spread over India, the land of serpents, they found the cult of these creatures diffused among the aborigines and adopted it from them." "In the later Vedas serpents are mentioned

Within the Indian tradition animals have a place in mythology and religion. The bull or cow is a sacred animal which may not be slain.

as a class of semidivine beings, along with the Gandharvas and others; in the Sūtras offerings to them are prescribed. In the latter works we meet for the first time with the Nāgas, really serpents and human only in the form" of the head. In post-Vedic times, serpent-worship is found all over India. Worship is habitually performed even now to the more common and dangerous snakes, especially the cobra, *pūjā*.

As for other creatures, "the wild goose or swan (*hamsa*), so familiar to the classical poets, is said to swim in the water and fly in a line, and the curious power of separating soma from water is attributed to it in the *White Yajurveda*, as that of extracting milk from water is in the later poetry. The latter faculty belongs also to the curlew (*krauñca*)." On the other hand, the *cakravāka*, the ruddy goose, is referred to as a model of conjugal love, peahens (*mayūri*) are spoken of as removing poison and devouring snakes, and parrots are described as "uttering human speech."

What can be noted in these instances is that, as another writer has said,

> more or less unconsciously behind all lies the motive power of the belief in transmigration, which presents to the mind of the worshipper the possibility that the living form may enshrine the spirit of a deceased father or other ancestor, who has chosen this as his temporary home. Nature and ancestor-worship are so intimately conjoined that it is often impossible with certainty to assign to one or the other the priority.[25]

Similarly, the deification of animals was common in primitive Japan. The forest, the tall grasses, were full of mysterious creatures which were regarded as "superior" beings — *kamis*. In Shintō mythology animals had the attributes of man, e.g., the gift of speech; but they also possessed rarer qualities, e.g., the toad knew things which even the gods did not know. It is not surprising, then, that the famous heroes of the legends often appeared as inferior to the animals they met. At the very least there was a close familiarity, a community of interests, based on the structure of nature between man and the animals as well as between the animals and the gods. This was the case with reptiles, birds, mammals (especially wolves), fishes, and even insects. (One story tells of a caterpillar which was worshiped like a real deity.)

Interaction between heaven and man

The Chinese elaborated an organic theory of a reciprocal relationship between heaven and man. In the period of the Chan Kuo (Warring States period, 481–221 B.C.), "scholars of the positive and negative principle" advocated a kind of nature worship which was carried into the Early Han period. According to this principle, natural phenomena and man-made institutions are mutually interrelated, and therefore if the king, who was the representative of man, governed the country well, the phenomena of nature such as weather, wind, and rain would be favorable to man, whereas if the reign of the king was bad, natural calamities would arise. This idea was strongly stressed by Tung Chung-shu (ca. 179–ca. 104 B.C.) of the Early Han dynasty, who thought that disasters were sent from heaven in order to admonish the king. The thought of *Ko-ming* (revolution), which means, literally, "to cut off (or take away) the mandate of Heaven from some particular ruler," played a role in checking or correcting the tyranny of aristocrats.

Buddhism also had sūtras which stated the theory of disaster and which were highly regarded by the Chinese. A typical example of these sūtras is the *Chin-kuang-ming* (Suvarna-prabhūsa, Golden Splendor) sūtra, which states in detail, in the 13th chapter, that if the king does not protect the *dharma* (religion, law), a terrible calamity will arise. That is to say, as the result of maladministration on the part of the emperor, falsehood and struggle will increase in his country and the ministers and subjects will rise against him. Furthermore, the deities will become angry; wars will break out; the enemy will overrun the country; family members will fight each other; nothing will be pleasant or comfortable for man. Natural occurrences will likewise be bad. Living beings will lack vigor, plagues will arise, and pestilence will sweep the land. Therefore, the emperor should strive to govern the country by the *dharma* (law).

Now this sūtra is unusual, as Buddhist sūtras seldom teach the theory that "disasters arise through poor government by the King." Yet Chinese Buddhists highly esteemed the theory in this sūtra, of which five different Chinese translations were made and on which many commentaries were composed.

Naturalized Buddhist monks from India propagated Buddhism in conformity with this organismic way of Chinese thinking. Guṇavarman, for example, taught Buddhism to the Emperor Wen of the Sung dynasty, saying: "The four seas are your land and all existences are your subjects. One pleasant word and all your subjects are happy. One good act brings harmony to the people. If you only punish wrong-doers without killing and do not impose heavy taxes, then nature will harmonize with man, and fruits and crops will ripen well."[26]

More investigation is necessary to know how long this organic form of ethical thought continued in China. It can be safely said, however, that the thought of reciprocity between Heaven and human deeds is not exclusive to the Chinese. It was taught not only in Buddhism but also in Indian and other ethical systems, that good natural developments generally spring from good deeds and that evil overcomes from evil deeds. Chinese "Pure Land" teachings themselves explained this ethical theory in terms of the relationship of reciprocity between Buddha's grace and nature, in line with the idea that there was a reciprocity between heaven and man. The same idea was introduced into Japan, where it was maintained by aristocrats of the imperial court, especially in the Heian period, and spread among the common people in later days.

Nature and natural law: in antiquity

The idea that there is a connection between cosmic and ritual order, between natural and moral law, had already been formed when the Indo-Aryans and the Iranians formed a single people (Vedic *ṛta* = Avestic *aṣa*). When the Vedic singer extols a god in song, he does not look up to the god with that shuddering awe and faith with which the Psalmist looks up to Yahweh. The Vedic poets stood on a more familiar footing with the gods whom they honored in songs, and from whom they asked rewards in an almost fawning manner. When they sang a song of praise to a god, they expected him to present them with wealth in sons, cows, food, etc.

One exception is the god Varuṇa. He is conceived as the king of all, both gods and men, the universal monarch. He is the upholder of both the physical and the moral orders. He is the great lord of the laws of nature. He established heaven and earth; he dwells in all the worlds; he is the guardian of the whole world and supporter of the earth and the heaven. By Varuṇa's ordinances the moon and the stars move and shine. He regulates the seasons and the months and also the waters that bring prosperity to the earth. Varuṇa concerns himself more with the moral ways of men than any other god. His anger is roused by sin, the infringement of his ordinances. He punishes sinners severely. He is an omniscient god and a constant witness of men's truth and falsehood. No creature can do, think, or devise anything without his being noticed, so great and so powerful is Varuṇa.

Varuṇa was regarded as the great upholder of physical and moral order (*ṛta*). His order is called cosmic law (*ṛta*). He is the chief guardian of this order.[27] He does not allow anybody, either god or man, to infringe upon it. His figure was connected with the regularly recurring celestial phenomena, recurrence being seen in the course of the heavenly bodies seen in the sky. It was believed that by the law of Varuṇa, heaven and earth are held apart.

This highly ethical god corresponds to the Avestic Ahura Mazdā, the "wise spirit," who is of the same character though not of the same name. Some traits of Varuṇa were such as would not fit in with the framework of the Iranian religion, however. In Varuṇa there was a quality predominantly "nocturnal," which made possible his assimilation to the demon "Vṛtra."[28] Further, Varuṇa was also a god of mercy, merciful to the penitent. "There is no hymn addressed to Varuṇa that does not contain a prayer for forgiveness of guilt," we are told. "The element of divine mercy thus finds a place in the Vedic religion, but was excluded in the Avestic system owing to the juristic character of that religion."[29]

As mentioned above, the cosmic law is called *asa* in the Zend-Avesta, which is of the same etymological origin as *ṛta.* In the qualities of the god Varuṇa we find the Vedic conception of cosmic or moral law (*ṛta*). It is the law which pervades the whole world, which not only men but even gods must obey. It furnishes us with the standard of morality. The way of life of good men who follow the path of *ṛta* is called *vrata.*[30] To the Ṛgvedic people the universe was an ordered whole. This notion was shared by the Greeks. Thus Plato says: "Philosophers tell us . . . that communion and friendship and orderliness and temperance and justice bind together heaven and earth and gods and men, and that this universe is therefore called Cosmos or order, not disorder or misrule."[31]

Ṛta has sometimes been compared to the Greek *moira*, and to the Chinese *tao.*[32] Like these, *ṛta* was never personified. The meaning of the word *ṛta* would seem to have passed through some such evolution as "motion, rhythmic notion, order, cosmic order, moral order, the right." The idea, which was held by the Aryans before their invasion into India, may with reasonable probability be traced back to the second or third millennium B.C. The use of the word died out in India before the time of the rise of Buddhism,[33] but the conception of cosmic law dominated later Indian thought, being expressed with other words *karma*, or *dharma.*[34]

In China, also, Confucius based his teaching on cosmic law. His elder rival, Lao-tzu, goes much farther. In the work attributed to Lao-tzu, the *Tao-te Ching*, the pregnant sayings are concerned almost exclusively with the *Tao*, or cosmic order. It is upon the *Tao* that Lao-tzu's ethics, religion, and philosophy are built.

This Chinese concept of Tao was subsequently taken over by the Japanese of the ancient period. In particular, the ethical and political theory of Confucianism, and the legal and educational institutions of China, all based upon the universal principle of Tao (*michi* in Japanese), exerted tremendous influence. The idea of a cosmic principle was asserted by Prince Shōtoku with strongly Confucian insights: "The lord is heaven," he writes, "the vassal is Earth. Heaven overspreads, Earth upbears. When this is so, the four seasons follow their due course, and the powers of Nature develop their efficacy."[35]

Nature and natural law in the modern period

What may be called the modern view of nature and natural law, both in the East and in the West, has emerged since medieval times. A general esteem for nature and its laws of course existed then, as it has in every philosophical age. But the explanation of natural processes was radically different. In the Indian Vedāntic period, nature was generally conceived as directed from without. This conception was consistent with that of the medieval West, which accepted an explanation of nature as independent of God's will. On the other hand, among mystics, both Eastern and Western, the belief was that god existed *in* nature, which was therefore conceived as directed by an internal principle, God being regarded as the self-nature of everything.

Differing from these ways of thinking about nature, the modern view seems to play down the role of a director of nature, whether it be internal or external. (God is sometimes given other interesting roles in modern thought, of course.) Nature conforms to its own laws in modern thought, and interest in these laws has led to scientific thinking, to an appreciation of measurement (e.g., mathematics, geometry, astronomy), and to systems of government and jurisprudence in the West. In the East, thinking of a similar kind, while present, has been concentrated for the most part on metaphysical and ethical issues, though a conception of society as having laws of its own is likewise to be found in Eastern countries.

In Western ancient philosophy, Aristotle thought that nature had to be observed firsthand if its laws were to be understood. For Aristotle, God was only a prime mover who, so to speak, started the ball rolling, but was not an ever-present director. Aristotle's view was revived in the later Middle Ages, when Thomas Aquinas included Aristotelianism in his scholastic synthesis. Scholasticism, though conservative, was argumentatively rigorous and probably produced the philosophical thinking which in time led to its demise. Men such as Copernicus, Galileo, and Kepler, who were all good observers, made discoveries about nature that contradicted religious dogma. Naturally, these finds had to be very carefully brought to light, and many were condemned as heresy. These thinkers included a great deal of metaphysical speculation in their work, so they were not scientific in the twentieth-century sense. But their ways of experimentation form the basis of modern thought.

Francis Bacon (1561–1626) is sometimes thought of as the first modern philosopher in the West. Inspired by the "scientific" discoveries that were finding their way into the open in his time, he advocated an "inductive" method of inquiry to be undertaken by observing, by analyzing the observed data, then by inferring hypotheses and verifying them through further observation. The result, he thought, would be a separation of the essential from the nonessential and a discovery of the underlying structure or form of the phenomena being observed. Yet he believed any notion of this would have to be considered tentative, because some contrary instances might have been overlooked. Bacon knew that investigating in such a manner would be slow. The main objection to the method was not its slowness, however, but the fact that, as Bacon thought, it was obstructed by prejudice. People cling to four idols (prejudices), he said: (1) Idols of the tribe, or human nature's inherent tendencies which impair objectivity, e.g., a naively realistic reliance on sense experience. (2) Idols of the den, or each man's individuality, which can hamper objectivity. (3) Idols of the marketplace, or prejudices inherent in our language(s). And (4) idols of the theater, or the "plays" that past philosophy has created to explain nature. Bacon's thought is indicative of the direction that European philosophy generally took afterward. Eastern thought on nature and its laws did not take the same turn until it had felt the effects of Western influence.

Indian views of natural law (*dharma* or *sanātona dharma*) were nearly the same from antiquity until the advent of Westernization. Future scholars may discern shifts of meaning that occurred, but such distinctions are too specialized for the present work. The paradigmatic thinkers on nature were the Chinese. Many opinions have come to the fore as a result of their work, some of which are only slightly pre-modern in flavor. Much of this thought was transmitted to Japan and subsequently individualized by thinkers there who shared the Chinese preoccupation with nature. All of the ensuing speculation, however, remained in the domain of ethics, metaphysics, or social law as related to natural law.

Chinese discussions of nature and natural law also became relevant to the problem of the law in society. But, as in Western philosophy, a more pluralistic conception was necessary than the monistic ones that equated nature with its law. Huang Tsung-hsi (1610–95) is notable as a thinker who, while still in the Confucian tradition, advanced an almost modern point of view regarding natural law. In traditional Confucianism, if a man's character was correctly developed, his relationships would be in harmony also (a situation capable of expanding to all the relationships in the empire, hence to perfect government). Huang Tsung-hsi, however, attached importance to the form or system of government rather than simply to the character of the men administering it. "If men (who govern) were of the right kind," he claimed, "the full intent of the law would be fulfilled; and even if they were of the wrong kind, it would be impossible for them to govern tyrannically and make the people suffer. Therefore I say we must first have laws which govern well and later we shall have men who govern well."[36]

In the minds of a significant few among Japanese thinkers of the Tokugawa period, the attitude to emphasize was that which recognized the substantiality, orderliness, and intelligibility of the natural world. This helped eventually to foster a new interest in the study of nature. More directly, however, it expressed itself in the concern for the study—for instance, among Chinese Confucianists—of human history as revealing the constant laws of human behavior and political morality. This positivistic and quasi-scientific approach was a notable characteristic of Japanese thought and scholarship in the Tokugawa period, which showed a new interest in observing the constant laws of nature and human society, in contrast with the medieval, Buddhistic view of the world as subject only to ceaseless change, the Law of Impermanence.[37]

The school of the Old Learning or Antiquity (Kogaku) of Japan was in a sense a protest movement against the tradition of Chu Hsi and other Neo-Confucianists. This school asserted that Neo-Confucianists had distorted the Confucian sages' dynamic view of the world and life. The main characteristic of the Kogaku was its monistic philosophy based on the identification of *li* (principle or reason) and *ch'i* (material force). According to this school everything and every reason is a direct manifestation of the vitality of the cosmos. Thus relating metaphysics to ethics, the Kogaku scholars advocated a universalistic philosophical principle as the basis for practical life. In other words, the aim of life is the realization and fulfillment of one's potentialities through following the law of cosmic life. According to Itō Jinsai (1627–1705), "the moral order is not a mere haphazard law, but a providential rule, based upon the inherent nature of things. The ruling of Heaven is in all things, punishing evil and rewarding good."[38]

Conformity to nature was emphasized by teachers of Mental Culture (Shingaku). According to them, the human soul of each individual is the reflex of the heavenly reason; our innermost soul gives unerring guidance to our life when it thinks and wills in accordance with the true nature of our existence. The training in conformity with our nature is true Mental Culture. Benevolence, patience, faithfulness, and vigilance are the cardinal virtues, the means as well as the aim of spiritual exercise and moral life. "Flowers bloom pink, willow leaves are green, each according to its nature; the crow caws and the sparrow twitters, each lives and moves by its nature. Why could not mankind alone among creatures behave similarly (according to nature)?" Thus preached the Shingaku masters. Man's true and original nature, they explained, consists in living a virtuous life, virtue being natural to him, yet he does otherwise because he is misguided by selfishness, the root of all vice and ills. Thus the Shingaku teachers identify human nature with natural order and the latter with moral order, because all the three amount to the life of the cosmic soul.[39]

Ishida Baigan, the founder of the Japanese Shingaku school, considered nature in terms of its forms, another area of the Neo-Confucianists in which Nature is called the Mind. "It is the Mind," he said,

> which identifies itself in the Forms. See how the Mind exists even in birds and animals! Frogs are naturally afraid of snakes. It is not surely a mother who teaches its offspring that snakes are dangerous and will gobble them up and, of course, tadpoles do not study and do not gradually learn all this. The fact is that if you are born under the Forms of a frog, the fear for snakes comes straight in the Mind from the Forms. Let us consider something analogous: a flea when summer comes clings to man's body. Here again do a flea's parents teach it to live by sucking men's blood? Is it taught if it sees a man's hand approach, it must jump away immediately lest it loses its life? The reason is that when a flea jumps away it acts in accordance with the Forms and not because it has learnt to do so.[40]

To which Baigan adds: "Birds and Beasts have no Personal Mind and therefore comply perfectly with the dictates of the Forms."[41] This emphasis on natural law may be compared with some continental rationalists as well as with Hegel.

The final goal of ethical conduct, according to Baigan, was to recover one's own original Mind. "To attain something by following the Law means to attain the Mind."[42] "If you just let yourself go, and become receptive, everything is natural, easy, evident."[43] It is interesting to observe that Baigan wanted to apply his theory to politics. "By ruling without knowing this Order (Principle) a ruler will not be able to govern his country.[44] Baigan's thought may sound too idealistic, but it is perhaps not so when a highly idealistic Western counterpart such as Fichte is considered.

Master Jiun, the pioneer of Sanskrit scholarship in Japan, stressed the idea of natural law from a rationalistic standpoint. "In this world there are the true Laws which benefit it always. Those who have open eyes can see these Laws as clearly as they see the sun and moon. Whether a Buddha appears or whether a Buddha does not appear (regardless of it) this world exists, and human beings exist. These Ten Virtues will always be manifest along them (i.e., so long as they exist)."[45]

Here one is reminded of the thought of Hugo Grotius (de Groot, 1583–1645), whose sharp distinction between inviolable natural law and ever mutable positive or civil law has had great effect on European jurisprudence. Grotius maintained that "natural law . . . originates in principles which would be valid, even were there no God."[46] There is a striking similarity here between Grotius's concept of natural law and that of Jiun. But Grotius was a Westerner, and he included in his belief the opinion that God may be called the author of natural law because He is the author of nature and therefore He wills this law to be valid. Jiun, on the other hand, held that nature and law are nothing but Buddha himself.

The doctrine of Jiun had considerable ethical consequences, for he found the essence of Buddhism in observing natural law, which could be termed the observance of the Ten Virtues. "It is true of only the teachings of the Ten Virtues that they never change. Throughout all the ages, both ancient and modern, and throughout all lands they constitute the suitable and true Path for both the wise and ignorant, the superior man and the inferior man, and for both men and women."[47] Jiun thought that his concept of natural law was of universal application, just as the law itself is universal, and that natural law should be the basis for ethical conduct throughout all countries. "Just as heaven and earth exist," he held,

> so also are there various countries in existence. Sun, moon, and star
> move according to the laws of heaven, while mountains and marshes,
> seas and rivers are governed by the laws of earth. As there are various
> countries, so there exist human beings to inhabit them. A country is

constituted with the relationships between lord and subject, superiors and subordinates. A family is constituted with the relationships of parents and children, husband and wife, and between brothers."[48]

Ninomiya Sontoku (1787–1856), the "Peasant Sage" of Japan, stressed the importance of nature to man and further the importance of possessing nothing and following the natural in man's relationships with his fellow beings. His teaching is called *Hōtoku*, or Recompense (or indebtedness), because it emphasizes the indebtedness of man's existence to nature and to fellowship among mankind.

In Ninomiya's view, the concept of natural laws in the ethical sense was predominant. But nature in the objective world should be viewed as it is and should be analyzed in terms of causal recurrence. In Japan, before the introduction of Western civilization on a large scale, some thinkers advocated the necessity of viewing things in the natural world objectively. On this, Miura Baien (1723–89) was outspoken. For Miura, the final source of knowledge is neither tradition nor the writings of men but nature and man himself. If one wants a true view of the universe, one must test in heaven what one believes true of heaven and test in man what one believes true of man. Readers of books must therefore check what they read by looking into the book of nature; if nature confirms it, they may accept it, but otherwise they must set it aside.

Asada Gōryū advocated the importance of the disinterested study of nature. He said that scholars who are proud of their love are "captives in the human prison; they have not penetrated into the heart of things." He adds: "Concern for the world and compassion for the masses is benevolent in motive, but the study of creation in human terms is not conducive to true knowledge." In a letter to Asada Gōryū, Miura advocates the necessity of viewing things as they are:

> Now the universe shelters all things in it, and man is just one of those
> things. As all things come into existence, they are provided with
> innumerable distinct natures. Though afforded the same means,
> children cannot be just like their parents; fire cannot be like water.
> The landlord (nature) provides what the tenant (man) occupies, but
> the landlord is not the tenant, and the tenant is not the landlord, each
> being different in character and capacity.... To know the world of
> Heaven (nature), therefore, man must put his own interests aside in
> order to enter into the world of Heaven. In order to know objects,
> man must again put his own interests aside and enter into the world of
> objects; only in that way can his intellect hope to comprehend
> Heaven-and-earth and understand all things.[49]

Before opening its closed door to the world, Japan produced a number of nationalistic thinkers who maintained the doctrine of natural law. But this way of thinking did not develop, owing to feudal influences.

Conformity to nature

Within the field of art history we can notice the contrast between the way nature appears in Eastern and Western visual art. Whereas the depiction of nature is a relatively late feature of Western painting, which up to the end of the seventeenth century was concerned for the most part with human (or divine) subject matter, and which showed the natural world, so far as it did at all, only as a background to its renderings of human forms, in Eastern art it has been the other way round, with nature being the primary concern up to relatively recent times, and with human subjects being of subordinate importance. This contrast we shall examine in more detail.

Chinese thought traditionally tended to consider that all things could exist only so far as they were in conformity with man. This gave rise to an attitude that esteemed the principle of nature which exists in the mind of man. From ancient times, the idea of Heaven (*T'ien*) was conceived by the Chinese as in close relation to that of man.[50] According to a poem composed in the ancient period of the early Chou dynasty, Heaven created man, and therefore, Heaven, as the ancestor of man, handed down moral precepts which man had to observe.[51] This idea was inherited by Confucius. He recommended acknowledging "the order of Heaven," which meant "one should follow the morality given to man by Heaven."[52] There was a general assumption that politics should follow laws based upon natural law.

Some modern Europeans were deeply stirred by the fact that ancient China, where Confucianism was recognized as the national ideology and politics was administered by its doctrine, followed laws based upon natural law. Undoubtedly, some similarities exist between the idea of natural law in Europe and that of ancient China.

The opinion that "man should follow his true nature" was also stated by other scholars in ancient China, and yet their meaning was different from that of Confucius. Mo-tzu taught that the ruler should follow what Heaven wished and not follow what it did not wish. Lao-tzu insisted that the correct way of man is to follow the way of Heaven; therefore, it can be said that the basis of the correct way of man is *T'ien-tao* (the Way of Heaven). Yang chu (who lived between the time of Mo-tzu and Mencius) stated, "The original nature for man desires only sex and food. Therefore, it is better for man not to have relations with others but only to satisfy his own desires." He also said: "It is a natural law that man does what he wants." Mencius taught that "the true character of man is good; however, the evil mind arises by the temptation of material desires. Therefore, man should cultivate his mind himself and exhibit his own true character."

Buddhism was also influenced by this current of thought. Buddhists did not look for truth in the phenomenal world but explored the inner world by concentration of mind. In Zen Buddhism, Chinese traditional thought

The depiction of nature in Western painting, seen above in *The Adoration of the Magi* by Hieronymus Bosch (ca. 1488–1516), is a relatively recent feature, with human or divine subject matter dominating until the end of the 17th century whereas in Eastern art nature has been of primary concern up to relatively recent times, with human subjects being of subordinate importance, as in Keishoki's *Bird* from the Muromachi Period (1333–1568).

is expressed in a peculiarly Chinese way: "If one realizes the truth that all existences are the same, he immediately returns to his true nature."[53] Both illusion and enlightenment of man were understood to be derived from the natural character of humanity: The mind is the ground and nature is the king. Where there is nature there is the king, and where there is no nature, there is no king. Where there is nature, there are the body and mind. Where no nature exists, there is neither body nor mind. Buddha is created by self-nature; therefore, one must not look for the Buddha through the body. If self-nature is an illusion, then the Buddha is merely a sentient being. If self-nature is enlightenment, then the sentient being is merely the Buddha.[54]

In Japan fine arts of Zen-style developed the idea of conformity with nature in combination with an attitude of esteem for natural beauty. The gardens of Zen temples represent rocks and streams which are supposed to be natural scenery in miniature. Zen people prefer drawings of rocks and waters. What have they to do with religion? "These nature pictures are also icons, and something more. That is to say, they are not merely symbols but ways of pointing immediately at what is called in Chinese the *Tao*."[55] With this conviction the Zen masters make gardens and draw paintings representing natural scenery.

There were other ways of representing the idea of conformity to nature. Kaibara Ekiken expresses a view of the interrelation of man and nature through the Supreme Confucian virtue of humanity or benevolence (Chinese, *jen*, Japanese, *jin*). In unity with nature, one can find what makes man truly man.

> Not only do all men at the outset come into being because of nature's law of life, Ekiken believes, but from birth till the end of life they are kept in existence by the support of heaven and earth. Man surpasses all other created things in the consciousness of his indebtedness to the limitless bounty of nature. Thus it will be seen that man's duty is not only to do his best to serve his parents, which is a matter of course, but also serve nature throughout his life in order to repay his immense debt. That is one thing all men should keep in mind constantly.
>
> As men mindful of their obligation constantly to serve nature in repayment of this great debt, they should not forget that, just as they manifest filial piety in the service of their own parents, so they should manifest to the full their benevolence toward nature. Benevolence means having a sense of sympathy within and bringing blessings to man and things. For those who have been brought up on the blessings of nature, it is the way to serve nature.

Here Ekiken finds the reason why man should love nature.

> Following the way of heaven, he should be humble and not arrogant toward others, control his desires and not be indulgent of his passions,

The gardens of Zen temples, which represent rocks and streams, are both icons and a way of pointing immediately at what is called the *Tao*.

cherish a profound love for all mankind born of nature's great love, and not abuse or mistreat them. Nor should he waste, just to gratify his personal desires, the five grains and other bounties which nature has provided for the sake of the people. Secondly, no living creatures such as birds, beasts, insects, and fish should be killed wantonly. Not even grass and trees should be cut down out of season. All of these are objects of nature's love, having been brought forth by her and nurtured by her. To cherish them and keep them is therefore the way to serve nature in accordance with the great heart of nature.[56]

However, in carrying out the virtue of benevolence, there should be a difference in priority based upon closeness to oneself. "Among human obligations there is first the duty to love our relatives, then to show sympathy for all other human beings, and then not to mistreat birds and beasts or any other living things. That is the proper order for the practise of benevolence in accordance with the great heart of nature. Loving other people to the neglect of parents, or loving birds and beasts to the neglect of human beings, is not benevolence."[57]

Such an assumption prevails even nowadays among present-day Japanese. Their persuasion seems quite different from that prevailing in the West.

Harmony with nature

One of the conspicuous features of Buddhist thought is its endeavor to be in harmony with nature. The enjoyment of natural beauty and the pleasure of living comfortably in natural surroundings was expressed by monks and nuns in the *Poems of the Elders* (*Theragāthā* and *Therigāthās*). This attitude was inherited from the ancient Indian hermit-sages (*ṛṣis*) described in the *Mahābhārata* and the *Rāmāyana*.

The same attitude is reflected in Japanese gardening. Japanese gardens that developed on the Chinese example greatly differ from their Western and Islamic counterparts, which concentrate on geometric patterns and symmetry. Japanese gardens, although artificially made by adept gardeners, give us the impression that they represent natural beauty as such and that we are really in the midst of this. Artifice and nature are not opposed. Indeed, the harmonious union of man and nature is the ideal of Buddhists.

In the most ancient poetic collection, the *Manyō-shu* (*Collection of a Myriad Leaves*, eighth century), we find numerous lyrical poems devoted to the celebration of the splendors of landscapes, from the lofty summit of Mount Fuji to the smallest herb of the plain. In these poetic pieces the Japanese show the particular sentiment they express in the phrase *mono no aware*, which consists in understanding the "melancholy of things" and which implies a sympathy with all creatures, a fellow-feeling with the sorrows of nature as well as with human sufferings. But the term is so difficult to translate that some Western scholar has rendered it simply with a newly coined word: "Ahness!"

Even rationalistic thinkers accept the idea of man's harmony with nature. To Kaibara Ekiken, "man and nature are allied and inseparable; an understanding of nature is indispensable to the understanding of man. In this respect it may be said that Kaibara still reflects the essential humanistic and ethical concerns of Confucianism, which distinguish him from the more independent "scientific" thinkers and "Dutch" schoolmen of the eighteenth century in Japan."[58]

According to the Eshin School of Japanese Tendai Buddhism, heaven and earth are different in name but harmonious in meaning. The sun, the moon, and the stars are different but hang in the same sky. Every entity is nominally distinct from every other, but they all exist in one reality.[59] Traditionally among the Japanese, harmony has been esteemed as the foremost virtue in human relations, beginning with the time of Prince Shotoku, and this idea seems to have been transferred to the relationship between man and nature, although the context is quite different.

Action and change as reality

The idea that lies at the root of Indian religions is the belief in power, or rather in many powers. (Potential powers were called "*śakti*," which concept was greatly stressed in the Tantric religion.) This underlies the phallic worship which is so prevalent in India. Such an idea implies that the Absolute exists in the phenomenal world. This is a fact among the traditional precepts of Japanese thought, and it has played an effective role in the assimilation of Zen as well. It assumes that the process of the phenomenal world is activity, self-actualization, a procreation in the creative power and freedom of sublime wonder.

In this way of thinking, the Absolute, being of the phenomenal world, comprehends time and change. Master Dōgen says, "Being is time, and time is being. With the realization of mutability or impermanence as a dynamic axis, being and time reveal themselves to be identical. Everything in the world is time at each moment." This is consistent with Buddhism. Dōgen said, "Birth and death is the life of Buddha." Just as all beings are the Buddha nature, so all times are the Buddha nature. Enlightenment is nothing but the realization that all natural phenomena change.

For Dōgen, impermanence is itself the absolute state, and this impermanence is not to be rejected but to be valued. To do so is to realize that time is the basis for all existences.

Even the self and its doubt are parts of the temporal order for the Zen Buddhist. "There is no world without this doubting self, for this self is the

The belief in power, or rather in many powers, which is at the root of Indian religions, underlies the phallic worship prevalent in India.

world itself. We must look on everything in this world as time. Each thing stands in unimpeded relation just as each moment stands unimpeded. Therefore (from the standpoint of time), the desire for enlightenment arises spontaneously; (from the standpoint of mind) time arises with the same mind. This applies also to training and enlightenment. Thus we see by entering within: the self is time itself."[60]

So for the natural world, it is regarded not only as *in* time but as identical *with* time. "The mountain is time; the ocean is time. If they were not, there would be no mountain and no ocean. You cannot say that there is no time in the absolute present of the mountain and ocean. If time decays, the mountain and ocean do not decay. Through this principle (the self-identity of time and things) eyes appear, the plucked flower appears—this is time. If it is not, all this is not."[61]

Itō Jinsai (1627–1705), the Japanese Confucianist, regards heaven and earth as the evolution of great activity, where nothing but eternal development exists, and completely denies what is called death. According to Itō the world of reality is nothing but change and action, and action is in itself good. All of the characteristically Japanese scholars believe in phenomena as the fundamental mode of existence, however. They unanimously reject the quietism of the neo-Confucianists of the Sung period.

Nature as the absolute

Nature as the absolute has been discussed by thinkers of East and West. The term *nature* occasionally means "the sum total of all things in time and space; the entire physical universe." Nature is the source of all things.

Sometimes the word *nature* is capitalized as "Nature." In this case the term means "the power," "force," "principle," etc., that seems to regulate nature; it is often personified.

When we discuss nature as "the absolute," we have to think of the problem (as presented by Spinoza) of "*natura naturans*" versus "*natura naturata*" in East and West.* This comes out also as the problem of "the classification of beings." Scotus Erigena set up four classes of being or nature:

1. *creant non creantur* (nature which creates and is not created).
2. *creantur et creant* (nature which is created and creates).
3. *creantur non creant* (nature which is created and does not create).
4. *neque creant neque creantur* (nature which does not create and is not created).

---

*In Spinoza the term *natura naturans* signifies Nature as God the Creator, infinite and beyond our comprehension; *natura naturata* signifies God as manifest *in* Nature, apprehensible by us in its various modes and bodies.—Ed.

This classification exactly corresponds with that set up by the Sāṃkhya philosophy. The primordial being is called "Nature" (*physis, natura = prakati*) in both systems. But the Sāṃkhya philosophy did not admit God as the creator. Thus, whereas in Erigena's philosophy nature which creates and is not created is God considered as the principle of things, in the Sāṃkhya philosophy it is the primordial matter or the material cause, not God.[62] In Erigena's philosophy, "nature which is not created and does not create is God considered as having ceased to create and entered into his rest";[63] in the Sāṃkhya philosophy it is individual spirits which, being separate entities, stay always in the state of rest.

The Sāṃkhya texts compare the soul with a looking glass in which the inner organ is reflected. It is interesting to note that the Neo-Platonist Plotinus not only compares soul with light, as the Sāṃkhya philosophy does, but also, in order to explain conscious knowledge, makes use of the other comparison of the looking glass in which the images of objects appear, just as it occurs in the Sāṃkhya texts. There may have been some connection between Neo-Platonic doctrine and the Sāṃkhya philosophy.[64]

In this connection we may note also that Primal Nature in the Sāṃkhya philosophy is called "non-evolute" (avyakta), and other things are called "evolute" (vyakta). These two are similar respectively to *natura naturans* and *natura naturata*. In the Vedānta School, Āsmarathya (ca. 350–250 B.C.) explained the relationship between Brahman and *ātman* as that of *natura naturans* and its evolutionary by-products (*prakati-vikāra-bhāva = natura naturata*), which may be compared to the relation between fire and sparks.

A similar thought can be found in the Shigon philosophy of Japan. In this system the substance is the six elements which are earth, water, fire, wind, space, and consciousness; in short, matter (comprising the first five elements) and mind (i.e., the consciousness). The five elements cannot exist without the consciousness, and the consciousness likewise cannot be without the five elements. The six elements can be examined from two perspectives, viz., the neutral or the unconditional state, and the conditional or the phenomenal state. The former refers to the eternal, unchanging substance; the latter, the ever-changing phenomena. The neutral state corresponds to the *natura naturans*; the conditional state, *natura naturata*.

The notions of *natura naturans, natura naturata* were not lost in the modern West. They were exemplified in the philosophy of Spinoza, who identified God with nature. Nature or God has two aspects for Spinoza. By *natura naturans* one understands God as an infinite substance with divine attributes. *Natura naturans* is a self-dependent and self-determined unique substance. By *natura naturata* one understands "creation," although one must not take the last term to mean that the world is distinct from God. This might be called the system of modes. In any case, all things exist *in* nature. Nature is an infinite system in which there is one infinite chain of particular causes, but the whole infinite chain exists only because Nature exists. There is only one order of Nature.

In China, Taoism likewise taught that nature is the absolute. Some Chinese maintained the notion of nature as *Tzu-Jan—natura naturans—*a self-determining emergent from the background of the Tao. But Chinese Pure Land teachings adopted the ideas of Taoism. Chinese Buddhists had to pass through a process of complicated thought before they acknowledged a Chinese naturalism. In this connection, Chi-tsang reasoned as follows:[65] Chinese philosophical thought, especially in Lao-tzu and Chuang-tzu, regarded existence as phenomena, and voidness as a substance other than existence. Therefore, voidness was not identifiable with existence. Buddhism, on the contrary, taught that phenomena are actually the manifestation of the Absolute. Therefore, the absolute significance of the phenomenal world cannot be recognized in actual life in the philosophy of Lao-tzu and Chuang-tzu. In Buddhism, however, one can accept the phenomenal world as an absolute state of existence, because actual life in this world is identical with absolute existence. Although this criticism by Chi-tsang may not be correct, at least he tried to recognize a significance in the life of this world.

The T'ien-t'ai and Hua-yen sects further expanded on this thought. According to the T'ien-tai sect, appearance and actuality are not different kinds of substances. Appearances are identical with reality. Therefore, "each existence in this world is the middle way." Each of the phenomenal forms of this world is a form of absolute existence. The Hua-yen sect developed the thought even further. That is to say, the theory of "mutual penetration and identification of all things with one another" is taught by this sect. The supreme meaning emerges when all phenomena are perfectly identified by their harmonious interrelationships. Therefore, nothing exists outside of phenomena and their diverse manifestations.

In Zen Buddhism the following answers were given to the question "What is absolute existence?" "It is the cypress tree in the garden" or "It is three pounds of hemp." The same idea is seen in Su Tung-p'o's poem: "The sound of the stream is the teaching or sermon of the Buddha, and the color of the mountain is the pure and True Body (Dharmakāya) of the Buddha." The conclusion is that each one of the existences of this world is, just as it appears, the manifestation of truth.

Zen monks, of course, opposed and rejected mere superficial naturalism. For example, Hui-hai stated: "Ignorant people do not realize the fact that the True Body (Dharmakāya) manifests its form in accordance with the object although it does not possess any form originally. Therefore, they say that the green bamboo tree is none other than the True Body (Dharmakāya) and the chrysanthemum is identical with Prajñā (wisdom). If the chrysanthemum is wisdom, then wisdom is the same as an insentient existence. If the green bamboo is the True Body (Dharmakāya), then the True Body is the same as the grass or the tree. If so, eating the bamboo-shoot carries the meaning of eating the True Body. Therefore, it is unworthy to think of such things."[66]

Nevertheless, the Chinese generally accepted the view that nature is the absolute. In the end, the T'ien-t'ai sect taught the theory that "all existences and even grass, trees, and earth can attain Buddhahood." That is to say, even physical matter existing in nature can realize enlightenment and become Buddha. Generally speaking, the tendency was to regard nature as the most beautiful and highest kind of existence, on an equal plane with human beings.

With this in mind, the Chinese Buddhists (especially Zen monks) tried to seek absolute significance in everyday life. "Those who wish to attain the state of the One Vehicle (Ekayāna) must not defile the six sensual objects (form, sound, smell, taste, touch, and ideas). If one does not defile the six sensual objects, then he is enlightened."[67] In other words, everyday life, just as it truly is, is identical with enlightenment. This thought is clearly found in the following questions and answers: "Chao-chou asked, 'What is Tao?' His master Nan-ch'uan answered, 'The mind in everyday life is Tao.'"[68] "The priest asked, 'What is the mind in everyday life?' His master answered, 'It is to sleep whenever necessary and to sit whenever necessary.' The priest said, 'I do not understand you.' Then the master said, 'It is to be cool when it is hot and warm when it is cold.'"[69]

The state of enlightenment is therefore none other than this actual world. A poem composed by Su Tung-p'o states that "Rain is falling at Mount Lu and the tides are full at Che-chiang bay." In other words, there is a unity in nature to be enjoyed. "Every day is a pleasant and good day for man."[70]

But the state of enlightenment seems externally to be indistinguishable from a state of ignorance. In the following questions and answers, this is shown very clearly and impressively.

> A priest: "What is Buddha?"
> Chao-Chou: "He is at Buddha's hall."
> A priest: "The Buddha at Buddha's hall is the Buddha image made of mud."
> Chao-Chou: "Yes, you are right."
> A priest: "Then what is the true Buddha?"
> Chao-Chou: "He is at Buddha's hall."[71]

The lesson here is that while the external appearance is not different in the states before and after enlightenment, the spiritual condition must be completely different from the state before enlightenment. When Chih-hsien was asked "What is enlightenment?" he answered, "It is the flute behind the dead tree" or "It is the eyes behind a skeleton."[72] These things are not lifeless. Those who have achieved enlightenment realize that truth can manifest the absolute light in things which seem unworthy or meaningless.[73] Zen monks, for example, expressed the state of enlightenment poetically by impressive examples.

The Chinese tend to regard nature as absolute existence. That they have seldom thought to manipulate nature may be the chief reason why scientifically the Chinese have lagged behind other countries in the modern world.

With their tendency to regard nature or actuality as absolute existence, the Chinese came to adopt an attitude of optimism. Believing that this world is a good place in which to live, they finally came to believe that perfect existence must exist in this world. Here, the idea of the "Sheng-jen" (sage) was established. He was the perfect person such as the Chou King or Confucius. The sage is not a god, but a man. However, he is in principle the ideal. In art, Wang I-chih (307?–365?) was called "the sage of writing" and Tu Fu "the sage of poetry." They were regarded as the perfect models of principle in art.[74]

One result of the Chinese identification of nature with man is that the long history of China has been comparatively peaceful. Undoubtedly there were wars in China. However, Derk Bodde, an American sinologue, notes that the military genius is praised and appreciated in Western literature much more than in Chinese literature, where the typical hero is the poor but virtuous scholar.

Similarly, as the Chinese seldom thought nature needed to be transformed by experimental manipulation in order to master her ways or laws, they were slow to develop natural science. That is perhaps the chief reason why scientifically China lagged behind other countries in the modern world. Leaders of the People's Republic of China recognize this fact and are trying to improve and develop natural science, although this may lead to a conflict with traditional values maintained by Taoist-minded people.

In some cases, however, conflict with traditional values prevents the development of technology. This is most conspicuous with the Jains of India, who prohibit killing animals and the use of any insecticide from a spirit of compassion toward all living creatures. They may not use animals for experiments; they may not even exploit marshes, because the enterprise will kill many small creatures living there. With the Sikhs and Parsis there are no such prohibitions, and that is why they have been ahead of others in the modernization of India. For Chinese, Japanese, and Koreans who profess Mahāyāna Buddhism, there is no problem of this kind.

If the Japanese are willing to accept the phenomenal world as Absolute, it is in part because of their disposition to lay a greater emphasis upon intuitive sensible concrete events than upon universals. It was characteristic of the religious views of the ancient Japanese that they believed spirits resided in things. They personified spirits other than those of human beings, considering them all as ancestral gods, and tended to view every spirit as a divine ghost. It is such a turn of thought that gave birth to the Shintō shrines, for in order to perform religious ceremonies the gods and spirits were fixed in certain specified places. The most primitive form of this practice consists in the invocation and worship of spirits in some specific natural object, as a mountain, a river, a forest, a tree, or a stone. Forms of worship of ancient times were generally of this character. Herein also lies the original significance of the "divine hedge"and "rock boundary."[75]

The belief that spirits reside in things gave birth to Shinto shrines, for in order to perform religious ceremonies the gods and spirits were fixed in certain specified places.

This way of thinking runs through the subsequent history of Shintōism down to the present day. "Nowhere is there a shadow in which a god does not reside: in peaks, ridges, pines, cryptomerias, mountains, rivers, seas, villages, plains, and fields, everywhere there is a god. We can receive the constant and intimate help of these spirits in our tasks."[76] Takasumi Senge, the priest of Shintōism of the Great Shrine of Izumo, praised such a pantheistic point of view as follows: "There is no place in which a god does not reside, even in the wild waves' eight hundred folds or in the wild mountain's bosom."[77]

But the Japanese identification of the Absolute with Nature is quite different from some Western and Indian identifications. Western thinkers, such as Spinoza, have tended toward the reduction of multiplicity to unity. They have tended to explain the existence and natures of finite things in terms of one ultimate causal factor. This trend has been shared by some Indian monist mystics also. On the contrary, Japanese thinkers tended to admit the absolute significance of the variety of phenomena in the natural world.

Divine and sentient surroundings

In the Vedānta philosophy that constitutes the main current in the philosophical tradition of India, natural surroundings were regarded as insentient (*acid*), although they are manifestations of the fundamental principle which is the spirit (*cid*). Now, in India, practically all the prominent and striking features of the countryside have come to be regarded as sacred, and in a sense are deified. In particular, prominent rocks or hills and stones remarkable for shape or situation have become the objects of a ritual worship that in its general character is similar throughout the country. For example, the śalāgrāma stone, a variety of black ammonite, is sacred to Viṣṇu.[78]

But the attitude of Indian poets was quite different. Kālidāsa says that man attains his true dignity only in realizing that he is not independent of and above the world that is not human: that ocean and the rivers, the mountains and the forests, the trees and flowers, the beasts and birds are as much conscious of a personal life as man, and therefore that they claim from him a recognition of their dignity and worth.[79] In the *Meghadūta*, all forms of Nature, from the sublimest mountain to the tiniest flower that blooms, have for Kālidāsa as conscious an individuality, as real a personal life, as men or gods. In the description of the route to be followed by the cloud, which we have already summarized above, the student will note how skillfully the poet has blended the portrayal of the various aspects of Nature with a delineation of the varying emotions of the human heart.[80]

In the Amaruśataka, "the plant and animal world plays an important part and is treated with much charm. Of flowers, the lotus is the most conspicuous. One stanza, for example, describes the day-lotuses as closing their calyx-eyes in the evening, because unwilling to see the sun, their spouse and benefactor, sink down bereft of his rays. Another describes with pathetic beauty the dream of a bee—'The night will pass, the fair dawn will come, the sun will rise, the lotuses will laugh!'"—while unseen from within the calyx, an elephant, alas! arrived to tear up the lotus plant.

"Various birds to which poetical myths are attached are frequently introduced as furnishing analogies to human life and love. The *cātaka,* which would rather die of thirst than drink aught but the raindrops from the cloud, affords an illustration of pride. The *cakora,* supposed to imbibe the rays of the moon, affords a parallel to the lover who with his eyes drinks in the beams of his beloved's face. The *cakravāka,* which, fabled to be condemned to nocturnal separation from his mate, calls to her with plaintive cry during the watches of the night, serves as an emblem of conjugal fidelity."[81]

In Japan, it was consciously asserted in later periods that everything in the natural world is divine. Relevant to such an idea was the conception prevalent in medieval Japan that even grass and trees have spirits and consequently are eligible for salvation. The idea that even the things of "no-heart" (the objects of nature that have no spirits) can become Buddhas, based upon the Tendai doctrines, was particularly emphasized in Japan.

The same idea constituted an important theme for study in the Japanese Tendai sect and was inherited also by the Nichiren sect. Nichiren (1222–82) sought the superiority of the *Hokke* (Lotus) *Sūtra* in its recognition of the eligibility of the grass and the trees to become Buddhas. There appear time and again among Japanese Buddhist writings the following lines: "When a Buddha, who has attained enlightenment, looks around the universe, the grass, trees, and lands, all become Buddhas." In *"Noh"* songs we often come across such an idea, which was taken for granted socially and religiously in those days. "The voice of Buddhahood of such a holy priest makes even the grass and trees predestined to become Buddhas. ... Even the grass and trees have attained the effect of becoming Buddhas being led by the power that mankind is bound to be reborn into the Pure Land only if they invoke the Buddha's name and practice nembutsu prayer.... Had it not been for the teachings of Buddhahood, the spirit of the decayed willow tree which is impermanent and soulless would not have attained the Buddhahood." ("*Yugyō Yanagi.*")

The oral tradition of the medieval Tendai sect of Japan pushed the idea of the grass and trees becoming Buddhas so far as to preach "the nonbecoming Buddhas of the grass and trees." According to this theory, everything is by nature a Buddha—that is to say, to attain enlightenment through ascetic practice is one and the same thing as being a Buddha without recourse to ascetic practice. Not only the grass and trees but also rivers,

In India prominent rocks or hills and stones remarkable for shape or situation have become objects of a ritual worship.

mountains, and the earth are themselves Buddhahood already possessed intact. There is no becoming a Buddha in the sense of coming to be something separate and different in nature. That is the reason why the non-becoming of Buddhahood was preached.[82] The logical conclusion of the acceptance of given reality is here definitely clearly crystallized.

Some Indian Buddhists also admit the spirituality of the grass and trees, along with the various schools of Indian philosophy that adopted such a view. But most of the Indian philosophies maintain that all living things attain the state of deliverance through enlightened intelligence (vidyā), and not that the grass and trees become Buddhas in their actual state, as they are.

Such a tendency of thinking as discussed above seems to be still effective among the Japanese, even in these days when the knowledge of natural science prevails. For instance, the Japanese generally use the honorific expression "o" prefixed to the names of various objects, as in the cases of "*o'cha*" (the honorific wording of tea) and "*o-mizu*" (the honorific wording of water). Probably there is no other nation on earth that uses an honorific expression prefixed to the names of everyday objects. This usage is not conceived to be anything extraordinary by the Japanese themselves. We should not regard it merely as an honorific expression but rather consider it as a manifestation of the way of thinking that seeks a *raison d'être* and sacredness in everything that exists. According to the comments made by Westerners, "everything is Buddha" to the minds of the Japanese.

Active exploitation of nature

The ancient Indians lacked a notion of order in the objective natural world. Since Indians emphasize the existence of a universal Being behind natural phenomena, they tend to minimize the distinction between these two kinds of existence, that is, between universal reality and things in the phenomenal world, so that they will not have to regard them as equally real. They also have a tendency to slight the distinction between things perceived directly and things perceived by means of inference and other secondary means of cognition.

Out of this cast of thought comes an imagination that ignores natural law. There is a tendency among the Indians, divested in general of the concept of a perceptible objective order, not to differentiate between the actual and the ideal, or between fact and fantasy. "If there were a place where the dreams of ideal existence cherished by mankind since primitive times were to be realized on earth, that place is India."[83]

The very rich and fanciful imagination characteristic of this way of thinking leads Indians to ignore the physical limitations of things in space and time. This tendency is particularly marked in the Mahāyāna scriptures and

A very rich and fanciful imagination characterizes Indian thinking.

the *Purāṇas*. Vimalakīrti in the *Vimalakīrti-nirdesa* is said to have welcomed 32,000 monks to his small room by means of his supernatural power. Once, when the Buddha Śākyamuni was preaching the *Saddharmapundarīka* (the Lotus Sūtra) at Mount Gṛdhrakūṭa, it is said that a tower, which was 500 *yojanas* high and 250 square *yojanas* at the base, decorated with jewels, and containing the holy relics of the entire *Tathāgata Prabhūta*, emerged from the earth all at once, and that from it voices praising the sermon of Śākyamuni and recognizing the authority of the *Saddharmapundarīka* were heard. In dealing with these fantasies, the Indians were not concerned about the contradictions that marked such fanciful descriptions of time and space. They ignored the laws of nature and remained unperturbed. Of course, something of the sort is common to all mythologies everywhere, but the Indian capacity for it is unrivaled. They say carelessly that big but finite numbers such as a million, or a billion, are "as many as the number of the sands of the Gangetic river." Thus the Indian mind will transcend the realm of experience, crushing and paralyzing ordinary powers of expression.

We seldom come across an attempt to describe or define in general terms the Hindu conception of nature as a whole, and its relation to mankind accurately. When we do, we are confronted with statements and beliefs which apparently are inconsistent both with one another and with any definite and settled cosmological ideas. We come upon the elusive and varying character of Hindu thought, which claims for itself the utmost liberty of speculation and fancy and is not troubled by demands for consistency or exactitude.

The ruling philosophical school of India denies the real existence of a world of nature in the thought that all the world is only *māyā*, "illusion." Therefore, any inquiry into the character or the structure of the world is ultimately unjustifiable as well as unproductive. Reason cannot be applied to the natural world—such was the attitude of Advaitins. But in order to live, men had to work on nature even in India. Thus the strange worship of the implements of trade or occupation came into existence, a practice which is observed more or less throughout India but is most prevalent where commerce has been most highly developed and organized. Its origin is probably to be traced to the influence of the trade guilds and the desire to provide for a distinct center of guild interest. We now have a situation in which "the tools which a man uses in his trade, the fire that warms him, the books out of which the school-boy learns his lessons, the pots with which the wife cooks the dinner, all have a part in this strange and elaborate deification, and become the objects of worship that is by no means confined to the lowest and most ignorant strata of the population."[84]

In the modern West, the necessity of modifying nature was keenly felt. According to Spinoza, "human beings act with an end in view. And this inclines them to interpret Nature in the light of themselves. If they do not know the cause or causes of some natural event," Spinoza says, "'nothing remains for them but to turn to themselves and reflect what could induce

The tools which a man uses in his trade, the fire that warms him, the books out of
which the school-boy learns his lessons, the pots with which the wife cooks the dinner,
all have a part in a strange and elaborate deification and become the objects of worship
that is by no means confined to the lowest and most ignorant of the population.

them personally to bring about such a thing, and thus they necessarily estimate other natures by their own.' Again, since they find many things in nature useful to them, men are inclined to imagine that these things must have been made for their use by a superhuman power. And when they find inconveniences in nature, like earthquakes and diseases, they attribute them to the divine displeasure. If it is pointed out that these inconveniences affect the pious and good as well as the impious and bad, they talk about the inscrutable judgments of God."[85]

The Chinese find this incomprehensible. Ch'en Tu-hsiu says:

> Man's happiness in life is the result of man's own effort and is neither
> the gift of God nor a spontaneous natural product. If it were the gift
> of God, how is it that He was so generous with people today and so
> stingy with people in the past? If it is a spontaneous, natural product,
> why is it that the happiness of the various peoples in the world is not
> uniform?[86]

The monks of Southern Asia did not want to be involved in productive work of any kind. They just practiced meditation without working physically. This attitude has been preserved throughout Asiatic countries except China and Japan. In China, wishing a dependable food supply, Zen priests began to cultivate fields attached to their own temples in the eighth century A.D. The motto, "if one does not work a day, one should not eat on that day," has become their favorite one. This motto has also been greatly encouraged by the Communist government under Mao Tse-tung.

In Japan monks of many sects went so far as to engage in such kinds of economic activity as constructing roads, resthouses, hospitals, ponds, harbors, and cultivating fields. Such philanthropic works were encouraged in Japan as rendering service to others, which was claimed to be the essence of Mahāyāna. For laymen, all sorts of productive work except slaying animals and selling wines or weapons were encouraged.

Exertion was encouraged by Master Dōgen as a fundamental virtue of man. He wrote:

> The great Way of the Buddha and the Patriarchs involves the highest
> form of exertion, which goes on unceasingly in cycles from the first
> dawning of religious truth, through the test of discipline and practice,
> to enlightenment and Nirvāna. It is sustained exertion . . . which is
> neither self-imposed nor imposed by others, but free and uncoerced.
> The merit of this exertion upholds me and upholds others. The truth
> is that the benefits of one's own sustained exertion are shared by all
> beings in the ten quarters of the world. . . . Buddhahood is realized,
> and those who do not make an exertion when exertion is possible are
> those who hate Buddha, hate serving the Buddha, and hate exertion;
> they do not want to live and die with Buddha, they do not want him as
> their teacher and companion. At this moment a flower blossoms, a leaf
> falls — it is a manifestation of sustained exertion. . . . Everything is

exertion. To attempt to avoid exertion is an impossible evasion, for the attempt itself is exertion. And to belabor oneself, because it is impossible to be otherwise than one is, is to be like the rich man's son who left home to seek his fortune, only to endure poverty in a foreign land.[87]

Utilizing and remodeling the natural world also is part of natural order, according to Ninomiya Sontoku. This creed, and the indefatigable labors of Ninomiya to rescue his fellow farmer from the vagaries of nature, won for him the affectionate title, "Peasant Sage of Japan." "A popular ivory image of Sontoku represents him as a hard-working and affable youth with a happy, smiling face. But a wooden portrait kept in his home and a drawing now placed in the Ninomiya shrine at Odawara represent him as a man of rugged physique and rough features, with a look of unshakable determination. This is the man to whom shrines have been built in the rural districts around modern Tokyo.

"At first glance it might seem hard to reconcile Ninomiya's deep sense of gratitude to nature with his constant emphasis on the need for planning against natural vagaries. But to his mind the seeming irregularities of nature are in no way arbitrary or capricious. Natural calamities indeed occur without regard to immediate human desires, but they are aspects of an inexorable natural order that works ultimately for the good of man, providing man does his share. Man cannot rescue himself from the miseries of a hazardous livelihood by crying out against nature. He must instead be ready to understand the conditions set by Nature, and take them into account in the planning of his life. This requires, above all and before all, the virtue of honesty (*shisei*), which to Ninomiya meant not only a recognition of law and order in human relationships but also a wholehearted acceptance of the order of Nature."[88]

It also requires effort. "One of the things which must be accepted as a law of the universe is the necessity for human labor," Ninomiya writes. "Hard work is just as much a part of the natural order as the rising and setting of the sun or the alternation of the seasons. Every year, every month, every day and every hour has an incalculable value to the forwarding of human life."[89] This is as much as to say that hard work fulfills nature's own plan. But Ninomiya stresses the maximum utilization of nature's gifts without accepting that man should seek to dominate or exploit nature. Thus, in contrast to Satō Nobuhiro, he thinks not in terms of technological progress but of fulfilling nature's own plan through rational management and human industry.

The best thing for a man to do is to cultivate rice, Ninomiya says. "Now rice culture follows the seasons. Seeding starts at the end of spring, and transplanting, hoeing, fertilizing, and other [tasks are done] in the summer. When the rice is ripe in autumn, it is cut and taken in before winter arrives. After threshing, apportionment of the grain is made so that there will be enough for needs throughout the year, avoiding excess now and deficiency later. This is the quickest way to get rice to eat," Ninomiya insists. "Though some might consider it too long a process, [he assures us] that there is no other proper way to obtain rice for the people. If you work hard and faithfully at this great task, you will be free from hunger and starvation from generation to generation. Do not ask for any short cut. In the final analysis, Heaven has its own natural way of doing things, and in order to obtain rice the only proper procedure is to cultivate rice plants. In the cultivation of rice plants, too, there is a proper procedure, with the sowing of seeds. Remember that rice plants never produce rice plants, and rice seeds never produce rice seeds. First the seeds must grow into plants and then the plants produce seeds. From the beginning of creation there has always been this endless process of transformation and transmigration."[90]

Human nature

The term *nature* often means "human nature," by which may be meant any or all of the human instincts, desires, appetites, and drives. A "natural" man may also be regarded as one who is uncultured or undisciplined and thus inferior. This last notion is, however, foreign to the Japanese, as they accept external and objective nature for what it is, so are they inclined to accept man's natural desires and sentiments for what they are, and do not strive to repress or fight against them.

For example, love was the favorite theme of ancient Japanese poetry. Love among the ancient Japanese was sensual and unrestrained, an expression of the true meaning of life. In general, their sentiments were direct and open, without suppression. This tendency underwent transformations which varied according to historical period and social class, but it remained a relatively distinctive characteristic of most of the people. Japanese poetry is accordingly rich in love poems and seems vastly different from the general tendency of the poetry of the Indians or the Chinese.

In ancient China there were also some love songs included in the Book of Poetry (Shih Ching), but later Confucianists did not want to admit that they were love songs and explained them away in this fashion: "These are not really love poems. They are poems composed by ancient sages to administer good politics, just using allusions to love affairs. They are political, not love songs."

Moto-ori Norinaga (1730–1801), the great scholar of Japanese classics, laughed at this moralistic attitude of the Chinese Confucianists. He recognized the distinction between the Japanese and the Chinese in this respect: "The fact that the Book of Poetry (Shih Ching) lacks love poems reveals something of the customs of the people of that country (China). They only make an outward show of manly appearance, concealing the womanishness of their real selves. In contrast, the abundance of love poems in our empire reveals the way to express one's genuine dispositions."[91]

In India, too, there is an abundance of love poems, but the Indians in general sought an ultimate and absolute meaning beyond the passions of love, which many of them were taught to annihilate. So the acceptance of natural love may be taken as a distinguishing characteristic of the Japanese compared with most of the other civilized peoples of Asia.

This tendency affects the Japanese way of adopting foreign cultures. The ethical theories of Confucianism tended originally to asceticism, which was no doubt inherited by the Japanese Confucianists. Among them, however, there were those who tried to accept man's natural dispositions. *The Tale of Genji* and *The Tale of Ise* were the favorite reading of such Confucian scholars as Ogyū Sorai (1666–1728) and Hori Keizan (1688–1757). Ogyū recognized the intrinisic value of these old literary works, a value that should not be obscured by their erotic contents. He also maintained that since poetry expressed natural feelings, the farfetched moralizing on the poems by the Chinese critics was not relevant. In this respect his attitude is in conformity with that of the scholars of Japanese classics.

Dazai Shundai (1680–1747) called man's natural feelings the only genuine ones, which he listed as "likes and dislikes, suffering and rejoicing, anxiety and pleasure, etc." He maintains that "there is not a single human being devoid of these feelings. For the noble or the low, there is no difference in this respect. Love of one's parents, wives, and children is also the same for all. Since these feelings originate from an innate truthfulness, never stained with falsity, they are called genuine feelings."[92] His point of view is that of pure naturalism.

For Dazai, there are no double-dealings in actions that flow from natural dispositions, wherein the inside and outside are so transparent that they are one and the same thing. The natural dispositions are the innate true nature of man. Those actions done without being taught, without learning, without force but with freedom from all thoughts, are the work of the natural dispositions. In the social realm there are certain regulations of conduct, to which one should conform. But within one's inner self, one can think whatever one pleases. Thus, according to the way of saints, one is said to be a man of noble character only if one does not act against propriety but "observes decorum concerning the body (regardless of) whether or not one sees a woman and imagines her lasciviously and takes delight in her beauty. That is exactly what it means to discipline one's mind through proper decorum."[93]

Apparently this is a metamorphosis of Confucianism in Japan, discarding the traditional attitude of the ancient Chinese Confucianism, which refused to interpret the love poems of the *Book of Poetry* as such and tried instead to interpret them as political and moral lessons. Dazai, the Japanese Confucianist, defiantly declared: "I would rather be a master of acrobatic feats, than a moralist."[94]

As to the proper behavior of a married couple, Chinese Confucianism taught that one should discriminate between man and wife, according to hierarchical order. Japanese Confucianists like Nakae Tōju (1608–48), however, emphasized rather the harmony of husband and wife. "The husband should be righteous, while the wife should be obedient, and when both are in this manner in perfect harmony, that is the meaning of the way of discrimination."[95] More generally, Hirata Atsutane (1776–1843), a nationalist who had little use for Chinese thought in general, nevertheless said:

> Anyone knows perfectly well by Nature, without borrowing others' teachings, that gods, the lords, and parents are respectable and the wife and children lovable. Teachings of the way of humanity, complex as they appear to be, do in fact originate from this simple fact. To illustrate this with a near-by example, our country-men are by nature brave, just, and straight, and that is what we call *Yamato-gokoro* (the spirit of Japan) or *Mikuni-damashii* (the soul of our country). ... Since the True Way is as facile a matter as this, one should indeed stop acting like a sage and completely abandon the so-called mind or the way of enlightenment. Let us, instead, not distort or forget this spirit of Japan, the soul of this country, but train and regulate it so that we may polish it up into a straight, just, pure, and good spirit of Japan.[96]

This naturalistic and nationalistic tendency represents also the Japanese mode of accepting Buddhism. Onkō (Jiun Sonja: 1718–1804), a Buddhist of the modern period, to whom credit should be given for propagating Buddhism among the common people, preached that morality means to follow man's natural dispositions. Onkō accepted these dispositions, but he also emphasized man's ability to control his lower desires and sentiments. And while it is true that the Ritsu sect, with its 250 precepts, was introduced into Japan, its ascetic practice never became as widespread as it was in India and China. (Incidentally, these ascetic practices are still observed today in Sri Lanka, Burma, Thailand, Cambodia, and Laos.) On the whole, Japanese Buddhism inclined toward peaceful and quiet enjoyment. The practice of prayer, for instance, was an occasion for the aristocrats of the Heian period to enjoy sensory pleasure. For them, a Buddhist mass conducted in this world was already the Pure Land of Paradise. In fact, it meant merely "to have a pleasant evening." Such a tendency finally led to the repudiation of disciplines, a step especially popular among the followers of Pure Land Buddhism. Thus it was said:

> Those who practice the invocation of Amitābha alone, say that by playing the game of *go* (checkers) or that of *sugoroku* (a kind of backgammon) they do not violate any of their teachings. Clandestine sexual relation or the eating of meat is no hindrance to rebirth into the Pure Land. The observance of disciplines in the age of degeneration is the tiger in the street. That ought to be dreaded; that ought to be detested. Should one be afraid of sins and shrink from

evils, such a one would certainly be a man who never believes in the Buddha.[97]

The tendency to ignore the disciplines seemed also to be evident within the Zen sect. The *Nomori Kagami* (literally, Field-watch Mirror), by Fujiwara-no-Arifusa, 1294, has the following passage of rebuke: "By abusing the precedents of those who had attained enlightenment and by taking wine, meat, the five spices, etc., even those who have not yet attained that stage dare do the same shamelessly."

It is a well-known fact that, after Japan opened to the world in 1868, practically all the sects of Japanese Buddhism broke away from the disciplines. As a result, for the followers of Pure Land Buddhism, it is enough only to invoke Amitābha; for the followers of the Nichiren sect, it is enough only to chant the title of the Lotus Sūtra; for some of the other sects, it is enough only to chant certain sūtras and to repeat prayers (dhāranīs).

The outstanding repudiation of the disciplines is of drinking. The Indian Buddhists considered drinking a very serious religious sin. That was why "no drinking" was counted among the five precepts and was ordained to be strictly observed not only by priests and ascetics but also by lay believers in general. In India the discipline of no drinking was well observed from the time of early Buddhism to that of Mahāyāna Buddhism. (The late degenerate period of esoteric Buddhism was an exception.) In China also, this discipline was strictly observed, but upon arrival in Japan, it was abandoned.

Together with drinking, sexual relations between men and women also had their place in Buddhism in Japan. A novel such as *The Tale of Genji* (ca. 1000) describes lascivious scenes and immoral characters, considered however to be not lacking in beauty. This is characteristic of Japanese literature, which in that respect is inconsistent with ethical Confucianism. The same can be said of Japanese Buddhism. Toward the period of the degeneration of Buddhism in India, certain immoral rituals were practiced by some Buddhists, but among the Buddhists in China such a thing almost never occurred. Even esoteric Buddhism was transmitted into China in its purified form, which was then transplanted by Kūkai into Japan. The Japanese followers of the Shingon sect, founded by Kūkai (Kōbō Daishi, 774–835), kept their purity in the daily practice of asceticism. Toward the end of the Heian period there emerged a heretical religion in the Tachikawa group which identified sexual intercourse with the secret meaning of becoming a Buddha alive in the human body. Such licentious secret rituals soon disappeared, however.

Even now, Shōten (Ganeśa) and Aizen Myō-ō (The God of Love) are widely worshiped as objects of popular religion for the consummation of love. Shōten, or the God of Ecstasy, who was originally Ganeśa in India, was adopted and metamorphosed by the esoteric Buddhists. The images of Gaṇeśa now existent in India, in contrast, are by no means obscene; the religious custom of worshiping the images of the elephant-faced god and goddess in an embrace is confined perhaps to Japan, Mongolia, and Tibet only.

In a similar manner, entirely different meanings were bestowed upon those phrases which originally signified the fundamental ideas of Buddhism. For example, pairs of lovers in Japan once practiced a special kind of suicide called shinjū. When their love was not permitted by their parents or their superiors, they committed suicide together as a consummation, the supreme and genuine form of expression of their love. The famous playwright Chikamatsu Monzaemon (1653–1724), describing lovers on their way to commit suicide, celebrates the beauty of their last moments as follows: "Adieu to this world, adieu to the night ... The remaining one toll is the last sound of the bell they hear on earth; 'tranquility is comfort' is its sound."[98] Shinjū is a phenomenon peculiar to Japan; it is impossible to convey its real sentiment with such Western translations as a "lovers' double suicide" or "Selbstmord eines Liebespaares." In any case, whereas in both India and China the phrase "tranquility is comfort" (*vyupaśamah sūkham*) meant originally the denial of worldly afflictions, it is now used in Japan for expressing the consummation of sexual love. The various literary works of the Tokugawa period (from 1603 to 1867) show that the words which originally stood for the sacred ideas of Buddhism came to be used cryptically to suggest scenes of lust and dissipation. Such instances of sacrilege never occurred either in India or in China, where most persons try to distinguish the world of religion from that of the flesh. But there is a latent tendency among the Japanese to identify the one with the other. In this way the same characteristics that mark the form in which Confucianism was accepted are also said to mark the acceptance in Japan of Buddhism.

Even the traditional and conservative Buddhists in India were aware of the fact that the disciplines are hard to observe strictly in their original form, and that they undergo changes according to differences of time and place. The possibility of modification was admitted in the *Book of Disciplines:* "The Buddha announced to the various monks, 'Although these disciplines are prescribed by me, it is not necessary that you should practice them all, if you find them not pure (not adequate or applicable) in other districts. As to the disciplines that are not established by me, you should not hesitate to practice them all, if it is necessary to do so in other districts.' "[99]

In spite of these concessions made by the Buddha, the Japanese are probably the only Asiatic people who have forsaken almost all of the Buddhist disciplines. How should we account for this fact?

Since olden days there has been a strong tendency among the Japanese to hold fast to a specific and closed social nexus or a community. The repudiation of disciplines may seem on the surface to be incompatible with such a tendency, but the two are not necessarily in conflict. Religious disciplines are not always in agreement with customary morality. Quite prevalent among the Japanese are dual attitudes that ignore the disciplines on the one hand and produce self-sacrificing devotion to the interests of the closed social nexus or community on the other. Such attitudes gave rise to the idea that the assertion of natural desires and the abandonment of the disciplines do not necessarily mean the abandonment of the moral order.

The state of man redeemed and unredeemed

In Christianity, "nature" means "the state of man unredeemed by grace." In Buddhism, especially in the Jōdo Shin sect of Japan, "natural" means the Way for Deliverance. When we realize the mercy of Amitābha Buddha, when we realize the warmth and the sternness of life, there remains no other way of living than praising the Buddha. The Nembutsu comes forth effortlessly and spontaneously through our lips. This is what Shinran meant when he said:[100] "At any rate, for rebirth in the Pure Land, cleverness is not necessary—just complete and unceasing absorption in gratitude to Amida. Only then does the Nembutsu come forth effortlessly. This is what is meant by naturalness." This statement may be likened to an exclamation, "Oh, what a mystic life!" or "Oh, what a wonderful world!" Shinran says elsewhere, "To call the Nembutsu is to praise Buddha."

According to Hōnen, the true way of passing our earthly life is to live so that we may naturally call the Nembutsu. "You must," he says, "do away with all that may hold you from calling the Nembutsu. If you cannot recite the Nembutsu because you live single, be married and call it. If you cannot say the Nembutsu because you are married, be divorced and say it. If you feel unable to recite the Nembutsu because you are settled in one place, go from one place to another and recite it. If you cannot voice the Nembutsu because you are travelling, fix your abode and voice it. If you cannot call the Nembutsu because you have to earn a living, beg and call it. If you are incapable of reciting the Nembutsu because you are alone, recite it with your friends. If you feel it is hard to say the Nembutsu because you are joined with your fellow seekers, go into your own room and say it."

If we allow ourselves to interpret Naturalness in our own way, it means living to the best of our ability, in whatever place we live, so that we may be able to call the Nembutsu, to harmonize ourselves with the circumstances in which we live and also with the work in which we daily engage, and to feel unified with the world which surrounds us—these are the applications of the idea of naturalness (*Jinen-Hōni*) to our daily life.[101]

When this idea is realized, neither self-centeredness nor consciousness of duty infects our service to society. We remain thoroughly natural, and the naturalness lends itself to the construction of a peaceful society. Our life, which embraces *karma,* is now transcending the *karma.* We are choosing a great freedom wholly different from the small freedom preferred by our small self. When we love unmindful of how other people think of us, our life acquires the flavor of exquisite art and becomes a most suitable gift to Nature. No one regards enjoyment as a despicable thing once it becomes the natural state of mind named *Jinen-Hōni*. This is the life of perfect freedom. It is the way of spiritual liberation for ordinary people, not the Way of Saints.

Conclusions—contemporary implications

According to Buddhist philosophy, men constitute just one class of living beings. As such, they have no right to unlimited use of natural resources. Also, men have no right to unlimited exploitation of animal and plant life, which forms part of Nature. Until recently, Westerners or moderns tended to think that men were quite separate and different from the natural world. This assumption is ungrounded and unreasonable. It has brought about devastation. Now men incur retaliation by nature.

In order to deal with the difficult situation that has come about, we must seek a solution that is both objective and subjective. On the objective side, we must discard the arrogance of supposing that men are entitled to exploit the natural world at their own will, without limit and regardless of the consequences. It is not appropriate to maintain the idea of "conquering nature." Nature should be met with affection. In this connection, we emphasize that the world of nature should not be monopolized by a few countries. The whole natural world should be shared by all mankind. We cannot but feel anger at the small, limited number of countries which totally control the reserves of a limited energy supply, and which are extravagantly wasting what nature has entrusted to them. Just as individual egoism must be curtailed and placed under control, so national and ethnic egoism also should be restrained in the name of justice and respect for nature.

On the subjective side, there is need for correction of the opinion of moderns that the progress of mankind consists in the unlimited satisfaction of human desire for material objects. Buddhism taught satisfaction with what is given to men. "To know being satisfied" was thought to be the way to spiritual happiness. The key to the relationship between man and the environment may very well lie in the control of our desires according to this concept of satisfaction. For that purpose our desire should be scaled to the possibilities of nature conceived as supporting human existence. Nature is not an entity to confront as if it were quite different from us; it is something to embrace, as we might that from which we cannot separate. Admitting the distinction between man and nature, we have to think how to live with the knowledge that nature is necessary to us.

[1] *The Concise Encyclopedia of Living Faiths,* ed. R. C. Zaehner (New York: Hawthorn Books, Inc., 1959), p. 210.

[2] Arthur Anthony Macdonell, *Lectures on Comparative Religion* (University of Calcutta, 1925), p. 60.

[3] Arthur Anthony Macdonell, *A History of Sanskrit Literature* (New Delhi: Motilal Bunarsidass, 1971), p. 64.

[4] Ibid., pp. 64–65.

[5] Ibid., p. 66.

[6] Bertrand Russell, *A History of Western Philosophy,* fifth printing (New York: Simon and Schuster, 1945), p. 204.

[7] *Manyō-shū,* vols. 4; 6. Genchi Kato, *Shinto no Shūkyō Hattatushi teki Kenkyu* (Tokyo Chubunkan, 1935), pp. 38 f.

[8] Genchi Kato, pp. 38 f.

[9] Cf. Friedrich Max Müller, *India, What Can It Teach Us? A course of lectures delivered before the University of Cambridge* (London: Longmans, 1910), Lecture VI, pp. 189–92. Other instances of this kind are mentioned in this work.

[10] H. and H. A. Frankfurt, John A. Wilson, Th. Jacobson, *Before Philosophy; The Intellectual Adventure of Ancient Man. An essay on speculative thought in the Ancient Near East* (Middlesex: 1956; A Pelican Book), pp. 12–13.

[11] *Ṛgveda,* VI, 51, 5 etc.

[12] Discussed by T'ang Chun-i (The T'ien ming /Heavenly Ordinance/ in Be-Chin China, *Philosophy East and West,* vol. XI, no. 4, January 1962, pp. 195–218). Homer H. Dubs tries to find theism in pre-Han China ("Theism and Naturalism in Ancient Chinese Philosophy," *Philosophy East and West,* vol. IX, nos. 3 and 4, October 1959–January 1960, pp. 145–62).

[13] Hermann Oldenberg, *Ancient India: Its Language and Religions* (Chicago, London: Open Court Publishing Company, 1896), p. 71.

[14] Śaṅkara ad *Brahmasūtrabhāsya* I, 3, 28. Ānadāsrama Sanskrit Series, No. 21 (Poona: Anandasrama Press, 1900). Cf. Richard Garbe, *The Philosophy of Ancient India* (Chicago: The Open Court, 1899), p. 36.

[15] *Dīghanikāya* II, 88 f, in T. W. Rhys Davids, *Dialogues of the Buddha,* ii (Pali Text Society; 1910), pp. 93 f.

[16] M. Winternitz, *A History of Indian Literature,* vol. I (University of Calcutta, 1927), p. 7.

[17] A. A. Macdonell, *A History of Sanskrit Literature,* pp. 298–99.

[18] Ibid., p. 235.

[19] M. R. Kale, *The Meghadūta of Kālidāsa,* 6th ed. (Bombay: Booksellers' Publishing Co., n.d.), p. 14.

[20] A. A. Macdonell, *A History of Sanskrit Literature,* pp. 284–85.

[21] Ibid., p. 289.

[22] Cf. Yaichi Haga, *Kokuminsei Jūron* (Ten Lectures on the National Character) (Tokyo: Fuzambo, 1907), pp. 91 ff.

[23] R. H. Blyth, *Cultural East,* I (1947), p. 45.

[24] Dōgen, *Shōbōgenzō, Hotsumujōshin* (Manifestation of the Supreme Mind).

[25] A. S. Geden, "Nature (Hindu)," *Encyclopaedia of Religion and Ethics,* 3d ed., ed. James Hastings (Edinburgh: T. and T. Clark; New York: Charles Scribner's Sons, 1953), vol. IX, p. 232b.

[26] *Biographies of High Priests,* III (*Taishō Tripitaka,* Tokyo: Daizō Shuppan Kabushiki Kaisha, 1927), vol. 50, p. 341 a.

[27] In Egypt, truth and righteousness were personified as goddess *Maat,* the daughter of *Ra* and the wife of *Dhuti,* god of intelligence. This can be compared to *ṛta.* Cf. John B. Noss, *Man's Religions* (New York: Macmillan, 1956), p. 52.

[28] Mircea Eliade, *Images and Symbols. Studies in Religious Symbolism,* translated by Philip Mairet (New York: Sheed and Ward, 1961), p. 98.

[29] A. A. Macdonell, *Comparative Religion,* p. 62.

[30] *Ṛgveda,* IX, 121, 1; X, 37, 5.

[31] *Gorgias* 507–8, translated by Jowett (vol. II, p. 400) [*GBWW*, Vol. 7, p. 284 d].

[32] "The conception of natural or cosmic laws dominated the thought of common people even in recent times. Professor de Groot saw a boy with hare-lip, and this was explained to him by the father; who said that the mother of the boy had, during her pregnancy, accidentally made a cut in an old coat of the father's she was mending. Professor de Groot brings this brief under demonology. But is this really correct? There is not a word in the story, as he tells it, about any demon. Surely the only conclusion we are justified in drawing is that the Chinese father believed that given x, y would follow, and it would follow of itself. What is this but recognition of a law, a rule? (de Groot, *Religion of the Chinese* [New York, 1910], p. 12). We may not agree with it. The rule may seem to us foolishness. But we must add in simple justice to the Chinese father that similar ideas about experiences of a pregnant mother affecting the child are quite solemnly discussed in Europe at the present day. And the validity of the rule is not here in question. The point is that people believe that the event in question takes place without intervention of any soul or god." Cited from T. W. Rhys Davids, *Lectures on the Origin and Growth of Religion as Illustrated by Some Points in the History of Indian Buddhism* (London: Williams and Norgate, 1881), pp. 279–89.

[33] T. W. Rhys Davids, *Cosmic Law in Ancient Thought;* Proceedings of the British Academy, 1917–1918 (Rhys Davids, *Dialogues of the Buddha*, pp. 279–89).

[34] Of the pre-Buddhistic *Upanishads* it occurs only in one, the *Taittiriya*. In the peroration to that work Ṛta is placed above, before the gods. The word occurs, it is true, in three or four isolated passages of post-Buddhistic works, but these are archaisms. It has not been traced in either the Buddhist or the Jain canonical literature. (Rhys Davids.)

[35] *The Seventeen Article Constitution*, Article III.

[36] Joseph J. Spae, *Itō Jinsai* (Peiping: Catholic University of Peking, 1948), p. 205.

[37] W. T. De Bary et al., eds., *Sources of Japanese Tradition* (New York: Columbia University Press, 1958), p. 342.

[38] Joseph Spae, p. 205.

[39] Masaharu Anesaki, *A History of Japanese Religion*, (Rutland, Vt., and Tokyo: Charles E. Tuttle, 1963), p. 301.

[40] Ishida Baigan, *Seiri Mondō, Dialogue on Human Nature and Natural Order*, translated by Paolo Beonio-Brocchieri (Rome: Instituto per il Medio ed Estremo Oriente, 1961), p. 43.

[41] Ibid., p. 44.

[42] Ibid., p. 56.

[43] Ibid., p. 33.

[44] Ibid., p. 60.

[45] John Laidlaw Atkinson, "The Ten Buddhistic Virtues (Jūzen Hōgo)." A sermon preached in 1773 by Katsuragi Jiun. *Transactions of the Asiatic Society of Japan*, vol. XXXIII, 1905, pt. 2.

[46] Harald Hoffding, *A History of Modern Philosophy: A Sketch of the History of Philosophy from the Close of the Renaissance to Our Own Day*, translated from the German edition by B. E. Meyer (Dover Publications, 1955), vol. 1, p. 54.

[47] Jūzen Hōgo, p. 55.

[48] Jiun, *Jūzen Hōgo*, ed. Takuichi Kinami (Kyoto: Sanmitsudo Shoten, 1973), p. 41.

[49] De Bary et al., *Sources of Japanese Tradition*, p. 487.

[50] The ideogram *T'ien* is derived from the letter *Ta* by adding a line on the top. *Ta* is a hieroglyph which originally meant man. Therefore, one may imagine that this ideogram *T'ien* indicates the sky which is above man.

[51] Yoshio Takeuchi, *Shina Shisōshi*, (Tokyo: Iwanami Press, 1936), p. 9.

[52] Fung Yu-lan, *A Short History of Chinese Philosophy* (New York: Macmillan, 1958), pp. 44f.; cf. A. Forke, *Yang Chu's Garden of Pleasures*, and J. Legge, *The Chinese Classics*, II, pp. 92–99.

[53] *Hsin-hsin-ming* (Epigrams of Faith).

[54] The *Liu-Tsu Ta-shin fa-pao-f'an ching* (Jewelled Altar Sūtra, by the Sixth Patriarch) in Hakuji Ki, *Daini Zenshu-shi Kenkyū* (Tokyo: Iwanami Press, 1935), p. 149.

[55] Frederic Spiegelberg, *Zen, Rocks, and Waters* (New York: Random House, 1961), p. 19.

[56] De Bary et al., *Sources of Japanese Tradition*, pp. 367–68.

[57] Ibid., p. 377.

[58] Ibid., p. 366.

[59] Hakuju Ki, *A Study of Japanese Tendai Buddhism,* translated by Kansai Tamura, *Philosophical Studies of Japan,* The Japanese National Commission for UNESCO, vol. I, p. 69.

[60] Shōbō Genzō, Uji, *The Sōtō Approach to Zen,* translated by Reiho Masunaga (Tokyo: Layman Buddhist Society Press, 1958), pp. 82–83.

[61] Ibid., pp. 88–89.

[62] *Sāṃkhya-Kārikā* 3.

[63] E. Gilson, *History of Christian Philosophy in the Middle Ages* (New York: Random House, 1955), pp. 115–16.

[64] Richard Garbe, pp. 47f.

[65] The *San-lun* hsuan-i, 25.

[66] The *Tun-wu-ju-tao-men-lun,* 86.

[67] The *Hsin-hsin*-ming.

[68] The *Wu*-men-kuan, Chapter 19.

[69] The *Ching-te ch'uan-teng lu,* X (*Taishō Tripitaka,* vol. LI, p. 275a).

[70] The *Cheng-tao-ko.*

[71] The *Ching-te ch'uan-teng lu,* X, (*Taishō Tripitaka,* vol. LI, p. 277c).

[72] Ibid., XI (*Taisho,* LI, p. 284b).

[73] Ibid., SVII (*Taisho,* LI, p. 337a).

[74] Kōjiro Yoshikawa, *Chinese Classics and View of Life* (in Japanese; Tokyo: Chikuma Shobo, 1947), p. 28.

[75] Hajime Nakamura, *Ways of Thinking of Eastern Peoples* (Honolulu: East-West Center Press, 1964), p. 350.

[76] Yōkyoku, Ōyashiro (A Noh Song entitled "The Great Shrine").

[77] Hajime Nakamura, pp. 350–351.

[78] A. S. Geden, p. 233a.

[79] M. R. Kale: *Meghadūta,* p. 13.

[80] Ibid., p. 14.

[81] Arthur A. Macdonell, A History of Sanskrit Literature, p. 289.

[82] Hakuju Ui, *Bukkyō Hanron,* (In Japanese, *An Outline of Buddhism;* Tokyo: Iwanami Press, 1948), vol. II, p. 337.

[83] Romain Rolland, *La vie de Ramakrishna* (Paris, 1920), p. 31.

[84] A. S. Geden, *Studies in the Religions of the East,* pp. 406 f.

[85] Frederick Copleston, *A History of Philosophy,* vol. 4, p. 233.

[86] De Bary et al., *Sources of Chinese Tradition,* p. 831.

[87] *Shōbō Genzō,* Gyōji (De Bary et al., *Sources of Japanese Tradition,* p. 243–45).

[88] *Sources of Japanese Tradition,* compiled by Ryusaku Tsunoda, William Theodore de Bary, and Donald Keene (Columbia University Press, 1858), p. 579.

[89] De Bary, *Sources of Japanese Tradition,* p. 74.

[90] Ibid., p. 584.

[91] *Tamakatsuma* X.

[92] Deizai-roku (Essays on Economy), I, fol. 10.

[93] Ibid.

[94] *Gakusoku* 7.

[95] *Okina Mondō.*

[96] *Kodō Taii* 3.

[97] *Kōfukuji Sōjō.*

[98] *Sonezaki Shinjū.*

[99] *Shibunritsu* XXIII (*Taishō Tripitaka,* XXII, 153a).

[100] In the latter part of the *Tannishō.*

[101] Kenryo Kanamatsu, *Naturalness* (Los Angeles: The White Path Society, 1956), p. 133.

NOTE TO THE READER

Readers accustomed to Western terms will realize that in the Indian and Japanese traditions of which Professor Nakamura speaks, the idea of nature is difficult to distinguish from the ideas of God, of man, of art, and of morality, with each of which it tends to merge. The significance of this will be apparent if we recall the discussion in Chapter 60 of the *Syntopicon*, NATURE, where the point is made that the meaning of that term in our tradition is not so much in what it conveys by itself but is a function of the difference we feel there is, or that ages before our own felt there was, between it and other terms. In our tradition, God, man, nature, and art are with certain exceptions (which the chapter acknowledges) concepts so different that they cannot possibly be taken for one another; indeed, they derive their force as ideas precisely from that fact. And each one *has* force, as an idea, that it does not have, or does not appear to have, in the traditions of the East, where the conceptual differences which have been so important to us are regarded as unsophisticated or mistaken. This would seem the real distinction to be made between East and West in this matter, as Professor Nakamura himself implies in his long essay.

Among the relevant topics in the *Syntopicon* chapter mentioned above are 1*b*, where authors who nevertheless identify God, nature, and man (chief among them Spinoza, who is discussed, appropriately, by Professor Nakamura) are considered; Topics 2*a* and 2*b*, where the antithesis between nature and art and between nature and convention are discussed; Topics 5*a*, where readings on the subject of human nature are listed, and 5*d*, where passages dealing with nature as providing a canon of beauty for production or judgment are to be found; and Topics 6*a* and 6*b*, which deal with nature in relation to religion and theology.

Readers who own *Gateway to the Great Books* will find many short pieces worth reading in connection with Professor Nakamura's essay. Among them are Emerson, "Nature," Vol. 10, pp. 512–24; J. H. Fabre, "A Laboratory of the Open Fields: the Sacred Beetle," Vol. 8, pp. 97–119; J. B. S. Haldane, "On Being the Right Size," Vol. 8, pp. 148–54; Rudyard Kipling, "Mowgli's Brothers," Vol. 2, pp. 126–41; and Mark Twain, "Learning the River," from *Life on the Mississippi*, Vol. 6, pp. 50–98.

PART FOUR

Additions
to the
Great Books Library

Selected Essays

Arthur Schopenhauer

Editor's Introduction

The essays reprinted here are taken from the book which was the first to win any fame for Schopenhauer during his lifetime. When it appeared in 1851, under the title *Parerga and Paralipomena: Short Philosophical Essays,* he was already sixty-three years old and his major work, to which he owes his place in the history of philosophy, had been published thirty-three years before. *The World As Will and Idea* was first written in the years 1814–18, then later enlarged and published in a second edition in 1844. Neither edition attracted the slightest attention from either the learned world or the public at large. Yet the essays reprinted here, expressly called "Supplements and Remnants," and meant to be subsidiary to the earlier work, immediately won him worldwide attention. They called forth new editions of Schopenhauer's previous work, gave rise to courses in his philosophy in universities abroad as well as in Germany, and provided new inspiration for writers and artists; Wagner claimed that his opera *Tristan und Isolde* embodied musically Schopenhauer's theory of the world. Thus, from 1851 until his death in 1860, Schopenhauer enjoyed the fame that he had always desired and was convinced that he deserved.

By his early education he was a citizen of Europe. His father, of Dutch as well as German ancestry, was a rich merchant of Danzig, where his son, Arthur, was born February 22, 1788. When the city came under Prussian absolutism in 1793, the family moved to the free city of Hamburg. At the age of ten the boy was sent to live for two years with one of his father's business friends at Le Havre in order to learn the French language. Later he accompanied his parents on a prolonged tour of Belgium, England, France, Switzerland, and Austria. While in London, he attended school for several months, and, although hating school, did acquire English so that in later years he was a regular subscriber to "The Times." Acceding to his father's wishes, he reluctantly entered upon a business apprenticeship in Hamburg but abandoned this in 1805 upon his father's sudden death (apparently a suicide). His mother, a novelist, then moved with Schopenhauer's sister to Weimar, where she established a salon and joined the social circle of the poets Goethe and Wieland. Schopenhauer himself remained in Hamburg for a time, studying the classics, literature, and music, and then in 1807 joined his mother at Weimar, where he completed his preparatory studies for the university.

In 1809 he began his university career, matriculating at first as a medical student at Göttingen but soon transferring into the humanities. It was here that he began the study of Plato and Kant and discovered his vocation to philosophy. In 1811 he went to the University of Berlin, then the philosophical center of Germany. There he attended lectures of Fichte and Schleiermacher, but considered them of little worth, and preferred the lectures on classical philology and the natural sciences. In 1813, upon the completion of his dissertation, he received the degree of doctor of philosophy from the University of Jena.

From 1813 through 1819 he was engaged in pursuing his own studies and composing his major philosophical work. He did this first at Weimar, where he assisted Goethe in his work on the theory of color, intended as a refutation of Newton's theory. There Schopenhauer also began his study of Indian antiquity, which later resulted in his claim that the *Upanishads* together with the work of Plato and of Kant provided the foundation of his own philosophy. He soon left Weimar, breaking with his mother over her way of life, which he considered frivolous. He moved to Dresden where he completed the first exposition of his philosophical system.

His philosophy is succinctly expressed in the title that he gave the work. The world presents itself as phenomena in our ideas, structured by the mind's categories of space, time, and causality. But the underlying reality, the thing-in-itself, is will. Although we can grasp its individual manifestation in ourselves, will in itself is a universal tendency or drive that is unconscious, nonrational, beyond space and time, an eternal aimless and insatiable striving, inseparably united with misery and misfortune. The place that he assigns to aimless pain and suffering makes Schopenhauer the philosopher of pessimism, while the primary force attributed to blind survival is an anticipation of the Bergsonian *élan vital* and the Freudian *libido*.

The only escape that Schopenhauer provided from the merciless insistence of will lies in the fine arts and the pursuit of beauty, especially in music, since these, he claimed, can attain a level of experience that is contemplative, "will-less," and beyond the activity of the passions. In this, the arts, according to Schopenhauer, provide not only a distinct kind of knowledge but one that is superior to anything that the sciences have to offer.

In 1820, after a lengthy tour of Italy, Schopenhauer returned to the University of Berlin, where he qualified as a lecturer. After enjoying a triumphant dispute with Hegel, he was encouraged to make a further challenge by scheduling his lectures at the same time as those of that highly popular teacher. He received no takers, and soon thereafter he was spending more of his time in traveling than in lecturing. In 1833, upon the final settlement of his patrimony, he retired to Frankfurt, where he continued to write and to pursue his own cultural interests, with little or no recognition from the public until the publication of his essays in 1851. He died in Frankfurt, September 21, 1860.

On Books and Reading

Ignorance is degrading only when found in company with riches. The poor man is restrained by poverty and need: labor occupies his thoughts, and takes the place of knowledge. But rich men who are ignorant live for their lusts only, and are like the beasts of the field; as may be seen every day: and they can also be reproached for not having used wealth and leisure for that which gives them their greatest value.

When we read, another person thinks for us: we merely repeat his mental process. In learning to write, the pupil goes over with his pen what the teacher has outlined in pencil: so in reading; the greater part of the work of thought is already done for us. This is why it relieves us to take up a book after being occupied with our own thoughts. And in reading, the mind is, in fact, only the playground of another's thoughts. So it comes about that if anyone spends almost the whole day in reading, and by way of relaxation devotes the intervals to some thoughtless pastime, he gradually loses the capacity for thinking; just as the man who always rides, at last forgets how to walk. This is the case with many learned persons: they have read themselves stupid. For to occupy every spare moment in reading, and to do nothing but read, is even more paralyzing to the mind than constant manual labor, which at least allows those engaged in it to follow their own thoughts. A spring never free from the pressure of some foreign body at last loses its elasticity; and so does the mind if other people's thoughts are constantly forced upon it. Just as you can ruin the stomach and impair the whole body by taking too much nourishment, so you can overfill and choke the mind by feeding it too much. The more you read, the fewer are the traces left by what you have read: the mind becomes like a tablet crossed over and over with writing. There is no time for ruminating, and in no other way can you assimilate what you have read. If you read on and on without setting your own thoughts to work, what you have read can not strike root, and is generally lost. It is, in fact, just the same with mental as with bodily food: hardly the fifth part of what one takes is assimilated. The rest passes off in evaporation, respiration and the like.

The result of all this is that thoughts put on paper are nothing more than footsteps in the sand: you see the way the man has gone, but to know what he saw on his walk, you want his eyes.

There is no quality of style that can be gained by reading writers who possess it; whether it be persuasiveness, imagination, the gift of drawing comparisons, boldness, bitterness, brevity, grace, ease of expression or wit, unexpected contrasts, a laconic or naive manner, and the like. But if these qualities are already in us, exist, that is to say, potentially, we can call them forth and bring them to consciousness; we can learn the purposes to which they can be put; we can be strengthened in our inclination to use them, or get courage to do so; we can judge by examples the effect of applying them, and so acquire the correct use of them; and of course it is only when we have arrived at that point that we actually possess these qualities. The only way in which reading can form style is by teaching us the use to which we can put our own natural gifts. We must have these gifts before we begin to learn the use of them. Without them, reading teaches us nothing but cold, dead mannerisms and makes us shallow imitators.

The strata of the earth preserve in rows the creatures which lived in former ages; and the array of books on the shelves of a library stores up in like manner the errors of the past and the way in which they have been exposed. Like those creatures, they too were full of life in their time, and made a great deal of noise; but now they are stiff and fossilized, and an object of curiosity to the literary palaeontologist alone.

Herodotus relates that Xerxes wept at the sight of his army, which stretched further than the eye could reach, in the thought that of all these, after a hundred years, not one would be alive. And in looking over a huge catalogue of new books, one might weep at thinking that, when ten years have passed, not one of them will be heard of.

It is in literature as in life: wherever you turn, you stumble at once upon the incorrigible mob of humanity, swarming in all directions, crowding and soiling everything, like flies in summer. Hence the number, which no man can count, of bad books, those rank weeds of literature, which draw nourishment from the corn and choke it. The time, money and attention of the public, which rightfully belong to good books and their noble aims, they take for themselves: they are written for the mere purpose of making money or procuring places. So they are not only useless; they do positive mischief. Nine-tenths of the whole of our present literature has no other aim than to get a few shillings out of the pockets of the public; and to this end author, publisher and reviewer are in league.

Let me mention a crafty and wicked trick, albeit a profitable and successful one, practised by littérateurs, hack writers, and voluminous authors. In complete disregard of good taste and the true culture of the period, they have succeeded in getting the whole of the world of fashion into leading strings, so that they are all trained to read in time, and all the same thing, viz., *the newest books;* and that for the purpose of getting food for conversation in the circles in which they move. This is the aim served by bad novels, produced by writers who were once celebrated, as Spindler, Bulwer Lytton, Eugene Sue. What can be more miserable than the lot of a reading public like this, always bound to peruse the latest works of extremely commonplace persons who write for money only, and who are therefore never few in number? and for this advantage they are content to know by name only the works of the few superior minds of all ages and all countries. Literary newspapers, too, are a singularly cunning device for robbing the reading public of the time which, if culture is to be attained, should be devoted to the genuine productions of literature, instead of being occupied by the daily bungling commonplace persons.

Hence, in regard to reading, it is a very important thing to be able to refrain. Skill in doing so consists in not taking into one's hands any book merely because at the time it happens to be extensively read; such as political or religious pamphlets, novels, poetry, and the like, which make a noise, and may even attain to several editions in the first and last year of their existence. Consider, rather, that the man who writes for fools is always sure of a large audience; be careful to limit your time for reading, and devote it exclusively to the works of those great minds of all times and countries, who o'ertop the rest of humanity, those whom the voice of fame points to as such. These alone really educate and instruct. You can never read bad literature too little, nor good literature too much. Bad books are intellectual poison; they destroy the mind. Because people always read what is new instead of the best of all ages, writers remain in the narrow circle of the ideas which happen to prevail in their time; and so the period sinks deeper and deeper into its own mire.

There are at all times two literatures in progress, running side by side, but little known to each other; the one real, the other only apparent. The former grows into permanent literature; it is pursued by those who live *for* science or poetry; its course is sober and quiet, but extremely slow; and it produces in Europe scarcely a dozen works in a century; these, however, are permanent. The other kind is pursued by persons who live *on* science or poetry; it goes at a gallop with much noise and shouting of partisans; and every twelve-month puts a thousand works on the market. But after a few years one asks, Where are they? where is the glory which came so soon and made so much clamor? This kind may be called fleeting, and the other, permanent literature.

In the history of politics, half a century is always a considerable time; the matter which goes to form them is ever on the move; there is always something going on. But in the history of literature there is often a complete standstill for the same period; nothing has happened, for clumsy attempts don't count. You are just where you were fifty years previously.

To explain what I mean, let me compare the advance of knowledge among mankind to the course taken by a planet. The false paths on which humanity usually enters after every important advance are like the epicycles in the Ptolemaic system, and after passing through one of them, the world is just where it was before it entered it. But the great minds, who really bring the race further on its course do not accompany it on the epicycles it makes from time to time. This explains why posthumous fame is often bought at the expense of contemporary praise, and *vice versa*. An instance of such an epicycle is the philosophy started by Fichte and Schelling, and crowned by Hegel's caricature of it. This epicycle was a deviation from the limit to which philosophy had been ultimately brought by Kant; and at that point I took it up again afterwards, to carry it further. In the intervening period the sham philosophers I have mentioned and some others went through their epicycle, which had just come to an end; so that those who

went with them on their course are conscious of the fact that they are exactly at the point from which they started.

This circumstance explains why it is that, every thirty years or so, science, literature, and art, as expressed in the spirit of the time, are declared bankrupt. The errors which appear from time to time amount to such a height in that period that the mere weight of their absurdity makes the fabric fall; whilst the opposition to them has been gathering force at the same time. So an upset takes place, often followed by an error in the opposite direction. To exhibit these movements in their periodical return would be the true practical aim of the history of literature: little attention, however, is paid to it. And besides, the comparatively short duration of these periods makes it difficult to collect the data of epochs long gone by, so that it is most convenient to observe how the matter stands in one's own generation. An instance of this tendency, drawn from physical science, is supplied in the Neptunian geology of Werter.

But let me keep strictly to the example cited above, the nearest we can take. In German philosophy, the brilliant epoch of Kant was immediately followed by a period which aimed rather at being imposing than at convincing. Instead of being thorough and clear, it tried to be dazzling, hyperbolical, and, in a special degree, unintelligible: instead of seeking truth, it intrigued. Philosophy could make no progress in this fashion; and at last the whole school and its method became bankrupt. For the effrontery of Hegel and his fellows came to such a pass,—whether because they talked such sophisticated nonsense, or were so unscrupulously puffed, or because the entire aim of this pretty piece of work was quite obvious,—that in the end there was nothing to prevent charlatanry of the whole business from becoming manifest to everybody: and when, in consequence of certain disclosures, the favor it had enjoyed in high quarters was withdrawn, the system was openly ridiculed. This most miserable of all the meagre philosophies that have ever existed came to grief, and dragged down with it into the abysm of discredit, the systems of Fichte and Schelling which had preceded it. And so, as far as Germany is concerned, the total philosophical incompetence of the first half of the century following upon Kant is quite plain: and still the Germans boast of their talent for philosophy in comparison with foreigners, especially since an English writer has been so maliciously ironical as to call them "a nation of thinkers."

For an example of the general system of epicycles drawn from the history of art, look at the school of sculpture which flourished in the last century and took its name from Bernini, more especially at the development of it which prevailed in France. The ideal of this school was not antique beauty, but commonplace nature: instead of the simplicity and grace of ancient art, it represented the manners of a French minuet.

This tendency became bankrupt when, under Winkelman's direction, a return was made to the antique school. The history of painting furnishes an illustration in the first quarter of the century, when art was looked upon merely as a means and instrument of mediaeval religious sentiment, and its themes consequently drawn from ecclesiastical subjects alone: these, however, were treated by painters who had none of the true earnestness of faith, and in their delusion they followed Francesco Francia, Pietro Perugino, Angelico da Fiesole and others like them, rating them higher even than the really great masters who followed. It was in view of this terror, and because in poetry an analogous aim had at the same time found favor, that Goethe wrote his parable *Pfaffen-spiel*. This school, too, got the reputation of being whimsical, became bankrupt, and was followed by a return to nature, which proclaimed itself in *genre* pictures and scenes of life of every kind, even though it now and then strayed into what was vulgar.

The progress of the human mind in literature is similar. The history of literature is for the most part like the catalogue of a museum of deformities; the spirit in which they keep best is pigskin. The few creatures that have been born in goodly shape need not be looked for there. They are still alive, and are everywhere to be met with in the world, immortal, and with their years ever green. They alone form what I have called real literature; the history of which, poor as it is in persons, we learn from our youth up out of the mouths of all educated people, before compilations recount it for us.

As an antidote to the prevailing monomania for reading literary histories, in order to be able to chatter about everything, without having any real knowledge at all, let me refer to a passage in Lichtenberg's works (vol. II., p. 302), which is well worth perusal.

I believe that the over-minute acquaintance with the history of science and learning, which is such a prevalent feature of our day, is very prejudicial to the advance of knowledge itself. There is pleasure in following up this history; but as a matter of fact, it leaves the mind, not empty indeed, but without any power of its own, just because it makes it so full. Whoever has felt the desire, not to fill up his mind, but to strengthen it, to develop his faculties and aptitudes, and generally, to enlarge his powers, will have found that there is nothing so weakening as intercourse with a so-called littérateur, on a matter of knowledge on which he has not thought at all, though he knows a thousand little facts appertaining to its history and literature. It is like reading a cookery-book when you are hungry. I believe that so-called literary history will never thrive amongst thoughtful people, who are conscious of their own worth and the worth of real knowledge. These people are more given to employing their own reason than to troubling themselves to know how others have employed theirs. The worst of it is that, as you will find, the more knowledge takes the direction of literary research, the less the power of promoting knowledge becomes; the only thing that increases is pride in the possession of it. Such persons believe that they possess knowledge in a greater degree than those who really possess it. It is surely a well-founded remark, that knowledge never makes its possessor proud. Those alone let themselves be blown out with pride, who incapable of extending knowledge in their own persons, occupy themselves with clearing up dark points in its history, or are able to recount what others have done. They are proud, because they consider this occupation, which is mostly of a mechanical nature, the practice of knowledge. I could illustrate what I mean by examples, but it would be an odious task.

Still, I wish some one would attempt a *tragical* history of literature, giving the way in which the writers and artists, who form the proudest possession of the various nations which have given them birth, have been treated by them during their lives. Such a history would exhibit the ceaseless warfare, which what was good and genuine in all times and countries has had to wage with what was bad and perverse. It would tell of the martyrdom of almost all those who truly enlightened humanity, of almost all the great masters of every kind of art: it would show us how, with few exceptions, they were tormented to death, without recognition, without sympathy, without followers; how they lived in poverty and misery, whilst fame, honor, and riches, were the lot of the unworthy; how their fate was that of Esau, who while he was hunting and getting venison for his father, was robbed of the blessing by· Jacob, disguised in his brother's clothes, how, in spite of all, they were kept up by the love of their work, until at last the bitter fight of the teacher of humanity is over, until the immortal laurel is held out to him, and the hour strikes when it can be said:

*Der schwere Panzer wird zum Flügelkleide
Kurz ist der Schmerz, unendlich ist die Freude.*[*]

---

[*] The heavy armor becomes a cloak of flight;
Brief is the sorrow, unending the delight.
(Schiller: *Maid of Orleans*)

On Style

Style is the physiognomy of the mind, and a safer index to character than the face. To imitate another man's style is like wearing a mask, which, be it never so fine, is not long in arousing disgust and abhorrence, because it is lifeless; so that even the ugliest living face is better. Hence those who write in Latin and copy the manner of ancient authors, may be said to speak through a mask; the reader, it is true, hears what they say, but he cannot observe their physiognomy too; he cannot see their *style*. With the Latin works of writers who think for themselves, the case is different, and their style is visible; writers, I mean, who have not condescended to any sort of imitation, such as Scotus Erigena, Petrarch, Bacon, Descartes, Spinoza, and many others. An affectation in style is like making grimaces. Further, the language in which a man writes is the physiognomy of the nation to which he belongs; and here there are many hard and fast differences, beginning from the language of the Greeks, down to that of the Caribbean islanders.

To form a provincial estimate of the value of a writer's productions, it is not directly necessary to know the subject on which he has thought, or what it is that he has said about it; that would imply a perusal of all his works. It will be enough, in the main, to know *how* he has thought. This, which means the essential temper or general quality of his mind, may be precisely determined by his style. A man's style shows the *formal* nature of all his thoughts—the formal nature which can never change, be the subject or the character of his thoughts what it may: it is, as it were, the dough out of which all the contents of his mind are kneaded. When Eulenspiegel was asked how long it would take to walk to the next village, he gave the seemingly incongruous answer: *Walk.* He wanted to find out by the man's pace the distance he would cover in a given time. In the same way, when I have read a few pages of an author, I know fairly well how far he can bring me.

Every mediocre writer tries to mask his own natural style, because in his heart he knows the truth of what I am saying. He is thus forced, at the outset, to give up any attempt at being frank or naïve—a privilege which is thereby reserved for superior minds, conscious of their own worth, and therefore sure of themselves. What I mean is that these everyday writers are absolutely unable to resolve upon writing just as they think; because they have a notion that, were they to do so, their work might possibly look very childish and simple. For all that, it would not be without its value. If they would only go honestly to work, and say, quite simply, the things they have really thought, and just as they have thought them, these writers would be readable and, within their own proper sphere, even instructive.

But instead of that, they try to make the reader believe that their thoughts have gone much further and deeper than is really the case. They say what they have to say in long sentences that wind about in a forced and unnatural way; they coin new words and write prolix periods which go round and round the thought and wrap it up in a sort of disguise. They tremble between the two separate aims of communicating what they want to say and of concealing it. Their object is to dress it up so that it may look learned or deep, in order to give people the impression that there is very much more in it than for the moment meets the eye. They either jot down their thoughts bit by bit, in short, ambiguous, and paradoxical sentences, which apparently mean much more than they say,—of this kind of writing Schelling's treatises on natural philosophy are a splendid instance; or else they hold forth with a deluge of words and the most intolerable diffusiveness, as though no end of fuss were necessary to make the reader understand the deep meaning of their sentences, whereas it is some quite simple if not actually trivial idea,—examples of which may be found in plenty in the popular works of Fichte, and the philosophical manuals of a hundred other miserable dunces not worth mentioning; or, again, they try to write in some particular style which they have been pleased to take up and think very grand, a style, for example, *par excellence* profound and scientific, where the reader is tormented to death by the narcotic effect of long-spun periods without a single idea in them,—such as are furnished in a special measure by those most impudent of all mortals, the Hegelians; or it may be that it is an intellectual style they have striven after, where it seems as though their object were to go crazy altogether; and so on in many other cases. All these endeavors to put off the *nascetur ridiculus mus*—to avoid showing the funny little creature that is born after such mighty throes—often make it difficult to know what it is that they really mean. And then, too, they write down words, nay, even whole sentences, without attaching any meaning to them themselves, but in the hope that some one else will get sense out of them.

And what is at the bottom of all this? Nothing but the untiring effort to sell words for thoughts; a mode of merchandise that is always trying to make fresh openings for itself, and by means of odd expressions, turns of phrase, and combinations of every sort, whether new or used in a new sense, to produce the appearance of intellect in order to make up for the very painfully felt lack of it.

It is amusing to see how writers with this object in view will attempt first one mannerism and then another, as though they were putting on the mask of intellect! This mask may possibly deceive the inexperienced for a while, until it is seen to be a dead thing, with no life in it at all; it is then laughed at and exchanged for another. Such an author will at one moment write in a dithyrambic vein as though he were tipsy; at another, nay, on the very next page, he will be pompous, severe, profoundly learned and prolix, stumbling on in the most cumbrous way and chopping up everything very small; like the late Christian Wolf, only in a modern dress. Longest of all lasts the mask of unintelligibility; but this is only in Germany, whither it was introduced by Fichte, perfected by Schelling, and carried to its highest pitch in Hegel—always with the best results.

And yet nothing is easier than to write so that no one can understand; just as contrarily, nothing is more difficult than to express deep things in such a way that every one must necessarily grasp them. All the arts and tricks I have been mentioning are rendered superfluous if the author really has any brains; for that allows him to show himself as he is, and confirms to all time Horace's maxim that good sense is the source and origin of good style:

Scribendi recte sapere est et principium et fons.

But those authors I have named are like certain workers in metal, who try a hundred different compounds to take the place of gold—the only metal which can never have any substitute. Rather than do that, there is nothing against which a writer should be more upon his guard than the manifest endeavor to exhibit more intellect than he really has; because this makes the reader suspect that he possesses very little; since it is always the case that if a man affects anything, whatever it may be, it is just there that he is deficient.

That is why it is praise to an author to say that he is *naïve;* it means that he need not shrink from showing himself as he is. Generally speaking, to be naïve is to be attractive; while lack of naturalness is everywhere repulsive. As a matter of fact we find that every really great writer tries to express his thoughts as purely, clearly, definitely and shortly as possible. Simplicity has always been held to be a mark of truth; it is also a mark of genius. Style receives its beauty from the thought it expresses; but with sham-thinkers the thoughts are supposed to be fine because of the style. Style is nothing but the mere silhouette of thought; and an obscure or bad style means a dull or confused brain.

The first rule, then, for a good style is that *the author should have something to say;* nay, this is in itself almost all that is necessary. Ah, how much it means! The neglect of this rule is a fundamental trait in the philosophical writing, and, in fact, in all the reflective literature, of my country, more especially since Fichte. These writers all let it be seen that they want to appear as though they had something to say; whereas they have nothing to say. Writing of this kind was brought in by the pseudo-philosophers at the Universities, and now it is current everywhere, even among the first literary notabilities of the age. It is the mother of that strained and vague style, where there seem to be two or even more meanings in the sentence; also of that prolix and cumbrous manner of expression, called *le stile empesé;* again, of that mere waste of words which consists in pouring them out like a flood; finally, of that trick of concealing the direst poverty of thought under a farrago of never-ending chatter, which clacks away like a windmill and quite stupefies one —stuff which a man may read for hours together without getting hold of a single clearly expressed and definite idea. However, people are easy-going, and they have formed the habit of reading page upon page of all sorts of such verbiage, without having any particular idea of what the author really means. They fancy it is all as it should be, and fail to discover that he is writing simply for writing's sake.

On the other hand, a good author, fertile in ideas, soon wins his reader's confidence that, when he writes, he has really and truly *something to say;* and this gives the intelligent reader patience to follow him with attention.

Such an author, just because he really has something to say, will never fail to express himself in the simplest and most straightforward manner; because his object is to awake the very same thought in the reader that he has in himself, and no other. So he will be able to affirm with Boileau that his thoughts are everywhere open to the light of the day, and that his verse always says something, whether it says it well or ill:

Ma pensée au grand jour partout s'offre et s'expose,
Et mon vers, bein ou mal, dit toujours quelque chose:

while of the writers previously described it may be asserted, in the words of the same poet, that they talk much and never say anything at all—*qui parlant beaucoup ne disent jamais rien.*

Another characteristic of such writers is that they always avoid a postitive assertion wherever they can possibly do so, in order to leave a loophole for escape in case of need. Hence they never fail to choose the more *abstract* way of expressing themselves; whereas intelligent people use the more *concrete;* because the latter brings things more within the range of actual demonstration, which is the source of all evidence.

There are many examples proving this preference for abstract expression; and a particularly ridiculous one is afforded by the use of the verb *to condition* in the sense of *to cause* or *to produce.* People say *to condition something* instead of *to cause it,* because being abstract and indefinite it says less; it affirms that *A* cannot happen without *B*, instead of that *A* is caused by *B.* A back door is always left open; and this suits people whose secret knowledge of their own incapacity inspires them with a perpetual terror of all positive assertion; while with other people it is merely the effect of that tendency by which everything that is stupid in literature or bad in life is immediately imitated—a fact proved in either case by the rapid way in which it spreads. The Englishman uses his own judgment in what he writes as well as in what he does; but there is no nation of which this eulogy is less true than of the Germans. The consequence of this state of things is that the word *cause* has of late almost disappeared from the language of literature, and people talk only of *condition*. The fact is worth mentioning because it is so characteristically ridiculous.

The very fact that these commonplace authors are never more than half-conscious when they write, would be enough to account for their dullness of mind and the tedious things they produce. I say they are only half-conscious, because they really do not themselves understand the meaning of the words they use: they take words ready-made and commit them to memory. Hence when they write, it is not so much words as whole phrases that they put together—*phrases banales*. This is the explanation of that palpable lack of clearly-expressed thought in what they say. The fact is that they do not possess the die to give this stamp to their writing; clear thought of their own is just what they have not got. And what do we find in its place?—a vague, enigmatical intermixture of words, current phrases, hackneyed terms, and fashionable expressions. The result is that the foggy stuff they write is like a page printed with very old type.

On the other hand, an intelligent author really speaks to us when he writes, and that is why he is able to rouse our interest and commune with us. It is the intelligent author alone who puts individual words together with a full consciousness of their meaning, and chooses them with deliberate design. Consequently, his discourse stands to that of the writer described above, much as a picture that has been really painted, to one that has been produced by the use of a stencil. In the one case, every word, every touch of the brush, has a special purpose; in the other, all is done mechanically. The same distinction may be observed in music. For just as Lichtenberg says that Garrick's soul seemed to be in every muscle in his body, so it is the omnipresence of intellect that always and everywhere characterizes the work of genius.

I have alluded to the tediousness which marks the works of these writers; and in this connection it is to be observed, generally, that tediousness is of two kinds; objective and subjective. A work is objectively tedious when it contains the defect in question; that is to say, when its author has no perfectly clear thought or knowledge to communicate. For if a man has any clear thought or knowledge in him, his aim will be to communicate it, and he will direct his energies to this end; so that the ideas he furnishes are everywhere clearly expressed. The result is that he is neither diffuse, nor unmeaning, nor confused, and consequently not tedious. In such a case, even though the author is at bottom in error, the error is at any rate clearly worked out and well thought over, so that it is at least formally correct; and thus some value always attaches to the work. But for the same reason a work that is objectively tedious is at all times devoid of any value whatever.

The other kind of tediousness is only relative: a reader may find a work dull because he has no interest in the question treated of in it, and this means that his intellect is restricted. The best work may, therefore, be tedious subjectively, tedious, I mean, to this or that particular person; just as, contrarily, the worst work may be subjectively engrossing to this or that particular person who has an interest in the question treated of, or in the writer of the book.

It would generally serve writers in good stead if they would see that, whilst a man should, if possible, think like a great genius, he should talk the same language as everyone else. Authors should use common words to say uncommon things. But they do just the opposite. We find them trying to wrap up trivial ideas in grand words, and to clothe their very ordinary thoughts in the most extraordinary phrases, the most far-fetched, unnatural, and out-of-the-way expressions. Their sentences perpetually stalk about on stilts. They take so much pleasure in bombast, and write in such a high-flown, bloated, affected, hyperbolical and acrobatic style that their prototype is Ancient Pistol, whom his friend Falstaff once impatiently told to say what he had to say *like a man of this world.*[1]

There is no expression in any other language exactly answering to the French *stile empesé;* but the thing itself exists all the more often. When associated with affectation, it is in literature what assumption of dignity, grand airs and primness are in society; and equally intolerable. Dullness of mind is fond of donning this dress; just as in ordinary life it is stupid people who like being demure and formal.

An author who writes in the prim style resembles a man who dresses himself up in order to avoid being confounded or put on the same level with a mob—a risk never run by the *gentleman,* even in his worst clothes. The plebeian may be known by a certain showiness of attire and a wish to have everything spick and span; and in the same way, the commonplace person is betrayed by his style.

Nevertheless, an author follows a false aim if he tries to write exactly as he speaks. There is no style of writing but should have a certain trace of kinship with the *epigraphic* or *monumental* style, which is, indeed, the ancestor of all styles. For an author to write as he speaks is just as reprehensible as the opposite fault, to speak as he writes; for this gives a pedantic effect to what he says, and at the same time makes him hardly intelligible.

An obscure and vague manner of expression is always and everywhere a very bad sign. In ninety-nine cases out of a hundred it comes from vagueness of thought; and this again almost always means that there is something radically wrong and incongruous about the thought itself—in a word, that it is incorrect. When a right thought springs up in the mind, it strives after expression and is not long in reaching it; for clear thought easily finds words to fit it. If a man is capable of thinking anything at all, he is also always able to express it in clear, intelligible, and unambiguous terms. Those writers who construct difficult, obscure, involved, and equivocal sentences, most certainly do not know aright what it is that they want to say: they have only a dull consciousness of it, which is still in the

stage of struggle to shape itself as thought. Often, indeed, their desire is to conceal from themselves and others that they really have nothing at all to say. They wish to appear to know what they do not know, to think what they do not think, to say what they do not say. If a man has some real communication to make, which will he choose—an indistinct or a clear way of expressing himself? Even Quintilian remarks that things which are said by a highly educated man are often easier to understand and much clearer; and that the less educated a man is, the more obscurely he will write—*plerumque accidit ut faciliora sint ad intelligendum et lucidiora multo que a doctissimo quoque dicuntur . . . . Erit ergo etiam obscurior quo quisque deterior.*

An author should avoid enigmatical phrases; he should know whether he wants to say a thing or does not want to say it. It is this indecision of style that makes so many writers insipid. The only case that offers an exception to this rule arises when it is necessary to make a remark that is in some way improper.

As exaggeration generally produces an effect the opposite of that aimed at; so words, it is true, serve to make thought intelligible—but only up to a certain point. If words are heaped up beyond it, the thought becomes more and more obscure again. To find where the point lies is the problem of style, and the business of the critical faculty; for a word too much always defeats its purpose. This is what Voltaire means when he says that *the adjective is the enemy of the substantive.* But, as we have seen, many people try to conceal their poverty of thought under a flood of verbiage.

Accordingly let all redundancy be avoided, all stringing together of remarks which have no meaning and are not worth perusal. A writer must make a sparing use of the reader's time, patience and attention; so as to lead him to believe that his author writes what is worth careful study, and will reward the time

---

[1] *King Henry IV.,* Part II. Act v. Sc. 3; *GBWW,* Vol. 26, p. 500 c.

spent upon it. It is always better to omit something good than to add that which is not worth saying at all. This is the right application of Hesiod's maxim, πλέον ἥμισυ πάντος—the half is more than the whole. *Le secret pour être ennuyeux, c'est de tout dire.** Therefore, if possible, the quintessence only! mere leading thoughts! nothing that the reader would think for himself. To use many words to communicate few thoughts is everywhere the unmistakable sign of mediocrity. To gather much thought into few words stamps the man of genius.

Truth is most beautiful undraped; and the impression it makes is deep in proportion as its expression has been simple. This is so, partly because it then takes unobstructed possession of the hearer's whole soul, and leaves him no by-thought to distract him; partly, also, because he feels that here he is not being corrupted or cheated by the arts of rhetoric, but that all the effect of what is said comes from the thing itself. For instance, what declamation on the vanity of human existence could ever be more telling than the words of Job? *Man that is born of woman hath but a short time to live and is full of misery. He cometh up, and is cut down, like a flower; he fleeth as it were a shadow, and never continueth in one stay.*

For the same reason Goethe's naïve poetry is incomparably greater than Schiller's rhetoric. It is this, again, that makes many popular songs so affecting. As in architecture an excess of decoration is to be avoided, so in the art of literature a writer must guard against all rhetorical finery, all useless amplification, and all superfluity of expression in general; in a word, he must strive after *chastity* of style. Every word that can be spared is hurtful if it remains. The law of simplicity and naïveté holds good of all fine art; for it is quite possible to be at once simple and sublime.

True brevity of expression consists in everywhere saying only what is worth saying, and in avoiding tedious detail about things which everyone can supply for himself. This involves correct discrimination between what is necessary and what is superfluous. A writer should never be brief at the expense of being clear, to say nothing of being grammatical. It shows lamentable want of judgment to weaken the expression of a thought, or to stunt the meaning of a period for the sake of using a few words less. But this is the precise endeavor of that false brevity nowadays so much in vogue, which proceeds by leaving out useful words and even by sacrificing grammar and logic. It is not only that such writers spare a word by making a single verb or adjective do duty for several different periods, so that the reader, as it were, has to grope his way through them in the dark; they also practice, in many other respects, an unseemly economy of speech, in the effort to effect what they foolishly take to be brevity of expression and conciseness of style. By omitting something that might have thrown a light over the whole sentence, they turn it into a conundrum, which the reader tries to solve by going over it again and again.[2]

It is wealth and weight of thought, and nothing else, that gives brevity to style, and makes it concise and pregnant. If a writer's ideas are important, luminous, and generally worth communicating, they will necessarily furnish matter and substance enough to fill out the periods which give them expression, and make these in all their parts both grammatically and verbally complete; and so much will this be the case that no one will ever find them hollow, empty or feeble. The diction will everywhere be brief and pregnant, and allow the thought to find intelligible and easy expression, and even unfold and move about with grace.

Therefore instead of contracting his words

---

* To be a bore the secret is: to say everything.

[2] *Translator's Note.*—In the original, Schopenhauer here enters upon a lengthy examination of certain common errors in the writing and speaking of German. His remarks are addressed to his own countrymen, and would lose all point, even if they were intelligible, in an English translation. But for those who practice their German by conversing or corresponding with Germans, let me recommend what he there says as a useful corrective to a slipshod style, such as can easily be contracted if it is assumed that the natives of a country always know their own language perfectly.

and forms of speech, let a writer enlarge his thoughts. If a man has been thinned by illness and finds his clothes too big, it is not by cutting them down, but by recovering his usual bodily condition, that he ought to make them fit him again.

Let me here mention an error of style, very prevalent nowadays, and, in the degraded state of literature and the neglect of ancient languages, always on the increase; I mean *subjectivity*. A writer commits this error when he thinks it enough if he himself knows what he means and wants to say, and takes no thought for the reader, who is left to get at the bottom of it as best he can. This is as though the author were holding a monologue; whereas, it ought to be a dialogue; and a dialogue, too, in which he must express himself all the more clearly inasmuch as he cannot hear the questions of his interlocutor.

Style should for this very reason never be subjective, but *objective;* and it will not be objective unless the words are so set down that they directly force the reader to think precisely the same thing as the author thought when he wrote them. Nor will this result be obtained unless the author has always been careful to remember that thought so far follows the law of gravity that it travels from head to paper much more easily than from paper to head; so that he must assist the latter passage by every means in his power. If he does this, a writer's words will have a purely objective effect, like that of a finished picture in oils; whilst the subjective style is not much more certain in its working than spots on the wall, which look like figures only to one whose phantasy has been accidentally aroused by them; other people see nothing but spots and blurs. The difference in question applies to literary method as a whole; but it is often established also in particular instances. For example, in a recently published work I found the following sentence: *I have not written in order to increase the number of existing books*. This means just the opposite of what the writer wanted to say, and is nonsense as well.

He who writes carelessly confesses thereby at the very outset that he does not attach much importance to his own thoughts. For it is only where a man is convinced of the truth and importance of his thoughts, that he feels the enthusiasm necessary for an untiring and assiduous effort to find the clearest, finest, and strongest expression for them,—just as for sacred relics or priceless works of art there are provided silvern or golden receptacles. It was this feeling that led ancient authors, whose thoughts, expressed in their own words, have lived thousands of years, and therefore bear the honored title of *classics,* always to write with care. Plato, indeed, is said to have written the introduction to his *Republic* seven times over in different ways.

As neglect of dress betrays want of respect for the company a man meets, so a hasty, careless, bad style shows an outrageous lack of regard for the reader, who then rightly punishes it by refusing to read the book. It is especially amusing to see reviewers criticising the works of others in their own most careless style—the style of a hireling. It is as though a judge were to come into court in dressing-gown and slippers! If I see a man badly and dirtily dressed, I feel some hesitation, at first, in entering into conversation with him: and when, on taking up a book, I am struck at once by the negligence of its style, I put it away.

Good writing should be governed by the rule that a man can think only one thing clearly at a time; and, therefore, that he should not be expected to think two or even more things in one and the same moment. But this is what is done when a writer breaks up his principal sentence into little pieces, for the purpose of pushing into the gaps thus made two or three other thoughts by way of parenthesis; thereby unnecessarily and wantonly confusing the reader. And here it is again my own countrymen who are chiefly in fault. That German lends itself to this way of writing, makes the thing possible, but does not justify it. No prose reads more easily or pleasantly than French, because, as a rule, it is free from the error in question. The Frenchman strings his thoughts together, as far as he can, in the most logical and natural order, and so lays them before his reader one after the other for convenient deliberation, so that every one of them may receive undivided attention. The German, on the other hand, weaves them together into a sentence which he twists and crosses, and crosses and twists again; because he wants to say six things all at once, instead of advancing them one by one. His aim should be to attract and hold the reader's attention; but, above and beyond neglect of this aim, he demands from the reader that he shall set the above mentioned rule at defiance, and think three or four different thoughts at one and the same time; or since that is impossible, that his thoughts shall succeed each other as quickly as the vibrations of a cord. In this way an author lays the foundation of his *stile empesé*, which is then carried to perfection by the use of high-flown, pompous expressions to communicate the simplest things, and other artifices of the same kind.

In those long sentences rich in involved parenthesis, like a box of boxes one within another, and padded out like roast geese stuffed with apples, it is really the *memory* that is chiefly taxed; while it is the understanding and the judgment which should be called into play, instead of having their activity thereby actually hindered and weakened.[3] This kind of sentence furnishes the reader with mere half-phrases, which he is then called upon to collect carefully and store up in his memory, as though they were the pieces of a torn letter, afterwards to be completed and made sense of by the other halves to which they respectively belong. He is expected to go on reading for a little without exercising any thought, nay, exerting only his memory, in the hope that, when he comes to the end of the sentence, he may see its meaning and so receive something to think about; and he is thus given a great deal to learn by heart before obtaining anything to understand. This is manifestly wrong and an abuse of the reader's patience.

The ordinary writer has an unmistakable preference for this style, because it causes the reader to spend time and trouble in understanding that which he would have understood in a moment without it; and this makes it look as though the writer had more depth and intelligence than the reader. This is, indeed, one of those artifices referred to above, by means of which mediocre authors unconsciously, and as it were by instinct, strive to conceal their poverty of thought and give an appearance of the opposite. Their ingenuity in this respect is really astounding.

It is manifestly against all sound reason to put one thought obliquely on top of another, as though both together formed a wooden cross. But this is what is done where a writer interrupts what he has begun to say, for the purpose of inserting some quite alien matter; thus depositing with the reader a meaningless half-sentence, and bidding him keep it until the completion comes. It is much as though a man were to treat his guests by handing them an empty plate, in the hope of something appearing upon it. And commas used for a similar purpose belong to the same family as notes at the foot of the page and parenthesis in the middle of the text; nay, all three differ only in degree. If Demosthenes and Cicero occasionally inserted words by ways of parenthesis, they would have done better to have refrained.

But this style of writing becomes the height of absurdity when the parenthesis are not even fitted into the frame of the sentence, but wedged in so as directly to shatter it. If, for instance, it is an impertinent thing to interrupt another person when he is speaking, it is no less impertinent to interrupt oneself. But all bad, careless, and hasty authors, who scribble with the bread actually before their eyes, use this style of writing six times on a page, and rejoice in it. It consists in—it is advisable to give rule and example together, wherever it is possible—breaking up one

---

[3] *Translator's Note.*—This sentence in the original is obviously meant to illustrate the fault of which it speaks. It does so by the use of a construction very common in German, but happily unknown in English; where, however, the fault itself exists none the less, though in different form.

On Men of Learning

When one sees the number and variety of institutions which exist for the purposes of education, and the vast throng of scholars and masters, one might fancy the human race to be very much concerned about truth and wisdom. But here, too, appearances are deceptive. The masters teach in order to gain money, and strive, not after wisdom, but the outward show and reputation of it; and the scholars learn, not for the sake of knowledge and insight, but to be able to chatter and give themselves airs. Every thirty years a new race comes into the world —a youngster that knows nothing about anything, and after summarily devouring in all haste the results of human knowledge as they have been accumulated for thousands of years, aspires to be thought cleverer than the whole of the past. For this purpose he goes to the University, and takes to reading books —new books, as being of his own age and standing. Everything he reads must be briefly put, must be new! he is new himself. Then he falls to and criticises. And here I am not taking the slightest account of studies pursued for the sole object of making a living.

Students, and learned persons of all sorts and every age, aim as a rule at acquiring *information* rather than insight. They pique themselves upon knowing about everything —stones, plants, battles, experiments, and all the books in existence. It never occurs to them that information is only a means of insight, and in itself of little or no value; that it is his way of *thinking* that makes a man a philosopher. When I hear of these portents of learning and their imposing erudition, I sometimes say to myself: Ah, how little they must have had to think about, to have been able to read so much! And when I actually find it reported of the elder Pliny that he was continually reading or being read to, at table, on a journey, or in his bath, the question forces itself upon my mind, whether the man was so very lacking in thought of his own that he had to have alien thought incessantly instilled into him; as though he were a consumptive patient taking jellies to keep himself alive. And neither his undiscerning credulity nor his inexpressibly repulsive and barely intelligible style—which seems like that of a man taking notes, and very economical of paper—is of a kind to give me a high opinion of his power of independent thought.

We have seen that much reading and learning is prejudicial to thinking for oneself; and, in the same way, through much writing and teaching, a man loses the habit of being quite clear, and therefore thorough, in regard to the things he knows and understands; simply because he has left himself no time to acquire clearness or thoroughness. And so, when clear knowledge fails him in his utterances, he is forced to fill out the gaps with words and phrases. It is this, and not the dryness of the subject-matter, that makes most books such tedious reading. There is a saying that a good cook can make a palatable dish even out of an old shoe; and a good writer can make the dryest things interesting.

With by far the largest number of learned men, knowledge is a means, not an end. That is why they will never achieve any great work; because, to do that, he who pursues knowledge must pursue it as an end, and treat everything else, even existence itself, as only a means. For everything which a man fails to pursue for its own sake is but half-pursued; and true excellence, no matter in what sphere, can be attained only where the work has been produced for its own sake alone, and not as a means to further ends.

And so, too, no one will ever succeed in doing anything really great and original in the way of thought, who does not seek to acquire knowledge for himself, and, making this the immediate object of his studies, decline to trouble himself about the knowledge of others. But the average man of learning studies for the purpose of being able to teach and write. His head is like a stomach and intestines which let the food pass through them undigested. That is just why his teaching and writing is of so little use. For it is not upon undigested refuse that people can be nourished, but solely upon the milk which secretes from the very blood itself.

The wig is the appropriate symbol of the man of learning, pure and simple. It adorns the head with a copious quantity of false hair, in lack of one's own: just as erudition means endowing it with a great mass of alien thought. This, to be sure, does not clothe the head so well and naturally, nor is it so generally useful, nor so suited for all purposes, nor so firmly rooted; nor when alien thought is used up, can it be immediately replaced by more from the same source, as is the case with that which springs from soil of one's own. So we find Sterne, in his *Tristram Shandy*, boldly asserting that *an ounce of a man's own wit is worth a ton of other people's.*

And in fact the most profound erudition is no more akin to genius than a collection of dried plants is like Nature, with its constant flow of new life, ever fresh, ever young, ever changing. There are no two things more opposed than the childish naïveté of an ancient author and the learning of his commentator.

Dilettanti, dilettanti! This is the slighting way in which those who pursue any branch of art or learning for the love and enjoyment of the thing,—*per il loro diletto,* are spoken of by those who have taken it up for the sake of gain, attracted solely by the prospect of money. This contempt of theirs comes from the base belief that no man will seriously devote himself to a subject, unless he is spurred on to it by want, hunger, or else some form of greed. The public is of the same way of thinking; and hence its general respect for professionals and its distrust of *dilettanti.* But the truth is that the *dilettante* treats his subject as an end, whereas the professional, pure and simple, treats it merely as a means. He alone will be really in earnest about a matter, who has a direct interest therein, takes to it because he likes it, and pursues it *con amore.* It is these, and not hirelings, that have always done the greatest work.

In the republic of letters it is as in other republics; favor is shown to the plain man— he who goes his way in silence and does not set up to be cleverer than others. But the abnormal man is looked upon as threatening danger; people band together against him, and have, oh! such a majority on their side.

The condition of this republic is much like that of a small State in America, where every man is intent only upon his own advantage, and seeks reputation and power for himself, quite heedless of the general weal, which then goes to ruin. So it is in the republic of letters; it is himself, and himself alone, that a man puts forward, because he wants to gain fame. The only thing in which all agree is in trying to keep down a really eminent man, if he should chance to show himself, as one who would be a common peril. From this it is easy to see how it fares with knowledge as a whole.

Between professors and independent men of learning there has always been from of old a certain antagonism, which may perhaps be likened to that existing between dogs and wolves. In virtue of their position, professors enjoy great facilities for becoming known to their contemporaries. Contrarily, independent men of learning enjoy, by their position, great facilities for becoming known to posterity; to which it is necessary that, amongst other and much rarer gifts, a man should have a certain leisure and freedom. As mankind takes a long time in finding out on whom to bestow its attention, they may both work together side by side.

He who holds a professorship may be said

to receive his food in the stall; and this is the best way with ruminant animals. But he who finds his food for himself at the hands of Nature is better off in the open field.

Of human knowledge as a whole and in every branch of it, by far the largest part exists nowhere but on paper,—I mean, in books, that paper memory of mankind. Only a small part of it is at any given period really active in the minds of particular persons. This is due, in the main, to the brevity and uncertainty of life; but it also comes from the fact that men are lazy and bent on pleasure. Every generation attains, on its hasty passage through existence, just so much of human knowledge as it needs, and then soon disappears. Most men of learning are very superficial. Then follows a new generation, full of hope, but ignorant, and with everything to learn from the beginning. It seizes, in its turn, just so much as it can grasp or find useful on its brief journey and then too goes its way. How badly it would fare with human knowledge if it were not for the art of writing and printing! This it is that makes libraries the only sure and lasting memory of the human race, for its individual members have all of them but a very limited and imperfect one. Hence most men of learning are as loth to have their knowledge examined as merchants to lay bare their books.

Human knowledge extends on all sides farther than the eye can reach; and of that which would be generally worth knowing, no one man can possess even the thousandth part.

All branches of learning have thus been so much enlarged that he who would "do something" has to pursue no more than one subject and disregard all others. In his own subject he will then, it is true, be superior to the vulgar; but in all else he will belong to it. If we add to this that neglect of the ancient languages, which is now-a-days on the increase and is doing away with all general education in the humanities—for a mere smattering of Latin and Greek is of no use—we shall come to have men of learning who outside their own subject display an ignorance truly bovine.

An exclusive specialist of this kind stands on a par with a workman in a factory, whose whole life is spent in making one particular kind of screw, or catch, or handle, for some particular instrument or machine, in which, indeed, he attains incredible dexterity. The specialist may also be likened to a man who lives in his own house and never leaves it. There he is perfectly familiar with everything, every little step, corner, or board; much as Quasimodo in Victor Hugo's *Nôtre Dame* knows the cathedral; but outside it, all is strange and unknown.

For true culture in the humanities it is absolutely necessary that a man should be many-sided and take large views; and for a man of learning in the higher sense of the word, an extensive acquaintance with history is needful. He, however, who wishes to be a complete philosopher, must gather into his head the remotest ends of human knowledge: for where else could they ever come together?

It is precisely minds of the first order that will never be specialists. For their very nature is to make the whole of existence their problem; and this is a subject upon which they will every one of them in some form provide mankind with a new revelation. For he alone can deserve the name of genius who takes the All, the Essential, the Universal, for the theme of his achievements; not he who spends his life in explaining some special relation of things one to another.

On Thinking for Oneself

A library may be very large; but if it is in disorder, it is not so useful as one that is small but well arranged. In the same way, a man may have a great mass of knowledge, but if he has not worked it up by thinking it over for himself, it has much less value than a far smaller amount which he has thoroughly pondered. For it is only when a man looks at his knowledge from all sides, and combines the things he knows by comparing truth with truth, that he obtains a complete hold over it and gets it into his power. A man cannot turn over anything in his mind unless he knows it; he should, therefore, learn something; but it is only when he has turned it over that he can be said to know it.

Reading and learning are things that anyone can do of his own free will; but not so *thinking*. Thinking must be kindled, like a fire by a draught; it must be sustained by some interest in the matter in hand. This interest may be of purely objective kind, or merely subjective. The latter comes into play only in things that concern us personally. Objective interest is confined to heads that think by nature; to whom thinking is as natural as breathing; and they are very rare. This is why most men of learning show so little of it.

It is incredible what a different effect is produced upon the mind by thinking for oneself, as compared with reading. It carries on and intensifies that original difference in the nature of two minds which leads the one to think and the other to read. What I mean is that reading forces alien thoughts upon the mind—thoughts which are as foreign to the drift and temper in which it may be for the moment, as the seal is to the wax on which it stamps its imprint. The mind is thus entirely under compulsion from without; it is driven to think this or that, though for the moment it may not have the slightest impulse or inclination to do so.

But when a man thinks for himself, he follows the impulses of his own mind, which is determined for him at the time, either by his environment or some particular recollection. The visible world of a man's surroundings does not, as reading does, impress a *single* definite thought upon his mind, but merely gives the matter and occasion which lead him to think what is appropriate to his nature and present temper. So it is, that much reading deprives the mind of all elasticity; it is like keeping a spring continually under pressure. The safest way of having no thoughts of one's own is to take up a book every moment one has nothing else to do. It is this practice which explains why erudition makes most men more stupid and silly than they are by nature, and prevents their writings obtaining any measure of success. They remain, in Pope's words:

For ever reading, never to be read.[1]

Men of learning are those who have done their reading in the pages of a book. Thinkers and men of genius are those who have gone straight to the book of Nature; it is they who have enlightened the world and carried humanity further on its way.

If a man's thoughts are to have truth and life in them, they must, after all, be his own fundamental thoughts; for these are the only ones that he can fully and wholly understand. To read another's thoughts is like taking the leavings of a meal to which we have not been

---

[1] *Dunciad,* iii, 194.

invited, or putting on the clothes which some unknown visitor has laid aside. The thought we read is related to the thought which springs up in ourselves, as the fossil-impress of some prehistoric plant to a plant as it buds forth in spring-time.

Reading is nothing more than a substitute for thought of one's own. It means putting the mind into leading-strings. The multitude of books serves only to show how many false paths there are, and how widely astray a man may wander if he follows any of them. But he who is guided by his genius, he who thinks for himself, who thinks spontaneously and exactly, possesses the only compass by which he can steer aright. A man should read only when his own thoughts stagnate at their source, which will happen often enough even with the best of minds. On the other hand, to take up a book for the purpose of scaring away one's own original thoughts is sin against the Holy Spirit. It is like running away from Nature to look at a museum of dried plants or gaze at a landscape in copper-plate.

A man may have discovered some portion of truth or wisdom, after spending a great deal of time and trouble in thinking it over for himself and adding thought to thought; and it may sometimes happen that he could have found it all ready to hand in a book and spared himself the trouble. But even so, it is a hundred times more valuable if he has acquired it by thinking it out for himself. For it is only when we gain our knowledge in this way that it enters as an integral part, a living member, into the whole system of our thought; that it stands in complete and firm relation with what we know; that it is understood with all that underlies it and follows from it; that it wears the color, the precise shade, the distinguishing mark, of our own way of thinking; that it comes exactly at the right time, just as we felt the necessity for it; that it stands fast and cannot be forgotten. This is the perfect application, nay, the interpretation, of Goethe's advice to earn our inheritance for ourselves so that we may really possess it:

Was du ererbt von deinen Vätern hast,
Erwirb es, um es zu besitzen.[2]

The man who thinks for himself, forms his own opinions and learns the authorities for them only later on, when they serve but to strengthen his belief in them and in himself. But the book-philosopher starts from the authorities. He reads other people's books, collects their opinions, and so forms a whole for himself, which resembles an automaton made up of anything but flesh and blood. Contrarily, he who thinks for himself creates a work like a living man as made by Nature. For the work comes into being as a man does; the thinking mind is impregnated from without, and it then forms and bears its child.

Truth that has been merely learned is like an artificial limb, a false tooth, a waxen nose; at best, like a nose made out of another's flesh; it adheres to us only because it is put on. But truth acquired by thinking of our own is like a natural limb; it alone really belongs to us. This is the fundamental difference between the thinker and the mere man of learning. The intellectual attainments of a man who thinks for himself resemble a fine painting, where the light and shade are correct, the tone sustained, the color perfectly harmonized; it is true to life. On the other hand, the intellectual attainments of the mere man of learning are like a large palette, full of all sorts of colors, which at most are systematically arranged but devoid of harmony, connection and meaning.

Reading is thinking with some one else's head instead of one's own. To think with one's own head is always to aim at developing a coherent whole—a system, even though it be not a strictly complete one; and nothing hinders this so much as too strong a current of others' thoughts, such as comes of continual reading. These thoughts, springing every one of them from different minds, belonging to different systems, and tinged with differ-

---

[2] *Faust*, I. 682–83; *GBWW*, Vol. 47, p. 18a.
All that you have, bequeathed you by your father,
Earn it in order to possess it.

ent colors, never of themselves flow together into an intellectual whole; they never form a unity of knowledge, or insight, or conviction; but, rather, fill the head with a Babylonian confusion of tongues. The mind that is overloaded with alien thought is thus deprived of all clear insight, and is well-nigh disorganized. This is a state of things observable in many men of learning; and it makes them inferior in sound sense, correct judgment and practical tact, to many illiterate persons, who, after obtaining a little knowledge from without, by means of experience, intercourse with others, and a small amount of reading, have always subordinated it to, and embodied it with, their own thought.

The really scientific *thinker* does the same thing as these illiterate persons, but on a larger scale. Although he has need for much knowledge, and so must read a great deal, his mind is nevertheless strong enough to master it all, to assimilate and incorporate it with the system of his thoughts, and so to make it fit in with the organic unity of his insight, which, though vast, is always growing. And in the process, his own thought, like the bass in an organ, always dominates everything and is never drowned by other tones, as happens with minds which are full of mere antiquarian lore; where shreds of music, as it were, in every key, mingle confusedly, and no fundamental note is heard at all.

Those who have spent their lives in reading, and taken their wisdom from books, are like people who have obtained precise information about a country from the descriptions of many travellers. Such people can tell a great deal about it; but, after all, they have no connected, clear, and profound knowledge of its real condition. But those who have spent their lives in thinking, resemble the travellers themselves; they alone really know what they are talking about; they are acquainted with the actual state of affairs, and are quite at home in the subject.

The thinker stands in the same relation to the ordinary book-philosopher as an eye-witness does to the historian; he speaks from direct knowledge of his own. That is why all those who think for themselves come, at bottom, to much the same conclusion. The differences they present are due to their different points of view; and when these do not affect the matter, they all speak alike. They merely express the result of their own objective perception of things. There are many passages in my works which I have given to the public only after some hesitation, because of their paradoxical nature; and afterwards I have experienced a pleasant surprise in finding the same opinion recorded in the works of great men who lived long ago.

The book-philosopher merely reports what one person has said and another meant, or the objections raised by a third, and so on. He compares different opinions, ponders, criticises, and tries to get at the truth of the matter; herein on a par with the critical historian. For instance, he will set out to inquire whether Leibnitz was not for some time a follower of Spinoza, and questions of a like nature. The curious student of such matters may find conspicuous examples of what I mean in Herbart's *Analytical Elucidation of Morality and Natural Right,* and in the same author's *Letters on Freedom.* Surprise may be felt that a man of the kind should put himself to so much trouble; for, on the face of it, if he would only examine the matter for himself, he would speedily attain his object by the exercise of a little thought. But there is a small difficulty in the way. It does not depend upon his own will. A man can always sit down and read, but not—think. It is with thoughts as with men; they cannot always be summoned at pleasure; we must wait for them to come. Thought about a subject must appear of itself, by a happy and harmonious combination of external stimulus with mental temper and attention; and it is just that which never seems to come to these people.

This truth may be illustrated by what happens in the case of matters affecting our own personal interest. When it is necessary to come to some resolution in a matter of that kind, we cannot well sit down at any given moment and think over the merits of the case and make up our mind; for, if we try to do so, we often find ourselves unable, at that particular moment, to keep our mind fixed upon the subject; it wanders off to other things. Aversion to the matter in question is sometimes to blame for this. In such a case we should not use force, but wait for the proper frame of mind to come of itself. It often comes unexpectedly and returns again and again; and the variety of temper in which we approach it at different moments puts the matter always in a fresh light. It is this long process which is understood by the term *a ripe resolution.* For the work of coming to a resolution must be distributed; and in the process much that is overlooked at one moment occurs to us at another; and the repugnance vanishes when we find, as we usually do, on a closer inspection, that things are not so bad as they seemed.

This rule applies to the life of the intellect as well as to matters of practice. A man must wait for the right moment. Not even the greatest mind is capable of thinking for itself at all times. Hence a great mind does well to spend its leisure in reading, which, as I have said, is a substitute for thought; it brings stuff to the mind by letting another person do the thinking; although that is always done in a manner not our own. Therefore, a man should not read too much, in order that his mind may not become accustomed to the substitute and thereby forget the reality; that it may not form the habit of walking in well-worn paths; nor by following an alien course of thought grow a stranger to its own. Least of all should a man quite withdraw his gaze from the real world for the mere sake of reading; as the impulse and the temper which prompt to thought of one's own come far oftener from the world of reality than from the world of books. The real life that a man sees before him is the natural subject of thought; and in its strength as the primary element of existence, it can more easily than anything else rouse and influence the thinking mind.

After these considerations, it will not be matter for surprise that a man who thinks for himself can easily be distinguished from the book-philosopher by the very way in which he talks, by his marked earnestness, and the originality, directness, and personal conviction that stamp all his thoughts and expressions. The book-philosopher, on the other hand, lets it be seen that everything he has is second-hand; that his ideas are like the lumber and trash of an old furniture-shop, collected together from all quarters. Mentally, he is dull and pointless—a copy of a copy. His literary style is made up of conventional, nay, vulgar phrases, and terms that happen to be current; in this respect much like a small State where all the money that circulates is foreign, because it has no coinage of its own.

Mere experience can as little as reading supply the place of thought. It stands to thinking in the same relation in which eating stands to digestion and assimilation. When experience boasts that to its discoveries alone is due the advancement of the human race, it is as though the mouth were to claim the whole credit of maintaining the body in health.

The works of all truly capable minds are distinguished by a character of *decision* and *definiteness,* which means they are clear and free from obscurity. A truly capable mind always knows definitely and clearly what it is that it wants to express, whether its medium is prose, verse, or music. Other minds are not decisive and not definite; and by this they may be known for what they are.

The characteristic sign of a mind of the highest order is that it always judges at first hand. Everything it advances is the result of thinking for itself; and this is everywhere evident by the way in which it gives its thoughts utterance. Such a mind is like a Prince. In the realm of intellect its authority is imperial, whereas the authority of minds of a lower order is delegated only; as may be seen in their style, which has no independent stamp of its own.

Every one who really thinks for himself is so far like a monarch. His position is undelegated and supreme. His judgments, like royal decrees, spring from his own sovereign power and proceed directly from himself. He acknowledges authority as little as a monarch admits a command; he subscribes to nothing but what he has himself authorized. The multitude of common minds, laboring under all sorts of current opinions, authorities, prejudices, is like the people, which silently obeys the law and accepts orders from above.

Those who are so zealous and eager to settle debated questions by citing authorities, are really glad when they are able to put the understanding and the insight of others into the field in place of their own, which are wanting. Their number is legion. For, as Seneca says, there is no man but prefers belief to the exercise of judgment—*unusquisque mavult credere quam judicare.* In their controversies such people make a promiscuous use of the weapon of authority, and strike out at one another with it. If any one chances to become involved in such a contest, he will do well not to try reason and argument as a mode of defence; for against a weapon of that kind these people are like Siegfrieds, with a skin of horn, and dipped in the flood of incapacity for thinking and judging. They will meet his attack by bringing up their authorities as a way of abashing him—*argumentum ad verecundiam,* and then cry out that they have won the battle.

In the real world, be it never so fair, favorable and pleasant, we always live subject to the law of gravity which we have to be constantly overcoming. But in the world of intellect we are disembodied spirits, held in bondage to no such law, and free from penury and distress. Thus it is that there exists no happiness on earth like that which, at the auspicious moment, a fine and fruitful mind finds in itself.

The presence of a thought is like the presence of a woman we love. We fancy we shall never forget the thought nor become indifferent to the dear one. But out of sight, out of mind! The finest thought runs the risk of being irrevocably forgotten if we do not write it down, and the darling of being deserted if we do not marry her.

There are plenty of thoughts which are valuable to the man who thinks them; but only few of them which have enough strength to produce repercussive or reflex action—I mean, to win the reader's sympathy after they have been put on paper.

But still it must not be forgotten that a true value attaches only to what a man has thought in the first instance *for his own case.* Thinkers may be classed according as they think chiefly for their own case or for that of others. The former are the genuine independent thinkers; they really think and are really independent; they are the true *philosophers;* they alone are in earnest. The pleasure and the happiness of their existence consists in thinking. The others are the *sophists;* they want to seem that which they are not, and seek their happiness in what they hope to get from the world. They are in earnest about nothing else. To which of these two classes a man belongs may be seen by his whole style and manner. Lichtenberg is an example for the former class; Herder, there can be no doubt, belongs to the second.

When one considers how vast and how close to us is *the problem of existence*—this equivocal, tortured, fleeting, dream-like existence of ours—so vast and so close that a man no sooner discovers it than it overshadows and obscures all other problems and aims; and when one sees how all men, with few and rare exceptions, have no clear consciousness of the problem, nay, seem to be quite unaware of its presence, but busy themselves with everything rather than with this, and live on, taking no thought but for the passing day and the hardly longer span of their own personal future, either expressly discarding the problem or else over-ready to come to terms with it by adopting some system of popular metaphysics and letting it satisfy them; when, I say, one takes all this to heart, one may come to the opinion that man may be said to be *a thinking being* only in a very remote sense, and henceforth feel no special surprise at any trait of human thoughtlessness or folly; but know, rather, that the normal man's intellectual range of vision does indeed extend beyond that of the brute, whose whole existence is, as it were, a continual present, with no consciousness of the past or the future, but not such an immeasurable distance as is generally supposed.

This is, in fact, corroborated by the way in which most men converse; where their thoughts are found to be chopped up fine, like chaff, so that for them to spin out a discourse of any length is impossible.

If this world were peopled by really thinking beings, it could not be that noise of every kind would be allowed such generous limits, as is the case with the most horrible and at the same time aimless form of it.[3] If Nature had meant man to think, she would not have given him ears; or, at any rate, she would have furnished them with airtight flaps, such as are the enviable possession of the bat. But, in truth, man is a poor animal like the rest, and his powers are meant only to maintain him in the struggle for existence; so he must needs keep his ears always open, to announce of themselves, by night as by day, the approach of the pursuer.

---

[3] *Translator's Note.*—Schopenhauer refers to the cracking of whips. See the essay *On Noise* in *Studies in Pessimism*.

On Criticism

The following brief remarks on the critical faculty are chiefly intended to show that, for the most part, there is no such thing. It is a *rara avis;* almost as rare, indeed, as the phoenix, which appears only once in five hundred years.

When we speak of *taste*—an expression not chosen with any regard for it—we mean the discovery, or, it may be only the recognition, of what is *right aesthetically,* apart from the guidance of any rule; and this, either because no rule has as yet been extended to the matter in question, or else because, if existing, it is unknown to the artist, or the critic, as the case may be. Instead of *taste,* we might use the expression *aesthetic sense,* if this were not tautological.

The perceptive critical taste is, so to speak, the female analogue to the male quality of productive talent or genius. Not capable of *begetting* great work itself, it consists in a capacity of *reception,* that is to say, of recognizing as such what is right, fit, beautiful, or the reverse; in other words, of discriminating the good from the bad, of discovering and appreciating the one and condemning the other.

In appreciating a genius, criticism should not deal with the errors in his productions or with the poorer of his works, and then proceed to rate him low; it should attend only to the qualities in which he most excels. For in the sphere of intellect, as in other spheres, weakness and perversity cleave so firmly to human nature that even the most brilliant mind is not wholly and at all times free from them. Hence the great errors to be found even in the works of the greatest men; or as Horace puts it, *quandoque bonus dormitat Homerus.*[*]

That which distinguishes genius, and should be the standard for judging it, is the height to which it is able to soar when it is in the proper mood and finds a fitting occasion —a height always out of the reach of ordinary talent. And, in like manner, it is a very dangerous thing to compare two great men of the same class; for instance, two great poets, or musicians, or philosophers, or artists; because injustice to the one or the other, at least for the moment, can hardly be avoided. For in making a comparison of the kind the critic looks to some particular merit of the one and at once discovers that it is absent in the other, who is thereby disparaged. And then if the process is reversed, and the critic begins with the latter and discovers his peculiar merit, which is quite of a different order from that presented by the former, with whom it may be looked for in vain, the result is that both of them suffer undue depreciation.

There are critics who severally think that it rests with each one of them what shall be accounted good, and what bad. They all mistake their own toy-trumpets for the trombones of fame.

A drug does not effect its purpose if the dose is too large; and it is the same with censure and adverse criticism when it exceeds the measure of justice.

The disastrous thing for intellectual merit is that it must wait for those to praise the good who have themselves produced nothing but what is bad; nay, it is a primary misfortune that it has to receive its crown at the hands of the critical power of mankind—a

---

[*] *Ars poetica* 359: Sometimes even great Homer nods.

quality of which most men possess only the weak and impotent semblance, so that the reality may be numbered amongst the rarest gifts of nature. Hence La Bruyère's remark is, unhappily, as true as it is neat. *Après l'esprit de discernement,* he says, *ce qu'il y a au monde de plus rare, ce sont les diamans et les perles.** The spirit of discernment! the critical faculty! it is these that are lacking. Men do not know how to distinguish the genuine from the false, the corn from the chaff, gold from copper; or to perceive the wide gulf that separates a genius from an ordinary man. Thus we have that bad state of things described in an old-fashioned verse, which gives it as the lot of the great ones here on earth to be recognized only when they are gone:

Es ist nun das Geschick der Grossen hier auf Erden,
Erst wann sie nicht mehr sind, von uns erkannt zu
  werden.

When any genuine and excellent work makes its appearance, the chief difficulty in its way is the amount of bad work it finds already in possession of the field, and accepted as though it were good. And then if, after a long time, the new comer really succeeds, by a hard struggle, in vindicating his place for himself and winning reputation, he will soon encounter fresh difficulty from some affected, dull, awkward imitator, whom people drag in, with the object of calmly setting him up on the altar beside the genius; not seeing the difference and really thinking that here they have to do with another great man. This is what Yriarte means by the first lines of his twenty-eighth Fable, where he declares that the ignorant rabble always sets equal value on the good and the bad:

Siempre acostumbra hacer el vulgo necio
  De lo bueno y lo malo igual aprecio.

So even Shakespeare's dramas had, immediately after his death, to give place to those of Ben Jonson, Massinger, Beaumont and Fletcher, and to yield the supremacy for a hundred years. So Kant's serious philosophy was crowded out by the nonsense of Fichte, Schelling, Jacobi, Hegel. And even in a sphere accessible to all, we have seen unworthy imitators quickly diverting public attention from the incomparable Walter Scott. For, say what you will, the public has no sense for excellence, and therefore no notion how very rare it is to find men really capable of doing anything great in poetry, philosophy, or art, or that their works are alone worthy of exclusive attention. The dabblers, whether in verse or in any other high sphere, should be every day unsparingly reminded that neither gods, nor men, nor booksellers have pardoned their mediocrity:

mediocribus esse poetis
Non homines, non Dî, non concessere columnae.[1]

Are they not the weeds that prevent the corn coming up, so that they may cover all the ground themselves? And then there happens that which has been well and freshly described by the lamented Feuchtersleben,[2] who died so young: how people cry out in their haste that nothing is being done, while all the while great work is quietly growing to maturity; and then, when it appears, it is not seen or heard in the clamor, but goes its way silently, in modest grief:

"Ist doch,"—rufen sie vermessen—
"Nichts im Werke, nichts gethan!"
Und das Grosse, reift indessen
Still heran.
Es ersheint nun: niemand sieht es,
Niemand hört es im Geschrei
Mit bescheid'ner Trauer zieht es
Still vorbei.

---

* The rarest things in the world after the spirit of discernment are diamonds and pearls.

[1] Horace, *Ars Poetica*, 372.

[2] *Translator's Note.*—Ernst Freiherr von Feuchtersleben (1806–49), an Austrian physician, philosopher, and poet, and a specialist in medical psychology. The best known of his songs is that beginning *"Es ist bestimmt in Gottes Rath,"* to which Mendelssohn composed one of his finest melodies.

This lamentable death of the critical faculty is not less obvious in the case of science, as is shown by the tenacious life of false and disproved theories. If they are once accepted, they may go on bidding defiance to truth for fifty or even a hundred years and more, as stable as an iron pier in the midst of the waves. The Ptolemaic system was still held a century after Copernicus had promulgated his theory. Bacon, Descartes and Locke made their way extremely slowly and only after a long time; as the reader may see by d'Alembert's celebrated Preface to the *Encyclopedia.* Newton was not more successful; and this is sufficiently proved by the bitterness and contempt with which Leibnitz attacked his theory of gravitation in the controversy with Clarke. Although Newton lived for almost forty years after the appearance of the *Principia,* his teaching was, when he died, only to some extent accepted in his own country, whilst outside England he counted scarcely twenty adherents; if we may believe the introductory note to Voltaire's exposition of his theory. It was, indeed, chiefly owing to this treatise of Voltaire's that the system became known in France nearly twenty years after Newton's death. Until then a firm, resolute, and patriotic stand was made by the Cartesian *Vortices;* whilst only forty years previously, this same Cartesian philosophy had been forbidden in the French schools; and now in turn d'Agnesseau, the Chancellor, refused Voltaire the *Imprimatur* for his treatise on the Newtonian doctrine. On the other hand, in our day Newton's absurd theory of color still completely holds the field, forty years after the publication of Goethe's. Hume, too, was disregarded up to his fiftieth year, though he began very early and wrote in a thoroughly popular style. And Kant, in spite of having written and talked all his life long, did not become a famous man until he was sixty.

Artists and poets have, to be sure, more chance than thinkers, because their public is at least a hundred times as large. Still, what was thought of Beethoven and Mozart during their lives? what of Dante? what even of Shakespeare? If the latter's contemporaries had in any way recognized his worth, at least one good and accredited portrait of him would have come down to us from an age when the art of painting flourished; whereas we possess only some very doubtful pictures, a bad copperplate, and a still worse bust on his tomb. And in like manner, if he had been duly honored, specimens of his handwriting would have been preserved to us by the hundred, instead of being confined, as is the case, to the signatures to a few legal documents. The Portuguese are still proud of their only poet Camoëns. He lived, however, on alms collected every evening in the street by a black slave whom he had brought with him from the Indies. In time, no doubt, justice will be done everyone; *tempo è galant' uomo;* but it is as late and slow in arriving as in a court of law, and the secret condition of it is that the recipient shall be no longer alive. The precept of Jesus the son of Sirach is faithfully followed: *Judge none blessed before his death.*[3] He, then, who has produced immortal works, must find comfort by applying to them the words of the Indian myth, that the minutes of life amongst the immortals seem like years of earthly existence; and so, too, that years upon earth are only as the minutes of the immortals.

This lack of critical insight is also shown by the fact that, while in every century the excellent work of earlier time is held in honor, that of its own is misunderstood, and the attention which is its due is given to bad work, such as every decade carries with it only to be the sport of the next. That men are slow to recognize genuine merit when it appears in their own age, also proves that they do not understand or enjoy or really value the long-acknowledged works of genius, which they honor only on the score of authority. The crucial test is the fact that bad work—Fichte's philosophy, for example—if it wins any reputation, also maintains it for one or two generations; and only when its public is very large does its fall follow sooner.

Now, just as the sun cannot shed its light

---

[3] *Ecclesiasticus,* xi. 28.

but to the eye that sees it, nor music sound but to the hearing ear, so the value of all masterly work in art and science is conditioned by the kinship and capacity of the mind to which it speaks. It is only such a mind as this that possesses the magic word to stir and call forth the spirits that lie hidden in great work. To the ordinary mind a masterpiece is a sealed cabinet of mystery,—an unfamiliar musical instrument from which the player, however much he may flatter himself, can draw none but confused tones. How different a painting looks when seen in a good light, as compared with some dark corner! Just in the same way, the impression made by a masterpiece varies with the capacity of the mind to understand it.

A fine work, then, requires a mind sensitive to its beauty; a thoughtful work, a mind that can really think, if it is to exist and live at all. But alas! it may happen only too often that he who gives a fine work to the world afterwards feels like a maker of fireworks, who displays with enthusiasm the wonders that have taken him so much time and trouble to prepare, and then learns that he has come to the wrong place, and that the fancied spectators were one and all inmates of an asylum for the blind. Still even that is better than if his public had consisted entirely of men who made fireworks themselves; as in this case, if his display had been extraordinarily good, it might possibly have cost him his head.

The source of all pleasure and delight is the feeling of kinship. Even with the sense of beauty it is unquestionably our own species in the animal world, and then again our own race, that appears to us the fairest. So, too, in intercourse with others, every man shows a decided preference for those who resemble him: and a blockhead will find the society of another blockhead incomparably more pleasant than that of any number of great minds put together. Every man must necessarily take his chief pleasure in his own work, because it is the mirror of his own mind, the echo of his own thought; and next in order will come the work of people like him; that is

to say, a dull, shallow and perverse man, a dealer in mere words, will give his sincere and hearty applause only to that which is dull, shallow, perverse or merely verbose. On the other hand, he will allow merit to the work of great minds only on the score of authority, in other words, because he is ashamed to speak his opinion; for in reality they give him no pleasure at all. They do not appeal to him; nay, they repel him; and he will not confess this even to himself. The works of genius cannot be fully enjoyed except by those who are themselves of the privileged order. The first recognition of them, however, when they exist without authority to support them, demands considerable superiority of mind.

When the reader takes all this into consideration, he should be surprised, not that great work is so late in winning reputation, but that it wins it at all. And as a matter of fact, fame comes only by a slow and complex process. The stupid person is by degrees forced, and as it were, tamed, into recognizing the superiority of one who stands immediately above him; this one in his turn bows before some one else; and so it goes on until the weight of votes gradually prevail over their number; and this is just the condition of all genuine, in other words, deserved fame. But until then, the greatest genius, even after he has passed his time of trial, stands like a king amidst a crowd of his own subjects, who do not know him by sight and therefore will not do his behests; unless, indeed, his chief ministers of state are in his train. For no subordinate official can be the direct recipient of the royal commands, as he knows only the signature of his immediate superior; and this is repeated all the way up into the highest ranks, where the undersecretary attests the minister's signature, and the minister that of the king. There are analogous stages to be passed before a genius can attain widespread fame. This is why his reputation most easily comes to a standstill at the very outset; because the highest authorities, of whom there can be but few, are most frequently not to be found; but the further down he goes in the scale the more numerous are those who take the word from above, so that his fame is no more arrested.

We must console ourselves for this state of things by reflecting that it is really fortunate that the greater number of men do not form a judgment on their own responsibility, but merely take it on authority. For what sort of criticism should we have on Plato and Kant, Homer, Shakespeare and Goethe, if every man were to form his opinion by what he really has and enjoys of these writers, instead of being forced by authority to speak of them in a fit and proper way, however little he may really feel what he says. Unless something of this kind took place, it would be impossible for true merit, in any high sphere, to attain fame at all. At the same time it is also fortunate that every man has just so much critical power of his own as is necessary for recognizing the superiority of those who are placed immediately over him, and for following their lead. This means that the many come in the end to submit to the authority of the few; and there results that hierarchy of critical judgments on which is based the possibility of a steady, and eventually wide-reaching, fame.

The lowest class in the community is quite impervious to the merits of a great genius; and for these people there is nothing left but the monument raised to him, which, by the impression it produces on their senses, awakes in them a dim idea of the man's greatness.

Literary journals should be a dam against the unconscionable scribbling of the age, and the ever-increasing deluge of bad and useless books. Their judgments should be uncorrupted, just and rigorous; and every piece of bad work done by an incapable person; every device by which the empty head tries to come to the assistance of the empty purse, that is to say, about nine-tenths of all existing books, should be mercilessly scourged. Literary journals would then perform their duty, which is to keep down the craving for writing and put a check upon the deception of the public, instead of furthering these evils by a miserable toleration, which plays into the hands of author and publisher, and robs the reader of his time and his money.

If there were such a paper as I mean, every bad writer, every brainless compiler, every plagiarist from other's books, every hollow and incapable place-hunter, every sham-philosopher, every vain and languishing poetaster, would shudder at the prospect of the pillory in which his bad work would inevitably have to stand soon after publication. This would paralyze his twitching fingers, to the true welfare of literature, in which what is bad is not only useless but positively pernicious. Now, most books are bad and ought to have remained unwritten. Consequently praise should be as rare as is now the case with blame, which is withheld under the influence of personal considerations, coupled with the maxim *accedas socius, laudes lauderis ut absens.**

It is quite wrong to try to introduce into literature the same toleration as must necessarily prevail in society towards those stupid, brainless people who everywhere swarm in it. In literature such people are impudent intruders; and to disparage the bad is here duty towards the good; for he who thinks nothing bad will think nothing good either. Politeness, which has its source in social relations, is in literature an alien, and often injurious, element; because it exacts that bad work shall be called good. In this way the very aim of science and art is directly frustrated.

The ideal journal could, to be sure, be written only by people who joined incorruptible honesty with rare knowledge and still rarer power of judgment; so that perhaps there could, at the very most, be one, and even hardly one, in the whole country; but there it would stand, like a just Areopagus, every member of which would have to be elected by all the others. Under the system that prevails at present, literary journals are carried on by a clique, and secretly perhaps also by booksellers for the good of the trade;

_____
* Present or absent, sing the praises of your associate.

and they are often nothing but coalitions of bad heads to prevent the good ones succeeding. As Goethe once remarked to me, nowhere is there so much dishonesty as in literature.

But, above all, anonymity, that shield of all literary rascality, would have to disappear. It was introduced under the pretext of protecting the honest critic, who warned the public, against the resentment of the author and his friends. But where there is one case of this sort, there will be a hundred where it merely serves to take all responsibility from the man who cannot stand by what he has said, or possibly to conceal the shame of one who has been cowardly and base enough to recommend a book to the public for the purpose of putting money into his own pocket. Often enough it is only a cloak for covering the obscurity, incompetence and insignificance of the critic. It is incredible what impudence these fellows will show, and what literary trickery they will venture to commit, as soon as they know they are safe under the shadow of anonymity. Let me recommend a general *Anti-criticism,* a universal medicine or panacea, to put a stop to all anonymous reviewing, whether it praises the bad or blames the good: *Rascal! your name!* For a man to wrap himself up and draw his hat over his face, and then fall upon people who are walking about without any disguise—this is not the part of a gentleman, it is the part of a scoundrel and a knave.

An anonymous review has no more authority than an anonymous letter; and one should be received with the same mistrust as the other. Or shall we take the name of the man who consents to preside over what is, in the strict sense of the word, *une société anonyme* as a guarantee for the veracity of his colleagues?

Even Rousseau, in the preface to the *Nouvelle Héloïse,* declares *tout honnête homme doit avouer les livres qu'il publie;* which in plain language means that every honorable man ought to sign his articles, and that no one is honorable who does not do so. How much truer this is of polemical writing, which is the general character of reviews! Riemer was quite right in the opinion he gives in his *Reminiscences of Goethe:*[4] *An overt enemy,* he says, *an enemy who meets you face to face, is an honorable man, who will treat you fairly, and with whom you can come to terms and be reconciled: but an enemy who conceals himself is a base, cowardly scoundrel, who has not courage enough to avow his own judgment; it is not his opinion that he cares about, but only the secret pleasures of wreaking his anger without being found out or punished.* This will also have been Goethe's opinion, as he was generally the source from which Riemer drew his observations. And, indeed, Rousseau's maxim applies to every line that is printed. Would a man in a mask ever be allowed to harangue a mob, or speak in any assembly; and that, too, when he was going to attack others and overwhelm them with abuse?

Anonymity is the refuge for all literary and journalistic rascality. It is a practice which must be completely stopped. Every article, even in a newspaper, should be accompanied by the name of its author; and the editor should be made strictly responsible for the accuracy of the signature. The freedom of the press should be thus far restricted; so that when a man publicly proclaims through the far-sounding trumpet of the newspaper, he should be answerable for it, at any rate with his honor, if he has any; and if he has none, let his name neutralize the effect of his words. And since even the most insignificant person is known in his own circle, the result of such a measure would be to put an end to two-thirds of the newspaper lies, and to restrain the audacity of many a poisonous tongue.

---

[4] Preface, p. xxix.

On Genius

No difference of rank, position, or birth, is so great as the gulf that separates the countless millions who use their head only in the service of their belly, in other words, look upon it as an instrument of the will, and those very few and rare persons who have the courage to say: No! it is too good for that; my head shall be active only in its own service; it shall try to comprehend the wondrous and varied spectacle of this world, and then reproduce it in some form, whether as art or as literature, that may answer to my character as an individual. These are the truly noble, the real *noblesse* of the world. The others are serfs and go with the soil—*glebae adscripti.* Of course, I am here referring to those who have not only the courage, but also the call, and therefore the right, to order the head to quit the service of the will; with a result that proves the sacrifice to have been worth the making. In the case of those to whom all this can only partially apply, the gulf is not so wide; but even though their talent be small, so long as it is real, there will always be a sharp line of demarcation between them and the millions.[1]

The works of fine art, poetry and philosophy produced by a nation are the outcome of the superfluous intellect existing in it.

For him who can understand aright—*cum grano salis**—the relation between the genius and the normal man may, perhaps, be best expressed as follows: A genius has a double intellect, one for himself and the service of his will; the other for the world, of which he becomes the mirror, in virtue of his purely objective attitude towards it. The work of art or poetry or philosophy produced by the genius is simply the result, or quintessence, of this contemplative attitude, elaborated according to certain technical rules.

The normal man, on the other hand, has only a single intellect, which may be called *subjective* by contrast with the *objective* intellect of genius. However acute this subjective intellect may be—and it exists in very various degrees of perfection—it is never on the same level with the double intellect of genius; just as the open chest notes of the human voice, however high, are essentially different from the falsetto notes. These, like the two upper octaves of the flute and the harmonics of the violin, are produced by the column of air dividing itself into two vibrating halves, with a node between them; while the open chest notes of the human voice and the lower octave of the flute are produced by the undivided column of air vibrating as a whole. This illustration may help the reader to understand that specific peculiarity of genius which is unmistakably stamped on the works, and even on the physiognomy, of him who is gifted with it. At the same time it is obvious that a double intellect like this must, as a rule, obstruct the service of the will; and this explains the poor capacity often shown by genius in the conduct of life. And what specially

---

[1] The correct scale for adjusting the hierarchy of intelligences is furnished by the degree in which the mind takes merely individual or approaches universal views of things. The brute recognizes only the individual as such: its comprehension does not extend beyond the limits of the individual. But man reduces the individual to the general; herein lies the exercise of his reason; and the higher his intelligence reaches, the nearer do his general ideas approach the point at which they become universal.

* With a grain of salt.

characterizes genius is that it has none of that sobriety of temper which is always to be found in the ordinary simple intellect, be it acute or dull.

The brain may be likened to a parasite which is nourished as a part of the human frame without contributing directly to its inner economy; it is securely housed in the topmost story, and there leads a self-sufficient and independent life. In the same way it may be said that a man endowed with great mental gifts leads, apart from the individual life common to all, a second life, purely of the intellect. He devotes himself to the constant increase, rectification and extension, not of mere learning, but of real systematic knowledge and insight; and remains untouched by the fate that overtakes him personally, so long as it does not disturb him in his work. It is thus a life which raises a man and sets him above fate and its changes. Always thinking, learning, experimenting, practicing his knowledge, the man soon comes to look upon this second life as the chief mode of existence, and his merely personal life as something subordinate, serving only to advance ends higher than itself.

An example of this independent, separate existence is furnished by Goethe. During the war in the Champagne, and amid all the bustle of the camp, he made observations for his theory of color; and as soon as the numberless calamities of that war allowed of his retiring for a short time to the fortress of Luxembourg, he took up the manuscript of his *Farbenlehre*. This is an example which we, the salt of the earth, should endeavor to follow, by never letting anything disturb us in the pursuit of our intellectual life, however much the storm of the world may invade and agitate our personal environment; always remembering that we are the sons, not of the bondwoman, but of the free. As our emblem and coat of arms, I propose a tree mightily shaken by the wind, but still bearing its ruddy fruit on every branch; with the motto *Dum convellor mitescunt,* or *Conquassata sed ferax.**

That purely intellectual life of the in-

dividual has its counterpart in humanity as a whole. For there, too, the real life is the life of the *will*, both in the empirical and in the transcendental meaning of the word. The purely intellectual life of humanity lies in its effort to increase knowledge by means of the sciences, and its desire to perfect the arts. Both science and art thus advance slowly from one generation to another, and grow with the centuries, every race as it hurries by furnishing its contribution. This intellectual life, like some gift from heaven, hovers over the stir and movement of the world; or it is, as it were, a sweet-scented air developed out of the ferment itself—the real life of mankind, dominated by will; and side by side with the history of nations, the history of philosophy, science and art takes its innocent and bloodless way.

The difference between the genius and the ordinary man is, no doubt, a *quantitative* one, insofar as it is a difference of degree; but I am tempted to regard it also as *qualitative,* in view of the fact that ordinary minds, notwithstanding individual variation, have a certain tendency to think alike. Thus on similar occasions their thoughts at once all take a similar direction, and run on the same lines; and this explains why their judgments constantly agree—not, however, because they are based on truth. To such lengths does this go that certain fundamental views obtain amongst mankind at all times, and are always being repeated and brought forward anew, whilst the great minds of all ages are in open or secret opposition to them.

A genius is a man in whose mind the world is presented as an object is presented in a mirror, but with a degree more of clearness and greater distinction of outline than is attained by ordinary people. It is from him that humanity may look for most instruction; for the deepest insight into the most important matters is to be acquired, not by an observant attention to detail, but by a close study

---

* While I am shaken, they ripen, or, Shaken but fruitful.

of things as a whole. And if his mind reaches maturity, the instruction he gives will be conveyed now in one form, now in another. Thus genius may be defined as an eminently clear consciousness of things in general, and therefore, also of that which is opposed to them, namely, one's own self.

The world looks up to a man thus endowed, and expects to learn something about life and its real nature. But several highly favorable circumstances must combine to produce genius, and this is a very rare event. It happens only now and then, let us say once in a century, that a man is born whose intellect so perceptibly surpasses the normal measure as to amount to that second faculty which seems to be accidental, as it is out of all relation to the will. He may remain a long time without being recognized or appreciated, stupidity preventing the one and envy the other. But should this once come to pass, mankind will crowd round him and his works, in the hope that he may be able to enlighten some of the darkness of their existence or inform them about it. His message is, to some extent, a revelation, and he himself a higher being, even though he may be but little above the ordinary standard.

Like the ordinary man, the genius is what he is chiefly for himself. This is essential to his nature: a fact which can neither be avoided nor altered. What he may be for others remains a matter of chance and of secondary importance. In no case can people receive from his mind more than a reflection, and then only when he joins with them in the attempt to get his thought into their heads; where, however, it is never anything but an exotic plant, stunted and frail.

In order to have original, uncommon, and perhaps even immortal thoughts, it is enough to estrange oneself so fully from the world of things for a few moments, that the most ordinary objects and events appear quite new and unfamiliar. In this way their true nature is disclosed. What is here demanded cannot, perhaps, be said to be difficult; it is not in our power at all, but is just the province of genius.

By itself, genius can produce original thoughts just as little as a woman by herself can bear children. Outward circumstances must come to fructify genius, and be, as it were, a father to its progeny.

The mind of genius is among other minds what the carbuncle is among precious stones: it sends forth light of its own, while the others reflect only that which they have received. The relation of the genius to the ordinary mind may also be described as that of an idio-electrical body to one which merely is a conductor of electricity.

The mere man of learning, who spends his life in teaching what he has learned, is not strictly to be called a man of genius; just as idio-electrical bodies are not conductors. Nay, genius stands to mere learning as the words to the music in a song. A man of learning is a man who has learned a great deal; a man of genius, one from whom we learn something which the genius has learned from nobody. Great minds, of which there is scarcely one in a hundred millions, are thus the lighthouses of humanity; and without them mankind would lose itself in the boundless sea of monstrous error and bewilderment.

And so the simple man of learning, in the strict sense of the word—the ordinary professor, for instance—looks upon the genius much as we look upon a hare, which is good to eat after it has been killed and dressed up. So long as it is alive, it is only good to shoot at.

He who wishes to experience gratitude from his contemporaries, must adjust his pace to theirs. But great things are never produced in this way. And he who wants to do great things must direct his gaze to posterity, and in firm confidence elaborate his work for coming generations. No doubt, the result may be that he will remain quite unknown to his contemporaries, and comparable to a man who, compelled to spend his life upon a lonely island, with great effort sets up a monument there, to transmit to future seafarers the knowledge of his existence. If he thinks it a hard fate, let him console himself with the reflection that the ordinary man who lives for practical aims only, often suffers a like fate, without having any compensation to hope for; inasmuch as he may, under favorable conditions, spend a life of material production, earning, buying, building, fertilizing, laying out, founding, establishing, beautifying with daily effort and unflagging zeal, and all the time think that he is working for himself; and yet in the end it is his descendants who reap the benefit of it all, and sometimes not even his descendants. It is the same with the man of genius; he, too, hopes for his reward and for honor at least; and at last finds that he has worked for posterity alone. Both, to be sure, have inherited a great deal from their ancestors.

The compensation I have mentioned as the privilege of genius lies, not in what it is to others, but in what it is to itself. What man has in any real sense lived more than he whose moments of thought make their echoes heard through the tumult of centuries? Perhaps, after all, it would be the best thing for a genius to attain undisturbed possession of himself, by spending his life in enjoying the pleasure of his own thoughts, his own works, and by admitting the world only as the heir of his ample existence. Then the world would find the mark of his existence only after his death, as it finds that of the Ichnolith.

It is not only in the activity of his highest powers that the genius surpasses ordinary people. A man who is unusually well-knit, supple and agile, will perform all his movements with exceptional ease, even with comfort, because he takes a direct pleasure in an activity for which he is particularly well-equipped, and therefore often exercises it without any object. Further, if he is an acrobat or a dancer, not only does he take leaps which other people cannot execute, but he also betrays rare elasticity and agility in those easier steps which others can also perform, and even in ordinary walking. In the same way a man of superior mind will not only produce thoughts and works which could never have come from another; it will

not be here alone that he will show his greatness; but as knowledge and thought form a mode of activity natural and easy to him, he will also delight himself in them at all times, and so apprehend small matters which are within the range of other minds, more easily, quickly and correctly than they. Thus he will take a direct and lively pleasure in every increase of knowledge, every problem solved, every witty thought, whether of his own or another's; and so his mind will have no further aim than to be constantly active. This will be an inexhaustible spring of delight; and boredom, that spectre which haunts the ordinary man, can never come near him.

Then, too, the masterpieces of past and contemporary men of genius exist in their fullness for him alone. If a great product of genius is recommended to the ordinary, simple mind, it will take as much pleasure in it as the victim of gout receives in being invited to a ball. The one goes for the sake of formality, and the other reads the book so as not to be in arrear. For La Bruyère was quite right when he said: *All the wit in the world is lost upon him who has none.* The whole range of thought of a man of talent, or of a genius, compared with the thoughts of the common man, is, even when directed to objects essentially the same, like a brilliant oil-painting, full of life, compared with a mere outline or a weak sketch in water-color.

All this is part of the reward of genius, and compensates him for a lonely existence in a world with which he has nothing in common and no sympathies. But since size is relative, it comes to the same thing whether I say, Caius was a great man, or Caius has to live amongst wretchedly small people: for Brobdingnack and Lilliput vary only in the point from which they start. However great, then, however admirable or instructive, a long posterity may think the author of immortal works, during his lifetime he will appear to his contemporaries small, wretched, and insipid in proportion. This is what I mean by saying that as there are three hundred degrees from the base of a tower to the summit, so there are exactly three hundred from the summit to the base. Great minds thus owe little ones some indulgence; for it is only in virtue of these little minds that they themselves are great.

Let us, then, not be suprised if we find men of genius generally unsociable and repellent. It is not their want of sociability that is to blame. Their path through the world is like that of a man who goes for a walk on a bright summer morning. He gazes with delight on the beauty and freshness of nature, but he has to rely wholly on that for entertainment; for he can find no society but the peasants as they bend over the earth and cultivate the soil. It is often the case that a great mind prefers soliloquy to the dialogue he may have in this world. If he condescends to it now and then, the hollowness of it may possibly drive him back to his soliloquy; for in forgetfulness of his interlocutor, or caring little whether he understands or not, he talks to him as a child talks to a doll.

Modesty in a great mind would, no doubt, be pleasing to the world; but, unluckily, it is a *contradictio in adjecto.*[*] It would compel a genius to give the thoughts and opinions, nay, even the method and style, of the million preference over his own; to set a higher value upon them; and, wide apart as they are, to bring his views into harmony with theirs, or even suppress them altogether, so as to let the others hold the field. In that case, however, he would either produce nothing at all, or else his achievements would be just upon a level with theirs. Great, genuine and extraordinary work can be done only in so far as its author disregards the method, the thoughts, the opinions of his contemporaries, and quietly works on, in spite of their criticism, on his side despising what they praise. No one becomes great without arrogance of this sort. Should his life and work fall upon a time which cannot recognize and appreciate him, he is at any rate true to himself; like some noble traveler forced to pass the night in a miserable inn; when morning comes, he contentedly goes his way.

A poet or philosopher should have no fault to find with his age if it only permits him to do his work undisturbed in his own corner; nor with his fate if the corner granted him allows of his following his vocation without having to think about other people.

For the brain to be a mere laborer in the service of the belly, is indeed the common lot of almost all those who do not live on the work of their hands; and they are far from being discontented with their lot. But it strikes despair into a man of great mind, whose brain-power goes beyond the measure necessary for the service of the will; and he prefers, if need be, to live in the narrowest circumstances, so long as they afford him the free use of his time for the development and application of his faculties; in other words, if they give him the leisure which is invaluable to him.

It is otherwise with ordinary people: for them leisure has no value in itself, nor is it, indeed, without its dangers, as these people seem to know. The technical work of our time, which is done to an unprecedented perfection, has, by increasing and multiplying objects of luxury, given the favorites of fortune a choice between more leisure and culture upon the one side, and additional luxury and good living, but with increased activity, upon the other; and, true to their character, they choose the latter, and prefer champagne to freedom. And they are consistent in their choice; for, to them, every exertion of the mind which does not serve the aims of the will is folly. Intellectual effort for its own sake, they call eccentricity. Therefore, persistence in the aims of the will and the belly will be concentricity; and, to be sure, the will is the centre, the kernel of the world.

But in general it is very seldom that any such alternative is presented. For as with money, most men have no superfluity, but only just enough for their needs, so with intelligence; they possess just what will suffice for the service of the will, that is, for the

---

[*] A contradiction between an adjective and its noun.

carrying on their business. Having made their fortune, they are content to gape or to indulge in sensual pleasures or childish amusements, cards or dice; or they will talk in the dullest way, or dress up and make obeisance to one another. And how few are those who have even a little superfluity of intellectual power! Like the others they too make themselves a pleasure; but it is a pleasure of the intellect. Either they will pursue some liberal study which brings them in nothing, or they will practice some art; and in general, they will be capable of taking an objective interest in things, so that it will be possible to converse with them. But with the others it is better not to enter into any relations at all; for, except when they tell the results of their own experience or give an account of their special vocation, or at any rate impart what they have learned from some one else, their conversation will not be worth listening to; and if anything is said to them, they will rarely grasp or understand it aright, and it will in most cases be opposed to their own opinions. Balthazar Gracian describes them very strikingly as men who are not men—*hombres che non lo son.* And Giordano Bruno says the same thing: *What a difference there is in having to do with men compared with those who are only made in their image and likeness!* And how wonderfully this passage agrees with that remark in the Kurral: *The common people look like men but I have never seen anything quite like them.* If the reader will consider the extent to which these ideas agree in thought and even in expression, and in the wide difference between them in point of date and nationality, he cannot doubt but that they are at one with the facts of life. It was certainly not under the influence of those passages that, about twenty years ago, I tried to get a snuff-box made, the lid of which should have two fine chestnuts represented upon it, if possible in mosaic; together with a leaf which was to show that they were horse-chestnuts. This symbol was meant to keep the thought constantly before my mind. If anyone wishes for entertainment, such as will prevent him

feeling solitary even when he is alone, let me recommend the company of dogs, whose moral and intellectual qualities may almost afford delight and gratification.

Still, we should always be careful to avoid being unjust. I am often surprised by the cleverness, and now and again by the stupidity of my dog; and I have similar experiences with mankind. Countless times, in indignation at their incapacity, their total lack of discernment, their bestiality, I have been forced to echo the old complaint that folly is the mother and the nurse of the human race:

Humani generis mater nutrixque profecto
Stultitia est.

But at other times I have been astounded that from such a race there could have gone forth so many arts and sciences, abounding in so much use and beauty, even though it has always been the few that produce them. Yet these arts and sciences have struck root, established and perfected themselves: and the race has with persistent fidelity preserved Homer, Plato, Horace and others for thousands of years, by copying and treasuring their writings, thus saving them from oblivion, in spite of all the evils and atrocities that have happened in the world. Thus the race has proved that it appreciates the value of these things, and at the same time it can form a correct view of special achievements or estimate signs of judgment and intelligence. When this takes place amongst those who belong to the great multitude, it is by a kind of inspiration. Sometimes a correct opinion will be formed by the multitude itself; but this is only when the chorus of praise has grown full and complete. It is then like the sound of untrained voices; where there are enough of them, it is always harmonious.

Those who emerge from the multitude, those who are called men of genius, are merely the *lucida intervalla* of the whole human race. They achieve that which others could not possibly achieve. Their originality is so great that not only is their divergence from others obvious, but their individuality is expressed with such force, that all the men of genius who have ever existed show, every one of them, peculiarities of character and mind; so that the gift of his works is one which he alone of all men could ever have presented to the world. This is what makes that simile of Ariosto's so true and so justly celebrated: *Natura lo fece e poi ruppe lo stampo.* After Nature stamps a man of genius, she breaks the die.

But there is always a limit to human capacity; and no one can be a great genius without having some decidedly weak side, it may even be, some intellectual narrowness. In other words, there will be some faculty in which he is now and then inferior to men of moderate endowments. It will be a faculty which, if strong, might have been an obstacle to the exercise of the qualities in which he excels. What this weak point is, it will always ⁚be hard to define with any accuracy even in a given case. It may be better expressed indirectly; thus Plato's weak point is exactly that in which Aristotle is strong, and *vice versa;* and so, too, Kant is deficient just where Goethe is great.

Now, mankind is fond of venerating something; but its veneration is generally directed to the wrong object, and it remains so directed until posterity comes to set it right. But the educated public is no sooner set right in this, than the honor which is due to genius degenerates; just as the honor which the faithful pay to their saints easily passes into a frivolous worship of relics. Thousands of Christians adore the relics of a saint whose life and doctrine are unknown to them; and the religion of thousands of Buddhists lies more in veneration of the Holy Tooth or some such object, or the vessel that contains it, or the Holy Bowl, or the fossil footstep, or the Holy Tree which Buddha planted, than in the thorough knowledge and faithful practice of his high teaching. Petrarch's house in Arqua; Tasso's supposed prison in Ferrara; Shakespeare's house in Stratford, with his chair; Goethe's house in Weimar,

with its furniture; Kant's old hat; the autographs of great men; these things are gaped at with interest and awe by many who have never read their works. They cannot do anything more than just gape.

The intelligent amongst them are moved by the wish to see the objects which the great man habitually had before his eyes; and by a strange illusion, these produce the mistaken notion that with the objects they are bringing back the man himself, or that something of him must cling to them. Akin to such people are those who earnestly strive to acquaint themselves with the subject-matter of a poet's works, or to unravel the personal circumstances and events in his life which have suggested particular passages. This is as though the audience in a theatre were to admire a fine scene and then rush upon the stage to look at the scaffolding that supports it. There are in our day enough instances of these critical investigators, and they prove the truth of the saying that mankind is interested, not in the *form* of a work, that is, in its manner of treatment, but in its actual matter. All it cares for is the theme. To read a philosopher's biography, instead of studying his thoughts, is like neglecting a picture and attending only to the style of its frame, debating whether it is carved well or ill, and how much it cost to gild it.

This is all very well. However, there is another class of persons whose interest is also directed to material and personal considerations, but they go much further and carry it to a point where it becomes absolutely futile. Because a great man has opened up to them the treasures of his inmost being, and, by a supreme effort of his faculties, produced works which not only redound to their elevation and enlightenment, but will also benefit their posterity to the tenth and twentieth generation; because he has presented mankind with a matchless gift, these varlets think themselves justified in sitting in judgment upon his personal morality, and trying if they cannot discover here or there some spot in him which will soothe the pain they feel at the sight of so great a mind, compared with the overwhelming feeling of their own nothingness.

This is the real source of all those prolix discussions, carried on in countless books and reviews, on the moral aspect of Goethe's life, and whether he ought not to have married one or other of the girls with whom he fell in love in his young days; whether, again, instead of honestly devoting himself to the service of his master, he should not have been a man of the people, a German patriot, worthy of a seat in the *Paulskirche,* and so on. Such crying ingratitude and malicious detraction prove that these self-constituted judges are as great knaves morally as they are intellectually, which is saying a great deal.

A man of talent will strive for money and reputation; but the spring that moves genius to the production of its works is not as easy to name. Wealth is seldom its reward. Nor is it reputation or glory; only a Frenchman could mean that. Glory is such an uncertain thing, and, if you look at it closely, of so little value. Besides it never corresponds to the effort you have made:

Responsura tuo nunquam est par fama labori.

Nor, again, is it exactly the pleasure it gives you; for this is almost outweighed by the greatness of the effort. It is rather a peculiar kind of instinct, which drives the man of genius to give permanent form to what he sees and feels, without being conscious of any further motive. It works, in the main, by a necessity similar to that which makes a tree bear its fruit; and no external condition is needed but the ground upon which it is to thrive.

On a closer examination, it seems as though, in the case of a genius, the will to live, which is the spirit of the human species, were conscious of having, by some rare chance, and for a brief period, attained a greater clearness of vision, and were now trying to secure it, or at least the outcome of it, for the whole species, to which the individual genius in his inmost being belongs; so that the light which he sheds about him may pierce the darkness and dullness of ordinary human consciousness and there produce some good effect.

Arising in some such way, this instinct drives the genius to carry his work to completion, without thinking of reward or applause or sympathy; to leave all care for his own personal welfare; to make his life one of industrious solitude, and to strain his faculties to the utmost. He thus comes to think more about posterity than about contemporaries; because, while the latter can only lead him astray, posterity forms the majority of the species, and time will gradually bring the discerning few who can appreciate him. Meanwhile it is with him as with the artist described by Goethe; he has no princely patron to prize his talents, no friend to rejoice with him:

Ein Fürst der die Talente schätzt,
Ein Freund, der sich mit mir ergötzt,
Die haben leider mir gefehlt.

His work is, as it were, a sacred object and the true fruit of his life, and his aim in storing it away for a more discerning posterity will be to make it the property of mankind. An aim like this far surpasses all others, and for it he wears the crown of thorns which is one day to bloom into a wreath of laurel. All his powers are concentrated in the effort to complete and secure his work; just as the insect, in the last stage of its development, uses its whole strength on behalf of a brood it will never live to see; it puts its eggs in some place of safety, where, as it well knows, the young will one day find life and nourishment, and then dies in confidence.

On the Sufferings of the World

Unless *suffering* is the direct and immediate object of life, our existence must entirely fail of its aim. It is absurd to look upon the enormous amount of pain that abounds everywhere in the world, and originates in needs and necessities inseparable from life itself, as serving no purpose at all and the result of mere chance. Each separate misfortune, as it comes, seems, no doubt, to be something exceptional; but misfortune in general is the rule.

I know of no greater absurdity than that propounded by most systems of philosophy in declaring evil to be negative in its character. Evil is just what is positive; it makes its own existence felt. Leibnitz is particularly concerned to defend this absurdity; and he seeks to strengthen his position by using a palpable and paltry sophism.[1] It is the good which is negative; in other words, happiness and satisfaction always imply some desire fulfilled, some state of pain brought to an end.

This explains the fact that we generally find pleasure to be not nearly so pleasant as we expected, and pain very much more painful.

The pleasure in this world, it has been said, outweighs the pain; or, at any rate, there is an even balance between the two. If the reader wishes to see shortly whether this statement is true, let him compare the respective feelings of two animals, one of which is engaged in eating the other.

The best consolation in misfortune or affliction of any kind will be the thought of other people who are in a still worse plight than yourself; and this is a form of consolation open to every one. But what an awful fate this means for mankind as a whole!

We are like lambs in a field, disporting themselves under the eye of the butcher, who chooses out first one and then another for his prey. So it is that in our good days we are all unconscious of the evil Fate may have presently in store for us—sickness, poverty, mutilation, loss of sight or reason.

No little part of the torment of existence lies in this, that Time is continually pressing upon us, never letting us take breath, but always coming after us, like a taskmaster with a whip. If at any moment Time stays his hand, it is only when we are delivered over to the misery of boredom.

But misfortune has its uses; for, as our bodily frame would burst asunder if the pressure of the atmosphere were removed, so, if the lives of men were relieved of all need, hardship and adversity; if everything they took in hand were successful, they would be so swollen with arrogance that, though they might not burst, they would present the spectacle of unbridled folly—nay, they would go mad. And I may say, further, that a certain amount of care or pain or trouble is necessary for every man at all times. A ship without ballast is unstable and will not go straight.

Certain it is that *work, worry, labour* and *trou-*

---

[1] *Translator's Note*, cf. *Théod,* § 153. Leibnitz argued that evil is a negative quality—*i.e.,* the absence of good; and that its active and seemingly positive character is an incidental and not an essential part of its nature. Cold, he said, is only the absence of the power of heat, and the active power of expansion in freezing water is an incidental and not an essential part of the nature of cold. The fact is, that the power of expansion in freezing water is really an increase of repulsion amongst its molecules; and Schopenhauer is quite right in calling the whole argument a sophism.

ble, form the lot of almost all men their whole life long. But if all wishes were fulfilled as soon as they arose, how would men occupy their lives? what would they do with their time? If the world were a paradise of luxury and ease, a land flowing with milk and honey, where every Jack obtained his Jill at once and without any difficulty, men would either die of boredom or hang themselves; or there would be wars, massacres, and murders; so that in the end mankind would inflict more suffering on itself than it has now to accept at the hands of Nature.

In early youth, as we contemplate our coming life, we are like children in a theatre before the curtain is raised, sitting there in high spirits and eagerly waiting for the play to begin. It is a blessing that we do not know what is really going to happen. Could we foresee it, there are times when children might seem like innocent prisoners, condemned, not to death, but to life, and as yet all unconscious of what their sentence means. Nevertheless, every man desires to reach old age; in other words, a state of life of which it may be said: "It is bad to-day, and it will be worse to-morrow; and so on till the worst of all."

If you try to imagine, as nearly as you can, what an amount of misery, pain and suffering of every kind the sun shines upon in its course, you will admit that it would be much better if, on the earth as little as on the moon, the sun were able to call forth the phenomena of life; and if, here as there, the surface were still in a crystalline state.

Again, you may look upon life as an unprofitable episode, disturbing the blessed calm of non-existence. And, in any case, even though things have gone with you tolerably well, the longer you live the more clearly you will feel that, on the whole, life is a *disappointment, nay, a cheat.*

If two men who were friends in their youth meet again when they are old, after being separated for a life-time, the chief feeling they will have at the sight of each other will be one of complete disappointment at life as a whole; because their thoughts will be carried back to that earlier time when life seemed so fair as it lay spread out before them in the rosy light of dawn, promised so much—and then performed so little. This feeling will so completely predominate over every other that they will not even consider it necessary to give it words; but on either side it will be silently assumed, and form the ground-work of all they have to talk about.

He who lives to see two or three generations is like a man who sits some time in the conjurer's booth at a fair, and witnesses the performance twice or thrice in succession. The tricks were meant to be seen only once; and when they are no longer a novelty and cease to deceive, their effect is gone.

While no man is much to be envied for his lot, there are countless numbers whose fate is to be deplored.

Life is a task to be done. It is a fine thing to say *defunctus est;* it means that the man has done his task.

If children were brought into the world by an act of pure reason alone, would the human race continue to exist? Would not a man rather have so much sympathy with the coming generation as to spare it the burden of existence? or at any rate not take it upon himself to impose that burden upon it in cold blood.

I shall be told, I suppose, that my philosophy is comfortless—because I speak the truth; and people prefer to be assured that everything the Lord has made is good. Go to the priests, then, and leave philosophers in peace! At any rate, do not ask us to accommodate our doctrines to the lessons you have been taught. That is what those rascals of sham philosophers will do for you. Ask them for any doctrine you please, and you will get it. Your University professors are bound to preach optimism; and it is an easy and agreeable task to upset their theories.

I have reminded the reader that every state of welfare, every feeling of satisfaction, is negative in its character; that is to say, it consists in freedom from pain, which is the positive element of existence. It follows, therefore, that the happiness of any given life is to be measured, not by its joys and pleasures, but by the extent to which it has been free from suffering—from positive evil. If this is the true standpoint, the lower animals appear to enjoy a happier destiny than man. Let us examine the matter a little more closely.

However varied the forms that human happiness and misery may take, leading a man to seek the one and shun the other, the material basis of it all is bodily pleasure or bodily pain. This basis is very restricted: it is simply health, food, protection from wet and cold, the satisfaction of the sexual instinct; or else the absence of these things. Consequently, as far as real physical pleasure is concerned, the man is not better off than the brute, except in so far as the higher possibilities of his nervous system make him more sensitive to every kind of pleasure, but also, it must be remembered, to every kind of pain. But then compared with the brute, how much stronger are the passions aroused in him! what an immeasurable difference there is in the depth and vehemence of his emotions!—and yet, in the one case, as in the other, all to produce the same result in the end: namely, health, food, clothing, and so on.

The chief source of all this passion is that thought for what is absent and future, which, with man, exercises such a powerful influence upon all he does. It is this that is the real origin of his cares, his hopes, his fears—emotions which affect him much more deeply than could ever be the case with those present joys and sufferings to which the brute is confined. In his powers of reflection, memory and foresight, man possesses, as it were, a machine for condensing and storing up his pleasures and his sorrows. But the brute has nothing of the kind; whenever it is in pain, it is as though it were suffering for the first time, even though the same thing should have previously happened to it times out of number. It has no power of summing up its feelings. Hence its careless and placid temper: how much it is to be envied! But in man reflection comes in, with all the emotions to

which it gives rise; and taking up the same elements of pleasure and pain which are common to him and the brute, it develops his susceptibility to happiness and misery to such a degree that, at one moment the man is brought in an instant to a state of delight that may even prove fatal, at another to the depths of despair and suicide.

If we carry our analysis a step farther, we shall find that, in order to increase his pleasures, man has intentionally added to the number and pressure of his needs, which in their original state were not much more difficult to satisfy than those of the brute. Hence luxury in all its forms; delicate food, the use of tobacco and opium, spirituous liquors, fine clothes and the thousand and one things that he considers necessary to his existence.

And above and beyond all this, there is a separate and peculiar source of pleasure, and consequently of pain, which man has established for himself, also as the result of using his powers of reflection; and this occupies him out of all proportion to its value, nay, almost more than all his other interests put together—I mean ambition and the feeling of honour and shame; in plain words, what he thinks about the opinion other people have of him. Taking a thousand forms, often very strange ones, this becomes the goal of almost all the efforts he makes that are not rooted in physical pleasure or pain. It is true that besides the sources of pleasure which he has in common with the brute, man has the pleasures of the mind as well. These admit of many gradations, from the most innocent trifling or the merest talk up to the highest intellectual achievements; but there is the accompanying boredom to be set against them on the side of suffering. Boredom is a form of suffering unknown to brutes, at any rate in their natural state; it is only the very cleverest of them who show faint traces of it when they are domesticated; whereas in the case of man it has become a downright scourge. The crowd of miserable wretches whose one aim in life is to fill their purses but never to put anything into their heads, offers a singular instance of this torment of boredom. Their wealth becomes a punishment by delivering them up to the misery of having nothing to do; for, to escape it, they will rush about in all directions, travelling here, there and everywhere. No sooner do they arrive in a place than they are anxious to know what amusements it affords; just as though they were beggars asking where they could receive a dole! Of a truth, need and boredom are the two poles of human life. Finally, I may mention that as regards the sexual relation, man is committed to a peculiar arrangement which drives him obstinately to choose one person. This feeling grows, now and then, into a more or less passionate love,[2] which is the source of little pleasure and much suffering.

It is, however, a wonderful thing that the mere addition of thought should serve to raise such a vast and lofty structure of human happiness and misery; resting, too, on the same narrow basis of joy and sorrow as man holds in common with the brute, and exposing him to such violent emotions, to so many storms of passion, so much convulsion of feeling, that what he has suffered stands written and may be read in the lines on his face. And yet, when all is told, he has been struggling ultimately for the very same things as the brute has attained, and with an incomparably smaller expenditure of passion and pain.

But all this contributes to increase the measure of suffering in human life out of all proportion to its pleasures; and the pains of life are made much worse for man by the fact that death is something very real to him. The brute flies from death instinctively without really knowing what it is, and therefore without ever contemplating it in the way natural to a man, who has this prospect always before his eyes. So that even if only a few brutes die a natural death, and most of them live only just long enough to transmit their species, and then, if not earlier, become the prey of some other animal,—whilst man, on the other hand, manages to make so-called natural death the rule, to which, however, there are a good many exceptions—the advantage is

on the side of the brute, for the reason stated above. But the fact is that man attains the natural term of years just as seldom as the brute; because the unnatural way in which he lives, and the strain of work and emotion, lead to a degeneration of the race; and so his goal is not often reached.

The brute is much more content with mere existence than man; the plant is wholly so; and man finds satisfaction in it just in proportion as he is dull and obtuse. Accordingly, the life of the brute carries less of sorrow with it, but also less of joy, when compared with the life of man; and while this may be traced, on the one side, to freedom from the torment of *care* and *anxiety*, it is also due to the fact that *hope*, in any real sense, is unknown to the brute. It is thus deprived of any share in that which gives us the most and the best of our joys and pleasures, the mental anticipation of a happy future, and the inspiriting play of phantasy, both of which we owe to our power of imagination. If the brute is free from care, it is also, in this sense, without hope; in either case because its consciousness is limited to the present moment, to what it can actually see before it. The brute is an embodiment of present impulses, and hence what elements of fear and hope exist in its nature—and they do not go very far—arise only in relation to objects that lie before it and within reach of those impulses: whereas a man's range of vision embraces the whole of his life, and extends far into the past and the future.

Following upon this, there is one respect in which brutes show real wisdom when compared with us—I mean, their quiet, placid enjoyment of the present moment. The tranquillity of mind which this seems to give them often puts us to shame for the many times we allow our thoughts and our cares to make us restless and discontented. And, in fact, those pleasures of hope and anticipation which I have been mentioning are not to be had for nothing. The delight which a man has in hop-

[2] I have treated this subject at length in a special chapter of the second volume of my chief work.

ing for and looking forward to some special satisfaction is a part of the real pleasure attaching to it enjoyed in advance. This is afterwards deducted; for the more we look forward to anything, the less satisfaction we find in it when it comes. But the brute's enjoyment is not anticipated and therefore suffers no deduction; so that the actual pleasure of the moment comes to it whole and unimpaired. In the same way, too, evil presses upon the brute only with its own intrinsic weight; whereas with us the fear of its coming often makes its burden ten times more grievous.

It is just this characteristic way in which the brute gives itself up entirely to the present moment that contributes so much to the delight we take in our domestic pets. They are the present moment personified, and in some respects they make us feel the value of every hour that is free from trouble and annoyance, which we, with our thoughts and preoccupations, mostly disregard. But man, that selfish and heartless creature, misuses this quality of the brute to be more content than we are with mere existence, and often works it to such an extent that he allows the brute absolutely nothing more than mere, bare life. The bird which was made so that it might rove over half the world, he shuts up into the space of a cubic foot, there to die a slow death in longing and crying for freedom; for in a cage it does not sing for the pleasure of it. And when I see how man misuses the dog, his best friend; how he ties up this intelligent animal with a chain, I feel the deepest sympathy with the brute and burning indignation against its master.

We shall see later that by taking a very high standpoint it is possible to justify the sufferings of mankind. But this justification cannot apply to animals, whose sufferings, while in a great measure brought about by men, are often considerable even apart from their agency.[3] And so we are forced to ask, Why and for what purpose does all this torment and agony exist? There is nothing here to give the will pause; it is not free to deny itself and so obtain redemption. There is

only one consideration that may serve to explain the sufferings of animals. It is this: that the will to live, which underlies the whole world of phenomena, must in their case satisfy its cravings by feeding upon itself. This it does by forming a gradation of phenomena, every one of which exists at the expense of another. I have shown, however, that the capacity for suffering is less in animals than in man. Any further explanation that may be given of their fate will be in the nature of hypothesis, if not actually mythical in its character; and I may leave the reader to speculate upon the matter for himself.

Brahma is said to have produced the world by a kind of fall or mistake; and in order to atone for his folly, he is bound to remain in it himself until he works out his redemption. As an account of the origin of things, that is admirable! According to the doctrines of *Buddhism*, the world came into being as the result of some inexplicable disturbance in the heavenly calm of Nirvana, that blessed state obtained by expiation, which had endured so long a time—the change taking place by a kind of fatality. This explanation must be understood as having at bottom some moral bearing; although it is illustrated by an exactly parallel theory in the domain of physical science, which places the origin of the sun in a primitive streak of mist, formed one knows not how. Subsequently, by a series of moral errors, the world became gradually worse and worse—true of the physical orders as well—until it assumed the dismal aspect it wears to-day. Excellent! The *Greeks* looked upon the world and the gods as the work of an inscrutable necessity. A passable explanation: we may be content with it until we can get a better. Again, *Ormuzd* and *Ahriman* are rival powers, continually at war. That is not bad. But that a God like Jehovah should have created this world of misery and woe, out of pure caprice, and because he enjoyed doing it, and should then have clapped his hands in praise of his own work,

---

[3] Cf. *Welt als Wille und Vorstellung*, vol. ii. p. 404.

and declared everything to be very good—that will not do at all! In its explanation of the origin of the world, Judaism is inferior to any other form of religious doctrine professed by a civilised nation; and it is quite in keeping with this that it is the only one which presents no trace whatever of any belief in the immortality of the soul.

Even though Leibnitz' contention, that this is the best of all possible worlds, were correct, that would not justify God in having created it. For he is the Creator not of the world only, but of possibility itself; and, therefore, he ought to have so ordered possibility as that it would admit of something better.

There are two things which make it impossible to believe that this world is the successful work of an all-wise, all-good, and, at the same time, all-powerful Being; firstly, the misery which abounds in it everywhere; and secondly, the obvious imperfection of its highest product, man, who is a burlesque of what he should be. These things cannot be reconciled with any such belief. On the contrary, they are just the facts which support what I have been saying; they are our authority for viewing the world as the outcome of our own misdeeds, and therefore, as something that had better not have been. Whilst, under the former hypothesis, they amount to a bitter accusation against the Creator, and supply material for sarcasm; under the latter they form an indictment against our own nature, our own will, and teach us a lesson of humility. They lead us to see that, like the children of a libertine, we come into the world with the burden of sin upon us; and that it is only through having continually to atone for this sin that our existence is so miserable, and that its end is death.

There is nothing more certain than the general truth that it is the grievous *sin of the world* which has produced the grievous *suffering of the world*. I am not referring here to the physical connection between these two things lying in the realm of experience; my meaning is metaphysical. Accordingly, the sole thing that reconciles me to the Old Testament is the story of the Fall. In my eyes, it is the only metaphysical truth in that book, even though it appears in the form of an allegory. There seems to me no better explanation of our existence than that it is the result of some false step, some sin of which we are paying the penalty. I cannot refrain from recommending the thoughtful reader a popular, but, at the same time, profound treatise on this subject by Claudius[4] which exhibits the essentially pessimistic spirit of Christianity. It is entitled: *Cursed is the ground for thy sake.*

Between the ethics of the Greeks and the ethics of the Hindoos, there is a glaring contrast. In the one case (with the exception, it must be confessed, of Plato), the object of ethics is to enable a man to lead a happy life; in the other, it is to free and redeem him from life altogether—as is directly stated in the very first words of the *Sankhya Karika.*

Allied with this is the contrast between the Greek and the Christian idea of death. It is strikingly presented in a visible form on a fine antique sarcophagus in the gallery at Florence, which exhibits, in relief, the whole series of ceremonies attending a wedding in ancient times, from the formal offer to the evening when Hymen's touch lights the happy couple home. Compare with that the Christian coffin, draped in mournful black and surmounted with a crucifix! How much significance there is in these two ways of finding comfort in death. They are opposed to each other, but each is right. The one points to the *affirmation* of the will to live, which remains sure of life for all time, however rapidly its forms may change. The other, in the symbol of suffering and death, points to the *denial* of the will to live, to redemption from this world, the domain of death and devil. And in the question between the affirmation and the denial of the will to

---

[4] *Translator's Note.* Matthias Claudius (1740–1815), a popular poet, and friend of Klopstock, Herder and Lessing. He edited the *Wandsbecker Bote,* in the fourth part of which appeared the treatise mentioned above. He generally wrote under the pseudonym of *Asmus,* and Schopenhauer often refers to him by this name.

live, Christianity is in the last resort right.

The contrast which the New Testament presents when compared with the old, according to the ecclesiastical view of the matter, is just that existing between my ethical system and the moral philosophy of Europe. The Old Testament represents man as under the dominion of Law, in which, however, there is no redemption. The New Testament declares Law to have failed, frees man from its dominion,[5] and in its stead preaches the kingdom of grace, to be won by faith, love of neighbour and entire sacrifice of self. This is the path of redemption from the evil of the world. The spirit of the New Testament is undoubtedly asceticism, however your protestants and rationalists may twist it to suit their purpose. Asceticism is the denial of the will to live; and the transition from the Old Testament to the New, from the dominion of Law to that of Faith, from justification by works to redemption through the Mediator, from the domain of sin and death to eternal life in Christ, means, when taken in its real sense, the transition from the merely moral virtues to the denial of the will to live. My philosophy shows the metaphysical foundation of justice and the love of mankind, and points to the goal to which these virtues necessarily lead, if they are practised in perfection. At the same time it is candid in confessing that a man must turn his back upon the world, and that the denial of the will to live is the way of redemption. It is therefore really at one with the spirit of the New Testament, whilst all other systems are couched in the spirit of the Old; that is to say, theoretically as well as practically, their result is Judaism —mere despotic theism. In this sense, then, my doctrine might be called the only true Christian philosophy—however paradoxical a statement this may seem to people who take superficial views instead of penetrating to the heart of the matter.

If you want a safe compass to guide you through life, and to banish all doubt as to the right way of looking at it, you cannot do better than accustom yourself to regard this world as a penitentiary, a sort of penal colony, or $\dot{\epsilon}\rho\gamma\alpha\sigma\tau\dot{\eta}\rho\iota o\nu$, as the earliest philosophers called it. Amongst the Christian Fathers, Origen, with praiseworthy courage, took this view,[6] which is further justified by certain objective theories of life. I refer, not to my own philosophy alone, but to the wisdom of all ages, as expressed in Brahmanism and Buddhism, and in the sayings of Greek philosophers like Empedocles and Pythagoras; as also by Cicero, in his remark that the wise men of old used to teach that we come into this world to pay the penalty of crime committed in another state of existence—a doctrine which formed part of the initiation into the mysteries. And Vanini— whom his contemporaries burned, finding that an easier task than to confute him—puts the same thing in a very forcible way. *Man,* he says, *is so full of every kind of misery that, were it not repugnant to the Christian religion, I should venture to affirm that if evil spirits exist at all, they have passed into human form and are now atoning for their crimes.* And true Christianity—using the word in its right sense—also regards our existence as the consequence of sin and error.

If you accustom yourself to this view of life you will regulate your expectations accordingly, and cease to look upon all its disagreeable incidents, great and small, its sufferings, its worries, its misery, as anything unusual or irregular; nay, you will find that everything is as it should be, in a world where each of us pays the penalty of existence in his own peculiar way. Amongst the evils of a penal colony is the society of those who form it; and if the reader is worthy of better company, he will need no words from me to remind him of what he has to put up with at present. If he has a soul above the common, or if he is a man of genius, he will occasionally feel like some noble prisoner of state, condemned to work in the galleys with common criminals; and he will follow his example and try to isolate himself.

---

[5] Cf. Romans vii; Galatians ii. iii.

[6] Augustine, *De Civitate Dei,* L. xi. c. 23; *GBWW,* Vol. 19, p. 335a.

In general, however, it should be said that this view of life will enable us to contemplate the so-called imperfections of the great majority of men, their moral and intellectual deficiencies and the resulting base type of countenance, without any surprise, to say nothing of indignation; for we shall never cease to reflect where we are, and that the men about us are beings conceived and born in sin, and living to atone for it. That is what Christianity means in speaking of the sinful nature of man.

Pardon's the word to all![7] Whatever folly men commit, be their shortcomings or their vices what they may, let us exercise forbearance; remembering that when these faults appear in others, it is our follies and vices that we behold. They are the shortcomings of humanity, to which we belong; whose faults, one and all, we share; yes, even those very faults at which we now wax so indignant, merely because they have not yet appeared in ourselves. They are faults that do not lie on the surface. But they exist down there in the depths of our nature; and should anything call them forth, they will come and show themselves, just as we now see them in others. One man, it is true, may have faults that are absent in his fellow; and it is undeniable that the sum total of bad qualities is in some cases very large; for the difference of individuality between man and man passes all measure.

In fact, the conviction that the world and man is something that had better not have been, is of a kind to fill us with indulgence towards one another. Nay, from this point of view, we might well consider the proper form of address to be, not *Monsieur, Sir, mein Herr,* but *my fellow-sufferer, Soci malorum, compagnon de misères!* This may perhaps sound strange, but it is in keeping with the facts; it puts others in a right light; and it reminds us of that which is after all the most necessary thing in life—the tolerance, patience, regard, and love of neighbour, of which everyone stands in need, and which, therefore, every man owes to his fellow.

---

[7] "Cymbeline," Act v. Sc. 5, 422; *GBWW*, Vol. 27, p. 488b.

The Vanity of Existence

This vanity finds expression in the whole way in which things exist; in the infinite nature of Time and Space, as opposed to the finite nature of the individual in both; in the ever-passing present moment as the only mode of actual existence; in the interdependence and relativity of all things; in continual Becoming without ever Being; in constant wishing and never being satisfied; in the long battle which forms the history of life, where every effort is checked by difficulties, and stopped until they are overcome. Time is that in which all things pass away; it is merely the form under which the will to live—the thing-in-itself and therefore imperishable— has revealed to it that its efforts are in vain: it is that agent by which at every moment all things in our hands become as nothing, and lose any real value they possess.

That which *has been* exists no more; it exists as little as that which has *never* been. But of everything that exists you must say, in the next moment, that it has been. Hence something of great importance now past is inferior to something of little importance now present, in that the latter is a *reality*, and related to the former as something to nothing.

A man finds himself, to his great astonishment suddenly existing, after thousands and thousands of years of non-existence: he lives for a little while; and then, again, comes an equally long period when he must exist no more. The heart rebels against this, and feels that it cannot be true. The crudest intellect cannot speculate on such a subject without having a presentiment that Time is something ideal in its nature. This ideality of Time and Space is the key to every true system of metaphysics; because it provides for quite another order of things than is to be met with in the domain of nature. This is why Kant is so great.

Of every event in our life we can say only for one moment that it *is*; for ever after, that it *was*. Every evening we are poorer by a day. It might, perhaps, make us mad to see how rapidly our short span of time ebbs away; if it were not that in the furthest depths of our being we are secretly conscious of our share in the inexhaustible spring of eternity, so that we can always hope to find life in it again.

Considerations of the kind touched on above might, indeed, lead us to embrace the belief that the greatest *wisdom* is to make the enjoyment of the present the supreme object of life; because that is the only reality, all else being merely the play of thought. On the other hand, such a course might just as well be called the greatest *folly:* for that which in the next moment exists no more, and vanishes utterly, like a dream, can never be worth a serious effort.

The whole foundation on which our existence rests is the present—the ever-fleeting present. It lies, then, in the very nature of our existence to take the form of constant motion, and to offer no possibility of our ever attaining the rest for which we are always striving. We are like a man running downhill, who cannot keep on his legs unless he runs on, and will inevitably fall if he stops; or, again, like a pole balanced on the tip of one's finger; or like a planet, which would fall into its sun the moment it ceased to hurry forward on its way. Unrest is the mark of existence.

In a world where all is unstable, and nought can endure, but is swept onwards at once in the hurrying whirlpool of change; where a man, if he is to keep erect at all, must always be advancing and moving, like an acrobat on a rope—in such a world, happiness is inconceivable. How can it dwell where, as Plato says, *continual Becoming and never Being* is the sole form of existence? In the first place, a man never is happy, but spends his whole life in striving after something which he thinks will make him so; he seldom attains his goal, and when he does, it is only to be disappointed; he is mostly shipwrecked in the end, and comes into harbour with masts and rigging gone. And then, it is all one whether he has been happy or miserable; for his life was never anything more than a present moment always vanishing; and now it is over.

At the same time it is a wonderful thing that, in the world of human beings as in that of animals in general, this manifold restless motion is produced and kept up by the agency of two simple impulses—hunger and the sexual instinct; aided a little, perhaps, by the influence of boredom, but by nothing else; and that, in the theatre of life, these suffice to form the *primum mobile* of how complicated a machinery, setting in motion how strange and varied a scene!

On looking a little closer, we find that inorganic matter presents a constant conflict between chemical forces, which eventually works dissolution; and on the other hand, that organic life is impossible without continual change of matter, and cannot exist if it does not receive perpetual help from without. This is the realm of *finality;* and its opposite would be *an infinite existence,* exposed to no attack from without, and needing nothing to support it; ἀεὶ ὡσαύτως ὄν, the realm of eternal peace; οὔτε γιγνόμενον οὔτε ἀπολλύμενον, some timeless, changeless state, one and undiversified; the negative knowledge of which forms the dominant note of the Platonic philosophy. It is to some such state as this that the denial of the will to live opens up the way.

The scenes of our life are like pictures done in rough mosaic. Looked at close, they produce no effect. There is nothing beautiful to be found in them, unless you stand some distance off. So, to gain anything we have

longed for is only to discover how vain and empty it is; and even though we are always living in expectation of better things, at the same time we often repent and long to have the past back again. We look upon the present as something to be put up with while it lasts, and serving only as the way towards our goal. Hence most people, if they glance back when they come to the end of life, will find that all along they have been living *ad interim:* they will be surprised to find that the very thing they disregarded and let slip by unenjoyed, was just the life in the expectation of which they passed all their time. Of how many a man may it not be said that hope made a fool of him until he danced into the arms of death!

Then again, how insatiable a creature is man! Every satisfaction he attains lays the seeds of some new desire, so that there is no end to the wishes of each individual will. And why is this? The real reason is simply that, taken in itself, Will is the lord of all worlds: everything belongs to it, and therefore no one single thing can ever give it satisfaction, but only the whole, which is endless. For all that, it must rouse our sympathy to think how very little the Will, this lord of the world, really gets when it takes the form of an individual; usually only just enough to keep the body together. This is why man is so very miserable.

Life presents itself chiefly as a task—the task, I mean, of subsisting at all, *gagner sa vie.* If this is accomplished, life is a burden, and then there comes the second task of doing something with that which has been won—of warding off boredom, which, like a bird of prey, hovers over us, ready to fall wherever it sees a life secure from need. The first task is to win something; the second, to banish the feeling that it has been won; otherwise it is a burden.

Human life must be some kind of mistake. The truth of this will be sufficiently obvious if we only remember that man is a compound of needs and necessities hard to satisfy; and that even when they are satisfied, all he obtains is a state of painlessness, where nothing remains to him but abandonment to boredom. This is direct proof that existence has no real value in itself; for what is boredom but the feeling of the emptiness of life? If life—the craving for which is the very essence of our being—were possessed of any positive intrinsic value, there would be no such thing as boredom at all: mere existence would satisfy us in itself, and we should want for nothing. But as it is, we take no delight in existence except when we are struggling for something; and then distance and difficulties to be overcome make our goal look as though it would satisfy us—an illusion which vanishes when we reach it; or else when we are occupied with some purely intellectual interest—where in reality we have stepped forth from life to look upon it from the outside, much after the manner of spectators at a play. And even sensual pleasure itself means nothing but a struggle and aspiration, ceasing the moment its aim is attained. Whenever we are not occupied in one of these ways, but cast upon existence itself, its vain and worthless nature is brought home to us; and this is what we mean by boredom. The hankering after what is strange and uncommon—an innate and ineradicable tendency of human nature—shows how glad we are at any interruption of that natural course of affairs which is so very tedious.

That this most perfect manifestation of the will to live, the human organism, with the cunning and complex working of its machinery, must fall to dust and yield up itself and all its strivings to extinction—this is the naïve way in which Nature, who is always so true and sincere in what she says, proclaims the whole struggle of this will as in its very essence barren and unprofitable. Were it of any value in itself, anything unconditioned and absolute, it could not thus end in mere nothing.

If we turn from contemplating the world as a whole, and, in particular, the generations of men as they live their little hour of mock-existence and then are swept away in rapid succession; if we turn from this, and look at life in its small details, as presented, say, in a comedy, how ridiculous it all seems! It is like a drop of water seen through a microscope, a single drop teeming with *infusoria;* or a speck of cheese full of mites invisible to the naked eye. How we laugh as they bustle about so eagerly, and struggle with one another in so tiny a space! And whether here, or in the little span of human life, this terrible activity produces a comic effect.

It is only in the microscope that our life looks so big. It is an indivisible point, drawn out and magnified by the powerful lenses of Time and Space.

On Suicide

As far as I know, none but the votaries of monotheistic, that is to say, Jewish religions, look upon suicide as a crime. This is all the more striking, inasmuch as neither in the Old nor in the New Testament is there to be found any prohibition or positive disapproval of it; so that religious teachers are forced to base their condemnation of suicide on philosophical grounds of their own invention. These are so very bad that writers of this kind endeavour to make up for the weakness of their arguments by the strong terms in which they express their abhorrence of the practice; in other words, they declaim against it. They tell us that suicide is the greatest piece of cowardice; that only a madman could be guilty of it; and other insipidities of the same kind; or else they make the nonsensical remark that suicide is *wrong;* when it is quite obvious that there is nothing in the world to which every man has a more unassailable title than to his own life and person.

Suicide, as I have said, is actually accounted a crime; and a crime which, especially under the vulgar bigotry that prevails in England, is followed by an ignominious burial and the seizure of the man's property; and for that reason, in a case of suicide, the jury almost always bring in a verdict of insanity. Now let the reader's own moral feelings decide as to whether or not suicide is a criminal act. Think of the impression that would be made upon you by the news that some one you know had committed the crime, say, of murder or theft, or been guilty of some act of cruelty or deception; and compare it with your feelings when you hear that he has met a voluntary death. While in the one case a lively sense of indignation and extreme re-

sentment will be aroused, and you will call loudly for punishment or revenge, in the other you will be moved to grief and sympathy; and mingled with your thoughts will be admiration for his courage, rather than the moral disapproval which follows upon a wicked action. Who has not had acquaintances, friends, relations, who of their own free will have left this world; and are these to be thought of with horror as criminals? Most emphatically No! I am rather of opinion that the clergy should be challenged to explain what right they have to go into the pulpit, or take up their pens, and stamp as a crime an action which many men whom we hold in affection and honour have committed; and to refuse an honourable burial to those who relinquish this world voluntarily. They have no Biblical authority to boast of, as justifying their condemnation of suicide; nay, not even any philosophical arguments that will hold water; and it must be understood that it is arguments we want, and that we will not be put off with mere phrases or words of abuse. If the criminal law forbids suicide, that is not an argument valid in the Church; and besides, the prohibition is ridiculous; for what penalty can frighten a man who is not afraid of death itself? If the law punishes people for trying to commit suicide, it is punishing the want of skill that makes the attempt a failure.

The ancients, moreover, were very far from regarding the matter in that light. Pliny says: *Life is not so desirable a thing as to be protracted at any cost. Whoever you are, you are sure to die, even though your life has been full of abomination and crime. The chief of all remedies for a troubled mind is the feeling that among the blessings which Nature gives to man, there is none greater than an opportune death; and the best of it is that every one can avail himself of it.* And elsewhere the same writer declares: *Not even to God are all things possible; for he could not compass his own death, if he willed to die, and yet in all the miseries of our earthly life, this is the best of his gifts to man.* Nay, in Massilia and on the isle of Ceos, the man who could give valid reasons for relinquishing his life, was handed the cup of hemlock by the magistrate; and that, too, in public. And in ancient times, how many heroes and wise men died a voluntary death. Aristotle, it is true, declared suicide to be an offence against the State, although not against the person;[1] but in Stobaeus' exposition of the Peripatetic philosophy there is the following remark: *The good man should flee life when his misfortunes become too great; the bad man, also, when he is too prosperous.* And similarly: *So he will marry and beget children and take part in the affairs of the State, and, generally, practise virtue and continue to live; and then, again, if need be, and at any time necessity compels him, he will depart to his place of refuge in the tomb.* And we find that the Stoics actually praised suicide as a noble and heroic action, as hundreds of passages show; above all in the works of Seneca, who expresses the strongest approval of it. As is well known, the Hindoos look upon suicide as a religious act, especially when it takes the form of self-immolation by widows; but also when it consists in casting oneself under the wheels of the chariot of the god at Juggernaut, or being eaten by crocodiles in the Ganges, or being drowned in the holy tanks in the temples, and so on. The same thing occurs on the stage—that mirror of life. For example, in *L'Orphelin de la Chine,* a celebrated Chinese play, almost all the noble characters end by suicide; without the slightest hint anywhere, or any impression being produced on the spectator, that they are committing a crime. And in our own theatre it is much the same —Palmira, for instance, in *Mahomet,* or Mortimer in *Maria Stuart,* Othello, Countess Terzky.[2] Is Hamlet's monologue the meditation of a criminal? He merely declares that if we had any certainty of being annihilated by it, death would be infinitely preferable to the world as it is. But *there lies the rub!*

The reasons advanced against suicide by the clergy of monotheistic, that is to say, Jewish religions, and by those philosophers who adapt themselves thereto, are weak sophisms which can easily be refuted.[3] The most thorough-going refutation of them is given by Hume in his *Essay on Suicide.* This did not appear until after his death, when it was immediately suppressed, owing to the scandalous bigotry and outrageous ecclesiastical tyranny that prevailed in England; and hence only a very few copies of it were sold under cover of secrecy and at a high price. This and another treatise by that great man have come to us from Basle, and we may be thankful for the reprint.[4] It is a great disgrace to the English nation that a purely philosophical treatise, which, proceeding from one of the first thinkers and writers in England, aimed at refuting the current arguments against suicide by the light of cold reason, should be forced to sneak about in that country, as though it were some rascally production, until at last it found refuge on the Continent. At the same time it shows what a good conscience the Church has in such matters.

In my chief work I have explained the only valid reason existing against suicide on the score of morality. It is this: that suicide thwarts the attainment of the highest moral aim by the fact that, for a real release from this world of misery, it substitutes one that is merely apparent.[5] But from a *mistake* to a

---

[1] *Eth. Nichom.,* v. 11; *GBWW,* Vol. 9, p. 386b.

[2] *Translator's Note.* Palmira: a female slave in Goethe's play of *Mahomet.* Mortimer: a would-be lover and rescuer of Mary in Schiller's *Maria Stuart.* Countess Terzky: a leading character in Schiller's *Wallenstein's Tod.*

[3] See my treatise on the *Foundation of Morals,* § 5.

[4] *Essays on Suicide* and the *Immortality of the Soul,* by the late David Hume, Basle, 1799.

[5] *Translator's Note.* Schopenhauer refers to *Die Welt als Wille und Vorstellung,* vol. i., § 69, where the reader may find the same argument stated at somewhat greater length. According to Schopenhauer, moral freedom—the highest ethical aim— is to be obtained only by a denial of the will to live. Far from being a denial, suicide is an emphatic assertion of this will. For it is in fleeing from the pleasures, not from the sufferings of life, that this

crime is a far cry; and it is as a crime that the clergy of Christendom wish us to regard suicide.

The inmost kernel of Christianity is the truth that suffering—*the Cross*—is the real end and object of life. Hence Christianity condemns suicide as thwarting this end; whilst the ancient world, taking a lower point of view, held it in approval, nay, in honour. But if that is to be accounted a valid reason against suicide, it involves the recognition of asceticism; that is to say, it is valid only from a much higher ethical standpoint than has ever been adopted by moral philosophers in Europe. If we abandon that high standpoint, there is no tenable reason left, on the score of morality, for condemning suicide. The extraordinary energy and zeal with which the clergy of monotheistic religions attack suicide is not supported either by any passages in the Bible or by any considerations of weight; so that it looks as though they must have some secret reason for their contention. May it not be this—that the voluntary surrender of life is a bad compliment for him who said that *all things were very good?* If this is so, it offers another instance of the crass optimism of these religions,—denouncing suicide to escape being denounced by it.

It will generally be found that, as soon as the terrors of life reach the point at which they outweigh the terrors of death, a man will put an end to his life. But the terrors of death offer considerable resistance; they stand like a sentinel at the gate leading out of this world. Perhaps there is no man alive who would not have already put an end to his life, if this end had been of a purely negative character, a sudden stoppage of existence. There is something positive about it; it is the destruction of the body; and a man shrinks from that, because his body is the manifestation of the will to live.

However, the struggle with that sentinel is, as a rule, not so hard as it may seem from a long way off, mainly in consequence of the antagonism between the ills of the body and the ills of the mind. If we are in great bodily pain, or the pain lasts a long time, we become indifferent to other troubles; all we think about is to get well. In the same way great mental suffering makes us insensible to bodily pain; we despise it; nay, if it should outweigh the other, it distracts our thoughts, and we welcome it as a pause in mental suffering. It is this feeling that makes suicide easy; for the bodily pain that accompanies it loses all significance in the eyes of one who is tortured by an excess of mental suffering. This is especially evident in the case of those who are driven to suicide by some purely morbid and exaggerated ill-humour. No special effort to overcome their feelings is necessary, nor do such people require to be worked up in order to take the step; but as soon as the keeper into whose charge they are given leaves them for a couple of minutes, they quickly bring their life to an end.

When, in some dreadful and ghastly dream, we reach the moment of greatest horror, it awakes us; thereby banishing all the hideous shapes that were born of the night. And life is a dream: when the moment of greatest horror compels us to break it off, the same thing happens.

Suicide may also be regarded as an experiment—a question which man puts to Nature, trying to force her to an answer. The question is this: What change will death produce in a man's existence and in his insight into the nature of things? It is a clumsy experiment to make; for it involves the destruction of the very consciousness which puts the question and awaits the answer.

---

denial consists. When a man destroys his existence as an individual, he is not by any means destroying his will to live. On the contrary, he would like to live if he could do so with satisfaction to himself; if he could assert his will against the power of circumstance; but circumstance is too strong for him.

On Education

The human intellect is said to be so constituted that *general ideas* arise by abstraction from *particular observations,* and therefore come after them in point of time. If this is what actually occurs, as happens in the case of a man who has to depend solely upon his own experience for what he learns — who has no teacher and no book, — such a man knows quite well which of his particular observations belong to and are represented by each of his general ideas. He has a perfect acquaintance with both sides of his experience, and accordingly, he treats everything that comes in his way from a right standpoint. This might be called the *natural* method of education.

Contrarily, the *artificial* method is to hear what other people say, to learn and to read, and so to get your head crammed full of general ideas before you have any sort of extended acquaintance with the world as it is, and as you may see it for yourself. You will be told that the particular observations which go to make these general ideas will come to you later on in the course of experience; but until that time arrives, you apply your general ideas wrongly, you judge men and things from a wrong standpoint, you see them in a wrong light, and treat them in a wrong way. So it is that education perverts the mind.

This explains why it so frequently happens that, after a long course of learning and reading, we enter upon the world in our youth, partly with an artless ignorance of things, partly with wrong notions about them; so that our demeanor savors at one moment of a nervous anxiety, at another of a mistaken confidence. The reason of this is simply that our head is full of general ideas which we are now trying to turn to some use, but which we hardly ever apply rightly. This is the result of acting in direct opposition to the natural development of the mind by obtaining general ideas first, and particular observations last: it is putting the cart before the horse. Instead of developing the child's own faculties of discernment, and teaching it to judge and think for itself, the teacher uses all his energies to stuff its head full of the ready-made thoughts of other people. The mistaken views of life, which spring from a false application of general ideas, have afterwards to be corrected by long years of experience; and it is seldom that they are wholly corrected. This is why so few men of learning are possessed of common-sense, such as is often to be met with in people who have had no instruction at all.

To acquire a knowledge of the world might be defined as the aim of all education; and it follows from what I have said that special stress should be laid upon beginning to acquire this knowledge *at the right end.* As I have shown, this means, in the main, that the particular observation of a thing shall precede the general idea of it; further, that narrow and circumscribed ideas shall come before ideas of a wide range. It means, therefore, that the whole system of education shall follow in the steps that must have been taken by the ideas themselves in the course of their formation. But whenever any of these steps are skipped or left out, the instruction is defective, and the ideas obtained are false; and finally, a distorted view of the world arises, peculiar to the individual himself — a view such as almost everyone entertains for some time, and most men for as long as they live. No one can look into his own mind without seeing that it was only after reaching a very mature age, and in some cases when he least expected it, that he came to a right understanding or a clear view of many matters in his life, that, after all, were not very difficult or complicated. Up till then, they were points in his knowledge of the world which were still obscure, due to his having skipped some particular lesson in those early days of his education, whatever it may have been like—whether artificial and conventional, or of that natural kind which is based upon individual experience.

It follows that an attempt should be made to find out the strictly natural course of knowledge, so that education may proceed methodically by keeping to it; and that children may become acquainted with the ways of the world, without getting wrong ideas into their heads, which very often cannot be got out again. If this plan were adopted, special care would have to be taken to prevent children from using words without clearly understanding their meaning and application. The fatal tendency to be satisfied with words instead of trying to understand things —to learn phrases by heart, so that they may prove a refuge in time of need, exists, as a rule, even in children; and the tendency lasts on into manhood, making the knowledge of many learned persons to consist in mere verbiage.

However, the main endeavor must always be to let particular observations precede general ideas and not *vice versa,* as is usually and unfortunately the case; as though a child should come feet foremost into the world, or a verse be begun by writing down the rhyme! The ordinary method is to imprint ideas and opinions, in the strict sense of the word, *prejudices,* on the mind of the child, before it has had any but a very few particular observations. It is thus that he afterwards comes to view the world and gather experience through the medium of those ready-made ideas, rather than to let his ideas be formed for him out of his own experience of life, as they ought to be.

A man sees a great many things when he looks at the world for himself, and he sees them from many sides; but this method of learning is not nearly so short or so quick as the method which employs abstract ideas and makes hasty generalizations about everything. Experience, therefore, will be a long time in correcting preconceived ideas, or perhaps never bring its task to an end; for wherever a man finds that the aspect of things seems to contradict the general ideas he has formed, he will begin by rejecting the evidence it offers as partial and one-sided; nay, he will shut his eyes to it altogether and deny that it stands in any contradiction at all with his preconceived notions, in order that he may thus preserve them uninjured. So it is that many a man carries about a burden of wrong notions all his life long—crotchets, whims, fancies, prejudices, which at last become fixed ideas. The fact is that he has never tried to form his fundamental ideas for himself out of his own experience of life, his own way of looking at the world, because he has taken over his ideas ready-made from other people; and this it is that makes him— as it makes how many others!—so shallow and superficial.

Instead of that method of instruction, care should be taken to educate children on the natural lines. No idea should ever be established in a child's mind otherwise than by what the child can see for itself, or at any rate it should be verified by the same means; and the result of this would be that the child's ideas, if few, would be well-grounded and accurate. It would learn how to measure things by its own standard rather than by another's; and so it would escape a thousand strange fancies and prejudices, and not need to have them eradicated by the lessons it will subsequently be taught in the school of life. The child would, in this way, have its mind once for all habituated to clear views and thorough-going knowledge; it would use its own judgment and take an unbiased estimate of things.

And, in general, children should not form their notions of what life is like from the copy before they have learned it from the original, to whatever aspect of it their attention may be directed. Instead, therefore, of hastening to place *books,* and books alone, in their hands, let them be made acquainted, step by step, with *things*—with the actual circumstances of human life. And above all let care be taken to bring them to a clear and objective view of the world as it is, to educate them always to derive their ideas directly from real life, and to shape them in conformity with it—not to fetch them from other sources, such as books, fairy tales, or what people say—then to apply them ready-made to real life. For this will mean that their heads are full of wrong notions, and that they will either see things in a false light or try in vain to *remodel the world* to suit their views, and so enter upon false paths; and that, too, whether they are only constructing theories of life or engaged in the actual business of it. It is incredible how much harm is done when the seeds of wrong notions are laid in the mind in those early years, later on to bear a crop of prejudice; for the subsequent lessons, which are learned from real life in the world have to be devoted mainly to their extirpation. *To unlearn the evil* was the answer, according to Diogenes Laertius, Antisthenes gave, when he was asked what branch of knowledge was most necessary; and we can see what he meant.

No child under the age of fifteen should receive instruction in subjects which may possibly be the vehicle of serious error, such as philosophy, religion, or any other branch of knowledge where it is necessary to take large views; because wrong notions imbibed early can seldom be rooted out, and of all the intellectual faculties, judgment is the last to arrive at maturity. The child should give its attention either to subjects where no error is possible at all, such as mathematics, or to those in which there is no particular danger in making a mistake, such as languages, natural science, history and so on. And in general, the branches of knowledge which are to be studied at any period of life should be such as the mind is equal to at that period and can perfectly understand. Childhood and youth

form the time for collecting materials, for getting a special and thorough knowledge of the individual and particular things. In those years it is too early to form views on a large scale; and ultimate explanations must be put off to a later date. The faculty of judgment, which cannot come into play without mature experience, should be left to itself; and care should be taken not to anticipate its action by inculcating prejudice, which will paralyze it for ever.

On the other hand, the memory should be specially taxed in youth, since it is then that it is strongest and most tenacious. But in choosing the things that should be committed to memory the utmost care and forethought must be exercised; as lessons well learnt in youth are never forgotten. This precious soil must therefore be cultivated so as to bear as much fruit as possible. If you think how deeply rooted in your memory are those persons whom you knew in the first twelve years of your life, how indelible the impression made upon you by the events of those years, how clear your recollection of most of the things that happened to you then, most of what was told or taught you, it will seem a natural thing to take the susceptibility and tenacity of the mind at that period as the groundwork of education. This may be done by a strict observance of method, and a systematic regulation of the impressions which the mind is to receive.

But the years of youth allotted to a man are short, and memory is, in general, bound within narrow limits; still more so, the memory of any one individual. Since this is the case, it is all-important to fill the memory with what is essential and material in any branch of knowledge, to the exclusion of everything else. The decision as to what is essential and material should rest with the master-minds in every department of thought; their choice should be made after the most mature deliberation, and the outcome of it fixed and determined. Such a choice would have to proceed by sifting the things which it is necessary and important for a man to know in general, and then, necessary and important for him to know in any particular business or calling. Knowledge of the first kind would have to be classified, after an encyclopædic fashion, in graduated courses, adapted to the degree of general culture which a man may be expected to have in the circumstances in which he is placed; beginning with a course limited to the necessary requirements of primary education, and extending upwards to the subjects treated of in all the branches of philosophical thought. The regulation of the second kind of knowledge would be left to those who had shown genuine mastery in the several departments into which it is divided; and the whole system would provide an elaborate rule or canon for intellectual education, which would, of course, have to be revised every ten years. Some such arrangement as this would employ the youthful power of the memory to best advantage, and supply excellent working material to the faculty of judgment, when it made its appearance later on.

A man's knowledge may be said to be mature, in other words, it has reached the most complete state of perfection to which he, as an individual, is capable of bringing it, when an exact correspondence is established between the whole of his abstract ideas and the things he has actually perceived for himself. This will mean that each of his abstract ideas rests, directly or indirectly, upon a basis of observation, which alone endows it with any real value; and also that he is able to place every observation he makes under the right abstract idea which belongs to it. Maturity is the work of experience alone; and therefore it requires time. The knowledge we derive from our own observation is usually distinct from that which we acquire through the medium of abstract ideas; the one coming to us in the natural way, the other by what people tell us, and the course of instruction we receive, whether it is good or bad. The result is, that in youth there is generally very little agreement or correspondence between our abstract ideas, which are merely phrases in the mind, and that real knowledge which we have obtained by our own observation. It is

only later on that a gradual approach takes place between these two kinds of knowledge, accompanied by a mutual correction of error; and knowledge is not mature until this coalition is accomplished. This maturity or perfection of knowledge is something quite independent of another kind of perfection, which may be of a high or a low order—the perfection, I mean, to which a man may bring his own individual faculties; which is measured, not by any correspondence between the two kinds of knowledge, but by the degree of intensity which each kind attains.

For the practical man the most needful thing is to acquire an accurate and profound knowledge of *the ways of the world*. But this, though the most needful, is also the most wearisome of all studies, as a man may reach a great age without coming to the end of his task; whereas, in the domain of the sciences, he masters the more important facts when he is still young. In acquiring that knowledge of the world, it is while he is a novice, namely, in boyhood and in youth, that the first and hardest lessons are put before him; but it often happens that even in later years there is still a great deal to be learned.

The study is difficult enough in itself; but the difficulty is doubled by *novels,* which represent a state of things in life and the world, such as, in fact, does not exist. Youth is credulous, and accepts these views of life, which then become part and parcel of the mind; so that, instead of a merely negative condition of ignorance, you have positive error—a whole tissue of false notions to start with; and at a later date these actually spoil the schooling of experience, and put a wrong construction on the lessons it teaches. If, before this, the youth had no light at all to guide him, he is now misled by a will-o'-the-wisp; still more often is this the case with a girl. They have both had a false view of things foisted on them by reading novels; and expectations have been aroused which can never be fulfilled. This generally exercises a baneful influence on their whole life. In this respect those whose youth has allowed them no time or opportunity for reading novels—

Of Women

S chiller's poem in honor of women, *Würde der Frauen*, is the result of much careful thought, and it appeals to the reader by its antithetic style and its use of contrast; but as an expression of the true praise which should be accorded to them, it is, I think, inferior to these few words of Jouy's: *Without women, the beginning of our life would be helpless; the middle, devoid of pleasure; and the end, of consolation.* The same thing is more feelingly expressed by Byron in *Sardanapalus:*

> *The very first*
> *Of human life must spring from woman's breast,*
> *Your first small words are taught you from her lips,*
> *Your first tears quench'd by her, and your last sighs*
> *Too often breathed out in a woman's hearing,*
> *When men have shrunk from the ignoble care*
> *Of watching the last hour of him who led them.*
>   (Act I. Scene 2.)

These two passages indicate the right standpoint for the appreciation of women.

You need only look at the way in which she is formed, to see that woman is not meant to undergo great labor, whether of the mind or of the body. She pays the debt of life not by what she does, but by what she suffers; by the pains of child-bearing and care for the child, and by submission to her husband, to whom she should be a patient and cheering companion. The keenest sorrows and joys are not for her, nor is she called upon to display a great deal of strength. The current of her life should be more gentle, peaceful and trivial than man's, without being essentially happier or unhappier.

Women are directly fitted for acting as the nurses and teachers of our early childhood by the fact that they are themselves childish, frivolous and short-sighted; in a word, they are big children all their life long—a kind of intermediate stage between the child and the full-grown man, who is man in the strict sense of the word. See how a girl will fondle a child for days together, dance with it and sing to it; and then think what a man, with the best will in the world, could do if he were put in her place.

With young girls Nature seems to have had in view what, in the language of the drama, is called *a striking effect;* as for a few years she dowers them with a wealth of beauty and is lavish in her gift of charm, at the expense of all the rest of their life; so that during those years they may capture the fantasy of some man to such a degree that he is hurried away into undertaking the honorable care of them, in some form or other, as long as they live—a step for which there would not appear to be any sufficient warranty if reason only directed his thoughts. Accordingly, Nature has equipped woman, as she does all her creatures, with the weapons and implements requisite for the safeguarding of her existence, and for just as long as it is necessary for her to have them. Here, as elsewhere, Nature proceeds with her usual economy; for just as the female ant, after fecundation, loses her wings, which are then superfluous, nay, actually a danger to the business of breeding; so, after giving birth to one or two children, a woman generally loses her beauty; probably, indeed, for similar reasons.

And so we find that young girls, in their hearts, look upon domestic affairs or work of any kind as of secondary importance, if not actually as a mere jest. The only business that really claims their earnest attention is love, making conquests, and everything connected with this—dress, dancing, and so on.

The nobler and more perfect a thing is, the later and slower it is in arriving at maturity. A man reaches the maturity of his reasoning powers and mental faculties hardly before the age of twenty-eight; a woman at eighteen. And then, too, in the case of woman, it is only reason of a sort—very niggard in its dimensions. That is why women remain children their whole life long; never seeing anything but what is quite close to them, cleaving to the present moment, taking appearance for reality, and preferring trifles to matters of the first importance. For it is by virtue of his reasoning faculty that man does not live in the present only, like the brute, but looks about him and considers the past and the future; and this is the origin of prudence, as well as of that care and anxiety which so many people exhibit. Both the advantages and the disadvantages which this involves, are shared in by the woman to a smaller extent because of her weaker power of reasoning. She may, in fact, be described as intellectually short-sighted, because, while she has an intuitive understanding of what lies quite close to her, her field of vision is narrow and does not reach to what is remote; so that things which are absent, or past, or to come, have much less effect upon women than upon men. This is the reason why women are more often inclined to be extravagant, and sometimes carry their inclination to a length that borders upon madness. In their hearts, women think that it is men's business to earn money and theirs to spend it—if possible during their husband's life, but, at any rate, after his death. The very fact that their husband hands them over his earnings for purposes of housekeeping strengthens them in this belief.

However many disadvantages all this may involve, there is at least this to be said in its favor; that the woman lives more in the present than the man, and that, if the present is at all tolerable, she enjoys it more eagerly. This is the source of that cheerfulness which is peculiar to women, fitting her to amuse man in his hours of recreation, and, in case of need, to console him when he is borne down by the weight of his cares.

It is by no means a bad plan to consult women in matters of difficulty, as the Germans used to do in ancient times; for their way of looking at things is quite different from ours, chiefly in the fact that they like to take the shortest way to their goal, and, in general, manage to fix their eyes upon what lies before them; while we, as a rule, see far beyond it, just because it is in front of our noses. In cases like this, we need to be brought back to the right standpoint, so as to recover the near and simple view.

Then, again, women are decidedly more sober in their judgment than we are, so that they do not see more in things than is really there; whilst, if our passions are aroused, we are apt to see things in an exaggerated way, or imagine what does not exist.

The weakness of their reasoning faculty also explains why it is that women show more sympathy for the unfortunate than men do, and so treat them with more kindness and interest; and why it is that, on the contrary, they are inferior to men in point of justice, and less honorable and conscientious. For it is just because their reasoning power is weak that present circumstances have such a hold over them, and those concrete things, which lie directly before their eyes, exercise a power which is seldom counteracted to any extent by abstract principles of thought, by fixed rules of conduct, firm resolutions, or, in general, by consideration for the past and the future, or regard for what is absent and remote. Accordingly, they possess the first and main elements that go to make a virtuous character, but they are deficient in those secondary qualities which are often a necessary instrument in the formation of it.[1]

Hence, it will be found that the fundamental fault of the female character is that it has

---

[1] In this respect they may be compared to an animal organism which contains a liver but no gall-bladder. Here let me refer to what I have said in my treatise on *The Foundation of Morals.* § 17.

no sense of justice. This is mainly due to the fact, already mentioned, that women are defective in the powers of reasoning and deliberation; but it is also traceable to the position which Nature has assigned to them as the weaker sex. They are dependent, not upon strength, but upon craft; and hence their instinctive capacity for cunning, and their ineradicable tendency to say what is not true. For as lions are provided with claws and teeth, and elephants and boars with tusks, bulls with horns, and cuttle fish with its clouds of inky fluid, so Nature has equipped woman, for her defence and protection, with the arts of dissimulation; and all the power which Nature has conferred upon man in the shape of physical strength and reason, has been bestowed upon women in this form. Hence, dissimulation is innate in woman, and almost as much a quality of the stupid as of the clever. It is as natural for them to make use of it on every occasion as it is for those animals to employ their means of defence when they are attacked; they have a feeling that in doing so they are only within their rights. Therefore a woman who is perfectly truthful and not given to dissimulation is perhaps an impossibility, and for this very reason they are so quick at seeing through dissimulation in others that it is not a wise thing to attempt it with them. But this fundamental defect which I have stated, with all that it entails, gives rise to falsity, faithlessness, treachery, ingratitude, and so on. Perjury in a court of justice is more often committed by women than by men. It may, indeed, be generally questioned whether women ought to be sworn in at all. From time to time one finds repeated cases everywhere of ladies, who want for nothing, taking things from shop-counters when no one is looking, and making off with them.

Nature has appointed that the propagation of the species shall be the business of men who are young, strong and handsome; so that the race may not degenerate. This is the firm will and purpose of Nature in regard to the species, and it finds its expression in the passions of women. There is no law

that is older or more powerful than this. Woe, then, to the man who sets up claims and interests that will conflict with it; whatever he may say and do, they will be unmercifully crushed at the first serious encounter. For the innate rule that governs women's conduct, though it is secret and unformulated, nay, unconscious in its working, is this: *We are justified in deceiving those who think they have acquired rights over the species by paying little attention to the individual, that is, to us. The constitution and, therefore, the welfare of the species have been placed in our hands and committed to our care, through the control we obtain over the next generation, which proceeds from us; let us discharge our duties conscientiously.* But women have no abstract knowledge of this leading principle; they are conscious of it only as a concrete fact; and they have no other method of giving expression to it than the way in which they act when the opportunity arrives. And then their conscience does not trouble them so much as we fancy; for in the darkest recesses of their heart, they are aware that in committing a breach of their duty towards the individual, they have all the better fulfilled their duty towards the species, which is infinitely greater.[2]

And since women exist in the main solely for the propagation of the species, and are not destined for anything else, they live, as a rule, more for the species than for the individual, and in their hearts take the affairs of the species more seriously than those of the individual. This gives their whole life and being a certain levity; the general bent of their character is in a direction fundamentally different from that of man; and it is this which produces that discord in married life which is so frequent, and almost the normal state.

The natural feeling between men is mere indifference, but between women it is actual enmity. The reason of this is that trade-jealousy—*odium figulinum*—which, in the case of

---

[2] A more detailed discussion of the matter in question may be found in my chief work, *Die Welt als Wille und Vorstellung*, vol. ii, ch. 44.

men does not go beyond the confines of their own particular pursuit; but, with women, embraces the whole sex; since they have only one kind of business. Even when they meet in the street, women look at one another like Guelphs and Ghibellines. And it is a patent fact that when two women make first acquaintance with each other, they behave with more constraint and dissimulation than two men would show in a like case; and hence it is that an exchange of compliments between two women is a much more ridiculous proceeding than between two men. Further, whilst a man will, as a general rule, always preserve a certain amount of consideration and humanity in speaking to others, even to those who are in a very inferior position, it is intolerable to see how proudly and disdainfully a fine lady will generally behave towards one who is in a lower social rank (I do not mean a woman who is in her service), whenever she speaks to her. The reason of this may be that, with women, differences of rank are much more precarious than with us; because, while a hundred considerations carry weight in our case, in theirs there is only one, namely, with which man they have found favor; as also that they stand in much nearer relations with one another than men do, in consequence of the one-sided nature of their calling. This makes them endeavor to lay stress upon differences of rank.

It is only the man whose intellect is clouded by his sexual impulses that could give the name of *the fair sex* to that under-sized, narrow-shouldered, broad-hipped, and short-legged race; for the whole beauty of the sex is bound up with this impulse. Instead of calling them beautiful, there would be more warrant for describing women as the unæsthetic sex. Neither for music, nor for poetry, nor for fine art, have they really and truly any sense or susceptibility; it is a mere mockery if they make a pretense of it in order to assist their endeavor to please. Hence, as a result of this, they are incapable of taking a *purely objective interest* in anything; and the reason of it seems to me to be as follows. A man tries to acquire *direct* mastery over things,

either by understanding them, or by forcing them to do his will. But a woman is always and everywhere reduced to obtaining this mastery *indirectly,* namely, through a man; and whatever direct mastery she may have is entirely confined to him. And so it lies in woman's nature to look upon everything only as a means for conquering man; and if she takes an interest in anything else, it is simulated—a mere roundabout way of gaining her ends by coquetry, and feigning what she does not feel. Hence, even Rousseau declared: *Women have, in general, no love for any art; they have no proper knowledge of any; and they have no genius.*[3]

No one who sees at all below the surface can have failed to remark the same thing. You need only observe the kind of attention women bestow upon a concert, an opera, or a play—the childish simplicity, for example, with which they keep on chattering during the finest passages in the greatest masterpieces. If it is true that the Greeks excluded women from their theatres they were quite right in what they did; at any rate you would have been able to hear what was said upon the stage. In our day, besides, or in lieu of saying, *Let a woman keep silence in the church,* it would be much to the point to say *Let a woman keep silence in the theatre.* This might, perhaps, be put up in big letters on the curtain.

And you cannot expect anything else of women if you consider that the most distinguished intellects among the whole sex have never managed to produce a single achievement in the fine arts that is really great, genuine, and original; or given to the world any work of permanent value in any sphere. This is most strikingly shown in regard to painting, where mastery of technique is at least as much within their power as within ours— and hence they are diligent in cultivating it; but still, they have not a single great painting to boast of, just because they are deficient in that objectivity of mind which is so directly indispensable in painting. They never get beyond a subjective point of view. It is quite

---

[3] Lettre à d'Alembert. Note xx.

in keeping with this that ordinary women have no real susceptibility for art at all; for Nature proceeds in strict sequence—*non facit saltum*. And Huarte[4] in his *Examen de ingenios para las scienzias*—a book which has been famous for three hundred years—denies women the possession of all the higher faculties. The case is not altered by particular and partial exceptions; taken as a whole, women are, and remain, thorough-going Philistines, and quite incurable. Hence, with that absurd arrangement which allows them to share the rank and title of their husbands they are a constant stimulus to his ignoble ambitions. And, further, it is just because they are Philistines that modern society, where they take the lead and set the tone, is in such a bad way. Napoleon's saying—that *women have no rank*—should be adopted as the right standpoint in determining their position in society; and as regards their other qualities Chamfort makes the very true remark: *They are made to trade with our own weaknesses and our follies, but not with our reason. The sympathies that exist between them and men are skin-deep only, and do not touch the mind or the feelings or the character.* They form the *sexus sequior*—the second sex, inferior in every respect to the first; their infirmities should be treated with consideration; but to show them great reverence is extremely ridiculous, and lowers us in their eyes. When Nature made two divisions of the human race, she did not draw the line exactly through the middle. These divisions are polar and opposed to each other, it is true; but the difference between them is not qualitative merely, it is also quantitative.

This is just the view which the ancients took of woman, and the view which people in the East take now; and their judgment as to her proper position is much more correct than ours, with our old French notions of gallantry and our preposterous system of reverence—that highest product of Teutonico-Christian stupidity. These notions have served only to make women more arrogant and overbearing; so that one is occasionally reminded of the holy apes in Benares, who in the consciousness of their sanctity and in-

violable position, think they can do exactly as they please.

But in the West, the woman, and especially the *lady*, finds herself in a false position; for woman, rightly called by the ancients, *sexus sequior*, is by no means fit to be the object of our honor and veneration, or to hold her head higher than man and be on equal terms with him. The consequences of this false position are sufficiently obvious. Accordingly, it would be a very desirable thing if this Number-Two of the human race were in Europe also relegated to her natural place, and an end put to that lady nuisance, which not only moves all Asia to laughter, but would have been ridiculed by Greece and Rome as well. It is impossible to calculate the good effects which such a change would bring about in our social, civil and political arrangements. There would be no necessity for the Salic law: it would be a superfluous truism. In Europe the *lady*, strictly so-called, is a being who should not exist at all; she should be either a housewife or a girl who hopes to become one; and she should be brought up, not to be arrogant, but to be thrifty and submissive. It is just because there are such people as *ladies* in Europe that the women of the lower classes, that is to say, the great majority of the sex, are much more unhappy than they are in the East. And even Lord Byron says: *Thought of the state of women under the ancient Greeks—convenient enough. Present state, a remnant of the barbarism of the chivalric and the feudal ages—artificial and unnatural. They ought to mind home—and be well fed and clothed—but not mixed in society. Well educated, too, in religion—but to read neither poetry nor politics—nothing but books of piety and cookery. Music—drawing—dancing—also a little gardening and ploughing now and then. I have seen them mending the roads in Epirus with good success. Why not, as well as hay-making and milking?*

The laws of marriage prevailing in Europe

---

[4] *Translator's Note.*—Juan Huarte (1520?–1590) practised as a physician at Madrid. The work cited by Schopenhauer is well known, and has been translated into many languages.

consider the woman as the equivalent of the man—start, that is to say, from a wrong position. In our part of the world where monogamy is the rule, to marry means to halve one's rights and double one's duties. Now, when the laws gave women equal rights with man, they ought to have also endowed her with a masculine intellect. But the fact is, that just in proportion as the honors and privileges which the laws accord to women, exceed the amount which nature gives, is there a diminution in the number of women who really participate in these privileges; and all the remainder are deprived of their natural rights by just so much as is given to the others over and above their share. For the institution of monogamy, and the laws of marriage which it entails, bestow upon the woman an unnatural position of privilege, by considering her throughout as the full equivalent of the man, which is by no means the case; and seeing this, men who are shrewd and prudent very often scruple to make so great a sacrifice and to acquiesce in so unfair an arrangement.

Consequently, whilst among polygamous nations every woman is provided for, where monogamy prevails the number of married women is limited; and there remains over a large number of women without stay or support, who, in the upper classes, vegetate as useless old maids, and in the lower succumb to hard work for which they are not suited; or else become *filles de joie,* whose life is as destitute of joy as it is of honor. But under the circumstances they become a necessity; and their position is openly recognized as serving the special end of warding off temptation from those women favored by fate, who have found, or may hope to find, husbands. In London alone there are 80,000 prostitutes. What are they but the women, who, under the institution of monogamy have come off worse? Theirs is a dreadful fate: they are human sacrifices offered up on the altar of monogamy. The women whose wretched position is here described are the inevitable set-off to the European lady with her arrogance and pretension. Polygamy is therefore a real benefit to the female sex if it is taken as a whole. And, from another point of view, there is no true reason why a man whose wife suffers from chronic illness, or remains barren, or has gradually become too old for him, should not take a second. The motives which induce so many people to become converts to Mormonism appear to be just those which militate against the unnatural institution of monogamy.

Moreover, the bestowal of unnatural rights upon women has imposed upon them unnatural duties, and, nevertheless, a breach of these duties makes them unhappy. Let me explain. A man may often think that his social or financial position will suffer if he marries, unless he makes some brilliant alliance. His desire will then be to win a woman of his own choice under conditions other than those of marriage, such as will secure her position and that of the children. However fair, reasonable, fit and proper these conditions may be, and the woman consents by foregoing that undue amount of privilege which marriage alone can bestow, she to some extent loses her honor, because marriage is the basis of civic society; and she will lead an unhappy life, since human nature is so constituted that we pay an attention to the opinion of other people which is out of all proportion to its value. On the other hand, if she does not consent, she runs the risk either of having to be given in marriage to a man whom she does not like, or of being landed high and dry as an old maid; for the period during which she has a chance of being settled for life is very short. And in view of this aspect of the institution of monogamy, Thomasius' profoundly learned treatise, *de Concubinatu,* is well worth reading; for it shows that, amongst all nations and in all ages, down to the Lutheran Reformation, concubinage was permitted; nay, that it was an institution which was to a certain extent actually recognized by law, and attended with no dishonor. It was only the Lutheran Reformation that degraded it from this position. It was seen to be a further justification for the marriage of the clergy; and then, after that, the Catholic

Church did not dare to remain behind-hand in the matter.

There is no use arguing about polygamy; it must be taken as *de facto* existing everywhere, and the only question is as to how it shall be regulated. Where are there, then, any real monogamists? We all live, at any rate, for a time, and most of us, always, in polygamy. And so, since every man needs many women, there is nothing fairer than to allow him, nay, to make it incumbent upon him, to provide for many women. This will reduce woman to her true and natural position as a subordinate being; and the *lady*— that monster of European civilization and Teutonico-Christian stupidity—will disappear from the world, leaving only *women,* but no more *unhappy women,* of whom Europe is now full.

In India, no woman is ever independent, but in accordance with the law of Manu,[5] she stands under the control of her father, her husband, her brother or her son. It is, to be sure, a revolting thing that a widow should immolate herself upon her husband's funeral pyre; but it is also revolting that she should spend her husband's money with her paramours—the money for which he toiled his whole life long, in the consoling belief that he was providing for his children. Happy are those who have kept the middle course— *medium tenuere beati.*

The first love of a mother for her child is, with the lower animals as with men, of a purely *instinctive* character, and so it ceases when the child is no longer in a physically helpless condition. After that, the first love should give way to one that is based on habit and reason; but this often fails to make its appearance, especially where the mother did not love the father. The love of a father for his child is of a different order, and more likely to last; because it has its foundation in the fact that in the child he recognizes his own inner self; that is to say, his love for it is metaphysical in its origin.

In almost all nations, whether of the ancient or the modern world, even amongst the Hottentots, property is inherited by the male descendants alone; it is only in Europe that a departure has taken place; but not amongst the nobility, however. That the property which has cost men long years of toil and effort, and been won with so much difficulty, should afterwards come into the hands of women, who then, in their lack of reason, squander it in a short time, or otherwise fool it away, is a grievance and a wrong as serious as it is common, which should be prevented by limiting the right of women to inherit. In my opinion, the best arrangement would be that by which women, whether widows or daughters, should never receive anything beyond the interest for life on property secured by mortgage, and in no case the property itself, or the capital, except where all male descendants fail. The people who make money are men, not women; and it follows from this that women are neither justified in having unconditional possession of it, nor fit persons to be entrusted with its administration. When wealth, in any true sense of the word, that is to say, funds, houses or land, is to go to them as an inheritance they should never be allowed the free disposition of it. In their case a guardian should always be appointed; and hence they should never be given the free control of their own children, wherever it can be avoided. The vanity of women, even though it should not prove to be greater than that of men, has this much danger in it, that it takes an entirely material direction. They are vain, I mean, of their personal beauty, and then of finery, show and magnificence. That is just why they are so much in their element in society. It is this, too, which makes them so inclined to be extravagant, all the more as their reasoning power is low. Accordingly we find an extravagant nature—Γυνὴ τὸ σύνολον ἐστι δαπανηρὸν Φύσει.[6] But with men vanity often takes the direction of non-material advantages, such as intellect, learning, courage.

In the *Politics*[7] Aristotle explains the great

---

[5] Ch. V., v. 148.

[6] Brunck's *Gnomici poetae graeci*, v. 115.

[7] Bk. II. ch. 8; *GBWW*, Vol. 9, p. 464a.

disadvantage which accrued to the Spartans from the fact that they conceded too much to their women, by giving them the right of inheritance and dower, and a great amount of independence; and he shows how much this contributed to Sparta's fall. May it not be the case in France that the influence of women, which went on increasing steadily from the time of Louis XIII., was to blame for that gradual corruption of the Court and the Government, which brought about the Revolution of 1789, of which all subsequent disturbances have been the fruit? However that may be, the false position which women occupy, demonstrated as it is, in the most glaring way, by the institution of the *lady*, is a funda-mental defect in our social scheme, and this defect, proceeding from the very heart of it, must spread its baneful influence in all directions.

*   *   *

That woman is by nature meant to obey may be seen by the fact that every woman who is placed in the unnatural position of complete independence, immediately attaches herself to some man, by whom she allows herself to be guided and ruled. It is because she needs a lord and master. If she is young, it will be a lover; if she is old, a priest.

Human Nature

Truths of the physical order may possess much external significance, but internal significance they have none. The latter is the privilege of intellectual and moral truths, which are concerned with the objectivation of the will in its highest stages, whereas physical truths are concerned with it in its lowest.

For example, if we could establish the truth of what up till now is only a conjecture, namely, that it is the action of the sun which produces thermo-electricity at the equator; that this produces terrestrial magnetism; and that this magnetism, again, is the cause of the *aurora borealis*, these would be truths externally of great, but internally of little, significance. On the other hand, examples of internal significance are furnished by all great and true philosophical systems; by the catastrophe of every good tragedy; nay, even by the observation of human conduct in the extreme manifestations of its morality and immorality, of its good and its evil character. For all these are expressions of that reality which takes outward shape as the world, and which, in the highest stages of its objectivation, proclaims its innermost nature.

To say that the world has only a physical and not a moral significance is the greatest and most pernicious of all errors, the fundamental blunder, the real perversity of mind and temper; and, at bottom, it is doubtless the tendency which faith personifies as Anti-Christ. Nevertheless, in spite of all religions —and they are systems which one and all maintain the opposite, and seek to establish it in their mythical way—this fundamental error never becomes quite extinct, but raises its head from time to time afresh, until universal indignation compels it to hide itself once more.

Yet, however certain we may feel of the moral significance of life and the world, to explain and illustrate it, and to resolve the contradiction between this significance and the world as it is, form a task of great difficulty; so great, indeed, as to make it possible that it has remained for me to exhibit the true and only genuine and sound basis of morality everywhere and at all times effective, together with the results to which it leads. The actual facts of morality are too much on my side for me to fear that my theory can ever be replaced or upset by any other.

However, so long as even my ethical system continues to be ignored by the professorial world, it is Kant's moral principle that prevails in the universities. Among its various forms the one which is most in favour at present is "the dignity of man." I have already exposed the absurdity of this doctrine in my treatise on the *Foundation of Morality*.[1] Therefore I will only say here that if the question were asked on what the alleged dignity of man rests, it would not be long before the answer was made that it rests upon his morality. In other words, his morality rests upon his dignity, and his dignity rests upon his morality.

But apart from this circular argument it seems to me that the idea of dignity can be applied only in an ironical sense to a being whose will is so sinful, whose intellect is so limited, whose body is so weak and perishable as man's. How shall a man be proud, when his conception is a crime, his birth a penalty, his life a labour, and death a necessity!—

---

[1] § 8.

Quid superbit homo? cujus conceptio culpa,
Nasci poena, labor vita, necesse mori!

Therefore, in opposition to the above-mentioned form of the Kantian principle, I should be inclined to lay down the following rule: When you come into contact with a man, no matter whom, do not attempt an objective appreciation of him according to his worth and dignity. Do not consider his bad will, or his narrow understanding and perverse ideas; as the former may easily lead you to hate and the latter to despise him; but fix your attention only upon his sufferings, his needs, his anxieties, his pains. Then you will always feel your kinship with him; you will sympathise with him; and instead of hatred or contempt you will experience the commiseration that alone is the peace to which the Gospel calls us. The way to keep down hatred and contempt is certainly not to look for a man's alleged "dignity," but, on the contrary, to regard him as an object of pity.

The Buddhists, as the result of the more profound views which they entertain on ethical and metaphysical subjects, start from the cardinal vices and not the cardinal virtues; since the virtues make their appearance only as the contraries or negations of the vices. According to Schmidt's *History of the Eastern Mongolians* the cardinal vices in the Buddhist scheme are four: Lust, Indolence, Anger, and Avarice. But probably instead of Indolence, we should read Pride; for so it stands in the *Lettres édifiantes et curieuses*,[2] where Envy, or Hatred, is added as a fifth. I am confirmed in correcting the statement of the excellent Schmidt by the fact that my rendering agrees with the doctrine of the Sufis, who are certainly under the influence of the Brahmins and Buddhists. The Sufis also maintain that there are four cardinal vices, and they arrange them in very striking pairs, so that Lust appears in connection with Avarice, and Anger with Pride. The four cardinal virtues opposed to them would be Chastity and Generosity, together with Gentleness and Humility.

When we compare these profound ideas of morality, as they are entertained by oriental nations, with the celebrated cardinal virtues of Plato, which have been recapitulated again and again — Justice, Valour, Temperance, and Wisdom — it is plain that the latter are not based on any clear, leading idea, but are chosen on grounds that are superficial and, in part, obviously false. Virtues must be qualities of the will, but Wisdom is chiefly an attribute of the Intellect. $\Sigma\omega\phi\rho\sigma\acute{\nu}\nu\eta$, which Cicero translates *Temperantia*, is a very indefinite and ambiguous word, and it admits, therefore, of a variety of applications: it may mean discretion, or abstinence, or keeping a level head. Courage is not a virtue at all; although sometimes it is a servant or instrument of virtue; but it is just as ready to become the servant of the greatest villainy. It is really a quality of temperament. Even Geulinx (in the preface to his *Ethics*) condemned the Platonic virtues and put the following in their place: Diligence, Obedience, Justice and Humility; which are obviously bad. The Chinese distinguish five cardinal virtues: Sympathy, Justice, Propriety, Wisdom, and Sincerity. The virtues of Christianity are theological, not cardinal: Faith, Love, and Hope.

Fundamental disposition towards others, assuming the character either of Envy or of Sympathy, is the point at which the moral virtues and vices of mankind first diverge. These two diametrically opposite qualities exist in every man; for they spring from the inevitable comparison which he draws between his own lot and that of others. According as the result of this comparison affects his individual character does the one or the other of these qualities become the source and principle of all his action. Envy builds the wall between *Thee* and *Me* thicker and stronger; Sympathy makes it slight and transparent; nay, sometimes it pulls down the wall altogether; and then the distinction between self and not-self vanishes.

Valour, which has been mentioned as a virtue, or rather the Courage on which it is based (for valour is only courage in war),

---

[2] Edit. of 1819, vol. vi., p. 372.

deserves a closer examination. The ancients reckoned Courage among the virtues, and cowardice among the vices; but there is no corresponding idea in the Christian scheme, which makes for charity and patience, and in its teaching forbids all enmity or even resistance. The result is that with the moderns Courage is no longer a virtue. Nevertheless it must be admitted that cowardice does not seem to be very compatible with any nobility of character—if only for the reason that it betrays an overgreat apprehension about one's own person.

Courage, however, may also be explained as a readiness to meet ills that threaten at the moment, in order to avoid greater ills that lie in the future; whereas cowardice does the contrary. But this readiness is of the same quality as *patience*, for patience consists in the clear consciousness that there exist greater evils than those which are present, and that any violent attempt to flee from or guard against the ills we have may bring the others upon us. Courage, then, would be a kind of patience; and since it is patience that enables us to practise forbearance and self control, Courage is, through the medium of patience, at least akin to virtue.

But perhaps Courage admits of being considered from a higher point of view. The fear of death may in every case be traced to a deficiency in that natural philosophy—natural, and therefore resting on mere feeling— which gives a man the assurance that he exists in everything outside him just as much as in his own person; so that the death of his person can do him little harm. But it is just this very assurance that would give a man heroic Courage; and therefore, as the reader will recollect from my *Ethics*, Courage comes from the same source as the virtues of Justice and Humanity. This is, I admit, to take a very high view of the matter; but apart from it I cannot well explain why cowardice seems contemptible, and personal courage a noble and sublime thing; for no lower point of view enables me to see why a finite individual who is everything to himself—nay, who is himself even the very fundamental condition of the existence of the rest of the world—should not put his own preservation above every other aim. It is, then, an insufficient explanation of Courage to make it rest only on utility, to give it an empirical and not a transcendental character. It may have been for some such reason that Calderon once uttered a sceptical but remarkable opinion in regard to Courage, nay, actually denied its reality; and put his denial into the mouth of a wise old minister, addressing his young sovereign. "Although," he observed, "natural fear is operative in all alike, a man may be brave in not letting it be seen; and it is this that constitutes Courage":

Que aunque el natural temor
En todos obra igualmente,
No mostrarle es ser valiente
Y esto es lo que hace el valor.[3]

In regard to the difference which I have mentioned between the ancients and the moderns in their estimate of Courage as a virtue, it must be remembered that by Virtue, *virtus*, ἀρετή, the ancients understood every excellence or quality that was praiseworthy in itself, it might be moral or intellectual, or possibly only physical. But when Christianity demonstrated that the fundamental tendency of life was moral, it was moral superiority alone that henceforth attached to the notion of Virtue. Meanwhile the earlier usage still survived in the elder Latinists, and also in Italian writers, as is proved by the well-known meaning of the word *virtuoso*. The special attention of students should be drawn to this wider range of the idea of Virtue amongst the ancients, as otherwise it might easily be a source of secret perplexity. I may recommend two passages preserved for us by Stobaeus, which will serve this purpose. One of them is apparently from the Pythagorean philosopher Metopos, in which the fitness of every bodily member is declared to be a virtue. The other pronounces that the virtue of a shoemaker is to

---

[3] *La Hija del Aire,* ii., 2.

make good shoes. This may also serve to explain why it is that in the ancient scheme of ethics virtues and vices are mentioned which find no place in ours.

As the place of Courage amongst the virtues is a matter of doubt, so is that of Avarice amongst the vices. It must not, however, be confounded with greed, which is the most immediate meaning of the Latin word *avaritia*. Let us then draw up and examine the arguments *pro et contra* in regard to Avarice, and leave the final judgment to be formed by every man for himself.

On the one hand it is argued that it is not Avarice which is a vice, but extravagance, its opposite. Extravagance springs from a brutish limitation to the present moment, in comparison with which the future, existing as it does only in thought, is as nothing. It rests upon the illusion that sensual pleasures possess a positive or real value. Accordingly, future need and misery is the price at which the spendthrift purchases pleasures that are empty, fleeting, and often no more than imaginary; or else feeds his vain, stupid self-conceit on the bows and scrapes of parasites who laugh at him in secret, or on the gaze of the mob and those who envy his magnificence. We should, therefore, shun the spendthrift as though he had the plague, and on discovering his vice break with him betimes, in order that later on, when the consequences of his extravagance ensue, we may neither have to help to bear them, nor, on the other hand, have to play the part of the friends of Timon of Athens.

At the same time it is not to be expected that he who foolishly squanders his own fortune will leave another man's intact, if it should chance to be committed to his keeping; nay, *sui profusus* and *alieni appetens* are by Sallust very rightly conjoined. Hence it is that extravagance leads not only to impoverishment but also to crime; and crime amongst the moneyed classes is almost always the result of extravagance. It is accordingly with justice that the *Koran* declares all spendthrifts to be "brothers of Satan."

But it is superfluity that Avarice brings in its train, and when was superfluity ever unwelcome? That must be a good vice which has good consequences. Avarice proceeds upon the principle that all pleasure is only negative in its operation and that the happiness which consists of a series of pleasures is a chimæra; that, on the contrary, it is pains which are positive and extremely real. Accordingly, the avaricious man forgoes the former in order that he may be the better preserved from the latter, and thus it is that *bear and forbear—sustine et abstine—*is his maxim. And because he knows, further, how inexhaustible are the possibilities of misfortune, and how innumerable the paths of danger, he increases the means of avoiding them, in order, if possible, to surround himself with a triple wall of protection. Who, then, can say where precaution against disaster begins to be exaggerated? He alone who knows where the malignity of fate reaches its limit. And even if precaution were exaggerated it is an error which at the most would hurt the man who took it, and not others. If he will never need the treasures which he lays up for himself, they will one day benefit others whom nature has made less careful. That until then he withdraws the money from circulation is no misfortune; for money is not an article of consumption: it only represents the good things which a man may actually possess, and is not one itself. Coins are only counters; their value is what they represent; and what they represent cannot be withdrawn from circulation. Moreover, by holding back the money, the value of the remainder which is in circulation is enhanced by precisely the same amount. Even though it be the case, as is said, that many a miser comes in the end to love money itself for its own sake, it is equally certain that many a spendthrift, on the other hand, loves spending and squandering for no better reason. Friendship with a miser is not only without danger, but it is profitable, because of the great advantages it can bring. For it is doubtless those who are nearest and dearest to the miser who on his death will reap the fruits of the self-control which he exercised; but even in his lifetime, too, something may be expected of him in cases of great need. At any rate one can always hope for more from him than from the spendthrift, who has lost his all and is himself helpless and in debt. *Mas dà el duro que el desnudo*, says a Spanish proverb; the man who has a hard heart will give more than the man who has an empty purse. The upshot of all this is that Avarice is not a vice.

On the other side, it may be said that Avarice is the quintessence of all vices. When physical pleasures seduce a man from the right path, it is his sensual nature—the animal part of him—which is at fault. He is carried away by its attractions, and, overcome by the impression of the moment, he acts without thinking of the consequences. When, on the other hand, he is brought by age or bodily weakness to the condition in which the vices that he could never abandon end by abandoning him, and his capacity for physical pleasure dies—if he turns to Avarice, the intellectual desire survives the sensual. Money, which represents all the good things of this world, and is these good things in the abstract, now becomes the dry trunk overgrown with all the dead lusts of the flesh, which are egoism in the abstract. They come to life again in the love of the Mammon. The transient pleasure of the senses has become a deliberate and calculated lust of money, which, like that to which it is directed, is symbolical in its nature, and, like it, indestructible.

This obstinate love of the pleasures of the world—a love which, as it were, outlives itself; this utterly incorrigible sin, this refined and sublimated desire of the flesh, is the abstract form in which all lusts are concentrated, and to which it stands like a general idea to individual particulars. Accordingly, Avarice is the vice of age, just as extravagance is the vice of youth.

This *disputatio in utramque partem*—this debate for and against—is certainly calculated to drive us into accepting the *juste milieu* morality of Aristotle; a conclusion that is also supported by the following consideration.

Every human perfection is allied to a defect into which it threatens to pass; but it is also true that every defect is allied to a perfection. Hence it is that if, as often happens, we make a mistake about a man, it is because at the beginning of our acquaintance with him we confound his defects with the kinds of perfection to which they are allied. The cautious man seems to us a coward; the economical man, a miser; the spendthrift seems liberal; the rude fellow, downright and sincere; the foolhardy person looks as if he were going to work with a noble self-confidence; and so on in many other cases.

No one can live among men without feeling drawn again and again to the tempting supposition that moral baseness and intellectual incapacity are closely connected, as though they both sprang direct from one source. That that, however, is not so, I have shown in detail.[4] That it seems to be so is merely due to the fact that both are so often found together; and the circumstance is to be explained by the very frequent occurrence of each of them, so that it may easily happen for both to be compelled to live under one roof. At the same time it is not to be denied that they play into each other's hands to their mutual benefit; and it is this that produces the very unedifying spectacle which only too many men exhibit, and that makes the world to go as it goes. A man who is unintelligent is very likely to show his perfidy, villainy and malice; whereas a clever man understands how to conceal these qualities. And how often, on the other hand, does a perversity of heart prevent a man from seeing truths which his intelligence is quite capable of grasping!

Nevertheless, let no one boast. Just as every man, though he be the greatest genius, has very definite limitations in some one sphere of knowledge, and thus attests his common origin with the essentially perverse and stupid mass of mankind, so also has every man something in his nature which is positively evil. Even the best, nay the noblest,

---

[4] In my chief work, vol. ii., ch. xix.

character will sometimes surprise us by isolated traits of depravity; as though it were to acknowledge his kinship with the human race, in which villainy—nay, cruelty—is to be found in that degree. For it was just in virtue of this evil in him, this bad principle, that of necessity he became a man. And for the same reason the world in general is what my clear mirror of it has shown it to be.

But in spite of all this the difference even between one man and another is incalculably great, and many a one would be horrified to see another as he really is. Oh, for some Asmodeus of morality, to make not only roofs and walls transparent to his favourites, but also to lift the veil of dissimulation, fraud, hypocrisy, pretence, falsehood and deception, which is spread over all things! to show how little true honesty there is in the world, and how often, even where it is least to be expected, behind all the exterior outwork of virtue, secretly and in the innermost recesses, unrighteousness sits at the helm! It is just on this account that so many men of the better kind have four-footed friends: for, to be sure, how is a man to get relief from the endless dissimulation, falsity and malice of mankind, if there were no dogs into whose honest faces he can look without distrust?

For what is our civilised world but a big masquerade? where you meet knights, priests, soldiers, men of learning, barristers, clergymen, philosophers, and I don't know what all! But they are not what they pretend to be; they are only masks, and, as a rule, behind the masks you will find money-makers. One man, I suppose, puts on the mask of law, which he has borrowed for the purpose from a barrister, only in order to be able to give another man a sound drubbing; a second has chosen the mask of patriotism and the public welfare with a similar intent; a third takes religion or purity of doctrine. For all sorts of purposes men have often put on the mask of philosophy, and even of philanthropy, and I know not what besides. Women have a smaller choice. As a rule they avail themselves of the mask of morality, modesty,

domesticity, and humility. Then there are general masks, without any particular character attaching to them like dominoes. They may be met with everywhere; and of this sort is the strict rectitude, the courtesy, the sincere sympathy, the smiling friendship, that people profess. The whole of these masks as a rule are merely, as I have said, a disguise for some industry, commerce, or speculation. It is merchants alone who in this respect constitute any honest class. They are the only people who give themselves out to be what they are; and therefore they go about without any mask at all, and consequently take a humble rank.

It is very necessary that a man should be apprised early in life that it is a masquerade in which he finds himself. For otherwise there are many things which he will fail to understand and put up with, nay, at which he will be completely puzzled, and that man longest of all whose heart is made of better clay—

Et meliore luto finxit praecordia Titan.[5]

Such for instance is the favour that villainy finds; the neglect that merit, even the rarest and the greatest, suffers at the hands of those of the same profession; the hatred of truth and great capacity; the ignorance of scholars in their own province; and the fact that true wares are almost always despised and the merely specious ones in request. Therefore let even the young be instructed betimes that in this masquerade the apples are of wax, the flowers of silk, the fish of pasteboard, and that all things—yes, all things—are toys and trifles; and that of two men whom he may see earnestly engaged in business, one is supplying spurious goods and the other paying for them in false coin.

But there are more serious reflections to be made, and worse things to be recorded. Man is at bottom a savage, horrible beast. We know it, if only in the business of taming and

---

[5] Juvenal, *Sat.* 14, 34.

restraining him which we call civilisation. Hence it is that we are terrified if now and then his nature breaks out. Wherever and whenever the locks and chains of law and order fall off and give place to anarchy, he shows himself for what he is. But it is unnecessary to wait for anarchy in order to gain enlightenment on this subject. A hundred records, old and new, produce the conviction that in his unrelenting cruelty man is in no way inferior to the tiger and the hyaena. A forcible example is supplied by a publication of the year 1841 entitled *Slavery and the Internal Slave Trade in the United States of North America: being replies to questions transmitted by the British Anti-slavery Society to the American Anti-slavery Society*. This book constitutes one of the heaviest indictments against the human race. No one can put it down without a feeling of horror, and few without tears. For whatever the reader may have ever heard, or imagined, or dreamt, of the unhappy condition of slavery, or indeed of human cruelty in general, it will seem small to him when he reads of the way in which those devils in human form, those bigoted, church-going, strictly Sabbatarian rascals—and in particular the Anglican priests among them—treated their innocent black brothers, who by wrong and violence had got into their diabolical clutches.

Other examples are furnished by Tshudi's *Travels in Peru,* in the description which he gives of the treatment of the Peruvian soldiers at the hands of their officers; and by Macleod's *Travels in Eastern Africa,* where the author tells of the cold-blooded and truly devilish cruelty with which the Portuguese in Mozambique treat their slaves. But we need not go for examples to the New World, that obverse side of our planet. In the year 1848 it was brought to life that in England, not in one, but apparently in a hundred cases within a brief period, a husband had poisoned his wife or *vice versâ*, or both had joined in poisoning their children, or in torturing them slowly to death by starving and ill-treating them, with no other object than to get the money for burying them which they had insured in the Burial Clubs against their death. For this purpose a child was often insured in several, even in as many as twenty clubs at once.

Details of this character belong, indeed, to the blackest pages in the criminal records of humanity. But, when all is said, it is the inward and innate character of man, this god *par excellence* of the Pantheists, from which they and everything like them proceed. In every man there dwells, first and foremost, a colossal egoism, which breaks the bounds of right and justice with the greatest freedom, as everyday life shows on a small scale, and as history on every page of it on a large. Does not the recognised need of a balance of power in Europe, with the anxious way in which it is preserved, demonstrate that man is a beast of prey, who no sooner sees a weaker man near him than he falls upon him without fail? and does not the same hold good of the affairs of ordinary life?

But to the boundless egoism of our nature there is joined more or less in every human breast a fund of hatred, anger, envy, rancour and malice, accumulated like the venom in a serpent's tooth, and waiting only for an opportunity of venting itself, and then, like a demon unchained, of storming and raging. If a man has no great occasion for breaking out, he will end by taking advantage of the smallest, and by working it up into something great by the aid of his imagination; for, however small it may be, it is enough to rouse his anger—

Quantulacunque adeo est occasio, sufficit irae[6]—

and then he will carry it as far as he can and may. We see this in daily life, where such outbursts are well known under the name of "venting one's gall on something." It will also have been observed that if such outbursts meet with no opposition the subject of them feels decidedly the better for them after-

---

[6] Juvenal, *Sat.* 13, 183.

wards. That anger is not without its pleasure is a truth that was recorded even by Aristotle;[7] and he quotes a passage from Homer, who declares anger to be sweeter than honey. But not in anger alone—in hatred too, which stands to anger like a chronic to an acute disease, a man may indulge with the greatest delight:

Now hatred is by far the longest pleasure,
Men love in haste, but they detest at leisure.[8]

Gobineau in his work *Les Races Humaines* has called man *l'animal méchant par excellence.* People take this very ill, because they feel that it hits them; but he is quite right, for man is the only animal which causes pain to others without any further purpose than just to cause it. Other animals never do it except to satisfy their hunger, or in the rage of combat. If it is said against the tiger that he kills more than eats, he strangles his prey only for the purpose of eating it; and if he cannot eat it, the only explanation is, as the French phrase has it, that *ses yeux sont plus grands que son estomac.* No animal ever torments another for the mere purpose of tormenting, but man does it, and it is this that constitutes the diabolical feature in his character which is so much worse than the merely animal. I have already spoken of the matter in its broad aspect; but it is manifest even in small things, and every reader has a daily opportunity of observing it. For instance, if two little dogs are playing together—and what a genial and charming sight it is—and a child of three or four years joins them, it is almost inevitable for it to begin hitting them with a whip or stick, and thereby show itself, even at that age, *l'animal méchant par excellence.* The love of teasing and playing tricks, which is common enough, may be traced to the same source. For instance, if a man has expressed his annoyance at any interruption or other petty inconvenience, there will be no lack of people who for that very reason will bring it about: *animal méchant par excellence!* This is so certain that a man should be careful not to express any annoyance at small evils. On the other

hand he should also be careful not to express his pleasure at any trifle, for, if he does so, men will act like the jailer who, when he found that his prisoner had performed the laborious task of taming a spider, and took a pleasure in watching it, immediately crushed it under his foot: *l'animal méchant par excellence!* This is why all animals are instinctively afraid of the sight, or even of the track of a man, that *animal méchant par excellence!* nor does their instinct play them false; for it is man alone who hunts game for which he has no use and which does him no harm.

It is a fact, then, that in the heart of every man there lies a wild beast which only waits for an opportunity to storm and rage, in its desire to inflict pain on others, or, if they stand in his way, to kill them. It is this which is the source of all the lust of war and battle. In trying to tame and to some extent hold it in check, the intelligence, its appointed keeper, has always enough to do. People may, if they please, call it the radical evil of human nature—a name which will at least serve those with whom a word stands for an explanation. I say, however, that it is the will to live, which, more and more embittered by the constant sufferings of existence, seeks to alleviate its own torment by causing torment in others. But in this way a man gradually develops in himself real cruelty and malice. The observation may also be added that as, according to Kant, matter subsists only through the antagonism of the powers of expansion and contraction, so human society subsists only by the antagonism of hatred, or anger, and fear. For there is a moment in the life of all of us when the malignity of our nature might perhaps make us murderers, if it were not accompanied by a due admixture of fear to keep it within bounds; and this fear, again, would make a man the sport and laughing stock of every boy, if anger were not lying ready in him, and keeping watch.

But it is *Schadenfreude,* a mischievous delight in the misfortunes of others, which re-

---

[7] *Rhet.,* i., 11; ii., 2.
[8] Byron, *Don Juan,* c. xiii. 6.

mains the worst trait in human nature. It is a feeling which is closely akin to cruelty, and differs from it, to say the truth, only as theory from practice. In general, it may be said of it that it takes the place which pity ought to take—pity which is its opposite, and the true source of all real justice and charity.

Envy is also opposed to pity, but in another sense; envy, that is to say, is produced by a cause directly antagonistic to that which produces the delight in mischief. The opposition between pity and envy on the one hand, and pity and the delight in mischief on the other, rests, in the main, on the occasions which call them forth. In the case of envy it is only as a direct effect of the cause which excites it that we feel it at all. That is just the reason why envy, although it is a reprehensible feeling, still admits of some excuse, and is, in general, a very human quality; whereas the delight in mischief is diabolical, and its taunts are the laughter of hell.

The delight in mischief, as I have said, takes the place which pity ought to take. Envy, on the contrary, finds a place only where there is no inducement to pity, or rather an inducement to its opposite; and it is just as this opposite that envy arises in the human breast; and so far, therefore, it may still be reckoned a human sentiment. Nay, I am afraid that no one will be found to be entirely free from it. For that a man should feel his own lack of things more bitterly at the sight of another's delight in the enjoyment of them, is natural; nay, it is inevitable; but this should not rouse his hatred of the man who is happier than himself. It is just this hatred, however, in which true envy consists. Least of all should a man be envious, when it is a question, not of the gifts of fortune, or chance, or another's favour, but of the gifts of nature; because everything that is innate in a man rests on a metaphysical basis, and possesses justification of a higher kind; it is, so to speak, given him by Divine grace. But, unhappily, it is just in the case of personal advantages that envy is most irreconcilable. Thus it is that intelligence, or even genius, cannot get on in the world without begging

pardon for its existence, wherever it is not in a position to be able, proudly and boldly, to despise the world.

In other words, if envy is aroused only by wealth, rank, or power, it is often kept down by egoism, which perceives that, on occasion, assistance, enjoyment, support, protection, advancement, and so on, may be hoped for from the object of envy or that at least by intercourse with him a man may himself win honour from the reflected light of his superiority; and here, too, there is the hope of one day attaining all those advantages himself. On the other hand, in the envy that is directed to natural gifts and personal advantages, like beauty in women, or intelligence in men, there is no consolation or hope of one kind or the other; so that nothing remains but to indulge a bitter and irreconcilable hatred of the person who possesses these privileges; and hence the only remaining desire is to take vengeance on him.

But here the envious man finds himself in an unfortunate position; for all his blows fall powerless as soon as it is known that they come from him. Accordingly he hides his feelings as carefully as if they were secret sins, and so becomes an inexhaustible inventor of tricks and artifices and devices for concealing and masking his procedure, in order that, unperceived, he may wound the object of his envy. For instance, with an air of the utmost unconcern he will ignore the advantages which are eating his heart out; he will neither see them, nor know them, nor have observed or even heard of them, and thus make himself a master in the art of dissimulation. With great cunning he will completely overlook the man whose brilliant qualities are gnawing at his heart, and act as though he were quite an unimportant person; he will take no notice of him, and, on occasion, will have even quite forgotten his existence. But at the same time he will before all things endeavour by secret machination carefully to deprive those advantages of any opportunity of showing themselves and becoming known. Then out of his dark corner he will attack these qualities with censure, mockery, ridicule and calumny, like the toad which spurts its poison from a hole. No less will he enthusiastically praise unimportant people, or even indifferent or bad performances in the same sphere. In short, he will become a Proteas in stratagem, in order to wound others without showing himself. But what is the use of it? The trained eye recognises him in spite of it all. He betrays himself, if by nothing else, by the way in which he timidly avoids and flies from the object of his envy, who stands the more completely alone, the more brilliant he is; and this is the reason why pretty girls have no friends of their own sex. He betrays himself, too, by the causeless hatred which he shows—a hatred which finds vent in a violent explosion at any circumstance however trivial, though it is often only the product of his imagination. How many such men there are in the world may be recognised by the universal praise of modesty, that is, of a virtue invented on behalf of dull and commonplace people. Nevertheless, it is a virtue which, by exhibiting the necessity for dealing considerately with the wretched plight of these people, is just what calls attention to it.

For our self-consciousness and our pride there can be nothing more flattering than the sight of envy lurking in its retreat and plotting its schemes; but never let a man forget that where there is envy there is hatred, and let him be careful not to make a false friend out of any envious person. Therefore it is important to our safety to lay envy bare; and a man should study to discover its tricks, as it is everywhere to be found and always goes about *incognito;* or as I have said, like a venomous toad it lurks in dark corners. It deserves neither quarter nor sympathy; but as we can never reconcile it let our rule of conduct be to scorn it with a good heart, and as our happiness and glory is torture to it we may rejoice in its sufferings:

Den Neid wirst nimmer du versöhnen;
So magst du ihn getrost verhöhnen.
Dein Glück, dein Ruhm ist ihm ein Leiden:
Magst drum an seiner Quaal dich weiden.*

We have been taking a look at the *depravity* of man, and it is a sight which may well fill us with horror. But now we must cast our eyes on the *misery* of his existence; and when we have done so, and are horrified by that too, we must look back again at his depravity. We shall then find that they hold the balance to each other. We shall perceive the eternal justice of things; for we shall recognise that the world is itself the Last Judgment on it, and we shall begin to understand why it is that everything that lives must pay the penalty of its existence, first in living and then in dying. Thus the evil of the penalty accords with the evil of the sin—*malum poenae* with *malum culpae.* From the same point of view we lose our indignation at that intellectual incapacity of the great majority of mankind which in life so often disgusts us. In this *Sansara,* as the Buddhists call it, human misery, human depravity and human folly correspond with one another perfectly, and they are of like magnitude. But if, on some special inducement, we direct our gaze to one of them, and survey it in particular, it seems to exceed the other two. This, however, is an illusion, and merely the effect of their colossal range.

All things proclaim this *Sansara;* more than all else, the world of mankind; in which, from a moral point of view, villainy and baseness, and from an intellectual point of view, incapacity and stupidity, prevail to a horrifying extent. Nevertheless, there appear in it, although very spasmodically, and always as a fresh surprise, manifestations of honesty, of goodness, nay, even of nobility; and also of great intelligence, of the thinking mind of genius. They never quite vanish, but like single points of light gleam upon us out of the great dark mass. We must accept them as a pledge that this *Sansara* contains a good and redeeming principle, which is capable of

---

* Envy you must never appease;
So you may confidently deride it.
Your fortune, your fame are its pain:
You may feast then on its torment.

breaking through and of filling and freeing the whole of it.

The readers of my *Ethics* know that with me the ultimate foundation of morality is the truth which in the *Vedas* and the *Vedanta* receives its expression in the established, mystical formula, *Tat twam asi (This is thyself)*, which is spoken with reference to every living thing, be it man or beast, and is called the *Mahava-kya*, the great word.

Actions which proceed in accordance with this principle, such as those of the philanthropist, may indeed be regarded as the beginning of mysticism. Every benefit rendered with a pure intention proclaims that the man who exercises it acts in direct conflict with the world of appearance; for he recognises himself as identical with another individual, who exists in complete separation from him. Accordingly, all disinterested kindness is inexplicable; it is a mystery; and hence in order to explain it a man has to resort to all sorts of fictions. When Kant had demolished all other arguments for theism, he admitted one only, that it gave the best interpretation and solution of such mysterious actions, and of all others like them. He therefore allowed it to stand as a presumption unsusceptible indeed of theoretical proof, but valid from a practical point of view. I may, however, express my doubts whether he was quite serious about it. For to make morality rest on theism is really to reduce morality to egoism; although the English, it is true, as also the lowest classes of society with us, do not perceive the possibility of any other foundation for it.

The above-mentioned recognition of a man's own true being in another individual objectively presented to him, is exhibited in a particularly beautiful and clear way in the cases in which a man, already destined to death beyond any hope of rescue, gives himself up to the welfare of others with great solicitude and zeal, and tries to save them. Of this kind is the well-known story of a servant who was bitten in a courtyard at night by a mad dog. In the belief that she was beyond hope, she seized the dog and dragged it into a stable, which she then locked, so that no one else might be bitten. Then again there is the incident in Naples, which Tischbein has immortalised in one of his *aquarelles*. A son, fleeing from the lava which is rapidly streaming toward the sea, is carrying his aged father on his back. When there is only a narrow strip of land left between the devouring elements, the father bids the son put him down, so that the son may save himself by flight, as otherwise both will be lost. The son obeys, and as he goes casts a glance of farewell on his father. This is the moment depicted. The historical circumstance which Scott represents in his masterly way in *The Heart of Midlothian*, chap. ii., is of a precisely similar kind; where, of two delinquents condemned to death, the one who by his awkwardness caused the capture of the other happily sets him free in the chapel by overpowering the guard after the execution-sermon, without at the same time making any attempt on his own behalf. Nay, in the same category must also be placed the scene which is represented in a common engraving, which may perhaps be objectionable to western readers—I mean the one in which a soldier, kneeling to be shot, is trying by waving a cloth to frighten away his dog who wants to come to him.

In all these cases we see an individual in the face of his own immediate and certain destruction no longer thinking of saving himself, so that he may direct the whole of his efforts to saving some one else. How could there be a clearer expression of the consciousness that what is being destroyed is only a phenomenon, and that the destruction itself is only a phenomenon; that, on the other hand, the real being of the man who meets his death is untouched by that event, and lives on in the other man, in whom even now, as his action betrays, he so clearly perceives it to exist? For if this were not so, and it was his real being which was about to be annihilated, how could that being spend its last efforts in showing such an ardent sympathy in the welfare and continued existence of another?

There are two different ways in which a man may become conscious of his own existence. On the one hand, he may have an empirical perception of it, as it manifests itself externally—something so small that it approaches vanishing point; set in a world which, as regards time and space, is infinite; one only of the thousand millions of human creatures who run about on this planet for a very brief period and are renewed every thirty years. On the other hand, by going down into the depths of his own nature, a man may become conscious that he is all in all; that, in fact, he is the only real being; and that, in addition, this real being perceives itself again in others, who present themselves from without, as though they formed a mirror of himself.

Of these two ways in which a man may come to know what he is, the first grasps the phenomenon alone, the mere product of *the principle of individuation;* whereas the second makes a man immediately conscious that he is *the thing-in-itself.* This is a doctrine in which, as regards the first way, I have Kant, and as regards both, I have the *Vedas,* to support me.

There is, it is true, a simple objection to the second method. It may be said to assume that one and the same being can exist in different places at the same time, and yet be complete in each of them. Although, from an empirical point of view, this is the most palpable impossibility—nay, absurdity—it is nevertheless perfectly true of the thing-in-itself. The impossibility and absurdity of it, empirically, are only due to the forms which phenomena assume, in accordance with the principle of individuation. For the thing-in-itself, the will to live, exists whole and undivided in every being, even in the smallest, as completely as in the sum-total of all things that ever were or are or will be. This is why every being, even the smallest, says to itself, So long as I am safe, let the world perish—*dum ego salvus sim, pereat mundus.* And, in truth, even if only one individual were left in the world, and all the rest were to perish, the one that remained would still possess the whole self-being of the world, uninjured and undiminished, and would laugh at the destruction of the world as an illusion. This conclusion *per impossibile* may be balanced by the counter-conclusion, which is on all fours with it, that if that last individual were to be annihilated in and with him the whole world would be destroyed. It was in this sense that the mystic Angelus Silesius declared that God could not live for a moment without him, and that if he were to be annihilated God must of necessity give up the ghost:

Ich weiss dass ohne mich Gott nicht ein Nu kann leben;
Werd' ich zunicht, er muss von Noth den Geist aufgeben.

But the empirical point of view also to some extent enables us to perceive that it is true, or at least possible, that our self can exist in other beings whose consciousness is separated and different from our own. That this is so is shown by the experience of somnambulists. Although the identity of their ego is preserved throughout, they know nothing, when they awake, of all that a moment before they themselves said, did or suffered. So entirely is the individual consciousness a phenomenon that even in the same ego two consciousnesses can arise of which the one knows nothing of the other.

Free Will and Fatalism

No thoughtful man can have any doubt, after the conclusions reached in my prize-essay on *Moral Freedom,* that such freedom is to be sought, not anywhere in nature, but outside of it. The only freedom that exists is of a metaphysical character. In the physical world freedom is an impossibility. Accordingly, while our several actions are in no wise free, every man's individual character is to be regarded as a free act. He is such and such a man, because once for all it is his will to be that man. For the will itself, and in itself, and also insofar as it is manifest in an individual, and accordingly constitutes the original and fundamental desires of that individual, is independent of all knowledge, because it is antecedent to such knowledge. All that it receives from knowledge is the series of motives by which it successively develops its nature and makes itself cognisable or visible; but the will itself, as something that lies beyond time, and so long as it exists at all, never changes. Therefore every man, being what he is and placed in the circumstances which for the moment obtain, but which on their part also arise by strict necessity, can absolutely never do anything else than just what at that moment he does do. Accordingly, the whole course of a man's life, in all its incidents great and small, is as necessarily predetermined as the course of a clock.

The main reason of this is that the kind of metaphysical free act which I have described tends to become a knowing consciousness — a perceptive intuition, which is subject to the forms of space and time. By means of those forms the unity and indivisibility of the act are represented as drawn asunder into a series of states and events, which are subject to the Principle of Sufficient Reason in its four forms — and it is this that is meant by *necessity.* But the result of it all assumes a moral complexion. It amounts to this, that by what we do we know what we are, and by what we suffer we know what we deserve.

Further, it follows from this that a man's *individuality* does not rest upon the principle of individuation alone, and therefore is not altogether phenomenal in its nature. On the contrary, it has its roots in the thing-in-itself, in the will which is the essence of each individual. The character of this individual is itself individual. But how deep the roots of individuality extend is one of the questions which I do not undertake to answer.

In this connection it deserves to be mentioned that even Plato, in his own way, represented the individuality of a man as a free act.[1] He represented him as coming into the world with a given tendency, which was the result of the feelings and character already attaching to him in accordance with the doctrine of metempsychosis. The Brahmin philosophers also express the unalterable fixity of innate character in a mystical fashion. They say that Brahma, when a man is produced, engraves his doings and sufferings in written characters on his skull, and that his life must take shape in accordance therewith. They point to the jagged edges in the sutures of the skull-bones as evidence of this writing; and the purport of it, they say, depends on his previous life and actions. The same view appears to underlie the Christian, or rather, the Pauline, dogma of Predestination.

But this truth, which is universally confirmed by experience, is attended with another result. All genuine merit, moral as

---

[1] *Phaedrus* and *Laws, bk. x; GBWW,* Vol. 7.

well as intellectual, is not merely physical or empirical in its origin, but metaphysical; that is to say, it is given *à priori* and not *à posteriori;* in other words, it lies innate and is not acquired, and therefore its source is not a mere phenomenon, but the thing-in-itself. Hence it is that every man achieves only that which is irrevocably established in his nature, or is born with him. Intellectual capacity needs, it is true, to be developed just as many natural products need to be cultivated in order that we may enjoy or use them; but just as in the case of a natural product no cultivation can take the place of original material, neither can it do so in the case of intellect. That is the reason why qualities which are merely acquired, or learned, or enforced—that is, qualities *à posteriori,* whether moral or intellectual—are not real or genuine, but superficial only, and possessed of no value. This is a conclusion of true metaphysics, and experience teaches the same lesson to all who can look below the surface. Nay, it is proved by the great importance which we all attach to such innate characteristics as physiognomy and external appearance, in the case of a man who is at all distinguished; and that is why we are so curious to see him. Superficial people, to be sure,—and, for very good reasons, commonplace people too,—will be of the opposite opinion; for if anything fails them they will thus be enabled to console themselves by thinking that it is still to come.

The world, then, is not merely a battlefield where victory and defeat receive their due recompense in a future state. No! the world is itself the Last Judgment on it. Every man carries with him the reward and the disgrace that he deserves; and this is no other than the doctrine of the Brahmins and Buddhists as it is taught in the theory of metempsychosis.

The question has been raised, What two men would do, who lived a solitary life in the wilds and met each other for the first time. Hobbes, Pufendorf, and Rousseau have given different answers. Pufendorf believed that they would approach each other as friends; Hobbes, on the contrary, as enemies; Rousseau, that they would pass each other by in

silence. All three are both right and wrong. This is just a case in which the incalculable difference that there is in innate moral disposition between one individual and another would make its appearance. The difference is so strong that the question here raised might be regarded as the standard and measure of it. For there are men in whom the sight of another man at once rouses a feeling of enmity, since their inmost nature exclaims at once: That is not me! There are others in whom the sight awakens immediate sympathy; their inmost nature says: *That is me over again!* Between the two there are countless degrees. That in this most important matter we are so totally different is a great problem, nay, a mystery.

In regard to this *à priori* nature of moral character there is matter for varied reflection in a work by Bastholm, a Danish writer, entitled *Historical Contributions to the Knowledge of Man in the Savage State.* He is struck by the fact that intellectual culture and moral excellence are shown to be entirely independent of each other, inasmuch as one is often found without the other. The reason of this, as we shall find, is simply that moral excellence in no wise springs from reflection, which is developed by intellectual culture, but from the will itself, the constitution of which is innate and not susceptible in itself of any improvement by means of education. Bastholm represents most nations as very vicious and immoral; and on the other hand he reports that excellent traits of character are found amongst some savage peoples; as, for instance, amongst the Orotchyses, the inhabitants of the island Savu, the Tunguses, and the Pelew islanders. He thus attempts to solve the problem, How it is that some tribes are so remarkably good, when their neighbours are all bad.

It seems to me that the difficulty may be explained as follows: Moral qualities, as we know, are heritable, and an isolated tribe, such as is described, might take its rise in some one family, and ultimately in a single ancestor who happened to be a good man, and then maintain its purity. Is it not the case, for instance, that on many unpleasant occasions, such as repudiation of public debts, filibustering raids and so on, the English have often reminded the North Americans of their descent from English penal colonists? It is a reproach, however, which can apply only to a small part of the population.

It is marvellous how *every man's individuality* (that is to say, the union of a definite character with a definite intellect) accurately determines all his actions and thoughts down to the most unimportant details, as though it were a dye which pervaded them; and how, in consequence, one man's whole course of life, in other words, his inner and outer history, turns out so absolutely different from another's. As a botanist knows a plant in its entirety from a single leaf; as Cuvier from a single bone constructed the whole animal, so an accurate knowledge of a man's whole character may be attained from a single characteristic act; that is to say, he himself may to some extent be constructed from it, even though the act in question is of very trifling consequence. Nay, that is the most perfect test of all, for in a matter of importance people are on their guard; in trifles they follow their natural bent without much reflection. That is why Seneca's remark, that even the smallest things may be taken as evidence of character, is so true: *argumenta morum ex minimis quoque licet capere*. If a man shows by his absolutely unscrupulous and selfish behaviour in small things that a sentiment of justice is foreign to his disposition, he should not be trusted with a penny unless on due security. For who will believe that the man who every day shows that he is unjust in all matters other than those which concern property, and whose boundless selfishness everywhere protrudes through the small affairs of ordinary life which are subject to no scrutiny, like a dirty shirt through the holes of a ragged jacket—who, I ask, will believe that such a man will act honourably in matters of *meum* and *tuum* without any other incentive but that of justice? The man who has no conscience in small things will be a scoundrel in big things. If we neglect small traits of

character, we have only ourselves to blame if we afterwards learn to our disadvantage what this character is in the great affairs of life. On the same principle, we ought to break with so-called friends even in matters of trifling moment, if they show a character that is malicious or bad or vulgar, so that we may avoid the bad turn which only waits for an opportunity of being done us. The same thing applies to servants. Let it always be our maxim: Better alone than amongst traitors.

Of a truth the first and foremost step in all knowledge of mankind is the conviction that a man's conduct, taken as a whole, and in all its essential particulars, is not governed by his reason or by any of the resolutions which he may make in virtue of it. No man becomes this or that by wishing to be it, however earnestly. His acts proceed from his innate and unalterable character, and they are more immediately and particularly determined by motives. A man's conduct, therefore, is the necessary product of both character and motive. It may be illustrated by the course of a planet, which is the result of the combined effect of the tangential energy with which it is endowed, and the centripetal energy which operates from the sun. In this simile the former energy represents character, and the latter the influence of motive. It is almost more than a mere simile. The tangential energy which properly speaking is the source of the planet's motion, whilst on the other hand the motion is kept in check by gravitation, is, from a metaphysical point of view, the will manifesting itself in that body.

To grasp this fact is to see that we really never form anything more than a conjecture of what we shall do under circumstances which are still to happen; although we often take our conjecture for a resolve. When, for instance, in pursuance of a proposal, a man with the greatest sincerity, and even eagerness, accepts an engagement to do this or that on the occurrence of a certain future event, it is by no means certain that he will fulfil the engagement; unless he is so constituted that the promise which he gives, in itself and as such, is always and everywhere a motive sufficient for him, by acting upon him, through considerations of honour, like some external compulsion. But above and beyond this, what he will do on the occurrence of that event may be foretold from true and accurate knowledge of his character and the external circumstances under the influence of which he will fall; and it may with complete certainty be foretold from this alone. Nay, it is a very easy prophecy if he has been already seen in a like position; for he will inevitably do the same thing a second time, provided that on the first occasion he had a true and complete knowledge of the facts of the case. For, as I have often remarked, a final cause does not impel a man by being real, but by being known; *causa finalis non movet secundum suum esse reale, sed secundum esse cognitum.* Whatever he failed to recognise or understand the first time could have no influence upon his will; just as an electric current stops when some isolating body hinders the action of the conductor. This unalterable nature of character, and the consequent necessity of our actions, are made very clear to a man who has not, on any given occasion, behaved as he ought to have done, by showing a lack either of resolution or endurance or courage, or some other quality demanded at the moment. Afterwards he recognises what it is that he ought to have done; and, sincerely repenting of his incorrect behaviour, he thinks to himself, *If the opportunity were offered to me again, I should act differently.* It is offered once more; the same occasion recurs; and to his great astonishment he does precisely the same thing over again.[2]

The best examples of the truth in question are in every way furnished by Shakespeare's plays. It is a truth with which he was thoroughly imbued, and his intuitive wisdom expressed it in a concrete shape on every page. I shall here, however, give an instance of it in a case in which he makes it remarkably clear, without exhibiting any design or affectation in the matter; for he was a real artist and never set out from general ideas. His method was obviously to work up to the

psychological truth which he grasped directly and intuitively, regardless of the fact that few would notice or understand it, and without the smallest idea that some dull and shallow fellows in Germany would one day proclaim far and wide that he wrote his works to illustrate moral commonplaces. I allude to the character of the Earl of Northumberland, whom we find in three plays in succession, although he does not take a leading part in any one of them; nay, he appears only in a few scenes distributed over fifteen acts. Consequently, if the reader is not very attentive, a character exhibited at such great intervals, and its moral identity, may easily escape his notice, even though it has by no means escaped the poet's. He makes the earl appear everywhere with a noble and knightly grace, and talk in language suitable to it; nay, he sometimes puts very beautiful and even elevated passages into his mouth. At the same time he is very far from writing after the manner of Schiller, who was fond of painting the devil black, and whose moral approval or disapproval of the characters which he presented could be heard in their own words. With Shakespeare, and also with Goethe, every character, as long as he is on the stage and speaking, seems to be absolutely in the right, even though it were the devil himself. In this respect let the reader compare Duke Alba as he appears in Goethe with the same character in Schiller.

We make the acquaintance of the Earl of Northumberland in the play of *Richard II.,* where he is the first to hatch a plot against the King in favour of Bolingbroke, afterwards Henry IV., to whom he even offers some personal flattery (Act II., Sc. 3). In the following act he suffers a reprimand because, in speaking of the King he talks of him as "Richard," without more ado, but protests that he did it only for brevity's sake. A little later his insidious words induce the King to surrender. In the following act, when the King renounces the crown, Northumberland

---

[2] Cf. *World as Will [Die Welt als Wille und Vorstellung],* ii., pp. 251 ff. *sqq.* (third edition).

treats him with such harshness and contempt that the unlucky monarch is quite broken, and losing all patience once more exclaims to him: *Fiend, thou torment'st me ere I come to hell!* At the close, Northumberland announces to the new King that he has sent the heads of the former King's adherents to London.

In the following tragedy, *Henry IV.,* he hatches a plot against the new King in just the same way. In the fourth act we see the rebels united, making preparations for the decisive battle on the morrow, and only waiting impatiently for Northumberland and his division. At last there arrives a letter from him, saying that he is ill, and that he cannot entrust his force to any one else; but that nevertheless the others should go forward with courage and make a brave fight. They do so, but, greatly weakened by his absence, they are completely defeated; most of their leaders are captured, and his own son, the valorous Hotspur, falls by the hand of the Prince of Wales.

Again, in the following play, the *Second Part of Henry IV.,* we see him reduced to a state of the fiercest wrath by the death of his son, and maddened by the thirst for revenge. Accordingly he kindles another rebellion, and the heads of it assemble once more. In the fourth act, just as they are about to give battle, and are only waiting for him to join them, there comes a letter saying that he cannot collect a proper force, and will therefore seek safety for the present in Scotland; that, nevertheless, he heartily wishes their heroic undertaking the best success. Thereupon they surrender to the King under a treaty which is not kept, and so perish.

So far is character from being the work of reasoned choice and consideration that in any action the intellect has nothing to do but to present motives to the will. Thereafter it looks on as a mere spectator and witness at the course which life takes, in accordance with the influence of motive on the given character. All the incidents of life occur, strictly speaking, with the same necessity as the movement of a clock. On this point let me refer to my prize-essay on *The Freedom of the Will.* I have there explained the true meaning and origin of the persistent illusion that the will is entirely free in every single action; and I have indicated the cause to which it is due. I will only add here the following teleological explanation of this natural illusion.

Since every single action of a man's life seems to possess the freedom and originality which in truth only belong to his character as he apprehends it, and the mere apprehension of it by his intellect is what constitutes his career; and since what is original in every single action seems to the empirical consciousness to be always being performed anew, a man thus receives in the course of his career the strongest possible moral lesson. Then, and not before, he becomes thoroughly conscious of all the bad sides of his character. Conscience accompanies every act with the comment: *You should act differently,* although its true sense is: *You could be other than you are.* As the result of this immutability of character on the one hand, and, on the other, of the strict necessity which attends all the circumstances in which character is successively placed, every man's course of life is precisely determined from Alpha right through to Omega. But, nevertheless, one man's course of life turns out immeasurably happier, nobler and more worthy than another's, whether it be regarded from a subjective or an objective point of view, and unless we are to exclude all ideas of justice, we are led to the doctrine which is well accepted in Brahmanism and Buddhism, that the subjective conditions in which, as well as the objective conditions under which, every man is born, are the moral consequences of a previous existence.

Macchiavelli, who seems to have taken no interest whatever in philosophical speculations, is drawn by the keen subtlety of his very unique understanding into the following observation, which possesses a really deep meaning. It shows that he had an intuitive knowledge of the entire necessity with which, characters and motives being given, all actions take place. He makes it at the beginning of the prologue to his comedy *Clitia.*

If, he says, *the same men were to recur in the world in the way that the same circumstances recur, a hundred years would never elapse without our finding ourselves together once more, and doing the same things as we are doing now—Se nel mondo tornassino i medesimi uomini, como tornano i medesimi casi, non passarebbono mai cento anni che noi non ci trovassimo un altra volta insieme, a fare le medesime cose che hora.* He seems however to have been drawn into the remark by a reminiscence of what Augustine says in his *De Civitate Dei,* bk. xii., ch. xiii.[*]

Again, Fate, or the εἱμαρμένη of the ancients, is nothing but the conscious certainty that all that happens is fast bound by a chain of causes, and therefore takes place with a strict necessity; that the future is already ordained with absolute certainty and can undergo as little alteration as the past. In the fatalistic myths of the ancients all that can be regarded as fabulous is the prediction of the future; that is, if we refuse to consider the possibility of magnetic clairvoyance and second sight. Instead of trying to explain away the fundamental truth of Fatalism by superficial twaddle and foolish evasion, a man should attempt to get a clear knowledge and comprehension of it; for it is demonstrably true, and it helps us in a very important way to an understanding of the mysterious riddle of our life. Predestination and Fatalism do not differ in the main. They differ only in this, that with Predestination the given character and external determination of human action proceed from a rational Being, and with Fatalism from an irrational one. But in either case the result is the same: that happens which must happen.

On the other hand the conception of *Moral Freedom* is inseparable from that of *Originality.* A man may be said, but he cannot be conceived, to be the work of another, and at the same time be free in respect of his desires and acts. He who called him into existence out of nothing in the same process created and determined his nature—in other words, the whole of his qualities. For no one can create without creating a something, that is to say, a being determined throughout and

in all its qualities. But all that a man says and does necessarily proceeds from the qualities so determined; for it is only the qualities themselves set in motion. It is only some external impulse that they require to make their appearance. As a man is, so must he act; and praise or blame attaches, not to his separate acts, but to his nature and being.

That is the reason why Theism and the moral responsibility of man are incompatible; because responsibility always reverts to the creator of man and it is there that it has its centre. Vain attempts have been made to make a bridge from one of these incompatibles to the other by means of the conception of moral freedom; but it always breaks down again. What is *free* must also be *original.* If our will is *free,* our will is also *the original element,* and conversely. Pre-Kantian dogmatism tried to separate these two predicaments. It was thereby compelled to assume two kinds of freedom, one cosmological, of the first cause, and the other moral and theological, of human will. These are represented in Kant by the third as well as the fourth antinomy of freedom.

On the other hand, in my philosophy the plain recognition of the strictly necessary character of all action is in accordance with the doctrine that what manifests itself even in the organic and irrational world is *will.* If this were not so, the necessity under which irrational beings obviously act would place their action in conflict with will; if, I mean, there were really such a thing as the freedom of individual action, and this were not as strictly necessitated as every other kind of action. But, as I have just shown, it is this same doctrine of the necessary character of all acts of will which makes it needful to regard a man's existence and being as itself the work of his freedom, and consequently of his will. The will, therefore, must be self-existent; it must possess so-called *a-se-ity.* Under the opposite supposition all responsibility, as I have shown, would be at an end, and the moral like the physical world would be a mere ma-

---

[*] *GBWW,* Vol. 18, p. 350a.

chine, set in motion for the amusement of its manufacturer placed somewhere outside of it. So it is that truths hang together, and mutually advance and complete one another; whereas error gets jostled at every corner.

What kind of influence it is that *moral instruction* may exercise on conduct, and what are the limits of that influence, are questions which I have sufficiently examined in the twentieth section of my treatise on the *Foundation of Morality*. In all essential particulars an analogous influence is exercised by *example,* which, however, has a more powerful effect than doctrine, and therefore it deserves a brief analysis.

In the main, example works either by restraining a man or by encouraging him. It has the former effect when it determines him to leave undone what he wanted to do. He sees, I mean, that other people do not do it; and from this he judges, in general, that it is not expedient; that it may endanger his person, or his property, or his honour. He rests content, and gladly finds himself relieved from examining into the matter for himself. Or he may see that another man, who has not refrained, has incurred evil consequences from doing it; this is example of the deterrent kind. The example which encourages a man works in a two-fold manner. It either induces him to do what he would be glad to leave undone, if he were not afraid lest the omission might in some way endanger him, or injure him in others' opinion; or else it encourages him to do what he is glad to do, but has hitherto refrained from doing from fear of danger or shame; this is example of the seductive kind. Finally, example may bring a man to do what he would have otherwise never thought of doing. It is obvious that in this last case example works in the main only on the intellect; its effect on the will is secondary, and if it has any such effect, it is by the interposition of the man's own judgment, or by reliance on the person who presented the example.

The whole influence of example—and it is very strong—rests on the fact that a man has,

as a rule, too little judgment of his own, and often too little knowledge, to explore his own way for himself, and that he is glad, therefore, to tread in the footsteps of some one else. Accordingly, the more deficient he is in either of these qualities, the more is he open to the influence of example; and we find, in fact, that most men's guiding star is the example of others; that their whole course of life, in great things and in small, comes in the end to be mere imitation; and that not even in the pettiest matters do they act according to their own judgment. Imitation and custom are the spring of almost all human action. The cause of it is that men fight shy of all and any sort of reflection, and very properly mistrust their own discernment. At the same time this remarkably strong imitative instinct in man is a proof of his kinship with apes.

But the kind of effect which example exercises depends upon a man's character, and thus it is that the same example may possibly seduce one man and deter another. An easy opportunity of observing this is afforded in the case of certain social impertinences which come into vogue and gradually spread. The first time that a man notices anything of the kind, he may say to himself: *For shame! how can he do it! how selfish and inconsiderate of him! really, I shall take care never to do anything like that.* But twenty others will think: *Aha! if he does that, I may do it too.*

As regards morality, example, like doctrine, may, it is true, promote civil or legal amelioration, but not that inward amendment which is, strictly speaking, the only kind of moral amelioration. For example always works as a personal motive alone, and assumes, therefore, that a man is susceptible to this sort of motive. But it is just the predominating sensitiveness of a character to this or that sort of motive that determines whether its morality is true and real; though, of whatever kind it is, it is always innate. In general it may be said that example operates as a means of promoting the good and the bad qualities of a character, but it does not create them; and so it is that Seneca's maxim, *velle non discitur—will cannot be learned*—also holds good here. But the innateness of all truly moral qualities, of the good as of the bad, is a doctrine that consorts better with the metempsychosis of the Brahmins and Buddhists, according to which a man's good and bad deeds follow him from one existence to another like his shadow, than with Judaism. For Judaism requires a man to come into the world as a moral blank, so that, in virtue of an inconceivable free will, directed to objects which are neither to be sought nor avoided —*liberum arbitrium indifferentiae*—and consequently as the result of reasoned consideration, he may choose whether he is to be an angel or a devil, or anything else that may lie between the two. Though I am well aware what the Jewish scheme is, I pay no attention to it; for my standard is truth. I am no professor of philosophy, and therefore I do not find my vocation in establishing the fundamental ideas of Judaism at any cost, even though they for ever bar the way to all and every kind of philosophical knowledge. *Liberum arbitrium indifferentiae* under the name of *moral freedom* is a charming doll for professors of philosophy to dandle; and we must leave it to those intelligent, honourable and upright gentlemen.

On the Comparative Place of Interest and Beauty in Works of Art

In the productions of poetic genius, especially of the epic and dramatic kind, there is, apart from Beauty, another quality which is attractive: I mean Interest.

The beauty of a work of art consists in the fact that it holds up a clear mirror to certain *ideas* inherent in the world in general; the beauty of a work of poetic art in particular is that it renders the ideas inherent in mankind, and thereby leads it to a knowledge of these ideas. The means which poetry uses for this end are the exhibition of significant characters and the invention of circumstances which will bring about significant situations, giving occasion to the characters to unfold their peculiarities and show what is in them; so that by some such representation a clearer and fuller knowledge of the many-sided idea of humanity may be attained. Beauty, however, in its general aspect, is the inseparable characteristic of the idea when it has become known. In other words, everything is beautiful in which an idea is revealed; for to be beautiful means no more than clearly to express an idea.

Thus we perceive that beauty is always an affair of *knowledge,* and that it appeals to *the knowing subject,* and not to *the will;* nay, it is a fact that the apprehension of beauty on the part of the subject involves a complete suppression of the will.

On the other hand, we call drama or descriptive poetry interesting when it represents events and actions of a kind which necessarily arouse concern or sympathy, like that which we feel in real events involving our own person. The fate of the person represented in them is felt in just the same fashion as our own: we await the development of events with anxiety; we eagerly follow their course; our hearts quicken when the hero is threatened; our pulse falters as the danger reaches its acme, and throbs again when he is suddenly rescued. Until we reach the end of the story we cannot put the book aside; we lie awake far into the night sympathising with our hero's troubles as though they were our own. Nay, instead of finding pleasure and recreation in such representations, we should feel all the pain which real life often inflicts upon us, or at least the kind which pursues us in our uneasy dreams, if in the act of reading or looking at the stage we had not the firm ground of reality always beneath our feet. As it is, in the stress of a too violent feeling, we can find relief from the illusion of the moment, and then give way to it again at will. Moreover, we can gain this relief without any such violent transition as occurs in a dream, when we rid ourselves of its terrors only by the act of awaking.

It is obvious that what is affected by poetry of this character is our *will,* and not merely our intellectual powers pure and simple. The word *interest* means, therefore, that which arouses the concern of the individual will, *quod nostrâ interest;* and here it is that beauty is clearly distinguished from interest. The one is an affair of the intellect, and that, too, of the purest and simplest kind. The other works upon the will. Beauty, then, consists in an apprehension of ideas; and knowledge of this character is beyond the range of the principle that nothing happens without a cause. Interest, on the other hand, has its origin nowhere but in the course of events; that is to say, in the complexities which are possible only through the action of this principle in its different forms.

We have now obtained a clear conception of the essential difference between the beauty and the interest of a work of art. We have recognised that beauty is the true end of every art, and therefore, also, of the poetic art. It now remains to raise the question whether the interest of a work of art is a second end, or a means to the exhibition of its beauty; or whether the interest of it is produced by its beauty as an essential concomitant, and comes of itself as soon as it is beautiful; or whether interest is at any rate compatible with the main end of art; or, finally, whether it is a hindrance to it.

In the first place, it is to be observed that the interest of a work of art is confined to works of poetic art. It does not exist in the case of fine art, or of music or architecture. Nay, with these forms of art it is not even conceivable, unless, indeed, the interest be of an entirely personal character, and confined to one or two spectators; as, for example, where a picture is a portrait of some one whom we love or hate; the building, my house or my prison; the music, my wedding dance, or the tune to which I marched to the war. Interest of this kind is clearly quite foreign to the essence and purpose of art; it disturbs our judgment insofar as it makes the purely artistic attitude impossible. It may be, indeed, that to a smaller extent this is true of all interest.

Now, since the interest of a work of art lies in the fact that we have the same kind of sympathy with a poetic representation as with reality, it is obvious that the representation must deceive us for the moment; and this it can do only by its truth. But truth is an element in perfect art. A picture, a poem, should be as true as nature itself; but at the same time it should lay stress on whatever forms the unique character of its subject by drawing out all its essential manifestations, and by rejecting everything that is unessential and accidental. The picture or the poem will thus emphasize its *idea,* and give us that *ideal truth* which is superior to nature.

Truth, then, forms the point that is common both to interest and beauty in a work of art, as it is its truth which produces the illusion. The fact that the truth of which I speak is *ideal truth* might, indeed, be detrimental to the illusion, since it is just here that we have the general difference between poetry and reality, art and nature. But since it is possible for reality to coincide with the ideal, it is not actually necessary that this difference should destroy the illusion. In the case of fine arts there is, in the range of the means which art adopts, a certain limit, and beyond it illusion is impossible. Sculpture, that is to say, gives us mere colourless form; its figures are without eyes and without movement; and painting provides us with no more than a single view, enclosed within strict limits, which separate the picture from the adjacent reality. Here, then, there is no room for illusion, and consequently none for that interest or sympathy which resembles the interest we have in reality; the will is at once excluded, and the object alone is presented to us in a manner that frees it from any personal concern.

It is a highly remarkable fact that a spurious kind of fine art oversteps these limits, produces an illusion of reality, and arouses our interest; but at the same time it destroys the effect which fine art produces, and serves as nothing but a mere means of exhibiting the beautiful, that is, of communicating a knowledge of the ideas which it embodies. I refer to *waxwork.* Here, we might say, is the dividing line which separates it from the province of fine art. When waxwork is properly executed, it produces a perfect illusion; but for that very reason we approach a wax figure as we approach a real man, who, as such, is for the moment an object presented to our will. That is to say, he is an object of interest; he arouses the will, and consequently stills the intellect. We come up to a wax figure with the same reserve and caution as a real man would inspire in us: our will is excited; it waits to see whether he is going to be friendly to us, or the reverse, fly from us, or attack us; in a word, it expects some action of him. But as the figure, nevertheless, shows no sign of life, it produces the impression which is so very disagreeable, namely, of a corpse. This is a case where the interest is of the most complete kind, and yet where there is no work of art at all. In other words, interest is not in itself a real end of art.

The same truth is illustrated by the fact that even in poetry it is only the dramatic and descriptive kind to which interest attaches; for if interest were, with beauty, the aim of art, poetry of the lyrical kind would, for that very reason, not take half so great a position as the other two.

In the second place, if interest were a means in the production of beauty, every interesting work would also be beautiful. That, however, is by no means the case. A drama or a novel may often attract us by its interest, and yet be so utterly deficient in any kind of beauty that we are afterwards ashamed of having wasted our time on it. This applies to many a drama which gives no true picture of the real life of man; which contains characters very superficially drawn, or so distorted as to be actual monstrosities, such as are not to be found in nature; but the course of events and the play of the action are so intricate, and we feel so much for the hero in the situation in which he is placed, that we are not content until we see the knot untangled and the hero rescued. The action is so cleverly governed and guided in its course that we remain in a state of constant curiosity as to what is going to happen, and we are utterly unable to form a guess; so that between eagerness and surprise our interest is kept active; and as we are pleasantly entertained, we do not notice the lapse of time. Most of Kotzebue's plays are of this character. For the mob this is the right thing: it looks for amusement, something to pass the time, not for intellectual perception. Beauty is an affair of such perception; hence sensibility to beauty varies as much as the intellectual faculties themselves. For the inner truth of a representation, and its correspondence with the real nature of humanity, the mob has no sense at all. What is flat and superficial it can grasp, but the depths of human nature are opened to it in vain.

It is also to be observed that dramatic representations which depend for their value on their interest lose by repetition, because they are no longer able to arouse curiosity as to their course, since it is already known. To see them often, makes them stale and tedious. On the other hand, works of which the value lies in their beauty gain by repetition, as they are then more and more understood.

Most novels are on the same footing as dramatic representations of this character. They are creatures of the same sort of imagination as we see in the story-teller of Venice and Naples, who lays a hat on the ground and waits until an audience is assembled. Then he spins a tale which so captivates his hearers that, when he gets to the catastrophe, he makes a round of the crowd, hat in hand, for contributions, without the least fear that his hearers will slip away. Similar story-tellers ply their trade in this country, though in a less direct fashion. They do it through the agency of publishers and circulating libraries. Thus they can avoid going about in rags, like their colleagues elsewhere; they can offer the children of their imagination to the public under the title of novels, short stories, romantic poems, fairy tales, and so on; and the public, in a dressing-gown by the fireside, sits down more at its ease, but also with a greater amount of patience, to the enjoyment of the interest which they provide.

How very little aesthetic value there generally is in productions of this sort is well known; and yet it cannot be denied that many of them are interesting; or else how could they be so popular?

We see, then, in reply to our second question, that interest does not necessarily involve beauty; and, conversely, it is true that beauty does not necessarily involve interest. Significant characters may be represented, that open up the depths of human nature, and it may all be expressed in actions and sufferings of an exceptional kind, so that the real nature of humanity and the world may stand forth in the picture in the clearest and most forcible lines; and yet no high degree of interest may be excited in the course of events by the continued progress of the action, or by the complexity and unexpected solution of the plot. The immortal masterpieces of Shakespeare contain little that excites interest; the action does not go forward in one straight line, but falters, as in *Hamlet,* all through the play; or else it spreads out in breadth, as in *The Merchant of Venice,* whereas length is the proper dimension of interest; or the scenes hang loosely together, as in *Henry IV.* Thus it is that Shakespeare's dramas produce no appreciable effect on the mob.

The dramatic requirement stated by Aristotle, and more particularly the unity of action, have in view the interest of the piece rather than its artistic beauty. It may be said, generally, that these requirements are drawn up in accordance with the principle of sufficient reason to which I have referred above. We know, however, that the *idea,* and, consequently, the beauty of a work of art, exist only for the perceptive intelligence which has freed itself from the domination of that principle. It is just here that we find the distinction between interest and beauty; as it is obvious that interest is part and parcel of the mental attitude which is governed by the principle, whereas beauty is always beyond its range. The best and most striking refutation of the Aristotelian unities is Manzoni's. It may be found in the preface to his dramas.

What is true of Shakespeare's dramatic works is true also of Goethe's. Even *Egmont* makes little effect on the public, because it contains scarcely any complication or development; and if *Egmont* fails, what are we to say of *Tasso* or *Iphigenia?* That the Greek tragedians did not look to interest as a means of working upon the public, is clear from the fact that the material of their masterpieces was almost always known to every one: they selected events which had often been treated dramatically before. This shows us how sensitive was the Greek public to the beautiful, as it did not require the interest of unexpected events and new stories to season its enjoyment.

Neither does the quality of interest often attach to masterpieces of descriptive poetry. Father Homer lays the world and humanity before us in its true nature, but he takes no trouble to attract our sympathy by a complexity of circumstance, or to surprise us by unexpected entanglements. His pace is lingering; he stops at every scene; he puts one picture after another tranquilly before us, elaborating it with care. We experience no passionate emotion in reading him; our demeanour is one of pure perceptive intelligence; he does not arouse our will, but sings it to rest; and it costs us no effort to break off in our reading, for we are not in condition of eager curiosity. This is all still more true of Dante, whose work is not, in the proper sense of the word, an epic, but a descriptive poem. The same thing may be said of the four immortal romances: *Don Quixote, Tristram Shandy, La Nouvelle Heloïse,* and *Wilhelm Meister.* To arouse our interest is by no means the chief aim of these works; in *Tristram Shandy* the hero, even at the end of the book, is only eight years of age.

On the other hand, we must not venture to assert that the quality of interest is not to be found in masterpieces of literature. We have it in Schiller's dramas in an appreciable degree, and consequently they are popular; also in the *Oedipus Rex* of Sophocles. Amongst masterpieces of description, we find it in Ariosto's *Orlando Furioso;* nay, an example of a high degree of interest, bound up with the beautiful, is afforded in an excellent novel by Walter Scott—*The Heart of Midlothian.* This is the most interesting work of fiction that I know, where all the effects due to interest, as I have given them generally in the preceding remarks, may be most clearly observed. At the same time it is a very beautiful romance throughout; it shows the most varied pictures of life, drawn with striking truth; and it exhibits highly different characters with great justice and fidelity.

Interest, then, is certainly compatible with beauty. That was our third question. Nevertheless, a comparatively small admixture of the element of interest may well be found to be most advantageous as far as beauty is concerned; for beauty is and remains the end of art. Beauty is in twofold opposition with interest; firstly, because it lies in the perception of the idea, and such perception takes its object entirely out of the range of the forms enunciated by the principle of sufficient reason; whereas interest has its sphere mainly in circumstance, and it is out of this principle that the complexity of circumstance arises. Secondly, interest works by exciting the will; whereas beauty exists only for the pure perceptive intelligence, which has no will. However, with dramatic and descriptive literature an admixture of interest is necessary, just as a volatile and gaseous substance requires a material basis if it is to be preserved and transferred. The admixture is necessary, partly, indeed, because interest is itself created by the events which have to be devised in order to set the characters in motion; partly because our minds would be weary of watching scene after scene if they had no concern for us, or of passing from one significant picture to another if we were not drawn on by some secret thread. It is this that we call interest; it is the sympathy which the event in itself forces us to feel, and which, by riveting our attention, makes the mind obedient to the poet, and able to follow him into all the parts of his story.

If the interest of a work of art is sufficient to achieve this result, it does all that can be required of it; for its only service is to connect the pictures by which the poet desires to communicate a knowledge of the idea, as if they were pearls, and interest were the thread that holds them together, and makes an ornament out of the whole. But interest is prejudicial to beauty as soon as it oversteps this limit; and this is the case if we are so led away by the interest of a work that whenever we come to any detailed description in a novel, or any lengthy reflection on the part of a character in a drama, we grow impatient and want to put spurs to our author, so that we may follow the development of events with greater speed. Epic and dramatic writings, where beauty and interest are both present in a high degree, may be compared to the working of a watch, where interest is the spring which keeps all the wheels in motion. If it worked unhindered, the watch would run down in a few minutes. Beauty, holding us in the spell of description and reflection, is like the barrel which checks its movement.

Or we may say that interest is the body of a poetic work, and beauty the soul. In the epic and the drama, interest, as a necessary quality of the action, is the matter; and beauty, the form that requires the matter in order to be visible.

A Doll's House

Henrik Ibsen

Editor's Introduction

Acknowledged as one of the pioneers of the modern European theater, one who in his plays explored such universal themes as freedom versus responsibility, idealism versus reality, and the individual's discovery of self, Henrik Ibsen is one of the handful of playwrights who have achieved world reputation. Yet he always referred to himself as a poet and to his plays as books. He wrote several volumes of lyric poetry (in addition, six of his plays are in verse), and his first publication, in 1849 when he was twenty-one, was a poem called "To Autumn." His career as a dramatist spanned almost fifty years, beginning in 1850 with his first published play, *Catilina,* and ending with *When We Dead Awaken* in 1899. *A Doll's House,* here reprinted, dates from about the middle of that period.

Ibsen was born on March 20, 1828, in Skien, Norway, a small trading town of nearly 3,000 inhabitants one hundred miles southwest of the capital, Christiania (now Oslo). His father, Knud Ibsen, began as a successful merchant who ran the general store and imported goods from such places as Bordeaux, London, and Hamburg; he had five sons (the first died in infancy, making Henrik the oldest) and one daughter by Marichen Altenburg, a lively, sensitive woman whose favorite son is said to have been Henrik. For his first seven years Henrik enjoyed the benefits of a relatively carefree family life. In 1834, however, financial troubles began that would plague his parents for the rest of their lives. His father had to sell everything, including his domestic animals, and by 1835 was left with only his house and his family. This unfortunate turn of events, as well as the open circulation of a rumor, later on in his teens, that he was not really Knud Ibsen's son but that of an old admirer of his mother, affected Henrik deeply; themes of bankruptcy and illegitimacy recur often enough in his works to convince us that their inspiration was at least partly personal.

Details of Ibsen's early schooling are scarce. He began to read the Bible, his favorite book, at age six or seven and reportedly attended church regularly with his mother. We do not know what amount of theater he saw as a child in Skien, but the plays that were produced there during the 1830s and 1840s are almost exactly parallel to the plays he chose some ten and twenty years later for the theaters in Bergen and Christiania where he served as director. He loved to paint and read, and was painstaking about habits of dress, both for himself and for certain dolls he had made as puppets for large crowds of admirers in Skien in the early 1840s. This was one of his favorite hobbies; he seemed to have little interest in sports except fishing and swimming.

At the age of thirteen, Ibsen enrolled at a small private school, where his favorite subjects were history and religion. He also learned German and Latin. At this time he is said to have been hasty-tempered, sharp-tongued, and satirical, yet sometimes sociable and even friendly. In later years, however, he became more and more withdrawn; as a man he was socially formal and obsessively interested in dress. In looks he resembled his father, having the same short build and the face of a sea captain, and he had his mother's dark coloring. The few photographs there are of him show him as very serious, burly and gruff with a heavy beard, and somewhat menacing.

He left school at fifteen and was confirmed in the church at Gjerpen; a year later he left Skien to become an apprentice pharmacist in Grimstad, a town of about 800 which was apparently as grim as its name. The job appealed to Ibsen for two reasons: he was interested in medicine and was glad to have the experience, and he was anxious to leave his father's house.

He began to develop what became a characteristic sense of alienation and detachment, not only from that childhood home, which had become combative and bitter in the throes of financial difficulty and social disgrace, but also from his country. Perhaps no world literary figure ever arose from such a meager background. At the time of Ibsen's birth, Norway was still quite primitive: many houses in the rural area had no windows, only a hole in the roof to let smoke out; farming methods were extremely outdated; fishermen used inexpensive line instead of the more effective and costly net; cases of leprosy were still to be found along the west coast. Ibsen was a grown man before the first railway was seen in Norway. Nor had the country known any true independence for nearly 450 years. In the shadow of Danish rule from 1387 to 1814 when it was ceded to Sweden, Norway was culturally a province of Denmark, but politically a province of Sweden. Not until 1905, one year before Ibsen's death, did the Norwegian Parliament, called Storting, declare an end to the union of Sweden and Norway, and Prince Charles of Denmark became Haakon VII, king of Norway. Consistent with this political and economic backwardness, the amount of Norwegian literature was small, having only one writer, Ludvig Holberg (1684–1754), who was born in Norway but wrote in Denmark for Danish readers, and two poets, Henrik Wergeland (1808–1845) and J. S. Welhaven (1807–1873), of international repute.

During the six years he worked and lived in Grimstad, Ibsen read works by Dickens, Scott, Holberg, and Voltaire. He studied at night in order to get a Norwegian medical degree at the University. He also fathered an illegitimate son, Hans Jacob Henrickson, by a servant woman ten years his senior, and paid some form of child support for the next fourteen years. Hans Jacob became an interesting man of varied pursuits who nonetheless had nothing but a brief glimpse during his long life of his famous father.

Ibsen was offered a job as producer with the theater in Bergen in 1851, having failed his arithmetic, Greek, and oral Latin entrance exams at the University, where as a result he never became a fully matriculated student. He would hardly have had time, for he participated in no less than 145 different plays while he worked at the theater in Bergen.

In 1853 he became engaged to Rikke Holst, to whom he wrote and sent many poems, but whose father made sure that she finally had nothing to do with the young poet, whom he chased away with clenched fists. Again engaged in 1856, Ibsen married Suzannah Thoresen in 1858; she bore him one son, Sigurd, in 1859.

Following a job as artistic director of the Norwegian Theater (until 1862 when it went bankrupt), and as literary adviser for another theater, Ibsen left Norway for Rome in 1864. He returned only twice, for very short visits, in the next twenty-seven years, during which he lived in Rome, Dresden, and Munich. It was in Rome, at the age of thirty-seven, having already written countless poems and some even marginally successful plays, that he wrote and in 1866 published *Brand,* the play that brought him international renown. This was given a successful first performance in Stockholm in 1885, where even with cuts it ran for 6½ hours. *Peer Gynt* followed in 1867. These two plays, which are still frequently produced, were not only successful attempts at closet drama (drama, that is, written to be read rather than staged) but powerful polemics against what Ibsen felt was a narrow and complacent Norwegian life and people.

Ibsen moved to Dresden in 1868, where he stayed until 1875, when he moved to Munich. He spent his summer months out of town in the Tirol, where he met both the young Helene Raff, who became a frequent but barely tolerated guest (by Mrs. Ibsen) at their home, and Emilie Bardach, an eighteen-year-old Viennese girl of whom Ibsen was very fond. These incidents have echoes in both *Hedda Gabler* and *The Master Builder.*

Not until 1891, more than twenty-five years after he had left Christiania, did Ibsen come back to Norway as a world-famous author. He wrote four more plays after his return, the tone of which changed from the expressly social, moral, or political concerns of his previous plays to something more psychological and visionary yet at the same time intensely personal. He had a stroke in 1900, another in 1901, and finally died an invalid on May 23, 1906.

A Doll's House was finished in September 1879 and published that year. By April of 1880 there had been two new editions. Four years later it had been translated into Finnish, English, Polish, Russian, and Italian and had been performed in Stockholm, Oslo, Helsinki, Munich, Leningrad, and Warsaw. One of Ibsen's biographers, Michael Meyers, says that as of about 1890 "No play had ever contributed so momentously to social debate, been so widely and furiously received among people not normally interested in theatrical or even artistic matters." Critical reaction to *A Doll's House* was often violent. Ibsen himself rewrote his original ending for German directors who thought Nora's abandonment of her children immoral and "dangerous." Even today, the issue of a person's self-discovery and development in the face of social, familial, and emotional responsibilities remains a controversial one when it is considered with something like Ibsen's interest in human beings and their destinies, in such a film, for instance, as *Kramer vs. Kramer.*

Well before he died, Ibsen had become an influence not only on the theater audience in many countries but upon certain young intellectuals who became his champions. Among these was James Joyce, who at seventeen discovered Ibsen (whom he later characterized as "the most enduring influence of my life") and wrote an essay, his first published work, on *When We Dead Awaken* for the *Fortnightly Review.* Again, in an early work Freud wrote that *Rosmersholm* showed how perceptively Ibsen had treated an instance of the Oedipus complex. The best known of the "Ibsenites," however, was Bernard Shaw, who in 1890 commenced a distinguished career as a dramatic critic with a lecture called "The Quintessence of Ibsenism" delivered to the Fabian Society. This was later published as a book (1891) and subsequently (1913) enlarged to take account of Ibsen's later plays. What Shaw heard in Ibsen was a voice, which he called a Socialist one, that challenged Victorian complacencies and vital lies, and that promised to free the theater, as in fact it did, from the paralyzing conventions that still largely hobbled it in the last decade of the nineteenth century.

Ibsen's *Enemy of the People* is in *Gateway to the Great Books,* Volume 4, pages 164–246. Useful biographies and reference works are: *Henrik Ibsen: The Making of a Dramatist, 1828–1864* by Michael Meyer (1967); *Ibsen* by Harold Clurman (1977); *Life of Ibsen* by Halvdan Koht (1971); and *Ibsen's Drama: Author to Audience* by Einar Haugen (1979).

Dramatis Personae

TORVALD HELMER

NORA, his wife

DOCTOR RANK

MRS LINDE

NILS KROGSTAD

HELMER'S THREE YOUNG CHILDREN

ANNE, their nurse

A HOUSEMAID

A PORTER

(The action takes place in Helmer's house.)

ACT I

(SCENE.—*A room furnished comfortably and tastefully, but not extravagantly. At the back, a door to the right leads to the entrance-hall, another to the left leads to Helmer's study. Between the doors stands a piano. In the middle of the left-hand wall is a door, and beyond it a window. Near the window are a round table, arm-chairs, and a small sofa. In the right-hand wall, at the farther end, another door; and on the same side, nearer the footlights, a stove, two easy chairs, and a rocking-chair; between the stove and the door, a small table. Engravings on the walls; a cabinet with china and other small objects; a small book-case with well-bound books. The floors are carpeted, and a fire burns in the stove. It is winter.*

A bell rings in the hall; shortly afterwards the door is heard to open. Enter NORA, *humming a tune and in high spirits. She is in outdoor dress and carries a number of parcels; these she lays on the table to the right. She leaves the outer door open after her, and through it is seen a* PORTER *who is carrying a Christmas-tree and a basket, which he gives to the* MAID *who has opened the door.*)

NORA. Hide the Christmas-tree carefully, Helen. Make sure the children don't see it till this evening, when it is decorated. (*To the* PORTER, *taking out her purse.*) How much?

PORTER. Sixpence.

NORA. There is a shilling. No, keep the change. (*The* PORTER *thanks her, and goes out.* NORA *shuts the door. She is laughing to herself, as she takes off her hat and coat. She takes a packet of macaroons from her pocket and eats one or two; then goes cautiously to her husband's door and listens.*) Yes, he is in. (*Still humming, she goes to the table on the right.*)

HELMER (*calls out from his room*). Is that my little lark twittering out there?

NORA (*busy opening some of the parcels*). Yes, it is!

HELMER. Is it my little squirrel scurrying around?

NORA. Yes!

HELMER. When did my squirrel come home?

NORA. Just now. (*Puts the bag of macaroons into her pocket and wipes her mouth.*) Come in here, Torvald, and see what I have bought.

HELMER. Don't disturb me. (*A little later, he opens the door and looks into the room, pen in hand.*) Bought, did you say? All these things? Has my little spendthrift been wasting money again?

NORA. Yes but, Torvald, this year we really can let ourselves go a little. This is the first Christmas that we have not needed to economize.

HELMER. Still, you know, we can't spend money recklessly.

NORA. Yes, Torvald, we can be a wee bit more reckless now, can't we? Just a tiny wee bit! You are going to have a big salary and earn lots and lots of money.

HELMER. Yes, after the New Year; but then it will be a whole quarter before the salary is due.

NORA. Pooh! we can borrow till then.

HELMER. Nora! (*Goes up to her and takes her playfully by the ear.*) The same little featherbrain! Suppose, now, that I borrowed fifty pounds to-day, and you spent it all in the Christmas week, and then on New Year's Eve a slate fell on my head and killed me, and——

NORA (*putting her hands over his mouth*). Oh! don't say such horrid things.

HELMER. Still, suppose that happened—what then?

NORA. If that were to happen, I don't suppose I should care whether I owed money or not.

HELMER. Yes, but what about the people who had lent it?

NORA. Them? Who would bother about them? I shouldn't know who they were.

HELMER. That is like a woman! But seriously, Nora, you know what I think about that. No debt, no borrowing. There can be no freedom or beauty about a home life that depends on borrowing and debt. We two have kept bravely on the straight road so far, and we will go on the same way for the short time longer that there need be any struggle.

NORA (*moving towards the stove*). As you please, Torvald.

HELMER (*following her*). Come, come, my little skylark must not droop her wings. What is this! Is my little squirrel upset? (*Taking out his purse.*) Nora, what do you think I have got here?

NORA (*turning round quickly*). Money!

HELMER. There you are. (*Gives her some money.*) Do you think I don't know what a lot is wanted for housekeeping at Christmas-time?

NORA (*counting*). Ten shillings—a pound—two pounds! Thank you, thank you, Torvald; that will keep me going for a long time.

HELMER. Indeed it must.

NORA. Yes, yes, it will. But come here and let me show you what I have bought. And all so cheap! Look, here is a new suit for Ivar, and a sword; and a horse and a trumpet for Bob; and a doll and a doll's bed for Emmy—they are very plain, but anyway she will soon break them to pieces. And here are dress-lengths and handkerchiefs for the maids; old Anne ought really to have something better.

HELMER. And what is in this parcel?

NORA (*crying out*). No, no! you mustn't see that till this evening.

HELMER. Very well. But now tell me, you extravagant little person, what would you like for yourself?

NORA. For myself? Oh, I am sure I don't want anything.

HELMER. Yes, but you must. Tell me something reasonable that you would particularly like to have.

NORA. No, I really can't think of anything—unless, Torvald——

HELMER. Yes?

NORA (*playing with his coat buttons, and without raising her eyes to his*). If you really want to give me something, you might—you might——

HELMER. Well, out with it!

NORA (*speaking quickly*). You might give me money, Torvald. Only just as much as you can afford; and then one of these days I will buy something with it.

HELMER. But, Nora——

NORA. Oh, do! dear Torvald; please, please do! Then I will wrap it up in a beautiful gilt paper and hang it on the Christmas-tree. Wouldn't that be fun?

HELMER. What are little people called that are always wasting money?

NORA. Spendthrifts—I know. Let's do as you suggest, Torvald, and then I shall have time to think what I am most in need of. That is a very sensible plan, isn't it?

HELMER (*smiling*). Indeed it is—that is to say, if you were really to save out of the money I give you, and then really buy something for yourself. But if you spend it all on the housekeeping and any number of unnecessary things, then I merely have to pay up again.

NORA. Oh but, Torvald——

HELMER. You can't deny it, my dear little Nora. (*Puts his arm round her waist.*) It's a sweet little spendthrift, but she uses up a lot of money. It's almost unbelievable how expensive such little persons are!

NORA. You shouldn't say that. I do really save all I can.

HELMER (*laughing*). That's very true—all you can. But you can't save anything!

NORA (*smiling quietly and happily*). You haven't any idea how many expenses we skylarks and squirrels have, Torvald.

HELMER. You are an odd little soul. Very like your father. You always find some new way of wheedling money out of me, and, as soon as you have got it, it seems to melt in your hands. You never know where it has gone. Still, one must take you as you are. It's in the blood; for it is true that you can inherit these things, Nora.

NORA. Oh, I wish I had inherited many of father's qualities.

HELMER. And I would not wish you to be anything but just what you are, my sweet little skylark. But, you know, it strikes me that you are looking rather—what shall I say—rather uneasy to-day?

NORA. Do I?

HELMER. You do, really. Look straight at me.

NORA (*looks at him*). Well?

HELMER (*wagging his finger at her*). Hasn't Miss Sweet-Tooth been breaking rules in town to-day?

NORA. No; what makes you think that?

HELMER. Hasn't she paid a visit to the confectioner's?

NORA. No, I assure you, Torvald——

HELMER. Not been nibbling sweets?

NORA. No, certainly not.

HELMER. Not even taken a bite at a macaroon or two?

NORA. No, Torvald, I assure you really——

HELMER. There, there, you know I was only joking.

NORA (*going to the table on the right*). I shouldn't think of going against your wishes.

HELMER. No, I am sure of that; besides, you gave me your word—— (*Going up to her.*) Keep your little Christmas secrets to yourself, my darling. They will all be revealed to-night when the Christmas-tree is lit, no doubt.

NORA. Did you remember to invite Doctor Rank?

HELMER. No. But there is no need; he will come to dinner with us as a matter of course. However, I will ask him when he comes in this morning. I have ordered some good wine. Nora, you can't think how I am looking forward to this evening.

NORA. So am I! And how the children will enjoy themselves, Torvald!

HELMER. It is wonderful to feel that one has a perfectly safe job, and a big enough income. It's delightful to think of, isn't it?

NORA. It's wonderful!

HELMER. Do you remember last Christmas? For quite three weeks beforehand you shut yourself up every evening till long after midnight, making ornaments for the Christmas-tree, and all the other fine things that were to be a surprise to us. It was the dullest three weeks I ever spent!

NORA. I didn't find it dull.

HELMER (*smiling*). But there was precious little result, Nora.

NORA. Oh, you shouldn't tease me about that again. How could I help the cat's going in and tearing everything to pieces?

HELMER. Of course you couldn't, poor little girl. You had the best of intentions to please us all, and that's the main thing. But it is a good thing that our hard times are over.

NORA. Yes, it is really wonderful.

HELMER. This time I needn't sit here and be dull all alone, and you needn't ruin your dear eyes and your pretty little hands——

NORA (*clapping her hands*). No, Torvald, I needn't any longer, need I! It's wonderfully lovely to hear you say so! (*Taking his arm.*) Now I will tell you how I have been thinking we ought to arrange things, Torvald. As soon as Christmas is over—— (*A bell rings in the hall.*) There's the bell. (*She tidies the room a little.*) There's someone at the door. What a nuisance!

HELMER. If it is a caller, remember I am not at home.

MAID (*in the doorway*). A lady to see you, ma'am—a stranger.

NORA. Ask her to come in.

MAID (*to* HELMER). The doctor came at the same time, sir.

HELMER. Did he go straight into my room?

MAID. Yes, sir.

(HELMER *goes into his room. The* MAID *ushers in* MRS LINDE, *who is in outdoor clothes, and shuts the door.*)

MRS LINDE (*in a dejected and timid voice*). How do you do, Nora?

NORA (*doubtfully*). How do you do——

MRS LINDE. You don't recognize me, I suppose.

NORA. No, I don't know—yes, of course, I seem to—— (*Suddenly.*) Yes! Christine! Is it really you?

MRS LINDE. Yes, it is I.

NORA. Christine! To think of my not recognizing you! And yet how could I—— (*In a gentle voice.*) How you have altered, Christine!

MRS LINDE. Yes, I have indeed. In nine, ten long years——

NORA. Is it so long since we met? I suppose it is. The last eight years have been a happy time for me, I can tell you. And so now you have come into the town, and have taken this long journey in winter—that was brave of you.

MRS LINDE. I arrived by steamer this morning.

NORA. To have some fun at Christmas-time, of course. How lovely! We'll have such fun together! But take off your things. You are not cold, I hope. (*Helps her.*) Now let's sit down by the stove, and be cosy. No, take this arm-chair; I'll sit here in the rocking-chair. (*Takes her hands.*) Now you look like your old self again; it was only the first moment—— You are a little paler, Christine, and perhaps a little thinner.

MRS LINDE. And much, much older, Nora.

NORA. Perhaps a little older; very, very little; certainly not much. (*Stops suddenly and speaks seriously.*) What a thoughtless creature I am, chattering away like this. My poor, dear Christine, do forgive me.

MRS LINDE. What do you mean, Nora?

NORA (*gently*). Poor Christine, you are a widow.

MRS LINDE. Yes; it is three years ago now.

NORA. Yes, I knew; I saw it in the papers. I assure you, Christine, I meant ever so often to write to you at the time, but I always put it off and something always prevented me.

MRS LINDE. I quite understand, dear.

NORA.   It was very bad of me, Christine. Poor thing, how you must have suffered. And he left you nothing?

MRS LINDE.   No.

NORA.   And no children?

MRS LINDE.   No.

NORA.   Nothing at all, then.

MRS LINDE.   Not even any sorrow or grief to live upon.

NORA (*looking incredulously at her*).   But, Christine, is that possible?

MRS LINDE (*smiles sadly and strokes her hair*).   It sometimes happens, Nora.

NORA.   So you are quite alone. How dreadfully sad that must be. I have three lovely children. You can't see them just now. They are out with their nurse. But now you must tell me all about it.

MRS LINDE.   No, no; I want to hear about you.

NORA.   No, you must begin. I mustn't be selfish to-day; to-day I must only think of your affairs. But there is one thing I must tell you. Do you know we have just had a great piece of good luck?

MRS LINDE.   No, what is it?

NORA.   Imagine, my husband has been made manager of the Bank!

MRS LINDE.   Your husband? What good luck!

NORA.   Yes, tremendous! A barrister's profession is such an uncertain thing, especially if he won't undertake unsavoury cases; and naturally Torvald has never been willing to do that, and I quite agree with him. You can imagine how pleased we are! He is to take up his work in the Bank at the New Year, and then he will have a big salary and lots of commissions. After this we can live quite differently — we can do just as we like. I feel so relieved and so happy, Christine! It will be wonderful to have heaps of money and no worries, won't it?

MRS LINDE.   Yes, anyhow I think it would be delightful to have what one needs.

NORA.   No, not only what one needs, but heaps and heaps of money.

MRS LINDE (*smiling*).   Nora, Nora, haven't you learnt sense yet? At school you were always a great spendthrift.

NORA (*laughing*).   Yes, that is what Torvald says now. (*Wags her finger at her.*) But 'Nora, Nora' is not so silly as you think. We have not been in a position for me to waste money. We have both had to work.

MRS LINDE.   You too?

NORA.   Yes; odds and ends, needlework, crochet-work, embroidery, and that kind of thing. (*Dropping her voice.*) And other things as well. You know Torvald left his office when we were married? There was no prospect of promotion there, and he had to try and earn more than before. But during the first year he overworked himself dreadfully. You see, he had to make money every way he could, and he worked early and late; but he couldn't stand it, and became dreadfully ill, and the doctors said he must go south.

MRS LINDE.   You spent a whole year in Italy, didn't you?

NORA.   Yes. It was no easy matter to get away, I can tell you. It was just after Ivar was born; but naturally we had to go. It was a wonderfully beautiful journey, and it saved Torvald's life. But it cost a tremendous lot of money, Christine.

MRS LINDE.   So I should think.

NORA.   It cost about two hundred and fifty pounds. That's a lot, isn't it?

MRS LINDE.   Yes, and in emergencies like that it is lucky to have the money.

NORA.   I ought to tell you that we had it from father.

MRS LINDE.   Oh, I see. It was just about that time that he died, wasn't it?

NORA.   Yes; and do you know, I couldn't go and nurse him. I was expecting little Ivar's birth every day and I had my poor sick Torvald to look after. My dear, kind father—I never saw him again, Christine. That was the saddest time I have known since our marriage.

MRS LINDE.   I know how fond you were of him. And then you went off to Italy?

NORA.   Yes; you see we had money then, and the doctors insisted on our going, so we started a month later.

MRS LINDE.   And your husband came back quite well?

NORA.   As sound as a bell!

MRS LINDE.   But—the doctor?

NORA.   What doctor?

MRS LINDE.   I thought your maid said the gentleman who arrived here just as I did was the doctor?

NORA.   Yes, that was Doctor Rank, but he doesn't come here professionally. He is our greatest friend, and comes in at least once every day. No, Torvald has not had an hour's illness since then, and our children are strong and healthy and so am I. (*Jumps up and claps her hands.*) Christine! Christine! it's good to be alive and happy!—But how horrid of me; I am talking of nothing but my own affairs. (*Sits on a stool near her, and rests her arms on her knees.*) You mustn't be angry with me. Tell me, is it really true that you did not love your husband? Why did you marry him?

MRS LINDE.   My mother was alive then, and was bedridden and helpless, and I had to provide for my two younger brothers; so I did not think I was justified in refusing his offer.

NORA.   No, perhaps you were quite right. He was rich at that time, then?

MRS LINDE.   I believe he was quite well off. But his business was a precarious one; and, when he died, it all went to pieces and there was nothing left.

NORA.   And then?——

MRS LINDE.   Well, I had to turn my hand to anything I could find—first a small shop, then a small school, and so on. The last three years have seemed like one long working-day, with no rest. Now it is ended, Nora. My poor mother needs me no more, she is gone; and the boys do not need me either; they have got jobs and can fend for themselves.

NORA.   What a relief you must feel it——

MRS LINDE.   No, indeed; I only feel my life unspeakably empty. No one to live for any more. (*Gets up restlessly.*) That was why I could not stand the life in my little backwater any longer. I hope it may be easier here to find something which will busy me and occupy my thoughts. If only I could be lucky enough to get some regular work—office work of some kind——

NORA.   But, Christine, that is so frightfully tiring, and you look tired out now. You had far better go away to the seaside.

MRS LINDE (*walking to the window*).   I have no father to give me money for a journey, Nora.

NORA (*rising*).   Oh, don't be angry with me.

MRS LINDE (*going up to her*).   It is you that must not be angry with me, dear. The worst of a position like mine is that it makes one so bitter. No one to work for, and yet obliged to be always on the look-out for chances. One must live, and so one becomes selfish. When you told me of the happy turn your fortunes have taken—you will hardly believe it—I was delighted not so much on your account as on my own.

NORA. How do you mean?—Oh, I understand. You mean that perhaps Torvald could get you something to do.

MRS LINDE. Yes, that was what I was thinking of.

NORA. He must, Christine. Just leave it to me; I will broach the subject very cleverly—I will think of something that will please him very much. It will make me so happy to be of some use to you.

MRS LINDE. How kind you are, Nora, to be so anxious to help me! It is doubly kind in you, for you know so little of the burdens and troubles of life.

NORA. I——? I know so little of them?

MRS LINDE (smiling). My dear! Small household cares and that sort of thing!—You are a child, Nora.

NORA (tosses her head and crosses the stage). You ought not to be so superior.

MRS LINDE. No?

NORA. You are just like the others. They all think that I am incapable of anything really serious——

MRS LINDE. Come, come——

NORA. —that I have gone through nothing in this world of cares.

MRS LINDE. But, my dear Nora, you have just told me all your troubles.

NORA. Pooh!—those were trifles. (Lowering her voice.) I have not told you the important thing.

MRS LINDE. The important thing? What do you mean?

NORA. You look down upon me altogether, Christine—but you ought not to. You are proud, aren't you, of having worked so hard and so long for your mother?

MRS LINDE. Indeed, I don't look down on anyone. But it is true that I am both proud and glad to think that I was privileged to make the end of my mother's life almost free from care.

NORA. And you are proud to think of what you have done for your brothers.

MRS LINDE. I think I have the right to be.

NORA. I think so, too. But now, listen to this; I too have something to be proud and glad of.

MRS LINDE. I have no doubt you have. But what do you refer to?

NORA. Speak quietly. Suppose Torvald were to hear! He mustn't on any account—no one in the world must know, Christine, except you.

MRS LINDE. But what is it?

NORA. Come here. (Pulls her down on the sofa beside her.) Now I will show you that I too have something to be proud and glad of. It was I who saved Torvald's life.

MRS LINDE. 'Saved'? How?

NORA. I told you about our trip to Italy. Torvald would never have recovered if he had not gone there——

MRS LINDE. Yes, but your father gave you the necessary funds.

NORA (smiling). Yes, that is what Torvald and all the others think, but——

MRS LINDE. But——

NORA. Father didn't give us a shilling. I was the one who found the money.

MRS LINDE. You? All that large sum?

NORA. Two hundred and fifty pounds. What do you think of that?

MRS LINDE. But, Nora, how could you possibly do it? Did you win a prize in the Lottery?

NORA (contemptuously). In the Lottery? There would have been no credit in that.

MRS LINDE.　But where did you get it from, then?

NORA (*humming and smiling with an air of mystery*).　Hm, hm! Aha!

MRS LINDE.　Because you couldn't have borrowed it.

NORA.　Couldn't I? Why not?

MRS LINDE.　No, a wife cannot borrow without her husband's consent.

NORA (*tossing her head*).　Oh, if it is a wife who has any head for business—a wife who has the wit to be a little bit clever——

MRS LINDE.　I don't understand it at all, Nora.

NORA.　There is no need for you to. I never said I had borrowed the money. I may have got it some other way. (*Lies back on the sofa.*) Perhaps I got it from some other admirer. When anyone is as attractive as I am—— .

MRS LINDE.　You are a mad creature.

NORA.　Now, you know you're full of curiosity, Christine.

MRS LINDE.　Listen to me, Nora dear. Haven't you been a little bit imprudent?

NORA (*sits up straight*).　Is it imprudent to save your husband's life?

MRS LINDE.　It seems to me imprudent, without his knowledge, to——

NORA.　But it was absolutely necessary that he should not know! My goodness, can't you understand that? It was necessary he should have no idea what a dangerous condition he was in. It was to me that the doctors came and said that his life was in danger, and that the only thing to save him was to live in the south. Do you suppose I didn't try, first of all, to get what I wanted as if it were for myself? I told him how much I should love to travel abroad like other young wives; I tried tears and entreaties with him; I told him that he ought to remember the condition I was in, and that he ought to be kind and indulgent to me; I even hinted that he might raise a loan. That nearly made him angry, Christine. He said I was thoughtless, and that it was his duty as my husband not to indulge me in my whims and caprices—as I believe he called them. Very well, I thought, you must be saved—and that was how I came to devise a way out of the difficulty——

MRS LINDE.　And did your husband never get to know from your father that the money had not come from him?

NORA.　No, never. Father died just at that time. I had meant to let him into the secret and beg him never to reveal it. But he was so ill then—there never was any need to tell him.

MRS LINDE.　And since then have you never told your secret to your husband?

NORA.　Good Heavens, no! How could you think I would? A man who has such strong views about these things! And besides, how painful and humiliating it would be for Torvald, with his manly independence, to know that he owed me anything! It would upset our mutual relations altogether; our beautiful happy home would no longer be what it is now.

MRS LINDE.　Do you never mean to tell him about it?

NORA (*meditatively, and with a half smile*).　Yes—some day, perhaps, after many years, when I am no longer as pretty as I am now. Don't laugh at me! I mean, of course, when Torvald is no longer as devoted to me as he is now; when my dancing and dressing-up and reciting have palled on him; then it may be a good thing to have something in reserve—— (*Breaking off.*) What nonsense! That time will never come. Now, what do you think of my great secret, Christine? Do you still think I am useless? I can tell you, too, that this affair has been terribly worrying. It has been by no means easy for me to meet my commitments punctually. I may tell you that there is something that is called, in business, quarterly interest, and another thing called payment in instalments, and it is always so dreadfully difficult to manage them. I have had to save a little here and there, where I could, you understand. I haven't been able to put aside much from my housekeeping money, for Torvald likes good food. I couldn't let my children be shabbily dressed; I have felt I must use up all he gave me for them, the sweet little darlings!

MRS LINDE. So it has all had to come out of your own necessaries of life, poor Nora?

NORA. Of course. Besides, I was the one responsible for it. Whenever Torvald has given me money for new dresses and things like that, I have never spent more than half of it; I have always bought the simplest and cheapest things. Thank Heaven, any clothes look well on me, and so Torvald has never noticed it. But it was often very hard on me, Christine—because it is so nice to be really well dressed, isn't it?

MRS LINDE. Yes, of course.

NORA. Well, then I have found other ways of earning money. Last winter I was lucky enough to get a lot of copying to do; so I locked myself up and sat writing every evening until quite late at night. Often I was desperately tired; but all the same it was a tremendous pleasure to sit there working and earning money. It was like being a man.

MRS LINDE. How much have you been able to pay off in that way?

NORA. I can't tell you exactly. You see, it is difficult to keep an account of a business matter of that kind. I only know that I have paid every penny that I could scrape together. Quite often I was at my wits' end. (*Smiles.*) Then I used to sit here and imagine that a rich old gentleman had fallen in love with me——

MRS LINDE. What! Who was it?

NORA. Be quiet!—that he had died; and that when his will was opened it contained, written in big letters, the instruction: 'The lovely Mrs Nora Helmer is to have all I possess paid over to her at once in cash.'

MRS LINDE. But, my dear Nora—who could the man be?

NORA. Good gracious, can't you understand? There was no old gentleman at all; it was only something that I used to sit here and imagine, when I couldn't think of any way of procuring money. But it doesn't matter now; the tiresome old man can stay where he is, as far as I am concerned; I don't bother about him or his will either. I am free from care now. (*Jumps up.*) My goodness, it's wonderful to think of, Christine! Free from care! To be able to be free from care, quite free from care; to be able to play and romp with the children; to be able to keep the house beautifully and have everything just as Torvald likes it! And, think of it, soon the spring will come and the big blue sky! Perhaps we shall be able to take a little trip—perhaps I shall see the sea again! Oh, it's a wonderful thing to be alive and be happy. (*A bell is heard in the hall.*)

MRS LINDE (*rising*). There is the bell; perhaps I had better go.

NORA. No, don't go; no one will come in here; it is sure to be for Torvald.

SERVANT (*at the hall door*). Excuse me, ma'am—there is a gentleman to see the master, and as the doctor is with him——

NORA. Who is it?

KROGSTAD (*at the door*). It is I, Mrs Helmer. (MRS LINDE *starts, trembles, and turns to the window.*)

NORA (*takes a step towards him, and speaks in a strained, low voice*). You? What is it? What do you want to see my husband about?

KROGSTAD. Bank business—in a way. I have a small post in the Bank, and I hear your husband is to be our chief now——

NORA. Then it is——

KROGSTAD. Nothing but dry business matters, Mrs. Helmer; absolutely nothing else.

NORA. Will you please go into the study, then. (*She bows indifferently to him and shuts the door into the hall; then comes back and makes up the fire in the stove.*)

MRS LINDE. Nora—who was that man?

NORA. A lawyer, of the name of Krogstad.

MRS LINDE. Then it really was he.

NORA. Do you know the man?

MRS LINDE. I used to—many years ago. At one time he was a solicitor's clerk in our town.

NORA. Yes, he was.

MRS LINDE. He has altered a lot.

NORA. He made a very unhappy marriage.

MRS LINDE. He is a widower now, isn't he?

NORA. With several children. There now, it is burning up. (*Shuts the door of the stove and moves the rocking-chair aside.*)

MRS LINDE. They say he carries on various kinds of business.

NORA. Really! Perhaps he does; I don't know anything about it. But don't let us think of business; it is so tiresome.

DOCTOR RANK (*comes out of* HELMER's *study. Before he shuts the door he calls to him*). No, my dear fellow, I won't disturb you; I would rather go in to your wife for a little while. (*Shuts the door and sees* MRS LINDE.) I beg your pardon; I am afraid I am disturbing you too.

NORA. No, not at all. (*Introducing him.*) Doctor Rank, Mrs Linde.

RANK. I have often heard Mrs Linde's name mentioned here. I think I passed you on the stairs when I arrived, Mrs Linde?

MRS LINDE. Yes, I go up very slowly; I can't manage stairs well.

RANK. Ah! some slight internal weakness?

MRS LINDE. No, the fact is I have been overworking myself.

RANK. Nothing more than that? Then I suppose you have come to town to amuse yourself with our entertainments?

MRS LINDE. I have come to look for work.

RANK. Is that a good cure for overwork?

MRS LINDE. One must live, Doctor Rank.

RANK. Yes, the general opinion seems to be that it is necessary.

NORA. Look here, Doctor Rank—you know you want to live.

RANK. Certainly. However wretched I may feel, I want to prolong the agony as long as possible. All my patients are like that. And so are those who are morally diseased; one of them, and a bad case too, is at this very moment with Helmer——

MRS LINDE (*sadly*). Ah!

NORA. Whom do you mean?

RANK. A lawyer by the name of Krogstad, a fellow you don't know at all. He suffers from a diseased moral character, Mrs Helmer; but even he began talking of its being highly important that he should live.

NORA. Did he? What did he want to speak to Torvald about?

RANK. I have no idea; I only heard that it was something about the Bank.

NORA. I didn't know this—what's his name—Krogstad had anything to do with the Bank.

RANK. Yes, he has some sort of post there. (*To* MRS LINDE.) I don't know whether you find also in your part of the world that there are certain people who go zealously snuffing about to smell out moral corruption, and, as soon as they have found some, put the person concerned into some lucrative position where they can keep their eye on him. Healthy natures are left out in the cold.

MRS LINDE. Still I think the sick are those who most need taking care of.

RANK (*shrugging his shoulders*). Yes, there you are. That is the sentiment that is turning Society into a sick-house.

> (NORA, *who has been absorbed in her thoughts, breaks out into smothered laughter and claps her hands.*)

RANK. Why do you laugh at that? Have you any notion what Society really is?

NORA. What do I care about silly old Society? I am laughing at something quite different, something extremely amusing. Tell me, Doctor Rank, are all the people who are employed in the Bank dependent on Torvald now?

RANK. Is that what you find so extremely amusing?

NORA (*smiling and humming*). That's my affair! (*Walking about the room.*) It's perfectly glorious to think that we have—that Torvald has so much power over so many people. (*Takes the packet from her pocket.*) Doctor Rank, what do you say to a macaroon?

RANK. What, macaroons? I thought they were forbidden here.

NORA. Yes, but these are some Christine gave me.

MRS LINDE. What! I——

NORA. Oh, well, don't be alarmed! You couldn't know that Torvald had forbidden them. I must tell you that he is afraid they will spoil my teeth. But, gracious!—once in a way—— That's so, isn't it, Doctor Rank? Excuse me! (*Puts a macaroon into his mouth.*) You must have one too, Christine. And I shall have one, just a little one—or at most two. (*Walking about.*) I am tremendously happy. There is just one thing in the world now that I should dearly love to do.

RANK. Well, what is that?

NORA. It's something I should dearly love to say, if Torvald could hear me.

RANK. Well, why can't you say it?

NORA. No, I daren't; it's so shocking.

MRS LINDE. Shocking?

RANK. Well, I should not advise you to say it. Still, with us you might. What is it you would so much like to say if Torvald could hear you?

NORA. I should just love to say—Well, I'm damned!

RANK. Are you mad?

MRS LINDE. Nora, dear——!

RANK. Say it, here he is!

NORA (*hiding the packet*). Hush! Hush! Hush!

> (HELMER *comes out of his room, with his coat over his arm and his hat in his hand.*)

NORA. Well, Torvald dear, have you got rid of him?

HELMER. Yes, he has just gone.

NORA. Let me introduce you—this is Christine, who has come to town.

HELMER. Christine——? I'm sorry, but I don't know——

NORA. Mrs Linde, dear; Christine Linde.

HELMER. Of course. A school friend of my wife's, I presume?

MRS LINDE. Yes, we have known each other since then.

NORA. And just think, she has come a long way in order to see you.

HELMER. What do you mean?

MRS LINDE. No, really, I——

NORA. Christine is tremendously clever at book-keeping, and she is frightfully anxious to work under some clever man, so as to perfect herself——

HELMER. Very sensible, Mrs Linde.

NORA. And when she heard you had been appointed manager of the Bank—the news was telegraphed, you know—she travelled here as quick as she could. Torvald, I am sure you will be able to do something for Christine, for my sake, won't you?

HELMER. Well, it is not altogether impossible. I presume you are a widow, Mrs Linde?

MRS LINDE. Yes.

HELMER. And have had some experience of book-keeping?

MRS LINDE. Yes, a fair amount.

HELMER. Ah! well, it's very likely I may be able to find something for you——

NORA (*clapping her hands*). What did I tell you? What did I tell you?

HELMER. You have just come at a fortunate moment, Mrs Linde.

MRS LINDE. How am I to thank you?

HELMER. There is no need. (*Puts on his coat.*) But to-day you must excuse me——

RANK. Wait a minute; I will come with you. (*Brings his fur coat from the hall and warms it at the fire.*)

NORA. Don't be away long, Torvald dear.

HELMER. About an hour, not more.

NORA. Are you going too, Christine?

MRS LINDE (*putting on her cloak*). Yes, I must go and look for a room.

HELMER. Oh, well then, we can walk down the street together.

NORA (*helping her*). What a pity it is we are so short of space here; I am afraid it is impossible for us——

MRS LINDE. Please don't think of it! Good-bye, Nora dear, and many thanks.

NORA. Good-bye for the present. Of course you will come back this evening. And you too, Dr Rank. What do you say? If you are well enough? Oh, you must be! Wrap yourself up well.

    (*They go to the door all talking together. Children's voices are heard on the staircase.*)

NORA. There they are! There they are! (*She runs to open the door. The* NURSE *comes in with the children.*) Come in! Come in! (*Stoops and kisses them.*) Oh, you sweet blessings! Look at them, Christine! Aren't they darlings?

RANK. Don't let us stand here in the draught.

HELMER. Come along, Mrs Linde; the place will only be bearable for a mother now!

    (RANK, HELMER, *and* MRS LINDE *go downstairs. The* NURSE *comes forward with the children;* NORA *shuts the hall door.*)

NORA. How fresh and well you look! Such red cheeks!—like apples and roses. (*The children all talk at once while she speaks to them.*) Have you had great fun? That's splendid! What, you pulled both Emmy and Bob along on the sledge?—both at once?—that *was* good. You are a clever boy, Ivar. Let me take her for a little, Anne. My sweet little baby doll! (*Takes the baby from the* MAID *and dances it up and down.*) Yes, yes, mother will dance with Bob too. What! Have you been snowballing? I wish I had been there too! No, no, I'll take their things off, Anne; please let me do it, it is such fun. Go in now, you look half frozen. There is some hot coffee for you on the stove.

(*The* NURSE *goes into the room on the left.* NORA *takes off the children's things and throws them about, while they all talk to her at once.*)

NORA. Really! Did a big dog run after you? But it didn't bite you? No, dogs don't bite nice little dolly children. You mustn't look at the parcels, Ivar. What are they? Ah, I dare say you would like to know. No, no—it's something nasty! Come, let us have a game! What shall we play at? Hide and Seek? Yes, we'll play Hide and Seek. Bob shall hide first. Must I hide? All right, I'll hide first.

(*She and the children laugh and shout, and romp in and out of the room; at last* NORA *hides under the table, the children rush in and out, looking for her, but do not see her; they hear her smothered laughter, run to the table, lift up the cloth, and find her. Shouts of laughter. She crawls forward and pretends to frighten them. Fresh laughter. Meanwhile there has been a knock at the hall door, but none of them has noticed it. The door is half opened, and* KROGSTAD *appears. He waits a little; the game goes on.*)

KROGSTAD. Excuse me, Mrs Helmer.

NORA (*with a stifled cry, turns round and gets up on to her knees*). Oh! what do you want?

KROGSTAD. Forgive me, the outer door was ajar; I suppose someone forgot to shut it.

NORA (*rising*). My husband is out, Mr Krogstad.

KROGSTAD. I know that.

NORA. What do you want here, then?

KROGSTAD. A word with you.

NORA. With me?—— (*To the children, gently.*) Go in to nurse. What? No, the strange man won't do mother any harm. When he has gone we will have another game. (*She takes the children into the room on the left, and shuts the door after them.*) You want to speak to me?

KROGSTAD. Yes, I do.

NORA. To-day? It is not the first of the month yet.

KROGSTAD. No, it's Christmas Eve, and it will depend on *you* what sort of a Christmas you will spend.

NORA. What do you mean? To-day it is absolutely impossible for me——

KROGSTAD. We won't talk about that till later on. This is something different. I presume you can give me a moment?

NORA. Yes—yes, I can—although——

KROGSTAD. Good. I was in Olsen's Restaurant and saw your husband going down the street——

NORA. Yes?

KROGSTAD. With a lady.

NORA. What then?

KROGSTAD. May I inquire if it was a Mrs Linde?

NORA. It was.

KROGSTAD. Just arrived in town?

NORA. Yes, to-day.

KROGSTAD. She is a great friend of yours, isn't she?

NORA. She is. But I don't see——

KROGSTAD. I knew her too, once upon a time.

NORA. I am aware of that.

KROGSTAD. Are you? So you know all about it; I thought as much. Then I can ask you, without beating about the bush—is Mrs Linde to have a job in the Bank?

NORA. What right have you to question me, Mr Krogstad?—You, one of my husband's subordinates! But since you ask, you shall know. Yes, Mrs Linde *is* to have a job. And it was I who pleaded her cause, Mr Krogstad, let me tell you that.

KROGSTAD. I was right in what I thought, then.

NORA (*walking up and down the stage*). Sometimes one has a tiny little bit of influence, I should hope. Because one is a woman, it does not necessarily follow that—— When anyone is in a subordinate position, Mr Krogstad, they should really be careful to avoid offending anyone who—who——

KROGSTAD. Who has influence?

NORA. Exactly.

KROGSTAD (*changing his tone*). Mrs Helmer, you will kindly use your influence on my behalf.

NORA. What? What do you mean?

KROGSTAD. You will kindly see that I am allowed to keep my subordinate position in the Bank.

NORA. What do you mean by that? Who proposes to take your post away from you?

KROGSTAD. Oh, there is no necessity to keep up the pretence of ignorance. I can quite understand that your friend is not very anxious to expose herself to the chance of rubbing shoulders with me; and I quite understand, too, whom I have to thank for being turned off.

NORA. But I assure you——

KROGSTAD. Very likely; but, to come to the point, the time has come when I should advise you to use your influence to prevent that.

NORA. But, Mr Krogstad, I *have* no influence.

KROGSTAD. Haven't you? I thought you said yourself just now——

NORA. Naturally I did not mean you to put that construction on it. I! What should make you think I have any influence of that kind with my husband?

KROGSTAD. Oh, I have known your husband from our student days. I don't suppose he is any more unassailable than other husbands.

NORA. If you speak slightingly of my husband, I shall turn you out of the house.

KROGSTAD. You are bold, Mrs Helmer.

NORA. I am not afraid of you any longer. As soon as the New Year comes, I shall be free of the whole thing in a very short time.

KROGSTAD (*controlling himself*). Listen to me, Mrs Helmer. If necessary, I am prepared to fight for my small job in the Bank as if I were fighting for my life.

NORA. So it seems.

KROGSTAD. It's not only for the sake of the money; as a matter of fact, that weighs least with me in the matter. There is another reason—well, I may as well tell you. My position is this. I dare say you know, like everybody else, that once, many years ago, I was guilty of an indiscretion.

NORA. I think I have heard something of the kind.

KROGSTAD. The matter never came into court; but every way seemed to be closed to me after that. So I took to the business that you know of. I had to do something; and, honestly, I don't think I've been one of the worst. But now I must cut myself free from all that. My sons are growing up; for their sake I must try and win back as much respect as I can in the town. This job in the Bank was like the first step up for me—and now your husband is going to kick me downstairs again into the mud.

NORA. But you must believe me, Mr Krogstad; it is not in my power to help you at all.

KROGSTAD. Then it is because you haven't the will; but I have means to compel you.

NORA. You don't mean that you will tell my husband that I owe you money?

KROGSTAD. Hm!—suppose I were to tell him?

NORA. It would be perfectly infamous of you. (*Sobbing*.) To think of his learning my secret, which has been my pride and joy, in such an ugly, clumsy way—that he should learn it from you! And it would put me in a horribly disagreeable position——

KROGSTAD. Only disagreeable?

NORA (*impetuously*). Well, do it, then!—and it will be the worse for you. My husband will see for himself what a blackguard you are, and you certainly won't keep your job then.

KROGSTAD. I asked you if it was only a disagreeable scene at home that you were afraid of?

NORA. If my husband does get to know of it, of course he will at once pay you what is still owing, and we shall have nothing more to do with you.

KROGSTAD (*coming a step nearer*). Listen to me, Mrs Helmer. Either you have a very bad memory or you know very little of business. I shall have to remind you of a few details.

NORA. What do you mean?

KROGSTAD. When your husband was ill, you came to me to borrow two hundred and fifty pounds.

NORA. I didn't know anyone else to go to.

KROGSTAD. I promised to get you that amount——

NORA. Yes, and you did so.

KROGSTAD. I promised to get you that amount, on certain conditions. Your mind was so taken up with your husband's illness, and you were so anxious to get the money for your journey, that you seem to have paid no attention to the conditions of our bargain. Therefore it will not be amiss if I remind you of them. Now, I promised to get the money on the security of a bond which I drew up.

NORA. Yes, and which I signed.

KROGSTAD. Good. But below your signature there were a few lines constituting your father a surety for the money; those lines your father should have signed.

NORA. Should? He did sign them.

KROGSTAD. I had left the date blank; that is to say, your father should himself have inserted the date on which he signed the paper. Do you remember that?

NORA. Yes, I think I remember——

KROGSTAD. Then I gave you the bond to send by post to your father. Isn't that so?

NORA. Yes.

KROGSTAD. And you naturally did so at once, because five or six days afterwards you brought me the bond with your father's signature. And then I gave you the money.

NORA. Well, haven't I been paying it off regularly?

KROGSTAD. Fairly regularly, yes. But—to come back to the matter in hand—that must have been a very trying time for you, Mrs Helmer?

NORA. It was, indeed.

KROGSTAD. Your father was very ill, wasn't he?

NORA. He was very near his end.

KROGSTAD. And died soon afterwards?

NORA. Yes.

KROGSTAD. Tell me, Mrs Helmer, can you by any chance remember what day your father died?—on what day of the month, I mean.

NORA. Father died on the 29th of September.

KROGSTAD. That is correct; I have ascertained it for myself. And, as that is so, there is a discrepancy (*taking a paper from his pocket*) which I cannot account for.

NORA. What discrepancy? I don't know——

KROGSTAD. The discrepancy consists, Mrs Helmer, in the fact that your father signed this bond three days after his death.

NORA. What do you mean? I don't understand——

KROGSTAD. Your father died on the 29th of September. But, look here; your father has dated his signature the 2nd of October. It is a discrepancy, isn't it? (NORA *is silent.*) Can you explain it to me? (NORA *is still silent.*) It is a remarkable thing, too, that the words '2nd of October,' as well as the year, are not written in your father's handwriting but in one that I think I know. Well, of course it can be explained; your father may have forgotten to date his signature, and someone else may have dated it haphazard before they knew of his death. There is no harm in that. It all depends on the signature of the name; and *that* is genuine, I suppose, Mrs Helmer? It was your father himself who signed his name here?

NORA (*after a short pause, throws her head up and looks defiantly at him*). No, it was not. It was I who wrote father's name.

KROGSTAD. Are you aware that is a dangerous confession?

NORA. In what way? You shall have your money soon.

KROGSTAD. Let me ask you a question; why did you not send the paper to your father?

NORA. It was impossible; father was so ill. If I had asked him for his signature, I should have had to tell him what the money was to be used for; and when he was so ill himself I couldn't tell him that my husband's life was in danger—it was impossible.

KROGSTAD. It would have been better for you if you had given up your trip abroad.

NORA. No, that was impossible. That trip was to save my husband's life; I couldn't give that up.

KROGSTAD. But did it never occur to you that you were committing a fraud on me?

NORA. I couldn't take that into account; I didn't trouble myself about you at all. I couldn't bear you, because you put so many heartless difficulties in my way, although you knew what a dangerous condition my husband was in.

KROGSTAD. Mrs Helmer, you evidently do not realize clearly what it is that you have been guilty of. But I can assure you that my one false step, which lost me all my reputation, was nothing more or nothing worse than what you have done.

NORA. You? Do you ask me to believe that you were brave enough to run a risk to save your wife's life?

KROGSTAD. The law cares nothing about motives.

NORA. Then it must be a very foolish law.

KROGSTAD. Foolish or not, it is the law by which you will be judged, if I produce this paper in court.

NORA. I don't believe it. Is a daughter not to be allowed to spare her dying father anxiety and care? Is a wife not to be allowed to save her husband's life? I don't know much about law; but I am certain that there must be laws permitting such things as that. Have you no knowledge of such laws—you who are a lawyer? You must be a very poor lawyer, Mr Krogstad.

KROGSTAD. Maybe. But matters of business—such business as you and I have had together—do you think I don't understand that? Very well. Do as you please. But let me tell you this—if I lose my position a second time, you shall lose yours with me. (*He bows, and goes out through the hall.*)

NORA (*appears buried in thought for a short time, then tosses her head*). Nonsense! Trying to frighten me like that!—I am not as silly as he thinks. (*Begins to busy herself putting the children's things in order.*) And yet——? No, it's impossible! I did it for love's sake.

THE CHILDREN (*in the doorway on the left*). Mother, the stranger man has gone out through the gate.

NORA. Yes, dears, I know. But, don't tell anyone about the stranger man. Do you hear? Not even father.

CHIDREN. No, mother; but will you come and play again?

NORA. No, no—not now.

CHILDREN. But, mother, you promised us.

NORA. Yes, but I can't now. Run along in; I have such a lot to do. Run along in, my sweet little darlings. (*She gets them into the room by degrees and shuts the door on them; then sits down on the sofa, takes up a piece of needlework, and sews a few stitches, but soon stops.*) No! (*Throws down the work, gets up, goes to the hall door, and calls out.*) Helen! bring the tree in. (*Goes to the table on the left, opens a drawer, and stops again.*) No, no! it is quite impossible!

MAID (*coming in with the tree*). Where shall I put it, ma'am?

NORA. Here, in the middle of the floor.

MAID. Shall I get you anything else?

NORA. No, thank you. I have all I want. (*Exit* MAID.)

NORA (*begins decorating the tree*). A candle here—and flowers here—— The horrible man! It's all nonsense—there's nothing wrong. The tree shall be marvellous! I will do everything I can think of to please you, Torvald!—I will sing for you, dance for you—— (HELMER *comes in with some papers under his arm.*) Oh! are you back already?

HELMER. Yes. Has anyone been here?

NORA. Here? No.

HELMER. That's strange. I saw Krogstad going out of the gate.

NORA. Did you? Oh yes, I forgot, Krogstad was here for a moment.

HELMER. Nora, I can see from your manner that he has been here begging you to say a good word for him.

NORA. Yes.

HELMER. And you were to appear to do it of your own accord; you were to conceal from me the fact of his having been here; didn't he beg that of you too?

NORA. Yes, Torvald, but——

HELMER. Nora, Nora, and you would be a party to that sort of thing? To have any talk with a man like that, and give him any sort of promise? And to tell me a lie into the bargain?

NORA. A lie——?

HELMER. Didn't you tell me no one had been here? (*Shakes his finger at her.*) My little song-bird must never do that again. A song-bird must have a clean beak to chirp with—no false notes! (*Puts his arm round her waist.*) That is so, isn't it? Yes, I am sure it is. (*Lets her go.*) We will say no more about it. (*Sits down by the stove.*) How warm and snug it is here! (*Turns over his papers.*)

NORA (*after a short pause, during which she busies herself with the Christmas-tree*).   Torvald!

HELMER.   Yes.

NORA.   I am looking forward tremendously to the fancy-dress ball at the Stenborgs' the day after to-morrow.

HELMER.   And I am tremendously curious to see what you are going to surprise me with.

NORA.   It was very silly of me to want to do that.

HELMER.   What do you mean?

NORA.   I can't hit upon anything that will do; everything I think of seems so silly and insignificant.

HELMER.   Does my little Nora acknowledge that at last?

NORA (*standing behind his chair with her arms on the back of it*).   Are you very busy, Torvald?

HELMER.   Well——

NORA.   What are all those papers?

HELMER.   Bank business.

NORA.   Already?

HELMER.   I have got authority from the retiring manager to undertake the necessary changes in the staff and in the rearrangement of the work; and I must make use of the Christmas week for that, so as to have everything in order for the new year.

NORA.   Then that was why this poor Krogstad——

HELMER.   Hm!

NORA (*leans against the back of his chair and strokes his hair*).   If you hadn't been so busy I should have asked you a tremendously big favour, Torvald.

HELMER.   What is that? Tell me.

NORA.   There is no one has such good taste as you. And I do so want to look nice at the fancy-dress ball. Torvald, couldn't you take me in hand and decide what I shall go as, and what sort of a dress I shall wear?

HELMER.   Aha! so my obstinate little woman is obliged to get someone to come to her rescue?

NORA.   Yes, Torvald, I can't get along a bit without your help.

HELMER.   Very well, I will think it over, we shall manage to hit upon something.

NORA.   That is nice of you. (*Goes to the Christmas-tree. A short pause.*) How pretty the red flowers look—— But, tell me, was it really something very bad that this Krogstad was guilty of?

HELMER.   He forged someone's name. Have you any idea what that means?

NORA.   Isn't it possible that he was driven to do it by necessity?

HELMER.   Yes; or, as in so many cases, by imprudence. I am not so heartless as to condemn a man altogether because of a single false step of that kind.

NORA.   No, you wouldn't, would you, Torvald?

HELMER.   Many a man has been able to retrieve his character, if he has openly confessed his fault and taken his punishment.

NORA.   Punishment——?

HELMER.   But Krogstad did nothing of that sort; he got himself out of it by a cunning trick, and that is why he has gone under altogether.

NORA.   But do you think it would——?

HELMER.   Just think how a guilty man like that has to lie and play the hypocrite with everyone, how he has to wear a mask in the presence of those near and dear to him, even before his own wife and children. And about the children—that is the most terrible part of it all, Nora.

NORA. How?

HELMER. Because such an atmosphere of lies infects and poisons the whole life of a home. Each breath the children take in such a house is full of the germs of evil.

NORA (*coming nearer him*). Are you sure of that?

HELMER. My dear, I have often seen it in the course of my life as a lawyer. Almost everyone who has gone to the bad early in life has had a deceitful mother.

NORA. Why do you only say—mother?

HELMER. It seems most commonly to be the mother's influence, though naturally a bad father's influence would have the same result. Every lawyer is familiar with the fact. This Krogstad, now, has been persistently poisoning his own children with lies and dissimulation; that is why I say he has lost all moral character. (*Holds out his hands to her.*) That is why my sweet little Nora must promise me not to plead his cause. Give me your hand on it. Come, come, what is this? Give me your hand. There now, that's settled. I assure you it would be quite impossible for me to work with him; I literally feel physically ill when I am in the company of such people.

NORA (*takes her hand out of his and goes to the opposite side of the Christmas-tree*). It's terribly hot in here; and I have such a lot to do.

HELMER (*getting up and putting his papers in order*). Yes, and I must try and read through some of these before dinner; and I must think about your costume, too. And it is just possible I may have something ready in gold paper to hang up on the tree. (*Puts his hand on her head.*) My precious little singing-bird! (*He goes into his room and shuts the door after him.*)

NORA (*after a pause, whispers*). No, no—it isn't true. It's impossible; it must be impossible.

(*The* NURSE *opens the door on the left.*)

NURSE. The little ones are begging so hard to be allowed to come in to mother.

NORA. No, no, no! Don't let them come in to me! You stay with them, Anne.

NURSE. Very well, ma'am. (*Shuts the door.*)

NORA (*pale with terror*). Deprave my little children? Poison my home? (*A short pause. Then she tosses her head.*) It's not true. It can't possibly be true.

ACT II

(THE SAME SCENE.—*The Christmas-tree is in the corner by the piano, stripped of its ornaments and with burnt-down candle-ends on its dishevelled branches.* NORA'S *cloak and hat are lying on the sofa. She is alone in the room, walking about uneasily. She stops by the sofa and takes up her cloak.*)

NORA (*drops her cloak*). Someone is coming now! (*Goes to the door and listens.*) No—it's no one. Of course, no one will come to-day, Christmas Day—nor to-morrow either. But, perhaps—(*opens the door and looks out*). No, nothing in the letter-box; it's quite empty. (*Comes forward.*) What rubbish! of course he can't be in earnest about it. Such a thing couldn't happen; it is impossible—I have three little children.

(*Enter the* NURSE *from the room on the left, carrying a big cardboard box.*)

NURSE. At last I have found the box with the fancy dress.

NORA. Thanks; put it on the table.

NURSE (*doing so*). But it is very much in need of mending.

NORA. I should like to tear it into a hundred thousand pieces.

NURSE. What an idea! It can easily be put in order—just a little patience.

NORA. Yes, I will go and get Mrs Linde to come and help me with it.

NURSE. What, out again? In this horrible weather? You will catch cold, ma'am, and make yourself ill.

NORA. Well, worse than that might happen. How are the children?

NURSE. The poor little souls are playing with their Christmas presents, but——

NORA. Do they ask much for me?

NURSE. You see, they are so accustomed to have their mother with them.

NORA. Yes, but, nurse, I shall not be able to be so much with them now as I was before.

NURSE. Oh well, young children easily get accustomed to anything.

NORA. Do you think so? Do you think they would forget their mother if she went away altogether?

NURSE. Good heavens!—went away altogether?

NORA. Nurse, I want you to tell me something I have often wondered about—how could you have the heart to put your own child out among strangers?

NURSE. I was obliged to, if I wanted to be little Nora's nurse.

NORA. Yes, but how could you be willing to do it?

NURSE. What, when I was going to get such a good place by it? A poor girl who has got into trouble should be glad to. Besides, that wicked man didn't do a single thing for me.

NORA. But I suppose your daughter has quite forgotten you.

NURSE. No, indeed she hasn't. She wrote to me when she was confirmed, and when she was married.

NORA (*putting her arms round her neck*). Dear old Anne, you were a good mother to me when I was little.

NURSE. Little Nora, poor dear, had no other mother but me.

NORA. And if my little ones had no other mother, I am sure you would—— What nonsense I am talking! (*Opens the box.*) Go in to them. Now I must—— You will see to-morrow how lovely I shall look.

NURSE. I am sure there will be no one at the ball as lovely as you, ma'am. (*Goes into the room on the left.*)

NORA (*begins to unpack the box, but soon pushes it away from her*). If only I dared go out. If only no one would come. If only I could be sure nothing would happen here in the meantime. How absurd! No one will come. Only I mustn't think about it. I will brush my muff. What pretty, pretty gloves! Out of my thoughts, out of my thoughts! One, two, three, four, five, six—— (*Screams.*) Oh! there is someone coming—— (*Makes a movement towards the door, but stands irresolute.*)

(*Enter* MRS LINDE *from the hall, where she has taken off her cloak and hat.*)

NORA. Oh, it's you, Christine. There is no one else out there, is there? How good of you to come!

MRS LINDE. I heard you were up asking for me.

NORA. Yes, I was passing by. As a matter of fact, it is something you could help me with. Let us sit down here on the sofa. Look here. To-morrow evening there is to be a fancy-dress ball at the Stenborgs', who live above us; and Torvald wants me to go as a Neapolitan fisher-girl, and dance the Tarantella that I learnt at Capri.

MRS LINDE. I see; you are going to keep up the character.

NORA. Yes, Torvald wants me to. Look, here is the dress; Torvald had it made for me there, but now it is all so torn, and I haven't any idea——

MRS LINDE. We will easily put that right. It is only some of the trimming come unsewn here and there. Needle and cotton? Now then, that's all we want.

NORA. It *is* nice of you.

MRS LINDE (*sewing*). So you are going to be dressed up to-morrow, Nora. I'll tell you what—I shall come in for a moment and see you in your fine feathers. But I have completely forgotten to thank you for a delightful evening yesterday.

NORA (*gets up, and crosses the stage*). Well, I don't think yesterday was as pleasant as usual. You ought to have come to town a little earlier, Christine. Certainly Torvald does understand how to make a house dainty and attractive.

MRS LINDE. And so do you, it seems to me; you are not your father's daughter for nothing. But tell me, is Doctor Rank always as depressed as he was yesterday?

NORA. No; yesterday it was very noticeable. You see he suffers from a very dangerous disease. He has tuberculosis of the spine, poor creature. His father was a horrible man who committed all sorts of excesses; and that is why his son was sickly from childhood, do you understand?

MRS LINDE (*dropping her sewing*). But, my dearest Nora, how do you know anything about such things?

NORA (*walking about*). Pooh! When you have three children, you get visits now and then from—from married women, who know something of medical matters, and they talk about one thing and another.

MRS LINDE (*goes on sewing. A short silence*). Does Doctor Rank come here every day?

NORA. Every day regularly. He is Torvald's most intimate friend, and a great friend of mine too. He is just like one of the family.

MRS LINDE. But tell me this—is he perfectly sincere? I mean, isn't he the kind of man who is very anxious to make himself agreeable?

NORA. Not in the least. What makes you think that?

MRS LINDE. When you introduced him to me yesterday, he declared he had often heard my name mentioned in this house; but afterwards I noticed that your husband hadn't the slightest idea who I was. So how could Doctor Rank——?

NORA. That's quite right, Christine. Torvald is so absurdly fond of me that he wants me absolutely to himself, as he says. At first he used to seem almost jealous if I mentioned any of the dear folk at home, so naturally I gave up doing so. But I often talk about such things with Doctor Rank, because he likes hearing about them.

MRS LINDE. Listen to me, Nora. You are still very like a child in many things, and I am older than you in many ways and have a little more experience. Let me tell you this—you ought to make an end of it with Doctor Rank.

NORA. What ought I to make an end of?

MRS LINDE. Of two things, I think. Yesterday you talked some nonsense about a rich admirer who was to leave you money——

NORA. An admirer who doesn't exist, unfortunately! But what then?

MRS LINDE. Is Doctor Rank a man of means?

NORA. Yes, he is.

MRS LINDE. And has no one to provide for?

NORA. No, no one; but——

MRS LINDE. And comes here every day?

NORA. Yes, I told you so.

MRS LINDE. But how can this well-bred man be so tactless?

NORA. I don't understand you at all.

MRS LINDE. Don't prevaricate, Nora. Do you suppose I don't guess who lent you the two hundred and fifty pounds?

NORA. Are you out of your senses? How can you think of such a thing! A friend of ours, who comes here every day! Do you realize what a horribly painful position that would be?

MRS LINDE. Then it really isn't him?

NORA. No, certainly not. It would never have entered my head for a moment. Besides, he had no money to lend then; he came into his money afterwards.

MRS LINDE. Well, I think that was lucky for you, my dear Nora.

NORA. No, it would never have come into my head to ask Doctor Rank. Although I am quite sure that if I had asked him——

MRS LINDE. But of course you won't.

NORA. Of course not. I have no reason to think it could possibly be necessary. But I am quite sure that if I told Doctor Rank——

MRS LINDE. Behind your husband's back?

NORA. I must make an end of it with the other one, and that will be behind his back too. I *must* make an end of it with him.

MRS LINDE. Yes, that is what I told you yesterday, but——

NORA (*walking up and down*). A man can put a thing like that straight much easier than a woman——

MRS LINDE. One's husband, yes.

NORA. Nonsense! (*Standing still.*) When you pay off a debt you get your bond back, don't you?

MRS LINDE. Yes, as a matter of course.

NORA. And can tear it into a hundred thousand pieces, and burn it up—the nasty dirty paper!

MRS LINDE (*looks hard at her, lays down her sewing, and gets up slowly*). Nora, you are concealing something from me.

NORA. Do I look as if I were?

MRS LINDE. Something has happened to you since yesterday morning. Nora, what is it?

NORA (*going nearer to her*). Christine! (*Listens.*) Hush! there's Torvald come home. Do you mind going in to the children for the present? Torvald can't bear to see dressmaking going on. Let Anne help you.

MRS LINDE (*gathering some of the things together*). Certainly—but I am not going away from here till we have had it out with one another. (*She goes into the room on the left, as* HELMER *comes in from the hall.*)

NORA (*going up to* HELMER). I have wanted you so much, Torvald dear.

HELMER. Was that the dressmaker?

NORA. No, it was Christine; she is helping me to put my dress in order. You will see I shall look quite smart.

HELMER. Wasn't that a happy thought of mine, now?

NORA. Splendid! But don't you think it is nice of me, too, to do as you wish?

HELMER. Nice?—because you do as your husband wishes? Well, well, you little rogue, I am sure you didn't mean it in that way. But I am not going to disturb you; you will want to be trying on your dress, I expect.

NORA.   I suppose you are going to work.

HELMER.   Yes. (*Shows her a bundle of papers.*) Look at that. I have just been into the Bank. (*Turns to go into his room.*)

NORA.   Torvald.

HELMER.   Yes.

NORA.   If your little squirrel were to ask you for something very, very prettily——?

HELMER.   What then?

NORA.   Would you do it?

HELMER.   I should like to hear what it is, first.

NORA.   Your squirrel would run about and do all her tricks if you would be nice, and do what she wants.

HELMER.   Speak plainly.

NORA.   Your skylark would chirp about in every room, with her song rising and falling——

HELMER.   Well, my skylark does that anyhow.

NORA.   I would play the fairy and dance for you in the moonlight, Torvald.

HELMER.   Nora—you surely don't mean that request you made to me this morning?

NORA (*going near him*).   Yes, Torvald, I beg you so earnestly——

HELMER.   Have you really the courage to open up that question again?

NORA.   Yes, dear, you *must* do as I ask; you *must* let Krogstad keep his post in the Bank.

HELMER.   My dear Nora, it is his post that I have arranged Mrs Linde shall have.

NORA.   Yes, you have been awfully kind about that; but you could just as well dismiss some other clerk instead of Krogstad.

HELMER.   This is simply incredible obstinacy! Because you chose to give him a thoughtless promise that you would speak for him, I am expected to——

NORA.   That isn't the reason, Torvald. It is for your own sake. This fellow writes in the most scurrilous newspapers; you have told me so yourself. He can do you an unspeakable amount of harm. I am frightened to death of him——

HELMER.   Ah, I understand; it is recollections of the past that scare you.

NORA.   What do you mean?

HELMER.   Naturally you are thinking of your father.

NORA.   Yes—yes, of course. Remember what these malicious creatures wrote in the papers about father, and how horribly they slandered him. I believe they would have procured his dismissal if the Ministry hadn't sent you over to inquire into it, and if you hadn't been so kindly disposed and helpful to him.

HELMER.   My little Nora, there is an important difference between your father and me. Your father's reputation as a public official was not above suspicion. Mine is, and I hope it will continue to be so, as long as I hold my office.

NORA.   You never can tell what mischief these men may contrive. We ought to be so well off, so snug and happy here in our peaceful home, and have no cares—you and I and the children, Torvald! That is why I beg you so earnestly——

HELMER.   And it is just by interceding for him that you make it impossible for me to keep him. It is already known at the Bank that I mean to dismiss Krogstad. Is it to get about now that the new manager has changed his mind at his wife's bidding——

NORA.   And what if it did?

HELMER.   Of course!—if only this obstinate little person can get her way! Do you suppose I am going to make myself ridiculous before my whole staff, to let people think that I am a man to be swayed by all sorts of outside influence? I should very soon feel the consequences of it, I can tell you! And besides, there is one thing that makes it quite impossible for me to have Krogstad in the Bank as long as I am manager.

NORA.   Whatever is that?

HELMER.   His moral failings I might perhaps have overlooked, if necessary——

NORA.   Yes, you could—couldn't you?

HELMER.   And I hear he is a good worker, too. But I knew him when we were boys. It was one of those rash friendships that so often prove an embarrassment later. I may as well tell you plainly, we were once on very intimate terms with one another. But this tactless fellow has no restraint when other people are present. On the contrary, he thinks it gives him the right to adopt a familiar tone with me, and every minute it is 'I say, Helmer, old fellow!' and that sort of thing. I assure you it is extremely painful for me. He would make my position in the Bank intolerable.

NORA.   Torvald, I don't believe you mean that.

HELMER.   Don't you? Why not?

NORA.   Because it is such a narrow-minded way of looking at things.

HELMER.   What are you saying? Narrow-minded? Do you think I am narrow-minded?

NORA.   No, just the opposite, dear—and it is exactly for that reason.

HELMER.   It's the same thing. You say my point of view is narrow-minded, so I must be so too. Narrow-minded! Very well—I must put an end to this. (*Goes to the hall door and calls.*) Helen!

NORA.   What are you going to do?

HELMER (*looking among his papers*).   Settle it. (*Enter* MAID.) Look here; take this letter and go downstairs with it at once. Find a messenger and tell him to deliver it, and be quick. The address is on it, and here is the money.

MAID.   Very well, sir. (*Exit with the letter.*)

HELMER (*putting his papers together*).   Now then, little Miss Obstinate.

NORA (*breathlessly*).   Torvald—what was that letter?

HELMER.   Krogstad's dismissal.

NORA.   Call her back, Torvald! There is still time. Oh Torvald, call her back! Do it for my sake—for your own sake—for the children's sake! Do you hear me, Torvald? Call her back! You don't know what that letter can bring upon us.

HELMER.   It's too late.

NORA.   Yes, it's too late.

HELMER.   My dear Nora, I can forgive the anxiety you are in, although really it is an insult to me. It is, indeed. Isn't it an insult to think that I should be afraid of a starving pen-pusher's vengeance? But I forgive you nevertheless, because it is such eloquent witness to your great love for me. (*Takes her in his arms.*) And that is as it should be, my own darling Nora. Come what will, you may be sure I shall have both courage and strength if they be needed. You will see I am man enough to take everything upon myself.

NORA (*in a horror-stricken voice*).   What do you mean by that?

HELMER.   Everything, I say——

NORA (*recovering herself*).   You will never have to do that.

HELMER. That's right. Well, we will share it, Nora, as man and wife should. That is how it shall be. (*Caressing her.*) Are you content now? There! there!—not these frightened dove's eyes! The whole thing is only the wildest fancy!——Now, you must go and play through the Tarantella and practise with your tambourine. I shall go into the inner office and shut the door, and I shall hear nothing; you can make as much noise as you please. (*Turns back at the door.*) And when Rank comes, tell him where he will find me. (*Nods to her, takes his papers and goes into his room, and shuts the door after him.*)

NORA (*bewildered with anxiety, stands as if rooted to the spot, and whispers*). He was capable of doing it. He will do it. He will do it in spite of everything.—No, not that! Never, never! Anything rather than that! Oh, for some help, some way out of it! (*The doorbell rings.*) Doctor Rank! Anything rather than that—anything, whatever it is!

> (*She puts her hands over her face, pulls herself together, goes to the door, and opens it.* RANK *is standing outside, hanging up his coat. During the following dialogue it begins to grow dark.*)

NORA. Good afternoon, Doctor Rank. I knew your ring. But you mustn't go in to Torvald now; I think he is busy with something.

RANK. And you?

NORA (*brings him in and shuts the door after him*). Oh, you know very well I always have time for you.

RANK. Thank you. I shall make use of as much of it as I can.

NORA. What do you mean by that? As much of it as you can?

RANK. Well, does that alarm you?

NORA. It was such a strange way of putting it. Is anything likely to happen?

RANK. Nothing but what I have long been prepared for. But I certainly didn't expect it to happen so soon.

NORA (*gripping him by the arm*). What have you found out? Doctor Rank, you must tell me.

RANK (*sitting down by the stove*). It is all up with me. And it can't be helped.

NORA (*with a sigh of relief*). Is it about yourself?

RANK. Who else? It is no use lying to one's self. I am the most wretched of all my patients, Mrs Helmer. Lately I have been taking stock of my internal economy. Bankrupt! Probably within a month I shall lie rotting in the churchyard.

NORA. What an ugly thing to say!

RANK. The thing itself is cursedly ugly, and the worst of it is that I shall have to face so much more that is ugly before that. I shall only make one more examination of myself; when I have done that, I shall know pretty certainly when it will be that the horrors of dissolution will begin. There is something I want to tell you. Helmer's refined nature gives him an unconquerable disgust at everything that is ugly; I won't have him in my sickroom.

NORA. Oh, but, Doctor Rank——

RANK. I won't have him there. Not on any account. I bar my door to him. As soon as I am quite certain that the worst has come, I shall send you my card with a black cross on it, and then you will know that the loathsome end has begun.

NORA. You are quite absurd to-day. And I wanted you so much to be in a really good humour.

RANK. With death stalking beside me?—To have to pay this penalty for another man's sin! Is there any justice in that? And in every single family, in one way or another, some such inexorable retribution is being exacted——

NORA (*putting her hands over her ears*).   Rubbish! Do talk about something cheerful.

RANK.   Oh, it's a mere laughing matter, the whole thing. My poor innocent spine has to suffer for my father's youthful amusements.

NORA (*sitting at the table on the left*).   I suppose you mean that he was too partial to asparagus and pâté de foie gras, don't you?

RANK.   Yes, and to truffles.

NORA.   Truffles, yes. And oysters too, I suppose?

RANK.   Oysters, of course, that goes without saying.

NORA.   And heaps of port and champagne. It is sad that all these nice things should take their revenge on our bones.

RANK.   Especially that they should revenge themselves on the unlucky bones of those who have not had the satisfaction of enjoying them.

NORA.   Yes, that's the saddest part of it all.

RANK (*with a searching look at her*).   Hm!——

NORA (*after a short pause*).   Why did you smile?

RANK.   No, it was you that laughed.

NORA.   No, it was you that smiled, Doctor Rank!

RANK (*rising*).   You are a greater rascal than I thought.

NORA.   I am in a silly mood to-day.

RANK.   So it seems.

NORA (*putting her hands on his shoulders*).   Dear, dear Doctor Rank, death mustn't take you away from Torvald and me.

RANK.   It is a loss you would easily recover from. Those who are gone are soon forgotten.

NORA (*looking at him anxiously*).   Do you believe that?

RANK.   People form new ties, and then——

NORA.   Who will form new ties?

RANK.   Both you and Helmer, when I am gone. You yourself are already on the high road to it, I think. What did that Mrs Linde want here last night?

NORA.   Oho!—you don't mean to say you are jealous of poor Christine?

RANK.   Yes, I am. She will be my successor in this house. When I am done for, this woman will——

NORA.   Hush! don't speak so loud. She is in that room.

RANK.   To-day again. There, you see.

NORA.   She has only come to sew my dress for me. Good gracious, how unreasonable you are! (*Sits down on the sofa.*) Be nice now, Doctor Rank, and to-morrow you'll see how beautifully I shall dance, and you can imagine I am doing it all for you—and for Torvald too, of course. (*Takes various things out of the box.*) Doctor Rank, come and sit down here, and I will show you something.

RANK (*sitting down*).   What is it?

NORA.   Just look at those!

RANK.   Silk stockings.

NORA.   Flesh-coloured. Aren't they lovely? It is so dark here now, but to-morrow—— No, no, no! you must only look at the feet. Oh well, you may have permission to look at the legs too.

RANK.   Hm!——

NORA.   Why are you looking so critical? Don't you think they will fit me?

RANK.   I have no means of forming an opinion about that.

NORA (*looks at him for a moment*).   Shame on you! (*Hits him lightly on the ear with the stockings.*) That's to punish you. (*Folds them up again.*)

RANK. And what other nice things am I to be allowed to see?

NORA. Not a single thing more, for being so naughty. (*She looks among the things, humming to herself.*)

RANK (*after a short silence*). When I am sitting here, talking to you as intimately as this, I cannot imagine for a moment what would have become of me if I had never come into this house.

NORA (*smiling*). I believe you do feel thoroughly at home with us.

RANK (*in a lower voice, looking straight in front of him*). And to have to leave it all——

NORA. Nonsense, you are not going to leave it.

RANK (*as before*). And not be able to leave behind one the slightest token of one's gratitude, barely a fleeting regret even—nothing but an empty place which the first comer can fill as well as any other.

NORA. And if I asked you now for a——? No!

RANK. For what?

NORA. For a big proof of your friendship——

RANK. Yes, yes!

NORA. I mean a tremendously big favour——

RANK. Would you really make me so happy for once?

NORA. Ah, but you don't know what it is yet.

RANK. No—but tell me.

NORA. I really can't, Doctor Rank. It is something out of all reason; it means advice, and help, and a favour——

RANK. The bigger a thing it is the better. I can't conceive what it is you mean. Do tell me. Haven't I your confidence?

NORA. More than anyone else. I know you are my truest and best friend, and so I will tell you what it is. Well, Doctor Rank, it is something you must help me to prevent. You know how devotedly, how inexpressibly deeply Torvald loves me; he would never for a moment hesitate to give his life for me.

RANK (*leaning towards her*). Nora—do you think he is the only one——?

NORA (*with a slight start*). The only one——?

RANK. The only one who would gladly give his life for your sake.

NORA (*sadly*). Is that it?

RANK. I was determined you should know it before I went away, and there will never be a better opportunity than this. Now you know it, Nora. And now you know, too, that you can trust me as you would trust no one else.

NORA (*rises, deliberately and quietly*). Let me pass.

RANK (*makes room for her to pass him, but sits still*). Nora!

NORA (*at the hall door*). Helen, bring in the lamp. (*Goes over to the stove.*) Dear Doctor Rank, that was really horrid of you.

RANK. To have loved you as much as anyone else does? Was that horrid?

NORA. No, but to go and tell me so. There was really no need——

RANK. What do you mean? Did you know——? (MAID *enters with lamp, puts it down on the table, and goes out.*) Nora—Mrs Helmer—tell me, had you any idea of this?

NORA. Oh, how do I know whether I had or whether I hadn't? I really can't tell you—— To think you could be so clumsy, Doctor Rank! We were getting on so nicely.

RANK. Well, at all events you know now that you can command me, body and soul. So won't you speak out?

NORA (*looking at him*). After what happened?

RANK. I beg you to let me know what it is.

NORA. I can't tell you anything now.

RANK. Yes, yes. You mustn't punish me in that way. Let me have permission to do for you whatever a man may do.

NORA. You can do nothing for me now. Besides, I really don't need any help at all. You will find that the whole thing is merely fancy on my part. It really is so—of course it is! (*Sits down in the rocking-chair, and looks at him with a smile.*) You are a nice sort of man, Doctor Rank!—don't you feel ashamed of yourself, now the lamp has come?

RANK. Not a bit. But perhaps I had better go—for ever?

NORA. No, indeed, you shall not. Of course you must come here just as before. You know very well Torvald can't do without you.

RANK. Yes, but you?

NORA. Oh, I am always tremendously pleased when you come.

RANK. It is just that, that put me on the wrong track. You are a riddle to me. I have often thought that you would almost as soon be in my company as in Helmer's.

NORA. Yes—you see there are some people one loves best, and others whom one would almost always rather have as companions.

RANK. Yes, there is something in that.

NORA. When I was at home, of course I loved father best. But I always thought it tremendous fun if I could steal down into the maids' room, because they never moralized at all, and talked to each other about such entertaining things.

RANK. I see—it is *their* place I have taken.

NORA (*jumping up and going to him*). Oh, dear, nice Doctor Rank, I never meant that at all. But surely you can understand that being with Torvald is a little like being with father——

(*Enter* MAID *from the hall.*)

MAID. If you please, ma'am. (*Whispers and hands her a card.*)

NORA (*glancing at the card*). Oh! (*Puts it in her pocket.*)

RANK. Is there anything wrong?

NORA. No, no, not in the least. It is only something—it is my new dress——

RANK. What? Your dress is lying there.

NORA. Oh, yes, that one; but this is another. I ordered it. Torvald mustn't know about it——

RANK. Oho! Then that was the great secret.

NORA. Of course. Do go in to him; he is sitting in the inner room. Keep him as long as——

RANK. Don't worry; I won't let him escape. (*Goes into* HELMER's *room.*)

NORA (*to the* MAID). And he is standing waiting in the kitchen?

MAID. Yes; he came up the back stairs.

NORA. But didn't you tell him no one was in?

MAID. Yes, but it was no good.

NORA. He won't go away?

MAID. No; he says he won't until he has seen you, ma'am.

NORA. Well, let him come in—but quietly. Helen, you mustn't say anything about it to anyone. It is a surprise for my husband.

MAID. Yes, ma'am, I quite understand. (*Exit.*)

NORA. This dreadful thing is going to happen! It will happen in spite of me! No, no, no, it can't happen—it shan't happen!

> (*She bolts the door of* HELMER's *room. The* MAID *opens the hall door for* KROGSTAD *and shuts it after him. He is wearing a fur coat, high boots, and a fur cap.*)

NORA (*advancing towards him*). Speak quietly—my husband is at home.

KROGSTAD. I don't care about that.

NORA. What do you want of me?

KROGSTAD. An explanation of something.

NORA. Hurry up then. What is it?

KROGSTAD. You know, I suppose, that I have got my dismissal.

NORA. I couldn't prevent it, Mr Krogstad. I fought as hard as I could on your side, but it was no good.

KROGSTAD. Does your husband love you so little, then? He knows what I can expose you to, and yet he ventures——

NORA. How can you suppose that he has any knowledge of the sort?

KROGSTAD. I didn't suppose so at all. It would not be the least like our dear Torvald Helmer to show so much courage——

NORA. Mr Krogstad, a little respect for my husband, please.

KROGSTAD. Certainly—all the respect he deserves. But since you have kept the matter so carefully to yourself, I can only suppose that you have a little clearer idea, than you had yesterday, of what it actually is that you have done?

NORA. More than you could ever teach me.

KROGSTAD. Yes, such a bad lawyer as I am.

NORA. What is it you want of me?

KROGSTAD. Only to see how you were, Mrs Helmer. I have been thinking about you all day long. A mere cashier, a pen-pusher, a—well, a man like me—even he has a little of what is called feeling, you know.

NORA. Show it, then; think of my little children.

KROGSTAD. Have you and your husband thought of mine? But never mind about that. I only wanted to tell you that you need not take this matter too seriously. In the first place there will be no accusation made on my part.

NORA. No, of course not; I was sure of that.

KROGSTAD. The whole thing can be arranged amicably; there is no reason why anyone should know anything about it. It will remain a secret between us three.

NORA. My husband must never get to know anything about it.

KROGSTAD. How will you be able to prevent it? Am I to understand that you can pay the balance that is owing?

NORA. No, not just at present.

KROGSTAD. Or perhaps that you have some expedient for raising the money soon?

NORA. No expedient that I mean to make use of.

KROGSTAD. Well, in any case, it would have been of no use to you now. If you stood there with ever so much money in your hand, I would never part with your bond.

NORA. Tell me what purpose you mean to put it to.

KROGSTAD. I shall only preserve it—keep it in my possession. No one who is not concerned in the matter shall have the slightest hint of it. So that if the thought of it has driven you to any desperate resolution——

NORA. It has.

KROGSTAD. If you had it in your mind to run away from your home——

NORA. I had.

KROGSTAD. Or even something worse——

NORA. How could you know that?

KROGSTAD. Give up the idea.

NORA. How did you know I had thought of *that*?

KROGSTAD. Most of us think of that at first. I did, too—but I hadn't the courage.

NORA (*faintly*). Nor had I.

KROGSTAD (*in a tone of relief*). No, that's it, isn't it—you hadn't the courage either?

NORA. No, I haven't—I haven't.

KROGSTAD. Besides, it would have been a very foolish thing. Once the first storm at home is over—— I have a letter for your husband in my pocket.

NORA. Telling him everything?

KROGSTAD. In as lenient a manner as I possibly could.

NORA (*quickly*). He mustn't get the letter. Tear it up. I'll find some means of getting money.

KROGSTAD. Excuse me, Mrs Helmer, but I think I told you just now——

NORA. I am not speaking of what I owe you. Tell me what sum you are asking my husband for, and I will get the money.

KROGSTAD. I am not asking your husband for a penny.

NORA. What do you want, then?

KROGSTAD. I will tell you. I want to rehabilitate myself, Mrs Helmer; I want to get on; and in that your husband must help me. For the last year and a half I have not had a hand in anything dishonourable, and all that time I have been struggling in most restricted circumstances. I was content to work my way up step by step. Now I am turned out, and I am not going to be satisfied with merely being taken into favour again. I want to get on, I tell you. I want to get into the Bank again, in a higher position. Your husband must make a place for me——

NORA. That he will never do!

KROGSTAD. He will; I know him; he dare not protest. And as soon as I am in there again with him, then you will see! Within a year I shall be the manager's right hand. It will be Nils Krogstad and not Torvald Helmer who manages the Bank.

NORA. That's a thing you will never see!

KROGSTAD. Do you mean that you will——?

NORA. I have courage enough for it now.

KROGSTAD. Oh, you can't frighten me. A fine, spoilt woman like you——

NORA. You will see, you will see.

KROGSTAD. Under the ice, perhaps? Down into the cold, coal-black water? And then, in the spring, to float up to the surface, all horrible and unrecognizable, with your hair fallen out——

NORA. You can't frighten me.

KROGSTAD. Nor you me. People don't do such things, Mrs Helmer. Besides, what use would it be? I should have him completely in my power all the same.

NORA. Afterwards? When I am no longer——

KROGSTAD. Have you forgotten that it is I who have the keeping of your reputation? (NORA *stands speechlessly looking at him.*) Well, now, I have warned you. Don't do anything foolish. When Helmer has had my letter, I shall expect a message from him. And be sure you remember that it is your husband himself who has forced me into such ways as this again. I will never forgive him for that. Good-bye, Mrs Helmer. (*Exit through the hall.*)

NORA (*goes to the hall door, opens it slightly, and listens*). He is going. He is not putting the letter in the box. Oh no, no! that's impossible! (*Opens the door by degrees.*) What is that? He is standing outside. He is not going downstairs. Is he hesitating? Can he——?

> (*A letter drops into the box; then* KROGSTAD'S *footsteps are heard, till they die away as he goes downstairs.* NORA *utters a stifled cry, and runs across the room to the table by the sofa. A short pause.*)

NORA. In the letter-box. (*Steals across to the hall door.*) It's lying there—Torvald, Torvald, there is no hope for us now!

> (MRS LINDE *comes in from the room on the left, carrying the dress.*)

MRS LINDE. There, I can't see anything more to mend now. Would you like to try it on——?

NORA (*in a hoarse whisper*). Christine, come here.

MRS LINDE (*throwing the dress down on the sofa*). What is the matter with you? You look so agitated!

NORA. Come here. Do you see that letter? There, look—you can see it through the glass in the letter-box.

MRS LINDE. Yes, I see it.

NORA. That letter is from Krogstad.

MRS LINDE. Nora—it was Krogstad who lent you the money!

NORA. Yes, and now Torvald will know all about it.

MRS LINDE. Believe me, Nora, that's the best thing for both of you.

NORA. You don't know all. I forged a name.

MRS LINDE. Good heavens——!

NORA. I only want to say this to you, Christine—you must be my witness.

MRS LINDE. Your witness? What do you mean? What am I to——?

NORA. If I should go out of my mind—and it might easily happen——

MRS LINDE. Nora!

NORA. Or if anything else should happen to me—anything, for instance, that might prevent my being here——

MRS LINDE. Nora! Nora! you are quite out of your mind.

NORA. And if it should happen that there were someone who wanted to take all the responsibility, all the blame, you understand——

MRS LINDE. Yes, yes—but how can you suppose——?

NORA. Then you must be my witness, that it is not true, Christine. I am not out of my mind at all; I am in my right senses now, and I tell you no one else has known anything about it; I, and I alone, did the whole thing. Remember that.

MRS LINDE. I will, indeed. But I don't understand all this.

NORA. How should you understand it? A wonderful thing is going to happen!

MRS LINDE. A wonderful thing?

NORA. Yes, a wonderful thing!—But it is so terrible, Christine; it *mustn't* happen, not for all the world.

MRS LINDE. I will go at once and see Krogstad.

NORA. Don't go to him; he will do you some harm.

MRS LINDE. There was a time when he would gladly do anything for my sake.

NORA. He?

MRS LINDE. Where does he live?

NORA. How should I know——? Yes (*feeling in her pocket*), here is his card. But the letter, the letter——!

HELMER (*calls from his room, knocking at the door*). Nora!

NORA (*cries out anxiously*). Oh, what's that? What do you want?

HELMER. Don't be so frightened. We are not coming in; you have locked the door. Are you trying on your dress?

NORA. Yes, that's it. I look so nice, Torvald.

MRS LINDE (*who has read the card*). I see he lives at the corner here.

NORA. Yes, but it's no use. It is hopeless. The letter is lying there in the box.

MRS LINDE. And your husband keeps the key?

NORA. Yes, always.

MRS LINDE. Krogstad must ask for his letter back unread, he must find some excuse——

NORA. But it is just at this time that Torvald generally——

MRS LINDE. You must delay him. Go in to him in the meantime. I'll come back as soon as I can. (*She goes out hurriedly through the hall door.*)

NORA (*goes to* HELMER'*s door, opens it, and peeps in*). Torvald!

HELMER (*from the inner room*). Well? May I venture at last to come into my own room again? Come along, Rank, now you will see—— (*Halting in the doorway.*) But what is this?

NORA. What is what, dear?

HELMER. Rank led me to expect a splendid transformation.

RANK (*in the doorway*). I understood so, but evidently I was mistaken.

NORA. Yes, nobody is to have the chance of admiring me in my dress until to-morrow.

HELMER. But, my dear Nora, you look so worn out. Have you been practising too much?

NORA. No, I have not practised at all.

HELMER. But you will need to——

NORA. Yes, indeed I shall, Torvald. But I can't get on a bit without you to help me; I have absolutely forgotten the whole thing.

HELMER. Oh, we will soon work it up again.

NORA. Yes, help me, Torvald. Promise that you will! I am so nervous about it—all the people—— You must give yourself up to me entirely this evening. Not the tiniest bit of business—you mustn't even take a pen in your hand. Will you promise, Torvald dear?

HELMER. I promise. This evening I will be wholly and absolutely at your service, you helpless little mortal. Ah, by the way, first of all I will just—— (*Goes towards the hall door.*)

NORA. What are you going to do there?

HELMER. Only to see if any letters have come.

NORA. No, no! don't do that, Torvald!

HELMER. Why not?

NORA. Torvald, please don't. There is nothing there.

HELMER. Well, let me look. (*Turns to go to the letter-box.* NORA, *at the piano, plays the first bars of the Tarantella.* HELMER *stops in the doorway.*) Aha!

NORA. I can't dance to-morrow if I don't practise with you.

HELMER (*going up to her*). Are you really so afraid of it, dear?

NORA. Yes, so dreadfully afraid of it. Let me practise at once; there is time now, before we go to dinner. Sit down and play for me, Torvald dear; criticize me, and correct me as you play.

HELMER. With great pleasure, if you wish me to. (*Sits down at the piano.*)

NORA (*takes out of the box a tambourine and a long variegated shawl. She hastily drapes the shawl round her. Then she springs to the front of the stage and calls out*).   Now play for me! I am going to dance!

> (HELMER *plays and* NORA *dances.* RANK *stands by the piano behind* HELMER, *and looks on.*)

HELMER (*as he plays*).   Slower, slower!

NORA.   I can't do it any other way.

HELMER.   Not so violently, Nora!

NORA.   This is the way.

HELMER (*stops playing*).   No, no—that is not a bit right.

NORA (*laughing and swinging the tambourine*).   Didn't I tell you so?

RANK.   Let me play for her.

HELMER (*getting up*).   Yes, do. I can correct her better then.

> (RANK *sits down at the piano and plays.* NORA *dances more and more wildly.* HELMER *has taken up a position beside the stove, and during her dance gives her frequent instructions. She does not seem to hear him; her hair comes down and falls over her shoulders; she pays no attention to it, but goes on dancing. Enter* MRS LINDE.)

MRS LINDE (*standing as if spell-bound in the doorway*).   Oh!——

NORA (*as she dances*).   Such fun, Christine!

HELMER.   My dear darling Nora, you are dancing as if your life depended on it.

NORA.   So it does.

HELMER.   Stop, Rank; this is sheer madness. Stop, I tell you! (RANK *stops playing, and* NORA *suddenly stands still.* HELMER *goes up to her.*) I could never have believed it. You have forgotten everything I taught you.

NORA (*throwing away the tambourine*).   There, you see.

HELMER.   You will want a lot of coaching.

NORA.   Yes, you see how much I need it. You must coach me up to the last minute. Promise me that, Torvald!

HELMER.   You can depend on me.

NORA.   You must not think of anything but me, either to-day or to-morrow; you mustn't open a single letter—not even open the letter-box——

HELMER.   Ah, you are still afraid of that fellow——

NORA.   Yes, indeed I am.

HELMER.   Nora, I can tell from your looks that there is a letter from him lying there.

NORA.   I don't know; I think there is; but you mustn't read anything of that kind now. Nothing horrid must come between us till this is all over.

RANK (*whispers to* HELMER).   You mustn't contradict her.

HELMER (*taking her in his arms*).   The child shall have her way. But to-morrow night, after you have danced——

NORA.   Then you will be free.

> (*The* MAID *appears in the doorway to the right.*)

MAID.   Dinner is served, ma'am.

NORA.   We will have champagne, Helen.

MAID.   Very good, ma'am. (*Exit.*)

HELMER.   Hallo!—are we going to have a banquet?

NORA.   Yes, a champagne banquet till the small hours. (*Calls out.*) And a few macaroons, Helen—lots, just for once!

HELMER.   Come, come, don't be so wild and nervous. Be my own little skylark, as you used.

NORA.   Yes, dear, I will. But go in now, and you too, Doctor Rank. Christine, you must help me to do up my hair.

RANK (*whispers to* HELMER *as they go out*).   I suppose there is nothing—she is not expecting anything?

HELMER.   Far from it, my dear fellow; it is simply nothing more than this childish nervousness I was telling you of.

> (*They go into the right-hand room.*)

NORA.   Well!

MRS LINDE.   Gone out of town.

NORA.   I could tell from your face.

MRS LINDE.   He is coming home to-morrow evening. I wrote a note for him.

NORA.   You should have let it alone; you must prevent nothing. After all, it is splendid to be waiting for a wonderful thing to happen.

MRS LINDE.   What is it that you are waiting for?

NORA.   Oh, you wouldn't understand. Go in to them, I will come in a moment. (MRS LINDE *goes into the dining-room.* NORA *stands still for a little while, as if to compose herself. Then she looks at her watch.*) Five o'clock. Seven hours till midnight; and then twenty-four hours till the next midnight. Then the Tarantella will be over. Twenty-four and seven? Thirty-one hours to live.

HELMER (*from the doorway on the right*).   Where's my little skylark?

NORA (*going to him with her arms outstretched*).   Here she is!

ACT III

(THE SAME SCENE.—*The table has been placed in the middle of the stage, with chairs round it. A lamp is burning on the table. The door into the hall stands open. Dance music is heard in the room above.* MRS LINDE *is sitting at the table idly turning over the leaves of a book; she tries to read, but does not seem able to collect her thoughts. Every now and then she listens intently for a sound at the outer door.*)

MRS LINDE (*looking at her watch*).   Not yet—and the time is nearly up. If only he does not—— (*Listens again.*) Ah, there he is. (*Goes into the hall and opens the outer door carefully. Light footsteps are heard on the stairs. She whispers.*) Come in. There is no one here.

KROGSTAD (*in the doorway*).   I found a note from you at home. What does this mean?

MRS LINDE.   It is absolutely necessary that I should have a talk with you.

KROGSTAD.   Really? And is it absolutely necessary that it should be here?

MRS LINDE.   It is impossible where I live; there is no private entrance to my rooms. Come in; we are quite alone. The maid is asleep, and the Helmers are at the dance upstairs.

KROGSTAD (*coming into the room*).   Are the Helmers really at a dance to-night?

MRS LINDE.   Yes, why not?

KROGSTAD.   Certainly—why not?

MRS LINDE.   Now, Nils, let us have a talk.

KROGSTAD.   Can we two have anything to talk about?

MRS LINDE.   We have a great deal to talk about.

KROGSTAD.   I shouldn't have thought so.

MRS LINDE.   No, you have never properly understood me.

KROGSTAD.   Was there anything else to understand except what was obvious to all the world—a heartless woman jilts a man when a more lucrative chance turns up?

MRS LINDE.   Do you believe I am as absolutely heartless as all that? And do you believe that I did it with a light heart?

KROGSTAD.   Didn't you?

MRS LINDE.   Nils, did you really think that?

KROGSTAD.   If it were as you say, why did you write to me as you did at the time?

MRS LINDE.   I could do nothing else. As I had to break with you, it was my duty also to put an end to all that you felt for me.

KROGSTAD (*wringing his hands*).   So that was it. And all this—only for the sake of money!

MRS LINDE.   You mustn't forget that I had a helpless mother and two little brothers. We couldn't wait for you, Nils; your prospects seemed hopeless then.

KROGSTAD.   That may be so, but you had no right to throw me over for anyone else's sake.

MRS LINDE.   I really don't know. Often I used to ask myself if I had the right to do it.

KROGSTAD (*more gently*).   When I lost you, it was as if all the solid ground went from under my feet. Look at me now—I am a shipwrecked man clinging to a bit of wreckage.

MRS LINDE.   But help may be near.

KROGSTAD.   It *was* near; but then you came and stood in my way.

MRS LINDE.   Unintentionally, Nils. It was only to-day that I learnt it was your place I was going to take in the Bank.

KROGSTAD.   I believe you, if you say so. But now that you know it, are you not going to give it up to me?

MRS LINDE.   No, because that wouldn't benefit you in the least.

KROGSTAD.   Oh, benefit, benefit—I would have done it, benefit or not.

MRS LINDE.   I have learnt to act prudently. Life, and hard, bitter necessity have taught me that.

KROGSTAD.   And life has taught me not to believe in fine speeches.

MRS LINDE.   Then life has taught you something very sensible. But deeds you must believe in?

KROGSTAD.   What do you mean by that?

MRS LINDE.   You said you were like a shipwrecked man clinging to some wreckage.

KROGSTAD.   I had good reason to say so.

MRS LINDE.   Well, I am like a shipwrecked woman clinging to some wreckage—no one to mourn for, no one to care for.

KROGSTAD.   It was your own choice.

MRS LINDE.   There was no choice—then.

KROGSTAD.   Well, what now?

MRS LINDE.   Nils, how would it be if we two shipwrecked people could join forces?

KROGSTAD.   What are you saying?

MRS LINDE.   Two on the same piece of wreckage would stand a better chance than each on their own.

KROGSTAD.   Christine!

MRS LINDE.   What do you suppose brought me to town?

KROGSTAD.   Do you mean that you gave me a thought?

MRS LINDE. I could not endure life without work. All my life, as long as I can remember, I have worked, and it has been my greatest and only pleasure. But now I am quite alone in the world—my life is so dreadfully empty and I feel so forsaken. There is not the least pleasure in working for one's self. Nils, give me someone and something to work for.

KROGSTAD. I don't trust that. It is nothing but a woman's overstrained sense of generosity that prompts you to make such an offer of yourself.

MRS LINDE. Have you ever noticed anything of the sort in me?

KROGSTAD. Could you really do it? Tell me—do you know all about my past life?

MRS LINDE. Yes.

KROGSTAD. And do you know what they think of me here?

MRS LINDE. You seemed to me to imply that with me you might have been quite another man.

KROGSTAD. I am certain of it.

MRS LINDE. Is it too late now?

KROGSTAD. Christine, are you saying this deliberately? Yes, I am sure you are. I see it in your face. Have you really the courage, then——?

MRS LINDE. I want to be a mother to someone, and your children need a mother. We two need each other. Nils, I have faith in your real character—I can dare anything together with you.

KROGSTAD (*grasps her hands*). Thanks, thanks, Christine! Now I shall find a way to clear myself in the eyes of the world. Ah, but I forgot——

MRS LINDE (*listening*). Hush! The Tarantella! Go, go!

KROGSTAD. Why? What is it?

MRS LINDE. Do you hear them up there? When that is over, we can expect them back.

KROGSTAD. Yes, yes—I'll go. But it's all no use. Of course you don't know what steps I have taken in the matter of the Helmers.

MRS LINDE. Yes, I know all about that.

KROGSTAD. And in spite of that have you the courage to——?

MRS LINDE. I understand very well to what lengths a man like you might be driven by despair.

KROGSTAD. If I could only undo what I have done!

MRS LINDE. You cannot. Your letter is lying in the letter-box now.

KROGSTAD. Are you sure of that?

MRS LINDE. Quite sure, but——

KROGSTAD (*with a searching look at her*). Is that what it all means?—that you want to save your friend at any cost? Tell me frankly. Is that it?

MRS LINDE. Nils, a woman who has once sold herself for another's sake, doesn't do it a second time.

KROGSTAD. I will ask for my letter back.

MRS LINDE. No, no.

KROGSTAD. Yes, of course I will. I will wait here till Helmer comes; I will tell him he must give me my letter back—that it only concerns my dismissal—that he is not to read it——

MRS LINDE. No, Nils, you must not recall your letter.

KROGSTAD. But, tell me, wasn't it for that very purpose that you asked me to meet you here?

MRS LINDE. In my first moment of fright, it was. But twenty-four hours have passed since then, and in that time I have witnessed incredible things in this house. Helmer must know all about it. This unhappy secret must be disclosed; they must have a complete understanding between them, which is impossible with all this concealment and falsehood going on.

KROGSTAD.   All right, if you will take the responsibility. But there is one thing I can do in any case, and I shall do it at once.

MRS LINDE (*listening*).   You must be quick and go! The dance is over; we aren't safe a moment longer.

KROGSTAD.   I'll wait for you below.

MRS LINDE.   Yes, do. You must see me back to my door.

KROGSTAD.   I have never had such an amazing piece of good fortune in my life! (*Goes out through the outer door. The door between the room and the hall remains open.*)

MRS LINDE (*tidying up the room and laying her hat and cloak ready*).   What a difference! what a difference! Someone to work for and live for—a home to bring comfort into. That I will do, indeed. I wish they would be quick and come—— (*Listens.*) Ah, there they are now. I must put on my things.

> (*Takes up her hat and cloak.* HELMER's *and* NORA's *voices are heard outside; a key is turned, and* HELMER *brings* NORA *almost by force into the hall. She is in an Italian costume with a large black shawl round her; he has on evening dress, with a black domino [cloak] open over it.*)

NORA (*hanging back in the doorway, and struggling with him*).   No, no, no!—don't take me in. I want to go upstairs again; I don't want to leave so early.

HELMER.   But, my dearest Nora——

NORA.   Please, Torvald dear—please, *please*—only an hour more.

HELMER.   Not a single minute, my sweet Nora. You know that was our agreement. Come along into the room; you are catching cold standing there. (*He brings her gently into the room, in spite of her resistance.*)

MRS LINDE.   Good evening.

NORA.   Christine!

HELMER.   You here, so late, Mrs Linde?

MRS LINDE.   Yes, you must forgive me; I was so anxious to see Nora in her dress.

NORA.   Have you been sitting here waiting for me?

MRS LINDE.   Yes, unfortunately I came too late, you had already gone upstairs; and I thought I couldn't go away again without having seen you.

HELMER (*taking off* NORA's *shawl*).   Yes, take a good look at her. I think she is worth looking at. Isn't she charming, Mrs Linde?

MRS LINDE.   Yes, indeed she is.

HELMER.   Doesn't she look remarkably pretty? Everyone thought so at the dance. But she is terribly self-willed, this sweet little person. What are we to do with her? You'll hardly believe that I almost had to bring her away by force.

NORA.   Torvald, you will repent not having let me stay, even if it were only for half an hour.

HELMER.   Listen to her, Mrs Linde! She had danced her Tarantella, and it had been a tremendous success, as it deserved—although possibly the performance was a trifle too realistic—a little more so, I mean, than was strictly compatible with the limitations of art. But never mind about that! The chief thing is, she had made a success—she had made a tremendous success. Do you think I was going to let her remain there after that, and spoil the effect? No, indeed! I took my charming little Capri maiden—my capricious little Capri maiden, I should say—on my arm;

took one quick turn round the room; a curtsy on either side, and, as they say in novels, the beautiful apparition disappeared. An exit ought always to be effective, Mrs Linde; but that is what I cannot make Nora understand. Pooh! this room is hot. (*Throws his domino on a chair, and opens the door of his room.*) Hallo! it's all dark in here. Oh, of course—excuse me—— (*He goes in, and lights some candles.*)

NORA (*in a hurried and breathless whisper*). Well?

MRS LINDE (*in a low voice*). I have had a talk with him.

NORA. Yes, and——

MRS LINDE. Nora, you must tell your husband all about it.

NORA (*in an expressionless voice*). I knew it.

MRS LINDE. You have nothing to be afraid of as far as Krogstad is concerned; but you must tell him.

NORA. I won't tell him.

MRS LINDE. Then the letter will.

NORA. Thank you, Christine. Now I know what I must do. Hush——!

HELMER (*coming in again*). Well, Mrs Linde, have you admired her?

MRS LINDE. Yes, and now I will say good night.

HELMER. What, already? Is this yours, this knitting?

MRS LINDE (*taking it*). Yes, thank you, I had very nearly forgotten it.

HELMER. So you knit?

MRS LINDE. Of course.

HELMER. Do you know, you ought to embroider.

MRS LINDE. Really? Why?

HELMER. Yes, it's far more becoming. Let me show you. You hold the embroidery thus in your left hand, and use the needle with the right—like this—with a long, easy sweep. Do you see?

MRS LINDE. Yes, perhaps——

HELMER. But in the case of knitting—that can never be anything but ungraceful; look here—the arms close together, the knitting-needles going up and down—it has a sort of Chinese effect—— That was really excellent champagne they gave us.

MRS LINDE. Well—good night, Nora, and don't be self-willed any more.

HELMER. That's right, Mrs Linde.

MRS LINDE. Good night, Mr Helmer.

HELMER (*accompanying her to the door*). Good night, good night. I hope you will get home all right. I should be very happy to—but you haven't any great distance to go. Good night, good night. (*She goes out; he shuts the door after her, and comes in again.*) Ah!—at last we have got rid of her. She is a frightful bore, that woman.

NORA. Aren't you very tired, Torvald?

HELMER. No, not in the least.

NORA. Nor sleepy?

HELMER. Not a bit. On the contrary, I feel extraordinarily lively. And you?—you really look both tired and sleepy.

NORA. Yes, I am very tired. I want to go to sleep at once.

HELMER. There, you see it was quite right of me not to let you stay there any longer.

NORA. Everything you do is quite right, Torvald.

HELMER (*kissing her on the forehead*). Now my little skylark is speaking reasonably. Did you notice what good spirits Rank was in this evening?

NORA. Really? Was he? I didn't speak to him at all.

HELMER. And I very little, but I haven't for a long time seen him in such good form. (*Looks for a while at her and then goes nearer to her.*) It is wonderful to be at home by ourselves again, to be all alone with you—you fascinating, charming little darling!

NORA. Don't look at me like that, Torvald.

HELMER. Why shouldn't I look at my dearest treasure?—at all the beauty that is mine, all my very own?

NORA (*going to the other side of the table*). You mustn't say things like that to me to-night.

HELMER (*following her*). You have still got the Tarantella in your blood, I see. And it makes you more captivating than ever. Listen—the guests are beginning to go now. (*In a lower voice.*) Nora—soon the whole house will be quiet.

NORA. Yes, I hope so.

HELMER. Yes, my own darling Nora. Do you know, when I am out at a party with you like this, why I speak so little to you, why I keep away from you, and only send a stolen glance in your direction now and then?—do you know why I do that? It is because I make believe to myself that we are secretly in love, and you are my secretly promised bride, and that no one suspects there is anything between us.

NORA. Yes, yes—I know quite well your thoughts are with me all the time.

HELMER. And when we are leaving, and I am putting the shawl over your beautiful young shoulders—on your lovely neck—then I imagine that you are my young bride and that we have just come from the wedding, and I am bringing you for the first time into our home—to be alone with you for the first time—quite alone with my shy little darling! All this evening I have longed for nothing but you. When I watched the seductive figures of the Tarantella, my blood was on fire; I could endure it no longer, and that was why I brought you down so early——

NORA. Go away, Torvald! You must let me go. I won't——

HELMER. What's that? You're joking, my little Nora! You won't—you won't? Am I not your husband——? (*A knock is heard at the outer door.*)

NORA (*starting*). Did you hear——?

HELMER (*going into the hall*). Who is it?

RANK (*outside*). It's me. May I come in for a moment?

HELMER (*in a fretful whisper*). Oh, what does he want now? (*Aloud.*) Wait a minute! (*Unlocks the door.*) Well, that's kind of you not to pass by our door.

RANK. I thought I heard your voice, and felt as if I should like to look in. (*With a swift glance round.*) Ah, yes!—these dear familiar rooms. You are very happy and cosy in here, you two.

HELMER. It seems to me that you looked after yourself pretty well upstairs too.

RANK. Excellently. Why shouldn't I? Why shouldn't one enjoy everything in this world?—at any rate as much as one can, and as long as one can. The wine was capital——

HELMER. Especially the champagne.

RANK. So you noticed that too? It is almost incredible how much I managed to put away!

NORA. Torvald drank a great deal of champagne to-night too.

RANK. Did he?

NORA. Yes, and he is always in such good spirits afterwards.

RANK. Well, why should one not enjoy a merry evening after a well-spent day?

HELMER. Well spent? I am afraid I can't take credit for that.

RANK (*clapping him on the back*). But I can, you know!

NORA. Doctor Rank, you must have been occupied with some scientific investigation to-day.

RANK. Exactly.

HELMER. Just listen!—little Nora talking about scientific investigations!

NORA. And may I congratulate you on the result?

RANK. Indeed you may.

NORA. Was it favourable, then?

RANK. The best possible, for both doctor and patient—certainty.

NORA (*quickly and searchingly*). Certainty?

RANK. Absolute certainty. So wasn't I entitled to make a merry evening of it after that?

NORA. Yes, you certainly were, Doctor Rank.

HELMER. I think so too, so long as you don't have to pay for it in the morning.

RANK. Oh well, one can't have anything in this life without paying for it.

NORA. Doctor Rank—do you like fancy-dress balls?

RANK. Yes, if there is a fine lot of pretty costumes.

NORA. Tell me—what shall we two wear at the next?

HELMER. Little featherbrain!—are you thinking of the next already?

RANK. We two? Yes, I can tell you. You shall go as a good fairy——

HELMER. Yes, but what do you suggest as an appropriate costume for that?

RANK. Let your wife go dressed just as she is in everyday life.

HELMER. That was really very nicely said. But can't you tell us what you will be?

RANK. Yes, my dear friend, I have quite made up my mind about that.

HELMER. Well?

RANK. At the next fancy-dress ball I shall be invisible.

HELMER. That's a good joke!

RANK. There is a big black hat—have you never heard of hats that make you invisible? If you put one on, no one can see you.

HELMER (*suppressing a smile*). Yes, you are quite right.

RANK. But I am clean forgetting what I came for. Helmer, give me a cigar—one of the dark Havanas.

HELMER. With the greatest pleasure. (*Offers him his case.*)

RANK (*takes a cigar and cuts off the end*). Thanks.

NORA (*striking a match*). Let me give you a light.

RANK. Thank you. (*She holds the match for him to light his cigar.*) And now good-bye!

HELMER. Good-bye, good-bye, dear old man!

NORA. Sleep well, Doctor Rank.

RANK. Thank you for that wish.

NORA. Wish me the same.

RANK. You? Well, if you want me to sleep well! And thanks for the light. (*He nods to them both and goes out.*)

HELMER (*in a subdued voice*). He has drunk more than he ought.

NORA (*absently*). Maybe. (HELMER *takes a bunch of keys out of his pocket and goes into the hall.*) Torvald! what are you going to do there?

HELMER. Empty the letter-box; it's quite full; there will be no room to put the newspaper in to-morrow morning.

443

NORA. Are you going to work to-night?

HELMER. You know quite well I'm not. What's this? Someone has been at the lock.

NORA. At the lock——?

HELMER. Yes, someone has. What can it mean? I should never have thought the maid—— Here is a broken hairpin. Nora, it is one of yours.

NORA (*quickly*). Then it must have been the children——

HELMER. Then you must get them out of those ways. There, at last I have got it open. (*Takes out the contents of the letter-box, and calls to the kitchen.*) Helen!—Helen, put out the light over the front door. (*Goes back into the room and shuts the door into the hall. He holds out his hand full of letters.*) Look at that—look what a heap of them there are. (*Turning them over.*) What on earth is that?

NORA (*at the window*). The letter—No! Torvald, no!

HELMER. Two cards—of Rank's.

NORA. Of Doctor Rank's?

HELMER (*looking at them*). Doctor Rank. They were on the top. He must have put them in when he went out.

NORA. Is there anything written on them?

HELMER. There is a black cross over the name. Look there—what an uncomfortable idea! It looks as if he were announcing his own death.

NORA. It is just what he is doing.

HELMER. What? Do you know anything about it? Has he said anything to you?

NORA. Yes. He told me that when the cards came it would be his leave-taking from us. He means to shut himself up and die.

HELMER. My poor old friend! I knew of course we shouldn't have him very long with us. But so soon! And so he hides himself away like a wounded animal.

NORA. If it has to happen, it is best it should be without a word—don't you think so, Torvald?

HELMER (*walking up and down*). He had so grown into our lives. I can't think of him as having gone out of them. With his sufferings and his loneliness, he was like a cloudy background to our sunlit happiness. Well, perhaps it is best so. For him, anyway. (*Standing still.*) And perhaps for us too, Nora. We two are thrown quite upon each other now. (*Puts his arms round her.*) My darling wife, I don't feel as if I could hold you tight enough. Do you know, Nora, I have often wished that you might be threatened by some great danger, so that I might risk my life's blood, and everything, for your sake.

NORA (*disengages herself, and says firmly and decidedly*). Now you must read your letters, Torvald.

HELMER. No, no; not to-night. I want to be with you, my darling wife.

NORA. With the thought of your friend's death——

HELMER. You are right, it has affected us both. Something ugly has come between us—the thought of the horrors of death. We must try and rid our minds of that. Until then—we will each go to our own room.

NORA (*hanging on his neck*). Good night, Torvald—good night!

HELMER (*kissing her on the forehead*). Good night, my little singing-bird. Sleep well, Nora. Now I will read my letters through. (*He takes his letters and goes into his room, shutting the door after him.*)

NORA (*gropes distractedly about, seizes* HELMER's *domino, throws it round her, while she says in quick, hoarse, spasmodic whispers*). Never to see him again. Never! Never! (*Puts her shawl over her head.*) Never to see my children again either—never again. Never!

Never!—oh! the icy, black water—the bottomless depths—If only it were over! He has got it now—now he is reading it. Good-bye, Torvald, and my children!

(*She is about to rush out through the hall, when* HELMER *opens his door hurriedly and stands with an open letter in his hand.*)

HELMER. Nora!

NORA. Oh!——

HELMER. What is this? Do you know what is in this letter?

NORA. Yes, I know. Let me go! Let me get out!

HELMER (*holding her back*). Where are you going?

NORA (*trying to get free*). You shan't save me, Torvald!

HELMER (*reeling*). True? Is this true, that I read here? Horrible! No, no—it's impossible that it can be true.

NORA. It is true. I have loved you above everything else in the world.

HELMER. Oh, don't let us have any silly excuses.

NORA (*taking a step towards him*). Torvald——!

HELMER. Miserable creature—what have you done?

NORA. Let me go. You shall not suffer for my sake. You shall not take it upon yourself.

HELMER. No tragedy airs, please. (*Locks the hall door.*) Here you shall stay and give me an explanation. Do you understand what you have done? Answer me! Do you understand what you have done?

NORA (*looks steadily at him and says with a growing look of coldness in her face*). Yes, now I am beginning to understand thoroughly.

HELMER (*walking about the room*). What a horrible awakening! All these eight years— she who was my pride and joy—a hypocrite, a liar—worse, worse—a criminal! The unutterable ugliness of it all!—What disgraceful behaviour! (NORA *is silent and looks steadily at him. He stops in front of her.*) I ought to have suspected that something of the sort would happen. I ought to have foreseen it. All your father's want of principle—be silent!—all your father's want of principle has come out in you. No religion, no morality, no sense of duty—— How I am punished for having winked at what he did! I did it for your sake, and this is how you repay me.

NORA. Yes, that's just it.

HELMER. Now you have destroyed all my happiness. You have ruined all my future. It is horrible to think of! I am in the power of an unscrupulous man; he can do what he likes with me, ask anything he likes of me, give me any orders he pleases—I dare not refuse. And I must sink to such miserable depths because of a thoughtless woman!

NORA. When I am out of the way, you will be free.

HELMER. No fine speeches, please. Your father had always plenty of those ready, too. What good would it be to me if you were out of the way, as you say? Not the slightest. He can make the affair known everywhere; and if he does, I may be falsely suspected of having been a party to your criminal action. Very likely people will think I was behind it all—that it was I who prompted you! And I have to thank you for all this—you whom I have cherished during the whole of our married life. Do you understand now what it is you have done for me?

NORA (*coldly and quietly*). Yes.

HELMER. It is so incredible that I can't take it in. But we must come to some understanding. Take off that shawl. Take it off, I tell you. I must try and appease him some way or another. The matter must be hushed up at any cost. And as for you and me, it must appear as if everything between us were just as before—but naturally only in the eyes of the world. You will still remain in my house, that is a matter of course. But I shall not allow you to bring up the children; I dare not trust them to you. To think that I should have to say this to one whom I have loved so dearly, and whom I still——No, that is all over. From this moment happiness is not the question; all that concerns us is to save the remains, the fragments, the appearance——

> (*A ring is heard at the front-door bell.*)

HELMER (*with a start*). What is that? So late! Can the worst——? Can he——? Hide yourself, Nora. Say you are ill.

> (NORA *stands motionless.* HELMER *goes and unlocks the hall door.*)

MAID (*half-dressed, comes to the door*). A letter for the mistress.

HELMER. Give it to me. (*Takes the letter, and shuts the door.*) Yes, it is from him. You shall not have it; I will read it myself.

NORA. Yes, read it.

HELMER (*standing by the lamp*). I scarcely have the courage to do it. It may mean ruin for both of us. No, I must know. (*Tears open the letter, runs his eye over a few lines, looks at a paper enclosed, and gives a shout of joy.*) Nora! (*She looks at him questioningly.*) Nora!—No, I must read it once again—— Yes, it is true! I am saved! Nora, I am saved!

NORA. And I?

HELMER. You too, of course; we are both saved, both you and I. Look, he sends you your bond back. He says he regrets and repents—that a happy change in his life—never mind what he says! We are saved, Nora! No one can do anything to you. Oh, Nora, Nora!—no, first I must destroy these hateful things. Let me see—— (*Takes a look at the bond.*) No, no, I won't look at it. The whole thing shall be nothing but a bad dream to me. (*Tears up the bond and both letters, throws them all into the stove, and watches them burn.*) There—now it doesn't exist any longer. He says that since Christmas Eve you—— These must have been three dreadful days for you, Nora.

NORA. I have fought a hard fight these three days.

HELMER. And suffered agonies, and seen no way out but—— No, we won't call any of the horrors to mind. We will only shout with joy, and keep saying, 'It's all over! It's all over!' Listen to me, Nora. You don't seem to realize that it is all over. What is this?—such a cold, set face! My poor little Nora, I quite understand; you don't feel as if you could believe that I have forgiven you. But it is true, Nora, I swear it; I have forgiven you everything. I know that what you did, you did out of love for me.

NORA. That is true.

HELMER. You have loved me as a wife ought to love her husband. Only you had not sufficient knowledge to judge of the means you used. But do you suppose you are any the less dear to me, because you don't understand how to act on your own responsibility? No, no; just lean on me; I will advise you and direct you. I shouldn't be a man if this womanly helplessness did not actually give you a double attractiveness in my eyes. You mustn't think any more about the hard things I said in my first moment of consternation, when I thought everything was going to overwhelm me. I have forgiven you, Nora; I swear to you I have forgiven you.

NORA. Thank you for your forgiveness. (*She goes out through the door to the right.*)

HELMER. No, don't go—— (*Looks in.*) What are you doing in there?

NORA (*from within*).   Taking off my fancy dress.

HELMER (*standing at the open door*).   Yes, do. Try and calm yourself, and make your mind easy again, my frightened little singing-bird. Relax, and feel secure; I have broad wings to shelter you under. (*Walks up and down by the door.*) How warm and cosy our home is, Nora. Here is shelter for you; here I will protect you like a hunted dove that I have saved from a hawk's claws; I will bring peace to your poor beating heart. It will come, little by little, Nora, believe me. To-morrow morning you will look upon it all quite differently; soon everything will be just as it was before. Very soon you won't need me to assure you that I have forgiven you; you will yourself feel the certainty that I have done so. Do you imagine I should ever think of such a thing as repudiating you, or even reproaching you? You have no idea what a true man's heart is like, Nora. There is something so indescribably sweet and satisfying, to a man, in the knowledge that he has forgiven his wife— forgiven her freely, and with all his heart. It seems as if that had made her, as it were, doubly his own; he has given her a new life, so to speak; and she has in a way become both wife and child to him. So you shall be for me after this, my little scared, helpless darling. Have no anxiety about anything, Nora; just be frank and open with me, and I will serve as will and conscience both to you—— What is this? Not gone to bed? Have you changed your things?

NORA (*in everyday dress*).   Yes, Torvald, I have changed my things now.

HELMER.   But what for?—as late as this.

NORA.   I shan't sleep to-night.

HELMER.   But, my dear Nora——

NORA (*looking at her watch*).   It is not so very late. Sit down here, Torvald. You and I have a lot to say to one another. (*She sits down at one side of the table.*)

HELMER.   Nora—what is this?—this cold, set face?

NORA.   Sit down. It will take some time; I have a lot to talk over with you.

HELMER (*sits down at the opposite side of the table*).   You alarm me, Nora!—and I don't understand you.

NORA.   No, that is just it. You don't understand me, and I have never understood you either—before to-night. No, you mustn't interrupt me. You must simply listen to what I say. Torvald, this is a settling of accounts.

HELMER.   What do you mean by that?

NORA (*after a short silence*).   Isn't there one thing that strikes you as strange in our sitting here like this?

HELMER.   What is that?

NORA.   We have been married now eight years. Doesn't it occur to you that this is the first time we two, you and I, husband and wife, have had a serious conversation?

HELMER.   What do you mean by serious?

NORA.   In all these eight years—longer than that—from the very beginning of our acquaintance, we have never exchanged a word on any serious subject.

HELMER.   Was it likely that I would be continually and for ever telling you about worries that you could not help me to bear?

NORA.   I am not speaking about business matters. I say that we have never sat down in earnest together to try and get at the bottom of anything.

HELMER.   But, dearest Nora, would it have been any good to you?

NORA.   That is just it; you have never understood me. I have been greatly wronged, Torvald—first by father and then by you.

HELMER.   What! By us two—by us two, who have loved you better than anyone else in the world?

NORA (*shaking her head*).   You have never loved me. You have only thought it pleasant to be in love with me.

HELMER.   Nora, what do I hear you saying?

NORA.   It is perfectly true, Torvald. When I was at home with father, he told me his opinion about everything, and so I had the same opinions; and if I differed from him I concealed the fact, because he would not have liked it. He called me his doll-child, and he played with me just as I used to play with my dolls. And when I came to live with you——

HELMER.   What sort of an expression is that to use about our marriage?

NORA (*undisturbed*).   I mean that I was simply transferred from father's hands into yours. You arranged everything according to your own taste, and so I got the same tastes as you—or else I pretended to, I am really not quite sure which—I think sometimes the one and sometimes the other. When I look back on it, it seems to me as if I had been living here like a poor woman—just from hand to mouth. I have existed merely to perform tricks for you, Torvald. But you wanted it like that. You and father have committed a great sin against me. It is your fault that I have made nothing of my life.

HELMER.   How unreasonable and how ungrateful you are, Nora! Haven't you been happy here?

NORA.   No, I have never been happy. I thought I was, but it has never really been so.

HELMER.   Not—not happy!

NORA.   No, only merry. And you have always been so kind to me. But our home has been nothing but a playroom. I have been your doll-wife, just as at home I was father's doll-child; and here the children have been my dolls. I thought it great fun when you played with me, just as they thought it great fun when I played with them. That is what our marriage has been, Torvald.

HELMER.   There is some truth in what you say—exaggerated and strained as your view of it is. But in future it will be different. Playtime is over, and lesson-time will begin.

NORA.   Whose lessons? Mine, or the children's?

HELMER.   Both yours and the children's, my darling Nora.

NORA.   I'm afraid, Torvald, you are not the man to educate me into being a proper wife for you.

HELMER.   And you can say that!

NORA.   And I—how am I fitted to bring up the children?

HELMER.   Nora!

NORA.   Didn't you say so yourself a little while ago—that you dare not trust me to bring them up?

HELMER.   In a moment of anger! Why do you take any notice of that?

NORA.   Actually, you were perfectly right. I am not fit for the task. There is another task I must undertake first. I must try and educate myself—you are not the man to help me in that. I must do that for myself. And that is why I am going to leave you now.

HELMER (*springing up*).   What are you saying?

NORA.   I must stand quite alone, if I am to understand myself and everything about me. It is for that reason that I cannot remain with you any longer.

HELMER. Nora, Nora!

NORA. I am going away from here now, at once. I am sure Christine will take me in for the night——

HELMER. You are out of your mind! I won't allow it! I forbid you!

NORA. It is no use forbidding me anything any longer. I will take with me only what belongs to me. I will take nothing from you, either now or later.

HELMER. What sort of madness is this!

NORA. To-morrow I shall go home—I mean, to my old home. It will be easiest for me to find something to do there.

HELMER. You blind, foolish woman!

NORA. I must try and get some sense, Torvald.

HELMER. To desert your home, your husband, and your children! And you don't consider what people will say!

NORA. I cannot consider that at all. I only know that it is necessary for me.

HELMER. It's shocking. This is how you would neglect your most sacred duties.

NORA. What do you consider my most sacred duties?

HELMER. Do I need to tell you that? Are they not your duties to your husband and your children?

NORA. I have other duties just as sacred.

HELMER. Indeed you have not. What duties could those be?

NORA. Duties to myself.

HELMER. Before all else, you are a wife and a mother.

NORA. I don't believe that any longer. I believe that before all else I am a reasonable human being, just as you are—or, at all events, that I must try and become one. I know quite well, Torvald, that most people would think you right, and that views of that kind are to be found in books; but I can no longer content myself with what most people say, or with what is found in books. I must think over things for myself and get to understand them.

HELMER. Can you not understand your place in your own home? Have you not a reliable guide in such matters as that?—have you no religion?

NORA. I am afraid, Torvald, I do not exactly know what religion is.

HELMER. What are you saying?

NORA. I know nothing but what the clergyman said, when I went to be confirmed. He told us that religion was this, and that, and the other. When I am away from all this, and am alone, I will look into that matter too. I will see if what the clergyman said is true, or at all events if it is true for me.

HELMER. This is unheard of in a girl of your age! But if religion cannot lead you aright, let me try and awaken your conscience. I suppose you have some moral sense? Or—answer me—am I to think you have none?

NORA. I assure you, Torvald, that is not an easy question to answer. I really don't know. The thing perplexes me altogether. I only know that you and I look at it in quite a different light. I am learning, too, that the law is quite another thing from what I supposed; but I find it impossible to convince myself that the law is right. According to it a woman has no right to spare her old dying father, or to save her husband's life. I can't believe that.

HELMER. You talk like a child. You don't understand the conditions of the world in which you live.

NORA. No, I don't. But now I am going to try. I am going to see if I can make out who is right, the world or I.

HELMER. You are ill, Nora; you are delirious; I almost think you are out of your mind.

NORA. I have never felt my mind so clear and certain as to-night.

HELMER. And is it with a clear and certain mind that you forsake your husband and your children?

NORA. Yes, it is.

HELMER. Then there is only one possible explanation.

NORA. What is that?

HELMER. You do not love me any more.

NORA. No, that is just it.

HELMER. Nora!—and you can say that?

NORA. It gives me great pain, Torvald, because you have always been so kind to me, but I cannot help it. I don't love you any more.

HELMER (*regaining his composure*). Is that a clear and certain conviction too?

NORA. Yes, absolutely clear and certain. That is the reason why I will not stay here any longer.

HELMER. And can you tell me what I have done to forfeit your love?

NORA. Yes, indeed I can. It was to-night, when the wonderful thing did not happen; then I saw you were not the man I had thought you.

HELMER. Explain yourself better. I don't understand you.

NORA. I have waited so patiently for eight years; for, goodness knows, I knew very well that wonderful things don't happen every day. Then this horrible misfortune came upon me; and then I felt quite certain that the wonderful thing was going to happen at last. When Krogstad's letter was lying out there, never for a moment did I imagine that you would consent to accept this man's conditions. I was so absolutely certain that you would say to him: Publish the thing to the whole world. And when that was done——

HELMER. Yes, what then?—when I had exposed my wife to shame and disgrace?

NORA. When that was done, I was so absolutely certain, you would come forward and take everything upon yourself, and say: I am the guilty one.

HELMER. Nora——!

NORA. You mean that I would never have accepted such a sacrifice on your part? No, of course not. But what would my assurances have been worth against yours? That was the wonderful thing which I hoped for and feared; and it was to prevent that, that I wanted to kill myself.

HELMER. I would gladly work night and day for you, Nora—bear sorrow and want for your sake. But no man would sacrifice his honour for the one he loves.

NORA. It is a thing hundreds of thousands of women have done.

HELMER. Oh, you think and talk like a thoughtless child.

NORA. Maybe. But you neither think nor talk like the man I could bind myself to. As soon as your fear was over—and it was not fear for what threatened me, but for what might happen to you—when the whole thing was past, as far as you were concerned it was exactly as if nothing at all had happened. Exactly as before, I was your little skylark, your doll, which you would in future treat with doubly gentle care, because it was so brittle and fragile. (*Getting up.*) Torvald—it was then it dawned upon me that for eight years I had been living here with a strange man, and had borne him three children—— Oh, I can't bear to think of it! I could tear myself into little bits!

HELMER (*sadly*). I see, I see. An abyss has opened between us—there is no denying it. But, Nora, would it not be possible to fill it up?

NORA. As I am now, I am no wife for you.

HELMER. I have it in me to become a different man.

NORA. Perhaps—if your doll is taken away from you.

HELMER. But to part!—to part from you! No, no, Nora, I can't understand that idea.

NORA (*going out to the right*). That makes it all the more certain that it must be done. (*She comes back with her cloak and hat and a small bag which she puts on a chair by the table.*)

HELMER. Nora, Nora, not now! Wait till to-morrow.

NORA (*putting on her cloak*). I cannot spend the night in a strange man's room.

HELMER. But can't we live here like brother and sister——?

NORA (*putting on her hat*). You know very well that wouldn't last long. (*Puts the shawl round her.*) Good-bye, Torvald. I won't see the little ones. I know they are in better hands than mine. As I am now, I can be of no use to them.

HELMER. But some day, Nora—some day?

NORA. How can I tell? I have no idea what is going to become of me.

HELMER. But you are my wife, whatever becomes of you.

NORA. Listen, Torvald. I have heard that when a wife deserts her husband's house, as I am doing now, he is legally freed from all obligations towards her. In any case I set you free from all your obligations. You are not to feel yourself bound in the slightest way, any more than I shall. There must be perfect freedom on both sides. See, here is your ring back. Give me mine.

HELMER. That too?

NORA. That too.

HELMER. Here it is.

NORA. That's right. Now it is all over. I have put the keys here. The maids know all about everything in the house—better than I do. To-morrow, after I have left her, Christine will come here and pack up my own things that I brought with me from home. I will have them sent after me.

HELMER. All over! All over!—Nora, will you never think of me again?

NORA. I know I shall often think of you and the children and this house.

HELMER. May I write to you, Nora?

NORA. No—never. You must not do that.

HELMER. But at least let me send you——

NORA. Nothing—nothing——

HELMER. Let me help you if you are in want.

NORA. No. I can receive nothing from a stranger.

HELMER. Nora—can I never be anything more than a stranger to you?

NORA (*taking her bag*). Ah, Torvald, the most wonderful thing of all would have to happen.

HELMER. Tell me what that would be!

NORA. Both you and I would have to be so changed that—— Oh, Torvald, I don't believe any longer in wonderful things happening.

HELMER. But I will believe in it. Tell me! So changed that——?

NORA. That our life together would be a real marriage. Good-bye. (*She goes out through the hall.*)

HELMER (*sinks down on a chair at the door and buries his face in his hands*). Nora! Nora! (*Looks round, and rises.*) Empty. She is gone. (*A hope flashes across his mind.*) The most wonderful thing of all——? (*The sound of a door shutting is heard from below.*)

The Dynamo and the Virgin (1900)

Henry Adams

Editor's Introduction

Henry Adams (1838–1918), historian, biographer, and man of letters, was one of the Massachusetts Adamses, a grandson of the sixth president of the United States and a great-grandson of the second. As such, he was burdened (as he liked to say) with an inescapable past, which he carried with him, regarding it with an ironic detachment that became a mannerism, throughout a long life devoted to the study of power—political, religious, and scientific—in human affairs.

Born in Boston, where he grew up, and educated at Harvard College, from which he graduated in 1858, Adams had thoughts of a public career natural in a young man with such antecedents, and began to take courses in the civil law. These he abandoned without much regret when at the beginning of the Civil War his father, Charles Francis Adams, who had been appointed minister to England, asked him to become his private secretary. Henry Adams stayed in London for the duration of the War and three years besides, returning to the United States in 1868, when he was thirty, eager for some kind of public service. But the country he returned to was that of Grant's administration and the Gilded Age, the corruption and falsity of which were repellent to a young man schooled in an older politics and at home in a different world. There seemed no prospect of any sort of political career for Adams, who could only conceive of himself as a critic of the society and institutions he saw about him, and who began the study and writings, first of articles on economic subjects, that were to become the occupations of his life.

In 1870 Adams, having achieved reputation as a publicist in the reform political movement of his day, was made editor of the *North American Review*, a distinguished journal of opinion, and was also appointed professor of medieval history at Harvard. He remained in both positions for about seven years, after which he resigned to edit the papers of Albert Gallatin, Jefferson's secretary of the Treasury, of whom he also wrote the definitive biography. Subsequently he wrote a nine-volume *History of the United States of America* about the administrations of Jefferson and Madison, an elegantly crafted work of painstaking scholarship on which his reputation as an historian is chiefly based.

The ensuing portion of Adams's life was marked by prolonged grief at his wife's death through suicide (1885), and by an increasing concern with the unintelligibility, as he believed it to be, of the coming twentieth century, in which he thought he perceived the emergence of runaway forces that would carry the human race to catastrophe. Two speculative essays written toward the end of his life, "The Rule of Phase Applied to History" (1909), and *Letter to American Teachers of History* (1910), were inspired by this concern. So were two much longer works, *Mont-Saint-Michel and Chartres* (published in 1913), a study of medieval cathedrals and the force that made them, and the autobiographical *Education of Henry Adams* (published in 1918), in which Adams depicted himself as mystified and overwhelmed by what he regarded as the chaos of his own times. These are the books by which he is best known.

The chapter called "The Dynamo and the Virgin," here reprinted, is taken from *The Education* and contrasts what for Adams were the reigning symbols of the modern and the medieval worlds. The earlier of these periods had seen the construction of the great cathedrals of Europe, expressive, he said, of "an emotion, the deepest man ever felt—the struggle of his own littleness to grasp the infinite," which manifested itself in works of singular coherence and beauty. The modern period struck Adams as dominated by a different kind of force, infinite in another way, which expressed itself in multiplicity, the dispersal of energy, rather than in unity, the harmonious whole of Christian faith. Of this modern force the dynamo, a vast centrifuge humming all but silently as it generated energy in quantities undreamed of a generation earlier, seemed to Adams a perfect illustration as he contemplated it at the Paris Exposition of 1900. The mystery by which it converted mechanical to electrical power struck him as the modern equivalent of the Virgin's translation of faith to stone and appeared as terrifying as it was unfathomable. Something similar could be said also, he thought, of other modern inventions such as the Branly coherer, which allowed the reception of radio signals over long distances, and the discovery of radium, with its silent, secret, burning force. Adams took satisfaction in the fact that his friend, Samuel Pierpont Langley, an eminent scientist of the day who had done pioneer work in aeronautics and solar radiation, found it as difficult as he did to answer the philosophic questions that such scientific advances posed, and to suggest where they might end.

Adams's last years were passed quietly at his home in Washington, D.C., where he lived in a house built for him by the architect H. H. Richardson on the site of what is now the Hay-Adams hotel overlooking Lafayette Park and the White House. The historian took sardonic note of a succession of presidents who seemed to him no wiser than he was about the world they were called upon to govern. He died on March 27, 1918, and was buried in Rock Creek Cemetery beside his wife in a grave marked only by an untitled statue of a seated figure, the work of the sculptor Augustus Saint-Gaudens, which Adams had commissioned in 1891 after his wife's death to express what he called his acceptance of fate.

The Dynamo and the Virgin (1900)

Until the Great Exposition of 1900 closed its doors in November, Adams haunted it, aching to absorb knowledge, and helpless to find it. He would have liked to know how much of it could have been grasped by the best-informed man in the world. While he was thus meditating chaos, Langley came by, and showed it to him. At Langley's behest, the Exhibition dropped its superfluous rags and stripped itself to the skin, for Langley knew what to study, and why, and how; while Adams might as well have stood outside in the night, staring at the Milky Way. Yet Langley said nothing new, and taught nothing that one might not have learned from Lord Bacon, three hundred years before; but though one should have known the "Advancement of Science" as well as one knew the "Comedy of Errors," the literary knowledge counted for nothing until some teacher should show how to apply it. Bacon took a vast deal of trouble in teaching King James I and his subjects, American or other, towards the year 1620, that true science was the development or economy of forces; yet an elderly American in 1900 knew neither the formula nor the forces; or even so much as to say to himself that his historical business in the Exposition concerned only the economies or developments of force since 1893, when he began the study at Chicago.

Nothing in education is so astonishing as the amount of ignorance it accumulates in the form of inert facts. Adams had looked at most of the accumulations of art in the storehouses called Art Museums; yet he did not know how to look at the art exhibits of 1900. He had studied Karl Marx and his doctrines of history with profound attention, yet he could not apply them at Paris. Langley, with the ease of a great master of experiment, threw out of the field every exhibit that did not reveal a new application of force, and naturally threw out, to begin with, almost the whole art exhibit. Equally, he ignored almost the whole industrial exhibit. He led his pupil directly to the forces. His chief interest was in new motors to make his airship feasible, and he taught Adams the astonishing complexities of the new Daimler motor, and of the automobile, which, since 1893, had become a nightmare at a hundred kilometres an hour, almost as destructive as the electric tram which was only ten years older; and threatening to become as terrible as the locomotive steam-engine itself, which was almost exactly Adams's own age.

Then he showed his scholar the great hall of dynamos, and explained how little he knew about electricity or force of any kind, even of his own special sun, which spouted heat in inconceivable volume, but which, as far as he knew, might spout less or more, at any time, for all the certainty he felt in it. To him, the dynamo itself was but an ingenious channel for conveying somewhere the heat latent in a few tons of poor coal hidden in a dirty engine-house carefully kept out of sight; but to Adams the dynamo became a symbol of infinity. As he grew accustomed to the great gallery of machines, he began to feel the forty-foot dynamos as a moral force, much as the early Christians felt the Cross. The planet itself seemed less impressive, in its old-fashioned, deliberate, annual or daily revolution, than this huge wheel, revolving within arm's length at some vertiginous speed, and barely murmuring—scarcely humming an audible warning to stand a hair's-breadth further for respect of power

—while it would not wake the baby lying close against its frame. Before the end, one began to pray to it; inherited instinct taught the natural expression of man before silent and infinite force. Among the thousand symbols of ultimate energy, the dynamo was not so human as some, but it was the most expressive.

Yet the dynamo, next to the steam-engine, was the most familiar of exhibits. For Adams's objects its value lay chiefly in its occult mechanism. Between the dynamo in the gallery of machines and the engine-house outside, the break of continuity amounted to abysmal fracture for a historian's objects. No more relation could he discover between the steam and the electric current than between the Cross and the cathedral. The forces were interchangeable if not reversible, but he could see only an absolute *fiat* in electricity as in faith. Langley could not help him. Indeed, Langley seemed to be worried by the same trouble, for he constantly repeated that the new forces were anarchical, and especially that he was not responsible for the new rays, that were little short of parricidal in their wicked spirit towards science. His own rays, with which he had doubled the solar spectrum, were altogether harmless and beneficent; but Radium denied its God—or, what was to Langley the same thing, denied the truths of his Science. The force was wholly new.

A historian who asked only to learn enough to be as futile as Langley or Kelvin, made rapid progress under this teaching, and mixed himself up in the tangle of ideas until he achieved a sort of Paradise of ignorance vastly consoling to his fatigued senses. He wrapped himself in vibrations and rays which were new, and he would have hugged Marconi and Branly had he met them, as he hugged the dynamo; while he lost his arithmetic in trying to figure out the equation between the discoveries and the economies of force. The economies, like the discoveries, were absolute, supersensual, occult; incapable of expression in horse-power. What

mathematical equivalent could he suggest as the value of a Branly coherer? Frozen air, or the electric furnace, had some scale of measurement, no doubt, if somebody could invent a thermometer adequate to the purpose; but X-rays had played no part whatever in man's consciousness, and the atom itself had figured only as a fiction of thought. In these seven years man had translated himself into a new universe which had no common scale of measurement with the old. He had entered a supersensual world, in which he could measure nothing except by chance collisions of movements imperceptible to his senses, perhaps even imperceptible to his instruments, but perceptible to each other, and so to some known ray at the end of the scale. Langley seemed prepared for anything, even for an indeterminable number of universes interfused—physics stark mad in metaphysics.

Historians undertake to arrange sequences,—called stories, or histories—assuming in silence a relation of cause and effect. These assumptions, hidden in the depths of dusty libraries, have been astounding, but commonly unconscious and childlike; so much so, that if any captious critic were to drag them to light, historians would probably reply, with one voice, that they had never supposed themselves required to know what they were talking about. Adams, for one, had toiled in vain to find out what he meant. He had even published a dozen volumes of American history for no other purpose than to satisfy himself whether, by the severest process of stating, with the least possible comment, such facts as seemed sure, in such order as seemed rigorously consequent, he could fix for a familiar moment a necessary sequence of human movement. The result had satisfied him as little as at Harvard College. Where he saw sequence, other men saw something quite different, and no one saw the same unit of measure. He cared little about his experiments and less about his statesmen, who seemed to him quite as ignorant as himself and, as a rule, no more honest; but he insisted on a relation of sequence, and if he could not reach it by one method, he would try as many methods as science knew. Satisfied that the sequence of men led to nothing and that the sequence of their society could lead no further, while the mere sequence of time was artificial, and the sequence of thought was chaos, he turned at last to the sequence of force; and thus it happened that, after ten years' pursuit, he found himself lying in the Gallery of Machines at the Great Exposition of 1900, his historical neck broken by the sudden irruption of forces totally new.

Since no one else showed much concern, an elderly person without other cares had no need to betray alarm. The year 1900 was not the first to upset schoolmasters. Copernicus and Galileo had broken many professorial necks about 1600; Columbus had stood the world on its head towards 1500; but the nearest approach to the revolution of 1900 was that of 310, when Constantine set up the Cross. The rays that Langley disowned, as well as those which he fathered, were occult, supersensual, irrational; they were a revelation of mysterious energy like that of the Cross; they were what, in terms of mediæval science, were called immediate modes of the divine substance.

The historian was thus reduced to his last resources. Clearly if he was bound to reduce all these forces to a common value, this common value could have no measure but that of their attraction on his own mind. He must treat them as they had been felt; as convertible, reversible, interchangeable attractions on thought. He made up his mind to venture it; he would risk translating rays into faith. Such a reversible process would vastly amuse a chemist, but the chemist could not deny that he, or some of his fellow physicists, could feel the force of both. When Adams was a boy in Boston, the best chemist in the place had probably never heard of Venus except by way of scandal, or of the Virgin except as idolatry; neither had he heard of dynamos or automobiles or radium; yet his mind was ready to feel the force of all, though the rays were unborn and the women were dead.

Here opened another totally new education, which promised to be by far the most hazardous of all. The knife-edge along which he must crawl, like Sir Lancelot in the twelfth century, divided two kingdoms of force which had nothing in common but attraction. They were as different as a magnet is from gravitation, supposing one knew what a magnet was, or gravitation, or love. The force of the Virgin was still felt at Lourdes, and seemed to be as potent as X-rays; but in America neither Venus nor Virgin ever had value as force—at most as sentiment. No American had ever been truly afraid of either.

This problem in dynamics gravely perplexed an American historian. The Woman had once been supreme; in France she still seemed potent, not merely as a sentiment, but as a force. Why was she unknown in America? For evidently America was ashamed of her, and she was ashamed of herself, otherwise they would not have strewn fig-leaves so profusely all over her. When she was a true force, she was ignorant of fig-leaves, but the monthly-magazine-made American female had not a feature that would have been recognized by Adam. The trait was notorious, and often humorous, but any one brought up among Puritans knew that sex was sin. In any previous age, sex was strength. Neither art nor beauty was needed. Every one, even among Puritans, knew that neither Diana of the Ephesians nor any of the Oriental goddesses was worshipped for her beauty. She was goddess because of her force; she was the animated dynamo; she was reproduction—the greatest and most mysterious of all energies; all she needed was to be fecund. Singularly enough, not one of Adams's many schools of education had ever drawn his attention to the opening lines of Lucretius, though they were perhaps the finest in all Latin literature, where the poet invoked Venus exactly as Dante invoked the Virgin:—

"Quae quoniam rerum naturam sola *gubernas."**

The Venus of Epicurean philosophy survived in the Virgin of the Schools:—

> *"Donna, sei tanto grande, e tanto vali,*
> *Che qual vuol grazia, e a te non ricorre,*
> *Sua disianza vuol volar senz' ali."†*

All this was to American thought as though it had never existed. The true American knew something of the facts, but nothing of the feelings; he read the letter, but he never felt the law. Before this historical chasm, a mind like that of Adams felt itself helpless; he turned from the Virgin to the Dynamo as though he were a Branly coherer. On one side, at the Louvre and at Chartres, as he knew by the record of work actually done and still before his eyes, was the highest energy ever known to man, the creator of four-fifths of his noblest art, exercising vastly more attraction over the human mind than all the steam-engines and dynamos ever dreamed of; and yet this energy was unknown to the American mind. An American Virgin would never dare command; an American Venus would never dare exist.

The question, which to any plain American of the nineteenth century seemed as remote as it did to Adams, drew him almost violently to study, once it was posed; and on this point Langleys were as useless as though they were Herbert Spencers or dynamos. The idea survived only as art. There one turned as naturally as though the artist were himself a woman. Adams began to ponder, asking himself whether he knew of any American artist who had ever insisted on the power of sex, as every classic had always done; but he could think only of Walt Whitman; Bret Harte, as far as the magazines would let him venture; and one or two painters, for the flesh-tones. All the rest had used sex for sentiment, never for force; to them, Eve was a tender flower, and Herodias an unfeminine horror. American art, like the American language and American education, was as far as possible sexless. Society

regarded this victory over sex as its greatest triumph, and the historian readily admitted it, since the moral issue, for the moment, did not concern one who was studying the relations of unmoral force. He cared nothing for the sex of the dynamo until he could measure its energy.

Vaguely seeking a clue, he wandered through the art exhibit, and, in his stroll, stopped almost every day before St. Gaudens's General Sherman, which had been given the central post of honor. St. Gaudens himself was in Paris, putting on the work his usual interminable last touches, and listening to the usual contradictory suggestions of brother sculptors. Of all the American artists who gave to American art whatever life it breathed in the seventies, St. Gaudens was perhaps the most sympathetic, but certainly the most inarticulate. General Grant or Don Cameron had scarcely less instinct of rhetoric than he. All the others—the Hunts, Richardson, John La Farge, Stanford White— were exuberant; only St. Gaudens could never discuss or dilate on an emotion, or suggest artistic arguments for giving to his work the forms that he felt. He never laid down the law, or affected the despot, or became brutalized like Whistler by the brutalities of his world. He required no incense; he was no egoist; his simplicity of thought was excessive; he could not imitate, or give any form but his own to the creations of his hand. No one felt more strongly than he the strength of other men, but the idea that they could affect him never stirred an image in his mind.

This summer his health was poor and his spirits were low. For such a temper, Adams was not the best companion, since his own gaiety was not *folle;* but he risked going now and then to the studio on Mont Parnasse to draw him out for a stroll in the Bois de Bou-

---

* "Since thou then art sole mistress of the nature of things." (Lucretius, *On the Nature of Things*; *GBWW*, Vol. 12, p. 1.)

† "Lady, thou art so great, and so availest, that whoso would have grace, and has not recourse to thee, would have his desire fly without wings." (Dante, *Paradiso*, 33, 5; *GBWW*, Vol. 21, p. 156.)

logne, or dinner as pleased his moods, and in return St. Gaudens sometimes let Adams go about in his company.

Once St. Gaudens took him down to Amiens, with a party of Frenchmen, to see the cathedral. Not until they found themselves actually studying the sculpture of the western portal, did it dawn on Adams's mind that, for his purposes, St. Gaudens on that spot had more interest to him than the cathedral itself. Great men before great monuments express great truths, provided they are not taken too solemnly. Adams never tired of quoting the supreme phrase of his idol Gibbon, before the Gothic cathedrals: "I darted a contemptuous look on the stately monuments of superstition." Even in the footnotes of his history, Gibbon had never inserted a bit of humor more human than this, and one would have paid largely for a photograph of the fat little historian, on the background of Notre Dame of Amiens, try-ing to persuade his readers—perhaps him-self—that he was darting a contemptuous look on the stately monument, for which he felt in fact the respect which every man of his vast study and active mind always feels before objects worthy of it; but besides the humor, one felt also the relation. Gibbon ig-nored the Virgin, because in 1789 religious monuments were out of fashion. In 1900 his remark sounded fresh and simple as the green fields to ears that had heard a hun-dred years of other remarks, mostly no more fresh and certainly less simple. Without mal-ice, one might find it more instructive than a whole lecture of Ruskin. One sees what one brings, and at that moment Gibbon brought the French Revolution. Ruskin brought reac-tion against the Revolution. St. Gaudens had passed beyond all. He liked the stately monu-ments much more than he liked Gibbon or Ruskin; he loved their dignity; their unity; their scale; their lines; their lights and shad-ows; their decorative sculpture; but he was even less conscious than they of the force that created it all—the Virgin, the Woman—by whose genius "the stately monuments of superstition" were built, through which she

was expressed. He would have seen more meaning in Isis with the cow's horns, at Ed-foo, who expressed the same thought. The art remained, but the energy was lost even upon the artist.

Yet in mind and person St. Gaudens was a survival of the 1500; he bore the stamp of the Renaissance, and should have carried an im-age of the Virgin round his neck, or stuck in his hat, like Louis XI. In mere time he was a lost soul that had strayed by chance into the twentieth century, and forgotten where it came from. He writhed and cursed at his ignorance, much as Adams did at his own, but in the opposite sense. St. Gaudens was a child of Benvenuto Cellini, smothered in an American cradle. Adams was a quintessence of Boston, devoured by curiosity to think like Benvenuto. St. Gaudens's art was starved from birth, and Adams's instinct was blight-ed from babyhood. Each had but half of a nature, and when they came together before the Virgin of Amiens they ought both to have felt in her the force that made them one; but it was not so. To Adams she became more than ever a channel of force; to St. Gaudens she remained as before a channel of taste.

For a symbol of power, St. Gaudens in-stinctively preferred the horse, as was plain in his horse and Victory of the Sherman monument. Doubtless Sherman also felt it so. The attitude was so American that, for at least forty years, Adams had never realized that any other could be in sound taste. How many years had he taken to admit a notion of what Michael Angelo and Rubens were driving at? He could not say; but he knew that only since 1895 had he begun to feel the Virgin or Venus as force, and not every-where even so. At Chartres—perhaps at Lourdes—possibly at Cnidos if one could still find there the divinely naked Aphrodite of Praxiteles—but otherwise one must look for force to the goddesses of Indian mythology. The idea died out long ago in the German and English stock. St. Gaudens at Amiens was hardly less sensitive to the force of the female energy than Matthew Arnold at the Grande

Chartreuse. Neither of them felt goddesses as power—only as reflected emotion, human expression, beauty, purity, taste, scarcely even as sympathy. They felt a railway train as power; yet they, and all other artists, constantly complained that the power embodied in a railway train could never be embodied in art. All the steam in the world could not, like the Virgin, build Chartres.

Yet in mechanics, whatever the mechanicians might think, both energies acted as interchangeable forces on man, and by action on man all known force may be measured. Indeed, few men of science measured force in any other way. After once admitting that a straight line was the shortest distance between two points, no serious mathematician cared to deny anything that suited his convenience, and rejected no symbol, unproved or unproveable, that helped him to accomplish work. The symbol was force, as a compass-needle or a triangle was force, as the mechanist might prove by losing it, and nothing could be gained by ignoring their value. Symbol or energy, the Virgin had acted as the greatest force the Western world ever felt, and had drawn man's activities to herself more strongly than any other power, natural or supernatural, had ever done; the historian's business was to follow the track of the energy; to find where it came from and where it went to; its complex source and shifting channels; its values, equivalents, conversions. It could scarcely be more complex than radium; it could hardly be deflected, diverted, polarized, absorbed more perplexingly than other radiant matter. Adams knew nothing about any of them, but as a mathematical problem of influence on human progress, though all were occult, all reacted on his mind, and he rather inclined to think the Virgin easiest to handle.

The pursuit turned out to be long and tortuous, leading at last into the vast forests of scholastic science. From Zeno to Descartes, hand in hand with Thomas Aquinas, Montaigne, and Pascal, one stumbled as stupidly as though one were still a German student of 1860. Only with the instinct of despair could one force one's self into this old thicket of ignorance after having been repulsed at a score of entrances more promising and more popular. Thus far, no path had led anywhere, unless perhaps to an exceedingly modest living. Forty-five years of study had proved to be quite futile for the pursuit of power; one controlled no more force in 1900 than in 1850, although the amount of force controlled by society had enormously increased. The secret of education still hid itself somewhere behind ignorance, and one fumbled over it as feebly as ever. In such labyrinths, the staff is a force almost more necessary than the legs; the pen becomes a sort of blind-man's dog, to keep him from falling into the gutters. The pen works for itself, and acts like a hand, modelling the plastic material over and over again to the form that suits it best. The form is never arbitrary, but is a sort of growth like crystallization, as any artist knows too well; for often the pencil or pen runs into side-paths and shapelessness, loses its relations, stops or is bogged. Then it has to return on its trail, and recover, if it can, its line of force. The result of a year's work depends more on what is struck out than on what is left in; on the sequence of the main lines of thought, than on their play or variety. Compelled once more to lean heavily on this support, Adams covered more thousands of pages with figures as formal as though they were algebra, laboriously striking out, altering, burning, experimenting, until the year had expired, the Exposition had long been closed, and winter drawing to its end, before he sailed from Cherbourg, on January 19, 1901, for home.

PICTURE CREDITS

*Key to abbreviations used to indicate location of pictures on page: r.—right; l.—left; t.—top; b.—bottom; c.—center; *—courtesy. Abbreviations are combined to indicate unusual placement.*

—**FRONTISPIECE** Dan McCoy—Rainbow —**84** *New Realities* —**162** G. G. Brownlee, *Biochemical Society Transactions* (London) 7 (1979): 279–96. —**238** Ian Berry—Magnum —**239** Henri Cartier-Bresson—Magnum —**245** *The Metropolitan Museum of Art, Harris-Brisbane Dick Fund, 1929 —**246** Henri Cartier-Bresson—Magnum —**247** Elliott Erwitt—Magnum —**248** Werner Bischof—Magnum —**250–251** Burt Glinn—Magnum —**252** Josef Koudelka—Magnum —**254** Ian Berry—Magnum —**255** Burt Glinn—Magnum —**257, 259** Werner Bischof—Magnum —**270** *The Metropolitan Museum of Art, Kennedy Fund, 1912 —**271** *The Metropolitan Museum of Art, Gift of Nathan V. Hammer, 1953 —**273** Burt Glinn—Magnum —**276** Arthur Tress—Magnum —**281** Henri Cartier-Bresson—Magnum —**283** Norma Morrison —**286–287** Bernard Pierre Wolff—Magnum —**289** Marc Riboud—Magnum —**291** Marilyn Silverstone—Magnum —**306** Archiv für Kunst und Geschichte, Berlin-Nikolassee —**398** *Teaterhistorisk Museum, Copenhagen —**452** *Harvard University Archives

INDEX

The Great Ideas Today
1961-1980

This is a twenty-year cumulative index of *The Great Ideas Today*,
1961–1980. It is arranged in sections: AUTHORS, CONTENTS,
and TITLES. The entries in CONTENTS appear as they did in
the Table of Contents of each volume under various headings.
Titles in capital letters in the AUTHORS and TITLES sections are
of reprinted works, as distinct from original articles. The year
listed after such work refers to the issue of *The Great Ideas Today*
in which it appeared.

AUTHORS

CONTENTS

GREAT IDEA, CONTEMPORARY STATUS OF

GREAT BOOKS AND GREAT BOOKS' AUTHORS (variously listed under RECONSIDERATIONS, REFLECTIONS, or REVIEWS)

SYNTOPICON, ADDITIONS TO

SPECIAL FEATURES

EDITORS' REVIEW OF THE YEAR

TITLES

To extend the tradition of excellence of your Britannica Great Books educational program, you may also avail yourself of other aids for your home reference center.

Described on the next page is a companion product—the Britannica 3 bookcase—that is designed to help you and your family. It will add attractiveness and value to your home library, as it keeps it well organized.

Should you wish to order it, or to obtain further information, please write to us at

Britannica Home Library Service
Att: Year Book Department
P.O. Box 4928
Chicago, Illinois 60680

Britannica 3
custom-designed
BOOKCASE

- requires less than 1 x 3-ft. floor space

- laminated pecan finish resists burns, stains, scratches

- Early American styling enriches any setting

- case size: $35^3/_4''$ wide, $9^3/_4''$ deep, $27^5/_8''$ high

Authors

in Great Books of the Western World

Homer	Nicomachus
Aeschylus	Ptolemy
Sophocles	Marcus Aurelius
Herodotus	Galen
Euripides	Plotinus
Thucydides	Augustine
Hippocrates	Thomas Aquinas
Aristophanes	Dante
Plato	Chaucer
Aristotle	Machiavelli
Euclid	Copernicus
Archimedes	Rabelais
Apollonius	Montaigne
Lucretius	Gilbert
Virgil	Cervantes
Plutarch	Francis Bacon
Tacitus	Galileo
Epictetus	Shakespeare
	Kepler